HIGHLIGHTS FROM THE REVIEWS OF *The Letters of Samuel Beckett* *Volume I: 1929–1940*

"The most bracing read [of 2009] was *The Letters of Samuel Beckett, 1929–1940*, a portrait of the Dubliner as a young European with a hard gemlike gift for language, learning and mockery. Beckett's genius exercised itself most exuberantly in the correspondence with Thomas MacGreevy, another Irish poet more at home in Paris, his senior but his soulmate. Constantly Beckett is veering between certainty about his need to write and doubt about the results, all expressed in prose that is undoubting, delighted and demanding." Seamus Heaney in "Books of the year 2009," *The Times Literary Supplement*

"This edition of letters has been annotated with knowledge and care, using vast research. It will, for the most part, please admirers of Beckett's art and satisfy those who respect his wishes that only letters which have bearing on his work should appear." Colm Tóibín, *The London Review of Books*

"The editorial work behind this project has been immense in scale. Every book that Beckett mentions, every painting, every piece of music is tracked down and accounted for. His movements are traced from week to week. Everyone he alludes to is identified; his principal contacts earn potted biographies. When he writes in a foreign language, we are given both the original and an English translation . . . The standard of the commentary is of the highest . . . *The Letters of Samuel Beckett* is a model edition." J. M. Coetzee, *The New York Review of Books*

"One of the highlights of the year was the publication of *The Letters of Samuel Beckett Volume I: 1929–1940* . . . Every page is a hoot. Beckett comes across as even smarter, and more smarting, than one already knew." Paul Muldoon in "Books of the Year 2009," *The Times Literary Supplement*

"*Imagination Dead Imagine* is the title of one of his late pieces, but the point is that the Beckettian imagination continued lively to the very end. In that letter to Axel Kaun he placed himself on 'the road toward this, for me, very desirable literature of the non-word,' but a few lines later he states his program with a contrary succinctness: 'Word-storming in the name of beauty.' *The Letters of Samuel Beckett Volume I: 1929–1940* is a preliminary record of that storm." John Banville, *The New Republic*

"Can a writer's letters - occasional and ephemeral as these tend to be - really qualify as great literature? In Beckett's case, yes. For here is the most reticent of twentieth-century writers, one who refused to explain his plays and fictions, wrote almost no formal literary criticism, and refused to attend his own Nobel Prize ceremony - revealing himself in letter after letter as warm, playful, unfailingly polite even at his most vituperative and scatological, irreverent but never cynical, and, above all, a brilliant stylist whose learning is without the slightest pretension or preciosity." Marjorie Perloff, *Bookforum*

"This edition . . . is a triumph. The introductory and supplementary material is well judged and helpful, the annotations and identifications are tirelessly thorough. The later Beckett declared that 'every word is like an unnecessary stain on silence and nothingness,' but these letters are packed with wonderfully necessary words." Stefan Collini in "Books of the Year 2009", *The Times Literary Supplement*

"The editorial labor in this first volume is immensely impressive." Denis Donoghue, *The New Criterion*

"The first volume of Beckett's letters, *The Letters of Samuel Beckett Volume I: 1929–1940* (Cambridge), was the funniest, most intelligent and most poignant book I read this year, and since three more volumes are promised by Cambridge University Press we should be moved and entertained for some years to come." Gabriel Josipovici in "Books of the Year 2009," *The Times Literary Supplement*

"This first of a promised four volumes (to include 2,500 out of a total 15,000 items of correspondence) represents already a heroic achievement by the editors who embarked on the project nearly a quarter of a century ago . . . Each letter has demanded a dense undergrowth of notes in minuscule print, providing information on every allusion, every reference, even acknowledging where such information has been sought but not found . . . The editorial team deserves all our thanks for their patience, their stamina and their scholarly rigour." Nicholas Grene, *The Irish Times*

"An elating cultural moment is upon us. It is also a slightly surprising moment. Beckett, in his published output and authorial persona, was rigorously spare and self-effacing. Who knew that in his private writing he would be so humanly forthcoming? We always knew he was brilliant - but this brilliant? . . . The knowledge of what lay ahead for Beckett - the writing of the plays and the great prose fiction - makes one very impatient for the further volumes of letters, almost as if Beckett were in actual correspondence with oneself." Joseph O'Neill, *The New York Times Sunday Book Review* and *The International Herald Tribune*

HIGHLIGHTS FROM THE REVIEWS OF *The Letters of Samuel Beckett Volume II: 1941–1956*

"Here it is: just two years after the first volume, the second instalment of what promises to be one of the great productions of literary scholarship of our time, *The Letters of Samuel Beckett* . . . There is in this volume, Gunn tells us, 'a new absence of hostility and recrimination, a lack of grievance towards the world and its inhabitants.' That is true, and it is one of the reasons why this book is so much more enjoyable to read than the first volume . . . This magnificent volume of letters, so painstakingly prepared by the editors, takes us a bit closer to answering those questions." Nicholas Grene, *The Irish Times*

"Not to beat about the bush, here's the book of the year." David Sexton, *London Evening Standard*

"Few writers have been better served by their editors than Samuel Beckett. This sumptuous volume, *The Letters of Samuel Beckett Volume II: 1941–1956*, like its predecessor and the two that will follow, is beautifully designed and laid out, while the editorial apparatus includes lavishly detailed notes, yearly chronologies, an extensive biographical appendix and more than 90 pages of introductory matter, highlighted by a brilliant summary essay by editor Dan Gunn. The letters in French - at least half of them - are followed by English translations. Anyone who admires Beckett will want to read and own this book." Michael Dirda, *The Washington Post*

"This is the second volume of what looks set to be a major achievement of 21st-century publishing, an astonishing work of scholarship, appraisal and documentation . . . The erudite and indefatigable editors have put together an outstanding and illuminating selection from Beckett's correspondence with friends, acquaintances, publishers, translators, all kinds of business associates - all having a bearing, in some sense or other, on the imperishable work." Patricia Craig, *The Independent* (London)

"Few modernist writers speak with such intensity as Beckett does of what was his to love; or have felt so keenly the impossibility of speech and, at the same time, its beauties and exactions . . . The accompanying translations, introductions, notes . . . chronologies and profiles of the principal correspondents make of this volume, like its predecessor, an *embarras de richesses*. It is one for which we are greatly in the editors' debt." Alan Jenkins, *The Times Literary Supplement*

"One more masterly stroke in this landmark project . . . Whether the [subsequent] letters are as moving and entertaining as in the first two volumes remains to be seen. I for one can't wait." Gabriel Josipovici, *The Wall Street Journal*

"Annotated with generous and attentive scholarship . . . What is fascinating in these six hundred pages of correspondence with friends, lovers, publishers, translators, aspiring writers, critics and theatre directors, is the slow meshing in our minds of the Beckett narratives we know with the author's peculiar manner of dealing with people, and also with the aesthetic he sets out to define in pages of the most tortuous prose addressed to the art critic Georges Duthuit. The reader understands, that is, just how bound up with Beckett's personality the work is." Tim Parks, *The London Review of Books*

"A large proportion of the letters in this volume are in French. They are translated with scrupulous panache by George Craig, himself an Irishman, whose Englishing of Beckett's slangy and playful French is pitch-perfect, and whose sparkling 'Translator's Preface' is a highlight of the book . . . the personal, intimate affectionate side of Beckett is much in evidence . . . What these letters celebrate, and do justice to, is the sound of a unique voice, telling the truth." Roy Foster, *The New Republic*

"This is an important work of impeccable scholarship directed not only at Beckett academics but informed fans seeking the man behind *Godot*. This volume is a landmark in our quest to understand Beckett's great esoteric works and has definitely been worth the wait." Brian Odom, *Washington Independent Review of Books*

"Magisterially edited, with George Craig's splendid translations and Dan Gunn's really sensitive introductory essay, all forty pages of it, obvious highlights." John Pilling, *Journal of Beckett Studies*

"*The Letters of Samuel Beckett, Volume II: 1941–1956* is, like its predecessor, a model of editorial diligence and inspiration. The scholarly apparatus is impeccable. The range of citations of sources boggles the mind – is there *anything* these Four Masters have not followed up and tracked to its lair? And what a marvel the translator, George Craig, has wrought . . . No author, no letter-writer, could have been better served." John Banville, *The New York Review of Books*

THE LETTERS OF SAMUEL BECKETT

Volume I *The Letters of Samuel Beckett: 1929–1940*
Volume II *The Letters of Samuel Beckett: 1941–1956*
Volume III *The Letters of Samuel Beckett: 1957–1965*
Volume IV *The Letters of Samuel Beckett: 1966–1989*

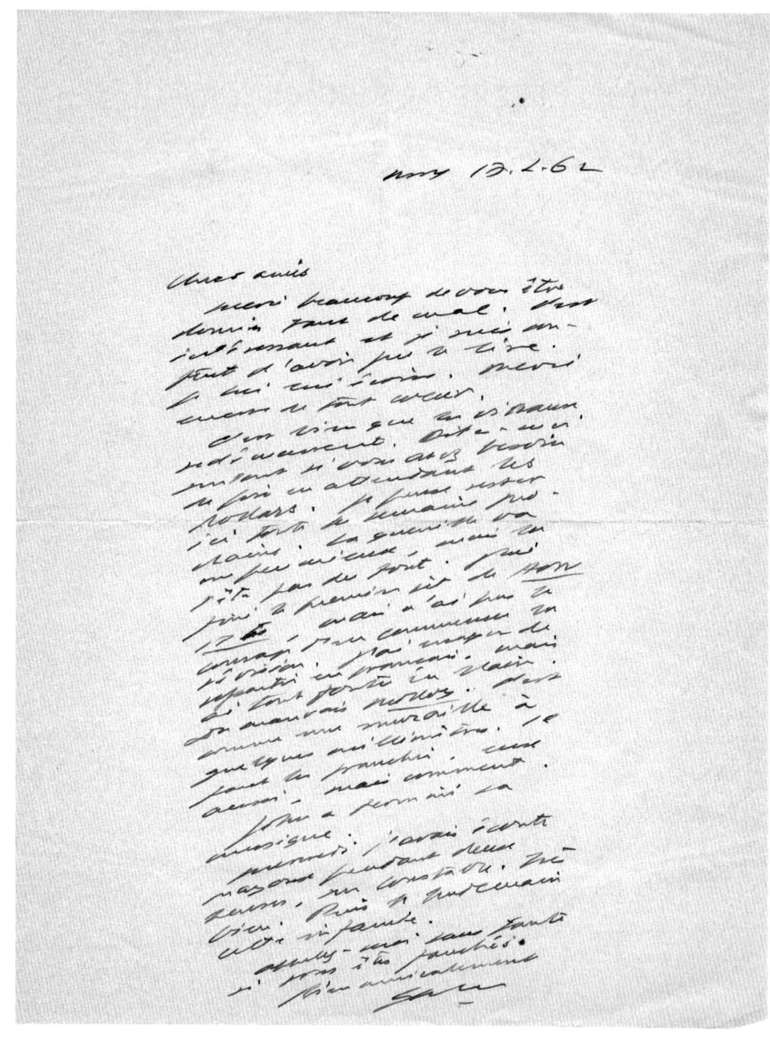

Letter from Samuel Beckett to Avigdor Arikha and Anne Atik,
17 February 1962.
Avigdor Arikha Collection, Lilly Library,
Indiana University, Bloomington, Indiana

THE LETTERS OF SAMUEL BECKETT

Volume III: 1957–1965

George Craig, *Editor and French Translator*

Martha Dow Fehsenfeld, *Founding Editor*

Dan Gunn, *Editor*

Lois More Overbeck, *General Editor*

CAMBRIDGE
UNIVERSITY PRESS

University Printing House, Cambridge CB2 8BS, United Kingdom

Cambridge University Press is part of the University of Cambridge.

It furthers the University's mission by disseminating knowledge in the pursuit of education, learning and research at the highest international levels of excellence.

www.cambridge.org

Information on this title: www.cambridge.org/9780521867955

First published 2014

Printed in the United States of America by Sheridan Books, Inc.

A catalogue record for this publication is available from the British Library

ISBN 978-0-521-86795-5 Hardback

Major support from The National Endowment for the Humanities (1991–1997, 2008–2011, 2011–2015) has facilitated the preparation of this edition. Any views, findings, or conclusions expressed in this publication do not necessarily reflect those of the National Endowment for the Humanities.

CONTENTS

ILLUSTRATIONS

GENERAL INTRODUCTION

Volume III of *The Letters of Samuel Beckett*, dealing as it does with the period 1957–1965, reveals a Beckett who, astonished by the critical and commercial success of his plays, finds himself having recourse more than ever before to letters as a way of conveying thoughts, intentions, projects, even aspirations, to his friends and to his ever more numerous colleagues and collaborators – as well as his by now customary doubts and hesitations, about his own work above all. Unlike its predecessor, Volume II, which began after the incomparably important interruption of the War years (during most of which Beckett was hardly able to write or send letters at all), the present volume's points of departure and of closure have something arbitrary about them: readers will find a continuity rather than a break with what comes before and after. Beckett, the author already known in France where he continues to reside, and internationally for the highly successful play *En attendant Godot* / *Waiting for Godot*, goes on during this period to become even more famous, even more admired – despite all his animadversions to the contrary – for this play and for the two long plays that follow it. The first, *Fin de partie* / *Endgame*, though already written by 1957, now receives its premiere; the second, *Happy Days* / *Oh les beaux jours*, occupies – from its composition to its staging – several of the central years and many of the central pages of the present volume. The playwright, recognized also for a series of challenging and obscure novels, goes on to translate much of his work, both from French into English and from English into French; he writes several more short prose works; and he writes an even more challenging novel, which is eventually given the title *Comment c'est* after much deliberation and discussion. He fears this work to be genuinely impenetrable, yet for him it represents the first major step out of an impasse in which he has felt trapped ever since completion of the third volume in his "trilogy" (a trilogy which, as he makes clear here, he did not wish to be called such), *L'Innommable* (*The Unnamable*). These are, after years of what were experienced as drought and blockage, years of comparative flow and expansiveness, years that see Beckett experimenting in new media too: radio, film, and later television.

There is, indeed, so much going on in Beckett's life during this period – so many productions, foreign visits, foreign guests, so many publications, translations, innovations – that it is at times hard for the reader of his letters to bear in mind the context within which Beckett was moving, the larger processes impinging upon the writer. There are at least two elements which merit mention here, not least because they appear only intermittently in the letters, and almost never in a manner that encourages Beckett himself to attempt an overview. The first of these is personal, and bears upon the possibility of having any sort of a *view*: the author's body, and the challenges it faces as it enters its fifties; Beckett's health problems affect his teeth, his ribs after he falls and breaks several of them, and most importantly of all – in that it afflicts a capacity crucial to a writer – his eyesight. The health worries – and they are set to become still more serious in the four years leading up to his being awarded the Nobel Prize in Literature in late 1969 – are the more worth mentioning here, in that Beckett himself, in stark contrast to his habit when he was a young man, when physical decrepitude was a major topic of his letters, makes only passing, and often joking, reference to his afflictions.

Nobody who has visited the archives to read Beckett's letters of this period in their original – or we should perhaps say *attempted to read* them – can fail to suspect that his weakening eyesight is a factor contributing to their illegibility. Not that his hand was ever an easy one to decipher; yet, aware of this, he referred to his own "foul fist" and could be seen to be making a conscious effort to write more legibly, or, better still from a reader's point of view, to use a typewriter. Whereas now – and the letters to Barbara Bray from the period of the present volume are the most extreme example of this in the entire corpus, nearly all of them being handwritten rather than typed – the words move across the page, frequently, in a series of strokes and flattening lines that it is hard to imagine even their author being able to discern clearly. And indeed Beckett admits as much, when, just two lines into a letter to Bray (on 17 October 1959) he writes: "At this point of my letter my eyes begin to go, an old trouble. It means a couple of hours mild migraine and semi-blindness. Never know why it comes on. I continue none the less, don't need a clear view of what I'm writing." That Beckett was able to write legibly is attested to by the very existence of the letters collected here, since they did reach their destination: the envelopes are almost invariably printed clearly. But deciphering has offered challenges to the editors beyond anything experienced heretofore, and has required hours and days and weeks of inspection, re-transcription, re-inspection, and re-re-transcription – indeed at times little short of inspiration – for the full text to reveal itself.

The second element in the larger context that it may be helpful to establish briefly here is not private, and it is one that appears only occasionally in the letters themselves, usually when Beckett is evincing concern for a friend. Whether one dates the origins of the war that pits France against those seeking Algerian independence to 1954, or later, what is certain is that these were violent years for anyone living, as Beckett did, in the French capital, years that led to what almost turned into civil war within France. The General Introduction to Volume II contained a section entitled "The War Years." Clearly, no event had anything like an impact upon Beckett that could compare with that of World War II (which also had the consequence for Beckett the correspondent of producing a four-year hiatus). Yet there is a sense in which "The War Years" would be a meaningful section header for the present volume too, since at least one half of the years covered here were marked, in France at least, by the fact – the brutal fact – of war.

From 1954, France was increasingly preoccupied with the rise of Algerian nationalism, its effects seen at first as no more than local skirmishing, but soon developing into a full-scale war, with the French Army pitted against the nationalists, above all the FLN (Front de Libération Nationale). France was recovering from the humiliating loss of its colonies in what was then called Indochina – Cambodia, Laos, and Vietnam – following the defeat of its Army at Dien Bien Phu. To many French people, Algeria was the most highly organized of its colonies, and its loss seemed unimaginable. The government of the day seemed powerless to control the situation, and in early 1958 there were rumours of a possible military coup in Metropolitan France (based on statements attributed to the parachutist General Massu, famous for having started one of these with the words "Moi, Général Massu," deliberately echoing an earlier historic speech by de Gaulle beginning "Moi, Général de Gaulle"). Responding to this crisis, General de Gaulle took power in May 1958, as he had done in the confusion of 1944. His military standing and unblemished reputation reassured many, but the violence continued, as did the tension between the large population of white settlers and the Algerian nationalists. As it became clear that the drive for independence might well succeed, many of the settlers, the "pieds noirs" as they were called, left Algeria for France, bitterly resentful, and convinced that they had been betrayed by their own government. They were not alone in thinking this.

Two factors emerged to create new dangers. One was evidence of the widespread use of torture by the French Army. The first overview came in Henri Alleg's *La Question* (1958, published by Jérôme Lindon and the Editions de Minuit). There followed book after book of personal testimony: the next was *La Gangrène* (1959), a collection of testimonies by tortured Algerian students, also published by Minuit. Both were seized by the authorities. The best known of these revelations was the earlier (1957) *Lieutenant en Algérie* by Jean-Jacques Servan-Schreiber, first Editor of the journal *L'Express*, who had been called up for service in Algeria. The effect of the overwhelming evidence was to divide the nation (in ways dismally reminiscent of the Dreyfus Affair), with conservative opinion on the side of the Army, and the views of intellectuals opposing that. The split was illustrated in the launching of a "Manifeste des 121," signed by that number of prominent intellectuals and artists opposed to the war, further inflaming conservative opinion.

The other important factor was the response of the "pieds noirs." The fiercest of them founded what in any other context would be called a "terrorist organization," the OAS (Organisation Armée Secrète). A catalogue of bomb attacks on those seen as sympathetic to the Algerian cause (and therefore anti-French) showed the lengths to which opponents of independence could go (even de Gaulle was not spared: the failed assassination evoked in *The Day of the Jackal* had a real basis). Two obvious targets were Lindon and the Editions de Minuit, subjected as they were to both legal process (he himself was charged with damaging Army morale) and direct attack by bombs. Others suffering similar attacks included academics such as Jean-Jacques Mayoux. Both these men were friends of Beckett; neither had been a political activist, both were motivated by principle. The recurrent expression of these ideological and political differences in public demonstrations brought in another factor: the almost ineradicable anti-Left attitudes of the police – even a conservative newspaper like *Le Figaro* could speak of the manifest enthusiasm with which the police attacked demonstrators. (One of the editors remembers a Philosophy student at the Ecole Normale Supérieure who took judo lessons solely in order to find a way of surviving the police treatment of demonstrators, especially young ones, all assumed to be "leftist.")

Beckett's characteristic reticence about public affairs cannot conceal the fact that these were years of real terror, not just in Paris. Memories of the Occupation were still fresh for all except the young, but the streets of the capital now were again dangerous, and the fate of the country worrying. Nothing changed until 1962, when the Accords d'Evian were signed and Algeria was granted independence. The war had ended, but not the divisions. Even Beckett with his characteristic reticence touches on the dire reality of those days, as when he speaks of Suzanne and himself listening out for the latest outrage, "the two of us with our ears glued to Europe No. 1 every hour," for a bulletin that might well signal a military coup; or mentions, to another friend, "Here apparently all quiet again. Tanks etc. gone. Great sigh of relief on coming back late from Odéon last night and hearing news on radio."[1] (That "Tanks etc. gone" must rank as one of Beckett's most remarkable understatements.) There were solid grounds for apprehension. In a desperate attempt to wrest control of Algeria from the French government, four senior officers rebelled on 22 April 1961, claiming that Algiers was now under their exclusive command: Generals Challe, Salan, Zeller (Army), and Jouhaud (Air Force). General de Gaulle invoked Emergency Powers and warned the French people of possible attacks. Support for the Government was widespread and immediate. Faced by this, Challe surrendered on 26 April.

For an understanding of these years, the three essential contextual factors are: (a) from the Algerian side, the gradual strengthening of the militant FLN, after bitter internal struggles among Algerian groups, and in particular its violent opposition to the French treatment of Algerian immigrants; (b) on the French side, the similarly violent response of the Paris police to any dissident, anti-Government activity by Algerians; and (c) the growing importance of the at least equally violent OAS in its total rejection of the idea of Algerian independence, before – and still more after – the signing of the Accords d'Evian, the official end of the war. The activities of the opposition, however fierce, were, of course, non-violent: letters, demonstrations, articles and editorials in the press, books. Each day brought new violence and new responses, not only from professional commentators, academics, and writers, but from priests, teachers, even serving soldiers. The testimony of many of these can be found in *Les belles lettres*, a remarkable, and deeply moving book put together by Charlotte Delbo, a survivor of Auschwitz, and published by the Editions de Minuit. Among the contributors, many previously unknown, are Jean-Paul Sartre, Claude Simon, and Graham

1 Letter to Robert Pinget, 6 February 1960; letter to Barbara Bray of 26 April 1961.

Greene. This was the world in which Beckett was living and working; it is hard not to see a grim relevance in the title of the novel he was writing at this time, *Comment c'est* (*How It Is*).

RESEARCH FOR VOLUME III

As the range and number of Beckett's contacts grows in the period presented here, so too have those of the editors, in their search first to locate the author's letters, then to understand the matter and people to which they make reference. In addition to the numerous libraries and archives mentioned in the Acknowledgments, the editors were often fortunate to receive help from the recipients of Beckett's letters themselves – more in the case of this volume than of earlier ones, for obvious reasons. The painter Avigdor Arikha, for example, in the two years before his death in 2010, devoted much time, and his remarkable memory, to assisting with comprehension of the context of the letters Beckett had addressed to him – assistance that was subsequently extended by his widow, the poet Anne Atik. Judith Schmidt worked in the Grove Press Record archives at Syracuse University alongside the editors before the Grove Press papers were fully catalogued. This was especially helpful as she understood the various stages of publication at the press; Beckett's letters were scattered throughout files related to translation, production, publicity, and reprint and performance rights.

SELECTION, PRESENTATION, AND ANNOTATION

While the principles guiding the editors' selection of the letters to be included in the edition are set out in full in Volume I, it may be helpful to indicate how these principles play out here, where the sheer quantity of materials is so much greater than it was in the early years of Beckett's correspondence. Where Volume I printed approximately 60 percent of the total corpus for the years 1929–1940, and Volume II approximately 40 percent for 1941–1956, here the percentage is a little over 20 percent. It can of course be hard for readers, keen to have access to every word Beckett wrote, to accept that so much has had to be sacrificed. And as it is hard for readers to enjoy the sacrifices, so it can be easy – certain reviews of Volume II indulged in this – to weave elaborate fantasies about the content of what has been lost: Beckett's letters on cricket, his love letters, his letters to his wife, and so on. It behoves the editors to be categorical in stating: first, that the option that might satisfy the truly hungry Beckett reader – doing a complete letters – was not one they had (not least for the obvious reason that it is too soon for this to be achieved, with letters still surfacing today); second, that they have not suppressed, or in the case of this volume been asked to suppress, any letters whatsoever; and third, that it is not the case (as certain reviewers of earlier volumes assumed) that by the current edition access is blocked to the corpus of letters that have *not* been selected, most of which exist in archives (signalled here) to which the truly curious and determined have access. The editors' choice, it should be repeated, has been made on the basis not of what to exclude, but of what best to *include*: while the latter implies the former, certainly, it nonetheless forms a different basis on which to work. This is so much the case, and the richness of materials is so great during the late 1950s and the 1960s, that the editors have chosen to restrict the range of the present volume to fewer years than originally advertised, ending in 1965 and not, as was earlier announced, in 1967.

This is an edition of Beckett's letters organized according to principles laid down by the author himself before his death, when he asked that letters "having bearing upon my work" be chosen. While the significance of this phrase "bearing upon my work" is endlessly debatable – especially with a writer such as Beckett for whom writing is never a profession but a need, a compulsion even, and where the work and the life are so inseparable – it is not the case that the selection made by the editors has been subject to other occult criteria. There is only a certain number of letters that can fit into four volumes, and in the present case into the nearly 900 pages between the front and the back covers. In response to a few examples that provoked speculation with respect to Volume II, let it be stated again (as it was there): if there are no letters here to the woman Beckett marries during the period covered by the present volume, Suzanne Deschevaux-Dumesnil, this is not because they have been removed by the editors or by the Beckett family, as being judged too private or revelatory; it is rather because, quite simply, these letters do not exist, to the best of the knowledge of both editors and the Beckett family. That Beckett wrote to his partner-then-wife is a certainty; that these letters no longer exist appears, if not a certainty, then at least a very strong probability.

When making their selection, the editors have understood "the work" to be above all the work *literary*. For of course during this period, as a direct consequence of his rapidly increasing popularity, there is an ever growing mass of letters that need to be written about other sorts of work – work that Beckett must do, however reluctantly. Though he may never have thought of himself as having a "career," he nonetheless does find himself having to manage what to all intents and purposes looks like a career. There are letters to be sent to agents, to publishers he barely knows, to actors he has never met, to enquirers looking for comment on countless subjects on which he has no wish to pronounce. Of the letters not selected for inclusion in the present volume, a high proportion bear upon that aspect of Beckett's work for which the author himself has little taste and at which he often confesses himself hopelessly incompetent, letters which may be summarized in the single word: *business*. This includes scores of letters about contracts, fees, royalties, manuscript sales, and so on. It is not that such letters, written by Beckett for whom no letter was ever wholly perfunctory, are entirely without interest; the information gleaned from them has been indispensable in establishing many of the notes to the letters which were indeed included. Rather, it is that such letters were judged to be less significant acts of writing in their own right, less in themselves literary, than many others, and in this sense less relevant to or revealing of the real *work*.

Rather less clear, and the subject of many letters that have been included as well as of many that have not, is that work which Beckett puts in, not to the composition of this or that story, novel, or play, but to the ways in which these are produced and disseminated. This can go from consideration of book covers, to inclusion of illustrations in his novels, to selection of a font or page size, to the choice of an actor for a particular role in one of his dramas, of a theatre director, or indeed of a theatre: choice, then, of the myriad other elements, as Beckett becomes more and more drawn toward the practicalities of directing his own plays, that turn a play from words on the page into an event on the stage. The quantity of letters in the corpus for this period dealing with matters theatrical is large. The editors have sought to provide a selection that is representative, that enables some narrative continuity to be achieved (and thereby a minimizing of the footnotes), that illustrates the vacillations in Beckett's own attitudes to his deepening involvement in theatre (from fascinated absorption at one extreme to disgusted rejection of the entire world of theatre at the other extreme), and that reveals how deeply enmeshed his affective life becomes with individuals – his preferred actors, of course, but also his producers and directors and set-designers – who themselves live in and for the theatre.

Fortunately, to offset all the work in the world, there is work in the room and on the page, most frequently carried out in the small house in Ussy-sur-Marne to which Beckett retreats. This is, as the Introduction to Volume III makes clear, a period of great and determined productivity for Beckett, often experienced by him as a return to basics, to essentials, to the writing that needs to be committed to paper for his other more worldly dealings to continue to matter. In letter after letter, and with an explicitness and consistency that is unprecedented in his correspondence, Beckett discusses his work in progress – or in regress as he regularly characterizes it, as he destroys draft after draft in order to start over again.

The relative openness with which Beckett writes about his own work here, when added to his increasing familiarity and friendship with many of his correspondents, as well as to the fact that an increasing number of his friends know each other, has two consequences in the presentation of the letters in this volume, of which the reader should be advised. The first consequence, and the less demanding of a reader's attention, is that Beckett makes many more allusions than he did previously to individuals whom he presumes his addressee to know, at times practically giving lists of friends and colleagues he has recently encountered. Letters in English preponderate in the present volume, and adding to the informality is the fact that in English the first name was (and still is) used more readily than in French, as well as the fact that standard practice in both languages over the decades has moved in the direction of greater informality. The result is a veritable proliferation of first names (and occasionally nicknames). It would quickly become tedious were every first name to receive a footnote indicating the family name, yet even an attentive reader can easily forget who is "George" or "Anne." It was judged prudent, therefore, to offer an index of first or familiar names, with surnames following, in the Appendix. It is hoped that in the cases of "Jean" (which can be the French male as it can be the English female first name) and of John (where there are four "John"s to whom Beckett refers), the context will make the individual's identity clear. Where there is a chance of doubt, the editors have erred on the side of caution and offered a footnote.

The second consequence of the increased informality, openness, and frequency of Beckett's letters is that it becomes harder – downright impracticable – to annotate each letter individually, as a discrete entity. Certain discussions, as for example the elaboration of *Comment c'est*, run for more than a year, while discussions of the production of *Warten auf*

Godot in Berlin in 1965 may not last as long but are spread over numerous correspondents. The editors have chosen to presume that, while a reader may sometimes wish to dip in and sample a letter here or there, the bulk of readers will wish to read sequentially; and that, therefore, an issue under discussion, whether a novel being written and re-written or a play being pulled apart as it is being produced, need not be explained or cross-referenced every time it appears. So, for example, when on 20 May 1961 Beckett says, "Poor John is still up to his neck in plaster, and will be for a long time yet," it is presumed that the reader will remember that it is John Beckett who has been injured in a car accident. When Jean-Jacques Mayoux's apartment is bombed in February 1962, the incident is given a full note in the first reference to it, in a letter to Mayoux himself; it goes footnote-free in subsequent mentions in letters to others. Beckett begins his letter of 30 March 1958 to Alan Schneider by saying he is "glad you like the monologue," and goes on to give several indications concerning his current work. As most of the explanatory details have already been furnished in previous letters (including those of 26 February and 7 March to Donald McWhinnie), the information is not given twice. The implication should be clear: the reader's first instinct, when something is judged insufficiently explicit in a letter or footnote, should be to read, or re-read, the letters immediately preceding; failing this, the Index of first names, as already mentioned, is there to help identify individuals; and this in turn can be supplemented by the Index proper which can further assist in the tracking of an individual's path through the volume.

There is one final aspect to Beckett's range of relationships that merits mention here, generative as it has been of hesitation and debate on the part of the editors - an awkwardness indeed (and one that pertains not only to Beckett). It is simply: how to call - what name to give to - the women who enter his life, when these women are more than "merely" friends or acquaintances? In 1961, Beckett marries the woman he has been living with since shortly before the Second World War, Suzanne Deschevaux-Dumesnil: the "companion" or "partner" becomes the "wife," that much is so ostensibly uncontroversial; though to anyone interested primarily in the biographical, even this simple fact and the terms it implies will beg for qualification. What name to give to the status of the woman he meets early in the present volume, Barbara Bray, with whom he will continue to spend at least part of his days and weeks and years up until his death in 1989? His "companion"? His "lover"? His "mistress"? His "principal mistress" (as one biographer of Beckett has called her)? Then, what name to give to the figure to whom he is increasingly drawn in the final year of the present volume, Jocelyn Herbert, and to whom he will become intimately attached in 1966? Then again, what name to give to the man in Jacoba van Velde's life when Beckett is writing to her during the years covered by the volume, or to the woman with whom Beckett's American publisher Barney Rosset was involved at the start of 1957? The modern resonances of the available terms, *companion/lover/partner/man-friend/mistress* (this last lacking its male counterpart), can be misleading. The editors have therefore gone back and forth, trying this term and then that, finally admitting a defeat whose sting has been mitigated only by their sense that defeat is perhaps inevitable when writing of an era when private lives could remain largely private, and when the individuals involved, not least Beckett himself, seem to have deployed considerable energy in attempting to prevent any of the convenient appellations from hardening into life-sentences.

Editorial policy has been, here as in earlier volumes, to publish certain letters that have already been published (often in less than ideal transcriptions), such as letters to Alan Schneider or to Barney Rosset. However, the fact of a letter's being publicly available in print has added a further chance of this letter's *not* being included, unless seen to be of particular interest – an interest offered here not least by the new context provided by the letters written to others that now surround it.

As in previous volumes, letters are presented here as they were written, and include Beckett's idiosyncratic spelling, his omissions – for example of diacritics in French (parait-il for paraît il, ca for ça) – and his punctuation preferences. There are frequent misspellings of proper names: McGowran for MacGowran; Jérome for Jérôme; Gauthier for Gautier; Hüsserl for Husserl. Beckett frequently uses a surname of a couple in the singular, sometimes following French practice to identify the couple, sometimes to identify only one of the couple: the Gilbert, the Hayden, the Barrault.

The letters, that is to say, appear as they were received, in their final state, by those to whom they were sent. Only when a correction made by Beckett is judged as being of special significance is the correction noted. Throughout, the editors have endeavoured to interrupt the flow of the letters as rarely and as little as possible. Their choice of whether to remark on an oddity within the body of a letter, using square brackets (as in [*for* clearer] or [sic]) or to relegate a comment or correction to a footnote has largely been dictated by this principle of minimizing interruption. Where the editors cannot be certain, either of their reading of a word or of an intended Beckett name or term, their interpolation is preceded by a question mark. Only in the case of letters from authors other than Beckett have trivial errors, such as typos, been silently corrected. In this volume, unlike in Volume II which contained whole letters from Suzanne Deschevaux-Dumesnil, all letters are from Beckett's own hand. However, some contain passages written by others, and these are signalled by their appearing in italics. Beckett received lists of questions, particularly from translators and bibliographers, and he often wrote his replies directly on the pages containing the lists; the questions are presented here in italics, and Beckett's responses in roman.

Every letter has, preceding it, the name of its addressee as well as of the place to which it was sent (where this is known). The date on which, and the place in which, the letter was composed are given as written, as is Beckett's signature. Postscripts appear after the signature, with their placement noted if it differs from this. A note following each letter provides a description of the physical document and of its current whereabouts. There follows, where relevant, a note concerning the letter's previous publication and an explanation of the date assigned to the letter where this is not explicit. Dating and place supplied by the editors are given within square brackets, with uncertainties acknowledged.

Where in previous volumes the editors' selection of letters and passages was not always accepted by the Samuel Beckett Estate, for this volume responsibility for the selection lies solely with the editors.

LACUNAE

While the editors have built up a corpus of copies of nearly 20,000 letters written by Samuel Beckett, it is certainly the case that there remain letters by and to him which have not yet surfaced. There are also certain – fortunately few – collections to which the editors have had no, or only limited, access. Such is the case with two letters to William York Tindall, Professor at Columbia University. In 1963, Tindall sent questions which appear to have been answered by Beckett in two parts. These letters are now in unidentified private hands, so the editors cannot consult, still less quote from, these. By far the most important collection to which the editors have not had access is constituted by the more than 300 letters addressed to Josette and Henri Hayden, sold at auction by Sotheby's in 2008. Through intermediaries, the editors have repeatedly asked the purchaser of this collection for access to it. Regrettably for the entire community of readers of Beckett, this access has been denied by the current owner, whose identity remains unknown both to the editors and to the Beckett Estate.

FRENCH TRANSLATOR'S PREFACE

Volume II of *The Letters of Samuel Beckett* began with Beckett in hiding in Unoccupied France, with no reliable means of support. Volume III brings a Beckett who has had four major prose works in French published, and one play both published and staged (the three *nouvelles*, the sequence of novels *Molloy, Malone meurt, L'Innommable*; *En attendant Godot*) – all to the astonished acclaim of serious critics: first in France; later, after translation, in England and the US. The play in particular will, after a shaky start, go on to draw audiences worldwide. What effect does all this have on Beckett's language?

The very words "Beckett's language" face me at once, as his translator, with a central question; might indeed be said to beg the question. In Volume II we were allowed, indeed required, to follow Beckett in the slow working out of his determination to write for publication in French. The size and quality of his achievement in the early 1950s might seem to have settled the issue: Beckett the anglophone writer has become a francophone writer. Neat, but profoundly mistaken. That there has been a change is obvious; how we are to understand this change, rather less so; how I as translator am to understand it, still less – even though it is of the first importance. One crude but useful way of representing the change might be to say that it is a move from "How does one say this in French?" to "How do the French say this?" This second phase is often referred to as "thinking in the new language", in this case French. A better formulation might be "How what to say in French stopped depending on translation from English." This has the advantage of keeping the word "translation" in front of me, because, in the case of Beckett, language (words, sentences) that has achieved this independence poses for the translator the same problem in reverse: how would Beckett the English-speaker have expressed this? The very fact of his investment in French brings me up against a fundamental but far more difficult question: what is Beckett's relation to either language? There is no neat answer here, but the letters keep in front of us the importance of the issue. Beckett the correspondent must open himself – daily, one might say – to the demands of both languages. There is no escaping the feelings that this generates. Taking up this language rather than that (even when the choice is forced on him from outside) is not like taking up this pen or that; it is re-entering each time a whole world structured by memory and desire.

Beckett himself, of course, enters the lists from time to time with what look very much like "neat answers" – famously, the dismissal of English that readers of Volume II will remember: "Horrible langue, que je sais encore trop bien" (Horrible language, which I still know too well).[1] I soon learned to be wary of these declarations. Consider, for example, the following three short statements. First, "If I am to do any more work in the coming years, and nothing at the moment seems less likely, I think it will be in English for the 3rd [Programme]."[2] Then this: "I feel no new work on the way. When it comes, if it does, it will almost certainly be in French."[3] And finally: "I'm trying to write in English, but to little purpose."[4] Examples could be multiplied. An obvious and easy explanation offers itself: he is telling some sort of story in order to get these people off his back.

But it won't do: there is indeed a "story", but it is the story he himself is caught up in. Easier even than lining up these apparent hesitations would be chronicling the unfavourable, hostile, occasionally vitriolic judgements he makes on his work. So pervasive is this that I have found myself setting it aside, and recognising that Beckett is a poor guide to his own work. Consider these examples, all concerning *Krapp's Last Tape*. First, a reference to the monologue, just written, which will become the play: "rather a sentimental affair in my best original English manner".[5] Then, in a letter to his American publisher, Barney Rosset: "In English I hate my guts and in French nothing more is possible."[6] Finally, when he has produced a French version (*La dernière bande*), this to a friend: "This evening I am having a reading with Blin of Krapp. Reading over the text this afternoon I thought it stank of translation."[7]

As he sees it – so differently from his readers – he is reluctantly engaged in a struggle that he knows he will never win, and is directly aware only

1 SB to Georges Duthuit, [? 28 June 1949].

2 SB to A. J. Leventhal and Ethna MacCarthy-Leventhal, 13 June 1957.

3 SB to Brendan Smith, [after 21 August 1957] (GEU, MSS 1221).

4 SB to Donald McWhinnie, 23 December 1957.

5 SB to Donald McWhinnie, 7 March 1958.

6 SB to Barney Rosset, 10 March 1958.

7 SB to Barbara Bray, 18 February 1960.

of how far his attempts fall short, as in this: "Sometimes I think I'm getting on, then realise how far I am from it still."[8] Or again this: "how sick and tired I am of translations and what a losing battle it is always".[9] And so he goes back once again to gardening – until the next time. In this perspective, even the notion of hesitation (with its hint of feebleness, dithering) has to be seriously modified. For Beckett there is, literally, no knowing what form the next prompting will take – if, that is, and as he will often say, there *is* another prompting. Moreover, when something does stir and he starts to write, there is no unstoppable flow. The new "work" is often abandoned, consigned to the waste-paper basket. Small wonder that he chooses as one of his titles "From an Abandoned Work".

But it is not only the general notion "my work" that undergoes this corrosive scrutiny. The two languages in which most of Beckett's work is written are also areas of intermittent uncertainty. In the euphoria of post-War freedom, he is flooded with French and it emerges gloriously in stories, novels, and plays. But, particularly when success comes, there can be no question of English falling away; not least since translation of the French texts brings a great increase in the number of serious anglophone correspondents. Just how the pull of the two languages, given his close relation with each, affects his judgement is evident from the glimpse he gives Alan Schneider of a work then in gestation: "I don't see the play at all clearly, but a little more so. The figure is a woman as far as I can see . . . I should like to try it in English but fear it will have to be French again."[10] And then we have the overwhelming *naturalness* of an utterance that draws on his awareness of the resources of the two languages – and of that third language which is his own writing. Two brief illustrations, both taken from a letter to the American academic Herbert Myron: the first where he speaks of "2 short pieces comportant musique by Mihalovici and John Beckett". The second has him, as he ends the letter, "Crawling out in the Homer mauve for a coupe and a blather at the Closerie" (the "Homer mauve" an adaptation of his own "Homer dusk", from the poem "Dortmunder"; the French "coupe" for the intended champagne; and the Irish colloquial "blather", or unrestrained chat).[11] As an Irishman I am tempted to say (restrainedly): "Choice of language, how are you?"

8 SB to Barbara Bray, 11 March 1959.
9 SB to Thomas MacGreevy, 30 January 1957 (TCD, MS 10402/202).
10 SB to Alan Schneider, 23 September 1960 (Burns Library, Samuel Beckett Collection, SB-AS).
11 SB to Herbert Myron, 18 September 1963.

Of course, the naturalness I have mentioned has its own drawbacks: the very ease with which the words come, in letters to people with whom Beckett is at ease, may turn off the internal scanner and let through words (or non-words) that do not quite fit – the set-designer he refers to as a "decorator" (the French "décorateur"); or the reference to the "diffusion" of a book when what he has in mind is its distribution or promotion.[12] It would be easy to lump these and other examples together under the label "Gallicism", but here I must tread carefully. One of the more obvious connotations of that word is "mistake"; I shall, I think, be well advised to look again before getting out the red pen or blue pencil. The "naturalness" of which I spoke affects a wide range of unusual words and constructions: from outright play (the unforgettable "abusive stationing," "stationnement abusif," parking offence) or the equally show-stopping "vows of prompt re-establishment" ("voeux de prompt rétablissement", wishes for a rapid recovery), to private preference: his occasional use of "renounce", as against "give up".[13] Sometimes indeed I am aware only of the presence of oddity, not, or at least not immediately, of what it is that is odd; as when, speaking of an actress's unimpressive performance, he says that it was "competent – without more".[14] For a moment I look about for another word, some substantive (more *what*?), before seeing that the description is based on "sans plus", literally "without more", where expectable English usage would have been "no more". A more obtrusive example (again rooted in private preference) is his frequent use of "(in) function of".[15] One strives to accommodate such forms, although in this case the expression, unnoticeable in educated French, does strain English usage. It is not that these oddities strike one as "mistakes"; rather one finds oneself wondering if, after all, the usage might not in fact be acceptable – made so, indeed, by Beckett's adoption of it. And all the time the sense that he knows exactly what he is doing, as when, referring to the work of an inept translator, he says "as traduced by".[16]

Above all, as translator, I must guard against the condescension of seeing these cases as instances of carelessness. Beckett never stops

12 SB to Reinhart Müller-Freienfels, 22 October 1965; SB to Christian Ludvigsen, 11 June 1957 (Ludvigsen Collection).

13 SB to Barbara Bray, 19 March 1960; SB to Thomas MacGreevy, 23 October 1961; SB to Barbara Bray, 28 October 1960.

14 SB to Matti Megged, 3 December 1962.

15 See, e.g., SB to Alan Simpson, 14 January 1957, SB to Barbara Bray, 17 November 1958.

16 SB to Barbara Bray, 6 September 1962 (TCD, MS 10948/1/192).

thinking about translation, whether his own or someone else's, and some of his reflections take us into a curious no-man's-land; a zone where there are no simple "rights" or "wrongs". It is worth considering one extended example. Beckett was so admiring of the work of the young Robert Pinget that he offered to translate one of his plays for BBC Radio and subsequent publication, and went on to do so. He is, predictably, uneasy about what he has done, and writes: "I shd. prefer if possible to avoid the word 'translation'. Perhaps 'English text' or just 'English' by SB. For Lindon's edition I'll put 'version anglaise' or 'texte anglais', not 'traduit par'."[17] Writing a few days later to Pinget himself, he puts it this way: "On ne peut pas dire 'traduit par', c'est vraiment trop libre. Es-tu d'accord avec 'texte anglais'? Suzanne aimerait mieux 'version anglaise', ça a un petit remugle scolaire qui me deplaît. Inutile de te dire que ma traduction ne me satisfait pas."[18] ("We can't say 'translated by': it's really too free. Can you agree to 'English text'? Suzanne would prefer 'English version', but that has a fusty schoolroom air that I dislike. No need to tell you that my translation doesn't satisfy me.") The final strand of this knot is in the reference to Suzanne's preference and Beckett's response to it, "schoolroom" and all: the technical name, in French schools and universities, for the exercise of translating into French, is 'version' (as contrasted with the translation of French into another language: "thème"). Outside the schoolroom context, these French words function exactly like their English equivalents "version" and "theme". Caveat traductor – atque lector.

It should go without saying that explicit references to and discussion of translation abound in the letters, but there is more than one reason for my drawing attention to them here. The first and most obvious one is the evidence of Beckett's own (predictably unflattering) view of his work as translator, memorably summarised in a Volume II letter: "my English is rusty, but I simply happen to be able still to write the queer kind of English that my queer French deserves".[19] And once at least we are given a glimpse of Beckett's response to the coexistence of English and French versions of his work: "I am not keen on bilingual edition either of the novels or the plays, but would not oppose it if my publishers agree it is desirable. It suggests an invitation to consider the work as a linguistic curiosity, or an adventure in self-translation, which does not

17 SB to Barbara Bray, 4 February 1960.
18 SB to Robert Pinget, 6 February 1960.
19 SB to Cyril Lucas, 4 January 1956.

appeal to me."[20] Once again, as in my earlier reference to Beckett's harsh judging of his own work, I am made aware of the gap between his experience and that of his readers. Will there really be verbal antique-dealers to hold up for dispassionate inspection this "linguistic curiosity"? I think not.

The second major reason why the continual reference to translation matters here is of course that it runs hard up against my own experience as translator. I do not simply stand by and chronicle or watch what Beckett does: every move of his requires a move of mine. The fact that many of these moves concern precisely what I am engaged in is the kind of irony that all translators will recognise: this is the translator as (more or less) dutiful servant, attentive only to His Master's Voice. Of course all I can capture is what I hear: my sense of what that voice is saying. This is *my* "adventure in translation".

But, precisely because all these references are, or appear to be, to textual matters, they focus attention on the page: on what we *read*. With Beckett, however, we are always involved in more than visual scanning. Here is a – by now famous – sentence to remind us forcibly of how much more: "My work is a matter of fundamental sounds (no joke intended), made as fully as possible, and I accept responsibility for nothing else."[21] The spoken dimension is everywhere in the published work – the prose works as well as the plays – but it matters too in the letters, and matters therefore in my attempt to translate them. A phrase quoted a little earlier makes the point: Beckett, writing to his friend Tom MacGreevy, "how sick and tired I am of translations and what a losing battle it is always". No one will have any difficulty in understanding it, but it contains one tiny oddity: the ending, with "always" as the final word, rather than the more expectable penultimate one. This, as so often in Beckett's letters, and always in those to Irish correspondents, is a *spoken* sentence: steady but perceptible rise to "losing battle", slight drop for "it is", bigger drop to "always". If I am to catch Beckett's meaning, I must listen out for his *voice*. Whatever he writes will also have been *said*. In the plays, this saying is of course crucial, the central reality. It is also an essential part of Beckett's work with his actors (even with Patrick Magee, whom he trusts and admires, he will find it necessary to "point" the text); but in everything he writes, including the letters, I must never lose . . . no: not "sight" – *sound* of it. Arranging my

20 SB to Peter du Sautoy, 17 April 1965.
21 SB to Alan Schneider, 29 December 1957.

words on the page is inviting, not just attention, but a particular enunciation.

This brings up, or brings back, the question of Beckett's English: specifically, the question of its greater or lesser Irishness. It is one that Beckett himself raises, as when, writing to the critic J. W. Lambert, he says: "I have not yet got down to the englishing, or anglo-irishing of *Fin de partie*."[22] Let us be clear, though. This does not signal for the translator that he should set about deploying "Begorrahs" and "Top of the mornings"; *Fin de partie*, like all Beckett texts, is the work of someone who loathed all forms of fake or self-conscious Irishry. What is at issue is not vocabulary but sentence-construction based on speech rhythms. Moreover, would a nimble polyglot be likely to produce a text which could be labelled on national lines, or seen as simply alien? Only very seldom do we find an expression which might bring the reader up short, as in the following example, from one of the *nouvelles*. An unnamed narrator, finding himself outside his house and wondering why he has gone there, asks "Was I hungry itself?"[23] The question requires a fixed pattern of utterance, rising in pitch from "Was" to the first syllable of "hungry", then falling away. It is this pattern which determines the meaning, taking in the unexpected (by English standards) "itself". That meaning could be put as "might it even be possible that I was hungry? Could that be the reason?" Instances such as this, needing explanation, are as I say rare. Most "departures" are of the kind shown in the example above, of "always" as the final word. It is this constant awareness of spoken values that matters in the "anglo-irishing" I am attempting, not, *above all* not the evoking of Ireland.

What I need to get to lies well below the surface text. I quoted just now Beckett's dismissive comment, on *La dernière bande*: it "stank of translation." The verb, forceful enough as it stands, hits harder in its echo of a much earlier cognate: Beckett's reaction (as far back as 1931) to a re-reading of *More Pricks Than Kicks*, where he was distressed to find "the stink of Joyce."[24] Here we touch on the long processes that took him away from Joyce, away above all from the temptations of verbal facility: of language as display. More is involved than breaking with habit or youthful readiness to show off, clinging as it were to Joyce's coat-tails. At work within him is the long elaboration of an aesthetic

22 SB to J. W. Lambert, 25 January 1957 (Bodleian, Ms Eng. C.2291, f.12).

23 "The Calmative," 26. It is worth noting that the French has the quite unexceptional "avais-je seulement faim?"

24 SB to Charles Prentice, 15 August 1931.

that is totally un-Joycean and based, not on inclusiveness but on ascesis: the aim of finding the fewest and simplest words to say what has to be said. As he puts it to Barbara Bray: "I only try to say as little more than I find as possible, that doesn't sound right somehow, and as little less."[25] One of the many factors indeed that led to his investment in French is that he would not have immediate access to the sort of huge word-hoard that he had in English. And if one had to name the French writer that best exemplified his new ideal, it would not be Flaubert, or Mallarmé, but Racine ("There too nothing happens, they just talk, but what talk, and how spoken", he says of a radio performance of *Bérénice*.)[26] Writing to Barbara Bray, he talks of "trying to find the rhythm and syntax of extreme weakness, penury perhaps I should say". He reacts with delight to another broadcast, of a work by a younger contemporary, then little known: "I heard on the air last week *Le Square* by Marguerite Duras . . . It is quite extraordinary. Just a little skivvy and a tired commercial sitting in a public square. No action whatsoever. Most marvellous and moving dialogue."[27] Such unqualified praise from Beckett is rare in the extreme – but then such spareness is itself rare. And I am sure he will have noticed how the "skivvy" and the "commercial" stand in for Racine's queen and king.

But if Beckett cannot be said to "possess" French in the way he does English, he writes now with total – and justified – assurance. And the word-hoard still has its uses. In the course of his translation of *Comment c'est* into *How It Is*, he finds seven different ways of rendering the phrase "si l'on veut": "if you want"; "at a pinch"; "manner of speaking"; "no objection"; "if you prefer"; "if it be kindly"; and "if you like."[28] And then three renderings of "A la bonne heure!": "cheers"; "God be praised"; and "bravo."[29] Quite apart from the intrinsic interest of the choices he makes, these examples, in their number and range, make abundantly clear Beckett's continuing attention to detail and nuance.

For the most part, I can hope to keep up with him, but some of what is in the letters simply defeats my attempts at translation: moments when Beckett identifies the precise phrasing that one language or the other offers him. This may be serious, as in the following example, where he

25 SB to Barbara Bray, 4 February 1959.

26 SB to Thomas MacGreevy, 27 September 1953.

27 SB to Alan Simpson, 14 January 1957.

28 *Comment c'est*, 65, 106, 151, 164, 192, 203, 208. *How It Is* (Grove) 42, 68, 96, 106, 123, 131, and 134.

29 *Comment c'est*, 67, 111, 162. *How It Is* (Grove), 43, 71, 105.

reaches back in memory: "Work no good, hammer hammer adamantine words, house inedible, hollow bricks, small old slates from demolished castle, second hand, couvreur fell off backward leaning scaffolding and burst, fat old man, instantaneous the things one has seen and not looked away."[30] These are his words; I know that I would never, as a translator, have hit on them. Serious there, but hilarious here, in this example: the French way of referring to the present month (the equivalent of our rather stuffy "inst.") is "courant", literally "running"; Beckett begins a letter, "Merci de votre lettre du 10 clopinant" (hobbling along).[31]

At moments, the assurance of which I spoke just now is such as to blur the distinction between the two languages. It is part of a process that will be familiar to anyone who is at ease in more than one language: one may not be immediately aware in which language a given communication, spoken or written, is being expressed. That is, one reacts to the words direct, not by reference to their Frenchness or Englishness, or whatever. In my *Writing Beckett's Letters*, I gathered many of the odder aspects of my experience of translating the letters; but one instance I did not mention is that of finding myself saying, as I do sometimes when working on these letters: "but surely I've read something like this already, just recently" – only to realise that what I am looking at is my own translation of a Beckett letter.[32] Something in me had registered familiarity, but not immediately identified it. There had, so to speak, been competition in my non-conscious memory between the French text and the English, but the outcome of the competition had been a tie, notable only for its effect on me: my version of that moment when, for the first time, two London Marathon runners reached the finishing line arm in arm. Such experiences are far more common for translators than the problem-solving which monoglots suppose to be what takes up their time.

Writing about the translation has entailed looking at, hearing, arguing about this word and that, this construction and that; in short, pausing over details, small parts of a whole, or, to put it less neutrally, nitpicking. But it is easy to banish the effects of that. All that is needed is to look at, listen to a page of Beckett. This brings back at once the only fact that really matters: Samuel Beckett is a great writer, and a part of his greatness is his sureness of linguistic touch. Whoever sets out to

30 SB to Jacoba van Velde, 19 October 1958 (BNF, 19794/56).
31 SB to Jacoba van Velde, 19 October 1958.
32 George Craig, *Writing Beckett's Letters*.

translate *him*: to catch the rhythms and sonorities of his prose, to represent the ebb and flow of his confidence, and to preserve his separateness (he is not *like* anybody) – well, any such venturer has to recognise that, quite simply, it cannot be done. The only parallel I can think of comes in the old carol: "Mark my footsteps, good my page / tread thou in them boldly. . ." As Beckett might have said: "Voire."

George Craig

EDITORIAL PROCEDURES

Letters are transcribed as written and presented as a clear text, that is, the final text as sent to the recipient. While some letters were repeatedly revised before being sent, letters to friends were not always checked. Inevitably, eccentricities appear: slips of the pen, typos, accidental substitutions, oddities of spelling, and persistent confusions (sent/send). To signal each one with "sic" or "for" would interfere with reading, hence only when Beckett's eccentricities might prevent or distort understanding are they noted.

Sequence Letters are presented chronologically. When more than one letter was written on the same day, the letters are ordered alphabetically by recipient's name, unless internal evidence or editorial necessity suggests another sequence. When the editors supply dating, the letter appears in sequence according to the date deduced. When Beckett sends a letter enclosing another letter, both letters are presented, with the enclosure following the letter itself.

Recipient The full name of the recipient, with a corporate identification if relevant, and the town or city to which the letter was sent, are indicated in small capitals as a header; these are editorial additions. Beckett himself seldom included a recipient's name and address in a letter; however, when he does, this is shown as written.

Date Dates are presented as written by Beckett, who most often follows European format (day, month, year), but placement is regularized. Beckett's notation separating the elements of a date (day, month, year) varies, but presentation is regularized here as dots ("1.7.64"). If the date, or any portion of it, is incomplete or incorrect, editorial emendation is given in square brackets; if a date, or any portion of it, is uncertain, this emendation is preceded by a question mark. The rationale for the dating is given, if needed, in the bibliographical note following the letter.

Place Place is presented as written, but placement is regularized. Where place is incomplete, editorial emendation is given in square brackets, preceded by a question mark if uncertain. Occasionally, the place of writing is not congruent with the place of mailing; for example, Beckett may write from Paris, but post the letter in La Ferté-sous-Jouarre. This is not corrected. When a letter is written on letterhead, that letterhead is presented in small capitals as the place of writing, even if Beckett inserts an additional indication of place.

Orthography Beckett's idiosyncratic spelling, capitalization, and abbreviation are preserved: this includes abbreviations without punctuation (wd, cd, yrs), varying presentation of superscripts (M$^{\underline{r}}$, Y^{r}, 14$^{\underline{me}}$), use of ampersands, contractions written without an apostrophe ("wont" for "won't"), and use of diacritics. Beckett's practice of indicating the titles of works is inconsistent: sometimes he underscores titles, sometimes he does not, sometimes he underscores partially.

Beckett often uses words or phrases from other languages when writing in English or French, but he seldom underscores such words or phrases. If Beckett's moves from one language to another produce what appears to be a variant spelling in the dominant language of the letter, this is marked or explained in a note.

Beckett frequently spells a name incorrectly. When a person's name, a title, or another reference is misspelled in the text of a letter, this is signaled in the notes. On occasions when the misspelled name is likely to confuse, its first use is corrected within square brackets in the text: e.g. "Marcel [*for* Maurice] Nadeau" and "Roland [*for* Ronald] Searle." When, as in a joke or pun made with a name, a misspelling is judged to be deliberate, it stands as written; standard spelling is given in the notes and the index.

Beckett presents ellipses with spaced dots; however, these are variously two dots or three dots. Beckett occasionally punctuates with a dash instead of a period at the end of a sentence.

Authorial emendation The results of Beckett's cancelations, insertions, and inversions are presented as a clear text. When a reading of an emendation by Beckett is uncertain, it is given within square brackets in the text, preceded by a question mark. Beckett often overwrites or overtypes to self-correct; when typing, he sometimes cancels a word or phrase if it does not fit the space on the page, and sometimes leaves it in partial form before writing it fully on the next line or page. Beckett changes his mind as he writes: sometimes omitting or inserting a word, phrase, or sentence; inverting word order; extending a thought in the margins. Typed letters may contain both typed and handwritten corrections. Drafts of letters show many more changes. Where Beckett's changes are judged to be illuminating – that is, not merely corrections of spelling or typos or false starts – these are presented in the notes. Scholars interested in the patterns of Beckett's changes will wish to consult the original manuscripts. When grammatical or spelling variants interfere with sense, these are editorially expanded or corrected within square brackets in the text, or are signaled in the notes.

Editorial emendation Editorial emendations to the text are supplied only when necessary to understanding and are shown within square brackets. Other than obvious typographical errors (overtypes, space slips, extra spacing, false starts), and the examples given above, there are no silent emendations. For the sake of readability, in the case of letters by writers other than Beckett, the editors have made silent corrections where there appeared to be trivial errors (typos, accidental omissions, etc.).

Placement and indentation of date and address have been regularized. Paragraph indentations are standardized. Line ends are marked only in the case of poetry. Postscripts are presented following the signature; if their original placement differs, this is described in a note.

Editorial ellipses in letters and other unpublished manuscripts are shown by three unspaced dots within square brackets; editorial ellipses in published materials are shown with three spaced dots.

Illegibility Illegibility is noted in square brackets [illeg]. If a reading is uncertain, it is given within square brackets and preceded by a question mark. Damage to the original manuscript that obscures or obliterates the text is described in the bibliographical note and is marked in the text as illegible. When the illegible words can be surmised, these are presented within square brackets within the text.

Signature The closing and signature lines are regularized. An autograph signature or initial can be assumed for an autograph letter; in a typed letter, the notation "s/" indicates a handwritten signature or initial. A typed letter may have both an autograph and a typed signature. When these are not identical, both are shown. When these are identical, the existence of an autograph signature is indicated only by "s/" and the typed signature is presented in the line that follows:

With best wishes
s/
Samuel Beckett

An unsigned carbon copy presents only a typed signature, but spacing allows for an autograph signature in the original:

With best wishes

Samuel Beckett

Other hands When part of a letter has been written by someone other than Beckett, that part is presented in italics, e.g. notes added to a letter by others, or queries written by others to which Beckett responds on the same page (Beckett's responses are presented in roman).

Bibliographical note Following each letter is a bibliographical note which gives a description of the letter. Description of the physical document may include an indication of letterhead, the image on a postcard, and enclosures. This description also includes the address on a postcard or envelope, the postmark, and any additional notation on the envelope, whether written by Beckett or in another hand (e.g. forwarding address, postal directives). Postmarks are indicated by city (not by post office) and date. Editorial markers are given in italics: e.g. *env to* M$^{\underline{rs}}$ Hutchinson; *pm* 15–2–57, Paris. The ownership of the physical property is given with the designated library abbreviation, collection name and accession information, or dealer's name; private ownership is indicated according to the owner's preference, by name or simply as "private collection." Previous publication is noted when the letter has been published in full or in a substantial portion (more than half); facsimile reproductions are indicated in this note.

Notations used in the bibliographical description indicate whether the letter is handwritten or typed; whether a letter, postcard, lettercard, telegram, or pneumatique; the bibliographical description indicates the number of leaves and sides, and whether the letter is signed, initialed, or unsigned. A leaf is a physical piece of paper; a side is a page written on, whether recto or verso. A postcard may bear an address on the recto (1 leaf, 1 side) or on the verso (1 leaf, 2 sides). Beckett sometimes folded a single piece of paper so that it had four sides (1 leaf, 4 sides). For the list of abbreviations, see "Abbreviations" below.

Discussion of dating When the date of a letter is corrected or derived from internal or external evidence, the rationale for the assigned date or date-range is given following the bibliographical note. Undated or partially dated letters are not unusual. Beckett may neglect to date a letter when it is part of a frequent exchange or when it follows or anticipates a personal meeting; he often misdates letters at the beginning of a new year. If envelopes clearly belong with the letter in question, the postmark may be helpful in dating. Some correspondence received by publishers and other businesses was routinely datestamped; this is signaled in the bibliographical note and may help with dating. While Beckett occasionally delivers a note personally, it is also the case that some stamped letters are sent without cancellation. Telegrams may bear only the date of receipt.

Translation Letters written entirely in a language other than English are translated immediately following the transcription of the original and its bibliographical note.

Translations of words or phrases are provided in the notes to the letter. Translations are given as in the following example: "Bon travail & bon sommeil" (work well & sleep well). The language of the original is not indicated in the translation unless there may be ambiguity; if required, the following abbreviations are used: colloq., colloquial; Fr., French; Ger., German; Gk., Greek; Ir., Irish; It., Italian; Lat., Latin; Sp., Spanish. Published translations are used for literary quotations, if available and deemed appropriate by the editors, and are so noted (see below).

Beckett may write the name of a German city with German, French, or English spelling; however, translations and editorial material present the English spelling of city and place names. Translations do not repeat Beckett's "mistakes." In the rare cases where spelling norms have changed (well into the 1950s Beckett wrote "to-day" and "to-morrow"), current practice is followed. Although Beckett practiced English-style capitalization when writing the titles of books in other languages, translations and notes use the capitalization practice of the language in which the book was written. In the translation of letters, all titles of books are indicated by italics.

Translators' initials are given when the translator is other than George Craig for French, Viola Westbrook for German, and Dan Gunn for Italian. Translation is provided in the notes for passages from corollary correspondences or printed sources when these are not in English.

ANNOTATIONS

In the chronologies, notes, and profiles, Samuel Beckett is referred to as "SB." Translations follow British spelling and punctuation practice; most other editorial materials follow American English spelling and punctuation. Although all letters are presented as written, in line with standard French practice the edition does not put accents on initial capitals in editorial matter. All other accents are displayed, even where, as in editorial headers, the material is represented in small capitals. This affects only editorial matter in French; other languages have other conventions.

Identifications of persons The first reference gives a person's name (including birth name and/or acquired appellations including pseudonyms and nicknames, where relevant). Identifications and life dates are not given for well-known figures such as William Shakespeare, René Descartes, or Dante Alighieri. Dates are given for less well-known public figures. Dates and a brief statement of identification are given for figures who, in the editors' judgment, may not be known to readers or about whom information is not readily available. Additional statements of identification may be given over the course of a volume, or over the four volumes, when a person's primary occupation, affiliation, or relationship to Samuel Beckett changes.

Names Names are not necessarily constant over time. Thomas McGreevy chose to change the spelling of his family name to "MacGreevy" in 1941; Beckett follows the new spelling, with occasional hesitations, and so editorially from Volume II onwards his name is spelled "MacGreevy." Members of MacGreevy's family retained the original spelling of the family name. As a result, the two spellings may appear in close succession. After World War II, Georges Pelorson changed his name to Georges Belmont. Some women assume their husband's surname when they marry: Mary Manning became Mary Manning Howe and then Mary Manning

Howe Adams, but she used her maiden name professionally. Jacoba van Velde is also known in the letters as Tonny and Tony Clerx (a married name). Suzanne Deschevaux-Dumesnil married Beckett in 1961, and is referred to thereafter as Suzanne Beckett. Editorial practice is to follow Beckett's spelling of the name at the time of writing (though not his misspellings), but also to refer to writers by the name given on the title page of their books.

Some persons become known by their initials, some by their nicknames, and some by both. Abraham Jacob Leventhal generally gives his name in publications as "A. J. Leventhal," but he is most often referred to in Beckett's letters by his nickname, "Con." Beckett's cousin Morris Sinclair may also be addressed as "Maurice," or by his family nickname "Sunny," which in German becomes "Sonny" (indeed he was the only son in the Sinclair family). In this volume, unlike in earlier volumes, SB makes very frequent use of first names and nicknames. So as to obviate the need for full names to be repeatedly given in the notes, an Index of first names is supplied in the Appendix.

When a name changes, a note signals this change. Both/all names are entered as one heading in the Index.

Dates Approximate dates are preceded by c. (circa), fl. (floruit), or a question mark; when dates are approximated as a range, the earliest birth year and the latest death year are given, preceded by c. to indicate approximation. If only the birth year or death year is known, it is given as, for example, (b. 1935) or (1852–?) or (d. 1956). Rarely, the only date known is a marriage date; this will be given as (m. 1933). When a date is unknown, it is indicated as (n.d.).

Titles In editorial material (introductions, translations, annotations, appendices), titles are presented with the capitalization and spelling conventions of the original language. The title of a work of art is italicized and commonly presented in English since the language of the artist may not be the same as the language of the museum or collections that have owned it. Generally, a catalogue raisonné gives titles in several languages. Titles of musical works are sometimes in the language of the composer and remain untranslated; however, lines from songs, recitatives, and arias are always translated. Titles of books that are referred to in the text appear in the notes in their original language, followed by date of first publication and title in English if there is a published translation, e.g. *Léviathan* (1929; *The Dark Journey*); if the English title is given in roman font, e.g. *Die notwendige Reise* (1932; The Necessary Journey), this indicates that no English translation has been found and that the translated title has been supplied by the editors.

For titles, dates, and names, including variant spellings of names, editorial practice has been to rely upon *The Grove Dictionary of Music*; *The Grove Dictionary of Art*; *The Cambridge Biographical Encyclopedia*, second edition; *The Dictionary of Irish Biography*; the catalogues of the Bibliothèque Nationale de France, the British Library, the National Library of Ireland, the Library of Congress, as well as other national libraries; and *The Oxford Dictionary for Writers and Editors*.

Glosses Unusual or archaic English words or foreign-language terms that have entered common English usage are not glossed if they can be found in the December 2013 electronic edition of *The Oxford English Dictionary*.

References References to unpublished materials give the archive and manuscript identification of the documents. References to published materials give a full bibliographical citation at the first mention, and a short-title reference thereafter. The Bibliography includes all published materials that are cited, with the exception of newspapers. Titles that are identified in the text but not cited do not appear in the Bibliography.

Cross-reference Cross-reference that refers back to specific material within the edition is given by indicating the date of the letter and the number of the pertinent note, e.g. 9 January 1936, n. 5. This holds for all volumes of the edition: cross-references do not include volume number. Cross-references are rarely given forward. It is presumed that most readers will read sequentially; those who wish to pursue a single figure or work will be able to do so by use of the Index.

Choice of editions Although it is necessary to select standard editions for editorial reference, these choices are not governed by a single rule. For example, most often the Bibliothèque de la Pléiade edition of French texts is used, or the more recent of these where two editions exist, because these editions take into account earlier editions. Exceptions have been made when a reference requires a first edition or an edition that Beckett refers to in a letter, or one he is known to have read, or the only one he could have read. The choice of edition may change over the course of the four volumes. Where there is no standard edition, editions are selected for their accessibility, for example the Riverside edition of Shakespeare's works. Biblical references are to the King James Version. Publication information is given for all first and subsequent editions of Beckett's texts, when this information is germane to the context of a letter; English-language quotations are generally taken from the first Grove Press editions.

Choice of translations Published English translations are provided for Beckett's foreign-language citations where these are available, unless the editors have determined that none of these is suitable. Beckett nearly always read in the original language, and so the choice of a translation is seldom directed by *his* reading.

Chronologies Chronologies precede each year of the letters in order to present an overview of the events mentioned in Beckett's letters; these include certain significant world events.

Profiles Biographical profiles of persons who have a continuing role in the narrative of *The Letters of Samuel Beckett* appear in the Appendix. Those who have a profile are indicated by an asterisk following their name in the first reference to them; this asterisk appears with their name in the Index. A profile presents a narrative of a person's life and work, with regard particularly to his or her association with Beckett. Profiles appear in the first volume of the letters in which the person becomes a figure of significance for Beckett. As profiles are not reprinted in successive volumes of the edition, they cover the historical range of a person's association with Beckett. Profiles given in other volumes are indicated, at the point of first reference in each volume, with the notation, e.g., "Profile, I." Profiles are also given for certain institutions, publications, and organizations.

ACKNOWLEDGMENTS

The family of Samuel Beckett has been welcoming as well as generous in sharing memories and documents. The editors warmly thank Edward and Felicity Beckett, Caroline and Patrick Murphy, Jill Babcock, Anne Sinclair, Frank Sinclair, and remember with gratitude the late Ann Beckett, John Beckett, Deirdre Hamilton, Sheila Page, and Morris Sinclair.

FUNDING AND CONTRIBUTIONS

The James T. Laney School of Graduate Studies of Emory University has supported the research for the edition, and its grant applications since 1990. The editing project at Emory, known as The Correspondence of Samuel Beckett, has been a laboratory for humanities research in which graduate students in several disciplines of the humanities are engaged. Emory faculty and staff colleagues have been willing partners as well.

The extensive process of gathering, organizing, and preparing documents and oral histories, fundamental to a such a project, was facilitated by major support from The National Endowment for the Humanities (1991 to 1997, 2009 to 2015). The research for this edition is international and cross-cultural. The Florence Gould Foundation supported the French and American partnership of this research (1995 through 2003). The James T. Laney School of Graduate Studies, Emory University, Emory College, and The American University of Paris contributed to cost-sharing for these grants.

The Mellon Foundation supported research at the Harry Ransom Center, University of Texas at Austin (1993–1994, 2011–2012, 2014–2015); the Huntington Library / British Academy Exchange Fellowship (1994–1995) supported research at the Huntington Library; the Everett Helm Visiting Fellowship supported research at the Lilly Library, Indiana University (1997–1998, 2002–2003, 2010–2011). The Rockefeller Foundation enabled the editorial team to meet at its Bellagio Study Center, Italy (2005), to work on the first two of the edition's four volumes. The Friends of the University of California San Diego Libraries supported research in the collections of the Mandeville Special Collections Library (2008).

The contributions of Emory Professors Alice N. Benston and the late George J. Benston to *The Letters of Samuel Beckett*, along with their intellectual mentorship and personal encouragement, have been and continue to be an immeasurable gift.

We are grateful for the efforts of Joseph Beck of Kilpatrick Stockton LLP, who has provided pro bono assistance to the edition in the area of copyright law.

The editors greatly appreciate the generous in-kind contributions of the following persons and the Emory Emeritus College: Deborah Ayer, Brenda Bynum, R. Cary Bynum, David Hesla, Linda Matthews, James Overbeck, Donald Saliers, Lynn Todd-Crawford, Molly Varene, and Holly York.

In this long-term research project, we thank especially those whose continuing financial and intellectual support has kept the edition moving forward toward completion; they are truly Sustaining Partners: H. Porter Abbott, Laura Barlament, Alice Benston and George Benston (d.), Jean (d.) and David (d.) Bergmark, Matthew and Natalie Bernstein, Brenda and R. Cary Bynum, Maydelle and Sam Fason, Martha Dow Fehsenfeld, Joan H. Hall, Christopher Herbert, David Hesla, William Hutchings, James Kimball King, Park Krausen, Alexis and Marilena Léon, Jay A. and Sandra Levy, Linda McCarter Matthews, Terence McQueeny, Marie Morris Nitschke and Eric R. Nitschke, Gregg and Sherry Orloff, Marjorie Perloff, Arvid Sponberg (d.), and Molly Stevens (matched by Google).

The edition has also been the beneficiary of gifts from individual donors, each of whom has additionally enriched this endeavor with his or her continuing interest: Philip M. Allen, Susan S. Ament, Catherine C. Aust, Frank Joseph Bennett, Brenda and R. Cary Bynum in memory of Max Aue, Claydean Cameron, Hilary Pyle Carey, James Ming Chen, Brian Cliff, Mary Evans Comstock, Barnaby Conrad III, Judith Schmidt Douw and John Douw, Rosemary F. Franklin, Robert D. Graff, Jennifer Jeffers, Anne Madden le Brocquy and Louis le Brocquy (d.), Eleanor Lee in honor of David Hesla, Jordan Lehning in honor of Ryan Lehning, Laura Sharon Levitt, Joanne Lincoln, Vicki L. Mead in honor of Ryan Lehning, Mary Lynn Morgan, Martin Muller, Suzann and John O'Neill (matched by The O'Neill Foundation), Victoria R. Orlowski, Frances L. Padgett in honor of Brenda Bynum, Ranny Riley (d.), Robert

Sandarg, David Schenck, Jason Daniel Schwartz, Lawrence Shainberg. Alan Teder, Arthur S. Williams, and Hersh Zeifman.

EMORY UNIVERSITY

The vision and support of the Deans of the James T. Laney School of Graduate Studies and Emory College have been instrumental in the research and preparation of the edition and the involvement of students in this work. The editors especially thank Lisa A. Tedesco, Vice Provost for Academic Affairs – Graduate Studies, Dean, James T. Laney School of Graduate Studies and Robin Forman, Dean of Emory College.

The editors wish to recognize the contributions of Viola Westbrook as German translator, and the Advisory Board at Emory University: Alice N. Benston (chair), Max Aue (d.), Geoffrey Bennington, and Ronald Schuchard.

Emory University Libraries have been at the heart of the research for the edition: in the Woodruff Library: Lloyd Busch, Joyce Clinkscales, Margaret Ellingson, Marie Hansen, Lisa A. Macklin, Alain St. Pierre, James Steffens, Sandra Still, Erich Wendt; in its Manuscript, Archives, and Rare Book Library (MARBL): Randall K. Burkett, Elizabeth Chase, Gabrielle Dudley, David Faulds, Christeene Fraser, Sara Logue, Susan Potts McDonald, Rosemary Magee, Sara Quigley, Elizabeth Russey, E. Kathleen Shoemaker, Ginger Cain Smith, Kevin Young; in the Woodruff Health Sciences Center Library: Kevin Bradford, Carolyn M. Brown, Kimberly R. Powell; in the Hugh F. MacMillan Law Library: Richelle Reid.

The dedicated support team in the editorial office at Emory has managed the demands of the edition with effectiveness and good humor: in addition to those named in Volumes I and II, Melissa Holm Shoemake and Kerry Higgins Wendt. The editors appreciate the assistance of Katie Busch, Donna Cunningham, Robin Harpak, Rosemary Hynes, Ulf Nilsson, José Rodriguez, and Geri Thomas in the James T. Laney School of Graduate Studies, as well as the technical assistance of Thomas Pierce and Judy Simmons.

Emory University Graduate Fellows have served the research of the project with thorough scholarship and ingenuity. In addition to those named in Volumes I and II: Levin Arnsperger, Lisa M. Chinn, Benjamin Clary, Stephanie Johnson, Catherene Ngoh, Lauren Upadhyay. Emory University Undergraduate Assistants have facilitated the research and record-keeping of the edition: in addition to those named in Volumes I and II, Narianna Kretschmer and Lindsay Lawson.

THE AMERICAN UNIVERSITY OF PARIS

The editors appreciate the assistance and support of President Celeste Schenck and former Dean Neil Gordon; and faculty colleagues Christine Baltay, Amanda Dennis, Geoff Gilbert, Daniel Medin, Roy Rosenstein, and Jula Wildberger. Thanks are due to librarians Isabelle Dupuy-Llorente, Ian Janes, and Jorge Sosa, and for the assistance of Béatrice Laplante and Brenda Torney. Student Interns have conducted effective research in Paris archives. In addition to those named in Volumes I and II, the editors thank Chauncey Allan, Chloe Elder, Hynd Lalam, Zoe Lockard, Mona Gainer-Salim, Alfredo Renteria, and Marion Tricoire.

ADVISORY TEAM

Gérard Kahn has given immensely valued support to the preparation of this volume. Other colleagues have served the edition in a significant advisory capacity, and the editors convey warm appreciation for their scholarship, counsel, and wisdom: Walter Asmus, Max Aue (d.), Alice N. Benston, Brenda Bynum, James Knowlson, Breon Mitchell, Mark Nixon, Ann Saddlemyer, Susan Schreibman, Ronald Schuchard, Dirk Van Hulle, and Barbara Wright.

For their insight and assistance with the research of *The Letters of Samuel Beckett 1957–1965*, the editors wish to thank:

Avigdor Arikha (d.), John Ashbery, Anne Atik. Michael Bakewell, András Barkóczi (Europa Konyvkiado), Anna Barry, Avis Berman, Anthony Bonner, Georges Borchardt, Barbara Bray (d.), Francesca Bray, Desmond Briscoe (d.), Terence Brown. John Calder, James Campbell, Nicolas Cavaillès, Eléonore Chatin, John Coffey, Robert Cohen, Stefan Collini, Sheila Colvin, Igor Cusack. Harriet Devine, John Douw, Judith Schmidt Douw, Barbara Duthuit, Claude Duthuit (d.). Roni Eshel, Martin Esslin (d.). Margaret Farrington, Raymond Federman (d.), Sherri Feldman, José Francisco Fernández, John Fletcher, Ted Flicker, Greta Foff, Samuel Foster, Robert Franzosi, Hagit Friedlander, Klaus Gerrit Friese. Antonia Rodríguez-Gago, William Gaskill, Joanna Gibson, David Gothard, Nicholas Grene, Paul Griffiths. Christine Hait, Lawrence Harvey (d.), Sheila Harvey, David Hayman, Jocelyn Herbert (d.),

Klaus Herm (d.), Aidan Higgins, Barbara Hogenson, Jakob Holder, Alannah Hopkin, Jacob Hovind, Michael Horovitz, Susan Howe. Marta Istomin, Benjamin Ivry. Bettina Jonič, Paul Joyce, Valerie Joynt. Michèle Kastner (Editions Benoît Jacob), Marek Kedzierski, S. B. Kennedy, Elizabeth Knowlson, Matthias Korn, Erika Kralik, Charles Krance. Alexis Léon, Ava Lehrer, Antoni Libera, Ross Lipman, Christopher Logue (d.), Sandra Lousada, Christian Ludvigsen, Silvia Habgerg Ludvigsen. Joe McCann, Caroline McGee, Mark McGee, Barry McGovern, James McGuire, Jack McReynolds, Paul McWhinnie, Pauline McWhinnie, Carol Maier, Franz Michael Maier, Alan Mandell, John Manning (d.), Charles Marowitz, Joanna Marston, Georges Matisse, Bennet Maxwell, James Mays, Deryk Mendel (d.), Jeremiah Mercurio, Georg S. Mueller, Marie-Christine Muller (International School of Geneva). Maurice Nadeau (d.). Shivaun O'Casey. Claire Paulhan, Marjorie Perloff, Alexis Péron, Giulio Pertile, Lino Pertile, Lynda Bellity Peskine, Rosemary Pountney. Heide Quittenbaüm. Nicholas Rawson, Robert Ryan. Bernard Schwartz, Maggie Sedwards, Maureen Simpson, Karen Smolens, Nina Soufy, Sandra Spanier, Daniel Spitzer, Philippe Staib, Malcolm Stanton, C. Wilson Sullivan, Sarah Swisher. Jerry Tallmer, Erika Tophoven, Jean Tormey, Derval Tubridy, David Tucker. Dirk van Hulle, Donald Verene, Pim Verhulst, Srdjan Vujic. Andrew Welsh, Jenny Lousada West, Georges Wildermeersch, Marc Wilkinson, Clas Zilliacus.

LIBRARIES AND ARCHIVES

In particular, the editors appreciate the efforts of the Beckett International Foundation at the University of Reading, to gather and organize a central archive of the papers of Samuel Beckett that has proven useful to generations of international scholars. The editors thank James Knowlson for his vision in building this collection and fostering the collaboration of Beckett scholars, and Mary Bryden, Sean Lawlor (d.), Mark Nixon, and John Pilling for their collegial assistance.

The editors acknowledge with gratitude colleagues in libraries, archives, museums, and other offices of record, who have assisted them with queries.

Akademie der Künste, Berlin: Stephan Dörschel, Ina Prescher. *Archives Nationales*, Paris: Clothilde Roullier. *Austrian Theatre Museum (Osterreiches Theatermuseum)*, Vienna: Othmar Barnert. *Ballet Ireland – the National Ballet of Ireland*, Dublin: Anne Maher. *Bibliothèque littéraire Jacques Doucet*:

Grégory Cingal. *Bibliothèque Nationale de France*: Iris Berbain; Département des Arts du Spectacle: Joëlle Garcia. *Bibliothèque de la SACD*, Paris: Florence Roth. *La Biennale di Venezia Archive*: Daniela Ducceschi. *Bolton Museum and Archives*: Caroline Furey, Julie Lamara. *Boston College*, John J. Burns Library: David Horn, Robert O'Neill, Justine Sundaram. *Boston University*, Howard Gotlieb Archival Research Center: Sean Noel. *BBC Sound Archive*: Gösta Johansson, Guinevere Jones. *BBC Written Archives*, Caversham: Katie Ankers, Samantha Blake, Trish Hayes, Jessica Hogg, Erin O'Neill, Julie Snelling, Monica Thapar, Jeff Walden. *British Library*: Jamie Andrews, Kathryn Johnson, Kate O'Brien.

College of Dance, Dublin: Joanna Banks. *Columbia University*, Butler Library, Rare Book and Manuscript Library: Carrie Hintz, Michael Ryan. *Dartmouth College*, Rauner Special Collections Library: Sarah I. Hartwell, Jay Satterfield, Morgan Swann. *Deutsche Oper Berlin*: Betting Raeder. *Deutsches Literaturarchiv, Abteilung Archiv*, Marbach: Jan Bürger, Anja Gomm, Regina Langer, Bastien Reinert, Martina Stecker. *The Dictionary of Irish Biography*: James McGuire. *Faber and Faber*, Archive: Robert Brown. *The Ford Foundation*: Jonathan Green. *Gallimard*: Eric Legendre. *Harvard University*, The Pusey Theatre Collection: Luke Dennis, Dale Stinchcomb. *Historisches Archiv SWR*, Baden-Baden: Jana Behrendt. *Historisches Archiv SWR*, Stuttgart: Tobias Fasora. *Indiana University*, Lilly Library: Rebecca Baumannn, Zachary T. Downey, Breon Mitchell, Isabel Planton, Joel Silver, Cherry Williams. *Institut Mémoires de l'édition contemporaine (IMEC)*: Yves Chèvrefils Desbiolles, André Derval, Albert Dichy, Catherine Josset, Nathalie Léger, Claire Paulhan, Sandrine Samson.

James Joyce Museum, Dublin: Robert Nicolson. *Library of Congress*, Department of Manuscripts: Alice Love Birney, Jeffrey M. Flannery, Thomas Mann. *Lucerne Festival*: Helmut Bachmann, Christina Bucher, Denise Mattich. *The Joan Mitchell Foundation*: Jen Dohne, Kira Osti, Carolyn Somers. *The Pierpont Morgan Library*, New York: Clara Drummond, Maria-Isabel Moestina. *National Library of Ireland*: Justin Furlong; Manuscripts Department: James Harte, Gerard Lyne, Evie Monaghan, Colette O'Daly. *New York Public Library*: Matthew J. Bolan, Sr.; Berg Collection: Rebecca Filner, Isaac Gewirtz; Billy Rose Theatre Division: Karen Nickeson, Annemarie Van Roessel. *New York University*: Erin Kimberly Shaw; Fales Library and Special Collections: Ann E. Butler, William J. Levay. *Northwestern University*, McCormick Library of Special Collections: Scott Krafft.

Ohio State University Libraries, Department of Rare Books and Manuscripts: Rebecca Jewett, Geoffrey D. Smith. *Paul Sacher Stiftung*, Basel: Robert Piencikowski, Heidy Zimmermann. *Prix Italia Archive*, Rome: Carla Teofani. *Radio Telefis Éireann (RTE)*, Dublin: Brian Lynch. *Royal National Theatre*, London: Gavin Clarke, Nicola Scadding. *Sotheby's*, London: Peter Beal, Gabrielle Heaton, Peter Selley. *Southern Illinois University at Carbondale*, Morris Library, Special Collections Research Center: James S. Bantin. *State University of New York at Buffalo*, The Poetry Collection: Michael Basinski, Robert J. Bertholf. *Stedelijk Museum*, Amsterdam: Chietra Chedam, Michiel Nijhoff. *Syracuse University Libraries*, The George Arents Research Center: Nicole C. Dittrich, Nicolette A. Dobrowolski, Kathleen Manwaring. *Theater Neumarkt*, Zurich: Bernhard Siebert. *Théâtre National de l'Odéon*: Juliette Caron, Patricia Gillet, Yvette Isselin. *Trinity College Dublin*, Graduate Records: Dolores Pocock; Library, Department of Manuscripts: Jane Maxwell, Bernard Meehan, Ellen O'Flaherty; Office of the Provost: Orlagh Ennis.

Ulster Museum, Belfast: S. B. Kennedy. *University of the Arts, Wimbledon College of Art*, Jocelyn Herbert Archive: Cathy Courtney. *University of California San Diego*, Mandeville Special Collections Library: Linda Corey Claassen. *University College Dublin*, Special Collections: Seamus Helferty. *University College London*, Archives: Gillian Furlong. *University of Delaware Libraries*, Special Collections: Jaime Margalotti, L. Rebecca Johnson Melvin, Timothy D. Murray. *University of Limerick*, The National Dance Archive of Ireland: Victoria O'Brien. *University of Oxford*, Bodleian Library: Christopher Fletcher. *University of Reading*, Beckett International Foundation (BIF); Special Collections Service: Guy Baxter, Brian Ryder, Charlotte Louise Murray. *University of Rochester*, Rush Rhees Library, Rare Books / Special Collections: Phyllis Andrews, Claire Webster. *University of Southern California*, Cinematic Arts Library: Ned Comstock. *University of Texas at Austin*, Harry Ransom Center: Steven Enniss, Patrice Fox, Elizabeth L. Garver, Richard Oram, Thomas Staley, Rick Watson, Richard Workman. *University of Tulsa*, McFarlin Library, Special Collections: Marc Carlson, Alison M. Greenlee, James Tindle. *Victoria and Albert Museum*, Theatre and Performance Collections: Janet Birkett, Kate Dorney. *Waddington Galleries*: Michelle Gower, Clare Preston, Leslie Waddington, Theo Waddington. *Washington University in St. Louis*, Olin Library, Special Collections: Joel Minor, Anne Posega, Kevin Ray. *Yale University*, Beinecke Library: Tim Young; Gilbert Music Library: Richard Boursey. *York Museums Trust, York Art Gallery*: Victoria Adams.

The following manuscript dealers have been helpful to the research for the edition,: Alan Clodd (d.); George J. Houle; Kennys Bookshop; Maggs Bros. Ltd.; Bertram Rota Ltd.; Sotheby's (London); Ulysses Books; Waiting for Godot Books.

PUBLISHERS

The editors appreciate the efforts of the late Barney Rosset on behalf of the edition as its original General Editor, as well as of all those at Grove Press who assisted with the research for the edition, with special mention of Judith Schmidt Douw, Fred Jordan, and Astrid Rosset. John Calder and his former associate Marion Boyars (d.), Beckett's London publisher of the poetry and prose, generously responded to research questions and provided assistance in contacting individuals. Faber and Faber, especially archivist Robert Brown, have made research in the firm's archives productive.

The editors wish to thank the editorial and production staff at Cambridge University Press, especially Anna Bond, Linda Bree, Paul Dobson, Leigh Muller, Thomas O'Reilly, and Kevin Taylor. It is a source of considerable sadness that Andrew Brown, who was responsible for bringing the Beckett Letters project to the Press and who supported it through thick and thin, did not live to see it to its completion.

The editors gratefully acknowledge the assistance of the many associates who read the manuscript of this volume and who made helpful suggestions; any errors that remain are the editors' responsibility.

PERMISSIONS

The editors and publishers acknowledge the following sources of copyrighted material. While every effort has been made, it has not always been possible to trace all copyright holders. If any omissions are brought to the editors' attention, these will be rectified in any subsequent editions.

Letters, manuscripts, and other documents written by Samuel Beckett are reproduced in this volume by permission of The Estate of Samuel Beckett.

Other letters and documents are reproduced with the kind permission of the following copyright holders: Dore Ashton; Anne Atik; Michael Bakewell; Edward Beckett; The Estate of John Beckett; Jacques Blin; Anthony Bonner; Francesca Bray; The BBC Written Archives Centre; Peter Brook; Jane Bullowa and Susan Bullowa; John Calder; Nicolas Cavaillès; John Coffey; Rosica Colin Ltd., London; The Curtis Brown Group Ltd.; the Estate of Suzanne Deschevaux-Dumesnil; Professor Harriet Devine; Judith Schmidt Douw; Françoise Duterte; Barbara Duthuit; The Estate of Martin Esslin; Ian von Franckenstein; Margaret Farrington and Robert Ryan; S. Fischer-Verlag GmbH, Frankfurt am Main; Ted Flicker; Patrick Gregory; Sir Peter Hall; Klaus Herm; Eva Hesse; Aidan Higgins; The Barbara Hogenson Agency, on behalf of Herbert Berghof; The International School of Geneva; Paul Joyce; Josef M. Keith; Eric Legendre, Editions Gallimard; The Estate of Christopher Logue; Christian Ludvigsen; Pauline McWhinnie; Patrick Mayoux; Les Editions de Minuit; Dr. Mark Nixon; Robert Pierret; Jacques Pinget; Antonia Fraser Pinter; Nicholas Rawson; Harry Ransom Center, University of Texas at Austin; Erik Reece; The Estate of Barney Rosset; The Royal Archives and the British Library, Department of Manuscripts; Jean Schneider; Eileen Simpson; Sandra Springs, trustee, the Estate of Ruby Cohn; Suhrkamp-Verlag GmbH, Berlin; Erika Tophoven; Jean Tormey; Hetty O. Staples; Sylvie Vereano; Marc Wilkinson.

The following individuals and institutions have granted permission for publication of documents (including letters and manuscripts) in their possession, or have expressed no objection to such publication: Theodor W. Adorno Archiv; Edward Albee; Fernando Arrabal; John Ashbery; Jill Babcock; Edward Beckett; Sophie Belmont; Bibliothèque littéraire Jacques Doucet; Bibliothèque Nationale de France: Département des Arts du Spectacle, and Département des Manuscrits; Bibliothèque de la Société des Auteurs et Compositeurs Dramatiques; Jacques Blin; Special Collections, The Bodleian Libraries; The Naughton Archive, Bolton Library and Museum Services; The John J. Burns Library, Boston College; The Howard Gotlieb Archival Research Center at Boston University; The BBC Written Archives Centre; The British Library Board; M. R. Büttner; Robert S. Cohen; Rosica Colin, Ltd.; Columbia University, Rare Books and Manuscripts Library; The Curtis Brown Group Ltd.; Dartmouth College Library; Deutsches Literaturarchiv, Marbach; Judith Schmidt Douw; The Manuscript, Archives and Rare Book Library (MARBL), Emory University; The Estate of Martin Esslin; Faber and Faber Ltd.; Margaret Farrington and Robert Ryan; S. Fischer Verlag GmbH, Frankfurt am Main; Editions Gallimard; Guardian News and Media Ltd; The Harvard Theatre Collection, Houghton Library, Harvard University; Jocelyn Herbert Estate; The Lilly Library, Indiana University; Fonds Samuel Beckett and Fonds Roger Blin, Archives, Institut Mémoires de l'édition contemporaine (IMEC); Paul Joyce; Valerie Joynt; S. B. Kennedy; Christian Ludvigsen; The William Ready Division of Archives and Research Collections, McMaster University Library; Jean Mascolo; the Meyers family; Les Editions de Minuit; The National Library of Ireland; The Kungliga Biblioteket, National Library of Sweden; The Henry W. and Albert A. Berg Collection of English and American Literature, The New York Public Library, Astor, Lenox and Tilden Foundations; Billy Rose Theatre Division, The New York Public Library for the Performing Arts; Rare Books and Manuscripts Library of the Ohio State University Libraries; Lois Overbeck; The Paul Sacher Foundation, Basel; Françoise Porte; Rosemary Pountney; Nicolas Putman; The Royal Archives and the British Library, Department of Manuscripts; Royal Court Theatre; Elliseva Sayers; Anne Sinclair and Frank Sinclair; Edith Smolens; Susan Solomons; Special Collections Research Center, Morris Library, Southern Illinois University Carbondale; Anne de Staël; SWR Historisches Archiv; Grove Press Records, Special Collections Research Center, Syracuse University; Erika Tophoven; The Board of Trinity College Dublin; The

Mandeville Special Collections Library, University of California, San Diego; Southern Historical Collection, Louis Round Wilson Special Collections Library, The University of North Carolina at Chapel Hill; Beckett International Foundation, The University of Reading; Harry Ransom Center, The University of Texas at Austin; McFarlin Library, University of Tulsa; Department of Special Collections, Washington University Libraries, Washington University in St. Louis; Wisconsin Historical Society; The Beinecke Rare Book and Manuscript Library, Yale University; The Gilmore Music Library, Yale University; C. Pierre Zaleski, Président, Société Historique Littéraire Polonaise, Director, Bibliothèque Polonaise de Paris.

ABBREVIATIONS

LIBRARY, MUSEUM, AND INSTITUTIONAL ABBREVIATIONS

AdK	Akademie der Künste, Berlin
Adorno Archiv	Theodor W. Adorno Archiv, Frankfurt
BBCWAC	British Broadcasting Corporation Written Archives Centre
BL	British Library
BNF	Bibliothèque Nationale de France
Bodleian	Bodleian Libraries, University of Oxford
Bolton	Bolton Museum and Archive Service
BP	Bibliothèque Polonaise, Paris
Burns Library	John J. Burns Library, Boston College,
AS-SB	Alan Schneider - Samuel Beckett
BR-SB	Barney Rosset - Samuel Beckett
SB-AS	Samuel Beckett - Alan Schneider
SB-BR	Samuel Beckett - Barney Rosset
SB-JD	Samuel Beckett - Judith Schmidt Douw
SB-RP	Samuel Beckett - Robert Pinget
C&B	Calder and Boyars
CtY, Beinecke	The Beinecke Rare Book and Manuscript Library, Yale University
CtY, Gilmore	Gilmore Music Library, Yale University
CUSD	Mandeville Special Collections Library, University of California San Diego
DLA	Deutsches Literaturarchiv, Marbach
Doucet	Bibliothèque littéraire Jacques Doucet
The Faber Archive	Faber and Faber Archive
Fischer Verlag	S. Fischer Verlag
GEU	Manuscript, Archives, and Rare Book Library (MARBL), Woodruff Library, Emory University
ICso	Special Collections Research Center, Morris Library, Southern Illinois University at Carbondale

IMEC	Institut Mémoires de l'édition contemporaine
InU	Lilly Library, Indiana University
MBU	Howard Gotlieb Archival Research Center, Boston University
McM	The William Ready Division of Archives and Research Collections, McMaster University
MHU	The Pusey Theatre Collection, Harvard University
MoSW	Special Collections, Olin Library, Washington University in St. Louis
NcU	Southern Historical Collection, Louis Round Wilson Special Collections Library, The University of North Carolina at Chapel Hill
NhD	Rauner Special Collections Library, Dartmouth College
NjP	Manuscripts Division, Department of Rare Books and Special Collections, Princeton University Library
NLI	Manuscripts Department, National Library of Ireland
NLS	The Kungliga Biblioteket, National Library of Sweden
NRU	Rare Books / Special Collections, Rush Rhees Library, University of Rochester
NSyU	Grove Press Records, The George Arents Research Center, Syracuse University Libraries
NTA	National Theatre Archives, London
NYCU	Columbia University, Butler Library, Rare Book and Manuscript Library
NyPL, Berg	Berg Collection, The New York Public Library
NyPL, Billy Rose	Billy Rose Theatre Division, The New York Public Library for the Performing Arts
OkTU	Special Collections, McFarlin Library, University of Tulsa
OSU	Rare Books and Manuscripts Library, Ohio State University, Columbus
Paul Sacher	Paul Sacher Stiftung, Paul Sacher Foundation, Basel
Prix Italia Archive	Prix Italia Archive, Rome
SACD	Bibliothèque de la Société des Auteurs et Compositeurs Dramatiques

Stedelijk	Bibliothek, Stedelijk Museum Amsterdam
SWR	Historisches Archiv, Sudwestrundfunk (SWR)
TCD	Manuscript Department, Library, Trinity College Dublin, when used with reference to manuscript identifications; in other instances, a short form for Trinity College Dublin
Tulsa	University of Tulsa
TxU	Harry Ransom Center, University of Texas at Austin
UAL Wimbledon	Jocelyn Herbert Archives, Wimbledon College of Art, University of the Arts London
UoR	Department of Special Collections, University of Reading
UoR, BIF	Beckett International Foundation, University of Reading
V and A	Theatre and Performance Collections, Victoria and Albert Museum
WHS	Wisconsin Historical Society

PRIVATE COLLECTIONS

Albee Collection	Collection of Edward Albee
Arrabal Collection	Collection of Fernando Arrabal
Ashbery Collection	Collection of John Ashbery
Babcock Collection	Collection of Jill Babcock
Edward Beckett Collection	Collection of Edward Beckett
Belmont Collection	Collection of Sophie Belmont
Bonner Collection	Collection of Anthony Bonner
Büttner Collection	Collection of the Estate of Gottfried Büttner
Cohen Collection	Collection of Robert S. Cohen
Rosica Colin Collection	Collection of Rosica Colin Ltd.
Cuming Collection	Collection of Melanie Daiken Cuming
Curtis Brown Collection	Collection of Curtis Brown Group Ltd.
De Staël Collection	Collection of Anne de Staël
Douw Collection	Collection of Judith Schmidt Douw
Esslin Collection	Collection of the Estate of Martin Esslin
Gallimard Archives	Collection of Editions Gallimard
Eva Hesse Collection	Collection of Eva Hesse
Paul Joyce Collection	Collection of Paul Joyce

Joynt Collection	Collection of Valerie Joynt
S. B. Kennedy Collection	Collection of S. B. Kennedy
Jerzy Kreczma	Private Collection
Lennon Collection	Collection of *The Guardian*
Ludvigsen Collection	Collection of Christian Ludvigsen
Mascolo Collection	Collection of Jean Mascolo
Mayoux Collection	Collection of Patrick Mayoux
Meyers Collection	Collection of the Sidney Meyers family
Overbeck Collection	Collection of Lois Overbeck
Özkök Collection	Collection of Lüfti Özkök
Porte Collection	Collection of Françoise Porte
Pountney Collection	Collection of Rosemary Pountney
Jacques Putman Collection	Collection of Nicolas Putman
Ryan Collection	Collection of Daphne Ryan
Sayers Collection	Collection of the Estate of Elliseva Sayers
Sinclair Collection	Collection of Anne and Frank Sinclair
Smolens Collection	Collection of Karen and Edith Smolens
Solomons Collection	Collection of Susan Solomons
Tophoven Collection	Collection of Erika Tophoven
Wilkinson Collection	Collection of Marc Wilkinson

ABBREVIATIONS FOR PUBLICATIONS

CSP Collected Shorter Plays

EDITORIAL ABBREVIATIONS

b.	born
c.	circa
colloq.	colloquial
d.	died
[illeg]	illegible word or words
ins	inserted
m.	before date of marriage or to indicate married name
n.d.	no date
np	no page
pseud.	pseudonym
s/	signed
sl.	slang

?	uncertain
< >	cancelled

ABBREVIATIONS IN BIBLIOGRAPHICAL NOTES

A	autograph
ACI	autograph card initialed
ACS	autograph card signed
AH	in another hand
AL draft	autograph letter draft
ALI	autograph letter initialed
ALS	autograph letter signed
AMS	autograph manuscript
AN	autograph note
ANI	autograph note initialed
ANS	autograph note signed
APCI	autograph postcard initialed
APCS	autograph postcard signed
APS	autograph postscript
corr	corrected
env	envelope
illeg	illegible
imprinted	imprinted with SB's name
Lettercard	folding lettercard
letterhead	imprinted letterhead (shown in small caps)
pm	postmark
Pneu	pneumatique
PS	postscript
T	typed
TL	typed letter
TLC	typed letter copy
TLcc	typed letter carbon copy
TLdraft	typed letter draft
TLI	typed letter initialed
TLS	typed letter signed
TMS	typed manuscript
TPC	typed postcard
TPCI	typed postcard initialed
TPCS	typed postcard signed

INTRODUCTION TO VOLUME III

"Dined with Arikhas last night. Then out with Avigdor. Anne not too well. Not more drink than usual but suddenly drunk. Don't remember driving home, him & self. Went down this morning to see if car there. Never better parked. Ran into Con & his white lipped Marion at one stage. Also Alberto with his latest. Checked & despatched all texts for Suhrkamp save Happy Days, Play & Words & Music which I must try & translate."[1] The single letter that contains this passage, sent by Samuel Beckett to Barbara Bray in April 1964 – and it is not untypical – would suffice to dispel whatever vestiges may remain of the myth of Beckett the hermit devoted exclusively to words on the page. Not that work is negligible or neglected: SB continues by discussing his obligations toward three of his plays then in various stages of production in French. However, the work has so proliferated, and its influence so grown, that its author finds himself drawn more and more irresistibly into the world, into the intensely sociable world of the theatre in particular. The consequence for Beckett the letter-writer is itself dramatic, as he strives to cope with the number and range of his contacts, with the requests for interviews, information, advice, support, the invitations to premieres, the offers of honors, the commissions of new texts.

Fresh ways need to be discovered to allow Beckett to say "No," to carve out for himself the time required for writing, including that writing demanded by the scrupulous correspondent he continues to be; while, when he and his work are enjoying such obvious public success, more and more refined ways need to be discovered to enable him convincingly to inhabit the position in which he has always appeared least uncomfortable, one in which defeat and impossibility are present *a priori*. From this particular letter to Barbara Bray, as it continues, a Beckett emerges very different not just from the hermit of legend, but from even the rather hesitant socializer evident in his own

1 SB to Barbara Bray, 21 April 1964.

letters of ten years previously, when success was being achieved through the international reception of *Godot*. Here, as he continues, is a Beckett fit to vie with Henry James on the density of his social calendar: "Dined with Hayden & Leslie Waddington who had just purchased another 4 1/2 millions 'worth'. Silly talk about 'success'. Started screaming. Off now to walk in Paris and bring Comédie to Lettres Nouvelles. Gisèle Freund this afternoon. Jesus." What the letters of the present volume illustrate is a writer who, despite an instinct for solitude, thrives on the intensity and multiplicity of his connections; who even while he is complaining about his social engagements is encouraging more and more people to write to him; who is forever asking his friends to inform him when they will next be in his home town, Paris, even while he is moaning about how overwhelmed he is by the demands being made upon him. "Am sorely tried with stupid mail that simply has to be dealt with daily," he grumbles in 1960; which by 1965 has him fantasizing that his old friend and helper Con Leventhal might be able to answer his mail for him – "Pity I couldn't train Con," he jokes.[2] Yet at the same time he can say, knowing that each letter deserves a reply, "Write whenever you like, I look forward to your letters."[3] The unreasonable demands are always being made by *others*; letters needing to be written may be "stupid," "fatuous," or even "impossible," but not *now*, never *this* letter.[4] He must constantly "try & catch up on mail which is a real burden," he explains, instantly qualifying his complaint – "I don't mean personal letters."[5] Beckett has a quite extraordinary ability, far beyond mere decorum, which he deploys here to full effect, to render virtually *all* his letters "personal," encouraging his interlocutor to feel that he or she could never be a bother, that the bother is always elsewhere.

The period from 1950 to 1956 was one which found Beckett, after completing *L'Innommable*, intensely frustrated with his literary production, while at the same time obliged to cope with mounting public interest in his work (and to a lesser extent in his life). "Between 1950 and last year," he explains in August 1957, "I was unable to write anything in French or English."[6] And while "anything" is an overstatement,

2 SB to Matti Megged, 21 November 1960; SB to Barbara Bray, [13 February 1965].

3 SB to Barbara Bray, 11 March 1959.

4 SB to Barbara Bray, 7 August 1959; SB to Barbara Bray, [13 February 1965]; SB to Alan Schneider, 26 November 1963.

5 SB to Barbara Bray, [6 May 1959] (TCD, MS 10948/1/31).

6 SB to Brendan Smith, [after 21 August 1957] (EMU, MS 1221).

it is a testament to what Beckett has felt to be a creative drought, one that ended – though as we shall see only partially – with the writing of *Fin de partie*. After the years of what was experienced as incapacitation, Beckett demonstrates in the letters here an immense impatience to be back to writing; while the works he has already let into the world demand his constant attention, through new editions and re-editions, through translations, productions, and revivals. It is in the tension between the old and the new, between the achieved and the only yet dimly perceived, the made and the making, as much as in the related tension between sociability and solitude, that the letters of the present volume are often composed and sent: a tension involving the very being of Beckett the writer – in rivalry as this regularly is with Beckett the manager of a prospering career as a dramatist. Only such an existential investment can explain how he could, at the very moment his work is achieving the recognition he has striven for, be intensely nostalgic for the period when the world was ignorant of him and of it. "I feel I'm getting more and more entangled in professionalism and self-exploitation," he protests to his American publisher Barney Rosset in November 1958; "What I really need is to get back into the state of mind of 1945 when it was write or perish."[7] Three days later, as if realizing the almost preposterous nature of this claim, especially when made to his publisher, he returns to the missing sense of urgency: "The only chance for me now as a writer is to go into retreat and put a stop to all this fucking élan acquis and get back down to the bottom of all the hills again, grimmer hills that [*for* than] in 45 of cherished memory and far less than then to climb with." The effect of such pronouncements on his devoted publisher cannot have been pleasant, even if Rosset was by then familiar with his author's propensity for – his courting of – impasse. Beckett continues: "It's not going to be easy, but it's definitely the only last gasp worth trying to pant as far as I'm concerned. So if all goes well no new work for a long time now, if ever."

Fortunately for Beckett's readers, for readers now of his letters, the "long time" he devotes to the work whose first flickers he has already sensed proves to be little over one year of his writing life. Even as he is writing the work that comes to be called *Comment c'est* Beckett senses – correctly, I imagine – that it will be one of the least read of his oeuvre to date. Not that, after *Fin de partie* is completed and then first performed, in 1957, Beckett has in fact been unproductive: there ensue his first

7 SB to Barney Rosset, 20 November 1958.

radio play, *All That Fall*, then *Krapp's Last Tape*, followed by – amongst other shorter works – the second radio play, *Embers*. Yet none of these satisfies Beckett's determination to issue "the only last gasp worth trying to pant," and it is not until *Comment c'est* that he feels he is moving on from the "sales draps" (the "sorry state") in which he was left by *L'Innommable* (to which he sometimes attaches *Textes pour rien*).[8] And how do we know this? We know it because the letters leading up to, then accounting for and discussing the writing of this text, are of a fullness and detail far in excess of anything ventured hitherto. If *Comment c'est* is a watershed for Beckett the writer, then it is as much for Beckett the letter-writer, for now he dares what never was dared before: to explain his intentions, offer long descriptions, discuss the process, outline the setbacks, translate passages from the unfinished text, choose extracts for stage presentation, hesitate over the title, send the completed work to friends and await their responses – all this before finally, hesitantly, delivering it to his publisher.

The reasons for this greater openness are numerous and complex, and I shall be able to suggest only some of them. But before attempting a fuller picture of the letters of this period, one feature deserves to be stressed: Beckett's expanded range of correspondents. When Beckett befriends someone it tends to be for life, hence many of the correspondents in this volume have mattered for years, even decades, such as Thomas MacGreevy, George Reavey, A. J. Leventhal, or Mary Manning Howe. Others are of more recent but durable acquaintance, often acting as intermediaries between his work on the page and its presentation to the public: such figures as his publishers Jérôme Lindon (in France), Barney Rosset (in the United States), Siegfried Unseld (in Germany), or John Calder (in the United Kingdom, whom he comes to know personally from 1957); or his translators Elmar Tophoven (for German), Jacoba van Velde (for Dutch), or Richard Seaver (for English); or theatre figures such as Roger Blin (director and actor), or Alan Schneider (his chief American director). To them and others who entered his life prior to 1957 the letters continue to issue, while many new figures enter Beckett's world, to whom, whether because they do not reside in Paris or because there is more to be said than can be conveyed in conversation, he feels the wish or need to write. These include a number of academics whose work he reads and responds to,

8 See SB to Jérôme Lindon, 10 April 1951.

including Theodor Adorno, Kay Boyle, Ruby Cohn, Martin Esslin, John Fletcher, Lawrence Harvey, and Hugh Kenner. He is approached by a number of aspiring authors whose work he is keen to back, even when he does not feel quite as convinced by it as he is by that of Robert Pinget (to whom he continues to write supportively): writers such as Aidan Higgins, Matti Megged, Harold Pinter, and Nicholas Rawson. His work in theatre brings him in touch with new actors whom he greatly admires, notably Patrick Magee, Jack MacGowran, Deryk Mendel; and with directors George Devine, Christian Ludvigsen, and Donald McWhinnie. Members of his family continue to pass away, eliciting letters of comfort and condolence, but his beloved nephew Edward (son of his brother Frank) grows to be of an age enabling correspondence to include discussion of the work. He finds, in the figure of Avigdor Arikha – whom he met in 1956 but with whom he becomes a friend during the years presented here – a man who combines a difficult past with a passionate present, an acute sensitivity to music, a fierce commitment to painting, a range of languages and an ability to cite from memory equal to his own – a peer, in short, to whom his letters flow in an utter trust and confidence. And above all, for the purposes of the present volume, through his work for the BBC he meets Barbara Bray, who, for reasons that his abundant letters to her will invite readers to divine, becomes his chief correspondent for this era, becomes the person to whom he can write about his work with an openness and directness never dared heretofore.

Only occasionally does Beckett write letters from within Paris to others in his home city, and these are usually formal acknowledgments or notes of thanks (for a review received or an appreciation enjoyed) or brief notes intended to set a rendez-vous. Most of his letters are sent either from Paris to some other town or city, from a foreign location he is visiting, or from his country cottage in Ussy-sur-Marne, to which he retreats on every available occasion – retreats, as it may almost at times appear, only so as to retreat from that retreat through the letters he writes there. The pattern, already established in the early 1950s, intensifies here: Paris is the city about which little good can be said but which he is drawn back to irresistibly, ground as it is of so much that is positive in his life even if it also exhausts him; while Ussy is where writing is possible. Not that Ussy offers a panacea: "I stay at this mournful address as much as possible," he writes to his old friend Ethna MacCarthy, "with occasional bouts in Paris trying to compress within a week a month's 'business' from which I think it is time I retired and became as before I went into it, with all past instead of in store."[9] Beckett's partner Suzanne Deschevaux-Dumesnil loses her taste for Ussy, adding to the risk and promise of isolation. "Hoping for some calm from the mild desolation peculiar to this place at this time," he writes to Barbara Bray; "Already the mouth opens to howl and closes as often as not without having done so, though none to hear."[10] If Ussy offers risk, it also offers reward: "A personage for next time – says nothing, just howls from time to time." Beckett's letters often appear to suggest that withdrawal to Ussy is even a form of self-punishment, one that is an obligatory prerequisite to work. As he puts it at one point: "The more I think of it all the more self-banishment seems the only way, with just a day or two off on, and off. A little longer here and I'd be driven to an attempt at new work or go quite mad, it's not so far."[11] And even work may constitute avoidance. Particularly oppressed by the Ussy isolation, he writes (to Barbara Bray), "The tomb will be lively after here and no pen and paper," going on in French in parody of Pascal: "J'ai découvert que tout le malheur des hommes vient d'une seule chose." The lack of that "single thing" is precisely what renders letters indispensable, with their own necessary journeys: "qui est de savoir demeurer au repos dans une chambre."[12]

When human company thins, the observation of nature – of birds in particular – becomes more acute, though it too may be tinged with a sense of the spectral or irreparable. "I find on the outer window sill a sparrow & mouse dead side by side," Beckett tells Barbara Bray after first reporting how "I haven't a ghost of new work in me."[13] He muses: "I supposed an owl had left them there uneaten or to be eaten later." Nature becomes a favored incipit to the reporting of loss or grief; Ussy (as I suggested in my Introduction to Volume II of the letters) turns into a privileged site of mourning. "The swallows have finished school and are making ready to depart," Beckett recounts, following this and finishing his letter – without one word of transition – by adding a sketch worthy of the Brothers Grimm: "Another funeral of an old woman I knew here. She was queer in the head, her bones went as brittle as pipe

9 SB to Ethna MacCarthy, 22 November 1957.

10 SB to Barbara Bray, 17 November 1958.

11 SB to Barbara Bray, 31 October 1961, cited in SB to Herbert Myron, 8 November 1961, n. 3.

12 SB to Barbara Bray, Friday [21 August 1964].

13 SB to Barbara Bray, 29 August 1961.

clay, she fell and broke everything."[14] The fairy-tale character can on occasion become himself – unless he is closer to a figure from Caspar David Friedrich (whose painting he so admires): "Lovely time I'm having. Lovely weather without, first crocuses – very small and pale. Slow walks in the gloaming with a crooked old stick."[15] And the writing process, Ussy's yoke, can itself take a magical turn, into some larger movement of nature, as here through the intervention of a peculiar class of "bird": "My companions are the ladybirds," he writes, "as every year at this time and other times I forget, suddenly on the paper I'm writing on, or typing on, then a little flight, then back."[16]

When writing flags, and contemplation cedes to the accursed restlessness, there is always, at Ussy, that outdoor activity which appeals more than any other, signaled metaphorically when he writes, "If I could dig in here, and only go to Paris occasionally, I'd be fine."[17] Dug in, he can get digging – "holes for winter plantation."[18] As the trees he has planted over the years have taken root and grown, the dynamic subtending digging can attain its apogee; but not before his own emptiness is asserted. "I am as hollow as an old radish," he tells Jacoba van Velde; "I would like to spend two months in the country digging holes, filling up each one as I go with the earth from the next one."[19] And the holes imagined in penitentiary futility can open, even for the "old radish," inwardly as well, through writing. In a letter to his old friend Nancy Cunard he tries to explain his fondness for Ussy: "Here is the best I have, not a sound and the Ile de France bowing itself out."[20] He follows with a part-truth, one whose potency is in any case being attenuated by this very act of communication: "I don't find solitude agonising, on the contrary"; before issuing a formulation on the no-place that this particular place appears to respect and require – "Holes in paper open and take me fathoms from anywhere."

Though only one hour's drive away from Ussy in the 2CV car that Beckett purchases, the pole that is Paris lures and menaces, all bustle and company; until, briefly, Paris changes. Beckett moves house only once in the years between his return from hiding during World War II

14 SB to Barbary Bray, 27 August 1959.
15 SB to Barbara Bray, 2 March 1959.
16 SB to Barbara Bray, 22 January 1960.
17 SB to Alan Schneider, 11 July 1962 (Burns Library, Samuel Beckett Collection, SB-AS).
18 SB to Barbara Bray, 4 August 1960.
19 SB to Jacoba van Velde, 2 August 1960.
20 SB to Nancy Cunard, 26 January 1959.

and his death in 1989. The apartment he has rented since before the War, at 6 Rue des Favorites, will be left in favor of an apartment in the process of construction which he purchases on the seventh floor at 38 Boulevard Saint-Jacques. He climbs the stairs and looks out the window at the view, the outward prospect leading inward: "perhaps I'll be able to write in Paris again," he muses.[21] Months later, the apartment still not habitable, the view has become less palatable, as he reports to Tom MacGreevy: "Perhaps it will be possible to work again in Paris and have a life a little less solitary when we move into the new place, though the view of the Santé Prison from the den I'll have is beginning to upset me in prospect!"[22] The antidote to the prison-house is anything but convincing when issued by one of Beckett's temperament and convictions, the names of the illustrious buildings turning ominous as he iterates them: "I'll learn to raise the eyes to Val de Grâce, Panthéon and the glimpse of Notre-Dame." The initial weeks in the new abode are anything but promising, too, with the noise of workmen and then neighbors. Yet the noises do subside, or Beckett gets used to them, to the point where, in an amazing volte-face, he announces he has decided to sell his Ussy house.[23] The resolution is short-lived, and in less than two months he is sounding his familiar note of renunciation: "Solution wd. be to live permanently here," he writes from Ussy, conjuring a further metaphor of emptiness, "and I think that's what it will have to come to before long, if I am to try and squeeze from this tired old flat tube what little is left in it."[24] Within four years, the view from the Paris apartment that promised escape has become a brutal superimposition of institution over institution, something like a private version of a Dantesque topography: Hell, Purgatory, Paradise. On Christmas Day 1965, he writes: "Through the open window I hear the Santé prisoners howling like beasts. And see beyond the Val de Grâce and Panthéon illuminated."[25]

The dialectic of come-and-go, to and from Paris, is altered by more than just the new apartment, as Beckett accepts more and more invitations to participate in production of his works abroad. London, to which he travels on several occasions, proves so sociable as to be almost unbearable. "Quite exhausted," he writes after a day rehearsing *Happy Days*. "Dread this week. Due with Sheila next Friday to

21 SB to Barbara Bray, 17 October 1959.

22 SB to Thomas MacGreevy, 7 February 1960.

23 SB to Barbara Bray, 6 April 1961; SB to Alan Schneider, 20 May 1961.

24 SB to Richard Seaver, 12 July 1961 (TxU, Seaver, R 16501).

25 SB to Thomas MacGreevy, 25 December 1965.

Monday. Little red agenda black with commitments."[26] In a reversal of Browning's "Oh to be in England" (Browning whose verses the play's protagonist Winnie also has going round her head), he exclaims "Oh to be in Paris now that the fug is here." He sees little of New York (which he only ever visits once, in 1964) beyond the set of *Film* and the cutting-room, yet the letters fly forth, and if the impressions are vivid they also resemble images plundered from the cutting-room floor: "Wearisome heat and humidity," he recounts to Robert Pinget; "I used to hang on to the strange letter boxes. Wonderful spurts along the rivers in open-topped Morgan Sport. Telephone pagodas in Chinatown. Ferocity of the taxi-drivers."[27] Even before arrival, the journey has offered a fresh experience of place, as he takes his first and only long-haul flight. Words issue more easily from this mid-flight place that is a non-place: a rare insouciance overtakes him, in which the journey that is a letter is itself already journeying. "Writing about 1/2 way across the pond," he tells Barbara Bray, continuing almost as in an intimate French whisper in her ear – "devant un cognac et même pas la mort dans l'âme."[28] For a moment, it is almost as if Beckett were himself his letter, contentedly defying his trans-Atlantic directionality: "Window & fools-cap, doesn't matter what happens now."

Not all travel is for work. This period sees Beckett establish a habit of taking regular holidays, usually beside the sea or in the mountains, that will in time take him to the Alps, the Dolomites, Liguria, Tunisia, Sardinia, Yugoslavia, Madeira, Portugal. From his holiday destinations he sends numerous letters, and an increasing number of picture post-cards inscribed either with simple greetings, or with condensed accounts of his news. Of foreign sites, it is, however, another city, Berlin, that proves most fertile of all for letters, a place that surprises him with the possibility of urban tranquility, where for once he is able to live *and* work. It is to his Berlin hosts' having taken seriously his request to be left to his own devices when not working that we owe the remarkable series of letters Beckett sends about his work assisting on the German production of *Godot*, letters reminiscent in their detail of those sent to Tom MacGreevy when he was visiting Germany and its art treasures nearly thirty years earlier. "I do nothing & go nowhere," he writes to Barbara Bray; "Wander round after the late lunch, then back

26 SB to Barbara Bray, [21 October 1962].
27 SB to Robert Pinget, 14 August 1964.
28 SB to Barbara Bray, 10 July 1964.

here to read till time to go out for dinner, then back & bed. Bought some paperbacks – & more Dew."[29]

Another form of journey, one that Beckett can practice while staying put in Ussy, is offered by the books that he reads. If there are fewer reports of paintings viewed or concerts attended in this volume of letters than in Volume II, the quantity of comment on books read is proportionately larger. "Have been in the country for a fortnight, and am going back to Paris tomorrow," he writes to Jacoba van Velde; "I am so fed up that I am re-reading Dante's *Paradiso*."[30] As when asked previously about his reading habits, in response to which question he claimed to be "a poor reader, incurably inattentive, on the look-out for an elsewhere," here too he can repeat the claim, in the teeth of evidence to the contrary: "I can read nothing any more and have no judgement."[31] Yet just two months before writing this: "am reading seriously for the 1st time La Jalousie."[32] Alain Robbe-Grillet, this novel's author, was one of Beckett's earliest champions and was also published by the Editions de Minuit; yet this leads to no suspension of judgment – on the contrary: "I'm afraid hallucination won't wash, here, except in so far as scrutiny at this intensity partakes of it. It is systematic Sachlichkeit, which of course has nothing to do with realism." In the sentence that follows, it is hard not to infer a note of self-chastisement for the highly theorized appraisal just proffered: "What worries me is all his own theorising, but the result belies it and is I think very imp[o]rtant and remarkable."

On established writers Beckett is often brief and humorous: "I have finished Pasternak with mixed feelings," he writes after plodding through *Doctor Zhivago*, "which is more than I hoped for."[33] The pressure he feels under to read the books recommended to him, by Barbara Bray especially, can show in the almost Gallic turn to a response: "This hurried line to thank you for letter, card and Hopkins which if I ever succeed in reading anything again I look forward to reading."[34] An even incomplete list of the established writers Beckett is reading yields its range: Barzini, Benn, Ernst Bloch, Kenneth Clark, Claudius, Creeley, Delacroix, Donne,

29 SB to Barbara Bray, Saturday [13 February 1965].

30 SB to Jacoba van Velde, 12 April 1958.

31 SB to Max Naumann, 17 February 1954; SB to Mary Hutchinson, 2 June 1959 (TxU, Hutchinson, 2.4).

32 SB to Barbara Bray, 26 March 1959.

33 SB to Barbara Bray, 4 February 1959.

34 SB to Barbara Bray, 4 October 1960.

Enzensberger, Flaubert, Fontane, Hopkins, Jarry, Dr Johnson ("I find it hard to resist anything to do with that old blusterer, especially his last years"), De Maistre, G. E. Moore, Renard ("For me it's as inexhaustible as Boswell"), Reverdy, Runciman, Sophocles, Stendhal, Wittgenstein (whom he claims not to have read, then claims not to have understood), W. B. Yeats (whose *Collected Poems* he admits he has been reading "with intense absorption").[35] He reads, re-reads, and diligently reports. Where once he soaked up "the divine Jane" and averred "she has much to teach me," now he sees cracks: "Poor Jane has got herself in a mess at the end of S. & S., the big scene between Elinor & Willoughby could hardly be worse."[36] And the list goes on, offered up with a schoolboy's anxiety at not keeping up: "I shd. like some time to read a play by Pinter. But not just now. I read Passage to India a long time, vague recollection like swallowing fine sand. Won't undertake it again just at the moment. Read the Amis without much difficulty, more trouble with the Red Badge but got to the end. Have not yet read the scripts."[37]

As mention of the as yet unread Pinter signals, it is not just classics or established writers that Beckett is reading; what often proves the case, in fact, is that the less established the writer, the fuller Beckett's comment. While this generosity does not extend to "these bastards of journalists," it does go out to academics whose work Beckett deems worthy.[38] Emblematic of his relationship to serious literary critics is how he responds to Kay Boyle. He begins by offering limited biographical and bibliographical information, then agrees to read an essay she has written on Joyce's story "The Boarding House" (from *Dubliners*). Again the asseveration of ignorance: "I know nothing about short story or any other aesthetics."[39] This is followed by an extended and rather scholarly warning about the dangers of allegorizing Joyce, before the further retreat from the critical stance, this time directed at what Boyle has written about his own early story "Dante and the Lobster" – "So regard all this as nothing more serious than the expression of a personal disability and blow up my lobster to whatever dimensions you fancy." Soon he is writing to Boyle to authorize her to circulate

35 SB to Barbara Bray, 26 March 1959; SB to Richard Roud, 12 January [1957]; SB to Thomas MacGreevy, 9 January 1961.

36 SB to Thomas MacGreevy, 14 February [1935]; SB to Barbara Bray, 16 January 1963.

37 SB to Barbara Bray, 4 February 1960.

38 SB to Alan Schneider, 29 December 1957.

39 SB to Kay Boyle, 28 May 1957.

his (out-of-print) story amongst her students. Then to praise her work on it: "It's one of the most sensitive, imaginative, inseeing, painstaking comments I've read. I came out of it almost beginning to like the story myself."[40] Further praise and encouragement follow, leading to an attempt, four years later, to answer her question about Willie's final gesture in *Happy Days*: is he reaching toward Winnie or toward her revolver? Beckett pretends ignorance. Yet as he continues he converts that ignorance into something other, into a precise object of intention, "ambiguity of motive" – this, for a writer, being the opposite of ignorance or uncertainty. "To cast the doubt was dramatically a chance not to be missed, not to be bungled either by resolving it."[41]

As well as being a critic, Kay Boyle was of course a novelist, and it may be for this reason that Beckett is especially responsive to her inquiries. Certainly it is to his fellow creators – the poets, novelists, dramatists, painters, musicians – that Beckett dispenses the most sympathetic attention. He hears Marguerite Duras's *Le Square* on the radio, then sees it at the theatre – "an infinitely affecting text" – and is in no doubt as to the appropriate action: "Something like this has to be supported."[42] Writers such as Ionesco or Genet are so well known that they require no support, but Beckett reads their new works, attends their productions, proposes their plays to share programs with his own. The latest play of the lesser-known Roland Dubillard elicits a delighted response.[43] Harold Pinter is eventually read, appreciated, encouraged, until Beckett helps to get a first play staged in Paris. He reads and attends the plays of the Spanish dramatist Fernando Arrabal.

The note of discriminating connoisseurship, so alien to him, becomes acceptable when in the service of one he admires. "I am glad you are giving some notice to Pinget," he writes to Mary Hutchinson, influential in the literary journal entitled *X*. "Of the younger writers whose work I know he seems to me by far the most interesting."[44] Beckett translates Pinget; Pinget translates Beckett. He offers the younger writer money when he figures him in need. And no doubt more valuable than any practical assistance was the certainty of having been read – read scrupulously, appreciatively, profoundly. One can only begin to imagine what phrases like the following must have

40 SB to Kay Boyle, 12 July 1957.
41 SB to Kay Boyle, 7 [*for* 6] October 1961.
42 SB to Avigdor Arikha, [6 May 1958].
43 SB to Alan Schneider, 6 February 1963.
44 SB to Mary Hutchinson, 2 June 1959.

meant to one such as Pinget, diffident, under-recognized, struggling in 1962, whose novel *L'Inquisitoire* had just been published: "Your book impressed and moved me tremendously," Beckett opens, following with a sentence that ends in one of his most unexpected metaphors: "Without talking about the writing, matchless in ease of flow and transparency, what struck me most is this sort of lighting of the light from within that enfolds all things and brings peace to all things, like the air of Umbria caressing an entombment."[45] The letter concludes on a verdict both literary and human: "It is the work of a great writer and a great heart."

Even as, in his discreet way, he is nurturing his circle of friends, admirers, fellow-artists near and distant, ensuring for himself and his work a kind of *company*, Beckett's wariness of the public domain does not abate. Indeed it increases in step with his understanding of the influence he may have. On more than one occasion he expresses himself to be an enthusiastic reader of the Scottish novelist Alexander Trocchi. "I like his work," he avers; but no sooner does so than he adds, "But I prefer my appreciations to remain private."[46] The line demarcating as "private" his ever-widening circle of friends and colleagues, of intellectual and even financial influence, is becoming increasingly hard to discern. "I'm not a critic, unless possibly the world's worst," he almost pleads to Richard Seaver, "and have no public comment to make on other writers" – in which phrase the notable newcomer is the word "public". In what follows there is an inflation almost proportional to the deflation that precedes it: "I've had to take a stand about this as about interviews, otherwise there's no end to it."

Beckett's risk of being publicly cited is thankfully reduced when his comment on his reading proves less positive; though, as distinct from formerly when he could be scathing, now when he indicates literary shortcomings it is usually to inform, redirect, bore into the writer's art to reach its mainsprings. To Tom MacGreevy, one of whose poems he has read, he doles out praise and encouragement: "Your quality and spirit, so uniquely yours and so difficulty [sic] to say exactly in what consisting, are there from beginning to end."[47] But he reveals his longing – an almost involuntary, even unreasonable, appetite – for something other, in the beautifully demanding sentence that follows: "There is inclination sometimes to ask for more labour towards that level of

45 SB to Robert Pinget, 8 April 1962; SB to John Calder, 19 December 1958.
46 SB to Richard Seaver, 30 January 1960.
47 SB to Thomas MacGreevy, 7 February 1960.

phrase and rhythm where magic necessity hides, then the thought that this might be the loss of something more precious and beyond the reach of form, sorrow and wisdom of spirit murmuring unwitnessed together." On behalf of the unpublished poet Nicholas Rawson, whose desperation he quickly senses, Beckett contacts friends and tries to place his poems in the journal *X*. Three years later, his ongoing worry about Rawson's well-being does not prevent him remarking to the poet, of his new work: "Odd things here and there that the cold eye crueller cast will better."[48] To the Israeli writer Matti Megged, who is beginning his career in 1960 and who has sent Beckett his novel, Beckett responds with a cavil about how "We must wait until we can meet again, with the Goddess Bottle between us, and have it all out in the give and take of talk."[49] Then, as if to disprove his own caveat, he issues as clear, emphatic, and directive a statement on "the relationship between living and writing" as is to be found anywhere in his writings. "Thus life in failure can hardly be anything but dismal at the best," he concludes, echoing the terms of his conversations with Georges Duthuit from a decade earlier, "whereas there is nothing more exciting for the writer, or richer in unexploited expressive possibilities, than the failure to express." To Aidan Higgins, another young writer, Irish this time, in whom he senses distress as well as literary talent, he invokes his customary let-out clause about his reluctance to comment, before issuing a detailed list of spelling errors and solecisms, and then determining that it is his duty as a friend to explain what is spoiling the text.[50] What ensues is so exacting, so penetrating an analysis of Higgins's prose, that it makes the refrain about the incapacity to comment almost laughable, however sincerely it may be meant. Or rather, what Beckett writes to Higgins reveals that comment does not emerge from a place different from the source of the writing that has made Beckett so important a figure for Higgins and many others by this time; as he protests to Con Leventhal when offered an honorary doctorate by Trinity College Dublin: "If I were a scholar or a man of letters it might be different. But what in God's name have doctoracy and literature to do with work like mine?"[51] After exposing what he sees as the shortcomings of Higgins's story, he tells him, "In you already, with the beginner, there's the old hand"; before exhorting him: "Work, work, writing for

48 SB to Nicholas Rawson, 25 December 1965.
49 SB to Matti Megged, 21 November 1960.
50 SB to Aidan Higgins, 22 April 1958.
51 SB to A. J. Leventhal, 3 February 1959.

nothing and yourself, don't make the silly mistake we all make of publishing too soon." Two years later, when Higgins's first collection is indeed published (with his mentor's assistance), Beckett again protests his inability to talk "about writing."[52] Notwithstanding which, he projects himself for Higgins's sake into a future perfect tense that is rich in his own astonishment at what has been achieved, against odds and expectations as well as inner convictions about failure – this, when conviction and dereliction are almost indistinguishable: "It's a fine start that's all I can say and some day perhaps many years hence from the terrible urgency of weakness, being and utterance all gone to the dogs, you'll come across it and say how the hell did I ever have the strength to do that."

If writing about what he has read poses for Beckett the challenge of writing *per se*, the problems are only aggravated when what he is reading (or re-reading) is his own prose, as is most patent when that reading is of the minute and fastidious sort required of the translator. By 1957, Beckett knows he must undertake, for his two chief languages, English and French, translations of his work himself. Consequently: "I am faced with deserts of self-translation from now to end of year."[53] The traffic goes both ways, with *Krapp's Last Tape*, *Happy Days*, *Play*, and *Eh Joe*, as well as several shorter pieces, passing into French; and *L'Innommable* and *Fin de partie* chief among the works requiring delivery into English. If, that is – and as George Craig discusses in his French translator's preface – "English" is the correct term for what Beckett is targeting: "I have not yet got down to the englishing, or anglo-irishing, of Fin de Partie," he writes.[54] The desirability of contaminating the national language with idiom, region, accent, Beckett's ambivalence toward the very Englishness of English, is nowhere clearer than when, in London, he finds himself assisting the actress Brenda Bruce who is to premiere the role of Winnie in *Happy Days*. For only when he deterritorializes her does he hear the voice that approximates to the one in his head. "The inflexions were quite wrong," he writes to Barbara Bray. "Got them I hope on the right track. Felt her English voice was wrong and for her to give an edge of her semi-native Scots. Great improvement."[55] When the director George Devine demurs, Beckett becomes adamant: "He has her

52 SB to Aidan Higgins, 7 February 1960.
53 SB to Arland Ussher, 14 April 1957.
54 SB to J. W. Lambert, 25 January 1957 (Bodleian, MS. Eng. C.2291, f.12).
55 SB to Barbara Bray, [8 October 1962].

back on her puke English – only dead flat – if you know what I mean. I'll get the Scots back or perish in the attempt."[56] When he translates Pinget's play *La Manivelle*, he starts by noting that "The rhythms are interesting and amusing trying to get them in English."[57] But by the time he has finished he admits, "I tried to keep down Irishism but it kept breaking through. Couldn't get his rhythms and loose syntax any other way."[58] A rhythm dictated less by words on the page than by spoken delivery is problematic, he knows, since he cannot simply reset Pinget's play in a real-world Ireland. When it comes to the play's publication, the very word "translation" appears hubristic to Beckett: "Perhaps 'English text' or just 'English' by SB"; while the inscription he requests for the French edition – "I'll put 'version anglaise' or 'texte anglais', not 'traduit par'" – only compounds the problem, "version" being the standard French term (as distinct from "thème") for translation into one's native language.[59] And when he is not translating his own work, or more rarely that of others, he is often encouraging and advising those who are rendering him into languages he knows less well or not at all. What he tells Matti Megged, who is proposing to translate the plays into Hebrew, might appear to be an invocation of a particular ease, but in it is implied the gauntlet that must be picked up by that special breed of translator that is a self-translator: "How difficult the transfer is, even into a kindred tongue, I know only too well. And I, when I can't translate, have the right to try and reinvent."[60] Rejection of the translator's conventional gold standard, that a translation should not read like a translation, is just the most obvious of the ways in which Beckett accepts the challenge, as when he comments gleefully on his rendering of *Imagination morte imaginez* into English: "Putting in plenty of Gallicisms. Reads weird."[61]

Revisiting his work with a view to translation may be easy, however, compared to having to read through work that he is pleased to have seen sink out of print, but which enthusiastic publishers and academics now seek to resuscitate. When Kay Boyle reaches back to his earliest published fiction, *More Pricks Than Kicks*, Beckett feels compelled to protest to her, as later to Barney Rosset. The resolution lasts some six

56 SB to Barbara Bray, [21 October 1962].
57 SB to Barbara Bray, 5 November 1959.
58 SB to Barbara Bray, [14 November 1959].
59 SB to Barbara Bray, 4 February 1960.
60 SB to Matti Megged, 3 December 1962.
61 SB to Barbara Bray, 7 July 1965.

years, until he finds himself reading the page proofs he has so dreaded. "I have broken down half way through galleys of More Pricks than Kicks," he tells Rosset: "I simply can't bear it. It was a ghastly mistake on my part to imagine, not having looked at it for a quarter of a century, that this old shit was revivable."[62] (Rosset will have to wait for another eight years before overcoming this particular authorial reluctance.) To John Calder he sends a refusal to allow his one published piece of sustained literary criticism, his *Proust*, to be translated and published in French.[63] He learns that his unpublished story "Premier amour" has been circulated to students, and later does what he can to suppress what he calls a "little piracy."[64] (It will take more than ten years for Jérôme Lindon to convince him to reverse his decision and allow the story to be published.) Almost as excruciatingly for Beckett, and all too menacingly for the present edition, he is obliged to revisit his own letters when he finds they are soon to be made public. "I am disturbed by the letter montage," he writes to Rosset, who has used extracts from the letters Alan Schneider has received from Beckett. "I dislike the ventilation of private documents. These throw no light on my work."[65] (It will take him even longer, nearly thirty years – years that include an appalled reading of the first biography of his life – to revise this particular opinion and to authorize the present edition.)[66]

Every time a revival is proposed of *Godot*, or later of *Endgame*, Beckett has to revisit the work, in his mind if not on the page: the oeuvre as albatross, when he says of that same oeuvre, "I am with it a little in the dark and fumbling of making, as long as that lasts, then no more" – the "no more" constantly menacing to become "ever after."[67] And to revivals are added the seemingly infinite adaptations, so that already by 1961 Beckett tells his German editor Stefani Hunzinger, who has inquired about a proposed television production of *Endgame*, "I would have to adapt it profoundly, something for which I have neither the time nor the desire."[68] He sums up: "More generally, I am going to be obliged from now on to hold out against any adaptations of this kind, so that

62 SB to Barney Rosset, 20 October 1964.
63 SB to John Calder, 23 November 1965.
64 SB to Barney Rosset, 8 April 1959.
65 SB to Barney Rosset, 8 January 1958.
66 Deirdre Bair, *Samuel Beckett: A Biography* (New York: Summit Books, 1990).
67 SB to Arland Ussher, 6 November 1962.
68 SB to Stefani Hunzinger, 14 October 1961.

only in the theatre will there be performances of plays for theatre, only on radio of those for radio." Yet however intensely felt, this impulse to blanket opposition is very far from the much more nuanced and endlessly revisable attitude that Beckett in fact finds himself adopting over years during which he makes compromise after compromise, often regretting it, at other times being delighted with the results. A single example may stand for the many. When Shivaun O'Casey proposes to present Beckett's story "From an Abandoned Work" on stage, its author is predictably opposed: "This is not at all the kind of dramatic writing I had in mind when we talked in Paris."[69] Beckett then lists at least three techniques for presentation – using a spotlit face, monologue text, an undramatized reading – which he believes will not be effective, before then offering what practically amounts to a new playlet, so detailed and innovative are the suggestions, beginning as they do: "Moonlight. Ashcan a little left of centre. Enter man left, limping, with stick, shadowy in faint general lighting alone." Nor is his imagination exhausted by what he offers. "If you like this idea you'll be able to improve on it," he concludes. "But keep it cool."

As media develop and mix, Beckett finds himself both seduced and repelled. Implacably opposed in 1954 to any musical setting for *Godot*, by 1959 he can report with equanimity spending an evening with the musician Marc Wilkinson who has set a passage of *Godot* for performance.[70] A film version of *Godot*, opposed in the past, is accepted in 1962 with the proviso that the script be identical to the play's text. "What a talky it will be," he wryly reflects.[71] He gives his permission for a television version of *Godot* too, and is unsurprised at the lamentable results. "The play does not lend itself to this medium," he writes to Christian Ludvigsen.[72] Yet once again he cannot avoid suggesting how it might indeed be *made to* lend itself, in a comment that surely adumbrates his own further work in this medium: "I think the problem is how to give the space on the small screen. Roughly speaking I think the solution is in a counterpoint of long shots and close-ups." Nor is his reaction to adaptation simply one of reluctant acquiescence followed by imaginative investment; when he knows and respects the artist proposing to do the adaptation he can be keen from the outset, as when he is

69 SB to Shivaun O'Casey, 13 January 1965.

70 See SB to Edouard Coester, 11 March 1954 and 23 March 1954; SB to Barbara Bray, 8 December 1959.

71 SB to Alan Clodd, 26 August 1962.

72 SB to Christian Ludvigsen, 30 August 1961, cited in SB to Judith Schmidt, 9 December 1961, n. 1.

approached by the French-Romanian musician Marcel Mihalovici who wants to make a chamber opera out of *Krapp*. So much that Beckett has expressed in his letters up to this point, not least about his abhorrence of "collaboration between the arts," his distaste for "Wagnerism," would lead to an expectation of curt refusal.[73] Yet soon he is working long days with Mihalovici, and is more than content with what he is discovering. His enthusiasm is such, indeed, that he breaks another rule, the one that has him avoid premieres, and travels to Bielefeld for the opening night, to be thrilled by what he hears.

Beckett's first drama for radio, *All That Fall*, receives its broadcast premiere in January 1957, and is followed by a second radio play, *Embers*, in 1959. It is the question of light that becomes the focus of his reaction to the avatars that are proposed for these two works. He learns through a cutting in the *New York Times* of a proposal to stage the earlier play and objects, to Barney Rosset, in the strongest terms: "Even the reduced visual dimension it will receive from the simplest and most static of readings . . . will be destructive of whatever quality it may have and which depends on the whole thing's coming out of the dark."[74] The play of light and dark is already present in the hesitations he manifests over the title of the latter work. He toys with *Ebb* and *Again the Last Ebb* before settling on *Embers*: "I decided on Embers," he explains, "because for one thing it receives light in the course of the piece and for another because embers are a better ebb than the sea's, because followed by no flow."[75] Any light must emerge *darkly*, as if in a photological equivalent of silence. "My own feeling," Beckett writes about *Embers* to Robert Farren of Radio Éireann, "is that it would have to be entirely reshaped and practically rewritten before it could face stage conditions."[76]

If the promise – or threat – of adaptation obliges Beckett to define the specificities of his several media, no such silver lining is detectable in that further revisiting of his own work enjoined this time by those whose form of adaptation is censorship. Although explicit political comment is almost as rare in the letters of this volume as it was in the previous ones, no reader of the letters that reveal the violence of Beckett's reaction to the censors can doubt that, despite his distaste for anything approaching public attitudinizing, despite his abhorrence

73 See SB to Georges Duthuit, 3 January 1951.
74 SB to Barney Rosset, 27 August 1957.
75 SB to Barbara Bray, 11 March 1959.
76 SB to Robert Farren, 9 January 1960.

of so much that constitutes politics, he was invested in his own form of political resistance. Asked by Kay Boyle to pronounce on the highly publicized trial taking place in Jerusalem in 1961, he writes, "Can't think of anything worth saying to say about Eichmann."[77] His comment that follows is typical, with its resistance to posture, its apprehension of reversals, its blend of deference, skepticism, understatement – by the time he writes this, Beckett is already a close friend of Avigdor Arikha, himself a Holocaust survivor: "Jewish friends here speak of him with indulgence. Just the I suppose flippant vision of his being sentenced to be treated kindly and shown in a comfortable cage on the fairgrounds of the world."

In the period covered by the present volume, there occur several international political crises; Beckett, an avid reader of the newspaper and listener to the radio, is very aware of these, while being equally aware of how little anything he might say about them would matter. The Algerian War of Independence impinges most immediately, with riots and bombings in Paris that endanger his friends, not least his publisher Jérôme Lindon. His letters from this period illustrate his concern for Lindon's well-being, a concern that is personal, certainly, but is not only that: Lindon, like Beckett himself, is a former *résistant*, his publishing house a former clandestine press from the period of the Occupation; along with many of Beckett's friends and associates he has signed the Manifeste des 121 opposing the war, and published the "Documents" series as well as several important novels denouncing French military torture in Algeria. As James Knowlson makes clear in his authorized biography, Beckett's room for public action, given he was not a French citizen and therefore liable to deportation, was seriously restricted (Beckett indeed remarks how he would surely have signed the Manifesto but for the fact that he is a foreigner).[78] When Lindon's home is bombed in December 1961, and then the offices of the Editions de Minuit, it is any note of hysteria that Beckett seems to be trying to avoid in his reports of the event, where the risk and the human cost are unadornedly stated. When the home of the critic Jean-Jacques Mayoux is bombed, his tone to Mary Hutchinson in London is almost determinedly matter-of-fact.[79] Yet it is in the context

77 SB to Kay Boyle, 30 October 1961.

78 See James Knowlson, *Damned to Fame: The Life of Samuel Beckett* (New York: Grove Press, 2004), 438–442. On the "Manifesto of the 121," see SB to Barbara Bray, 1 October 1960.

79 SB to Mary Hutchinson, 22 February 1962.

of such restraint that, in the report he offers of the same event to Avigdor Arikha, the final two words strike such a powerful note: "On Wednesday I had listened to Mayoux for two hours, on Constable. Very good. Then the next day, this unspeakable thing" – "cette infamie" is Beckett's original French.[80] When politics impinge on a domain where he believes he does have some influence and room for maneuver, Beckett can act and act decisively. Contacted by one Freda Troup about having his work staged in Apartheid South Africa, he responds: "I am in entire agreement with your views and prepared to refuse performance of my plays except before non-segregated audiences."[81] To Aidan Higgins, then resident in South Africa, he strikes an admonitory note about his place of residence.[82]

Beckett is of course no stranger to censorship, and his abhorrence of it doubtless contributed to his life decision – political too, in its way – to quit Ireland and vote with his feet by living in a country where writers such as the Marquis de Sade (whose work he so admires) were read and appreciated. The dust is still settling in 1957 from his altercation with Britain's public censor, the Lord Chamberlain, over cuts demanded from *Waiting for Godot*, and he will object repeatedly to the publishing of a bowdlerized version of this play in England. When he learns that the Dublin Theatre Festival, where his work was to be presented along with an adaptation of *Ulysses* and a new play by Sean O'Casey, is now hesitating because of opposition from Dublin's Roman Catholic Archbishop, he immediately declares his intention to withdraw his own work, describing the ensuing boycott of his fellow writers as "revolting."[83] And when it is proposed that his work be produced outside the festival, his position hardens. "As long as such conditions prevail in Ireland," he writes, "I do not wish my work to be performed there, either in festivals or outside them. If no protest is heard they will prevail for ever. This is the strongest I can make."[84] However, it is again in England that the censorship battle proves most protracted, as *Endgame* undergoes scrutiny. "But the Lord Cham[b]erlain is making his usual chamberpot storm, his stream being directed against two

80 SB to Avigdor Arikha, 17 February 1962.
81 SB to Freda Troup, 13 May 1963.
82 SB to Aidan Higgins, 7 February 1960.
83 SB to Alan Simpson, 17 February 1958.
84 SB to Carolyn Swift Simpson, 27 February 1958.

'pees', one 'balls', an 'arses' and the entire prayer scene!"[85] The moment in that prayer scene that becomes the bone of contention is when Hamm declares of God, "The bastard! He doesn't exist!"[86] Momentarily, the deity is revivified, as Beckett appeals to George Devine who is hoping to stage the play at London's Royal Court Theatre: "I have shown that I am prepared to put up with minor damage, which God knows is bad enough in this kind of fragile writing."[87] Concessions have their limits, however, for "no author can acquiesce in what he considers, rightly or wrongly, as grave injury to his work."[88] In a gesture that seems straight from a Beckett play, as a token of the spirit of compromise, six months later Beckett tells Devine: "I could accept, for example, 'The swine, he doesn't exist'."[89] But his patience, he makes clear in his very next letter to his director, has been stretched to breaking point, tired as he is of "buggering around with guardsmen, riflemen and hussars." It never takes much to convince Beckett that there are matters more important than the staging of the latest of his plays; and here he insists on a principle, one at the very heart of what it means to him to be a writer. No figure could be less Beckettian than Napoleon, yet it is the Napoleonic note that sounds in his exasperation: "I simply refuse to play along any further with these licensing grocers."[90] Extraordinary as the fact may seem a mere fifty years later, *Endgame* opened in London not just in club conditions, but played *in French* – where "Dieu" could be an unregenerate "salaud."[91]

Beckett's willingness to forgo the chance of having his play produced in a translation over which he has labored should not obscure the surge of interest he evinces during the years represented here in all aspects of stage production. If he was already familiar with many key figures – Roger Blin, Jean Martin, Alan Schneider – whose names will go on appearing, these are the years that also see him becoming close to the director Donald McWhinnie, the set designers Matias and Jocelyn Herbert, the actors Jack MacGowran, Patrick Magee, Delphine Seyrig, Madeleine Renaud, and Michael Lonsdale, to name just some of the

85 SB to Barney Rosset, 26 December 1957 (NSyU).
86 Samuel Beckett, *Endgame* (New York: Grove Press, 1958), 55.
87 SB to George Devine, 5 January 1957 [*for* 1958].
88 SB to George Devine, 5 January 1957 [*for* 1958].
89 SB to George Devine, 7 July 1958.
90 SB to George Devine, 28 July 1958.
91 Samuel Beckett, *Fin de partie*, in *Théâtre I* (Paris: Editions de Minuit, 1971), 190.

most significant. These are the years of Beckett's apprenticeship in the alchemy that turns a text into a successful stage production. Already he knows that no play script can be considered final until it has been internalized by actors and rehearsed on the boards. His willingness to modify, truncate, transform, is the exact opposite of rigid fidelity to sacrosanct text. He cuts the scene with the boy from *Endgame*, and when questioned about this explains that the cut is not definitive but depends rather on the cast and on the rhythms of any particular production. He often complains of the intense sociability of theatre, but the intensity of his longing to get involved in production is everywhere apparent. With *Krapp's Last Tape* written but not yet produced, he tells Barney Rosset: "I feel as clucky and beady and one-legged and bare-footed about this little text as an old hen with her last chick."[92] When the play is put on by Donald McWhinnie, it leads to Beckett's most satisfying experience in the theatre to date, with Patrick Magee being directed "marvellously," "unerringly," and – most revealing of the adverbs – "pitilessly" in the title role.[93]

Beckett's commitment is visible not least in his disappointment when he is asked by directors, both in England and in Germany, to absent himself so as to give the actors breathing-space. "They practically refused to listen to me," he reports to Barbara Bray after a particularly difficult rehearsal of *Krapp*, "so I lost my temper, said 'démerdez-vous' & swept out."[94] Though the resolution will not last, it is the single most important relation in the theatre that is jeopardized by Beckett's anger, as he continues, "I'm finished with Blin." In his dismissive judgment of the actor playing Krapp, a simple removal of the reiterated "no"s yields a precise vision of what its author considers to be required for success in this role: "Chauffard is quite unfitted for the part. No voice, no face, no eyes, no presence, no dexterity, no weight, no violence, no madness." When Patrick Magee is asked to attempt a dramatized reading from *Comment c'est*, translated for that purpose, Beckett offers to help by "pointing" the text, his determination to convey his vision being as strong as his contrary determination to permit his vision to be discovered only in performance. Pages and pages of his letters are devoted to instructing directors, Alan Schneider in particular, who is judged trustworthy not least because (like George Devine) he is biddable. When a

92 SB to Barney Rosset, 1 April 1958.

93 SB to George Reavey, 15 November 1958; SB to Barney Rosset, 20 November 1958; SB to Mary Manning Howe, 21 November 1958.

94 SB to Barbara Bray, 24 March 1960.

production is reported as deviating too far from his conception, he can be scathing, as when he learns of what has happened to the first German production of *Krapp*: "I dream sometimes of all German directors of plays with perhaps one exception united in one with his back to the wall and me shooting a bullet into his balls every five minutes till he loses his taste for improving authors."[95]

Yet if there is one thing more than any other that distinguishes the letters of the present volume from those of its predecessors, it is that here Beckett offers up a sense not just of his final view of whatever work is in progress (or in regress as he might be more likely to think of it), but also of its conception, gestation, birth pains, its first cautious steps. Even in his extraordinarily open and expansive letters to Georges Duthuit from the late 1940s there was, for example, almost no mention made of the process of writing *En attendant Godot*; the sequence of novels that starts with *Molloy* merits scarcely a mention to his friends until it is well and truly completed. For one for whom, as he puts it, "the making relation" is crucial, Beckett had a remarkable capacity to be taciturn about that making.[96] Already, in discussing the final changes to *Fin de partie* in 1957, he seems more voluble than previously, and this tendency is further discernible in how he discusses *All That Fall* and *Krapp's Last Tape*. But if what I suggested above is correct, it is with what will become the novel *Comment c'est* that Beckett lets his correspondents in to the writing process in a much fuller way, and this from the outset. And the confidence he establishes here, that a work unfinished – scarce glimpsed – can be shared without its evaporating into good intentions, carries over into his willingness to share his misgivings and excitements about what he will go on to write during the period: about *Happy Days*, *Play*, *Film*, and *Eh Joe*, as well as several shorter works. What the reader of his letters finds, as a result, is a lived apprehension of the work as it emerges, changes tack, almost sinks, recovers, stalls, then hauls itself toward its final shape.

As he sets out to commit himself to a new prose work that will take him forward from the impasse in which he has long felt stuck, the stakes could not be higher, as Beckett explains to Barbara Bray: "I am in acute crisis about my work (on the lines familiar to you by now) and have decided that I not merely can't but won't go on as I have been going more or less ever since the Textes pour Rien and must either get back to nothing again and the bottom of all the hills again like before

95 SB to Alan Schneider, 4 January 1960.
96 SB to Arland Ussher, 6 November 1962.

Molloy or else call it a day."[97] The most common word to describe his advance through the work that is provisionally entitled "Pim" is "struggling" – "struggling to struggle" as it even becomes – though "demolishing," "battering to bits," and "abandoning" all find their place.[98] Beckett rails against the obscurity of what he is producing, though when he does gain an insight into what he is seeking, it proves almost catastrophic.[99] He backtracks, apologizes for his stupidity ("I have to be like that so much for Pim"), complains, claims to have "lost touch, faith, interest"; but he does not give up on this "unabandoned work," describing the steps along the way in almost forensic detail.[100]

If the urgency of the need to move forward offers one possible reason for why *Comment c'est* yields such an unheralded wealth of writing about work in progress, in his French translator's preface George Craig suggests a relation to language whose shifts intimate other possible reasons. The post-War years saw a surge of energy into and through the French language, both in Beckett's texts and in his letters, so that by 1955, the year in which he returns to English to write "From an Abandoned Work" (his first work in English in approximately a decade), he has established himself as effectively a French – or French-language – writer. To Kay Boyle in 1957, shortly before writing *All That Fall* and *Krapp's Last Tape*, which together signal a full return to English, he writes: "now that I've forgotten half my English I feel like going back to it."[101] This impulse is later qualified, but even the reason behind his qualifications – the difficulty of achieving control in English, "A kind of lack of brakes" – points towards a revalorizing of his native language.[102] Not that Beckett did not write English-language letters before, but it may be from the gap between the language of composition – French for *Comment c'est* – and the language of the bulk of his letters during this period – English – that there emerges a certain freedom to expand upon the process, even if later he will regularly censure himself by remarking, "awful English this."[103] And of course the language of

97 SB to Barbara Bray, 29 November 1958.

98 SB to A. J. Leventhal, 3 February 1959; SB to Barney Rosset, 5 May 1959; SB to Barbara Bray, [6 May 1959] (TCD, MS 10948/1/31); SB to Barbara Bray, 13 November 1959.

99 See SB to Robert Pinget, 30 November 1959.

100 SB to Robert Pinget, 13 December 1959; SB to Barbara Bray, 24 March 1960.

101 SB to Kay Boyle, 26 July 1957.

102 SB to Barney Rosset, 26 December 1957, cited in SB to Donald McWhinnie, 13 January 1958, n. 4.

103 SB to Barbara Bray, [11 July 1960]; see also SB to Jocelyn Herbert, 8 November 1962; SB to Deryk Mendel, 13 May 1963.

address is ultimately indissociable from the identity of the addressee; this last comment being delivered most regularly to Beckett's chief correspondent of the period, perhaps the first person with whom he feels truly at ease in discussing his "making" – Barbara Bray.

During this era Beckett finds new friends and intimates who will remain close to him until the end of his days, and if Barbara Bray is the most important of them for the present collection she is far from being the only one. Just how precious are such new associations may better be appreciated when it is remembered that as he meets Bray, or writes the early letters of the present volume, he is already fifty years old; the shadow of mortality has hung over Beckett ever since his youth, but the shadow now has lengthened; the human connections made at this later age are precious not least because they are colored by the premonition of loss. Indeed, Beckett has ample opportunity during this period to measure just how much his friends mean to him: a past-master at the letter of condolence, he will repeatedly be called upon to apply the epistolary cataplasm to pain and grief. "I know your sorrow," he writes to Alan Schneider who has recently lost his father, "and I know that for the likes of us there is no ease for the heart to be had from words or reason and that in the very assurance of sorrow's fading there is more sorrow."[104] When he learns of the death of Denis Devlin, he writes that "it really knocked me all of a heap."[105] That most amenable of stage directors, George Devine, suffers a stroke when in his fifties. When he struggles to recover, Beckett writes to his partner Jocelyn Herbert, "You know what's in my heart for you and George, so I needn't try and say it" – following this with a turn of phrase that imposes just the pause required for the heart to make itself audible: "But you do, to you both, for me. You're with me here and I'm wishing for you hard."[106] Devine will die months later, at which point Beckett will overcome his reluctance to use the telephone and promise to call her; in time, the intimacy with – and in – grief will develop into an intimacy of a fuller kind, the letters eventuating from and sustaining this relationship being (as will be seen in Volume IV) among the most relaxed and smiling Beckett ever wrote. When his old friend Ethna MacCarthy falls terminally ill with cancer, he writes to her despite claiming he is unable to, then invites her widower to join him in Paris. Gone too in this period are his sister-in-law Jean Beckett, his old

104 SB to Alan Schneider, 19 November 1963.
105 SB to Thomas MacGreevy, 21 September 1959.
106 SB to Jocelyn Herbert, 15 September 1965.

Trinity College acquaintance H. O. White, his old friend the Irish poet and diplomat Denis Devlin: it is against the clamor of necrology that he often writes to his friends.

Letters may serve to slow the hurtle towards the cemetery; for the moribund deserve an especially patient attention, as do their survivors. It is no doubt in some way relevant that, shortly after Beckett meets her, Barbara Bray becomes a widow with two small children dependent upon her; his letter of condolence to her is one of his finest and most vividly felt.[107] While Beckett had important female correspondents before, such as Mary Manning Howe, Pamela Mitchell, Jacoba van Velde, and Mania Péron, only now, from 1958, does a woman become Beckett's chief correspondent; she it is who instructs him what to read, who is avid for details not just of the made but of the making. To her he can write in a manner both utterly personal and at the same time eminently suited to a collection (such as the present one) concerned principally with letters bearing upon his work, the liveliness of his expression lighting up even the most detailed description of literary or theatrical drudgery. "I at least understand," he writes to her after watching a production of *Krapp* with Cyril Cusack in the title role, "better than ever before which is saying something when and why its weakness, here and in my other plays, and made the new one seem quite impossible as planned."[108] The insight flickers with self-referentiality as he continues by writing once again, "awful English this." Or take an earlier, extraordinary letter, in which the sentences roll on in a manner hardly witnessed since the letters to Duthuit, almost never seen in English, and where the ostensible reason for the lack of inhibition – "still drunk" – accounts for only a fraction of the freedom, not least with memory's flotsam: "You shd. have gone to Lansdowne Road," he tells her, "charming venue, full of memories, cricket unexpectedly with brother's huge bat, hardly lift it, loss of railway ticket, fear of whiskered porter, walk home devious ways 10 miles, huge bag, father rampaging on Mrs Rooney's road, mother in furious swoon, police alerted in vain, midnight, foodless to bed, charming ground – Dicky Lloyd, Wakefield, Jaureguy, ape-armed uncle beating down umbrella's [sic] with short stick, part of boyhood, heroic days."[109] Readers of the letters may well wonder how exactly Beckett was able to sustain such intensity of connection while living with (and later

107 SB to Barbara Bray, 17 March 1958.

108 SB to Barbara Bray, 11 July 1960.

109 SB to Barbara Bray, 17 February 1959.

marrying) his long-term partner Suzanne Deschevaux-Dumesnil. As the letters to Suzanne have not survived, recourse will have to be made to Beckett's biography, as well as to *Play* with its classic lovers' triangle (turned into a line of heads facing forward). If the complexity does leave its mark on his letters, I would suggest one way it does so is through the increasingly telegraphic style in which he writes to Bray, in which pronouns become notable absentees. This allows him, when on holiday with his wife for example, to reduce the incidence of either "I" (which would be a very partial truth) or "we" (which might be hurtful, however fully aware Bray was of her lover's situation). "Bought six pairs of socks today in the Wednesday market," he writes from Courmayeur in the Alps. "Very colourful. Not the socks. 5 francs a pair."[110]

As his fame spreads, and as his private life becomes ever more complex, intersecting as it does with his writing life, explanations and solutions are demanded in frightening numbers, of a writer who feels constitutionally unsuited to offering these. He is called upon for a stage device, a clear-cut preference between German publishers, a definitive term in English for a notion he wishes to keep ambiguous, a means to finance a production, a substitute for a pregnant actress, a way of pronouncing an impossibly difficult text – and more. The letters gathered here offer Beckett's unflagging attempts, often against his grain, to be helpful. When a word or two of practical advice is not sufficient, he offers explanations that can be astonishingly explicit, as when he lays out his film, *Film*, beginning "The point of departure is the old metaphysical doctrine," and going on with an account that, if it were not so eloquent with its taxonomy of split personalities, would do service in any bluffer's guide.[111] But he never allows his readers to forget for long, as he dispenses advice, explanations, solutions, that these are only ever partial, provisional, and that what really matters is elsewhere, eluding any quick fixes.

Because of this same fame, his irrefutable public success, it is harder than ever for Beckett convincingly to be an advocate of failure, even when his attachment to failure arises from his deepest sense of what it is to be a writer, one whose role is not to sort or explain or even express things – neither in his literary texts nor in his letters. Incapacity needs to be ever more adventurously claimed, passivity stalked, by the writer who, at the end of the present volume, is only two years away from the

110 SB to Barbara Bray, 7 July 1965.
111 SB to Barney Rosset, 21 June 1963.

Nobel Prize. "I too at the foot of the cliff-blank-sheet," he puts it to fellow-writer Robert Pinget; "Without a glimmer, without a hope, but always in agreement with the Great Silent One."[112] To aspiring novelist Matti Megged he writes, in solidarity and admonishment both: "Writing I suppose for some of us – though most certainly not for all – is only possible in the last ditch and in complete désespoir de cause and at a depth where one's 'living' not only is gone, but never was."[113] At this level even encouragement might be a curse: "Either it comes to that or it doesn't – and one couldn't wish it for anyone."

Even as he is offering Barbara Bray support that is financial, emotional, practical, while she contemplates leaving London to move to Paris in 1960, Beckett is capable of no easy answers. "You have never understood what a rag I am," he writes to her, "and how little to be relied on and how little I can do for anyone and in brief how little there remains now of the being and the writer, how little of the little there ever was."[114] As he continues, the image he conjures up is almost the exact complement to those images encountered earlier in explanation of how writing might once again become authentic, of Sisyphus before the writing-hill, of the writer before the page-cliff: "It is like being in a wheel chair rolling slowly down and putting on the brakes every now and then to have a look round or just out of pusillanimity and then letting them off and waiting for the descent to resume, which it does not immediately the slope is still so gentle, and all the things one may say to oneself then, while waiting." What Beckett the successful author needs to remind his friends – and the more intimate the friend, the greater the need – is of that "gentle slope" which he is not disposed to avoid. For even as he is reaching out to help – and help he does, countless times over the course of the years recorded here – he is also, as he goes on to tell Bray at this momentous point in their lives, "a creature so committed already to the lying back & folded hands and closed eyes and gathering speed." He is, that is to say, a *writer* – his own sort of writer: "no place for that in solutions."

Dan Gunn

112 SB to Robert Pinget, 14 August 1964.
113 SB to Matti Megged, 3 December 1962.
114 SB to Barbara Bray, 10 October 1960.

LETTERS
1957–1965

CHRONOLOGY 1957

1957	4 January	SB writing "The Gloaming," a play for two actors (abandoned; later *Rough for Theatre I*).
	7 January	All police powers in Algiers taken over by General Massu.
	10–19 January	*Waiting for Godot* with an all black cast in previews at the Shubert Theatre in Boston. It opens on 21 January at the Ethel Barrymore Theatre, New York, but closes after five days.
	13 January	The BBC Third Programme broadcasts *All That Fall.*
	After 30 January	Publication of *Fin de partie* and *Acte sans paroles*, Editions de Minuit.
	February	SB begins English translation of *L'Innommable.*
	c. 11–15 February	John Beckett works with Deryk Mendel in Paris so that his music reflects Mendel's movements in *Acte sans paroles I.*
	Before 12 February	SB's first meeting with the Director of London's Royal Court Theatre, George Devine, in Paris.
	19 February	SB's first meeting with BBC radio producer Donald McWhinnie, in Paris.
	March	*Tous ceux qui tombent* published in *Les Lettres Nouvelles.*
	15 March	Grove Press publish *Murphy.*
	21 March	SB in London to supervise rehearsals of *Fin de partie* at the Royal Court Theatre for its world premiere.
	28 March	Death of Jack B. Yeats in Dublin; SB unable to attend the funeral.
	2 April	Gala performance of *Fin de partie*, as part of the French Festival Week in London.

3 April	SB leaves London for Paris.
26 April	Avant-première of *Fin de partie* at the Studio des Champs-Elysées, Paris; Générale (with critics), 30 April.
30 April	A. J. Leventhal talk on Beckett for the BBC Third Programme.
2 May	The BBC Third Programme broadcasts *Fin de partie* recorded with the original London cast.
7 May	SB begins English translation of *Fin de partie.*
22 May	The term "Le Nouveau Roman" is coined in *Le Monde* by Emile Henriot, reviewing works by Alain Robbe-Grillet and Nathalie Sarraute.
After 27 May	Publication of *Lieutenant en Algérie* by Jean-Jacques Servan-Schreiber, which denounces French military policy in Algeria.
24 August	SB has completed second mime, *Acte sans paroles II*, for Deryk Mendel.
30 August	Faber and Faber publish *All That Fall.*
20 September	SB goes to Etretat for two days, guest of Jérôme Lindon.
4 October	Launch of the first earth satellite, the Soviet Sputnik.
8 October	Alan Schneider in Paris for four days of discussions with SB about *Fin de partie*; they attend the Paris production together, twice.
12 October	*Fin de partie* closes after ninety-seven performances in Paris.
After 18 October	Publication of *Tous ceux qui tombent*, Editions de Minuit.
10 December	The BBC Third Programme broadcasts extracts from *Molloy*, read by Patrick Magee, with music by John Beckett.
14 December	The BBC Third Programme broadcasts "From an Abandoned Work," read by Patrick Magee.
20 December	Michel Butor's novel *La Modification* awarded the Prix Renaudot. Albert Camus awarded the Nobel Prize in Literature.

ADAM TARN
WARSAW

le 10 janvier 1957

6 Rue des Favorites
Paris 15me

Cher Adam Tarn

C'est avec beaucoup de peine et de déception que je me vois dans l'impossibilité de me rendre à votre émouvante invitation.[1] Les répétitions de ma nouvelle pièce m'accaparent, sans parler d'autres obligations et d'autres soucis qui me clouent ici.[2]

Je suis infiniment touché par l'amitié et la générosité auxquelles je dois d'être convié à la création de Godot à Varsovie et à un séjour dans votre pays et c'est de tout coeur que je vous adresse, à vous-même et aux dirigeants du Théâtre Wspolczesny, ma très vive reconnaissance et mon espoir de pouvoir un jour vous l'exprimer de vive voix, et mieux, en vous serrant la main, chez vous.

Avez-vous reçu le texte de All That Fall que j'avais prié Curtis Brown de vous envoyer? Sinon dites-le-moi et je vous l'enverrai moi-même.

J'ai été très heureux de rencontrer Julian Rogozinski et regrette seulement que ce ne fût pas plus longuement. Faites-lui mes amitiés.[3]

En vous renouvelant mes remerciements et mes regrets je vous prie de croire, cher Adam Tarn, à mes sentiments très amicaux.

s/
Samuel Beckett

TLS; 1 leaf, 1 side; BP.

10 January 1957 | 6 Rue des Favorites
Paris 15

Dear Adam Tarn,

To my great distress and disappointment, I find that it is impossible for me to accept your very moving invitation.[1] The rehearsals of my new play take up all my time, not to mention other obligations and concerns that keep me pinned here.[2]

I am greatly touched by the friendship and generosity to which I owe my being invited to see the first staging of *Godot* in Warsaw and to stay in your country, and I send, to you and to all those in charge of the Współczesny Theatre, my heartfelt thanks and my hope of being able one day to express them to you direct, and, better still, with a handshake, where you live.

Have you received the text of *All That Fall* that I had asked Curtis Brown to send you? If not, let me know and I will send it myself.

I was very glad to meet Julian Rogoziński and am only sorry that it was not for longer. Give him my regards.[3]

Once again my thanks, my regrets, and my warmest wishes.

s/

Samuel Beckett

1 Adam Tarn (1902–1975; Profile, II), Editor of *Dialog*, Warsaw, the first publisher of SB's work in Poland.

The Warsaw premiere of *Czekając na Godota*, directed by Jerzy Kreczmar (1902–1985), opened at the Teatr Współczesny on 26 January 1957. August Grodzicki commented: "Cela a été un véritable événement dans la vie théâtrale, culturelle et même politique du pays" (in Ahmad Kamyabi Mask, *Qu'attendent Eugène Ionesco et Samuel Beckett?* [Paris: A. Kamyabi Mask, 1991] 136) (This was a genuine event in the theatrical, cultural, and even political life of the country).

2 Rehearsals of *Fin de partie* had begun in anticipation of the Paris production at the Théâtre de l'Œuvre; the opening had been scheduled for 15 January, but it was postponed to 26 February (see 15 December 1956).

3 Julian Rogoziński (1912–1980) was the Polish translator of *En attendant Godot* (*Czekając na Godota*), and, later, of *Endgame* (*Końcówka*), *Act without Words I* (*Akt bez słów I*), and *Eh Joe* (*Słuchaj, Joe*). SB had met him and Adam Tarn in late 1956.

BARNEY ROSSET
GROVE PRESS, NEW YORK

January 11th 1956 or rather 57 — 6 Favorites
Paris 15

Dear Barney

Glad to have your long letter.[1] Bad news here. The Oeuvre has suddenly backed out of its engagements. Reason given: on the verge of bankruptcy they had to choose between selling the theatre and signing for a play with two cinema stars and strong financial backing.[2] To the latter spike their rectum has inclined, leaving us high, dry and theatreless. The rehearsals were well advanced. Blin and Martin are desolate. So it goes on this bitch of an earth.[3]

Thanks for figures. Very encouraging. Lindon received a whack from Saunders. Perhaps my personal was among it, for to me directly gar nix.[4]

Thanks for Canada dossier and for your efforts to edify the bastards.[5]

Glad you liked All That Fall. Rereading it I realize I wrote it too fast and missed a good few chances. First broadcast day after to-morrow evening from the 3rd. Second I am told the following Saturday or 19th. I hear from Curtis Brown that their New York agent is in touch with you. I know the BBC are broadcasting a recording and I am sure they would put the tape at your disposal. Would you like me to write myself to John Morris, director of the 3rd?[6] Tell me what you would like me to do and it will be done. Harper's Bazaar were after it too.[7] It is being translated into French at the moment, for publication in Nadeau's Lettres Nouvelles next month.[8] No objection at all to your publishing the Bones in the Evergreen, on the contrary. Please indicate date of composition, also of Dante and the L.[9] I feel very shaky about undertaking translation of Fin de Partie (of which I have just corrected second proofs), and wanted to see it here before doing so. But at the turn events now taking I think I shall have a shot without much further delay. The Royal Court Theatre, London (George Devine) want to do it in the Fall. I don't see how they can without cuts which I won't have.

Perhaps the new Watergate Theatre Club.[10] I have asked Lindon to let me have a few sets of proofs to send out - notably to you and to Germany - pending appearance of book.

Curious to hear about black Godot in Boston.[11] Première in Warsaw 26th inst. They very kindly invited me. But as usual I have had to decline.

So glad there is Linc whom salute from me.[12] And to you both all the best for the new jolt beginning of the buckled old wheel.

Yours ever s/ Sam

Suzanne has been very poorly. But a little better now.[13]

TLS, with APS; 1 leaf, 1 side; Burns Library, Samuel Beckett Collection, SB-BR.

1 Barney Rosset (1922–2012; Profile, II) was the Editor of Grove Press and SB's American publisher and theatrical agent.

2 The arrangement to produce *Fin de partie* at the Théâtre de l'Œuvre had been broken abruptly on 9 January ("Attestation" prepared for SB's signature, dated 1 February 1957; IMEC-Fonds Samuel Beckett, Boîte 11, *Fin de partie* divers). Jérôme Lindon (1925–2001; Profile, II), Director, Editions de Minuit, wrote to the Service Juridique of the Société des Auteurs et Compositeurs Dramatiques on 22 January: "Le préjudice causé à Samuel Beckett est évident" (The damage to Samuel Beckett is obvious). There had already been thirty rehearsals, and, by now, other Paris theatres were booked for the season (IMEC-Fonds Samuel Beckett, Boîte 11, *Fin de partie*, contrats, représentations [1]).

The Théâtre de l'Œuvre chose to produce *Vous qui nous jugez* by Robert Hossein (b. 1927), with Hossein as director and actor, and his wife Marina Vlady (b. 1938), a film star, in her first stage role. The play opened on 9 March.

3 Roger Blin (1907–1984; Profile, II) directed *Fin de partie* and played the role of Hamm; Jean Martin (1922–2009; Profile, II) played Clov.

4 Grove Press reported that 49 hardbound and 374 paperbound copies of *Molloy* had been sold in 1956. Grove Press paid royalties to Marion Saunders, the New York agent acting on behalf of Editions de Minuit and SB. She had sent a single payment to Lindon, publisher of the original French edition, which included the payment to SB as author and translator (Saunders Agency to Jérôme Lindon, 4 January 1957; IMEC-Fonds Samuel Beckett, Boîte 3, Correspondance 1957 – droits étrangers. Barney Rosset to SB, 14 January 1957; NSyU).

"Gar nix" combines English slang "nix" (nothing) with the German "gar nichts" (nothing whatsoever).

5 When the Canadian government prohibited the Grove edition of *Molloy*, Rosset demanded an explanation and threatened to make "the Canadian policy of cultural suppression" known to the press of Canada and the world (Raymond Labarge, Customs and Excise Division of the Department of National Revenue of Canada, to Barney Rosset, 10 December 1956; Rosset to Labarge, 25 December 1956; NSyU). On 27 December, Labarge replied that although *Molloy* had been considered indecent, Rosset's letter would be treated as an informal request for an appeal (NSyU). Rosset

sent copies of this correspondence to SB. The Canadian prohibition was rescinded on 29 January.

6 Rosset had sent SB a telegram on 19 December 1956: "RADIO SCRIPT MARVELOUS HOW CAN I OBTAIN PUBLISHING PHONOGRAPH AND PERFORMANCE RIGHTS" (NSyU).

John Morris (1895–1980; Profile, II) was Controller of the BBC Third Programme from 1952 to 1958.

7 Carmel Snow (1887–1961), who had met SB in Dublin in 1937, was Editor-in-Chief of *Harper's Bazaar* from 1932 through 1957. *Harper's Bazaar* had shown interest in publishing *Murphy* in 1946 (SB to Thomas McGreevy, 7 July 1937; TCD, MS 10402/128; 1 September 1946). Snow had arranged for SB to be photographed by Brassaï; the photograph was published in *Harper's Bazaar* (May 1957) 143.

8 Robert Pinget (1919–1997; Profile, II) wrote of the experience of working on the French translation of *All that Fall* with SB in his (unpublished) memoir written mostly in 1960 (Doucet, unclassified Pinget Collection, "Notre ami Samuel Beckett"):

> All That Fall est une petite pièce et c'est pour m'être utile qu'il m'a demandé ce service. Il me faisait l'honneur d'associer mon nom au sien pour la publication dans la revue des Lettres Nouvelles dont le directeur Maurice Nadeau lui avait demandé un texte. Cet honneur s'est renouvelé plusieurs fois par la suite. C'est tout juste si je m'en suis rendu compte sur le moment. Beckett est venu chez moi pour travailler à All That Fall: c'était la première fois que je le recevais. J'avais fait tant bien que mal une sorte de dégrossissage du texte et il me fallait son avis pour une multitude de choses. Il a ensuite entièrement repris ma traduction, ma connaissance de l'anglais étant encore plus que rudimentaire, ce qui lui aura donné double travail. Il a insisté pour que mon nom figure également sur la publication de Minuit. Ces sortes de gestes, quand on pense à l'importance qu'accorde Sam au moindre mot qu'il écrit, sont inoubliables. J'ai retiré un grand bénéfice de cette collaboration. L'honnêteté de ce travailleur acharné, sa précision, son refus de se laisser aller à la moindre faiblesse quand il s'agit d'écrire, m'ont confirmé ce que je savais sur le soin qu'on doit apporter à ce qu'on fait. Travail en profondeur, toujours plus en profondeur. (11–12.) (*All That Fall* is a small play, and it was to be helpful to me that he asked this favour of me. He was doing me the honour of putting my name alongside his for publication in the review *Les Lettres Nouvelles*, whose Editor, Maurice Nadeau, had asked him for a text. This honour has come my way more than once since then. I hardly took it in at the time. Beckett came to my flat to work on *All That Fall* – the first time he'd been there. I had done a first sort of run-through of the text, and needed his advice on heaps of things. He then went back over the whole of my translation, my knowledge of English being worse than rudimentary, which will have doubled his work. He insisted that my name too should appear on the Minuit publication. These sorts of gestures, when one thinks of the importance Sam gives to the slightest word he writes, are unforgettable. I benefited enormously from this collaboration. The honesty of this most determined of workers, his precision, his refusal to give in to the faintest weakness when it comes to writing, confirmed what I already knew of the care that must be taken in what one does. Work in depth, in ever greater depth.)

9 A selection of poems from SB's *Echo's Bones and Other Precipitates* (Paris: Europa Press, 1935) was published in the first issue of *Evergreen Review* (1.1 [December 1957]

179–192). In the same issue was published "Dante and the Lobster" (24–36), the first story in SB's *More Pricks Than Kicks* (London: Chatto & Windus, 1934).

SB's sentence about "Dante and the Lobster" appears in the top margin of the letter, with a line pointing to where it is to be inserted. Neither republication gives the date of composition.

10 George Devine (1910–1966; Profile, II) wished to produce *Fin de partie* in English at the Royal Court Theatre. As had been the case with *Waiting for Godot*, SB anticipated that the Lord Chamberlain's Office might refuse to grant a license for a London production unless there were cuts to the text. The New Watergate Theatre Club was formed in 1956 to present "outstanding plays ... for which no licence for public performance in this country has been granted" ("The Comedy as a Club Theatre," *The Times* 7 September 1956: 3).

11 Directed by Herbert Berghof (1909–1990), this new production of *Waiting for Godot* featured a black cast: Mantan Moreland (1902–1973) as Estragon, Earle Hyman (b. 1926) as Vladimir, Geoffrey Holder (b. 1930) as Lucky, Rex Ingram (1895–1969) as Pozzo, and Bert Chamberlain (n.d.) as the boy. It opened at the Shubert Theatre in Boston on 10 January.

12 Mary Lincoln Bonnell (1929–2013), a sculptor, was Rosset's companion at this time; here SB writes "Linc," but in subsequent letters she is referred to as "Link."

13 Suzanne Deschevaux-Dumesnil (1900–1989; Profile, I) was SB's partner.

MARGUERITE DURAS
PARIS

le 12 janvier 1957 Paris

Madame

Je n'avais pas été voir votre pièce au Studio. Je viens de l'écouter à la radio. Elle est merveilleuse, merveilleuse.[1]

Samuel Beckett

ALS; 1 leaf, 1 side; Mascolo Collection. Previous publication (facsimile and transcription): Marguerite Duras, *Romans, cinéma, théâtre, un parcours (1943–1993)* (Paris: Gallimard, 1997) 521.

12 January 1957 Paris

Dear Mme Duras

I had not been to see your play at the Studio. I have just been listening to it on the radio. It is marvellous, marvellous.[1]

Samuel Beckett

1 Marguerite Duras's play, which she adaped from her novel *Le Square*, had played at the Studio des Champs-Elysées from 18 September to 3 October 1956 with Ketty Albertini (1926–1986) as Elle, and René-Jacques Chauffard (1920–1972) as Lui, directed by Claude Martin (n.d.). It aired on Paris National Radio on 12 January with the same cast.

RICHARD ROUD
LONDON

12.1.56 [for 1957] Paris

Dear Round

Thanks for your letter. Sorry for the hitch.[1] Hope you'll be back soon.

Bad news here. The Oeuvre has suddenly backed out of its arrangements with us, preferring to Fin de Partie a God knows what with two film stars (Hossein & Vlady) and solid financial backing. So now we are theatreless. Blin & Martin are effondrés.[2] So it goes on this turd of an earth.

Suppose now publication will also be held up. I'll send you the book when it appears and let you know how things turn out.[3] Vague talk already of the Vieux Colombier (pure delirium) and The Mathurins (Popeye thinking).[4] Personally don't seem to care very much, except that I feel more like trying to translate the bloody thing here and now.

Glad you like the Renard. For me it's as inexhaustible as Boswell.[5]

Black Godot at Boston – of all tea-parties – last Thursday.[6] No news to date.

All the best
yrs. ever
Sam. Beckett

ALS; 1 leaf, 2 sides; Smolens Collection. *Dating*: The new production of *Waiting for Godot* with black actors opened in Boston on Thursday, 10 January 1957.

1 Richard Roud (1929–1989; Profile, II), whose name SB here writes as "Round," American film critic, at this time an Instructor of English in the University of Maryland Overseas Extension in England; he became Programme Director of the London Film

Festival in 1959, and founder of the New York Film Festival in 1963. Roud had asked SB if he could attend rehearsals of *Fin de partie* while he was in Paris, but this proved impossible (SB to Roud, 3 January 1957; Smolens Collection).

2 "Effondrés" (distraught).

3 *Fin de partie* was published as originally planned.

4 SB refers to the Théâtre du Vieux-Colombier and the Théâtre des Mathurins, Paris, and makes play with "Mathurin," the French name of the cartoon character "Popeye."

5 SB refers to Jules Renard's *Journal* (1887–1910) and to James Boswell's *Life of Johnson* (1791).

6 After meeting Michael Myerberg (1906–1974; Profile, II), the American producer of *Waiting for Godot*, SB wrote to Barney Rosset: "I mentioned to him that I thought Godot by an all negro cast would be interesting. He said he had had the same idea but was nervous about telling me, fearing I wd not like it [...] he is getting going with preparations for performance with all negro cast. This pleases me, rightly or wrongly, much." (20 August [1956]; NSyU.) Barney Rosset reported to SB on 14 January: "The Boston production went off very well. To me the new Vladimir is incomparable [...] and this greatly changes the whole play. The new Lucky is absolutely different [...] 'astounding.'" (14 January 1957; NSyU.) The production played at the Shubert Theatre in Boston from 10 to 19 January before moving to the Ethel Barrymore Theatre in New York where it opened on 21 January.

DONALD McWHINNIE
BBC, LONDON

December 14th 1956 [*for* 14 January 1957] 6 Rue des Favorites
Paris 15me

Dear Donald McWhinnie

Bien travaillé.[1] Though the reception on Sunday was very poor I heard well enough to realize what a good job. I did not agree with it all, who ever does, and perhaps I should have if I had lost less of the detail. Things I liked particularly: the double walk sound in the second half, Dan's YES and their wild laugh (marvellous). O'Farrell and Devlin I thought excellent most of the time, the latter a little perfunctory in parts (his long speeches), but this perhaps due to distortion. Miss Fitt very good indeed.[2] I didn't think the animals were right.[3] I shall send you more considered appreciation if I succeed in hearing it better on Saturday. In the meantime to yourself and the players and all others concerned my very warm thanks and congratulations.

I have read with much pleasure the Paddy Pedlar.[4] Do you want it back?

Yours ever
s/ Sam. Beckett

I heard on Paris National I think last Saturday Le Square by Maurgerite [sic] Duras. Quite wonderful. I suppose you know about it: presented at the Studio des C.-E. last autumn, crucified by the bleeders and taken off after a fortnight. Overwhelmingly moving – to me. Admirably spoken by Chauffard as the traveller.[5] Ideal – I imagine – for the 3rd, in French or translation. I don't know her. But you could write – if interested – c/o Gallimard, 5 Rue Sébastien-Bottin, Paris 7me.

TLS; 1 leaf, 1 side; *datestamped* 17 JAN 1957; BBCWAC, RCONT1, Samuel Beckett, Scriptwriter I. *Dating*: letter follows BBC broadcast of *All That Fall* (Sunday, 13 January 1957) and was received 17 January.

1 Donald McWhinnie (1920–1987; Profile, II)."Bien travaillé" (Well done).

2 J. G. Devlin (1907–1991) played Dan Rooney; Mary O'Farrell (1892–1968) played Mrs. Rooney; Sheila Ward (n.d.) played Miss Fitt.

3 *All That Fall* was "the first programme to contain what later came to be known as 'radiophonic' sound." Desmond Briscoe (1925–2006), Studio Manager of the BBC Radiophonic Workshop until 1983, said "we did away with natural sounds altogether, and simulated" (Desmond Briscoe and Roy Curtis-Bramwell, *The BBC Radiophonic Workshop: The First 25 Years* [London: British Broadasting Corporation, 1983] 14, 18). Donald McWhinnie explained why they did not use recorded animal sounds: "By using good mimics I think we can get real style and shape into the thing" (Donald McWhinnie to SB, 1 January 1957; BBCWAC, RCONT1, Samuel Beckett, Scriptwriter I).

4 Michael J. Molloy's *The Paddy Pedlar* (Dublin: Duffy, 1954) was adapted for broadcast and aired on the BBC Third Programme on 5 September 1956. The title is underscored by hand in the (typed) text of the letter.

5 A harsh review of *Le Square* by Marguerite Duras began in *Le Monde*: "Un moyen infaillible de précipiter la crise du théâtre, de le conduire aux derniers spasmes, serait de multiplier les représentations de pièces comme *le Square*" (R. K.[emp],"'Le Square' de Marguerite Duras," 19 September 1956: 8) (An infallible way of triggering a crisis in the theatre, of pushing it through to the final twitchings, would be to give a boost to the performing of plays like *Le Square*).

ALAN SIMPSON
PIKE THEATRE, DUBLIN

January 14th 1957

Rue des Favorites
Paris 15me

Dear Alan

Thanks for your letter.[1] The mime – Act Without Words – was to have been performed here at the Oeuvre with Fin de Partie at the end of next month. All sealed and signed, rehearsals (of the latter) well advanced. Last week the theatre suddenly backed out of its engagements, preferring to my black act a commercial play with film stars and financial backing. For the time being we are theatreless.

I have decided however not to hold up things abroad and not to insist on Paris priority. So you are welcome to the mime for your festival.[2] But before you take it on a few words on its nature and the complications arising therefrom.

It was written for a dancer and John's music is by no means a vague music of armosphere [sic] or background, but very closely tied up with the action of the mime.[3] This is not to say that the thing has to be danced, but simply that the movements of the player have to be very precise and rhythmical, at least whenever associated with the musical element which is intermittent, and indeed throughout if a tape-recording is used as is our intention here. The music (scored for piano, xylophone and drum) is not yet ready. It has to be composed in function of a stage, a player and accessories. John was to have come over to Paris end of this month to get it done. The music he would write for us here might not easily work at the Pike, though I suppose it could be made to. But the point that arises is this, that if things are held up here for long, as they may well be, John's music will have to be written in Dublin in function of Kelly and your stage and accessories and that the possibility of your producing the piece depends on his willingness to do this.[4] I am writing to him to explain the situation and suggest you get in touch with him yourself. Address: 7 Pembridge Crescent, London W.11.

It is all very complicated, but there it is. I intend now to get after the translation of the act, but don't know it [sic] if it's possible nor – if it is – when it will be ready.

I had made no financial arrangements with Edwards whom, as I think I told you, I had asked from the beginning to get your consent before doing anything about the mime.[5]

I heard on the air last week Le Square by Marguerite Duras, a one act played at the Studio des C.-E. last autumn, crucified by the bleeding crrritics and taken off after a fortnight. I did not – to my great regret see it then. It is quite extraordinary. Just a little skivvy and a tired commercial sitting in a public square talking. No action whatsoever. Most marvellous and moving dialogue. About 90 minutes. If you are interested write to her c/o Gallimard, 5 Rue Sébastien-Bottin, Paris 7me.

Remember me very kindly to Carol.[6]

Yours ever

s/ Sam

Glad to hear of the success of your revue.[7]

TLS, with APS; 1 leaf, 2 sides; TCD, MS 10731/44.

1 Alan Simpson (1920–1980; Profile, II), co-founder of the Pike Theatre.

2 Simpson wished to produce *Acte sans paroles I* with the actor Dermot Kelly, who had played Vladimir in the 1955 Pike Theatre production of *Waiting for Godot*, along with "one or two Ionesco plays" in the Dublin Festival in May 1957 (Simpson to SB, 10 January 1957; TCD, MS 10731/43).

3 *Acte sans Paroles I* was created for dancer Deryk Mendel (1921–2013; Profile, II), with music by SB's cousin John Beckett (1927–2007; Profile, II).

4 Writing to Alan Simpson on 19 January 1957, John Beckett explained that he preferred to "complete the work in terms of the [stage] dimension we originally had at our disposal, and likely will have again, in Paris, and of the type of movement envisaged by Mendel and me. Your stage is, of course much too small to provide the one, and, having seen him as Vladimir, I do not think that Dermot Kelly would be able to reproduce the other." (TCD, MS 10731/46.)

5 Hilton Edwards (1903–1982; Profile, I) had requested a short piece from SB to include in an "entertainment," *Tales from the Irish Hills*, that he was producing at the Gaiety Theatre, Dublin, in February (9 November 1956; GEU, MS 1221).

6 Carolyn Swift (1923–2002; Profile, II), co-founder of the Pike Theatre, was married to Alan Simpson.

7 Simpson wrote to SB of the success of the Pike Theatre's review *Say it with Follies* (10 January 1957; TCD, MS 10731/43; Carolyn Swift, *Stage by Stage* [Dublin: Poolbeg Press, 1985] 229).

ROSICA COLIN
LONDON

[after 18 January 1957] Paris

Thank you for yr. letter of Jan 18th to me.[1]

Sorry for the imbroglio. All those texts having been written directly in English did not go through Jérôme Lindon but were sent by me to Curtis Brown with instructions to them to handle all rights.[2]

I am extremely sorry if this puts you in a difficult situation, but I am afraid it is too late to do anything about it now.[3]

I shall reserve for you the handling of the U.K. publication rights of Fin de Partie. But I shall not authorize a bowdlerized edition. If I had known that Faber were going to bring out Godot in the Lord Chamberlain's text I should have refused my auth. But they did this without consulting me.[4] If I can only be published in England in an expurgated form, I prefer not to be published there at all. And I am fairly certain that F. & F. will not risk Fin de Partie as it stands, or withstands, if I ever succeed in translating it.[5]

It would give me great pleasure to meet you and I do hope you will not fail to look me up next time you are in Paris.[6]

AL draft; 1 leaf, 1 side; *on* Rosica Colin *to* SB, 18 January 1957 (TLS; 2 leaves, 2 sides); GEU, MS 1221.

1 Rosica Colin (1903–1983; Profile, II), SB's literary agent in London.

2 SB refers to *All That Fall*, written in English.
In her letter to SB of 18 January, Colin mentioned that Grove Press had a contract for publication of an eventual English translation of *Fin de partie*, and that she would also like to represent that text in England (Rosica Colin Collection; GEU, MS 1221). Jérôme Lindon, Editions de Minuit, handled the rights of all SB works written in French.

3 Lindon had asked Rosica Colin to represent SB's novels and *Waiting for Godot* in England; only after the theatrical agents Curtis Brown placed *Godot* with the Arts

Theatre, London, did Colin arrange for its publication by Faber and Faber. Both Curtis Brown and Rosica Colin wished to retain representation of SB's works.

4 SB inserts: "But they did this without consulting me." This is written in the right margin perpendicularly to the text. The Faber and Faber edition of *Waiting for Godot* (1955) reflected the cuts required by the Lord Chamberlain's Office for public performance.

5 When Faber and Faber agreed to publish *Fin de partie*, Colin assured Beckett on 20 February: "This time the full text, no Lord Chamberlain's cuts" (Rosica Colin Collection).

6 This last sentence is written in the left margin at a right angle to the text.

JACQUES PUTMAN
PARIS

5.2.57 Paris

Cher Jacques

On ne peut pas donner ce dialogue pour l'exposition de Bram.[1] C'est de l'algèbre de cirque. Ce serait lui rendre le pire des services. Demandez à Georges, il n'aurait qu'à développer ce qu'il dit sur lui dans son Musée.[2] Si je pouvais vous donner un petit texte ce serait avec joie. Mais il n'y a plus rien à tirer de moi et de ma pouffiasse de vie de chien de bâton de chaise mal percée. Un verre ensemble si vous voulez mardi prochain six heures à la terrasse de la Coupole.

Amitiés

s/ Sam

TLS; 1 leaf, 1 side; Porte Collection. Previous publication (facsimile): Claire Stoullig and Nathalie Schoeller, eds., *Bram van Velde* (Paris: Editions du Centre Georges Pompidou, 1989) 187.

5.2.57 Paris

Dear Jacques,

We can't put out this dialogue for the Bram exhibition.[1] It's convoluted nonsense. It would be doing him the worst of turns. Ask Georges – he would only have to work up what he says about him in his *Musée*.[2] If I could let you have a little text it would be with great pleasure. But there is nothing more to be got out of me or of my dirty bitch of a blundering life that palls between two not very close stools. A drink together if you like next Tuesday at 6 on the terrasse at the Coupole.

Best

s/ Sam

1 Bram van Velde (1895–1981; Profile, I) was to have an exhibition at the Galerie Michel Warren, 10 Rue des Beaux-Arts, Paris 7. In the catalogue, Jacques Putman (1926–1994), art critic, publisher, and champion of Van Velde's work, wished to publish a French translation of "Three Dialogues: Samuel Beckett and Georges Duthuit" (*Transition Forty-Nine*, no. 5 [December 1949] 97–103).

2 Georges Duthuit (1891–1973; Profile, II) makes a single brief mention of Bram van Velde in *Le Musée inimaginable*, II (Paris: J. Corti, 1956) 308.

ADAM TARN
WARSAW

le 5 février 1957

6 Rue des Favorites
Paris 15me

Cher Adam Tarn

Merci de votre lettre du 29 janvier. Je suis heureux que vous approuviez la mise en scène de Godot au Théâtre Wspolczesny. Je n'ai pas d'autres échos.

Je vous envoie cette semaine, à Rogozinski et à vous-même, vos exemplaires de Fin de Partie. La création à Paris est remise sine die à la suite d'une dispute avec le Théâtre de L'Oeuvre, où nous devions passer ce mois-ci.

Le texte du sermon est tiré des Psaumes de David, No. 145, verset 14. "Lead Kindly Light" et "Rock of Ages" sont des hymnes protestants.[1] "Sight [*for* Sigh] out etc." est d'un des singing-birds élisabéthains, je ne me rappelle plus lequel, ni le nom de la pièce. Peut-être Marston.[2] Je l'ai remplacé en français par du Ronsard: "Avant le temps, au lac qui erre Par le royaume de la nuit."[3] Le mot oublié par Maddy Rooney, et qu'elle remplace par "something something", est "lamentable[".] Curieux, qu'elle ait pu oublier ça. Entièrement à la disposition de R. pour d'autres éclaircissements.[4]

Croyez, cher Adam Tarn, à mes pensées sincèrement amicales.

s/

Samuel Beckett

TLS; 1 leaf, 1 side; BP.

5th February 1957

6 Rue des Favorites
Paris 15

Dear Adam Tarn,

Thank you for your letter of 29 January. I am glad that you approve of the production of *Godot* at the Współczesny Theatre. I have no other news of it.

This week I'll be sending you, Rogoziński and yourself, your copies of *Fin de partie*. The opening in Paris is postponed indefinitely, as a result of a dispute with the Théâtre de l'Œuvre, where we were due to go on this month.

The text of the sermon is taken from the Psalms of David, Psalm 145, verse 14. "Lead Kindly Light" and "Rock of Ages" are Protestant hymns.[1] "Sigh out" etc. is by one of the Elizabethan songbirds, I don't remember which, nor the name of the piece. Marston perhaps.[2] I have replaced it in French by some Ronsard: "Avant le temps, au lac qui erre Par le royaume de la nuit."[3] The word forgotten by Maddy Rooney that she replaces by "something something" is "lamentable." Odd that she should have forgotten that. Entirely at R's disposal for any other clarifications.[4]

With all good wishes

s/

Samuel Beckett

1 "The Lord upholdeth all that fall and raiseth up all those that be bowed down" (*All That Fall*, in *The Collected Shorter Plays of Samuel Beckett* [New York: Grove Weidenfeld, 1984] 38; hereafter *CSP*). "Lead Kindly Light," words (verses 1–3) by John Henry Newman; "Rock of Ages," words by Augustus M. Toplady (1740–1778).

2 The source for "Sigh out a something something tale of things, Done long ago and ill done" (*All That Fall*, *CSP*, 14) is in John Ford's *The Lover's Melancholy*

(1629): "Sigh out a lamentable tale of things, / Done long agoe and ill done" (Act IV.ii; rpt. *The English Experience: Its Records in Early Printed Books Published in Facsimile*, CCLXXI, ed. N. J. Norwood and W. J. Johnson [New York: Da Capo Press, 1970] 61).

3 Pierre de Ronsard's ode opens with the line: "Puis que la mort ne doit tarder" (Since death must soon come). SB uses the final two lines of the second verse: "Avant le temps au lac qui erre / Par le royaume de la Nuit" ([death … leads us] Before time to the lake / Which wanders through the realm of night) (*Ronsard: Œuvres Complètes*, I, ed. Gustave Cohen, Bibliothèque de la Pléiade [Paris: Gallimard, 1958] 968).

4 Julian Rogoziński.

EVA HESSE
MUNICH

14.2.57

6 Rue des Favorites
Paris 15me

Dear Miss Hesse

You have my heart-felt sympathy.

I hope enclosed notes will help you.[1]

Yours sincerely

Sam. Beckett

Note: Hesse's questions are presented in italics; SB's replies and headers, which are inserted in the left margin by hand, are shown in roman.

Queries

Enueg II

1. *breaking outside congress*

   Does congress imply (a) a coming together, (b) a building ? ?

   Congress: sexual coming together

2. *doch I assure thee/lying on O'Connell Bridge*

   Is the assurer or the assured lying on the bridge?

   The assurer. There should be a space between this line and the following.

Dortmunder

1. *sustaining the jade splinters*

   Does this mean simply that she's wearing jade trinkets?

   Enduring the jade splinters of the music.
2. *What is a signaculum?*

   Hymen in anatomical sense.
3. *in me, Habakkuk, mard of all sinners*

   What is mard? – mardochai? nard composite?

   Filth, merde.

Sanies I

1. *Donabate sad swans of Turvey Swords*

   Donabate a place name? sad swans of T. in Swords (nr Malahide) or Turvey Swords together a place name??

   Donabate: place north of Dublin. Swords: ditto. Sad swans of Turvey: old stone swans on gate pillars of old domain between Donabate and Swords.[2]
2. *tires bleeding voiding zeep the highway*

   voiding = avoiding? *zeep the noise made by the tires?*

   Voiding: emptying, expelling, as though road extruded by tires.
3. *potwalloping now through the promenaders*

   The conventional meaning of potwalloping doesn't fit in here; what is the intended meaning?

   Blundering heavily along.
4. *ah to be back in the caul with no trusts*

   What are trusts in this context?

   Responsibilities, commitments.
5. *Wild Woodbine – a cigarette? or flower?*

   Cheap cigarette.
6. *the tiger that funds ways home*

   What do you mean by funds?

   Merge together.

Sanies II

1. *What are skinnymalinks?*

   Skinny emaciated person.
2. *What are thongbells? thong = sound or voice?*

or thongbells a dialect word for some kind of flower?

Invented word: thong of whip – bells of tulips.

Alba

1. *so that there is no sun and no unveiling/and no host*

   What does host mean in this case? Stars? or theological host?

   Theological.

Echo's Bones

1. *the gantelope of sense and nonsense*

   Does gant allude to (a) glove, (b) Thos. Wolfe's Eugene Gant??

   Gauntlet, run the gauntlet.

Serena I

1. *Without the British Museum*

   without = outside (as considered from National History Museum), or sans??

   Outside. Gone from the BM where he was concerned with T. and the A.[3]

2. *oven strom*

   oven = hot strom = stroma (Greek)

   If not, what?

   Oven-hot cage. Strom: stream, as in maelstrom.

3. *screw me up Wren's giant bully*

   Wren's giant bully = cupola like gasometer?

   What's to be screwed up – the gasometer? or me?

   A tower in the City of London built by Wren and known as Wren's Bully. Or giant? Forget.[4] The narrow winding stairs suggest to him the thread of a screw. He screws himself up to top.

Serena II

1. *in the claws of the Pins*

   What are Pins in this connection?

   The Pins or Bens, a mountain range in Connemara, Ireland.

2. *Croagh Patrick waned Hindu*

   The "holy mountain" turns Hindu? Or what does waned mean?

   C.P., mountain of pilgrimage.[5] Waned: transformed by fading light.

3. *in a hag she drops her young*

   Hag has so many meanings: a bog, a soft place in a bog, a ravine?

I suppose you mean a bog as a composite of moor + toilet??

Soft place in bog. No toilet harmonics.

4. *the asphodels come running the flags after/she thinks*

   How to divide up the sentence: the asphodels (= forgetfulness)

   **come running (because) the flags (are approaching) *after she thinks. . . .*

   (a) *who comes running?*

   (b) *does after belong to the clause that follows one line lower?*

   The asphodels come running, the flags (reeds) come running after, she thinks she is dying, she is ashamed.

Serena III

1. *the Bull and Pool Beg*

   Is that the name of a tavern? Also Beg = small in gaelic . . .

   The Bull and the Pool Beg: two lights facing each other at the mouth of the Liffey and marking entrance of Dublin harbour.

2. *Merrion Flats*

   Are Flats flatlands or apartment blocks?

   Large expanse of dirty sand south of Dublin harbour, hardly covered by sea even at full tide.

3. *a thrillion sigmas*

   thrillion = trillion thrills?

   sigmas = small spikes of sponge? or milliseconds?

   scored with a thr. sigmas: scarred?

   Sigma: ~ Hogarth's "line of beauty" and symbol of Christ.[6]

   Scored: marked, furrowed. Thrillion: million, billion, thrillion.

4. *girls taken strippin*

   taken = taken out? or caught?

   strippin = stripping?

   Taken: surprised, caught

5. *the Rock = the Church?*

   The Rock: Blackrock, locality south of Dublin, often called the Rock. Rock of Ages harmonics.

Malacoda

1. *Malacoda refers to:*

   (a) *mucilage*

   (b) *mollusk*

   (c) *?*

2. *Malebranca is a stretcher??*
3. *What is Scarmilion? scar-vermilion sun?*

Malabranche, Malacoda, Scarmiglione: demons in Dante's Inferno.

Cascando

I have only a carbon copy of this poem, which I suspect may contain typographical errors. For instance, the 4th line reads:

1. *is it better abord than be barren*

Is abord spelt like that in the original, or is it a typing error?
abord = abort + bawd??

Read abort.

2. *bringing up the the bones the old loves*

Is "the the" in the original as an intended stutter, or did the person who typed up the poem put in an extra the by mistake??

One the only.

ACS; 1 leaf, 1 side; with TL enclosure containing questions (1 leaf, 1 side); Eva Hesse Collection.

1 For *Gedichte* (Wiesbaden: Limes Verlag, 1959), a German translation of SB's poems in French and English, Eva Hesse (b. 1925) translated those poems written in English. Elmar Tophoven (1923–1989; Profile, II) translated SB's poems written in French. Hesse indicated, "I mailed a list of queries relating to *Echo's Bones* to Beckett on 10 February 1957, to which he promptly replied" (Hesse to the editors, 18 November 1998).

2 Sir Patrick Barnewall had the mansion built in 1565 (*The Irish Times* 12 March 1999: 5).

3 The opening lines of "Serena I" allude to SB's reading in the British Library, then housed in the British Museum: "without the grand old British Museum / Thales and the Aretino"; for further discussion, see Knowlson, *Damned to Fame*, 157 and 648, n. 85.

4 Christopher Wren and Robert Hooke designed the Monument to the Great Fire (1671–1677), London. An inscription added to the Monument in 1681 suggested that Papists had caused the Great Fire, which provoked Alexander Pope to write: "Where London's column pointing at the skies, / Like a tall bully, lifts the head, and lyes" ("Epistle III to Allen Lord Bathurst," in *Moral Essays: Epistles to Several Persons*, ed. F. W. Bateson, The Twickenham Edition of the Poems of Alexander Pope [London: Methuen, 1951] 117).
SB inserts "Or giant? Forget." in left margin.

5 At Murrisk, near Westport in Co. Mayo, Croagh Patrick rises to 2,510 feet from the south shore of Clew Bay; as St. Patrick reputedly spent forty days fasting and praying on the mountain, it is the site of annual pilgrimages.

6 Hogarth defines the "line of beauty" as "the waving line, which is a line more productive of beauty than any of the former, as in flowers, and other forms of the ornamental kind" (William Hogarth, *The Analysis of Beauty, Written with a View of Fixing the Fluctuating Ideas of Taste* [London: J. Reaves, 1753] 38; rpt. Hogarth, *The Analysis of Beauty*, ed. Ronald Paulson [New Haven and London: Yale University Press: 1997] 42).

MARY HUTCHINSON
LONDON

14.2.57 Paris

Dear Mary

Thanks for your wire and letter. I shall be writing to George Devine. I do not think I shall try to translate the play.[1] I am overcome with stupid work and people to see. I hope to get away from Paris next week. I do not see any light any where and do not wish to see any. One is what one is and one's work what it is and the concern with approval small and with goodness and good people very weak. It will soon all be over and the foolishness as if never been. I do not want any one ever to move from his place on my account. I am very touched by your kindness and understanding.

Ever yours

Sam

ALS; 1 leaf, 1 side; *env to* Mrs Hutchinson, 21 Hyde Park Square, London W.2, Angleterre; *pm* 15-2-57, Paris; TxU, Hutchinson, 2.4.

1. Mary Hutchinson. Drawing by Henri Matisse

1 Mary Hutchinson (1889–1977; Profile, II), patron of the arts in London, had been encouraging George Devine to produce SB's work at the Royal Court Theatre. Devine

had written to her on 27 December 1956 to thank her for introducing him to SB, adding: "I am trying to persuade Beckett to translate Fin de Partie to make a complete Beckett programme" (TxU, Hutchinson, 10.8). Two days later, on 16 February, SB wrote to Devine to register his difficulties in doing the translation: "I feel more and more strongly that it is a hopeless undertaking. I cannot even translate 'vieux linge'." (TxU, English Stage Company, 1.2.)

KAY BOYLE
ROWAYTON, CONNECTICUT

4.3.57

6 rue des Favorites
Paris 15me

Dear Kay Boyle

I hear from Maria Jolas and from Laurence Vail that you are in search of information regarding my old book of short stories More Pricks Than Kicks.[1] I sent the information to Maria. Here it is again directly.

Published I think in 1934 or 35 by Chatto & Windus the book has been unobtainable since the war. The first story – Dante and the Lobster – appeared originally in Edward Titus's This Quarter, 1932 or 33, and I think has just appeared in U.S.A. in the new Grove Press magazine. Another – Yellow – was recently reprinted in New World Writing.[2]

I find these stories very unsatisfactory and do not propose to have them re-published.[3] Chatto & Windus have abandoned their rights.

I do not possess a copy of the book myself, but if you would write to Barney Rosset, Grove Press, 795 Broadway, New York, I am sure he would be able to place a copy at your disposal.

I am very pleased and flattered to hear that you are interested in my work. I should be happy to help with any biographical or bibliographical information that you may need.

With my kind regards to your husband, whom I met once at Mary Reynolds's house in Paris, I am[4]

yours sincerely
Sam. Beckett

ALS; 1 leaf, 1 side; *env to* Mrs Joseph Franckenstein, 188 Highland Avenue, Rowayton, Conn., U.S.A., *upper left corner* Avion; *pm* 4-3-57, Paris; TxU, Beckett Collection, 8.3.

1 American writer Kay Boyle* (1902–1992) was preparing to teach a course on the short story in the summer school of the University of Delaware (1957).

Maria Jolas (1893–1987; Profile, I). Laurence Vail (1891–1968) was from 1922 to 1928 the husband of Peggy Guggenheim (1898–1979; Profile, I) and, later, of Kay Boyle.

2 Samuel Beckett, "Dante and the Lobster," *This Quarter* 5.2 (December 1932) 222–236; in *More Pricks Than Kicks* 1–20; *Evergreen Review* 1.1 (December 1957) 24–36. Edward Titus (1870–1952; Profile, I).

Samuel Beckett, "Yellow," *More Pricks Than Kicks*, 227–252; rpt. in *New World Writing* 10 (November 1956) 108–119.

3 *More Pricks Than Kicks* was not reprinted by Grove Press until 1972; however, SB allowed an hors commerce mimeographed version, to give scholars access to this collection of stories (London: Calder and Boyars, 1966).

4 Joseph von Franckenstein (1909–1963), third husband of Kay Boyle.

American artist Mary Reynolds (1891–1950) was the partner of Marcel Duchamp in 1940; she and Duchamp had helped SB and Suzanne Deschevaux-Dumesnil in Arcachon following their flight from Paris at the time of the Occupation.

JACQUES PUTMAN
PARIS

dimanche [before 13 March 1957]

Cher Jacques

Ça ne peut pas marcher. Je ne peux pas rafistoler ça à la va[-]vite. J'ai des monceaux de gens sur le dos à en être malade. Il me faudrait huit jours de tranquillité pour en faire quelque chose d'à peu près compréhensible. Il faudrait changer, couper, ajouter, lier, presque refaire entièrement. En anglais ça tient le coup, en français c'est un désastre.[1] Ça ne pourrait que faire beaucoup de tort à Bram. Puisque ça presse tellement la meilleure solution serait peut-être de rédiger une courte note qui renvoie simplement à mes textes des Cahiers et de Pierre à Feu, au dialogue de Transition, aux textes de Duthuit dans les Cahiers et dans je ne sais plus quel panorama de la peinture moderne, et à tout autre texte sur lui que Bram jugera bon de faire citer.[2]

On pourrait peut-être se voir rapidement mardi. Je serai au Select à six heures.[3]

Amitiés

s/ Sam

TLS; 1 leaf, 1 side; Porte Collection. *Dating*: see 13 March 1957. Previous publication: Stoullig and Schoeller, eds., *Bram van Velde*, 187.

Sunday [before 13 March 1957]
Dear Jacques

It can't be done. I can't knock it into shape in a hurry. I've got loads of people pressing on me to the point where I feel ill. I would need a week's peace to make anything half-way comprehensible out of it. I'd have to change, cut, add, connect, almost rework completely. In English it holds up, in French it's a disaster.[1] It could only do serious harm to Bram. Since there's such a hurry, the best thing would perhaps be to write a short note referring readers to my texts in the *Cahiers* and *Pierre à Feu*, the dialogue in *Transition*, the Duthuit texts in the *Cahiers* and in I can't remember which panorama of modern painting, and any other text about him that Bram sees fit to have mentioned.[2]

We could perhaps get together briefly on Tuesday. I'll be in the Select at six.[3]

Best

s/ Sam

1 Translation of "Three Dialogues: Samuel Beckett and Georges Duthuit": SB to Jacques Putman, 5 February 1957, n. 1.

2 Samuel Beckett, "La Peinture des van Velde ou le monde et le pantalon" (*Cahiers d'Art*, 20–21 [1945–1946] 349–356; rpt. in Samuel Beckett, *Disjecta: Miscellaneous Writings and A Dramatic Fragment*, ed. Ruby Cohn [New York: Grove Press, 1984] 118–132); "Peintres de l'empêchement" (*Derrière le miroir* [*Pierre à Feu*], 11–12 [June 1948] 3, 4, 7); Georges Duthuit, "Maille à partir avec Bram van Velde" (*Cahiers d'Art*, 27.1 [July 1952] 79–81; rpt. in Stoullig and Schoeller, eds., *Bram van Velde*, 180).

3 Le Select, a café, 99 Boulevard du Montparnasse, Paris 6.

JACQUES PUTMAN
PARIS

13.3.57 Paris

Cher Jacques

Voici rafistolé le texte sur Bram.[1]

Il faut le montrer à Duthuit, qui ne sera peut-être pas d'accord.[2]

Il faudrait indiquer, au moyen d'un "chapeau", qu'il s'agit d'un texte rédigé en 49, en anglais.[3]

Je le trouve toujours très mauvais et de nature à nuire à Bram. Réfléchissez bien avant de le donner à Warren.

Merci de m'avoir fait envoyer une invitation par le Théâtre de la Cité Universitaire. Je serais allé volontiers, mais vendredi soir je suis pris.

Amitiés à vous tous.

s/ Sam

TLS; 1 leaf, 1 side; *enclosure* French TMS, *A corr* in other hands ["Three Dialogues: Samuel Beckett and Georges Duthuit"] (7 leaves, 7 sides); Jacques Putman Collection. Previous publication, letter only: Stoullig and Schoeller, eds., *Bram van Velde*, 189.

13.3.57 Paris

Dear Jacques

Here is the Bram text knocked into some sort of shape.[1]

You must show it to Duthuit, who may not agree.[2]

You should make it clear in an introductory note that it's something that was written in English in 1949.[3]

I still find it very bad, and likely to do harm to Bram. Think hard before you give it to Warren.

Thanks for getting an invitation from the Théâtre de la Cité Universitaire sent to me. I would gladly have gone, but I'm taken up on Friday evening.

Best to you all

s/ Sam

1 Publication by the Galerie Michel Warren of "Three Dialogues: Samuel Beckett and Georges Duthuit": 5 February 1957, n. 1. SB chose to publish only the third dialogue, on Bram van Velde, which he translated himself (*Bulletin de la Galerie Michel Warren* [Paris, 1957], np).

2 SB was right to doubt Georges Duthuit's reaction. A letter postmarked 16 January, from Duthuit to Mary Hutchinson, gives a sense of the distance that had grown between the two men, indeed of Duthuit's hostility to his former friend. Duthuit writes:

> J'ai reçu la dernière pièce de Beckett, "Fin de Partie", que je trouve imbécile et dégoûtante, pas dans le sens où il espérait que cette pièce le soit. Je n'ai pas eu le courage d'aller jusqu'à son histoire, dont vous me parlez pour la radio. En voilà un qui met trop de temps à mourir, et qui parle trop pour un silencieux. Il m'a envoyé une dédicace avec le mot "ami", mais c'est à choisir, ou les sentiments communs sont valables, ou comme il le considère, ils ne sont que farce macabre et honteuse absurdité, comme il le considère, tout à son avantage. J'en ai fini avec ces grosses ficelles irlandaises, trop bien ajustées, et je le lui ai fait savoir, en essayant de ne pas le blesser. Qu'il garde son public bourgeois. On finira par le voir à l'OTAN: c'est

tout indiqué. (Duthuit Collection.) (I have received Beckett's latest play, *Fin de Partie*, which I find mindless and nasty, not in the sense that he hoped this play would be. I didn't have the courage to go on to his story, the one you speak of, for radio. This is one man that is really too long a-dying, and talks too much for one given to silence. He sent me a dedicatory note with the word "friend" in it, but there's a choice to be made: either ordinary feelings are valid, or, as he sees it, they are no more than a macabre and shameful absurdity, as he sees it, to his own advantage. I've had enough of these thick Irish strings, pulled too tight, and I've told him so, trying not to hurt him. Let him hold on to his solid middle-class public. We'll end up seeing him in NATO, all indications point that way.)

Five years later, again to Mary Hutchinson, Duthuit expresses himself on the "Three Dialogues," describing their contents as "prétentieuses et ridicules, dans le genre noir" (pretentious and ridiculous, on the grim side), and as "pantalonnades esthétiques" (aesthetic posturings) (1 March 1962, Duthuit Collection). However, SB surely remained unaware of the extent of Duthuit's hostility to the "Three Dialogues," as he offered the dialogue on Bram van Velde in response to the request of Duthuit's son Claude for texts for a posthumous limited-edition tribute volume entitled *Georges Duthuit* (Paris: Flammarion, 1976) 57–62.

3 The note preceding the dialogue in the *Bulletin de la Galerie Michel Warren* reads: "Ce texte écrit en anglais en 1949, a été rédigé par Samuel Beckett" (np) (This text, written in English in 1949, was composed by Samuel Beckett).

JERZY KRECZMAR
WARSAW

le 20 mars 1957

6 Rue des Favorites
Paris 15me

Cher Jerzy Kreczmar

Je reçois à l'instant les photos de scène, programmes et affiche que vous avez eu la grande gentillesse de m'envoyer.[1]

Etant sans nouvelles de ma pièce à Varsovie, je pensais que cela avait dû mal marcher, et je suis très heureux d'apprendre que ce n'est pas le cas.[2]

Je trouve les photos absolument sensationnelles, de loin les meilleures que j'ai vues à ce jour. Vos comédiens ont tout à fait le physique de leur emploi. L'arbre est parfait (un peu trop de feuilles peut-être au second acte!). Les costumes aussi me plaisent beaucoup. Le garçon est très beau et son chapeau une vraie trouvaille.[3] Je ne vois pas de lune. L'avez-vous supprimée? Enfin tout cela me donne énormément de plaisir et je vous en remercie de tout coeur. Merci aussi à vos acteurs, à votre décorateur et à tous les autres sans qui il n'y a pas de spectacle possible et dont le programme ne parle jamais.

J'espère qu'un jour je pourrai aller à Varsovie vous rencontrer tous et vous voir travailler. Demain je pars pour Londres où nous allons présenter Fin de Partie en français (première mondiale) au Royal Court Theatre pendant huit jours.

Je n'arrive pas à déchiffrer votre adresse sur le papier d'emballage et par conséquent vous adresse cette lettre chez Julian Rogozinski à qui je vous prie de faire mes meilleures amitiés, ainsi qu'à Adam Tarn quand vous le verrez.

Une chaleureuse poignée de main à vous tous et encore merci pour le grand plaisir que vous venez de me faire.

s/
Samuel Beckett

TLS; 1 leaf, 1 side; Private Collection.

20th March 1957 — 6 Rue des Favorites
Paris 15

Dear Jerzy Krezcmar

I have just received the stage photos, programmes and poster that you were so kind as to send me.[1]

Having heard nothing of my play in Warsaw, I thought that it must have gone badly, and I am very glad to learn that this is not the case.[2]

I find the photos absolutely sensational - by far the best I have seen yet. Your actors look just right for their parts. The tree is perfect (perhaps a few leaves too many in the second act!). I greatly like the costumes too. The boy looks very good and his hat is a real find.[3] I don't see a moon. Did you cut it out? Anyway, it all gives me enormous pleasure, and I thank you most warmly. Thanks too to your actors, your set designer, and all the other people without whom no performance is possible, and who are never mentioned in the programme.

I hope that one day I shall be able to go to Warsaw to meet you all and see you at work. I leave tomorrow for London where we are going to put on *Fin de partie* in French (a world premiere) at the Royal Court Theatre for a week.

I am unable to make out your address on the wrapping paper, and so am addressing this letter c/o Julian Rogoziński, to whom I would ask you to pass on my best wishes, as well as to Adam Tarn when you see him.

A warm greeting to you all, and once again thank you for the great pleasure you have just given me.

s/
Samuel Beckett

1 Jerzy Kreczmar directed *Czekając na Godota* (see 10 January 1957).

2 Casimir Wierzynski (n.d.) wrote to Barney Rosset on 19 February 1957 for news of the Warsaw production, reporting that he had read an enthusiastic article in a Kracow literary paper published prior to the opening (NSyU).

3 Photos of the Teatr Współczesny production by photographer Edward Hartwig show the boy wearing a broad-brimmed straw hat and carrying a staff, Pozzo in a morning suit with spats, Lucky in a large checked jacket, Vladimir in dark clothing, Estragon in light. The tree of the second act has many leaves. (www.wspolczesny.pl/archiwum/spektakle/czekajac-na-godota, accessed 20 February 2014).

GEORGES BELMONT
PARIS

Mercredi [27 March 1957]

ROYAL COURT HOTEL,
SLOANE SQUARE,
LONDON, S. W. 1

cher Georges

Merci de ta lettre et des tuyaux qui – je l'espère – nous seront utiles. Je t'ai retenu une chambre ici à partir de vendredi et jusqu'au mardi suivant. Je suis très heureux que ce soit toi qui fasse[s] l'article pour Arts.[1] On nous annonce 13 critiques français, avec Gauthier sans doute derrière la mêlée.[2] Voici la table des préjouissances: samedi de 10 à 13 la pièce et de 14 à 16 le mime. Dimanche on travaillera dans les décors, le mime avec orchestre de 10 à 13 et la pièce l'après-midi. De quoi étoffer ton article, je te le promets. Lundi c'est la répétition générale devant le public (?). Mardi c'est le gala. Mercredi la presse.

J'ai coupé la scène du môme. L'essentiel reste, à savoir que Clov croit le voir et que Hamm n'y croit pas. Mais il y a un peu trop de conneries pp. 103–104, et je crois que nous gagnerons à les supprimer.[3]

Bien sûr, il ne faut pas traîner. Mais faut pas bâcler non plus. Je ne pense pas que la scène des poubelles soit trop longue, quand le climat y sera. Mais nous verrons.[4]

Je dois dîner avec des amis vendredi, mais si tu arrives tard, entre 23 et minuit par ex., j'aimerais aller t'accueillir à Waterloo.

Merci pour tout et à vendredi. Bien des choses à José.[5]

Sam

ALS; 1 leaf, 2 sides; *letterhead*; TxU, Belmont. *Dating*: SB rehearsing in London from 21 March; the Gala opening of *Fin de partie* in French took place on 2 April, and the public opening was 3 April.

Wednesday [27 March 1957]

ROYAL COURT HOTEL,
SLOANE SQUARE,
LONDON, S. W. 1

Dear Georges

Thank you for your letter and for the tips which, I hope, will be useful to us. I've booked a room for you here from Friday to the following Tuesday. I'm very glad that it's you who are doing the article for *Arts*.[1] We hear there are to be 13 French critics, with Gautier no doubt behind the scrum.[2] Here is the list of foreplay: Saturday 10 till 1 the play and 2 till 4 the mime. On Sunday we'll be working in the sets, mime with orchestra from 10 till 1 and the play in the afternoon. Just what you need to fill out your article, I promise. Monday is the public dress rehearsal (?). Tuesday is the gala. Wednesday the press.

I've cut the scene with the youngster. The essential is still there, i.e. that Clov thinks he sees him and Hamm does not, but there are too many silly things on pp. 103–104, and I think we will do well to cut them out.[3]

We mustn't of course drag it out, but we mustn't rush it either. I don't think the dustbin scene will be too long, when the atmosphere is right, but we'll see.[4]

I'm due to have dinner with friends on Friday, but if you get in late, say between 11 and midnight, I'd like to go and meet you at Waterloo.

Thank you for everything, and till Friday. Best wishes to José.[5]

Sam

1 Georges Belmont (1909–2008; Profile, I, as Georges Pelorson) reviewed the production in "Avec 'Fin de partie' Beckett a atteint la perfection classique," *Arts, Spectacles* 614 (10–16 April 1957) 1–2.

2 Jean-Jacques Gautier (1908–1986), whose name SB regularly spells "Gauthier," drama critic of *Le Figaro*, "had always been antagonistic toward Beckett" (Knowlson, *Damned to Fame*, 454). Other French reviews of the London premiere: Jacqueline Tourreil, "Création à Londres: Samuel Beckett décrit l'agonie des derniers humains," *Le Figaro* 4 April 1957: 14; Jean Wetz, "Samuel Beckett, auteur irlandais est très discuté par Londres," *Le Monde* 5 April 1957: 12.

3 Comparison of the French edition with the first English-language edition offers the closest definition of the cut (*Fin de partie* [Paris: Editions de Minuit, 1957] 103–104; *Endgame* [New York: Grove Press, 1958] 78); it is also consonant with the change described in Beckett's production notebook for *Endspiel* at the Schiller-Theater, Berlin, in 1975 (*Endgame, with a Revised Text*, ed. S. E. Gontarski, The Theatrical Notebooks of Samuel Beckett, II [New York: Grove Press, 1992] 264).

4 There are two dustbin scenes in *Fin de partie*: between Nell and Nagg, and among Hamm, Clov, and Nagg (*Fin de partie*, 29–39; 69–77).

5 Joséphine Caliot Belmont (1914–1988).

THOMAS MACGREEVY
DUBLIN

29 III 57

GREAT SORROW IMPOSSIBLE ATTEND PLEASE ARRANGE FLOWERS WRITING SAM[1]

Telegram; 1 leaf, 1 side; *pm* 29 III 57; TCD, MS 10402/205.

1 Thomas MacGreevy (1893–1967; Profile, I, as McGreevy), Director of the National Gallery of Ireland, and one of SB's closest friends.

SB is responding to MacGreevy's telegram announcing the death of Jack B. Yeats (1871–1957; Profile, I).

THOMAS MACGREEVY
DUBLIN

5.4 [1957] Paris

Bien cher Tom

Many thanks for your letter and telegram, which touched me greatly. We left London Wednesday afternoon, in an hour I leave for Ussy, quite tired out.[1]

I made a serious effort to get to Dublin for the funeral. Finally I had to accept that it was impossible. No seat on the Aer Lingus flight on the Friday afternoon. I should have had to travel by train and boat, which would have got me in in time. But I could get no assurance of a seat on the flight Dublin-London Saturday afternoon. I was very upset that I had to renounce, as I had always promised to myself I wd. go to Dublin again on that occasion. Many thanks for the flowers. Please tell me what I owe for them and I shall send you a cheque.[2]

Things in London were very difficult and exhausting, though everyone at the Royal Court Theatre was kindness itself and if the result is not what I hoped, the fault is mostly mine, and my text's. The mime went well. We resume here after Easter at the Studio des Champs-Elysées.[3] I am hoping to achieve a long spell now in the quiet of Ussy and piece together whatever bits remain.

I can imagine what an ordeal last week must have been for you. I hope things are better at the Gallery and that you are feeling the ease of your free evenings now.[4]

I really thought you wanted to be alone at the Invalides. Otherwise I should have been there to see you off, as I wanted to.[5]

Come back to us soon, dear Tom, and let us hear and say what friends like us have to say and hear.

Much love from us both.

Sam

ALS; 1 leaf, 1 side; TCD, MS 10402/206.

1 SB left London on 3 April, following the dress rehearsal on 1 April which he attended and the gala on 2 April which he did not attend.

2 The funeral of Jack B. Yeats was held in Dublin on the morning of Saturday 30 March. SB wrote to H. O. White (1885–1963; Profile II) on 15 April: "The light of Jack Yeats will always burn with me" (TCD, MS 3777/15).

3 *Acte sans paroles I* was performed by Deryk Mendel with music by John Beckett, following *Fin de partie*, at the Royal Court Theatre.

4 MacGreevy, a close friend and neighbor of Yeats on Fitzwilliam Square, had visited him and "spent every evening with him in his later years," even after Yeats moved permanently to the Portobello Nursing Home (Hilary Pyle, *Jack B. Yeats: A Biography* [London: Routledge and Kegan Paul, 1970] 170).

5 SB refers to the Air France coach terminal at Les Invalides in Paris.

GEORGES NEVEUX
PARIS

le 6 avril 1957

Ussy-sur-Marne
Seine-et-Marne

Cher Georges Neveux

Je vous remercie de tout cœur de votre lettre si amicale et si sensible.[1]

Je ne sais plus quoi penser de ce travail. On crie comme on peut, et voilà. Il est impossible que ça plaise, mais ça peut émouvoir. Je ne vise pas plus bas.

J'aimerais beaucoup vous rencontrer un jour, vous serrer la main et vous dire combien votre amitié m'est précieuse.

Samuel Beckett

ALS; 1 leaf, 1 side; SACD, Fonds Georges Neveux.

6 April 1957

Ussy-sur-Marne
Seine-et-Marne

Dear Georges Neveux,

Heartfelt thanks for your letter, so friendly and so sensitive.[1]

I don't know what to think of this work any more. We make the noises we can, that's all. It's not possible that people will like it. But it may move them. I aim no lower.

I should very much like to meet you one day, to shake your hand and tell you how precious your friendship is to me.

Samuel Beckett

1 On 23 February, SB had hand-delivered a copy of *Fin de partie* to critic Georges Neveux (1900–1982) who had been instrumental in obtaining a subvention for the first staging of *En attendant Godot* (see 28 February 1952). Neveux responded on 2 April:

> Cher Samuel Beckett, vous m'avez fait un très grand plaisir en m'envoyant votre Fin de Partie. Cette pièce va plus loin que Godot dans la projection qu'elle fait de notre néant sur la scène – mais les moyens qu'elle emploie sont moins simples. Elle aura donc contre elle, pour commencer, tous les admirateurs de Godot – c'est-à-dire tout le monde. Mais vos spectateurs après une bonne nuit d'insomnie, qu'ils vous devront, s'apercevront qu'ils sont pris à votre Fin de Partie comme des mouches sur un papier tue-mouches et, ils auront beau vous maudire, ils seront obligés de parler de vous et de compter avec cette effrayante et étouffante image d'eux-mêmes que vous avez déposée comme un œuf dans un coin de leurs cervelles. Vous gagnerez donc sûrement votre seconde partie, mais peut-être avec un peu de retard et quelques discussions. Pour ma part j'aurai du mal à oublier les parents dans leurs poubelles, cet aveugle tournant et ce mouchoir qui devient linceul, ce rideau qui devient nuit. Ils me poursuivent depuis trois jours.
>
> Je vous souhaite une mise en scène d'une nudité terrible pour bien perdre la 1ère manche et bien gagner la seconde – et la belle, dans nos mémoires. (SACD, Fonds Georges Neveux.)
>
> (Dear Samuel Beckett, you have given me great pleasure by sending me your *Fin de partie*. This play goes farther than *Godot* in the way it projects our nothingness on the stage – but the methods it employs are less simple. So it will have against it at the start all the admirers of *Godot* – that is, everyone. But your spectators, after one good sleepless night which they will owe you, will notice that they have been caught by your *Fin de partie* like flies on flypaper, and, no good their cursing you, they will be obliged to talk about you and reckon with this frightening and stifling image of themselves that you have lodged like an egg in a corner of their brain. So you will surely win your second game, but perhaps after a little delay and a few arguments. For my own part, I shall find it hard to forget the parents in their dustbins, this blind man turning and this handkerchief that becomes a shroud, this curtain that becomes the dark. They have been pursuing me for three days.
>
> I wish for you a production fearsome in its bareness, so that you may really lose the first set and really win the second – and the decider, in our memories.)

BARNEY ROSSET
GROVE PRESS, NEW YORK

April 6th 1957

Ussy-sur-Marne but as from
6 Rue des Favorites

Bien cher Barney

Here goes for one worthy of yours.

Your wire was phoned through to me here yesterday.[1] I got your long letter in London and apologize for not having answered it before now. I had a hard time there and left last Wednesday, before the première, quite tired out. My hopes now are to have a long spell here, but they are not high.

As you know I am incapable of understanding contracts. My "method" consists, when they are drawn up by those in whom I have confidence, in signing them without reading them. Any contract drawn up by you, and involving me alone, I shall sign in this fashion. Those involving Lindon and me I submit to him and sign when he tells me to. To the former category belong my translator's contracts with Grove and I leave it entirely to you to formulate them as you think fit. I know your friendship for me, and your probity, and the possibility of your deriving from them excessive benefits does not at any time cross my mind. When Faber offered to advance me money on the Fin de Partie translation I replied I was selling it to you, and I prefer it that way. This does not mean I am asking you for an advance, I am not. If I am short of money I shall tell you. I have undertaken to produce it before August and shall get going on it soon. I do not think there is anything in my contract with the Royal Court that infirms the above. They simply acquire the option to perform in the U.K. (exclusive I think of Canada) the play in English as translated by me.[2] I have the contract in Paris and shall check up on this, or have a copy made and send it to you.

Before going any further let me prepare you for an unsatisfactory job. The French is at least 20% undecantable into English and will forfeit that much of whatever edge and tension it may have. I am quite certain of this. My feeling throughout was not to translate it at all. But if I had not undertaken to do so, and given the option to the Royal Court, Fin de Partie could not have been created in London, and played there for a week only, for obvious financial reasons. So I committed myself, rightly or wrongly, in order to clinch the affair.

With regard to the American performance rights of the play and mime, nothing has yet been decided, and I have so far no contract with Curtis Brown concerning them. I am seriously considering offering you the control of these, and instructing Curtis Brown to handle the U.K. rights only. This would bring down, from Covent Garden and I suppose from Myerberg, thunderbolts upon my head, but the bloodiness and bowedness of that perishing appendix can hardly be augmented.[3] I have mentioned the idea to London [*for* Lindon], who approves of it. Let me know if you would be disposed to take it on.[4]

With regard to recordings, McWhinnie of the 3rd Programme and producer of All That Fall told me that their recording (disk) of same was almost ready, which means I suppose that it will soon be on the market.[5] I do not know if my transcription contract with the BBC preculudes [sic] you from making another recording. I should imagine not, but you would have to go into this with them. McWhinnie now is a very good friend and I think you might be well advised to write to him (Donald McW., BBC, London W.1.), for any information about All That Fall. The 3rd has also acquired for transmission Fin de Partie in French and the recording was made (or was to have been made when I left London, the actors having received their convocations) last Friday April 5th.[6] This certainly does not exclude a recording elsewhere and if you are prepared to pay for one in Paris it can easily be managed. I should be grateful if you would write to Lindon about this, as I hope to be as little as possible in Paris for some time.

Thanks for Evergreens. I did not see that composition dates were given of the story and poems, but they may have escaped me. Authors are sensitive – foolishly – about the chronos of their old vomit. By all means From an A.W. in 3, though it has appeared in Dublin (of all places).[7] I see nothing else.

Pleased that you should wish to publish my poems. The Limes Verlag, as I think I told you, are doing the French and English originals with German translation.[8] When you send me the odd ones you have collected, appart [sic] from Whoroscope and the Bones, I shall see if I can find any others in my chaotic archives. I have lost many and not all are worth reprinting. There is one wild love one called Cascando you might like. An American bitch.[9]

I have seen few of recent articles in French press. A very fine article indeed by Nadeau on Fin de Partie appeared in France-Observateur.[10] I shall ask Lindon to have copied whatever he has of interest and sent to you.

I sneaked away from London before the première. The dress rehearsal on the Monday, which I saw, and the gala on the Tuesday, which I did not, were not very satisfactory. But I am told the première went much better. It is an appallingly difficult text to play, and to find the style of, and the tone or tones for. The mime went well. My cousin did a fine job with the music and Deryk Mendel is absolutely remarkable. You will see a photo reportage of his performance in Life (I think).[11] We go on in Paris after Easter at the Studio des Champs-Elysées, by which time the performance will have much improved. The first reactions from London are violently antagonistic – "horrible evening... should never have left the garbage-bin... etc".[12] I am hoping for a little more understanding from the Observer and Sunday Times to-morrow.[13] Devine and his merry men were kindness and friendliness to an extreme degree. They follow my howls with Osborne's new play, The Entertainer, starring Olivier. The five weeks were booked out in 2 days.[14]

I arrived here yesterday, started up the 2-stroke mower-scyther and felled the deep grass for 2 hours, crucifying the blade on old mole-hills. A relief from life and letters. Endgame by August, Unnamable by Xmas, then maybe a few last years keeping bees and growing lavender. With with [sic] luck a week or so in East Hampton having the hell walloped out of me by B.R. at tennis and chess.

Greetings to Link.

Ever

s/ Sam

I have a telephone now in Paris. Blomet 09.11. Keep it under your hat for God's sake, I'm not in the book.

Many thanks for cheque and to Julia Schmidt for letter and poems.[15]

TLS; 2 leaves, 3 sides; Burns Library, Samuel Beckett Collection, SB-BR.

1 Rosset wired SB at the Royal Court Hotel on 4 April (NSyU).

2 The contract with the English Stage Company (at the Royal Court Theatre) was for the production of *Fin de partie* and *Acte sans paroles I*, with an option for subsequent production in English, specifying that SB prepare an English translation by August 1957 (SB to Pieter Rogers, Royal Court Theatre, 18 March 1957; GEU, MS 1221).

3 Curtis Brown, 6 Henrietta Street, Covent Garden, were SB's agents for *Waiting for Godot*. They had contracted with Michael Myerberg for the North American performance rights of the play. Myerberg had delayed the pre-Broadway tour of the play in Miami until January 1956, and further deferred the Broadway opening until 19 April 1956. No other productions were permitted in North America before completion of the Broadway run (see 1 April 1956).

4 Lindon wrote to Rosset on 2 April: "J'ai personnellement suggéré à Monsieur Beckett qu'il vous accorde, pour FIN DE PARTIE, non seulement les droits d'édition, mais également les droits de théâtre, de façon à éviter que la pièce soit montée dans de mauvaises conditions. Je crois que c'est aussi son idée [. . .] Il vous écrira dans ce sens." (NSyU.) (I have personally suggested to Mr Beckett that he should grant you, for *Fin de partie*, not only the publication rights but also the theatre rights, so as to avoid the play's being staged in unsatisfactory conditions. I believe that this is also his view [. . .] He will write to you to that effect.)

5 *All That Fall* was taped for original broadcast on 13 January by the BBC.

6 The BBC recorded a studio performance on 5 April of the French production directed by Roger Blin at the Royal Court Theatre.

7 *Evergreen Review* publication of "Dante and the Lobster" and selections from *Echo's Bones and Other Precipitates*: 11 January 1957, n. 9.

Samuel Beckett, "From an Abandoned Work," *Trinity News* 3.17 (7 June 1956) 4; a revised version was published by *Evergreen Review* 3 (1957) 83–91.

8 Samuel Beckett, *Gedichte* (Wiesbaden: Limes Verlag, 1959).

9 Samuel Beckett, "Cascando," *Dublin Magazine* 11.4 (October–December 1936) 3–4. James Knowlson suggests that the American woman was Elizabeth (Betty) Stockton (*Damned to Fame*, 214–215).

10 Maurice Nadeau, "Fin de partie de Samuel Beckett: La tragédie transposée en farce," *France-Observateur* 28 February 1957: 15; rpt. as "Beckett: La tragédie transposée en farce," *L'Avant-scène* 156 (1957) 4–6.

11 John Beckett composed the music for *Acte sans paroles I* and performed it with Jeremy Montagu (percussion) and T. G. Clubb (xylophone). Deryk Mendel performed in the mime; *Life* published a production photo of Nell and Nagg from *Fin de partie* ("Ash Can School of Drama," 22 April 1957: 143). A photo of the mime appeared in *Arts, Spectacles*, 10–16 April 1957: 1.

12 An unsigned review, "'Fin de partie' at Court Theatre," begins with "It is a rather horrible evening" (*The Times* 4 April 1957: 3).

13 The review of Harold Hobson (1904–1992; Profile, II), drama critic for *The Sunday Times*, was indeed positive ("Samuel Beckett's New Play," *The Sunday Times* 7 April 1957: 23). Kenneth Tynan's review was negative: "Last week's production, portentously stylised, piled on the agony until I thought my skull would split. Little variation, either of pace or emphasis, was permitted: a cosmic comedy was delivered as humourlessly as if its author had been Racine"; of *Acte sans paroles I*, he added: "This kind of facile pessimism is dismaying in an author of Beckett's stature." ("A Philosophy of Despair," *The Observer* 7 April 1957: 15.)

14 John Osborne's *The Entertainer*, with Laurence Olivier, was in rehearsal at the Royal Court Theatre during the run of *Fin de partie* (Knowlson, *Damned to Fame*, 392).

15 Payment for contributions to *Evergreen Review*. SB writes "Julia" for Judith Schmidt* (b. 1926).

ARLAND USSHER
DUBLIN

14.4.57

Ussy-sur-Marne
Seine et Marne

Dear Arland

Many thanks for your letter of February, with meditation on Godot, and for the Aphorisms and Thoughts, the former of which you had sent me, and the latter not. You pack a lot of wit and/or wisdom into a little room. Reading you the thought comes to me of Xenien linked in pairs in mutually annulling profundity. That would be very much your line of country I think.[1] What you say about loneliness and aloneness is very good (and true for some).[2] From the former I suffered much as a boy, but not much in the last 30 years, bending over me in my old dying-bed where I found me early and the last words unending. Jack Yeats's death had me in a lather in London trying to get over for the earthing and back all in the 24 hours, but it was impossible. I left quite tired out before the première of Fin de Partie and have been here in far east Ile de France, up in the wind above the loopy Marne, ever since. Con and Ethna were in London and I saw them too briefly. I missed Sean in Paris.[3] Aidan writes from the apartheid. His letters have become simple and warm and well worth having.[4] I am faced with deserts of self-translation from now to end of year. John did a good job on the mime. We go on at the Studio des Champs-Elysées at the end of this month.[5] I am tired of this blurring sheet behind the visions of old days, so away with it. Suzanne sends you her amitiés. Kind remembrance to Emily & Hetty. I remember a Tommy Staples, perhaps the brother.[6]

Affectionately

Sam

ALS; 1 leaf, 1 side; *env to* Arland Ussher Esq, 18 Green Road, Blackrock, Dublin, IRLANDE; *pm* 15-4-57, La Ferté-sous-Jouarre; TCD, MS 9031/49/1-2.

1 Percival Arland Ussher (1899–1980; Profile, I).

Ussher had sent two of his recent publications: *Alphabet of Aphorisms* (Dublin: The Dolmen Press, 1953) and *The Thoughts of Wi Wong* (Dublin: The Dolmen Press, 1956). With his letter to SB of 28 February, Ussher enclosed a piece he had written on *Waiting for Godot*, with the note: "Hope it doesn't infuriate you!" Ussher's piece has not been identified.

As early as 1938, SB had shared with Ussher his interest in the form of the Xenien (28 December 1938, n. 6). Xenien: a form of epigram developed in the late eighteenth century by Goethe and Schiller, on the model of the Latin poet Martial's *Xenia* (epigrams to accompany gifts).

2 In his letter of 28 February, Ussher wrote: "The problem of life: to convert loneliness (worst of conditions) into aloneness (which is the best). But when one has succeeded in this task one will of course be dead." (TCD, MS 9031/48.)

3 Abraham Jacob Leventhal (known as Con, 1896–1979; Profile, I) and his wife Ethna MacCarthy (1903–1959; Profile, I). SB probably refers to the artist Seán O'Sullivan (1906–1964; Profile, I).

4 Aidan Higgins (b. 1927; Profile, II) had been introduced to Ussher by SB; in his first letter to Higgins, SB wrote: "For wisdom see Arland Ussher" (17 September 1951; TxU, Higgins). Writing to SB about Higgins, Ussher described him as "A Rimbaud in search of an Africa (or a Verlaine). He speaks much of you, and more of Djuna Barnes, and Kafka the soul of the plot." (19 August [1953]; TCD, MS 9031-41/45/1.) At this time, Higgins was in Pretoria, South Africa, performing with the John Wright Marionettes (Higgins to Ussher, 14 April 1957; TCD, MS 1517).

5 John Beckett, who composed the music for *Acte sans paroles I*, was a friend of Aidan Higgins.

6 Emily Ussher (1898–1974), Arland's wife, and their daughter Henrietta Owen (Hetty, b. 1926, m. Staples). In his letter to SB of 28 February, Ussher mentioned that his son-in-law Gerald Staples (1909–1997) had attended Miss Elsner's Academy with SB; in fact, it was Gerald's sister Grace (1906–1997) who had attended Miss Elsner's Academy with SB, and his brother Thomas (1905–1999) who played cricket with SB at Earlsfort Terrace (Hetty Staples to the editors, June 1992).

CHRISTIAN LUDVIGSEN
HELLERUP, DENMARK

22.4.57

6 Rue des Favorites,
Paris 15e

Dear Mr Ludevigsen

Thanks for your letters, book, and everything, and for news of Godot in Copenhagen.[1] Fin de Partie is a different kettle of fish and much more difficult to play. But by all means, as far as I am concerned, let your student theatre have a shot at it.[2] We got a mixed reception in London. We go on at the Studio des Champs-Elysées, with the mime, next Friday 26th.

No, I have not read Wittgenstein.

My cordial greetings to your friends in the theatre and to yourself my thanks for your continued interest in my work.

Yours sincerely
Sam. Beckett

ALS; 1 leaf, 1 side; *env to* Mr Chr. Ludvigsen, C.V.E. Knutsvej 18a, Hellerup, DANEMARK; *pm* 23–4–57, La Ferté-sous-Jouarre; Ludvigsen Collection.

1 Christian Ludvigsen (b. 1930; Profile, II), whose name SB misspells here, was the translator of SB's work into Danish. *Vi venter på Godot*, in Ludvigsen's translation, opened at the Riddersalen in Copenhagen on 5 April 1957, directed by Inge Hvid-Møller and Niels Bing (Chr. Ludvigsen, *Det begyndte med Beckett – min egen teaterhistorie*, Aktuelle teaterproblemer, 42 [Aarhus: Institut for Dramaturgi, 1997] 17, 119). Ludvigsen was not involved in the Copenhagen production, which he called "half-hearted" and "entirely different" from the premiere at the Aarhus Teater on 10 April 1956 (Ludvigsen to the editors, 13 October 1997).

2 In March 1957, Den danske studenterscene performed Clov's opening mime and the dustbin scene between Nell and Nagg from *Fin de partie*, which was published as "Skraldespandsduetten: Scene af Skuespillet 'Fin de partie,'" tr. Christian Ludvigsen, *Perspectiv* 4.7 (1957) 14–16.

A. J. LEVENTHAL
DUBLIN

28.4.57 Paris

Dear Con

Thanks for your letter. Delighted to hear you are doing a causerie on this old bastard for the Third. I shall try and get in Tuesday evening, sometimes we can just hear.[1]

Thanks for Dub. Mag with your article which I liked very much. It is a difficult work to present, much less expound, and you give the "feeling" of it very well.[2] We got off to a good start at the Studio day before yesterday. "Avant-première" now till the "générale" next Tuesday. Blin has made enormous progress since London and gives now a quite extraordinary performance. The play gains greatly by the smallness and intimacy of the Studio.[3] I have now to tackle the horrible job of translation. Close of Play is not quite right for the title nor the American "The Game is Up". If I can use Endgame in the text phrase at the end, I shall use it for the title.

love to Ethna
yours ever
Sam

ALS; 1 leaf, 1 side; TxU, Leventhal Collection, 1.4.

1 A. J. Leventhal's talk "Samuel Beckett, Poet and Pessimist" was broadcast on 30 April 1957, and published in *The Listener* 57 (9 May 1957) 746–747.

2 Leventhal's article on *Fin de partie*: "Close of Play: Reflections on Samuel Beckett's New Work for the French Theatre," *Dublin Magazine* 32.2 (April–June 1957) 18–22.

3 *Fin de partie* would play at the Studio des Champs-Elysées, 15 Avenue Montaigne, Paris 8, a small theatre designed by Jacques Hébertot in 1922 to function as an

"atelier-laboratoire" (laboratory–workshop). The Générale took place on 30 April. Roger Blin continued in the role of Hamm.

DONALD McWHINNIE
BBC, LONDON

May 7th 1957 Paris

Dear Donald

Many thanks for your letter. I got snatches of Leventhal this day last week. I liked the way he read Alba. I couldn't hear the play two days later.[1] My cousin was here, cutting his tape to suit the Studio, and we talked of you and the 3rd and the possibility of doing something together. You are right in thinking there is little chance of my writing anything new for months to come. I suggested to John that he might do some music for a published text, the end of Part I of Molloy for example, i.e. from the shore to the ditch.[2] He thought it wd. be possible (on the lines of the Diary of a Madman production), and said he would look you up and talk it over with you.[3] He is at present in Dublin but will be back in London next week. This would be just conceivably better than nothing, though I doubt it.

We opened at the Studio Friday April 26th and have not yet been kicked out into the Avenue six storeys below.[4] The production has greatly improved since London and Blin gives now a very fine performance. The smaller theatre also helps. The mime suffers from being done with a recording purveyed by loudspeakers of extreme dilapidation. The press has been fairly good. I have not yet begun the translation. It is a hopeless undertaking.

I was in correspondence, pleasantly, with Roy Walker, worried by his imperfect French. He had a good and I think right idea about the play, but has not used it in his entertaining Listener comments on the broadcast, a copy of which he sent me. I liked his remarks on Landslide and John's production.[5]

Please thank Barbara for her letter which gave me great pleasure and tell her I shall be writing to her before the end of the week.

Forgive scrawl, I can't face the typewriter.

All the best, Donald, and to Barbara and John.[6]

Yours ever

Sam

ALS; 1 leaf, 1 side; BBCWAC, RCONT1, Samuel Beckett, Scriptwriter I.

1 Leventhal's talk on the BBC Third Programme on 30 April included a reading of SB's poem "Alba," from *Echo's Bones and Other Precipitates*, [18].

The BBC Third Programme broadcast of *Fin de partie*, recorded by the French cast in the BBC studio, was broadcast on 2 May.

2 John Beckett had been in Paris to adjust his music for *Acte sans paroles I* to the requirements of the stage space of the Studio des Champs-Elysées.

The BBC Third Programme accepted SB's suggestion (Donald McWhinnie to SB, 26 June 1957; BBCWAC, RCONT1, Samuel Beckett, Scriptwriter 1). SB later specified: "The passage I had in mind was from p. 103, 'And now my progress . . .', to end of Part I, with a cut, p. 107, line 25, 'Perhaps it is less to be thought . . .', to p. 108, line 5, 'Time will tell'. Olympia Press, Paris, edition, available in London." (SB to Donald McWhinnie, 30 June 1957, BBCWAC, RCONT1, Samuel Beckett, Scriptwriter I; *Molloy*, tr. Patrick Bowles in collaboration with the author [Paris: Olympia Press, 1955].)

3 Nikolai Gogol's short story "Diary of a Madman" was broadcast by the BBC Third Programme on 6 March 1957; Paul Scofield (1922–2008) "read the diary straight, and the music merely pointed the narrative, quietly and tactfully" (Michael Swan, "The Spoken Word: Language and Culture," *The Listener* 57 [14 March 1957] 452).

4 The Studio des Champs-Elysées is on the top floor of the Théâtre des Champs-Elysées.

5 Roy Walker, literary critic and contributor to *The Listener*, wrote about the broadcast of *Fin de partie* in his column "BBC Drama" ("Judge not . . ., " *The Listener* 57 [9 May 1957] 767–768). This article included a review of Ugo Betti's *Landslide*, directed by John Gibson (1924–1974) and broadcast by the BBC Third Programme on 28 April and 3 May.

6 Barbara Bray* (1924–2010), Script Editor for BBC Drama. John Morris.

BRAM VAN VELDE AND MARTHE ARNAUD-KUNTZ
? PARIS

22 mai 1957 Ussy-sur-Marne

Chers amis

Merci à Marthe pour sa lettre et à Bram pour cette exposition formidable.[1] J'ai été, longuement, la semaine dernière. Il n'y avait personne, ou presque, et ça a été merveilleux. J'y retournerai la semaine prochaine, et j'espère bien vous y rencontrer. Je m'occupe, comme vous, à me reposer. J'espère que vous y réussissez mieux que moi.

Affectueusement et à bientôt j'espère.

Sam

ALS; 1 leaf, 1 side; Jacques Putman Collection. Previous publication: Stoullig and Schoeller, eds., *Bram van Velde*, 189.

22 May 1957 Ussy-sur-Marne

Dear both

Thanks to Marthe for her letter and to Bram for that tremendous exhibition.[1] I was there for a long, long time last week. There was nobody, or hardly anybody there, and that was marvellous. I shall go back next week, and I hope I can meet you there. Like you, I'm working at resting. I hope you're having more success than I am.

Love, and till soon, I hope.

Sam

1 Marthe Arnaud-Kuntz (1887–1959) was Bram van Velde's companion. Bram van Velde's exhibition at the Galerie Michel Warren ran from 7 May to 1 June.

KAY BOYLE
ROWAYTON, CONNECTICUT

May 28th 1957 6 Rue des Favorites
Paris 15me

Dear Kay Boyle

Thank you for your letters and exegesis of The Boarding House. Se non è vero è ben trovato, and no doubt it is possible Joyce had some such allegory in mind. I simply feel it is not only unnecessary, but perhaps an injustice to him, to suppose so, and that the text could be shown to contain elements quite incompatible with your interpretation.[1] I do not agree that the first five paragraphs are relevant only in terms of an allegorical context. I know nothing about short story or any other aesthetics. But it seems normal to me, in exordium to the relation proper, to situate those whom it concerns and establish their climate. And I feel the butchery and cleavery have no other purpose than this, and that it is achieved.[2] "It was a bright morning etc" strikes me as more a novel opening than a short story one, there being leisure in the novel, and in the short story not, for the where and for whom to be dealt with later. But this is perhaps just my contrariness. It might also be enquired if these are short stories at all. They are chunks of Dublin, its air and light and scene and voices, and for me the only way to read them is right down in their immediacy. But that is the only way I can read the Vita Nuova, where allegory and anagogy are proclaimed intentions.[3] So regard all this as nothing more serious than the expression of a personal disability and blow up my lobster to whatever dimensions you fancy. All I know is the sudden stir of the bag that told me it was still alive - and suchlike particulars. The last words of my regrettable novel Watt are "no symbols where none intended". But I am willing to believe the offence is committed, maugre my . . . heart.[4]

It is not any unpublished texts of mine that they have at the Editions de Minuit, but simply clatters of critical articles, all blither and blather mostly. You're better off without them.[5]

Bien amicalement à vous.

s/ Sam. Beckett

TLS; 1 leaf, 1 side; *env to* Kay Boyle, 188 Highland Avenue, Rowayton, Conn., U.S.A., *upper left corner* Air Mail; *pm* 29-5-57, Paris; TxU, Boyle, 1.6. Previous publication: facsimile and transcription in "No Allegory Where None Intended: Beckett and Boyle on Joyce," *Joyce Studies Annual* (1991) 264-267.

1 Boyle's lecture "James Joyce's 'The Boarding House'" was being prepared for a summer course on the short story and contemporary short story writers at the University of Delaware (Sandra Whipple Spanier, *Kay Boyle: Artist and Activist* [Carbondale: Southern Illinois University Press, 1986] 179). Boyle sent a draft of the lecture to SB and to the Irish writer Padraic Colum (1881–1972); her transcriptions of their replies are included with the draft and the final typed manuscript (ICso, 90/88/11; all references are to this draft and the final TMS). In the first draft, Beckett's reply is

2. Kay Boyle

entitled "Beckett's Refutation of the Analysis of Joyce's 'The Boarding House,'" and in the final TMS, it is given as "From Samuel Beckett's Letter with Reference to My Comments on James Joyce's 'The Boarding House.'"

"Se non è vero è ben trovato" (If it's not true, it's well invented), an Italian saying.

2 Boyle places Joyce's story in the context of political protest, writing in her first draft, "If we recognize 'The Boarding House' as allegory, then the background of butchery is essential to the story." Boyle's lecture continues:

> Mrs. Mooney is the centuries' long British domination of Joyce's country, and the butcher history in which she is implicated both by father and husband is the history of the "Black and Tan." The cleaver with which her husband seeks to kill her is the instrument of that same history of violence, and the allegory is complete when Joyce writes that Mrs. Mooney "went to the priest and got a separation from him." Here is the sanction of the church on the separation not of husband and wife, but of England and Ireland.

Boyle responded to SB on 1 June: "After reading a good many of Joyce's letters recently, I realized even more how far from any semblance of truth my hoax analysis is" (TxU, Boyle, 1.6).

3 Although there are episodes and lyrics in Dante's *Vita Nuova* (*The New Life*) which can indeed be explained allegorically, nowhere in his book does he suggest it should be read in this way. The "Donna gentile" of *Vita Nuova* is, as SB implies, a real woman; it is elsewhere, for example in the *Convivio*, that Dante interprets her as an allegory of Philosophy (Dante Alighieri, *Convivio*, ed. Piero Cudini [Milan: Garzanti, 1980] I, 1, 16–18). Still less does Dante promote an anagogical reading of *Vita Nuova*, not mentioning anagogy there, and only once even in the *Convivio* (II, 1, 6) – and then in the technical context of the "celestial" sense of scriptural works. SB is presumably intending to refer in a loose way to Beatrice's angelical role in, and to the mystical dimension of, *Vita Nuova*.

4 "Dante and the Lobster," *More Pricks Than Kicks* (1934).

5 Editions de Minuit maintained dossiers de presse on SB's work; these are now housed at IMEC, Caen.

KAY BOYLE
ROWAYTON, CONNECTICUT

June 12th 1957

6 rue des Favorites
Paris 15e

Dear Kay Boyle

Thank you for your letter of June 1st. No, I hadn't properly realized what you were after. Quite agree and great relief.[1]

Of course you have my permission to have the story mimeographed whatever that is for your course and I am sure Rosset will not withhold his.[2]

Look forward to having text of your lecture and interpretation.[3]

I think all U.S. Godot performance rights are still in the clutches of

Michael Myerberg
234 N. 44th Street
New York 36

but perhaps better confirm with Barney Rosset.[4] All I am sure of is I have no word in the matter.

With best wishes
Yrs. sincerely.
Sam. Beckett

ALS; 1 leaf, 1 side; *env to* Kay Boyle, 188 Highland Avenue, Rowayton, Conn., U.S.A., *lower left corner* Air Mail; *pm* 12–6–57, La Ferté-sous-Jouarre; TxU, Beckett Collection, 8.3.

1 Fearing, from what SB had written in his letter to her of 28 May, that he had misunderstood her purpose in considering Joyce's story as allegory, Boyle replied on 1 June: "I am, in these analyses of short stories, trying to show how evil the allegory-symbol-seeking of the lifeless, bloodless, academically-paralyzed 'new critics' of our time can be if allowed a free hand. The things you have written to me are what I needed to confirm the point in this particular story." (TxU, Boyle, 1.6.)

2 At this time, SB's short story "Dante and the Lobster" from *More Pricks Than Kicks* was in print only in *Evergreen Review*, which was published by Grove Press.

3 Boyle's public lecture "The Tradition of Loneliness" discussed the "reasons for the self-exile, the literary revolt and the loneliness of individual writers in [the] Twenties, with particular reference to James Joyce and Samuel Beckett" ("Summer School Lecture Series," University of Delaware, Newark, University of Delaware news release, 9 July 1957).

4 SB writes "N." rather than "W. 44th Street."

ETHNA MACCARTHY-LEVENTHAL
DUBLIN

13.6.57 Ussy-sur-Marne

Dear Ethna

Many thanks for your letter and enclosure. The gallows times you do be having. I should like to hear how the Pike farce ends. Was edified to see that our old friend D. J. Reddin had issued the warrant for apprehension of Simpson.[1]

I am not so grand, though I spend most of my time in the quiet here, and expect shortly to have to undergo operation for removal of cyst shaped like Kelly's 3 balls in upper jaw and now thrusting hopefully, after I suppose 10 years surreptitious growth, against palate notably and sinuswards. My witch doctor is trying to reduce it by medical means, but I fear unsuccessfully. Ah well, I was always a great one for cysts. Bridges will be blown up in the process, and my surly gob more lopsided than ever.[2]

Fin de Partie and chaser still ambling at the Studio. Production greatly improved since Sloane Square. Their plans are to close July 10th and reopen in September. I have just finished first version of translation. Now the real fun begins. I am hoping John will be able to go to Berlin in September to look after mime music and play piano at Festival performances.[3]

I lunched with Sophie Jacobs who had depressing accounts of Stella, to whom my love when you see her.[4]

I tried to hear Con's broadcast on one but with scant success. There was an audible patch for his reading of Alba and I greatly liked the way he did it. The 3rd sent me the script and I should have written before now to thank him for the stout effort. It is not difficult to know more about me than I do, self-defence has plunged my head in my hands. But knowing so much and such friendship, that's Con.

If I am to do any new work in the coming years, and nothing at the moment seems less likely, I think it will be in English for the 3rd. If only they would evolve the radio voice.

End of my letter again now in the little empty house. To-morrow Paris and tribulation.

Love to the pair of you.

Ever

Sam

ALS; 1 leaf, 2 sides; *env to* Dr. Ethna MacCarthy-Leventhal, 35 Lower Baggot St., Dublin, IRLANDE; *pm* 13–6–57; TxU, Leventhal Collection, 1.7.

1 Ethna MacCarthy may have sent SB the account in *The Irish Times* of Alan Simpson's arrest: "'The Rose Tattoo' Producer Charged in Dublin Court" (25 May 1957: 5). The article indicates that the warrant was issued by District Justice Kenneth Reddin (1895–1967). SB had appeared in the court of Kenneth Reddin for a traffic violation (see 6 October 1937).

2 SB refers to the sign of Kelly's, a Dublin pawnbroker, 8 Westmoreland Street and 22/23 Fleet Street, and to Suzanne Deschevaux-Dumesnil's homeopathic doctor Roger Clarac (Knowlson, *Damned to Fame*, 394, 332).

3 The autograph manuscript of *Endgame* is dated as begun on 7 May 1957 and completed on 5 June 1957 (Carlton Lake, ed., with the assistance of Linda Eichhorn and Sally Leach, *No Symbols Where None Intended: A Catalogue of Books, Manuscripts, and Other Material Relating to Samuel Beckett in the Collections of the Humanities Research Center* [Austin: Humanities Research Center, University of Texas at Austin, 1984] 101).

4 Sophie Jacobs (1887–1972). Her sister was the artist Estella Solomons (1882–1968; Profile, I), who was married to Seumas O'Sullivan (pen name of James Starkey, 1879–1958; Profile, I), Editor of *Dublin Magazine*.

AVIGDOR ARIKHA
PARIS

22.6.57 Ussy-sur-Marne

Cher ami

Votre lettre à l'instant. Pas question de concentration. Je flotte affreusement dans une vraie vacance de l'esprit. Ça n'a jamais été à ce point.

J'aimerais beaucoup voir ce que vous faites pour les textes, que ce soit vous, et libre, il n'y a là rien à illustrer.[1]

Moi aussi, j'aime vraiment ce petit texte de Suzanne. Elle n'arrive que ce soir, elle sera contente que cela vous ait plu, personne ne l'a jamais remarqué.[2]

J'attends d'avoir le courage de reprendre ma traduction de Fin de Partie. Il faut que le texte définitif soit prêt pour la mi-août. C'est foutu d'avance, j'aurai du moins fini de perdre cette foutue partie-là.

Je pense être à Paris au début de juillet. Je vous ferai signe sans faute à ce moment-là.

Monsieur ?quist des Editions Bonnier est venu chez moi.[3] Il a parlé de vous et admiré votre tableau.

Bien amicalement de nous deux

Sam. Beckett

ALS; 1 leaf, 1 side; InU, Arikha.

22.6.57 Ussy-sur-Marne

Dear Avigdor

Your letter just now. No question of concentrating. I am floating horribly in real emptiness of mind. Never before so bad.

I would very much like to see what you're doing for the texts, that it's you who are doing it, and free: there's nothing there that needs illustrating.[1]

I too am really fond of that little text of Suzanne's. She only gets here this evening. She'll be very pleased that you liked it. No one has ever noticed it.[2]

I'm waiting to get up the courage to go back to my translation of *Fin de partie*. The final text has to be ready by mid-August. Fat chance of that. I will at least have ended losing that bloody game.

I should be in Paris in early July. I'll definitely get in touch then.

Mr ?quist from the Bonnier Editions came to see me.[3] He spoke of you and admired your picture.

All good wishes from us both.

Sam Beckett

1 Avigdor Arikha (1929–2010; Profile, II) had proposed to do drawings for the Minuit edition of SB's *Nouvelles et Textes pour rien*.

2 SB is probably referring to Suzanne Deschevaux-Dumesnil's short text published in *Transition Forty-Eight* no. 4 (January 1949) 19–21, entitled "F –." In the "Notes About Contributors," SB's companion is described briefly as "Forgotten in musical, unknown in literary circles" (151).

3 Åke Runnquist (1919–1991) was an editor and critic at Bonnier Förlag, SB's Swedish publisher.

KAY BOYLE
NEWARK, DELAWARE

July 12th 1957

6 Rue des Favorites
Paris 15me

Dear Kay Boyle

Thanks for letter and gloss. What's come over you? It's one of the most sensitive, imaginative, inseeing, painstaking comments I've read.[1] I came out of it almost beginning to like the story myself. Sorry to disappoint you and to have had this deplorable effect on your critical faculties. Et merci de tout coeur.[2]

s/ Sam. Beckett

TLS; 1 leaf, 1 side; T *env to* Kay Boyle, Alden Court, 54 E. Main Street, Newark, Delaware, U.S.A., *AN, upper left corner* Par avion; *pm* 12-7-57, Paris; TxU, Beckett Collection, 8.3.

1 SB refers to Boyle's lecture on him given at the University of Delaware. When Boyle wrote to SB on 1 June, she apologized: "Although my absurd interpretation of

your work - based on the identity of Belacqua - in my lecture entitled 'Samuel Beckett and the Tradition of Loneliness' is inexcusable, my feeling about your writing has a great part in my life" (TxU, Boyle, 1.6; in other places referred to as "The Tradition of Loneliness").

2 "Et merci de tout coeur" (And heartfelt thanks).

KAY BOYLE
NEWARK, DELAWARE

26.7.57

6 rue des Favorites
Paris 15me

Dear Kay - This exhausted bristol to thank you for and congratulate you on The Tradition of Loneliness which is very fine and gave me great pleasure. The Occupation interp. is perhaps a little tiré par le 2-Millimeterschnitt, but formidably ingenious (Pozzo-Bozzo gem) and after all for the likes of some of us it's that way always and no Nono zone inside or out.[1] Passage on switch to French very good too and probably true in the main, now that I've forgotten half my English I feel like going back to it.[2]

Bref brava and I clasp your hand.[3]

Sam Beckett

ACS; 1 leaf, 1 side; *env to* Kay Boyle, University of Delaware, Newark, Delaware, U.S.A., *lower left corner* Air mail; *pm* 26-7-57, Paris; TxU, Beckett Collection, 8.3.

1 In "The Tradition of Loneliness," Boyle quotes SB on his return to France in 1939: "'I preferred France in war to Ireland in peace. I made it just in time. I stayed in Paris until 1942, and then I had to leave - because of the Germans. I went to the Vaucluse'." Boyle expands:

> It should be recalled that the Germans entered Paris in the spring of 1940, and thus Beckett's casual remark that he stayed in Paris until 1942 covers more peril, more pain, and more actual hunger than many of us have ever known [. . .] it remained for others to say of him that after his work with the Resistance in France, "he looked haggard and ill on his return to Dublin in 1945, went back immediately to France and worked in an ambulance unit in a Red Cross hospital, and was decorated for his services."
>
> Because of the choices which define the acts of faith in Beckett's life [. . .] I have read Godot as Beckett's evaluation of the situation of France during the war. Vladimir and Estragon, who wait eternally, are no more than variations of the man in the street - of the man who is far worse off than in the street - the man in the gutter, actually, which is where in a military occupation he takes his

place. (ICso, Kay Boyle Collection; TMS 90/84/14; the unidentified source, incorrectly quoted here by Boyle, is Niall Montgomery, "No Symbols Where None Intended," *New World Writing* 5 [1954] 327.)

"Tiré par le 2-Millimeterschnitt": a Gallicism for the French idiom "tiré par les cheveux" (far-fetched, literally "pulled by the hair" – adapted for a comical German referent: "2-millimeter haircut," an extreme crew-cut).

Boyle writes: "Pozzo shouts out his name – P-O-Z-Z-O! – and Vladimir is not sure whether he has said 'Bozzo' or 'Pozzo.' It is well known that Prussians invariably pronounce 'B' as 'P' and 'P' as 'B.'" Boyle contrasts the food of the occupied (carrots and turnips) to that of the oppressor (chicken and wine). She writes: "Pozzo turns the bones with the end of his whip, and one's blood runs as cold as if one heard the commander of a concentration camp answer: 'Do I need the bones? No, personally, I do not need them any more.'" She also sees Lucky as "the concrete figure of the shackled will," and notes that inversion in Act II, where a blind Pozzo needs the help of Vladimir and Estragon, and provides them with an opportunity – as Vladimir says, "'Let us do something while we have the chance.'"

The "Nono zone" refers to a nickname given to the "Free Zone" which existed until November 1942: it is derived from "Zone non-O[ccupée]."

2 Boyle discusses SB's writing in French as an extrapolation of exile: "some left their native shores to escape the implications and confines of their native tongues [. . .] Beckett [escaped] through an abandoning of English entirely and an eventual writing of his books in French." Although she herself does not agree wholly with it, Boyle quotes a letter from an unidentified common friend:

> "For Sam, ours is a spiritually and aesthetically destitute age, one in which anything other than the meagrest and poorest means of expression are wholly out of place. His own language, because of the marvelous wealth of the English language, became for him too easy, too much of a temptation – and forcing himself to write in a foreign language that is at the same time a more formal and far less rich one, he felt he could better convey the sordidness and poverty of the epoch as he sees it." (6)

She adds to this Beckett's own words: "'It is worth while remarking that no language is so sophisticated as English. It is abstracted to death,'" as well as what he said to her in conversation: "'In 1942, I began writing in French. I just felt like it. It was a different experience from writing in English. It was more exciting for me'" (6–7).

3 "Bref" (In a word).

MARY HUTCHINSON
DALKEY, CO. DUBLIN, IRELAND

31 7 57 Ussy

Dear Mary

Thanks for your letter which I found here, yesterday, in the box, after some days in Paris. It is better you should write me Rue des

Favorites. Here a letter just lies in the box, if I am not here, unforwardable.

Many thanks indeed for Gascoyne's copy of More Pricks, which arrived this morning. Though I have not the courage to read it I am very glad to have it.[1]

I hope this reaches you at the Coliemore [*for* Colamore] Hotel, Dalkey. I can't think of anything, short of the continuance of some rocks in the mountains, that I want to hear about Dublin. Remember me to Joe and his wife if you get this line in time. I remember the house in Killiney well, if it is the one he used to live in 25 years ago. I used to go there when he was writing his book, with Rossi, on Swift. When I was a small boy a big bald man called Cream lived there. I think he is in Watt.[2]

I have a fortnight in which to finish Endgame for Faber & Devine. Many passages remain unsolved. It seems impossible to get a proper stretch here. But I look forward to a quiet winter here. I am fiddling with another mime for Mendel. Sonst gar nichts.[3]

Enjoy your stay in Ireland. I look forward to seeing you here. Let me know, if you can, a little in advance.

It is fine, after weeks of rain and grey, and I see the harvesters east, south and west, if I happen to look out of the windows.

Yours ever

Sam

ALS; 1 leaf, 1 side; *env* to Mrs Hutchinson, Coliemore Hotel, (Mrs Cullen), Coliemore Road, Dalkey, C^o Dublin, IRLANDE [*crossed out, AN AH* not known at this address, *AN Mary Hutchinson* but kept for me]; *pm* 31-7-57, La Ferté-sous-Jouarre, *verso pm* 20-8-57, Dun Laoghaire; TxU, Hutchinson, 2.4.

1 English poet David Gascoyne (1916–2001). *More Pricks Than Kicks* (1934) was out of print at this time.

2 SB refers to Joseph Maunsell Hone (1882–1959; Profile, I) and his wife Vera (1886–1971), whose home until 1940 was South Hill on the Killiney Road. SB visited Hone there in 1933 when the latter was collaborating with Italian scholar Mario Manlio Rossi on *Swift; or, the Egoist* (1934).

Mr. Cream is mentioned three times in *Watt* (New York: Grove Press, 1959): twice on p. 13, and again on p. 15.

3 By "another mime," SB refers to writing *Acte sans paroles II* for Deryk Mendel, about which he would write to Jérôme Lindon on 24 August: "J'ai fait un petit mime, très horizontal. Pas fameux. Mais Deryk m'écrit qu'il le trouve à son goût."

(IMEC-Fonds Samuel Beckett, Boîte 3, Correspondance 1957 – droits étrangers.) (I have done a little mime, very horizontal. Nothing much. But Deryk writes that it's his kind of thing.)

"Sonst gar nichts" (otherwise nothing at all).

CHRISTIAN LUDVIGSEN
HELLERUP, DENMARK

August 6th 1957

6 Rue des Favorites
Paris 15me

Dear Mr Ludvigsen

"The Lord upholdeth all that fall etc" is from the Old Testament, Psalm 145, verse 14.[1]

"Yep wiyya etc" is a phonetic transcription of an Irish yokel saying "get on with you out of that".

"Crucifying his gearbox" – no double meaning.

"Ramdam" – French slang meaning roughly fuss, uproar, hubbub, ado.

"Bawdy hour etc" – obscure obscene joke. Cf. Shakespeare's "bawdy hour of noon". Image of erection on way up (hour hand at nine) and on way down (hour hand at three).

Boghill – simply a typically Irish place name.

Effie and the Major – allusion to Theodor Fontane's novel Effie Briest.[2]

The title in French is Tous Ceux qui Tombent. The French translation, revised by me, appeared in a recent number of the Lettres Nouvelles (Nadeau's review). It might be a help to you and I am writing to ask them to send you a copy. There is a good German translation issued in brochure form by the Fischerverlag, Frankfurt am Main.[3] I am sure they would send you a copy if you asked them. There may be some delay with the Lettres Nouvelles, because of the vacation.

If I can be of any further help do not hesitate to ask me.

Yours sincerely
s/ Sam. Beckett

TLS; 1 leaf, 1 side; *T env to* Chr. Ludvigsen, C.V.E. Knuthsvej 18 a, Hellerup, Danemark; *pm* _-8-57; Ludvigsen Collection.

1 Ludvigsen's questions relate to *All That Fall* which he is translating into Danish as *Hvo som falder*.

2 From *All That Fall*: "Yep wiyya," *CSP*, 13; "crucifying his gearbox," 20; "ramdam," 25; "bawdy hour," 26; "Boghill," 27. SB echoes Mercutio's line: "for the bawdy hand of the dial is now upon the prick of noon" (William Shakespeare, *Romeo and Juliet*, II. iv.112–113, *The Riverside Shakespeare: The Complete Works*, ed. G. Blakemore Evans, assisted by J. J. M. Tobin, 2nd edn. [Boston: Houghton Mifflin, 1997]; all references to writings by Shakepeare are to this edition).

Theodor Fontane's *Effi Briest* (1898). Here, as in *All that Fall* and *Krapp's Last Tape*, SB adds an "e" to Effi's name (*CSP*, 29 and 62).

3 *Alle, die da fallen* translated by Erika Schöningh (b. 1931) and Elmar Tophoven was first published in *Die Neue Rundschau* 68.2 (1957) 255–282. This journal was a joint publication of Fischer Verlag and Suhrkamp Verlag. Fischer Verlag had published what SB here calls "the brochure" which served as an acting copy (Breon Mitchell to the editors, 9 February 2012).

STUART MAGUINNESS
LONDON

August 13th 1957 — Ussy-sur-Marne
Seine-et-Marne

Dear Stuart

Here this morning your Bérénice, Virgil studies and good letter.[1] Very many thanks. I am sadly far now from scholarship myself, but the touch of it brings me something of the old warmth and peace I ran away from so long ago, and often regret.

I shall send you the following works at least when my publisher returns from estivation, i.e. next month: L'Innommable, Nouvelles et Textes pour Rien and Fin de Partie. Ah yes, also Echo's Bones, which I remember you said you had not. There will be a rather high-falutin' edition soon of Godot, Fin de Partie, Acte sans Paroles and Tous Ceux Qui Tombent (All That Fall) which I should like to feel in the friends' corner of your shelves and shall not fail to send you when available.[2]

It was a good evening truly, all the time from out [*for* our] meeting outside to our parting within 69, and I walked back with a light step all the way via Montparno to Rue des Favorites (so rather disappointingly named, it may amuse you to know, from an old coaching enterprise that had its stables in Girard's Vale).[3] It is long since I spent such a short six hours and so lit by friendship and memory. Indeed may we soon have the same again.

I have finished at last and got off my translation, End-Game. Now the old waiting and listening again, a little hide and seek with another mime for Deryk Mendel and of course the Innommable for translation before the end of the year.[4] I shall I hope be here steadily into the winter, apart from some rerehearsing in September and a brief jaunt to Etretat.[5] But if you should write, write Rue des Favorites.

Have a happy trip, greet from me your wife and daughter, and believe me, dear Stuart,

Your affectionate friend

s/ Sam

TLS; 1 leaf, 1 side; UoR, BIF, MS 4199/1.

1 William Stuart Maguinness (1903–1983), who was at Trinity College Dublin with SB, won a gold medal both in Modern Languages and in Classics; he was the Head of the Department of Classics at King's College London from 1952 to 1972. Maguinness's school edition of Jean Racine's *Bérénice* was published by Manchester University Press in 1929 and reprinted in 1956. Maguinness published in the Virgil Society Papers series, "Some Reflections on the Aeneid," no. 1 (1951), "The Tragic Spirit of the Aeneid," no. 7 (1955), and "The Thirteenth Book of the Aeneid," no. 9 (1957); it is not known which of these he sent to SB.

2 Maguinness's copy of *Echo's Bones and Other Precipitates* (1935) was inscribed "September 1957" (*American Book Prices Current 1994–1995*, [Washington, CT: Bancroft-Parkman, 1995] 345). The individual titles were all published by Editions de Minuit, but the collected French edition described by SB was not published. Editions de Minuit sent *L'Innommable*, *Nouvelles et Textes pour rien*, and *Fin de partie* to Maguinness on 5 September (SB to Jérôme Lindon [before 5 September 1957], IMEC-Fonds Samuel Beckett, Boîte 3, Correspondance 1957 – droits étrangers).

3 Maguinness was staying at 69 Rue de la Tombe-Issoire, Paris 14, according to his card of 1 August to his wife Olive and daughter Juliet (b. 1939) (UoR, BIF, MS 4199/1). This was the home of Mania Péron (1900–1988; Profile, II). Maguinness had been a close friend of Alfred Péron (1904–1945, Profile, I) when they were both at Trinity College Dublin, and he was godfather to Michel Stuart Péron (b. 1932).

4 *Endgame* had been promised to Devine for mid-August. SB retained the hyphen in the title until returning page proofs, with a note that "Endgame is now to be printed without hyphen" (SB to Marilynn Meeker, 26 September 1957; NSyU).

5 Etretat, on the Normandy coast, was where the Lindon family had a holiday home.

CHRISTIAN LUDVIGSEN
HELLERUP, DENMARK

August 18th [1957] 6 Rue des Favorites
Paris 15me

Dear Mr Ludvigsen

Thank you for your letter of August 14th.

Glad mine was of help to you.

I asked Les Lettres Nouvelles to send you the issue and hope they did so.[1] No expense involved.

Yes, I refer to Schubert's Death and the Maiden and more precisely to the opening bars of the theme of the variations.[2]

"Lead Kindly Light" is a very well-known English Protestant hymn. "Rock of Ages" and "Nearer my God" are not the same. The choice of hymns is not very important. Use ones familiar in your country.

"Sigh out a lamentable tale of things
"Done long ago and ill done. . ."

is from a minor Elizabethan dramatist, I can't remember which, perhaps Marston. The French quotation is from Ronsard.[3] Try and supply an equivalent from your own literature.

The child falls out of the slow (down) train, probably shortly after it leaves the terminus. Someone gives the alarm, the train is stopped and signals are then set against all trains, including the up mail, until the mess is cleared up and traffic can be resumed.[4] I do not see your difficulty here. But perhaps in fact the situation is less plausible that [*for* than] it appears to me, or plausible only in terms of the Irish scene.

Yours sincerely

s/

Samuel Beckett

TLS; 1 leaf, 1 side; T *env to* Chr. Ludvigsen, C.V.E. Knuthsvej 18a, Hellerup Danemark; *pm* 19-8-57, La Ferté-sous-Jouarre; Ludvigsen Collection.

1 "Tous ceux qui tombent," *Les Lettres Nouvelles* 54.7 (March 1957) 321–351.

2 The slow movement of Schubert's String Quartet in D minor (1824) is a set of variations on his song "Der Tod und das Mädchen" ("Death and the Maiden") (1817).

3 "Lead Kindly Light" and "Rock of Ages"; "Sigh out . . ."; Ronsard: 5 February 1957 to Tarn, n. 1, n. 2, n. 3. The words of "Nearer my God to Thee" were written by Sarah Flower Adams (1805–1848) in 1840.

4 J. W. Lambert (1915–1986), Literary Editor of *The Sunday Times*, asked a question about the delay. SB replied: "Did old Dan push out the child? I have wondered extensively about this and can reach no conclusion." (SB to Lambert, 25 January 1957, Bodleian, MS. Eng. c.2291, f. 12.)

BARNEY ROSSET
GROVE PRESS, NEW YORK

August 27th 1957

6 Rue des Favorites
Paris 15me

Dear Barney

Thanks for your letter of August 23rd. By the same post copies of Banner agreement and of your letter to Collins of Curtis Brown and a cutting from the N.Y.T. announcing presentation of All That Fall.[1] These leave me worried and perplexed. All That Fall is a specifically radio play, or rather radio text, for voices, not bodies. I have already refused to have it "staged" and I cannot think of it in such terms. A perfectly straight reading before an audience seems to me just barely legitimate, though even on this score I have my doubts. But I am absolutely opposed to any form of adaptation with a view to its conversion into "theatre". It is no more theatre than End-Game is radio and to "act" it is to kill it. Even the reduced visual dimension it will receive from the simplest and most static of readings – and I am quite sure Berghof has no intention of leaving it at that – will be destructive of whatever quality it may have and which depends on the whole thing's coming out of the dark.[2] I think really we had better call it off, if it is not too late. I would have said all this before if I had known you had such a performance in mind and I am distressed at having to burst in on you with my wail at this late hour. But frankly the thought of All That Fall on a stage, however discreetly, is intolerable to me. If another radio performance could be given in the States, it goes without saying that I'd be very pleased.

Now for my sins I have to go on and say that I can't agree with the idea of Act Without Words as a film. It is not a film, not conceived in terms of cinema. If we can't keep our genres more or less distinct, or extricate them from the confusion that has them where they are, we might as well go home and lie down. Act Without Words is primitive theatre, or meant to be, and moreover, in some obscure way, a codicil to End-Game, and as such requires that this last extremity of human meat - or bones - be there, thinking and stumbling and sweating, under our noses, like Clov about Hamm, but gone from refuge.[3] The only point of making a film is to indicate, in the absence of Mendel or of John Beckett, the coordination of music and action. As I said, we have hopes of making the film. But if neither it nor Mendel nor John Beckett is available, then you'll simply have to do the play without the mime.

It is good news indeed that you're coming over soon. An evening with you would do me a power of good, and to thank you again better than in black and white for all you have done and are doing for me, and to hear you forgive me all the dirty cold water.

Ever

s/ Sam

I had a letter from Sarasota from a writer called (I think, having mislaid the letter) Wayne Davenport, in great distress over his failure to obtain recognition and asking my advice about periodicals, etc. He enclosed some poems which I thought were good. In my reply I suggested he might try, among other reviews, your Evergreen. Do what you can for him if he does. There is certainly talent there and he seems mortally disheartened.[4]

TLS; 1 leaf, 1 side; NSyU. Previous publication: "Rosset Remembers Beckett," *Theatre Week* (8–14 January 1990) 20.

1 *All That Fall* was to be presented at the Carnegie Hall Playhouse on 7 October by Banner Productions, which held an option for an additional night the following week (Barney Rosset to Alan C. Collins, Curtis Brown, 22 August 1957; NSyU).

2 Herbert Berghof, the director of the 1956 Broadway production of *Waiting for Godot* and the 1957 revival of the play, had been announced as the director of the staged reading.

3 In view of the problems in coordinating music and action in *Acte sans paroles I*, SB had mentioned to Rosset the possibility of "a sound film of the Paris performance. This does not exist, but we dream of making one." (12 August 1957; NSyU.)

SB told Deryk Mendel that the figure in *Act Without Words I* was "Clov thrown into the desert" (Mendel to the editors, 3 July 2002).

4 Wayne Davenport, *Portraits* (New York: Exposition Press, 1955). His work was not published in *Evergreen Review*.

FRANÇOIS BELOUX
PARIS

le 24 septembre 1957 — 6 Rue des Favorites
Paris 15me

Monsieur

J'ai lu avec un vif intérêt et vous renvoie ci-jointe l'adaptation cinématographique que vous avez faite de la moitié de mon roman Molloy.[1]

A mon grand regret, et malgré la valeur de votre travail, je ne peux pas vous donner l'autorisation que vous me demandez. Je ne désire pas que l'on tire des films de mes écrits et je m'y opposerai toujours.

Il m'est très pénible de penser qu'à cause de ce refus vous aurez fait tout ce travail pour rien et je regrette sincèrement que vous ne m'ayez pas consulté avant de l'entreprendre.

Croyez, Monsieur, à mes sentiments les meilleurs.

Samuel Beckett

TLcc; 1 leaf, 1 side; also AL draft, 1 leaf, 1 side *verso* François Beloux to SB, 21 September 1957; GEU, MS 1221.

24th September 1957 — 6 Rue des Favorites
Paris 15

Dear Mr Beloux

I have read with keen interest, and now return the enclosed cinema adaptation that you have made of half of my novel *Molloy*.[1]

To my great regret, and in spite of the value of your work, I cannot give you the authorisation that you are asking for. I do not want films to be made of my writings and I shall always hold out against it.

It pains me to think that because of this refusal you will have done all this work for nothing, and I am genuinely sorry that you did not consult me before undertaking it.

Yours sincerely
Samuel Beckett

1 French film and television producer François Beloux (1936–1972), graduate of the Institut des Hautes Etudes Cinématographiques, wrote on 21 September to request SB's permission to make a film of *Molloy*. He had adapted episodes of the novel: at the commissariat, the visit to his mother, the dog, and at Lousse's house.

HERBERT BERGHOF
NEW YORK

September 28th 1957

6 Rue des Favorites
Paris 15me

Dear Mr Berghof

In reply to yours of September 8th I was embarked on a difficult letter to you about All That Fall when I heard from Barney Rosset (to-day) that you had had a disagreement with the producer and were relinquishing the direction of the reading.[1] In these circumstances there does not seem much point in my completing and sending to you my remarks, of dubious interest in any case and (as always for me when I try to write about my work) an occasion of much labour and dissatisfaction. I hope we may meet some day and talk about these things, though I am not much good at that either. I know and am grateful to you for the great pains you took over Godot. Not having seen the production I have no comments to offer you. Friends in New York have spoken of it to me very highly.[2] If, as now seems likely, though no formal agreement has yet been reached, Alan Schneider is to direct Endgame, I beg you not to see in this circumstance any reflection on your own competence which both Barney Rosset and myself hold in great esteem. He just happens to be along first with a theatre and a producer and a definite offer. In his capacities too, having talked and worked with him here and in London, I have confidence, and I do not hold him at all responsible for the Miami fiasco.[3]

With best wishes,
Yours very cordially,

s/

Samuel Beckett

I do not know the poem of Matthias Claudius you refer to and should be grateful if you would send me a copy of it.[4]

TLS; 1 leaf, 1 side; NyPL, Billy Rose, Uta Hagen / Herbert Berghof Collection, T-MSS 2007-001, Box 77, F. 6.

1 On 8 September, Berghof had asked SB for assistance as he prepared to direct the reading of *All That Fall*: "I would rather be guided by you if this is not an imposition." Shortly afterward, however, Berghof withdrew; he explained to Sanford Friedman of Banner Productions that it was "devastating" to learn that SB considered a staged reading "'just barely legitimate'" (see 27 August 1957). Berghof continued: "I happen to agree. [. . .] I am in great awe of Samuel Beckett. You must not wonder if I feel miserable about it." (undated draft [after 8 September, before 28 September 1957]; NyPL, Billy Rose, Uta Hagen / Herbert Berghof Collection, T-MSS 2007-001, Box 77, F. 6.)

2 George Reavey (1907–1982; Profile, I) had written to SB about the Broadway production, and Barney Rosset had sent SB reviews (see [15 May 1956]).

3 Berghof had mentioned to SB, in his letter of 8 September, that Michael Myerberg had promised to let him direct *Endgame*, but was hesitant about doing the play; Berghof asked SB if he could acquire the rights for the play in New York were Myerberg not to do it. The "Miami fiasco" refers to the production of *Waiting for Godot* directed by Alan Schneider (1917–1984; Profile, II) in January 1956 (see 11 January 1956).

4 In closing his letter of 8 September, Berghof had written: "I wish there were your English words for the poem of Matthias Claudius which Schubert used at the crucial time of sickness – it is one of my favorites."

Berghof sent SB the poems of Matthias Claudius, and SB responded on 9 October with thanks, as well as his translation:

> Verso a poor translation of Schubert's poem.
>
> Death and the Maiden
> The Maiden
> Go, cruel scytheman, go
> Thy ways. I am yet but

A maid! Sweet scytheman, go
And touch me not!
Death
Give thy hand, tender fair,
I come in friendship, not to wound.
I am not cruel, be of good cheer,
Within my arms sleep sound.

for Herbert Berghof from
Samuel Beckett
Paris October 1957

SB also wrote: "I am distressed by your disappointment and the sadness of your letter. If you feel I have behaved badly towards you, please forgive me. Perhaps some day I shall have something to offer you, though I feel my work is nearly ended." (NyPL, Billy Rose, Uta Hagen / Herbert Berghof Collection, T-MSS 2007-001, Box 77, F. 6.)

JACOBA VAN VELDE AND FRITZ KUIPERS AMSTERDAM

31.10.57 Ussy sur Marne

Chers amis

Carte et lettre bien reçues, merci. Content de vous savoir si bien installés.[1] Je vous ai abonnés hier à "Arts" - pour 6 mois. C'est un infecte [sic] canard, mais je ne vois rien d'autre. Vous le recevrez sans doute à partir de la semaine prochaine.[2]

On n'a tiré aucune pièce de théâtre, à ma connaissance, de All That Fall, qui doit rester un texte radiophonique. J'aimerais que ce soit Tonny qui le traduise. Je crois que les droits sont libres pour la Hollande. Mais je n'en suis pas absolument sûr. Il faut demander ça à

CURTIS BROWN LTD
13 KING STREET
LONDON W.C.2

On ne joue plus Fin de Partie au Studio. Le dernier soir c'était plein à craquer. Il fallait donc l'arrêter.

Je suis jusqu'à la calvitie mourante dans la traduction de L'Innommable. A crever de rage et de honte.

Bram m'a donné une litho superbe. Je ne l'ai pas vu, ni Geer, ni Jacques, ni personne.[3]

Travaillez, Tonny. Cette sottise-là c'est ce que nous aurons eu de meilleur. Je vais rester ici et vomir mes dernières tripes.

Affectueusement à vous 2

Sam

ALS; 1 leaf, 1 side; BNF, 19794/47.

31.10.57 Ussy sur Marne

Dear both,

Received card and letter: thanks. Glad to know you're so comfortably settled.[1] I took out a subscription for you yesterday to "Arts" – for 6 months. It's a foul rag, but I can't think of another. You will be receiving it no doubt from next week.[2]

To my knowledge, no play has been made out of *All That Fall*, which must remain a text for radio. I would like it to be Tonny that translated it. I think that the rights are free for Holland. But I'm not absolutely sure. You must ask

CURTIS BROWN LTD
13 KING STREET
LONDON W.C.2

Endgame is no longer playing at the Studio. On the last evening the place was bursting at the seams. So they had to take it off.

I am in the last stages of baldness over the translation of L'Innommable. Feel like dying of rage and shame.

Bram has given me a superb litho. I haven't seen him, or Geer, or Jacques, or anyone.[3]

Keep working, Tonny. That particular lunacy will have been the best of us. I am going to stay on here and throw up the last of my guts.

Affectionately to the 2 of you

Sam

1 Jacoba van Velde (1913–1985; Profile, II) and her partner Frederik Carel Kuipers (known as Fritz, 1898–1973).

2 *Arts* was officially entitled *Arts, Spectacles* at this time.

3 SB possessed several lithographs by Bram van Velde; it is not known which litho is being referred to here. Bram's younger brother, the artist Geer van Velde (1898–1978, Profile, I).

SEBASTIAN RYAN
DUBLIN

November 11th 1957 — 6 Rue des Favorites
Paris 15me

Dear Sebastian[1]

Fin de Partie demands so much from its voices that I fear a performance by my compatriot foreigners, however good their French, is bound to be disastrous. It remains to try and decide whether this matters or not. I'm trying. In the meantime I'd like to know a little more about the theatre, I don't mean accommodation, but stage dimensions.[2] Also whether Alan Simpson, who has an option on Endgame, but cannot go on before the London opening, would have any objection to a performance in French in Dublin prior to his production. Consider also coldly with your friends the vulnerability of text and author.

Yours sincerely

s/

Samuel Beckett

TLS; 1 leaf, 1 side; Ryan Collection.

1 Sebastian Ryan (1932–1994), as a student at Trinity College Dublin, had published an essay, "Samuel Beckett," *Icarus* 3.11 (1953) 79–86. His father was journalist and author Desmond Ryan (1893–1964), a friend of SB.

2 Ryan had written to SB on 2 November seeking permission to put on *Fin de partie* in French, with Peter Murray (b. 1933, who used the name Paul Murray in his role as RTE radio producer) to direct and play Hamm, and John Edward Jordan (1930–1988) in the part of Clov. Mme D. Bannard Cogley (known as Toto, 1883–1965), founder of the Studio Theatre, 43 Upper Mount Street, was interested. This theatre lacked ceiling height over the stage, had limited stage lighting, and little wing space (Swift, *Stage by Stage*, 98).

ALAN SCHNEIDER
NEW YORK

November 21st 1957 Ussy-sur-Marne

Dear Alan

Forgive delay in replying to your letters. I am only just back in the country after another bout in Paris where I could not settle down to dealing with your queries.[1]

I hope the enclosed answers will help you.

Many thanks for good news of prospects and preparations.[2]

With regard to Godot complication, I confess I do not see exactly why such a revival should be damaging, but I take your word and Barney's that it would tend to.[3] I wrote forthwith to Curtis Brown (Kitty Black), asking if Myerberg has the right to do productions of Godot when, where and with whatever elements he likes without consulting me and whether I have or have not any contractual authority to intervene is [*for* in] such a matter. Also whether his control of Godot in US is everlasting or terminates after a specified period. So far no reply. Barney suggested I should write directly to Myerberg asking him to postpone his production till after Endgame opening. I think we should wait to have more definite information about his plans before I do this, also that there is little likelihood of his changing them just to please me. As soon as I hear from Kitty Black I shall let you know what she says. It goes without saying that I shall do whatever you and Barney think most advisable.

Blin is off to Vienna in a few days to direct Endgame in the German language production to be given there in January.[4] No news from Devine.

Salutations to Jean and daughter.[5]

Yours ever

s/ Sam

1. "Rag" is a printer's error for "rug". Blin didn't use one. Unimportant.[6]

2. I think in this text "end" is stronger than "die". As far as I remember Hamm and Clov never use "die" referring to themselves.

Their death is merely incidental to the end of "this... this... thing". But there is no system on my part here and the terms are used as naturally as possible. I do not say "deathgame" as I do not say that Mother Pegg "ended" of darkness.[7]

3. The French is "biscuit classique". If in US there is no particularly well known brand of dog biscuit you could fall back on "classic biscuit" or "standard biscuit" or "hard tack".[8]

4. In his kitchen it is his light, his life. To replace his by the normalizes and kills the line.[9]

9. Presumably in a dream – "last night" – he saw the inside of his chest.[10]

11. "All" because Nell has just told Clov to "desert".[11] "Us" means Hamm, Nagg and Nell.

12. I only know the one alluded to – his light dying. This if you like is an ironical allusion to Acts 2.17.[12] They endure their "thing" by projection away from it, Clov outwards towards going, Hamm inwards toward abiding. When Clov admits to having his visions less it means that his escape mechanism is breaking down. Dramatically this element allows his perception of life (boy) et [*for* at] the end and of course of the rat to be construed as hallucinations.[13]

15. What more can I say about Hamm's story? Technically it is the most difficult thing in the play because of the number of vocal levels. Dramatically it may be regarded as evoking events leading up to Clov's arrival, alone presumably the father having fallen by the way, and to the beginning of the particular horror to which this play is confined. It also allows Clov's "perception" of boy at end to be interpreted as vision of himself on last lap to "shelter" (which term use instead of "refuge" throughout if you wish).[14]

17. "Keep going etc" means "keep asking me about my story, don't let the dialogue die". Repeated ironically by Clov a little later with same meaning.[15] Cf. "return the ball" in Godot. I think this whole passage – up to recurrence of "end" motif – should be played as farcical parody of polite drawing-room conversation.[16]

19. Because Hamm is groggy.[17] Justify it if you like by Clov's refusal to touch him.

20. Hamm's voice spent after scream (second "What'll I do!"). Clov's "pity" means "pity you don't give me the opportunity of saying 'There are no more lozenges.'"[18]

Old Greek: I can't find my notes on the pre-Socratics. The arguments of the Heap and the Bald Head (which hair falling produces baldness) were used by all the Sophists and I think have been variously attributed to one or the other. They disprove the reality of mass in the same way and by means of the same fallacy as the arguments of the Arrow and Achilles and the Tortoise, invented a century earlier by Zeno the Eleatic, disprove the reality of movement. The leading Sophist, against whom Plato wrote his Dialogue, was Protagoras and he is probably the "old Greek" whose name Hamm can't remember.[19] One purpose of the image throughout the play is to suggest the impossibility logically, i.e. eristically, of the "thing" ever coming to an end. "The end is in the beginning and yet we go on."[20] In other words, the impossibility of catastrophe. Ended at its inception, and at every subsequent instant, it continues, ergo can never end. Don't mention any of this to your actors!

Clov's song: There is a quatrain by James Thompson might do the trick. I haven't got the text here and can't quite remember it:

Bid me sigh on from day to day
And wish and wish the soul away
Till hope (?) and youthful joys (?) are flown
And all the life of life is gone.

It figures in the "addenda" to Watt, so you can check above version with Barney. The trouble is that the air I used for the French song would be quite unsuitable for this. I don't mind if the song is cut. But if you like the idea of using the Thompson I'll ask John Beckett to do a setting for us. It's entirely as you wish.[21]

TLS; 2 leaves, 3 sides; *AN* red ink by Alan Schneider; Burns Library, Samuel Beckett Collection, SB-BR. Previous publication: Samuel Beckett and Alan Schneider, *No Author Better Served: The Correspondence of Samuel Beckett and Alan Schneider*, ed. Maurice Harmon (Cambridge, MA: Harvard University Press, 1998) 21–24.

1 SB replies to Schneider's letter of 8 November, written following their Paris meetings from 8 to 22 October (Beckett and Schneider, *No Author Better Served*, 17–21; Alan Schneider, 1957 Diary, WHS, Alan Schneider series 8, box 3; Alan Schneider, *Entrances: An American Director's Journey* [New York: Viking Press, 1986] 248–250).

2 In his letter of 8 November, Schneider reported on arrangements to open *Endgame* at the Cherry Lane Theatre at the end of January 1958.

3 On 12 November, Rosset had written to Kitty Black (1914–2006; Profile, II), Curtis Brown: "We feel that a re-opening of GODOT just prior to the opening of ENDGAME would detract a good deal from general interest in the new play" (NSyU).

4 Roger Blin had been invited to direct *Endspiel* at the Theater am Fleischmarkt, produced by Herbert Wochinz (b. 1925).

5 Eugenia (Jean) Muckle Schneider (b. 1923). Jean and Alan Schneider's daughter Viveca (b. 1955).

6 For the rest of this letter's notes, page references are to the 1958 Grove Press edition of *Endgame*.

Stage directions for Hamm (*Endgame*, 1). In the French premiere of *Fin de partie*, Blin wore a long robe draped over his legs.

7 "You know what she died of, Mother Pegg? Of darkness" (*Endgame*, 75).

8 Schneider's concern was that "Spratt's medium" was not a familiar term (*Endgame*, 10). In Schneider's production this became "hayden's biscuit, medium" (CUSD, MSS 103/12/12, p. 9).

9 "Your kitchen . . . Your light dying . . . *your* light" (*Endgame*, 12).

10 "Last night I saw inside my breast. There was a big sore." (*Endgame*, 32.)

11 *Endgame*, 23.

12 Schneider had asked about Clov's visions. Acts 2:17: "And it shall come to pass in the last days, saith God, I will pour out of my Spirit upon all flesh; and your sons and your daughters shall prophesy, and your young men shall see visions, and your old men shall dream dreams."

13 Clov's perception of the rat in his kitchen and the boy at the end of the play (*Endgame*, 54, 78).

14 Hamm's story (*Endgame*, 50–54).

15 Schneider had asked why Hamm's "Keep going . . ." is said "angrily" (*Endgame*, 59, 61).

16 *Waiting for Godot*, 9. The passage of drawing-room conversation parody: *Endgame*, 59–72.

17 Schneider asked about the line and stage directions that follow Clov's statement: "'If I don't kill that rat he'll die'." Hamm says, "That's right" (*Endgame*, 68).

18 SB replies to Schneider's question: "I don't know if I get why Clov says, 'Is your throat sore'"(*Endgame*, 72).

19 For the critical debate about the identity of the "Old Greek," see *Endgame*, ed. Gontarski, 46–47.

20 "The end is in the beginning and yet we go on," may allude to T. S. Eliot's "East Coker" (section I, lines 1 and 14) from *Four Quartets*.

21 Twice SB writes "Thompson" for "Thomson." The second stanza of "To Fortune" (1743), a poem by James Thomson (1700–1748) (*The Complete Poetical Works of James Thomson*, ed. J. Logie Robertson [Oxford: Oxford University Press, 1908] 427–428). The poem as cited in the "Addenda" to *Watt* (Grove) 248:

> Bid us sigh on from day to day,
> And wish and wish the soul away,
> Till youth and genial years are flown,
> And all the life of life is gone.

When SB sent *Endgame* to George Devine on 12 August, he said that he "couldn't do anything worth having with Clov's song so have suppressed it. No great loss." (TxU, English Stage Company, 1.2.) In *Endgame* as produced and published in English, Clov's song ("Joli oiseau, quitte ta cage, / Vole vers ma bien-aimée, / Niche-toi dans son corsage, / Dis-lui combien je suis emmerdé.") is cut (*Fin de partie*, 107; *Endgame*, 80).

The song as cited in Samuel Beckett, *Fin de partie*, Methuen's Twentieth Century Texts, Gen. Ed. W. J. Strachan (ed. John Fletcher, Beryl S. Fletcher, Barry Smith, Walter Bachem [London: Methuen Educational, 1970] 74, and 96–97), gives a tune supplied by Suzanne Beckett; however, John Beckett offered words and music from a music hall verse as the source for Clov's song, in which the notes and rhythm emphasize the final word – "emmerdé."

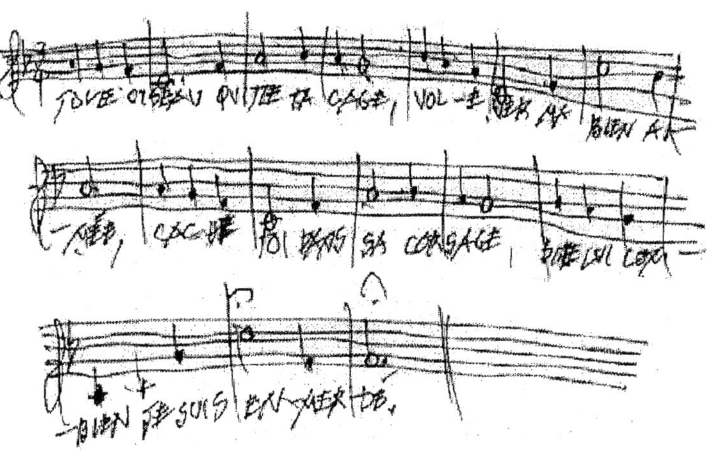

ETHNA MACCARTHY-LEVENTHAL
DUBLIN

22.11.57 Ussy sur Marne

Dear Ethna

It was good to have your letter. I should have written to Con to thank him for his good notice of ATF in the D.M. Will you please thank him for me. Sorry to hear of your slip followed by fall, I hope the surgical neck is up and about again.[1] My old cysts are still with me, but according to X Ray at a standstill. So I keep on trying to homeopathize them. Perhaps in this way I shall succeed in dying before an operation becomes necessary. I stay at this mournful address as much as possible, with occasional bouts in Paris trying to compress within a week a month's "business" from which I think it is time I retired and became as before I went into it, with all past instead of in store. It is like hanging from a ledge in a faint dream and a faint awareness of the three possibilities. To day since morning slow molten snow and the light hardly stronger than in the family vault. I am supposed to be translating L'Innommable, which is impossible. Not a sound all day and night but of the carts heaped high with the last mangels. No more heights, no more depths, the poldrums.[2] Poor Josette is reduced to 38 Kgs, 6/8 of tension and is to undergo some kind of deep sleep therapy. Henri did some very good work this summer not far from here.[3] Endgame is to open off-Broadway thank God in the Village next January. No news from Devine. I am trying to have him give the 2 parts to McGee and McGowran, but shall be surprised if he does.[4] Sebastian Ryan wrote asking permission for some friends to do it in French in some new Cogley joint (Mount St ?), I don't think this is to be encouraged. There is talk of a short programme of mimes at the next Dublin Festival, three in all, including the one you saw. I am not particularly keen.[5] John was in Greystones recently doing his music for a Molloy reading by the aforesaid McGee who I understand does it wonderfully.[6] A long letter from Cusack, after a long silence. His enormous book, Cadenza, finished at last, seems to be making a great stir among publishers' readers both sides of the Atlantic. I do hope he will have a success with it.[7] Good bye now for the present.

Love to you both

Sam

ALS; 1 leaf, 1 side; *env to* Dr. Ethna MacCarthy-Leventhal, 36 Lower Baggot Street, Dublin, IRLANDE; *pm* 23–11–57, place illeg; TxU, Leventhal Collection, 1.7.

1 A. J. Leventhal reviewed SB's *All That Fall* in "Dramatic Commentary," *Dublin Magazine* 32.4 (October–December 1957) 42–43.

2 "Poldrums": SB's invention, combining "polders" and "doldrums."

3 Josette Géraud Hayden (1913–2003), wife of the painter Henri Hayden (1883–1970; Profile, II). Hayden had painted landscapes of the countryside near his home in Reuil-en-Brie, not far from Ussy.

4 SB refers to actors Patrick Magee* (1922–1973) and Jack MacGowran* (1918–1973). SB writes "McGee," the spelling of the actor's family name, rather than "Magee," his stage name. He writes "McGowran" so regularly that this idiosyncracy will not henceforth be signalled.

5 Three mimes at the Dublin Festival: "A short programme of mime remains nevertheless a possibility. This does not involve writing. I have finished the one I mentioned to you when we met and could doubtless manage another by November. That is to say, with Act Without Words already performed, 3 mimes of simply 20 minutes each. The second is for 2 players and the third could be for one or two players." (SB to Brendan Smith, [after 21 August 1957], GEU, MS 1221.)

6 John Beckett praised Patrick Magee's readings of *Molloy* on the BBC Third Programme (SB to Barney Rosset, 21 November 1957; NSyU).

7 Married to SB's cousin Annabel Lilian Sinclair (known as Nancy, 1916–1969), Ralph Cusack (1912–1965) was also a painter, member of the White Stag group and the Dublin Society of Painters; he was a set designer, scene-painter, and the author of *Cadenza, An Excursion by Ralph Cusack* (London: Hamish Hamilton, 1958).

DONALD McWHINNIE
BBC, LONDON

11.12.57 Ussy

Dear Donald

I was in Paris last night and there listened to Molloy.[1] Reception execrable needless to say, but I got enough, knowing the text so well, to realize the extraordinary quality of Magee's performance. Please express to him my gratitude and congratulations. I trembled at the approach of certain passages in the tone he had committed himself to.[2] As far as I could hear he brought them off amazingly. I was also extremely pleased with the music. I had wondered a little if the text would take it. It not only did, it benefited by me, and as written by John it seems an indispensable part of the broadcast. It is obvious he and Magee came to a very good understanding. The points at which the music took over I thought very well chosen and its entry finely prepared by the voice.[3] To you, my dear Donald, for your direction my warmest thanks. The control and timing of the whole thing seemed to me faultless. If I could only have heard it properly, with the detail! My set here is more powerful and I am hoping to get it clearer on Friday, and on Saturday FAAW which I am waiting for with acute curiosity.[4] I'll write again at the beginning of next week.

Affectionately to you all

Sam

ACS; 1 leaf, 2 sides; OSU, Spec.rare.124, McWhinnie; T copy by McWhinnie for Patrick Magee (1 leaf, 1 side); BBCWAC, Central Artists, Patrick Magee I.

1 The reading from *Molloy* was recorded by the BBC Third Programme on 30 November, 1 and 2 December, and broadcast on 10 and 13 December.

2 Patrick Magee read the extract, taken from the second half of the first part of the novel, described by SB as "from shore to ditch" (see SB to McWhinnie, 7 May 1957, n. 2).

3 John Beckett and Donald McWhinnie worked on the music with Patrick Magee; it was scored for "three trumpets, three trombones, and three solo double basses" (John Beckett to McWhinnie, [before 6 November 1957]; BBCWAC, RCONT1, John Beckett, Composer I).

4 SB heard the re-broadcast of *Molloy* in Ussy on 13 December and the broadcasts of "From an Abandoned Work" on the BBC Third Programme on 14 and 19 December; both programs were produced by McWhinnie and read by Patrick Magee.

DONALD McWHINNIE
BBC, LONDON

23.12.57 Ussy

Dear Donald

Many thanks for your letter, scripts and – this morning – card of greeting. Mine to you all and the 3rd for Xmas and the next jolt of the old wheel.

I listened here to Molloy 2 and the two FAAWs. Alas no clearer than in Paris. More volume, but more interference. So I really can't comment relevantly. Magee's great quality and feeling came through again. If anything I think I prefer his Molloy to his FAAW which seemed a little rushed and telescoped at times and perhaps slightly over-querulous. But the distortion and fading and encroachments were such that this may very well be a false impression. And there is justification in the text for its being hurried, if it was. I did not hear "vero vero" which I have a weakness for, but it probably just got lost on the way to me.[1] I'd give a lot to have records, if this is not too greedy of me. Did John pass on to you Rosset's request for recordings? If you could oblige him I'd be grateful.[2] John wrote that he would do the music differently if he did it again. But I thought it was right, in a spirit not of reinforcement but of otherness, boots more by chance than design to the hero's arse, where thy boots are there will my arse be also. In short it's the lucky man I am to have had the three of you and great is my appreciation.[3] Endgame is running into trouble, which is all the more annoying as there seemed a good chance of Magee and McGowran. Devine wrote announcing he would present Endgame in March, not with the mime, but with A Resounding Tinkle. I find it impossible to leap at this and have said so, suggesting they forget all about me until I can offer, to complete the evening's misery, something else from my own muckheap more acceptable than the mime. This is not nosiness God knows and I have no doubt, having read Mr Tynan, that I would be in excellent company with Mr Simpson.[4] I simply prefer right or wrong to be unrelieved. This between ourselves. I'll let you know developments.

Thanks for giving FAAW to Faber. I couldn't find a copy for them.[5]

I shall be here till early in the New Year. I'm trying to write in English, but to little purpose.[6]

I hope Barbara received my feeble comments on her excellent translation and that there [*for* they] were of some use to her here and there.[7]

Affectionately to you all.

s/ Sam

TLS; 1 leaf, 1 side; *datestamped* 30 DEC 1957; OSU, Spec.rare.124, McWhinnie.

1 It was Mary Hutchinson who noted the absence of this passage in the broadcast of "From an Abandoned Work"; on 21 December, SB wrote to her: "I did not catch omission of "vero vero" which was certainly in their script" (TxU). The omitted passage: "Over, over, there is a soft place in my heart for all that is over, no, for the being over, I love the word, words have been my only loves, not many. Often all day long as I went along I have said it, and sometimes I would be saying vero, oh vero" (as published in "From an Abandoned Work," *Evergreen Review* 1.3 [1957] 90). The second sentence of this passage was indeed cut from the BBC script (BBCWAC, Tx, 14/12/57, p. 9).

2 John Beckett met McWhinnie to discuss commercial recordings. Rosset had suggested to SB that the cast "do the same recording twice"; he added, "there is

nothing to prevent the artist from immediately walking into an adjoining studio and doing the same thing over again. I will be happy to pay studio costs" (25 November 1957; NSyU).

3 John Beckett's letter to SB has not been found, but McWhinnie commented in his letter to SB of 31 December: "I thought John's notions for a different treatment for the music extremely interesting, but perhaps it might be more fruitful to apply them to other material?" (BBCWAC, RCONT1, Samuel Beckett, Scriptwriter I).

4 Kenneth Tynan wrote of N. F. Simpson's *A Resounding Tinkle*: "It does not belong in the English theatrical tradition at all ... He has voluntarily discarded most of the dramatist's conventional weapons." The affinity with Beckett is also remarked: "How, for so long, are we to keep ourselves amused? This is the problem that faced the tramps in 'Waiting for Godot'" (Kenneth Tynan, "The Hard Way," *The Observer* 8 December 1957: 15).

5 Rosica Colin wrote to SB on 3 December that Faber and Faber wished to include "From an Abandoned Work" in a volume with "another radio play" (Rosica Colin Collection; GEU, MS 1221). Beckett replied on 9 December:

> I feel from your letter that Faber and Faber have perhaps not read this fragment. It is a very loose monologue and has no pretensions to dramatic form of any kind. I feel therefore that it could hardly be included in a volume of radio writing. Its place would normally be in a collection of miscellanea, for which I have not at present, and perhaps may never have, the necessary material. (Rosica Colin Collection; AL draft, GEU, MS 1221.)

6 SB wrote to Rosset on 17 December: "I sometimes take a few hours off, from translation and supine brooding, to fiddle at the new radio text, and leave it down wishing I had complied with my father's wishes and gone into Guinness's Brewery" (NSyU).

7 In a letter of 6 December, SB had commented on Bray's translation and adaptation of *Le Square* (TCD, MS 10948/1/3).

GEORGE DEVINE
ROYAL COURT THEATRE, LONDON

December 26th 1957 — 6 Rue des Favorites
Paris 15me

Dear George

Thanks for your letter of December 21st. I am grateful for your understanding.[1]

I am willing for the play to be presented alone. This is what they are doing in New York, at the Cherry Lane, opening end of next month.

I am afraid I simply cannot accept omission or modification of the prayer passage which appears to me indispensable as it stands. And to play it in French would amount to an omission, for nine tenths of the audience. I think this does call for a firm stand. It is no more blasphemous than "My God, my god, why hast Thou forsaken me?"[2] The others are easy:

1. Replace "balls" by "botch" and, four lines later, "botches" by "ballockses". Or, if they object to "ballockses", simply replace "balls" by "hames".[3]

2. Replace "pee" by "urinate" or, if they object to "urinate", by "relieve myself".[4]

3. Replace "pee" by "urination" or, if they object to "urination", by "relief".[5]

5. [sic] It is a pity to lose "arses" because of its consonance with "ashes". "Rumps" I suppose would be the next best.[6]

I was very impressed by Magee's readings from my work and thought he would fit in well with McGowran. But I have not seen him in action and I need not say that I accept without question whatever you decide.

I have made a few inoffensive changes (including as it happens "ballockses" for "botches") when correcting proofs.[7] I shall send you a list of them, or a corrected script, in a few days.

Best wishes to you all.

Yours ever

s/ Sam

TLS; 1 leaf, 1 side; TxU, English Stage Company, 1.2.

1 In his letter of 21 December, Devine agreed to abide by SB's request not to put *Endgame* on a double bill with N. F. Simpson's *A Resounding Tinkle* (TxU, English Stage Company, 1.2).

2 Devine had sent SB a copy of a letter of 18 December from the Lord Chamberlain's Office which lists the passages deemed unacceptable in *Endgame* (Sir Norman W. Gwatkin, Assistant Comptroller, to Miriam Brickman, Royal Court Theatre; TxU, English Stage Company, 1.2). It demanded that the prayer passage be cut: "from 'Let us pray to God', down to 'he doesn't exist'" (*Endgame*, 54–55). In his letter to SB of 21 December, Devine suggested: "I did wonder if we should play the offending lines in French. We have a licence for this and I cannot see that he can object [. . .] The absurdity of his situation might make him relent but, in any case, it would become a

major issue as he has granted us a licence in French, which we hold." (TxU, English Stage Company, 1.2.)

3 Nagg's story of the tailor and the trousers (*Endgame*, 22–23).

4 Hamm: "I'd like to pee" (*Endgame*, 24).

5 Clov: "What about that pee?" (*Endgame*, 34).

6 Hamm: "Peace to our . . . arses" (*Endgame*, 82).

7 In Nagg's story of the tailor and the trousers, the tailor "ballockses the button-holes" (*Endgame*, 22).

ALAN SCHNEIDER
NEW YORK

29.12.57 Paris

Dear Alan

Thanks for your letter. You know how anxious I am to help you and Barney with that uncrackable nut. But I simply can't write about my work, or occasional stuff of any kind. Please forgive me.

It would be impertinent for me to advise you about the article you are doing and I don't intend to. But when it comes to these bastards of journalists I feel the only line is to refuse to be involved in exegesis of any kind. That's for those bastards of critics. And to insist on the extreme simplicity of dramatic situation and issue. If that's not enough for them, and it obviously isn't, or they don't see it, it's plenty for us, and we have no elucidations to offer of mysteries that are all of their making. My work is a matter of fundamental sounds (no joke intended), made as fully as possible, and I accept responsibility for nothing else. If people want to have headaches among the overtones, let them. And provide their own aspirin. Hamm as stated, and Clov as stated, together as stated, nec tecum nec sine te, in such a place, and in such a world, that's all I can manage, more than I could.[1]

I like the idea of the bare walls and the added space it gives. Paint the windows on them if you like. Glad you are pleased with your cast.[2]

In London the Lord Chamberpot demands inter alia the removal of the entire prayer scene! I've told him to buckingham off.

Congratulations on TV Great Cham. Yes, I always had a passion for that crazy old ruffian.[3]

Salutations to Jean and Vicky.

Ever

s/ Sam

TLS; 1 leaf, 1 side; Burns Library, Samuel Beckett Collection, SB-AS. Previous publication: "Beckett's Letters on Endgame: Extracts from His Correspondence with Director Alan Schneider," *The Village Voice*, 19 March 1958: 8, 15; rpt. as Beckett and Schneider, "On Endgame," *Village Voice Reader: A Mixed Bag from the Greenwich Village Newspaper*, ed. Daniel Wolf and Edwin Fancher (Garden City, NY: Doubleday, 1962) 185; rpt. Beckett, *Disjecta*, 108–109; Beckett and Schneider, *No Author Better Served*, 24–25.

1 From Martial's *Epigrams*, XII, 46: "Nec tecum possum vivere nec sine te" (Neither with you can I live nor without you).

2 The cast of this production: Clov, Alvin Epstein (b. 1925); Hamm, Lester Rawlins (1924–1988); Nagg, P. J. Kelly (n.d.); Nell, Nydia Westman (1902–1970).

3 Schneider directed *Life of Samuel Johnson*, adapted from Boswell's *Life of Samuel Johnson* by James Lee (1923–2002), produced by CBS-TV's *Omnibus* with Peter Ustinov (1921–2004); SB was very interested in learning how Lee had handled the relationship between Johnson and Mrs. Thrale (Schneider, *Entrances*, 245, 250).

CHRONOLOGY 1958

1958 2 January		Lord Chamberlain's Office demands cuts in text of *Endgame* before it will issue performance license for London production.
28 January		Premiere of *Endgame*, Cherry Lane Theatre, New York.
31 January		Launch of the first American earth satellite, Explorer 1.
by 17 February		SB withdraws his two mimes and a reading of *All That Fall* from the Dublin Theatre Festival.
23 February		Completes first draft of English translation, *The Unnamable*.
27 February		Withdraws all his work from Irish production.
6 March		Opening of *Endspiel* directed by Roger Blin at the Theater am Fleischmarkt, Vienna; Suzanne Deschevaux-Dumesnil and Jean Martin attend.
7 March		*Malone Dies* published by John Calder.
17 March		SB finishes writing *Krapp's Last Tape*.
25 April		Faber and Faber publish *Endgame, followed by Act Without Words I*.
5 May		SB meets Alain Resnais to discuss film of *Tous ceux qui tombent*. Attends performance of *Le Square* by Marguerite Duras at the Théâtre de Poche.
7–10 May		Visits Berne to attend Bram van Velde's retrospective.
13 May		"May 1958 Crisis" in Algeria. Charles de Gaulle declares his readiness to become head of government in France.

29 May	De Gaulle appointed Président du Conseil by President René Coty.
1 June	De Gaulle's cabinet approved by the Assemblée Nationale.
18 June	The BBC Third Programme broadcasts a selection from *Malone Dies* read by Patrick Magee, with music composed by John Beckett.
4 July	The Royal Court Theatre holds a private reading of *Endgame* for representatives of the Lord Chamberlain's Office.
8 July	SB begins a three-week holiday with Suzanne in Yugoslavia.
15 August	Dates early draft of an abandoned play, later *Rough for Theatre II*.
20 September	SB sees McWhinnie and Patrick Magee in Paris to discuss *Krapp's Last Tape*.
28 September	New French constitution adopted by referendum (79 percent in favor).
29 September	Grove Press publish *The Unnamable*.
21 October	SB goes to London for a week to assist with rehearsals of *Krapp's Last Tape* and *Endgame*.
23 October	Boris Pasternak awarded the Nobel Prize in Literature. He will refuse it, under pressure from Soviet authorities, on 29 October.
28 October	Premiere of *Krapp's Last Tape* as a curtain-raiser for *Endgame*, Royal Court Theatre, London.
1 November	SB completes English translation ("Text I") from *Textes pour rien*.
16 November	Symposium at the Royal Court Theatre on *Endgame* with Anthony Cronin and Donald McWhinnie.
before 23 November	Uncertain of its worth, SB asks Barbara Bray and Donald McWhinnie to read his "aborted radio script" (eventually entitled *Embers*).
December	Indiana University Press publish the *Anthology of Mexican Poetry*, translated by SB into English.

1 December	SB flies to Dublin for a week to see Ethna MacCarthy-Leventhal, who is dying of cancer, and Thomas MacGreevy, who has suffered a serious heart attack.
17 December	Begins "Pim" which eventually becomes part of *Comment c'est.*
29 December	Cardinal Roncalli is elected Pope, as John XXIII.

GEORGE DEVINE
ROYAL COURT THEATRE, LONDON

January 5th 1957 [*for* 1958]

6 Rue des Favorites
Paris 15me

Dear George

Thanks for your letter of January 3rd.

I am obliged to maintain the prayer passage as I wrote it.[1]

I have shown that I am prepared to put up with minor damage, which God knows is bad enough in this kind of fragile writing. But no author can acquiesce in what he considers, rightly or wrongly, as grave injury to his work.

I am extremely sorry to have to take this stand and I can assure you I do not do so lightly. I can only hope that you will not think me unreasonable and that Lord Scarborough may perhaps be induced to reconsider his decision.[2]

Yours ever
s/ Sam
Samuel Beckett

TLS; 1 leaf, 1 side; TxU, English Stage Company, 1.2. *Dating*: George Devine to SB, 3 January 1958.

1 Devine's letter to SB reported on his meeting with Sir Norman Gwatkin (d. 1971), Lord Chamberlain's Office, about the prayer passage in *Endgame*:

> The attitude seems to be entirely hypocritical, but I was given to understand that Lord Scarbrough had not written "alter" or "amend" against this passage, but "cut", which is supposed to be serious. However, the Assistant Comptroller feels that if we would follow his suggestions his Lordship might change his mind [. . .]

Cut the words "to God" after "Let us pray". Change Hamm's "God first" to something like "First things first". For Nag[g], cut the words "Our Father which art" and indicate in the stage directions that the words are not really distinguishable, and Hamm, change "the bastard" into "the swine". (3 January 1958; TxU, English Stage Company, 1.2.)

2 Lawrence Lumley (1896–1969), 11th Earl of Scarbrough, was the Lord Chamberlain from 1952 to 1965.

3. George Devine

MAURICE GIRODIAS
PARIS

le 7 janvier 1958

6 Rue des Favorites
Paris 15me

Cher Monsieur

Je vous remercie de votre lettre du 2 janvier.

Je déplore autant que vous l'état de nos rapports. Si j'y suis pour quelque chose, c'est bien involontairement, croyez-moi.[1]

Comme je vous l'ai déjà dit à plusieurs reprises, je suis incapable de m'occuper de l'aspect commercial de mon activité et j'y ai renoncé une fois pour toutes. Pour tout ce qui s'y rapporte je m'en remets entièrement à Monsieur Lindon.

Je lui ai parlé hier et il va se mettre en rapport avec vous.[2]

Je souhaite vivement que vous arriviez à un accord et que nos relations puissent reprendre dans la confiance et la cordialité.

Croyez, cher Monsieur, à mes sentiments les meilleurs.

Samuel Beckett

TLcc; 1 leaf, 1 side; *enclosure* with 7 January 1958 to Jérôme Lindon; IMEC-Fonds Samuel Beckett, Boîte 6, Editions de Minuit / The Olympia Press.

7 January 1958

6 Rue des Favorites
Paris 15me

Dear Monsieur Girodias

Thank you for your letter of 2nd January.

I deplore as much as you the state of our dealings. If I am the cause of any of that, it is wholly involuntarily, believe me.[1]

As I have said several times, I am not able to look after the commercial side of my activity, and I have abandoned that once and for all. In anything to do with it I rely entirely on Monsieur Lindon.

I spoke to him yesterday, and he will get in touch with you.[2]

It is my earnest wish that you will come to an agreement, and that our relations can be resumed, in trust and cordiality.

Yours sincerely

Samuel Beckett

1 Maurice Girodias (1919–1990; Profile, II), publisher of Olympia Press, wished to reconcile accounts and contracts for *Molloy* and *Watt*, which he published in English on behalf of Merlin Press for European distribution; the original publishing contracts were between SB and Alexander Trocchi (Merlin Press) for *Watt* and between Trocchi and Editions de Minuit for *Molloy*. Girodias wanted to annul contracts with Trocchi and establish a new contract for *Molloy* that would give Olympia Press exclusive sales in all countries except the United States and Canada, leaving SB free to establish a new contract for the French rights of *Watt* with Editions de Minuit. (IMEC-Fonds Samuel Beckett, Boîte 6, Editions de Minuit / The Olympia Press.)

2 Jérôme Lindon wrote to Girodias on 7 January to detail the steps that might be taken, including payments to Olympia Press, in view of the reassigned contracts (Girodias to SB, 2 January 1958; IMEC-Fonds Samuel Beckett, Boîte 6, Editions de Minuit / The Olympia Press).

BARNEY ROSSET
GROVE PRESS, NEW YORK

8.1.58

6 Rue des Favorites
Paris 15me

Dear Barney

Thanks for Endgame jacket. I like it very much.[1]

I am disturbed by the letter montage. You don't say what it's for, I suppose the programme. I dislike the ventilation of private documents. These throw no light on my work. At the same time I do not want to upset Alan if he is set on exhibiting them. In a word my embarrassment is extreme. I can't approve and I can't refuse. All I can say is this: if the publication of these extracts is of real importance to Alan (I can conceive it may be), go ahead with it; if not, let them remain private.[2]

The only thing I have or wish to offer to the public is my work. All the rest – photographs included – is none of its concern.

This in rueful haste because I must. Shall write soon again.

Ever

s/ Sam

TLS; 1 leaf, 1 side; Burns Library, Samuel Beckett Collection, SB-BR.

1 *Endgame* was published with only an acetate jacket; the cover was white, with a tan vertical band on which the title and the author's name were embossed (vertically). The Evergreen paperback used an image of Hamm with his "stancher."

2 *The New York Times* had requested an article on *Endgame* from Schneider, to be published on the Sunday before the play opened.

Copies of the letters to be included by Schneider had been sent by Rosset to SB.

ALAN SCHNEIDER
NEW YORK

9.1.58 Paris

Dear Alan

Your letter of Jan 5 today.[1] Shall answer it properly (?) tomorrow or this evening. This in haste to get something off my muckheap of a mind.

I received from Barney yesterday jacket of book and extracts from our letters, with no indication of what the latter was for. This disturbed me as I do not like publication of letters. I wrote to him at once saying I shd prefer the letters not to be used unless it was important for you that they should be. I see from your letter that it is and this is simply to say all right, go ahead. I may want to remove some phrases and shall indicate any corrections in my next letter. Thanks for the photos, they do me full justice.[2] Glad you are pleased with progress. Some of your questions look unanswerable. I have refused to allow the prayer passage to be touched in London and my feeling is it must not be. The bastard he does not exist is most important. More tomorrow and thanks for all your efforts. I like ashcan ad.[3]

Greetings to Jean and Vicky.

Ever

s/ Sam

TLS; 1 leaf, 1 side; Burns Library, Samuel Beckett Collection, SB-AS. Previous publication: "Beckett's Letters on 'Endgame'," *The Village Voice*: 15; Beckett and Schneider, "On Endgame," *Village Voice Reader*, 186; Beckett, *Disjecta*, 109; Beckett and Schneider, *No Author Better Served*, 28–29.

1 Schneider's letter to SB of 5 January: Beckett and Schneider, *No Author Better Served*, 25–28.

2 Schneider wrote to SB on 5 January: "I tried for weeks to write a conventional" essay. However, trying to please the paper, SB, Barney Rosset, the producer, and himself proved impossible. "Then I hit on the idea of showing the progression of

events leading up to the play (through our correspondence) and at the same time revealing things about the play and you indirectly and yet most truthful. This seemed to be an individual and important contribution." Schneider added, "if there is anything that bothers you, please let me know, and it can be eliminated" (Burns Library, Samuel Beckett Collection, AS-SB).

Photos had been taken by Schneider when he was in Paris with SB.

3 The advertisement for *Endgame* featured two cartoon figures in ash-cans.

ALAN SCHNEIDER
NEW YORK

10.1.58 Paris

Dear Alan

Here goes to elude your teasers:

1. Faces red and white probably like Werther's green coat, because the author saw them that way.[1] Don't seek deep motivation everywhere. If there is one here I'm unaware of it. Actually illogical that H and C, living in confinement, should have red faces. Scenically it serves to stress the couples and keep them apart.
2. Even if H uses rug throughout "give me a rug" is much better than "give me another rug". He is so cold he doesn't realize he has one already.[2]
3. I thought we had had this. Every man has his own light. Hamm, blind, is the the [sic] dark, his light has died. What he means is: "Think of me in my black world and don't come whining to me because yours is fading." I hope this accounts for importance of stressed "your".[3]
4. Yes, "that" is the shrinking of Clov.[4]
5. Typical illogism. Life is an asking for and a promising of what both asker and promiser know does not exist.
6. This is also related to 10. H does not know he is red. He thinks he is (bled) white (immediate cause of line being cold from open window if you like), as he thinks his eyes are white. That in reality his eyes are not white is unimportant. Blin also thought of

contact lenses. But this is the Antoine approach and wrong here. His preoccupation with white appears also in dog scene. The need of white and light of the blind.[5]

7. Perhaps "leching". Good strong old word and follows well on "lick your neighbour". I used "petting parties" for its sneer.[6]
8. To please Lord Scarborough I have consented to change "pee" to "relieve myself" and, when it occurs later as noun, to "relief", "arse" to "rump" and "balls (of the fly)" to "hames". But I have refused to touch the prayer passage the omission of which was demanded. It is indispensable this should be played as written. If you must change "pee" I prefer "leak" or "urinate" to "relief". "He doesn't exist" without "the bastard" is simply inacceptable to me.[7] Devine is coming over to see me. There are limits to the damage one can accept.
9. What H is doing here is putting off, with the help of such "business" as the gaff, toque, glasses, verse and story, the moment when he must whistle for Clov ("call") and call out to his father, I.e. [*for* i.e.] the moment of his definite dereliction. His whistling for Clov throughout play is with growing fear of its remaining unanswered (cf. notably at end of previous monologue beginning "you weep, and weep etc"). This time he feels certain that Clov will not "come-running" and that his father will not answer. But he cannot be <u>absolutely</u> certain until he has whistled and called in vain. (This also explains why Clov must enter throughout play immediately when whistled.)[8] It is this absolute and final certainty that H shrinks from with his "business". "Gags" is not good. In the English edition I changed it to "squirms", which is not good either but perhaps better expresses Hamm's situation. Perhaps "business" would be possible. "A little more business like that etc."[9]
10. Cf. 6.
11. Roger left for Vienna yesterday. Opening end of February.[10]
12. Thompson [*for* Thomson] quatrain: Line 1: read "us" instead of "me". Line 3: "Till youth and genial years are flown." Rest correct.

Bit late in the day to ask John for music now. Leave it to you. Or no song at all.[11]

13. Anemometer of course correct. My bad proof-correcting.[12]

With Blin gone to Vienna, probably with whistle, not much I can do about that. If I find another I'll send it on.[13]

Herewith letters with one or two cuts.[14]

Thanks for all you are doing and the great trouble you are taking. Greetings to the players.

All the best to Jean and Vicky.

Ever

s/ Sam

All I received from Barney was correspondence, not your connection stuff. In fact just 16 pages I am returning herewith.

TLS, with APS; 1 leaf, 2 sides; Burns Library, Samuel Beckett Collection, SB-AS. Previous publication: Beckett and Schneider, *No Author Better Served*, 29–31.

1 Werther's coat was blue (Johann Wolfgang von Goethe, *The Sorrows of Young Werther; Elective Affinities*; Novella, *Goethe's Collected Works*, XI, tr. Victor Lange and Judith Ryan, ed. David E. Wellbery [New York: Suhrkamp Publishers, 1988] 56).

2 *Endgame*, 67.

3 *Endgame*, 12.

4 *Endgame*, 28.

5 Schneider questions why Hamm asks: "Am I very white?" (*Endgame*, 64), and also whether SB and Blin had been concerned "with the problem of not seeing the irises" of Hamm's eyes (Beckett and Schneider, *No Author Better Served*, 27).

Hamm says of his eyes "It seems they've gone all white" (*Endgame*, 4). SB refers to Hamm's need for the dog to be white and for light ("Is Mother Pegg's light on?") (*Endgame*, 40, 41).

SB counsels against the kind of theatrical realism promoted by André Antoine (1858–1943), founder of the Théâtre Libre in 1887 and later Director of the Théâtre de l'Odéon (1906–1916).

6 *Endgame*, 69. Schneider suggested "orgies" as stronger than "petting parties" (Beckett and Schneider, *No Author Better Served*, 27).

7 While he thought he might be able to use "pee," Schneider believed that "The Bastard!" might need to be cut (Beckett and Schneider, *No Author Better Served*, 27; *Endgame*, 34, 55).

8 Schneider asked: "Why does he say ... 'and I'll call'" (Beckett and Schneider, *No Author Better Served*, 27). Hamm whistles for Clov repeatedly (*Endgame*, 3, 9, 23, 54, 70); he comes immediately, until the end (*Endgame*, 84). SB writes "throughout play" in the top margin with a line to its point of insertion.

Hamm calls his Father (*Endgame*, 66). "You weep, and weep" (*Endgame*, 68).

9 "Squirms" is eventually used (*Endgame*, 83).

10 Schneider had asked about *Endspiel* directed by Roger Blin at the Theater am Fleischmarkt in Vienna (Beckett and Schneider, *No Author Better Served*, 27).

11 Schneider was still considering use of the song, later cut (see 21 November 1957 to Schneider, n. 21).

12 Schneider noted that "anemometer" is misspelled as "anenometer" in the Grove edition (52).

13 Having looked for a whistle "that sounded as good as the one you had in Paris," Schneider asked if there was a possibility of getting another for the American production (Beckett and Schneider, *No Author Better Served*, 26).

14 SB's marked copy has not been found.

DONALD McWHINNIE
BBC, LONDON

13.1.58 Paris

Dear Donald

Thanks for your letter and cuttings. Also for the tapes which have arrived Av Hoche. I was speaking to Miss Reeves on the phone and hope to hear them next Thursday. Looking forward to this immensely.[1] Miss Colin gave me your message. If your doing Endgame depended on me alone I'd give you the green light straight away. But Devine's consent is necessary. I lunched with him yesterday. He was very understanding. A deadlock seems to have been reached with the prayer passage which I cannot alter and the Lord Chamberlain cannot pass. Devine said he may present the play at the Arts. I spoke to him of your suggestion. He seemed rather taken aback by the thought that you could do it without alteration and he not. He said he would get in touch with you on his return to London. He went back yesterday. I think it is quite possible he will assent to its transmission by the third.[2] He is very worked up about the LC's attitude and seems intent on making a shindy about it in London.[3] If he delays in contacting you don't hesitate to ring him, he is definitely anxious to see you about this. He said he had been very impressed by MacGowran and I think he will certainly offer him Clov. By Magee also, but rather disturbed by his "aloneness".

He suggested my writing a monologue for Magee to go with the play. I should like nothing better, but doubt if I can, my recent efforts having failed to produce anything worth having.[4] There is no need to commission me and I prefer not. What I have been trying to write is with thought of you and Magee and the Third.

I hope Barbara is quite well again. Affectionately to you both.

s/ Sam

TLS; 1 leaf, 1 side; *datestamped* 16 JAN 1958; BBCWAC, RCONT 1, Samuel Beckett, Scriptwriter I.

1 "John Beckett and Pat Magee did private recordings of the two readings" done for the BBC Third Programme, from *Molloy* and from "From an Abandoned Work" (SB to Barney Rosset, 20 January 1958, NSyU). Cecilia Reeves (later m. Gillie, 1907–1996) was on the staff of the BBC Paris Office. SB later wrote to McWhinnie: "I heard the tapes with the keenest enjoyment and appreciation. Magee's performance is unforgettable." (28 January 1958; OSU, Spec.rare.1924, McWhinnie.)

2 The Arts Theatre produced plays under club conditions and thereby evaded censorship (Raymond Mander and Joe Mitchenson, *The Theatres of London* [London: Rupert Hart-Davis, 1961] 259).

McWhinnie thought it might be possible that the BBC could broadcast *Endgame* and that broadcast might help "overcome certain obstacles which might arise in the theatre" (McWhinnie to SB, 31 December 1957; BBCWAC, RCONT 1, Samuel Beckett, Scriptwriter I).

3 Both Devine and the BBC saw the value in taking a public stand on censorship with productions of *Endgame*; censorship had not prevented production of the play in French at the Royal Court Theatre nor the broadcast in French on the BBC Third Programme in 1957. Devine had written to SB on 3 January: "We are all prepared to create a scandal if the play is finally stopped" (Internal memo from Richard D'Arcy Marriot, Assistant Director of Sound Broadcasting, to Lindsay Wellington, Director of Sound Broadcasting, 29 January 1958, BBCWAC, RCONT 1, Samuel Beckett, Scriptwriter I; TxU, English Stage Company, 1.2).

4 SB had written to Barney Rosset on 26 December 1957:

> Excited by Magee's readings I have been trying to write another radio script for the 3rd. It is not coming off. There is something in my English writing that infuriates me and I can't get rid of it. A kind of lack of brakes [. . .] I have laid it aside for the moment and am lashing and cursing about again in the Inno bracken. (NSyU.)

A note in French in a manuscript of *The Unnamable* indicates that SB resumed the translation after the failure of his radio play: "Reprise 21.1.58 après échec de Henry et Ada." (Restart 21.1.58 after failure of *Henry and Ada.*) (TxU, Beckett Collection / Works 5.9, The Unnamable, verso [21]; this note and the continuation of the translation are in red ink: "But let us go back as planned, afterwards we'll fall forward as projected" [22].)

BRENDAN SMITH
DUBLIN

January 20th 1958 | 6 Rue des Favorites
Paris 15me

Dear Mr Smith

I have been told that the Ulysses adaptation and the new O'Casey play will not be performed at your coming Festival, because of opposition from the Roman Catholic Archbishop of Dublin.[1]

I should be obliged if you would let me know if this is the case.

If it is I am afraid I shall have to withdraw my participation.

Yours sincerely
Samuel Beckett

TLcc; 1 leaf, 1 side; GEU, MS 1221.

1 Brendan Smith (1917–1989) was the Founder-Director of the Dublin Theatre Festival (An Tóstal) which planned to include a dramatization of James Joyce's *Ulysses* and a play by Sean O'Casey, *The Drums of Father Ned*. When Archbishop John McQuaid (1895–1973) refused to offer the votive mass to mark the public opening of the Festival, the Festival Council reconsidered its program ("Church Objection to Two Plays," *The Times* 8 January 1958: 4). Two days later, the Council decided that the plays would remain on the program ("Dublin Decision on Festival Plays: Production in Spite of Disapproval," *The Times* 10 January 1958: 5). One month later, the Tourist Board asked An Tóstal Council to withdraw Allan McClelland's *Bloomsday* ("Dublin Festival Plays Dropped; Effects of 'Public Controversy'," *The Times* 15 February 1958: 3).

ROGER BLIN
VIENNA

26.1.58 | Ussy

Cher Roger

Merci de ta lettre. J'espère que Hamm a pu se dégager et qu'il fait l'affaire, même sans favoris.[1] Je suis très heureux que tu sois là-bas, à condition que toi aussi tu le sois un peu, et d'avoir la certitude qu'il y aura eu en langue allemande au moins une mise en scène intelligente et intelligible. Ça ajoute encore à ce que je te dois et dont j'espère un jour pouvoir m'acquitter, avec une vraie pièce enfin.

Pour l'heure je me dépêche de finir la traduction de l'Innommable et ce n'est pas marrant je t'assure. Mais impossible de rien entreprendre vraiment avant de m'en être débarrassé.

Je suis peu à Paris. Suzanne a vu Nicole plusieurs fois et Marc est passé la voir hier. Quand elle pourra se mettre au traitement Clarac je suis sûr qu'elle ira vite mieux.[2]

La première à New York dans quelques jours. Je n'ai pas beaucoup de nouvelles. Paraît qu'ils ont un excellent Hamm, un Clov adéquat (le Lucky de Miami!) et deux "touchants" poubellicoles. Je m'attends au pire.[3]

Un grand article sur mézigue, de J.-J. Mayoux, dans les Etudes Anglaises. Bien, dans le style sorbonnagre, avec des rapprochements à faire bander un mort.[4]

Je ne te promets pas d'aller à Vienne. Je me sens bien moche. Mais tu auras de la visite. Dès que tu sauras la date fais-moi signe.

Salutations à Wochinz – et au plateau.[5]

Bien affectueusement à toi

Sam

ALS; 1 leaf, 1 side; *env* to Herrn Roger Blin, WIEN I, Theater am Fleischmarkt, Autriche; *verso*: Ex. BECKETT, 6 Rue des Favorites, Paris 15e; *pm* [torn out]; IMEC-Fonds Roger Blin.

26.1.58 Ussy

Dear Roger

Thank you for your letter. I hope that Hamm was able to make himself available, and that he does the trick even without sideburns.[1] I am very happy that you are there, provided you are too a little, and at having the certainty that there will have been at least one intelligent and intelligible production in German. It adds still more to my debt to you, which I hope one day to settle, with a real play at last.

For the moment I am hurrying to finish the translation of *L'Innommable*, and it is no joke, I can tell you. But impossible to take on anything until I have got rid of it.

I am seldom in Paris. Suzanne has seen Nicole several times, and Marc came round to see her yesterday. When she is able to get on to the Clarac treatment I am sure that she will improve rapidly.[2]

New York première in a few days' time. I have little in the way of news. Seems they have an excellent Hamm, an adequate Clov (the Lucky from Miami!) and two "touching" bin-minders. I expect the worst.[3]

Big article on My Nibs, by J.-J. Mayoux, in *Etudes Anglaises*. Fine, in the schullarly style, with links and parallels that would give a dead man a wet dream.[4]

I can't promise you to go to Vienna. I feel pretty awful. But you will have visitors. As soon as you know the date, let me know.

Greetings to Wochinz – and to the stage crew.[5]

Love

Sam

1 Georg Bucher (1905–1972) played Hamm in the production of *Endspiel* at the Theater am Fleischmarkt.

2 The actress Nicole Kessel (d. 2010) was Blin's partner. Marc Barbezat (1913–1999), founder of the review *L'Arbalète*, published from 1940 to 1948, and of Editions Arbalète, was the first editor of Jean Genet (Lynda Bellity Peskine to the editors, 16 November 2012). Suzanne Deschevaux-Dumesnil may have recommended treatment by her homeopathic doctor, Roger Clarac.

3 The cast of the Cherry Lane premiere of *Endgame*: 29 December 1957, n. 2. Alvin Epstein who played Clov had performed the role of Lucky in the Miami *Waiting for Godot*.

4 Jean-Jacques Mayoux, "Le Théâtre de Samuel Beckett," *Etudes Anglaises* 10.4 (October–November 1957) 350–366. Mayoux's high estimation of Beckett's work offers a huge range of alleged parallels (the "rapprochements"): from Epictetus to *Everyman* to Strindberg and Joyce, from Symbolism to the Absurd, from Mack Sennett to God and St. Veronica, and the suggestion that Pozzo is the symbol of capitalism.

5 Producer Wochinz: 21 November 1957 to Schneider, n. 4. Wander Bertoni (b. 1925) designed the set and costumes for the Vienna production of *Endspiel*.

ALAN SIMPSON
PIKE THEATRE, DUBLIN

January 28th 1958

6 Rue des Favorites
Paris 15me

Dear Alan

Thanks for your letter of January 21st.

By a straight reading I mean no props or make up or action of any kind, simply the players standing reading the text. The ideal for me would be a stage in darkness with a spot picking out the faces as required. It is a text written to come out of the dark and I suppose that is the nearest one could get to that with a stage reading. There could be a preliminary presentation of the characters, with lights on, by a speaker, who should also read the indications given in the text with regard to sounds, movements, etc., many of which I think could be omitted. No sound effects. In New York I am told they used a lectern from which the actors read as their turns came. I don't think this is a good idea. Don't think I'm imposing this form of presentation. Do it your own way. All I want you to observe is the strict limits of a reading. Within them you are free to use any method you like.[1]

I have heard from Kitty Black and am writing to her today to go ahead. The conditions she suggests are all right with me. If you find them too onerous I'll accept less.[2]

With regard to Endgame I'm afraid you'll have to wait till after the Royal Court production, unless of course in view of the deadlock with the LC George Devine abandons his rights, which is most unlikely. He told me he might do it at the Arts. I have not heard from him since I saw him in Paris a fortnight ago and confirmed to him that the incriminated passage would have to stand as written. The BBC is in touch with him about the possibility of their doing it on the 3rd without cuts. I shall let you know when I hear more.[3]

I heard a rumour that the Ulysses adaptation and O'Casey's new play had been withdrawn from the Festival programme because of opposition from McQuaid. If this is confirmed I won't have anything to do with it. I have written to Brendan Smith and hope to hear from him that there is nothing in it.

I know nothing about Pantagleize.[4]

Yours ever

s/ Sam

TLS; 1 leaf, 1 side; TCD, MS 10731/59.

1 SB had authorized the Pike Theatre to do a reading of *All That Fall* in his letter of 15 January to Simpson (TCD, MS 10731/56). When he wrote to SB on 21 January, Simpson proposed to present it "with little more than [. . .] a 'few props'" (TCD, MS 10731/58).

The New York reading of *All That Fall*: 27 August 1957.

2 Kitty Black would write to Simpson on 4 February to confirm arrangements for a "straight reading" of *All That Fall*, "avoiding all such elements as set, props, make-up, mime, etc." (Curtis Brown Collection).

3 Simpson had asked for a script of *Endgame*, saying "if George Devine can only do it in the Arts he might not mind if we did it for the Festival" (21 January 1958; TCD, MS 10731/58).

4 The Pike Theatre planned to produce *Pantagleize* by Michel de Ghelderode (1898–1962).

ALAN SCHNEIDER
NEW YORK

6.2.58

6 Rue des Favorites,
Paris 15me

Dear Alan This in haste to thank you for your letter with programme and the reviews which I here do solemnly declare well up to standard. I do hope they will not have too averse an effect on the booking and that you and your actors – to whom my warm greetings – will be repaid for all your work and enthusiasm by a reasonable canter.[1]

By all means "dustman". I am so glad you have been able to preserve the text in all its impurity.[2]

I can't write to commission and I declined to be commissioned by the BBC in the ordinary sense. I just promised I'd do my best and that's what I promise to you and Barney as soon as I get the Innommable finished. I must confess I feel the old tug to write in French again, where control is easier for me, and probably excessive. If my present presentiments are worth anything I probably won't succeed in writing in either. But I'll do my best.[3]

I liked the photo of Hamm and Clov and they sound fine.[4] Thank you again, dear Alan, for all you have done and are doing and will do.

Salutations to Jean and Vicky. Ever s/ Sam

TLS; 1 leaf, 1 side; Burns Library, Samuel Beckett Collection, SB-AS. Previous publication: "Beckett's Letters on 'Endgame'," *Village Voice*, 15; Beckett and Schneider, "On Endgame," *Village Voice Reader*, 186; Beckett, *Disjecta*, 109; Beckett and Schneider, *No Author Better Served*, 37.

1 Schneider describes the opening night of *Endgame* as well as the press following it in *Entrances* (256–258), as well as in his letter to SB of 30 January (Beckett and Schneider, *No Author Better Served*, 34–36). Brooks Atkinson's comment was positive: "Thanks largely to the bitterness of the direction and the acting, Samuel Beckett's second play turns out to be quite impressive" ("The Theatre: Beckett's 'Endgame'," *New York Times* 29 January 1958: 32). Other first-night reviews emphasized the play's bleakness: Walter Kerr, "Beckett's 'Endgame' Opens at Cherry Lane Theater," *New York Herald Tribune* 29 January 1958: 14; John Chapman, "Beckett's 'Endgame' is Off B'way and Out of One Reviewer's Mind," *Daily News* 29 January 1958: 50; Richard Watts Jr., "The Dark World of Samuel Beckett," *New York Post* 29 January 1958: 60.

2 Although he had resisted changing SB's text, Schneider said that right before the opening they "changed one word: NIGHTMAN (which no one understood) to DUSTMAN, which was clearer and had a similar beat … The rest remains as you wrote it." (30 January 1958; Burns Library, Samuel Beckett Collection, SB-AS; Beckett and Schneider, *No Author Better Served*, 36.)

3 Schneider had written: "Barney and I are already talking about getting you to write the next one in English. After all, if the BBC can commission you, so can we." (30 January 1958; Burns Library, Samuel Beckett Collection, AS-SB; Beckett and Schneider, *No Author Better Served*, 36.)

4 The photo sent to SB has not been identified.

DONALD McWHINNIE
LONDON

15.2.58 Paris

Dear Donald

Thanks for your letter. I have heard nothing from John Morris and hope he will let me know date of his arrival a little in advance, as

I plan to return to the country next week. If he asks for a cut which I have already accepted from the LC (I think I consented to change three words), there is of course no difficulty. But I obviously cannot move from my position with regard to the prayer passage.[1]

It is hard to find a passage in Malone, it is so broken. I suggest the following sequence, with perhaps a few staves from John between the sections:

Beginning	Ending
P.1: "I shall soon. ."	P.2: "Enough for this evening."
P.22: "My body does not. ."	P.23: "No, I want nothing."
P.30: "When I stop. . "	P.33: "colour to this view."
P.43 "Mortal tedium."	P.52: "nor to whom."

If this is too long it can be shortened. If there is any other passage, or combination of passages, you prefer, do not hesitate to let me know. You will require the authorisation of John Calder. I am seeing him tomorrow and shall mention it to him. I have just received an advance copy of his edition. If you decide to do this reading I should like to revise the text beforehand.[2] Some of it looks very clumsy to me now.

I rang up the Reeves again about the possibility of my acquiring for my personal delectation the Magee tapes. She said she had not yet had a decision from London. I feel I may have made an embarrassing request. If it's agin your regulations forget all about it.[3]

I have been working hard on L'Innommable and almost finished first draft. When I have I'll return to the radio text and see if there is anything to be saved from that wreck.[4] I look forward to seeing John G. Ask him to signal himself a little in advance. I hope Barbara is quite well again and that you'll both be over here soon again.

Affectionately to you both.

s/ Sam

So glad to see of the
Duras broadcast this
evening. Unfortunately shall
not hear it. She has a new

book just out with the Editions de Minuit. John has just rung up, we lunch together Monday.[5]

TLS; 1 leaf, 1 side; OSU, Spec.rare.124, McWhinnie.

1 John Morris's trip to Paris was anticipated in an inter-office memo of 12 February from L. Wellington to John Morris, the Controller of the Third Programme: "Will you ask Beckett, when you see him in Paris, whether he would agree to change or omit the word [bastard] for the purpose of broadcasting" (BBCWAC, RCONT 1, Samuel Beckett, Scriptwriter I).

2 SB's suggestions are passages from *Malone Dies* (London: John Calder, 1958).

3 Cecilia Reeves made the case for letting SB have copies of the tapes of *Molloy* and "From an Abandoned Work" read by Magee: "I think we can be absolutely sure that he would use them exclusively for his own private listening and I pass on the request because it is a service which would be of great value for him in future writing for radio" (Reeves to Donald McWhinnie, 4 February 1958; BBCWAC, RCONT 1, Samuel Beckett, Scriptwriter I).

4 SB would complete his first draft of *The Unnamable* on 23 February (Lake, *No Symbols Where None Intended*, 62). The radio play: 13 January 1958, n. 4.

5 John G. is John Gibson. The BBC Third Programme broadcast *The Square* on 15 February in Barbara Bray's adaptation and translation; Editions de Minuit had just published Marguerite Duras's *Moderato cantabile*.

The sentences following SB's signature are handwritten.

ALAN SIMPSON
PIKE THEATRE, DUBLIN

February 17th 1958

6 Rue des Favorites
Paris 15me

Dear Alan

After the revolting boycott of Joyce and O'Casey I don't want to have anything to do with the Dublin Theatre "Festival" and am withdrawing both mimes and All That Fall.[1] I have written to Brendan Smith to this effect. I am extremely sorry for any difficulties this may create for you. I know you will understand that it is quite impossible for me to do otherwise.[2]

Yours ever
s/ Sam

TLS; 1 leaf, 1 side; TCD, MS 10731/61.

1 On 12 February, it was reported that Sean O'Casey had withdrawn *The Drums of Father Ned* from the Dublin Festival after having been repeatedly asked to alter his play ("Play Withdrawn by Mr. Sean O'Casey," *The Times*: 3). On 15 February, it was reported that *Bloomsday*, the adaptation of *Ulysses* by Allan McClelland, had been withdrawn from the Dublin Festival at the request of the Tourist Board, sponsor of An Tóstal ("Dublin Festival Plays Dropped: Effects of 'Public Controversy'," *The Times*: 3). The Pike Theatre's reading of *All That Fall* was to have been a part of the Dublin Festival.

2 SB wrote to Barney Rosset: "The Roman Catholic bastards in Ireland yelped Joyce and O'Casey out of their 'Festival', so I withdrew my mimes and the reading of All That Fall to be given at the Pike. Now the whole thing seems to be off!" (20 February 1958, NSyU.)

THOMAS MACGREEVY
DUBLIN

February 18th 1958

6 Rue des Favorites
Paris 15me

Dear Tom

Thanks for your letters. Herewith copy of the list I have sent to Waddington. I suppose Jack Yeats will have his little purgatory on earth now for five or ten years. Waddington was over and I am glad to say bought about Fr 300.000 worth of pictures from Henri Hayden whom he intends soon to exhibit in London, either group or one-man. Hayden has been doing magnificent work and is getting some appreciation – at age of 73 or 74, though of course the work of his Cubist period still fetches high prices. Rouault's funeral was last Saturday, semi-national, and the traffic at St-Germain des Près [sic] was held up for hours. Billières made a pompous speech comparing him to Vigny's Moïse![1] It is good news that you may be in Paris in April. I shall certainly be here, or more likely at Ussy, so try and let me know a few days ahead to give the letter time to reach me and me to get in. By the way, in case you have not my phone numbers, they are Blomet 09.11 and Ussy-sur-Marne 18. I wish I were at the latter place at the moment, but it has been impossible to get away from Paris for the past fortnight and more. Suzanne was there alone for a few days and announced the first yellow crocus. I have been working hard on my translation of L'Innommable and a week in the country would see the first draft finished. I am sorry to feel the lonely evenings are getting you depressed, I know how hard they are to endure at times, but in the long run it's about the best we can do. I used to murder the Beethoven Violin Sonatas with Sonny Sinclair, so they are familiar. I always felt he treated the violin as a very poor relation and that this was very noticeable in the Kreutzer. The last performance of it I heard was by Heifetz and an indifferent pianist who drowned everything.[2] Suzanne is going to hear Schwarzkopf this evening at the Champs-Elysées. We went together last Monday to hear Marya Freund (aet. 82) give her cours d'interprétation at the Salle Debussy to a mere handful of girl students. They were doing Brahms. She sang very touchingly herself at the end Rain Lieder I hardly knew. I had not the cheek to pipe up and ask for Waldeinsamkeit or the Sapphische Ode. An American girl sang the Sally Gardens! Thinly, but Marya Freund was very pleased with it. She is an extraordinary old lady, told about the time she heard Brahms playing the piano at her parents' house in Poland. You may have heard her in Pierrot Lunaire.[3] We had a spell of wonderful summery days, now it is better [*for* bitter] cold again. 80% of the population have flu. Remember me very kindly to your sister and nieces.[4] Write again soon.

Much love from us both. Ever s/ Sam

Miss Rosica Colin, 45 Baron's Keep, London W.11

Charles Monteith, c/o Faber & Faber, 24 Russell Square, London W.C.1

George Devine, Royal Court Theatre, Sloane Square, London S.W.3

John Gibson, BBC (Drama Department), Broadcasting House, London W.1

Donald McWhinnie, BBC (Drama Department).

Mrs Hutchinson, 21 Hyde Park Square, London W.2

Harold Hobson, c/o Sunday Times

Mrs Jacobs, 30 Meadway, London N.W.11

Jack Lambert, c/o Sunday Times

Christopher Logue, 18 Denbigh Close, London W.11
Professor Stuart Maguinness, King's College, University of London, Strand, London W.C.2
Richard Roud, 13 Oakley Street, London, S.W.3
Ronald Searle, 22 Newton Road, London W.2
Jake Schwartz, 14 Chichester Terrace, Brighton, Sussex
Dr. A. G. Thompson, South Lodge, Squire's Mount, London N.W.3
Roy Walker, 111 Dartmouth Road, London N.W.2
Laz Aaronson, 26 Westbourne Terrace Road, London W.2
Mirion [*for* Miron] Grindea, Editor "Adam", 28 Emperor's Gate, London S.W.7
John Beckett, 18A Belsize Lane, London N.W.3
Leslie Daiken, 80 Regents Park Road, London N.W.1
Miss Kitty Black, c/o Curtis Brown Ltd, 13 King Street, London W.C.2

TLS; 1 leaf, 1 side; *enclosure*: list of names and addresses; TCD, MS 10402/210.

1 SB's list of invitees, as sent to Victor Waddington (1907–1981) for the exhibition of Later Works by Jack B. Yeats which would run from 6 March to 3 April, marked the move of the Waddington Galleries from Dublin to 2 Cork Street, London, W1.

Henri Hayden's next exhibition, at the Waddington Galleries in London, would take place from 12 February to 7 March 1959. Hayden's Cubist period: c. 1917–1922 (Henri Hayden, *Henri Hayden, His Cézannesque and Cubist Period* [London: Roland, Browse and Delbanco, 1966] [1–2]).

Georges Rouault died on 13 February. René Billières, Ministre de l'Education Nationale, had spoken at his funeral, and had compared the artist to *Moïse* (*Moses*) by Alfred de Vigny: "Le génie de Rouault se mesure à sa solitude, à cette gloire difficile et si rarement atteinte qui nimbera désormais son œuvre, sa vie, son nom . . . Puissant et solitaire tel le Moïse de Vigny." ("Les obsèques de Georges Rouault," *Combat*, 18 February 1958: 10.) (Rouault's genius is intimately related to his solitariness, and to this recondite glory, so rarely achieved, that will forever stand round his work, his life, his name . . . Powerful and solitary like Vigny's Moïse.) The state funeral took place at the Eglise Saint-Germain-des-Prés on Monday, 17 February (not on Saturday as indicated by SB).

2 SB's cousin, Morris Sinclair (known as Sunny or Sonny, 1918–2007; Profile, I) was an accomplished violinist.

Beethoven's Sonata for violin, no. 9, op. 47 (*The Kreutzer*). Jascha Heifetz played the piece with pianist Benno Moiseiwitsch; it was recorded in May 1951 (RCA Victor LM-1193; reissued as *Beethoven, Brahms, Franck*, Naxos Historical 8.110990).

3 Elisabeth Schwarzkopf's recital, with pianist Jacqueline Bonneau (1917–2007), was held at the Théâtre des Champs-Elysées on 18 February (*Officiel des Spectacles*, 587 [12–18 February 1958] 51).

The French soprano Marya Freund (1876–1966), who was born in Poland, was known for her performances of German Lieder and twentieth-century music; she sang in the French premiere of Arnold Schoenberg's *Pierrot lunaire* and collaborated with many contemporary composers. Johannes Brahms, Regenlieder (Rain Songs), Op. 59. *In Waldeinsamkeit*, op. 85, no. 6, and the *Sapphische Ode*, op. 94, were among SB's favorite Lieder by Brahms. "Down by the Salley Gardens," with words by W. B. Yeats, was set to music derived from an Irish traditional song, arranged by Herbert Hughes (1882–1937). SB writes "Sally" for "Salley."

4 MacGreevy lived with his widowed sister, Honora Phelan (known as Nora, 1891–1974); for a time, her daughters Elizabeth (1929–2003), Margaret (b. 1926), and Patricia (1925–2001) were part of the household.

DONALD McWHINNIE
BBC, LONDON

26.2.58 [*for* 25 February 1958]

6 Rue des Favorites
Paris 15me

Dear Donald

Thanks for your letter. I had two reasons for excluding the Sapo passages from my sequence, one, I don't like them, two, I think they are less suited to Magee than Malone's monologue proper.[1] The objection to omitting them is of course that you don't get the set-up of the work and that here and there an allusion by Malone to the story he is trying to tell will lose point. This could be overcome by a few lines of introduction which I could write for you. I propose therefore the following revised sequence, longer than the one I sent you and shorter than yours by five or six pages. Frankly I think 75 minutes is a bit on the long side.

Beginning	Ending
P. 1 "I shall soon"	P. 2 "this evening"
P. 5 "Present state"	P. 9 "present state"
P.18 "Live and invent"	P.19 "What an end"
P.20 "I have rummaged"	P.23 "want nothing"
P.30 "When I stop"	P.33 "to this view"
P.43 "Mortal tedium"	P.52 "nor to whom"

Perhaps it would be a good idea to get the reactions of Pat Magee and John Beckett to this choice of passages and to the excluding of

Sapo. If they agree with you that he should be included I'll propose another sequence including him.

Whatever sequence we finally choose, I should like to revise it before you start rehearsing with Magee.[2]

I am delighted at the thought of your coming over soon. I am just back from Ussy after a heavy bout of translating which has brought me to the end of L'Innommable, first draft. I have an exciting idea for a short stage monologue for Magee. But I know my exciting ideas and how depressing they can become.[3]

I am having lunch with John Morris tomorrow and shall add a scribble to this to tell you how it went.

Affectionately

s/ Sam

27.2.58 [*for* 26 February 1958] Just had lunch with JM. I confirmed to him that I couldn't touch the prayer passage nor suppress the two words that stand in the way of its being done on the 3rd. He was very nice about it and seemed to think there remains a possibility of your doing it as it stands.[4]

TLS, with APS; 1 leaf, 1 side; *datestamped* 27 FEB 1958; BBCWAC, RCONT I, Samuel Beckett, Scriptwriter I. *Dating*: This letter could not have been both written and received on 27 February; an inter-office memo from Leslie Stokes to the Assistant to Controller of the Third Programme dated 26 February indicates that John Morris had just rung up, following lunch with SB. Also following the meeting, SB reports to Rosica Colin on the same day that "the BBC cannot do the play as it stands either" (Rosica Colin Collection).

1 The Sapo passages: *Malone Dies*, 9–18.

2 The page numbers refer to the first English edition, published by John Calder (1958), of *Malone Dies*.

In his proposal to SB of 20 February, McWhinnie had suggested using pages 1–2, 5–16, 17–23, 43–52, or beginning with pages 1–23 and then going on with a later passage (BBCWAC, RCONT 1, Samuel Beckett, Scriptwriter I).

SB handwrites "Whatever . . . with Magee" in the left margin.

3 SB had written to Barney Rosset on 23 February: "I finished first draft of L'Inno this evening. A month to forget it, a fortnight to revise it, three weeks to retype it, you should have it sometime in the merry month." (NSyU.)

The Magee "stage monologue" was written at Devine's request "to go with Endgame in place of the mime" – "but ideas are easy and the writing of it will probably be too much for me" (SB to Barney Rosset, 20 February 1958, NSyU).

4 SB lunched with John Morris on 26 February (see dating note above).

The Lord Chamberlain's Office blocked performance of *Endgame*: "The principal objection by the censor is to a scene of about 30 lines in which three of the characters are seen in prayer. The official view is that this scene is blasphemous." ("Samuel

Beckett Play Refused Licence," *The Times* 10 February 1958: 3b.) SB reported to Rosset: "The Lord Chamberlain's ban on Endgame is now definite in London. This has caused a lot of outcry in the London papers. Devine writes he is trying to organize club conditions at the Royal Court." (20 February 1958, NSyU.) The outcry, stimulated by Devine's press release, pointed to the discrepancy between the Lord Chamberlain's Office's response to the French production in 1957 and the proposed English production:

> In its French version the play was passed by the Lord Chamberlain's office ... Does this mean that the LC considers all people who understand French beyond hope – unredeemable atheists or agnostics who need not be protected from blasphemy? Or does he believe that knowledge of the French language bestows immunity from corruption? ("Censor's Whim," *Evening Standard* 11 February 1958: 4.)

CAROLYN SWIFT
PIKE THEATRE, DUBLIN

February 27th 1958

6 Rue des Favorites
Paris 15me

Dear Carol

Thanks for your letter. I am very sorry to hear of Alan's great trouble. Please express to him my sincere sympathy.[1]

I am withdrawing altogether. As long as such conditions prevail in Ireland I do not wish my work to be performed there, either in festivals or outside them.

If no protest is heard they will prevail for ever. This is the strongest I can make.

I have therefore to cancel the permission I gave you to present All That Fall and Endgame.[2]

I hope you will forgive me.

My best wishes to you both and long flame to the Pike in that hideous gale.[3]

Yours ever
s/ Sam
Samuel Beckett

TLS; 1 leaf, 1 side; TCD, MS 10731/63.

1 Carolyn Swift's letter to SB of 22 February had mentioned the recent death of Alan Simpson's father (TCD, MS 10731/62).

2 Swift had written that she and Alan Simpson understood SB's withdrawal from the Dublin Theatre Festival, but she requested permission for the Pike Theatre to produce *All That Fall* during its autumn season. In his letter of 25 January 1957, SB had granted the Irish rights of *Endgame* to the Pike Theatre (TCD, MS 10731/49).

3 Alan Simpson was preparing an appeal against his prosecution for indecency over the Pike Theatre's production of Tennessee Williams's play *The Rose Tattoo* (Swift, *Stage by Stage*, 294–298).

RICHARD SEAVER
NEW YORK

March 5th 1958

6 Rue des Favorites
Paris 15me

Dear Seaver

Many thanks for your letter. If you have not succeeded in getting hold of a copy of Nouvelles et Textes pour Rien let me know and I'll send you one. The first edition is out of print and the second due now any day, with drawings by Avigdor Arikha.[1] There are only three stories - those you mention. A fourth, Premier Amour, written at the same time, never appeared anywhere, and I have scrapped it. I thought we had gone through pretty carefully together your translations of all three, but you must be right and it was only The End. I am in the country at the moment, so cannot tell you if I have Merlin 3.[2] If I find I haven't I'll ask you to send me a copy of your translation, with the other two. I think I shall try and translate the Textes pour Rien myself, they being in the idiom more or less of L'Innommable which I have just finished translating. My idea was for the book to appear with you figuring as translator of the stories and me as translator of the Textes. I should be very pleased if you would agree to this arrangement. If you do - and do not object to my fiddling about with your translations - I should of course insist on your receiving your share of translators' royalties (with Rosset a lump sum plus percentage on sales). There is not the least hurry, as I shall not be able to get working on the Textes before late autumn at the earliest. I do not remember if there are many changes as between the texts you worked with and those of the book. I should think not. Perhaps you might check up on this to begin with.[3]

Christopher was over not so long ago, in good form and talking much about getting married, which however he does not seem to have done. I had lunch with Pat, on a visit from Berlin, about a fortnight ago. He showed me his recent poems which I liked very much. I think he said you had read them.[4] Remember me to Trocchi if you write to him. Rosset was impressed by a story of his which I think is to appear in the next Evergreen.[5]

Yours ever
s/ Sam Beckett

TLS; 1 leaf, 1 side; TxU, Seaver, R 16501.

1 Richard Seaver (1916–2009; Profile, II). *Nouvelles et Textes pour rien* (Paris: Editions de Minuit, 1955) appeared in a second edition of 2,110 copies, with six 1957 pen-and-ink drawings by Arikha (printed, 20 June 1958).

2 "The End," tr. Richard Seaver with the author, appeared in *Merlin* 2.3 (Summer–Autumn 1954) 144–159. SB had asked Seaver to go on with the translation of "L'Expulsé" (see 12 November 1953, n. 2).

3 Prior to publication in *Nouvelles et Textes pour rien*, "L'Expulsé" was published in *Fontaine* (8.57 [December 1946 – January 1947] 685–708). SB's concern was that the French version of "La Fin" from which Seaver had worked might also have changed between the time he first worked on the translation in 1954 and its publication in book form in 1955.

4 Christopher Logue (1926–2011), one of the original Merlin group, had fallen in love with the writer Nell Dunn (b. 1936), but "his affection was not reciprocated" (Christopher Logue, *Prince Charming: A Memoir* [London: Faber and Faber, 1999] 227–228, 231, 244; "Christopher Logue," *The Daily Telegraph*, 6 December 2011: 37).

Patrick Bowles (1927–1995; Profile, II), translator with Beckett of *Molloy* into English, had published his translations of poems by Pablo Neruda: Pablo Neruda, Patrick Bowles, and Christopher Logue, *The Man Who Told His Love: 20 Poems Based on Pablo Neruda's Los Cantos d'amores*, an adaptation by Christopher Logue of an English translation by Patrick Bowles (Northwood: Scorpion Press, 1958). Bowles may have shown SB other poems as well.

5 Alexander Trocchi (1925–1984; Profile, II), former Editor of Merlin; *Evergreen Review* published an excerpt from his novel, *Cain's Book* (2.8 [Spring 1959] 109–118).

DONALD McWHINNIE
BBC, LONDON

March 7th 1958 | 6 Rue des Favorites
Paris 15me

Dear Donald

Your letter this morning. So be it. Straight through then, from the beginning to page 23 "No, I want nothing." If we definitely decide on this extract I shall want to revise it.[1]

I have written a short stage monologue for Magee (definitely non-radio). It involves a tape-recorder with the mechanics of which I am unfamiliar. I can't release it until I check up on some points. I have asked John B. to send me a book of the words (instructions for use). If he delays in doing so I may have to ask you to help me. Indeed if you happen to have such a thing handy you might send it along straight away. The monologue is rather a s[e]ntimental affair in my best original English manner. Begin to understand why I write in French.[2]

Photos of Magee from John G this morning.[3] Please thank them both. He's very like van Gogh with the beard. In the monologue he's 70.

In the States they call Endgame "The Dustman Cometh". Witty nation.[4]

Affectionately
s/ Sam

TLS; 1 leaf, 1 side; *datestamped* 11 MAR 1958; BBCWAC, RCONT 1, Samuel Beckett, Scriptwriter I.

1 Passages from *Malone Dies* for Patrick Magee's reading on the BBC: SB to Donald McWhinnie, 25 February 1958.

McWhinnie's letter to SB of 4 March had indicated that both he and John Beckett, who was composing music for the program, regretted the loss of the Sapo passages; McWhinnie also said he was "completely confident" that Magee could give "a highly effective interpretation" of them (Beckett, *Malone Dies*, 9–18; BBCWAC, RCONT 1, Samuel Beckett, Scriptwriter I).

2 The "Magee monologue" to which SB refers comes later to be entitled *Krapp's Last Tape*.

3 The photos of Patrick Magee sent by John Gibson have not been identified.

4 An article in the *Jacksonville Courier* (Illinois) reported that *Endgame* "is known familiarly as 'The Dustman Cometh' because two characters spend the whole

play sitting in a dust bin, which is English for garbage can" ("Bans [*for* Banned] English Version of Play Okayed in French," 10 February 1958: 7). The article is one of many that appeared in newspapers in the United Kingdom and the United States, all stimulated by George Devine's press release to the Associated Press, a part of a publicity "shindy" to protest against censorship of *Endgame* (see 13 January 1958, n. 3).

BARNEY ROSSET
GROVE PRESS, NEW YORK

March 10th 1958 Ussy

Dear Barney

Your letter and Judith Schmidt's this morning. Afraid I have nothing to say on the subject of the Artaud book. I'm sorry to be so eternally unsatisfactory.[1]

Glad you like the tapes.[2] I have finished the Magee monologue and sit looking at it with a fishy eye. In English I hate my guts and in French nothing more is possible. However I think I'll let it forth, in about a fortnight probably.

Sorry Endgame is limping so badly. Thanks for your efforts to keep it moving. Whatever you decide is right with me.[3]

I cannot have made myself clear on the subject of Seaver (to whom my warm greetings). I do not want him to do any more translating from me, but simply to produce the translations of the three Nouvelles he did with me in Paris years ago. If he has lost them, then no more about it. If he has them they would only need a last revision to be acceptable. The Textes I'll do myself - some day. If he has lost the translations of the Nouvelles I'll do them again myself - some day.

Back to Paris tomorrow, reluctantly. Bright sun, deep snow here.

I wanted to keep Sapo out of the Malone reading. But McWhinnie, John and Magee all want him in. So I let him in. And the extract will probably be the first 23 pages, ending "No, I want nothing".

Ever

s/ Sam

TLS; 1 leaf, 1 side; NSyU.

1 SB had received a copy of Antonin Artaud's *The Theatre and its Double*, translated by Mary Caroline Richards, which Grove Press would publish in August 1958.

2 Tapes of Patrick Magee reading from *Molloy* and "From an Abandoned Work": 15 February 1958 and n. 3.

3 Although Brooks Atkinson's positive second review appeared in the *New York Times* on 16 February, a major blizzard in New York limited its publicity value ("'Abstract Drama' Samuel Beckett's 'Endgame' is Staged with Ingenuity at the Cherry Lane," II, 1; Barney Rosset to SB, 17 February 1958, NSyU). Rosset had written to SB about the sagging attendance, and he had asked permission to cut royalties "to keep ENDGAME running as long as possible" (Rosset to SB, 3 March 1958, NSyU).

JAKE SCHWARTZ
BRIGHTON

March 15th 1958

6 Rue des Favorites
Paris 15me

Dear Jake

The Encyclopedia is now safely in my possession. It arrived in five parcels, one small and one large directly here and three large held up by the customs and which I have just cleared. It is a very beautiful edition and I am most happy to have it. My warmest thanks for your great generosity. I am not yet quite sure whether I shall keep it here or take it to the country, probably the latter, since most of my work now is done there and I have more room there. I know I shall have great pleasure from it, and instruction, in the years to come - if they do.[1]

I was much touched also by the Parnell autograph which I have tucked away in Dubliners with the Ivy Day. For this so friendly thought too all my thanks.[2]

I had not seen the clippings and was interested to read them. I am glad you enjoyed the Yeats show and that V.W. was friendly. From what I have heard the exhibition is a success and the new gallery well embarked.[3]

I have had a sharp spell of work and have not yet transcribed for you From An Abandoned Work. But I have not forgotten and shall do so on my return next week to the country. I am also keeping for you, if you would be interested, the MS of my translation of L'Innommable of which I have completed the first draft, and four states, in typescript, with copious and dirty corrections, of a short stage monologue I have just written (in English) for Pat Magee. This was composed on the machine from a tangle of old notes, so I have not the MS to offer you.[4]

I greatly enjoyed our evening at the Iles Marquises and hope we may soon have another such.[5]

Kind regards to Mrs Schwartz and again a thousand thanks for your munificent present.[6]

Ever

s/ Sam

I also received safely the Stanislaus book.[7]

TLS; 1 leaf, 1 side; TxU, Beckett Collection, 8.1. Previous publication: Lake, *No Symbols Where None Intended*, 90.

1 Jacob Schwartz* (n.d.), formerly a dentist, was at this time a rare book and manuscript dealer in Brighton, Sussex; he was known as "The Great Extractor." He had sent SB a copy of the *Encylopaedia Britannica*, 11th edition, which SB took with him to Ussy. Its twentieth volume was missing, as SB notes in his letter to Schwartz of 25 March (TxU, Beckett Collection, 8.1).

2 The autograph of Charles Stewart Parnell was later sent by SB, with his letter of 5 October 1966, to Jack MacGowran (TxU, Beckett Collection, 9.3). Parnell died on Ivy Day (6 October) and his memory figures in James Joyce's "Ivy Day in the Committee Room," *Dubliners*.

3 The clippings may have discussed the exhibition of Later Works by Jack B. Yeats at the Waddington Galleries in London, as did, for example, "Last Paintings of Jack B. Yeats" (*The Times* 11 March 1958: 3). V.W. is Victor Waddington.

4 Schwartz had asked SB for a fair copy of "From an Abandoned Work." This is now in the Harry Ransom Center, University of Texas (Beckett Collection, Works, 5.9 and 4.2).

5 SB's favorite restaurant in Montparnasse, Aux Iles Marquises, 15 Rue de la Gaîté, Paris 14.

6 Anita Sharp-Bolster (1895–1985), an Irish-born actress who had been a member of the Abbey Theatre company before embarking on a career in film, was married to Jake Schwartz.

7 Stanislaus Joyce, *My Brother's Keeper: James Joyce's Early Years* (London: Faber and Faber, 1958).

BARBARA BRAY
PURLEY, SURREY

March 17th 1958

6 Rue des Favorites
Paris 15me

Dear Barbara

Far from being troubled by your letter I am very touched that you should tell me about your great sorrow.[1] I wish I could find something to comfort you. All I could say, and much more, and much better, you will have said to yourself long ago. And I have so little light and wisdom in me, when it comes to such disaster, that I can see nothing for us but the old earth turning onward and time feasting on our suffering along with the rest. Somewhere at the heart of the gales of grief (and of love too, I've been told) already they have blown themselves out. I was always grateful for that humiliating consciousness and it was always there I huddled, in the innermost place of human frailty and lowliness. To fly there for me was not to fly far, and I'm not saying this is right for you. But I can't talk about solace of which I know nothing. And beyond all courage and reasonableness I am sure that for the likes of you and me at least it's the "death is dead and no more dying" that makes it possible (just) to go on living.[2] Forgive this wild stuff, I'm not a one to turn to in time of trouble. Work your head off and sleep at any price and leave the rest to the stream, to carry now away and bring you your other happy days.

Affectionately
s/ Sam

TLS; 1 leaf, 1 side; *env* to Mrs Barbara Bray, 121 Brighton Road, Purley, Surrey, Angleterre; *pm* 18-3-58, Paris; TCD, MS 10984/1/4.

1 SB had learned of the death in Cyprus of Bray's (estranged) husband John Bray, a former RAF prisoner of war whom she had married after graduating from Girton College, Cambridge, at the end of the war, and with whom she had spent three years teaching English literature in Cairo and Alexandria.

2 Bray was, like SB, no religious believer. SB adapts from the end of Shakespeare's Sonnet 146: "So shalt thou feed on Death, that feeds on men, / And Death once dead, there's no more dying then."

PATRICK MAGEE
LONDON

March 24th 1958 | 6 Rue des Favorites
Paris 15me

Dear Pat Magee

Herewith Molloy inadequately inscribed.

Donald McWhinnie will have told you how much I was moved by your readings, I look forward keenly to hearing you in Malone.[1]

I hope you like your monologue. If there is anything about it you want to ask me do not hesitate to write. I wish we could meet and go through it together.

Krapp's face as he listens is of course three quarters of that battle. I made no attempt to indicate its changes and unchangingness, feeling that these could safely be left to you.

With best wishes,
Yours sincerely
s/ Sam. Beckett

TLS; 1 leaf, 1 side; TCD, MS 11313/1.

1 Magee's readings from *Molloy* and "From an Abandoned Work."

ALAN SCHNEIDER
NEW YORK

March 30th 1958 | Ussy

Dear Alan

I'm glad you like the monologue. I think it would be a pity to rush it into production. It requires a pretty hefty actor and the magnetophonics very careful rehearsal. It could eventually raise the curtain for Endgame without any set complications, as the whole thing is played, apart from the two or three retreats backstage, in a small pool of light front centre, the rest of the stage being in darkness (I presume this is technically feasible). I have had no reaction from Devine so far, but if he wants to take it on and if he succeeds in organising club conditions at the Court for production of Endgame in May, I should be inclined to go to London and make a nuisance of myself at Krapp rehearsals and we could talk about it then.[1]

I'm told Clov carries skis at the end of Endgame. I think I understand your idea, but I feel this is wrong, stylistically and because "no more snow". Load him down as much as you like with shabby banal things, coats, bags and a pair of spare boots hanging down from his neck if you like, but not skis. He once asked Hamm for a pair and was told to get out to hell. I know it's only a wretched detail.[2]

I'm sorry you are losing Hiven [*for* Hiken] and having such tiresome juggling to attend to. I consider we shall have had a very good run – for such a beast![3]

Love to Jean and Vicki.

Ever

Sam

TLS; 1 leaf, 1 side; Burns Library, Samuel Beckett Collection, SB-AS. Previous publication: Beckett and Schneider, *No Author Better Served*, 44.

1 Schneider had written on 24 March that he was so excited about *Krapp's Last Tape* that he was "trying to convince producers to let me try it with the show for the next few weeks – subject to your approval" (Burns Library, Samuel Beckett Collection, AS-SB); Previous publication: Beckett and Schneider, *No Author Better Served*, 42.

2 "Clov appeared wearing the raincoat, carried a pair of skis in his right hand, a suitcase with a canoe paddle tied to it in his left, a knapsack on his back, and a climbing rope over his left shoulder" (*Endgame, with a revised text*, 60). Bicycles, not skis, are mentioned as lacking in the original text (6).

3 Gerald Hiken (b. 1927) achieved "a gradual strengthening of character in his portrayal of Clov," according to Jerry Tallmer ("'Endgame' Revisited," *The Village Voice* 2 April 1958: 11). Hiken had left the production on 20 March. After ninety-six performances at the Cherry Lane, *Endgame* would close on 20 April.

MICHAEL HOROVITZ
ENGLAND

April 1st 1958

6 Rue des Favorites
Paris 15me

Dear Mr Horovitz

Thank you for your letter and for your article which I have read with great interest and return to you herewith.[1]

My advice to you is to take further thought, and to read me further, before you undertake the inquiry you have in mind. There is writing, Joyce's for example, which repays such study, and writing which does not. I think mine is of the latter kind.

I do not see why you need my approval. You are quite free to write about me if you wish. I feel this is no business of mine.

I am not concerned with securing acceptance and understanding for my work. I find it impossible to approach it myself from this angle.

If you finally decide to go on with your idea I shall give you what help I can. It would consist mainly in biographical and bibliographical information, introductions to the few people I know likely to be of use to you and in making available for you my texts and the critical material in the possession of my publisher here. I could not go into discussions about the meaning of my work and my reactions to your findings would be feeble and unhelpful.

Yours sincerely
s/
Samuel Beckett

TLS; 1 leaf, 1 side: McM, Horovitz Collection, 1.24.

1 Poet and translator Michael Horovitz (b. 1935), who founded the journal *New Departures* in 1959, had asked Christopher Logue to forward a letter to SB. Logue advised Horovitz to "make a rough synopsis of your book. By rough I mean, minus detail. But be thorough as Beckett is a man of considerable academic learning and is likely to judge your seriousness closely." (Logue to Horovitz, 20 March 1958, TxU, New Departures, recip.) Horovitz published an essay: "Notes on 3 Novels by Samuel Beckett," *Tomorrow* 4 (1960) 57–59.

BARNEY ROSSET
GROVE PRESS, NEW YORK

April 1st 1958

6 Rue des Favorites
Paris 15me

Dear Barney

Thanks for yours of 28th. A letter from Alan too. Delighted that Krapp has this effect on you. I'd be grateful for an Evergreen proof.[1] I feel as clucky and beady and one-legged and bare-footed about this little text as an old hen with her last chick. I see the whole thing so clearly (appart [sic] from the changes of Krapp's white face as he listens) and realize now that this does not mean I have stated it clearly, though God knows I tried. I'd hate it to be made a balls of at the outset and that's why I question it's [sic] being let out to small groups beyond our controp [*for* control] before we get it done more or less right and set a standard of fidelity at least. Mary Manning is intelligent and knows the theatre, but I'm afraid her actor won't have the weight and authority that are needed. The magnetophonics too are difficult and will want great care and precision.[2] I have no news from Devine, but presumably Magee will do it in London before long. I'll certainly stick out my neck at those rehearsals and as Alan will be coming to London we could talk it over then. I know you're in a hurry to see it and it does my old heart good to feel your enthusiasm. Perhaps the whole thing is quite clear and simple and I fussing about nothing. Think it all over anyhow. The thing is frailer than perhaps it looks. I nearly entitled it "Ah Well". Would you have preferred that?

Ever
s/ Sam

TLS; 1 leaf, 1 side; NSyU.

1 Rosset had written to SB on 28 March: "We will pickle him first in the Evergreen Review . . . both Alan and my EVREV co-editor are krapping their hands in joy over Krapp" (NSyU).

2 Grove Press had already made arrangements with The Poets' Theatre, Cambridge, Massachusetts, to produce *Krapp's Last Tape*. SB's friend Mary Manning Howe (1905–1999; Profile, I) was involved with the company.

GEORGE DEVINE
ROYAL COURT THEATRE, LONDON

March 5th 1958 [*for* 5 April 1958] Ussy-sur-Marne

Dear George

Thanks for your letter. I saw Harold Hobson about a week ago. From what he said I hoped I would be seeing you here. Are you thinking of coming over soon? I hope so.

I'm glad you like Krapp. I think the recorder on the table should be a dummy and the recorded tape operated from the wings. This is probably too obvious to be worth saying, but when writing the thing I actually thought of the voice as coming from the visible machine! I suppose the little island of light in the midst of darkness is technically possible. It is of importance for the piece and means it can be played in the Endgame set. I made no attempt to describe Krapp's face as he listens, though this is a good half of the battle. Anyhow I didn't see it clearly. Expressiveness in blankness sums it up, I think, if that means anything.

I am naturally very excited at the thought of Guinness as Hamm.[1] I won't mention it.

Do try and get over. Vilar's Ubu is worth seeing.[2]

Greetings to all.

Yours ever

s/ Sam

TLS; 1 leaf, 1 side; TxU, English Stage Company, 1.2.

1 Alec Guinness declined the role of Hamm in the Royal Court Theatre production.

2 Jean Vilar's production of his edited version of *Ubu roi* by Alfred Jarry, entitled simply *Ubu*, had opened at the Théâtre National Populaire (TNP) on 5 March; Georges Wilson (1921–2010) played Père Ubu, and Rosy Varte (1923–2012) played Mère Ubu.

RICHARD ROUD
LONDON

7.4.58 Paris

Dear Roud

Thanks for your card. I note your new address. I'll never do the Johnson, in this or any other century.[1] Blin's conception of Hamm physical was influenced by Bacon's pope series. I'm sure he would do an excellent set and costumes for Endgame, but the theatre has kept the Noël set from last year.[2] I hear from Devine that his production (clubwise) will be either next month or in the early autumn. I have written a short stage monologue for Pat Magee which will be given with Endgame in place of the mime. I hope all goes well with you and that you'll be over soon. Vilar's Ubu is very Chaillot Jarry, but brilliant and definitely worth seeing.

Yours ever
s/ Sam. Beckett

TLS; 1 leaf, 1 side; T *env to* Richard Roud, Esq, 8 Bolton Studios, Gilston Road, London S.W.10, Angleterre; *pm* 8-4-58, La Ferté-sous-Jouarre; Smolens Collection.

1 SB's abandoned play on Samuel Johnson: 29 December 1957, n. 3.

2 Francis Bacon had created a series of paintings after Velázquez's *Portrait of Pope Innocent X* (Galleria Doria Pamphilj, Rome).

Jacques Noël (b. 1924) designed the set for *Fin de partie* and *Acte sans paroles I* in the 1955 London and the Paris productions. "Noël's set was very dour, rather like a tower made of stone . . . completely circular . . . dark grey" (Jocelyn Herbert, *Jocelyn Herbert: A Theatre Workbook*, ed. Cathy Courtney [London: Art Books International, 1993] 28).

MARY HUTCHINSON
LONDON

9.4.58 Ussy

Dear Mary – Thanks for your letter and enclosures. I am here today. The Abbey was founded by a protégé of St. Columban who passed through Ussy over thirteen centuries ago. The lady lying on her tomb just to be seen back centre is Ste. Ozanne, daughter of an Irish king. Agilbert also had a spell in Ireland.[1] Of course you may read the Magee monologue, ask George to lend you his copy. The lady birds have flown. It is so cold the sparrows have interrupted their nesting. There's hardly a leaf in the trees. I've been writing in French – for the waste-paper basket again – and reading Il Paradiso and trying again to understand Beatrice's explanation of the spots on the moon where the spirits appear to Dante as shadowy as "a pearl on a white forehead".[2]

yours ever Sam

APCS; 1 leaf, 1 side; "Jouarre (Seine-et-Marne), Ancienne Abbaye Notre-Dame, Crypte Saint-Paul. A droite, cénotaphe de Sainte Théodéchilde; à gauche, tombeau de Saint Agilbert (VIIe siècle)"; *to* Mrs Hutchinson, 21 Hyde Park Square, London W.2, Angleterre; *pm* 9-4-58, La Ferté-sous-Jouarre; TxU, Hutchinson, 2.4.

1 SB is accounting for the image on the picture postcard he is sending Mary Hutchinson. Irish monk Saint Columbanus (c. 540–615) undertook a mission to France in 590. He was received by Authair, whose son Adon (c. 600–670) founded Jouarre Abbey, which included a nunnery. Sainte-Ozanne, the daughter of an Irish king (*Encylopædia Universalis* says Scottish) was a nun there in the tenth century. Agilbert (d. c. 685) served in Wessex as a bishop; he resigned his See in 668 and was made Bishop of Paris (Alban Butler, *Butler's Lives of the Saints*, IV, ed. Herbert Thurston and Donald Attwater [New York: P. J. Kenedy and Sons, 1956] 87). According to Bede's *Historia ecclesiastica gentis Anglorum*, he had spent a long period studying in Ireland. He was buried at Jouarre Abbey.

2 As far back as 1934 (and as Mary Hutchinson was aware), SB had been pondering this passage from Canto III of Dante's *Paradiso*. He has his character Belacqua Shuah "stuck in the first of the canti of the moon" in "Dante and the Lobster," the opening story in his first published collection of stories, *More Pricks Than Kicks*. The story continues: "He was so bogged down that he could not move neither backward nor forward. Blissful Beatrice was there, Dante also, and she explained the spots on the moon to him. She had it from God, therefore he could rely on its being accurate in every particular" ([New York: Grove Press, 1972] 9). Dante's tercet runs: "tornan di nostri visi le postille / debili sì, che perla in bianca fronte / non vien men tosto alle nostre pupille" (the outlines of our faces return so faint that a pearl on a white brow does not come less quickly to our eyes) (Dante Alighieri, *The Divine Comedy of Dante Alighieri, Paradiso*, ed. and tr. John D. Sinclair [London: John Lane The Bodley Head, 1939; revised 1948] III.13–15). All references to Dante's *Divine Comedy* in translation are to this edition.

BARNEY ROSSET
GROVE PRESS, NEW YORK

10.4.58 Ussy

Dear Barney

Thanks for your letter with St Louis photos and to Judith Schmidt for hers with Krapp information and for cheque and royalty statements.[1]

This morning at the scream of dawn a hell-has-no-fury cable from Mary Manning. I replied confirming your withdrawal of Krapp from the Poets Theater.[2]

I feel we should not be in a hurry to find a theatre for Krapp. I can't see now how to write a play with intermission(s) and if I ever do another it will almost certainly be one act about Endgame length or a little shorter and thus in need of a curtain-raiser. We might keep Krapp for this purpose, though of course it would mean indefinite postponement. Or we might keep it for presentation with an eventual revival of Endgame or with the present production when it goes on tour. The ideal would be for Alan to see it in London (next month or in the early autumn, according to Devine) where I hope at least to get the mechanics of it right, and then go on from there.[3] This of course may not be possible and is not indispensable. The main thing is to take our time and get out of it whatever is in it. I feel – to a disturbing degree – the strangest of solicitudes for this little work.

I could no more take on Ted Flicker's commission than swim the Marne. The idea is interesting, and what he is doing at the Compass, but it's completely outside my possibilities.[4]

I am very pleased that Krapp is to appear in next Evergreen. A week with a proof is all I entreat.

I have been writing in French, for the waste-paper basket. And have received a proposal from Marcel Mihailovici to furnish him with the libretto of a half-hour opera! First line: "Je n'ai pas envie de chanter ce soir."[5]

Ever

s/ Sam

TLS; 1 leaf, 1 side; NSyU.

1 Rosset had sent photos of the production of *Waiting for Godot* at the Crystal Palace Theatre, a cabaret in St. Louis, which opened on 3 February. Judith Schmidt had sent SB statements of royalty payments on 3 April (NSyU).

2 In a second letter of 3 April, Schmidt explained that the Poets' Theatre, Cambridge, Massachusetts, had been given permission to produce *Krapp's Last Tape*, and then, in the face of SB's objection, that this permission had been withdrawn (see also 1 April 1958 to Barney Rosset, n. 2). SB responded on 10 April to Mary Manning Howe's telegram:

> I am very sorry about the Krapp misunderstanding and to have to disappoint you. The withdrawal from your theatre has nothing to do with your ability in which I have great confidence – though I think it unlikely you dispose of the kind of actor I have in mind. It is simply that for a number of reasons I do not want this piece rushed into production in the States. I am not even sure of the text. When I sent it to Barney Rosset I had no idea he would release it with such precipitation. If he had had time to consult me this unpleasant situation would not have arisen. It would be a pity if you were not to forgive me who for once am as innocent as the sperm unspilt. (TxU, Beckett Collection, 8.10.)

3 The Royal Court double bill, *Endgame* and *Krapp*, was delayed by the Lord Chamberlain's Office's refusal to grant a license for *Endgame*.

4 Theodore Jonas Flicker (b. 1930) had established the Crystal Palace Theater in St. Louis, then the only theatre in the United States staging plays in monthly repertory. Flicker asked SB to write "twenty-four hours of plays . . . as short as no words or as long as he wanted them to be. I would run them twenty-four hours a day." The audience members could come and leave at any time and would pay only for what they saw (Flicker to the editors, 4 October 2010).

5 Marcel Mihalovici* (known as Chip, 1898–1985), whose name SB spells here as "Mihailovici," French composer born in Romania; he and his wife, the pianist Monique Haas (1909–1987), were also friends of Thomas MacGreevy.

"Je n'ai pas envie de chanter ce soir" ("I don't feel like singing tonight").

PATRICK MAGEE
LONDON

April 11th 1958 — 6 Rue des Favorites
Paris 15me

Dear Pat Magee

Thanks for your letter. I'm glad you like Krapp. George Devine tells me he'll do it with Endgame next month or in the early autumn. Please God it doesn't clash with the Iceman.[1]

I'm afraid you'll have to draw attention to the first banana skin somehow, so as to be able to throw the second at the audience. All this business could be cut out of course, but I should prefer not. You have a precarious walk in any case and you needn't slip on the skin. A vague stumble yards from it would do, then you make it responsible. You are "drowned in dreams" here and a hitch in your locomotion should appear quite natural. It could be "prepared" on your way from table to front.[2]

You are quite right about the voice and I should have indicated its tone more precisely. The self-importance is mainly in relation to the "opus" and can therefore disappear in the canal and lake passages and reappear in the pier passage which the old Krapp finds so insufferable.[3]

The sour cud and iron stool are respectively the memories ("all that old misery") and the constipation ("my old weakness", "unattainable laxation").[4]

"Homework" is the old man's contemptuous description of the "opus magnum". He is overcome at the memory of his "farewell to love" (renouncement of Bianca and the girl in the punt) as liable to interfere with ("get in the way of") his intellectual activity.[5]

While I think of it a word to be brought out very strong is "burning" (page 7, line 1), in order that "fire" at the end may carry all its ambiguity.[6]

If any more queries occur to you I'll be very glad to answer them – or try to.

I hope you'll be able to get over and that we may have an evening together in Paris.

Yours sincerely
s/ Sam. Beckett

TLS; 1 leaf, 1 side; TCD, MS 11313/2.

1 Patrick Magee performed in Eugene O'Neill's *The Iceman Cometh* at the Arts Theatre from 29 January 1958; the play transferred to the Winter Garden Theatre on 29 March and ran until 3 May.

2 In the opening mime of *Krapp's Last Tape*, the stage directions read: "He treads on skin, slips, nearly falls, recovers himself, stoops and peers at skin and finally pushes it . . . over the edge of stage into pit" (Samuel Beckett, *Krapp's Last Tape and Other Dramatic Pieces* [New York: Grove Press, 1960] 11; all references are to this edition).

3 The opus magnum passage (17); the canal passage (17–20) and lake passages (21–23; 27); the pier passage (20–21).

4 "Sour cud and iron stool" (25); "All that old misery" (26); "my old weakness" (14, 26); "Unattainable laxation" (17).

5 "Homework" (24); "Farewell to love" (13); Bianca (16); girl in the punt (21–24, 27–28).

6 "Burning" (25); "fire" (28).

JACOBA VAN VELDE
AMSTERDAM

12.4.58 Ussy

Chère Tonny

Merci de votre carte. J'espère que vous avez pu travailler un peu et que vous êtes moins découragée. J'ai écrit un peu en français, encore pour rien. A la corbeille. Il y a deux moments qui valent la peine, dans le travail, celui de la mise en route et celui de la mise en corbeille. J'ai quand même écrit jusqu'au bout et laissé partir un petit monologue de scène en anglais qui sera donné avec Endgame à Londres à la place du mime dont personne n'a l'air de vouloir. Il est gentiment triste et sentimental, ça fera comme un petit coeur d'artichaut avant les tripes à la merde de Hamm et Clov, on dira, Tiens, il a le sang qui circule, on ne l'aurait jamais cru, ça doit être l'âge. La grande exposition de Bram à Berne le mois prochain (100 tableaux dont certains prêtés par Maeght!) se prépare. Jacques est passé chez nous pour faire photographier la gouache. Il m'invite à les accompagner en voiture, lui, Bram at [*for* et] Andrée.[1] J'aimerais beaucoup voir cette exposition, mais je serai peut-être obligé d'aller à Londres à cette époque. Je suis à la campagne depuis 15 jours et retourne à Paris demain. Je m'emmerde tellement que je relis le Paradis de Dante. On m'a donné l'édition 1911 de l'Encyclopédie Britannique. 28 volumes. Trop tard. On m'a demandé un livret d'opéra bouffe! J'ai écrit une ligne – "J'ai pas envie de chanter ce soir" – puis j'ai renoncé. Un temps de Terre Neuve, pas une feuille aux arbres. 52 ans demain, on arrive, j'ai reçu deux douzaines de vieux linges, va falloir que je me remette à pleurer.[2] Tous les amis sont à l'hôpital, je ferai bientôt une tournée pour leur fermer les yeux. J'ai rencontré Geneviève à Ubu au TNP. Dommage qu'elle n'ait pu aller à Bergen. Elle termine un roman. Je la reverrai la semaine prochaine.[3] Ce sera tout pour aujourd'hui.

Affectueusement à vous deux.

s/ Sam

TLS; 1 leaf, 1 side; BNF, 19794/53.

12.4.58 Ussy

Dear Tonny

Thank you for your card. I hope that you have been able to do some work, and that you are not so discouraged. I have written a little in French, again to no purpose. Into the waste-paper basket. There are two worthwhile moments in my work: the opening up and the basketing. Still, I did write on to the end, and let out a little stage monologue in English which will go on with *Endgame* in London, instead of the mime which no one seems to want. It is pleasantly sad and sentimental: a nice little entrée of artichoke hearts, to be followed by the tripe à la shit of Hamm and Clov. People will say, Well, well, he has blood in his veins, who would have thought it, it must be age. Bram's big exhibition in Berne next month (100 paintings, some of them lent by Maeght!) is being set up. Jacques called in to see to the photographing of the gouache. He is inviting me to go with them in the car, Bram, Andrée and him.[1] I would very much like to see this exhibition, but I may have to go to London at that time. Have been in the country for a fortnight, and am going back to Paris tomorrow. I am so fed up that I am re-reading Dante's *Paradiso*. I have been given the 1911 edition of the *Encyclopaedia Britannica*. 28 volumes. Too late. I have been asked for a libretto for a comic opera! I wrote one line: "I don't feel like singing tonight". Then I gave up. Newfoundland weather, not a leaf on the trees. 52 years old tomorrow, we're getting there. I have received two dozen old stanchers; I shall have to start crying again.[2] All my friends are in hospital, I shall soon be doing the rounds to close their eyes. I met Geneviève at *Ubu* in the TNP. Shame she was not able to go to Bergen. She is finishing a novel. I shall see her again next week.[3] That will be all for today.

Love to you both

Sam

1 The gouache photographed by Jacques Putman is likely to have been the one later donated to the Musée National d'Art Moderne, *Sans titre* ("Grande gouache bleue") 1939–1940 (AM 1982-243, reproduced in Rainer Michael Mason and Sylvie Ramond, eds., *Bram et Geer van Velde: Deux peintres, Un nom* [Paris: Editions Hazan, 2010] 327). Putman offered transport, along with his wife the designer Andrée Putman (1925–2013). The retrospective of Bram van Velde's work at the Kunsthalle in Berne would take place from 10 May to 15 June.

2 The previous day, SB wrote to Mary Hutchinson: "A thousand thanks for your present. You are very thoughtful to remember such a thing. I who never have a cold have one, so ça tombe à pic. They are very fine particularly the white one. I never had a handkerchief with my sigma before – that I can remember." (TxU, Hutchinson, 2.4.) "Ça tombe à pic" (perfect timing).

3 Geneviève Serreau (1915–1981) was a translator, theatre director, Secrétaire de la Rédaction at *Les Lettres Nouvelles*, and wife of theatre director Jean-Marie Serreau (1915–1973). SB encounters her attending *Ubu* put on by Jean Vilar's Théâtre National Populaire. Serreau would publish her novel *Le Fondateur*, in January the following year (Paris: Julliard, 1959).

MARIA JOLAS
? PARIS

April 16th 1958 — 6 Rue des Favorites
Paris 15me

Dear Maria

Thanks for your letter and extract from Critique.[1] If you see fit to use the clumsy and inadequate few lines herewith I shall be very pleased. If you prefer not to I shall understand. It is the best I can do. I am hopelessly bad about these things. For some strange reason I could not write it in French and cannot translate it into French.

I hope you are keeping well and that we may meet for a bit of a gosther soon.

Affectionately

s/ Sam

The little poem, and particularly the "fall", seemed in some way very true of him, or of part of him. It seemed to me at the time, as he said it, that he felt this himself. It was very moving. The poem is hard to find, even in the collected verse. Five lines, for ever in my head. If you don't know it and would like to have it I'll write it out for you.[2]

I shall always think of Gene Jolas with affection and gratitude. I recall with emotion his kindness to me, and his tolerance of me, when I was a very young man in Paris. He was the first to publish me. Our last talk was on the terrasse of Fouquet's, a year or two before his death. We said Goethe's marvellous lyric "Dem Geier gleich . . ." The last line, "schwebet mein Lied", will always sound for me with his voice, as he repeated it then, for himself, and bring me his face.[3]

Photocopy of TLS; 2 leaves, 2 sides; CtY, Beinecke, Gen Mss 108, series VII, 28.535.

1 Maria Jolas may have sent SB a copy of D. John Grossman's essay on Eugene Jolas (1894–1952): "Un poète international," *Critique* 62 (July 1952) 592–604. She asked SB to write a contribution to a 1958 "Radio Strasbourg Tribute: Remembrances of Eugene Jolas" (CtY, Beinecke, Gen Mss 108, series V, Box 26, Folder 499).

2 SB refers to the first stanza of Goethe's poem "Harzreise im Winter" that is mentioned in the tribute. SB writes "Schwebet" (hovers) instead of "Schwebe" in the last line:

> Dem Geier gleich,
> Der auf schweren Morgenwolken
> Mit sanftem Fittich ruhend
> Nach Beute schaut,
> Schwebe mein Lied.
>
> ("Like a hawk poised, with scarce-quivering wings, on lowering morning clouds, watching for prey, let my song hover.") (Johann Wolfgang von Goethe and David Luke, *Goethe: With Plain Prose Translations of Each Poem*, tr. and ed. David Luke, Penguin Classics [London: Penguin Books, 1964] 54.)

3 On 24 April, SB replied to Jolas's next letter concerning a German translation of what he had written: "I am glad you are pleased with my little text for Gene. Yes, I suppose I mean the 'letzte Zeile', but it's rather feeble. The statement is held up so long that it's like a resolution of harmonic tension. I don't know the German equivalent of 'fall' in that sense – 'chute'. There must be one. Perhaps Schluss would be better than 'letzte Zeile'. It's a detail." (CtY, Beinecke, Gen Mss 108, series VII, 28.535.)

"Letzte Zeile" (final line); "chute" (fall); "Schluss" (ending, closing).

One of James Joyce's preferred haunts, Fouquet's, 90 Avenue des Champs-Elysées, Paris 8.

AVIGDOR ARIKHA
PARIS

17.4.58 Paris

Cher ami

J'ai beaucoup parlé de vous hier à Bram van Velde et à Jacques Putman. Comme vous cherchez une galerie j'ai pensé que celle de Warren ferait peut-être l'affaire.[1] Van Velde et Putman aimeraient aller chez vous voir le travail.[2] Je ne sais vraiment pas si ça collera avec eux, j'ai plutôt l'impression que non. Mais je peux me tromper. A vous de décider. Si ça vous intéresse téléphonez à Putman vers midi (LAB 6184) pour prendre rendez-vous. Et si ça ne vous dit rien laissez tomber.

Suzanne est ravie de votre dessin.[3] Bravo pour le travail récent. Continuez.

Amitiés

s/ Sam

TLS; 1 leaf, 1 side; InU, Arikha.

17.4.58 Paris

Dear Avigdor

I talked a lot about you yesterday to Bram van Velde and Jacques Putman. As you're looking for a gallery it occurred to me that Warren's might do.[1] Van Velde and Putman would like to go to your place to see the work.[2] I don't know if it will work out with them. I rather think not, but I may be wrong. You decide. If it interests you, phone Putman round lunchtime (LAB 6184) to make an appointment. And if you don't feel like it, forget it.

Suzanne is delighted with your drawing.[3] Bravo for the recent work. Keep it up.

All best

s/ Sam

1 The Galerie Michel Warren had exhibited Bram van Velde's work in 1955 and 1957 (see SB to Jacques Putman, 5 February 1957, n. 1).

2 At this time Arikha was living and working in a rented apartment, 10 Villa d'Alésia, Paris 14.

3 The drawing to which SB refers has not been identified.

A. J. LEVENTHAL AND ETHNA MACCARTHY-LEVENTHAL DUBLIN

April 21st 1958 Ussy-sur-Marne

Dear Con and Ethna

Many thanks for your letters. I am glad to hear that Manchester approves of treatment. What I want to know is that there is no pain and that perhaps food and drink begin to taste again. I find it hard to write a "normal" letter. But I suppose there is nothing else for it and that in any case this is what you would prefer.[1]

I had not heard of Seumas's death before Con's letter. I enclose a nore [*for* note] of sympathy for Stella. As I do not know her address I should be grateful if you would send it on.[2]

I am surprised to hear of Ryan's project to invest money in the DM and can hardly believe that anything will come of it. I was told by friends he was ill and rang up Mary in some alarm. But there was confusion with Ralph Cusack who has been very ill (almost died). He has had, in a Nice hospital, a "Smithwick ectomy" for high blood pressure and is to have another in a month's time, according to Nancy. At the moment he is home in Spéracèdes. But you probably have his news from Scott and Ryan.[3]

I'm afraid what Con calls my "gesture" goes a little deeper than that, deep enough anyway for me not to want to be performed in Dublin, in festivals or otherwise. Foolish I suppose. But I was always that.[4]

Behan went barging and boozing through and according to an evening paper spent a night in quod for violence or threats thereof to air hostesses etc. I hear his play has been well translated by Boris Vian.[5]

Can't conceive by what stretch of ingenuity my work could be placed under sign of italianità. No doubt less is required. There are a number of Italian elements, of which I suppose the most tenacious is Belacqua (Purgatory, Canto 4, lines 106 et sqq). His attitude (which I discovered the other day in the Botticelli drawings for the Comedy, exactly as I had seen it) is certainly familiar to my creatures –

Ed un di loro, che me sembrava lasso,
Sedeva ed abbraciava le ginocchia,
Tenendo il viso giù tra esse basso –

and his weary "l'andare in su che porta?" For some strange reason I was certainly fascinated very early by the character and went to a lot of trouble to find out about him. But little seems to be known, except that he was a lute-maker in Florence, a friend of Dante and notorious for his indolence and apathy. There are a good many degrees between him and l'innommable, but it's the same engeance.[6] Perhaps a more interesting approach, from the technical view, is a line from Petrarch –

"Chi può dire com' egli arde è in picciol foco" –

arde being understood more generally, and less gallantly, that [*for* than] in the Canzoniere.[7] As thus solicited it can link up with the 3rd proposition (coup de grâce) of Gorgias in his Nonent:

1. Nothing is
2. If anything is, it cannot be known.
3. If anything is, and can be known, it cannot be expressed in speech.[8]

Leopardi was a strong influence when I was young (his pessimism, not his patriotism!) and his "fango è il mondo" serves you may remember as epigraph to the Proust essay (1931). I remember it's [sic] pleasing Joyce because of consonance between "il mondo" and "immonde". Might also be dragged in the Joyce essay in the Exagmination – "Dante, Bruno, Vico, Joyce". It's all rather beside the point, but it might be worth trying in an Italian embassy (the "great pun" on pietà too, mentioned I think in Dante and the L.) Don't quote any of the above, simply use it if you find it a help.[9]

I saw Thornton who simply wanted some bibliographical information which I was able to give him. He asked to see Eleuthéria and Mercier et Camier and I have promised to lend them to him if I can dig out the MSS.[10]

I have written a short stage monologue for Pat Magee. It will be given, in place of the mime, with Endgame as soon as club conditions are laid on at the Royal Court. Also been writing in French, but to absolutely no purpose.

Assez pour ce soir.[11]

Love. Bon courage. Write soon again.

s/ Sam

TLS; 1 leaf, 2 sides; TxU, Leventhal Collection, 1.4.

1 Ethna MacCarthy-Leventhal had throat cancer. The Christie Clinic in Manchester was (and remains) one of the leading centers for cancer research and treatment in the United Kingdom.

2 Seumas O'Sullivan was publisher of *Dublin Magazine* until his death on 24 March; SB's letter to his wife Estella Solomons is dated 20 April 1958:

> My mind goes back to Whitechurch and to his great kindness, and yours, to me there.
>
> All I can do now is to send you my loving thoughts and wishes that you may find comfort somewhere and strength to bear your great loneliness and sorrow. (Solomons Collection.)

The O'Sullivan family home was "Grange House," Whitechurch, Co. Dublin.

3 Although there was speculation about continuation of *Dublin Magazine* with the assistance of friends and "regular contributors" (among them A. J. Leventhal, Arland Ussher, Patrick McDonogh [1902–1961, also spelled McDonagh], and Pádraic Fallon [1905–1974]), the journal's final issue was that of June 1958 (Quidnunc, "An Irishman's Diary," *The Irish Times*, 31 March 1958: 8). Desmond and Mary Ryan; the Scott in question has not been identified. Ralph Cusack, who was married to SB's cousin Nancy Sinclair, had undergone a sympathectomy, developed by R. H. Smithwick to treat high blood pressure.

4 SB refers to his refusal to allow his plays to be performed in Ireland.

5 Brendan Behan (1923–1964) was in Paris to discuss the production of *The Quare Fellow*, translated by Jacqueline Sundstrom and Boris Vian as *Le Client du matin* (1959). On his return flight to Dublin, the plane's radio was struck by lightning and the pilot had to turn back to Orly. Behan complained so vociferously that he was arrested upon landing and spent the night in prison (Beatrice Behan with Des Hickey and Gus Smith, *My Life with Brendan* [Los Angeles: Nash Publishing, 1974] 120–123).

6 "Italianità" (Italianness). SB's affection for Belacqua: 9 April 1958, n. 2. Placed among the indolent, Belacqua is described in the lines cited by SB: "one of them, who

seemed to me weary, sat clasping his knees and holding his face low down between them" (Dante, *Purgatorio*, IV.106–109). When questioned by Dante as to why he does not advance up the mountain of Purgatory, Belacqua begins his reply, "O frate, l'andar su che porta?" (line 127) (O brother, what is the use of going up . . . ?). SB suggests that Belacqua is of "the same engeance" (the same breed) as his figure the Unnamable (in the work of that name).

7 SB cites the final line from poem 170 of Petrarch's *Canzoniere*, "Più volte già del bel sembiante umano," which concludes: "Et veggi' or ben che caritate accesa / lega la lingua altrui, gli spirti invola: / chi pò dir com' egli arde è 'n picciol foco." Robert Durling translates the sonnet as "Many times from her kind expression," and the second tercet: "And I see well how burning Love binds one's tongue, steals away one's breath: he who can say how he burns is in but a little fire" (*Petrarch's Lyric Poems: The Rime sparse and Other Poems*, tr. and ed. Robert Durling [Cambridge, MA: Harvard University Press, 1976] 317).

8 SB takes Petrarch's proposition about how passion expressed cannot be passion deeply felt, and gives it an ontological turn, invoking the sophist Gorgias of Lentini (c. 483 – c. 385 BC), whose lost work *On Nature or the Non-Existent* (the *Nonent*) is cited by Sextus Empiricus in *Against the Mathematicians* and by Pseudo-Aristoteles in *On Melissus, Xenophanes, and Gorgias*, as containing something close to the three propositions that SB in turn cites (see further Matthew Feldman, *Beckett's Books: A Cultural History of Samuel Beckett's "Interwar Notes"* [London and New York: Continuum, 2006], 76–77).

9 SB's quotation is from Leopardi's 1833 poem "A se stesso" ("To Himself"): "Amaro e noia / La vita, altro mai nulla; e fango è il mondo" ("Boredom and bitterness / Is life; and the rest nothing; the world is dirt") (*Selected Prose and Poetry*, ed. and tr. Iris Origo and John Heath-Stubbs, Oxford Library of Italian Classics [London: Oxford University Press, 1966], 280–281). "E fango è il mondo" served as an epigraph to SB's first published book, *Proust*. On the word-play between "il mondo" and "immonde," and Joyce's enjoyment of it, see 22 July 1955, and n. 4.

In "Dante and the Lobster," Belacqua's Italian teacher the Ottolenghi advises him: "'you might do worse than make up Dante's rare movements of compassion in Hell'." Belacqua responds: "'I recall one superb pun anyway: "*qui vive la pietà quando è ben morta*. . ."'" (*More Pricks Than Kicks* [New York: Grove Press, 1972] 19). The "great pun" is made up both of the contrast between "vive" and "è ben morta," and of the double sense of "pietà," signifying both "pity" (compassion for human suffering) and "piety" (respect for God and God's justice); so, when Virgil utters these words to the pilgrim Dante (in *Inferno*, XX.28), he can be understood to be saying several different things – things which, in the nature of puns, are strictly untranslatable (the reason, presumably, why the Ottolenghi questions Belacqua whether "'it is absolutely necessary to translate it?'"). Virgil can be variously understood to be meaning, for example, "Here pity lives when it is quite dead," as John D. Sinclair translates Dante's line; or "Here pity only lives when it is dead," as Allen Mandelbaum translates it (*Inferno* [New York: Bantam Classics, 1980]); or "Here piety lives when pity is quite dead," as Robert and Jean Hollander translate it (*The Inferno* [New York: Anchor Books, 2002]).

10 Thornton has not been identified.

11 "Assez pour ce soir" (Enough for tonight).

THOMAS MACGREEVY
DUBLIN

April 21st 1958

6 Rue des Favorites
Paris 15me Ussy

Dear Tom

It was good to have your letter and to feel you so much better as to fume at your inactivity. I had a very reassuring note from Alan. As I think you have probably left the Burlington I am sending this to your home address.[1] The Giorgione visitation is strange and interesting. I suppose this long preoccupation is the form you have found for some thing very deep and early in you, perhaps a kind of "besoin d'un frère", which would make the association with the 2nd Person shocking to you.[2]

I had a drink and pleasant chat with Chatelet [sic] at the Closerie. He agreed that an introduction from me to Marguerite Duthuit was unnecessary. He wants Matisse's private collection for exposition at Aix during the Festival. He has now made approach through the Tailleux at Aix.[3] We talked much of you, of Dante and of the Botticelli drawings for the Comdey [*for* Comedy] which I had been looking at a few days before when rereading the Paradise (with much the same reactions as 30 years ago, certainly not more understanding). I found Belacqua in a Purgatory drawing, in precisely the pose I had seen from Dante's line:

Ed un di loro, che me sembrava lasso,
Sedeva et abbraciava le ginocchia,
Tenendo il viso giù tra esse basso.

We talked also of Jouarre, near here, which he knew well. Columbanus passed through Ussy-sur-Marne at the beginning of the 7th and blessed Adon, lord of Ussy, who founded Jouarre. Agilbert (who was years in Ireland) is buried in the crypt and an Irish princess I never heard of, Ste-Ozanne.[4]

I got back here from Paris day before yesterday, relieved to enter the silence again. If Suzanne were with me she would add a line to this and thank you for writing to her, but she couldn't get away. I have half promised (and beginning to regret it) to go to Berne early next month to see a big Bram van Velde exhibition (100 works, pract[i]cally his life production!) at the Kunsthalle. I have lent my gouache and painting. As I feel now I'll probably cry off at the last moment. If I do go I may go on to see Giorgio.[5]

I have written in English a short stage dialogue which will be done in London with Endgame (in place of the mime) as soon as club conditions are available at the Royal Court. Have been writing in French too, but to no purpose. My batteries are badly in need of recharging. Marcel Mihalovici (Monsieur Monique Haas) has asked me to write him a libretto for a half hour opéra bouffe! We are dining with them at the end of this week and I'll find out more about it. But all commissions paralyse me.

It has been a harsh sad spring, but the last two days wonderful. One hasn't the heart for much.

Don't be tiring yourself with real letters. Just a few lines when you can, that I may know you are going on well.

Love ever, dear Tom.

s/ SAM

TLS; 1 leaf, 2 sides; TCD, MS 10402/213.

1 The Burlington Hotel, 27 Leeson Street Lower, Dublin 2, where MacGreevy was recovering from illness: "in 1958, I came for the first time in my life under doctor's orders for several months on end. The doctors were kind. But they insisted that I was to stop talking." (Thomas MacGreevy, *Nicolas Poussin* [Dublin: The Dolmen Press, 1960] v.) SB's friend, the physician Alan H. Thompson (1906–1996), had written to SB about MacGreevy.

2 MacGreevy had written to SB of a "visitation" that had come to him: "I had, all unconsciously, been looking for . . . a spirit, a temper, a human approach in which dream and reality, imagination and intellect, the transcendent and the immanent seemed, in perfect felicity, ideally, divinely as it might be, to blend" (Thomas MacGreevy, "Memoirs," 251–253; unpublished, Private Collection; Susan Schreibman to the editors, 1 April 2012).

"Besoin d'un frère" (need of a brother). Christ, the second person of the Trinity.

3 Art historian Albert Châtelet (b. 1928) was at this time Conservateur-adjoint of the Department of Paintings at the Louvre, and a good friend of MacGreevy (MacGreevy, *Nicolas Poussin*, vii). MacGreevy had suggested that Beckett introduce Châtelet to Marguerite Duthuit (1894–1982), wife of Georges Duthuit and daughter of Henri Matisse. SB had written to MacGreevy on 19 March: "Introduction for Châtelet embarrasses me slightly as I have altogether ceased from seeing the Duthuit, though

there has been no explicit breach" (TCD, MS 10402/211). By the time SB met Châtelet, the painter Francis Tailleux (1913–1981) had taken care of the introduction. The Aix-en-Provence Festival emphasized music, but the other arts also featured. La Closerie des Lilas, a restaurant, Boulevard du Montparnasse, Paris 6.

4 SB's cottage in Ussy was near La Ferté-sous-Jouarre. The Abbey of Jouarre: 9 April 1958, n. 1.

5 Bram van Velde's retrospective at the Kunsthalle in Berne exhibited sixty-three works (see 12 April 1958, n. 1).

Grande gouache bleue (see 12 April 1958, n. 1); *Sans titre* (1937).

Giorgio Joyce (1905–1976; Profile, I), son of James and Nora Joyce (1884–1951; Profile, I).

AIDAN HIGGINS
SOUTH AFRICA

April 22nd 1958

6 Rue des Favorites
Paris 15me

Dear Aidan

Thanks for your letters. Forgive my remissness. What happened was (roughly) this. I read your story, decided it was not for the Princess (Caetani), decided to read it again before writing to you, laid it aside, got deep into my troubles, couldn't find it when I wanted to go back to it, felt helpless before such a situation, etc. etc. I have now found it and reread it with great attention.[1]

My reluctance to comment has become overpowering. I hate the thought of the damage I may do from such unwillingness and such incapacity. If I were less concerned with you I should simply say it is very good, I like it very much, but don't see where to send it, and leave it at that. But I don't want to do that with you. And at the same time I know I can't go into it in a way profitable for you. This is not how writers help one another.

First some points of detail:

Pp. 1, 11, 13: "menacing as banners" . . . "cumbersome as manacles" . . . "ponderous as Juggernaut" . . . "colossal as a ship's hull" . . . "reckless as the sibyl of Cumae" . . . "Indelicate as chinaware" . . . "incorrigible as murder" . . . You want to be careful about that.[2]

P. 1: "phenominally" instead of "phenomenally".
P. 2: "relicti". I don't know the word in this sense. If it exists it should be "relicte". It suggests "relicts" – widows – which is not the case.
P. 3: "Portentious" instead of "portentous".
"âge dangereuse" instead of "âge dangereux". Not a very usual French expression.
P. 4: "Streben" instead of "streben".
"Uncommunitive". Deliberate invention?
P. 5: "Aggrevate" instead of "aggravate".
P. 7: "Hypertrophy of the prostate". Women don't have one (I'm sorry to say). No harm in that, as long as you make it clear you know. I have female haemophiles in Watt. But the footnote lets me out.
P.10: "Prunis" instead of "prunus".
P.11: "Indespensable" instead of "indispensable".
"Prunis" again.
P.12 "Prochet" ? My ignorance.
"Valarian" instead of "valerian".
"Bouyant" instead of "buoyant".
P.13: "Sibyl of Cumae's" instead of "sibyl of Cumae".
P.15: "Current" instead of "currant".
P.16: "Lebensgefuhl" instead of "Lebensgefühl". Not (I think) a very usual German term.[3]

All unimportant. But they had better be corrected before you send it out.

What I have to do now, and it's not easy, is to try and tell you what it is that spoils the text for me and obscures its great qualities. I think it is, briefly, a kind of straining towards depth and inwardness in certain passages. This begins after the pause on page 4.[4] Up to there I had read with only very trifling reserves and with admiration for the firmness and precision and rapidity of the writing. This quality is present throughout and I do not mean that those passages are devoid of it in which you quarry into the mind of Helen and the others. I simply feel a floundering and a labouring here and above all a falsening of position. I suppose it is too sweeping to say that expression of the within can only be from the within. There is in any case nothing more difficult and delicate than this discursive Auseinandersetzen of a world which is not to be revealed as object of speech, but as source of speech.[5] In other words, for you, chronicling in the third person, Helen (for example) is to be stated in two ways, through her physical being and through her own utterance. The memorable description of Emily May's service is more convincing, and more revealing of her "cose segrete" than your effort at incursion thereinto.[6] It is this discrepancy between two areas of statement and this relinquishing of what seems to me a legitimate mode, in which language has a chance, for one of mere literary convention, that weakness [*for* weakens] the story for me and finally leaves me outside it. The vision is so sensitive and the writing so effective when you stop blazing away at the microcosmic moon that results are likely to be considerable when you get to feel what is a possible prey and within the reach of words (yours) and what is not. I am not suggesting that words should not miss, that would ill become me, but the sitting rab[b]it, for near speechlessness, not with eloquence[,] what does not concern them. In you already, with the beginner, there's the old hand. Work, work, writing for nothing and yourself, don't make the silly mistake we all make of publishing too soon. What I have said is much too abstract and personal and black and white, that's what comes of trying to get down to the root. It's a terrible effort for me to write such stuff and I hope you disagree with it. Tired now, shall write you my gossip another time. Greetings to Jill.[7] Yours ever

s/ Sam

TLS; 1 leaf, 2 sides; T *env to* Mr Aidan Higgins, <c/o Anders, 63 Queen's Road, King William's Town, E. P., Afrique du Sud> AN AH c/o John Wright's Marionettes, P.O. Box 1273, Salisbury, S. Rhodesia; *upper left corner*, Par Avion; *pm* 23-4-58, La Ferté-sous-Jouarre; *pm* 30-4-58, King Williams' Town; TxU, Beckett Collection, 8.9. Previous publication: "Letter from Samuel Beckett Concerning Manuscript of Story 'Killachter Meadow'," *Review of Contemporary Fiction*, 3.1 (1983) 156–157.

1 Aidan Higgins later wrote to Arland Ussher, on 21 May: "I have sent a story via Sam to BOTTEGHE OSCURE but he kept it because he considered it unsuitable. He wrote an extensive criticism of it which was probably more helpful than publication." (TCD, MSS 9331-9041/1524.) Princess Marguerite Caetani (1890–1963) was the founder of *Botteghe Oscure* (1948–1960), an international literary magazine based in Rome.

2 The page numbers listed by SB in his letter refer to the manuscript version of the story later published in *Killachter Meadow* (New York: Grove Press, 1960).

3 In the published story Higgins adopted some but not all of SB's suggestions. "Lebensgefühl" (feeling of being alive).

4 The pause occurs in the published version before the section marked "I" (10–11).

5 "Auseinandersetzen" (here: explaining).

6 Helen Kervic is the third sister in Higgins's fictional family (13–14). Emily-May is the first-born sister, who is initially described serving a tennis ball (14).

SB adapts "cose segrete" from the moment when Virgil leads Dante through the gate of Hell. Dante writes: "E poi che la sua mano alla mia pose / con lieto volto, ond' io mi confortai, / mi mise dentro alle segrete cose" (And when he had laid his hand on mine with cheerful looks that gave me comfort, he led me in to the things that are hidden there) (*Inferno*, III.19–21).

7 Jill Damaris Anders (b. 1930) and Higgins were married in 1955.

AVIGDOR ARIKHA

Mardi [6 May 1958] Paris

Cher ami,

Merci de votre lettre.

Je pars en Suisse demain jusqu'à la fin de la semaine. Téléphonez-moi, si vous le voulez bien, lundi prochain le 12 vers midi.

J'ai vu hier soir Le Square de Marguerite Duras au Nouveau Théâtre de Poche, 65 Rue Rochechouart. Il ne faut pas rater ça. Ils ne peuvent pas faire de publicité et ça va se jouer (30 fois) pour ainsi dire sans qu'on le sache. Allez-y et dites à vos amis d'en faire autant. C'est (pour moi) un texte infiniment émouvant et Chauffard est ici remarquable. Il faut soutenir une chose pareille.[1]

J'espère pouvoir vous donner Krapp's Last Tape la semaine prochaine. Pour le moment je n'ai que ma copie personnelle dont je ne peux me séparer.

J'aurais grand plaisir à faire la connaissance de Cuny. Nous arrangerons ça à mon retour.[2]

4. Avigdor Arikha in his studio

Bien amicalement de nous deux.

Sam

ALS; 1 leaf, 1 side; InU, Arikha. Dating: opening of *Le Square*, 5 May 1958. Previous publication: Anne Atik, *How It Was: A Memoir of Samuel Beckett* (London: Faber and Faber, 2003) 50–51; transcribed here with variants.

Tuesday [6 May 1958] Paris

Dear AA

Thank you for your letter.

I leave for Switzerland tomorrow, till the end of the week. Phone me, if you would, next Monday 12th about noon.

Last night I saw *Le Square* by Marguerite Duras at the Nouveau Théâtre de Poche, 65 Rue Rochechouart. You mustn't miss it. They aren't able to do any publicity and it's going to be on (30 times) more or less unbeknown to anyone. Do go, and tell your friends to do the same. It is (for me) an infinitely affecting text, and Chauffard in this is most remarkable. Something like this has to be supported.[1]

I hope to be able to give you *Krapp's Last Tape* next week. For the moment I have only my own copy, which I can't let go of.

I would be very glad to meet Cuny. We'll arrange it on my return.[2]

All good wishes from both of us

Sam

1 SB had failed to see *Le Square* at the theatre when it was first produced (see 12 January 1957). It ran at the Nouveau Théâtre de Poche with the same cast and director as at the Studio des Champs-Elysées, but with the set redesigned by Jacques Noël for the smaller theatre. Claude Olivier summarized in his highly laudatory review: "La valeur de cette pièce ne tient nullement à ce qu'on pourrait appeler sa formule, sa structure. Si j'en juge en me référant aux critères habituels, je suis amené à conclure: ce n'est pas du théâtre, car il n'y a aucune action, aucune intrigue, pas de péripéties ni de mouvement." ("Je ne sais quel charme," *Les Lettres Françaises* 721 [8 May 1958] 10.) (The value of this play in no way depends on what one might call its formula, its structure. If I am to make a judgement by reference to the usual criteria, I am driven to concluding that it is not theatre at all, for there is no action, no plot, no ups and downs, no movement.)

2 After an early career as a set designer and painter, Alain Cuny (1908–1994) was by this time a well-established theatre and film actor. Arikha had met and become friends with him when working as a dubber of films.

ETHNA MACCARTHY-LEVENTHAL
DUBLIN

June 2nd 1958 Ussy-sur-Marne

Bien chère Ethna

Forgive my not having replied before now to your letter. I have been overwhelmed with work, finishing my translation of L'Innommable for the promised date. It goes off to NY today.[1]

Your clinical picture is grim, but no real pain are mighty words. I can't think or talk of it, you have my head, and eyes, in the sand.

I went to Berne for four days for a big rétrospective at the Kunsthalle of Bram van Velde. I was glad I went (driving with friends), but came back very tired with convivialities and Paul Klees.[2] I saw the bears, two babies being bottle-fed by the keeper, their mother or I suppose mothers have tried to eat them, and a pair of adults, in a corner, in the shadows, yawning, initiating an absent-minded copulation that looked as if it must last 48 hours at least. The Aare is green and foaming and all hairpin meanderings and from the terrace of the Federal Palace the Bernese Oberland jagged and dazzling. The devilish Föhn was doing its stuff, not blowing, just there, very limpifying and exasperating. Four days was plenty.[3]

I've written in English a stage monologue for Pat Magee which I think you will like if no one else. It will appear in the next number of the Evergreen Review and I'll send you a copy as soon as it's out.[4]

I haven't seen much of the Haydens lately. Waddington has been here and bought more from him and said he would give him a one-man in his new gallery next year. Josette mourante as usual, all dope and depression.[5]

I'm told Cusack is in Nice again for more ectomy. He had another attack of some kind. Poor man, what a state he must be in. Sally is with them.[6]

I don't know where to suggest you should go for sun, elephants and quiet. I needn't tell you my francs are yours, so don't let money considerations deter you.

Yod's film is on in Brussels and he wrote suggesting I should join him and her there, but I can't make it.[7] Godot is or was on there at the Rideau and a Frisco group is doing there the same old favourite in American, the same that played for the convicts in San Quentin. Good production, I'm told, but I won't go for it either. If I were a free agent I wouldn't stir from my little windy hill here until they came to fetch me. I've been a week here alone now, two words with the rural postman every second day.[8]

Fin de Partie is having a brief tour in Holland this month, Blin's production, then going on the the [sic] Venice Biennale, where I'm invited expenses paid but won't go either.[9]

Have now to try and excogitate a libretto for Marcel Mihalovici (bouffe!). So far can't get beyond the first line: "pas envie de chanter ce soir." Then I suppose translate Textes [p]our Rien. Che vitaccia!

Chère Ethna, je t'embrasse bien tendrement.[10]

Love to Con.

s/ Sam

TLS; 1 leaf, 2 sides; *env to* Mrs Leventhal, 35 Lr. Baggot St. Dublin IRLANDE; *pm* 3-6-58, La Ferté-sous-Jouarre; TxU, Leventhal Collection, 1.7.

1 On 20 May, SB wrote to Leslie Daiken (known as Yod, from his family name Yodaiken, 1912–1964; Profile, II) that he was "working like mad" on the translation (NLI, 22, 489 [Scrapbook], Daiken Collection). Five days later he wrote to Barney Rosset: "I prefer to send you the whole thing in one lot, so as to have the possibility of a final revision of first half in light of second. God knows what will happen between now and then, it looks like being touch and go." (NSyU.)

2 The Paul Klee Collection at the Kunsthalle in Berne is extensive.

3 The bear is the heraldic symbol for Berne. The Föhn is a downslope mountain wind which brings rapidly warming temperatures and fluctuating atmospheric pressure.

4 Knowlson suggests that Ethna is the girl in the punt in *Krapp's Last Tape* (*Damned to Fame*, 397–398).

5 Hayden's wife Josette was "mourante" (in the last stages).

6 Illness and treatment of Ralph Cusack: 21 April 1958 to Leventhal, n. 3. The sister of his wife Nancy was Sara Estella Sinclair Armstrong (known as Sally, 1910–1976).

7 Leslie Daiken's *One Potato, Two Potato* (1957), a film about London children at play, represented England in the Documentary class at the Festival mondial du film in Brussels; it received an Award of Merit.

8 *En attendant Godot* was performed from 16 April to 31 May at the Rideau Théâtre, Palais des Beaux-Arts, directed by André Deprez.

The San Francisco Actor's Workshop, founded in 1952 by Herbert Blau (1926–2013) and Jules Irving (1925–1979), was invited by the United States Department of State to represent "the American regional theatre movement at the 1958 International Exhibition in Brussels" (www.sanfranciscoactorsworkshop.com, accessed 15 March 2012). Blau, assisted by Alan Mandell (b. 1928), had directed the production of *Waiting for Godot* in the San Quentin State Prison, on 19 November 1957 to an audience of 1,000 ("Workshop Players Score Hit Here," *San Quentin News* 17.24, 26 November 1958: 1, 3); it played at the York Playhouse in New York for five weeks (5 August to 13 September) before opening in Brussels at the World's Fair in mid-September.

9 Blin's production of *Fin de partie* (with Jean Martin, Georges Adet, and Alice Reichen) was to be performed in Rotterdam, Scheveningen, and Amsterdam (21–25 June) as part of the Holland Festival 1958, and in Italy as part of the International Theatre Festival of the Venice Biennale on 3–4 July. The program included Deryk Mendel in *Acte sans paroles I* (IMEC-Fonds Samuel Beckett, Boîte 11, *Fin de Partie – Divers*; Beckett and Schneider, *No Author Better Served*, 45).

10 Libretto for Mihalovici: 10 April 1958, n. 5.
"Che vitaccia!" (Miserable life, wretched existence!)
"Chère Ethna, je t'embrasse bien tendrement" (Dear Ethna, a loving kiss).

THOMAS MACGREEVY
DUBLIN

June 2nd 1958 Ussy-sur-Marne

Dear Tom

Forgive my not having replied before now to your welcome letter. I have been overpowered with work finishing my translation of L'Innommable for the promised date. I dispatched it with relief to NY today and feel flat and tired after the effort and dissatisfied with the result.

I hope you have found satisfactory quarters on ground level somewhere less exposed to visits than the Burlington. The Lucan Spa seems a good idea. I often think of our jaunts there with JBY.[1]

I went to Berne (driving with Bram and friends) and stayed four days. The exhibition was very fine and our reception very magnificent. Too many more or less forced visits to private collections, too many Klees. The town is pleas[a]nt on the brisk green hairpin meandering Aare. From the terrace of the Federal Terrace clearly visible the Bernese Oberland with the Jungfraujoch. The horrible Föhn was blowing, blowing is not the word, one wished the damn thing would blow. Too many receptions and convivialities and people for me, never a moment alone, I was glad to get back. I met Frau Gideon (Joyce's friend) and a very pleasant Zurich doctor, I forget his name, who said that Joyce died in his arms, that but for misdiagnosis or tardy diagnosis he could have been saved and and [sic] even with that would have been saved today.[2] Both naturally hostile to Giorgio, who by the way is now in Munich, his doctoresse having set up there in practice.[3] Chagall's daughter Ida, married to Meyer director of the Kunsthalle, was our hostess, and a most agreeable one. Their hospitality was unbelievable.[4]

Suzanne who has been in Paris this past week received the visit (unannounced) of Stephen Joyce and his wife just back from Boston where he achieved a degree.[5]

I am urgently invited all expenses paid to Venice with Blin's production of Fin de Partie at the Biennale, but shall not go.

Edward has won the senior music cup at Columba's playing a Haendel flute sonata. A remarkable achievement considering he only started the flute 6 months ago, with a French teacher who plays in the Radio Eireann orchestra and whose name I forget, he used to know Rampal at the Conservatoire. Edward got 91%. He must really be talented. Jean is lepping with delight.[6]

We saw a wonderful Cézanne in Berne in a private collection (Mueller), a self-portrait painted at the very end. Overwhelmingly sad. A blind old broken man. You probably know it in reproduction.[7]

I am taking a week away from pen and paper in the open air, then I suppose back to them. They're a sorry pair, but finally I suppose about the best one has.

Write soon, dear Tom, with good news of yourself and your new surroundings. If Suzanne were here she would join me in the fond love I send you and wishes for a speedy return now to all your old activity.

Always

s/ Sam

TLS; 1 leaf, 2 sides; TCD, MS 10402/214.

1 The Burlington Hotel: 21 April 1958 to MacGreevy, n. 1. The Lucan Spa Hotel, Lucan Road, Dublin 20, was west of Phoenix Park; Yeats frequently sketched in the area (Pyle, *Jack B. Yeats: A Biography*, 162; Hilary Pyle, *Jack B. Yeats: His Watercolours, Drawings and Pastels* [Blackrock: Irish Academic Press, 1993] 193).

2 Carola Giedion-Welcker (1893–1979) was an art historian of modern sculpture; she married Sigfried Giedion (1888–1968), the author of *Space, Time and Architecture*. She had assisted in the arrangements for Joyce's return to Zurich in 1940. Dr H. Freysz was the surgeon who attended Joyce before his death (Richard Ellmann, *James Joyce, New and Revised Edition* [Oxford: Oxford University Press, 1982] 622, 739, 741). SB writes "Gideon" for "Giedion."

3 Giorgio Joyce married Dr. Asta Osterwalder Jahnke (1917–1993) in 1954.

4 SB received hospitality from Franz Meyer (1919–2007), then Director of the Kunsthalle in Zurich and Editor of the catalogue for the exhibition, and his wife Ida Chagall (1916–1994) (Knowlson, *Damned to Fame*, 408).

5 Stephen James Joyce (b. 1932) graduated from Harvard in 1958. SB had been witness at the wedding of Stephen Joyce and Solange Raytchine (n.d.) in April 1955.

6 The Dublin teacher of Edward Beckett* (b. 1943) was André Prieur (1921–2005), Principal Flautist with the RTE Symphony Orchestra. Prieur had studied with Marcel Moyse (1889–1984) at the Paris Conservatory and knew Jean-Pierre Rampal (1922–2000). Jean Wright Beckett (1906–1966).

7 Josef Mueller's collection included *Le Marin*, also known as *Le Jardinier Vallier vu de face* (1905), by Cézanne; the painting is also considered a self-portrait (John Rewald, *The Paintings of Paul Cézanne: A Catalogue Raisonné*, 2 vols. [New York: Harry N. Abrams, 1996] I, 333; II, 557–558).

MANIA PÉRON
PARIS

9.6.58 Ussy

Chère Mania

Je ne trouve pas grand'chose à redire à votre traduction.

Burns and thrills sont des verbes. On s'attendrait plutôt à "burn and thrill." "Qu'il n'en brûle" me paraît la meilleure traduction.[1]

Deux vers plus loin je crois qu'il faut lire "As they (absorb) the light etc." malgré la laideur syntaxique qui en résulte.[2]

"Myriad-moulded": vos deux interprétations se défendent et je ne sais vraiment pas laquelle est la bonne. "Multiforme" a l'avantage d'être presque aussi ambigu que l'original.[3]

"Lightning wrought and moulded" – pas question d'un trait d'union. Mais "of" peut exprimer l'agence et "par une pensée indomptable" est à envisager.[4]

"Clasp" est très fort, je vous propose donc "étreindre".[5]

Strophe 2, 6<u>me</u> vers, "aught" veut dire "<u>tout</u> ce que ton souffle est capable de lancer". J'ai donc ajouté "tous" aux "traits".[6]

Dernier vers de la même strophe: il veut dire "la mort n'est pour rien dans sa gloire". Je préfère donc "part" à "rôle".[7]

"Irremeable": rien à voir avec "irremediable" et vous l'avez bien traduit. "Meare" en latin veut dire "passer". Cf. "meatus" = passage. "Remeant" = "returning" existe également, quoique rare.[8]

Affreux poème en effet.

Très heureux que vous l'ayez échappé tellement belle.

Je viens de terminer ma traduction de L'Innommable et ne m'en suis pas encore relevé.

affectueusement Sam

ALS; 1 leaf, 1 side; *env to* Madame Péron, 69 Rue de la Tombe-Issoire, Paris 14me; *pm* 9-6-58, La Ferté-sous-Jouarre; TxU, Beckett (Lake) Collection, 17.21.

9.6.58 Ussy

Dear Mania

I have little in the way of criticisms to make of your translation.

Burns and *thrills* are verbs. One would expect rather *burn* and *thrill*. *Qu'il n'en brûle* seems to me the best translation.[1]

Two lines further on I think that one has to read "As they (absorb) the light etc.", in spite of the syntactic ugliness that results.[2]

"Myriad-moulded": a case could be made for both your interpretations, and I really do not know which is the right one. "Multiforme" has the advantage of being nearly as ambiguous as the original.[3]

"Lightning wrought and moulded" – no question of a hyphen. But "of" can express agency, and "par une pensée indomptable" could be considered.[4]

"Clasp" is very strong, so I would propose "étreindre" to you.[5]

Stanza 2, line 6, "aught" means "*tout* ce que ton souffle est capable de lancer". So I have added "tous" to "traits".[6]

Last line of the same stanza: it means "la mort n'est pour rien dans sa gloire". And so I prefer "part" to "role".[7]

"Irremeable": no connection with "irremediable", and your translation was good. "Meare" in Latin means "to pass". Cf. "meatus" = passage. "Remeant" = "returning" also exists, although rare.[8]

Dreadful poem, indeed.

Very glad that you had such a lucky escape.

I have just finished my translation of *L'Innommable* and still haven't got over it.

Love

Sam

1 Mania Péron has been translating "A Sequence of Sonnets on the Death of Robert Browning" by Algernon Charles Swinburne, probably for her class at the Lycée Buffon; SB comments here on Sonnet 1 which says of Browning's eyes: "they read / With sense more keen and spirit of sight more true / Than burns and thrills in sunrise" (lines 1–3) (Algernon Charles Swinburne, *The Complete Works*, VI, ed. Sir Edmund Gosse and Thomas James Wise [London: William Heinemann, 1925] 145; all citations are to this edition).

2 The two lines in question run: "and absorbs the glory round it shed, / As they the light of ages quick and dead" (145).

3 Sonnet 1, lines 12–13: "Stand fast and shine and smile, assured that nought / may fade of all their myriad-moulded fame" (145).

4 Sonnet 1, lines 9–10: "The works of words whose life seems lightning wrought, / And moulded of unconquerable thought" (145).

5 Sonnet 1, line 14: "Nor England's memory clasp not Browning's name" (145).

6 The line runs: "And bright as hope, can aught thy breath may dart" (146).

7 Sonnet 2, line 14: "What part hast thou then in his glory, Death?" (146).

8 Sonnet 4, line 4: "Beyond the irremeable outer seas that shine" (146).

RICHARD SEAVER
NEW YORK

June 21st 1958 Ussy-sur-Marne

Dear Seaver

Thanks for your letter of June 15th. I am glad you are agreeable to a joint translation of the Nouvelles & Textes. Only the latter are meant to be for nothing, so perhaps we should translate "et" by "followed by".[1] I have not yet recovered from The Unnamable and shall not start on my part for some months to come. I should prefer to receive the stories in one batch and I think for you too this may well prove to be more convenient, because of the recurrence of certain rhythms and formulae not only within one story, but throughout the three. I think "L'Expulsé" may be simply translated "The Expelled". "Calmant" I translated "pain-killer" in Endgame and "anodyne" in The Unnamable, but I think here, because of the way it comes into The End, "sedative" would perhaps be preferable to either.[2]

I read Trocchi's piece in the last Evergreen and liked it very much indeed.[3]

The Mexican Anthology is a purely alimentary job I was reduced to doing for UNESCO in 1950. I was rather handicapped by my ignorance of Spanish. But most of the poems chosen by Octavio Paz are so extremely bad that not much is lost.[4]

I am sorry to have missed you when you were over. I am only an hour out of town and would have gladly taken a day off from my Marne void if I had known you were in Paris.[5]

Pat did a brief talk on my work the other day for the Third Programme, but inaudible here.[6]

Yours ever
s/ Sam Beckett

TLS; 1 leaf, 1 side; TxU, Seaver, R 16501.

1 Seaver had written to SB indicating that he expected to finish translation of "The End" by the end of the month (TxU, R 16501L, Seaver to Beckett, 1958–1975).

2 SB translates "calmant" as "pain-killer" in *Endgame*, where it appears ten times. In *L'Innommable*, the term "calmant" is not used (Samuel Beckett, *L'Innommable* [Paris: Editions de Minuit, 1953]; this edition is referred to below, as is the English translation, *The Unnamable* [New York: Grove Press, 1958]). SB translates "analgésiques" (Minuit, 67) as "pain-killers" (Grove, 45), and "me prodiguant les soins indispensables" (Minuit, 69) becomes "taking my anodynes" (Grove, 46). "Laudanum" is the same in both editions (Minuit, 68; Grove, 45).

In "The End," the word "calmant" is used at the close of the story where it is translated as "calmative" (*Nouvelles et Textes pour rien*, 122; Samuel Beckett, *Stories and Texts for Nothing* [New York: Grove Weidenfeld, 1967] 72).

3 An excerpt, "From Cain's Book," by Alexander Trocchi, was published in *Evergreen Review* 1.4 (1957) 48–74.

4 SB's translations for the *Anthology of Mexican Poetry* edited by Octavio Paz: 27 February 1950, n. 5, and SB to Edith Greenburg, 20 October 1956.

5 Seaver had been in Europe one month earlier.

6 Patrick Bowles gave a radio talk on 15 June on the BBC Third Programme: "'Molloy': A Masterwork of Disillusion"; this was published as "How Samuel Beckett Sees the Universe," *The Listener* 59 (19 June 1958) 1011–1012.

MARC WILKINSON
LONDON

June 28th 1958

6 Rue des Favorites
Paris 15me

Dear Mr Wilkinson

Thank you for your most interesting letter of June 20th.[1]

I'm afraid the kind of text you have in mind is quite beyond my powers. I am incapable of such organised or pre-organised writing and little capable, I fear also, of creative collaboration.

I wrote recently, in English, a short stage monologue (20 minutes) of which Time is the indubitable villain. It will be produced (some day) with Endgame by George Devine. The text is to appear in the coming number of the Evergreen Review which is distributed in England by John Calder. It might conceivably, in a small way, lend itself to such musical treatment as you expound in your letter.[2]

I really do not know what other writer to suggest. Jean Genêt [sic]?

I look forward to hearing your "Voices" and to meeting you when you come to Paris.

Yours sincerely

s/

Samuel Beckett

TLS, 1 leaf, 1 side; Wilkinson Collection.

1 Marc Wilkinson* (b. 1929) composed music for theatre, film, and television; he later became resident composer of the National Theatre (1963–1974).

2 Wilkinson had requested SB's permission to "set to music an extract from Godot"; SB had replied on 21 March, "There is no objection on my part" (Wilkinson Collection). This piece was *Voices*, for soprano and chamber orchestra (Marc Wilkinson and Samuel Beckett, *Voices: From the Play Waiting for Godot* [London: Universal Edition, 1960]).

BARBARA BRAY
PURLEY, SURREY

July 6th 1958 | 6 Rue des Favorites

Dear Barbara

Many thanks for your good letter.

The Malone tapes have arrived Av Hoche and I am to hear them tomorrow afternoon.[1]

The next day I fly, without zest, to Belgrade, to get rid of my Godot and Molloy dinars. Ten days should do the trick. Then back to Paris and Ussy.[2]

I wish I could do another radio script for you. I have tried, without result. All my work for some time past leaves me with the feeling of "restes accom[m]odés". I can't go on with that cookery. I feel a last zone just there beside me, perhaps some day I'll stumble into it.[3]

I find Adamov neither gentle nor charming, but he may well be both.[4]

I hear Devine is reduced to trying to get the LC to change his "mind". Sounds like statistical physics. He must have abandoned his idea of a Royal Court Club.[5] Blin and his merry men have been touring Endgame in Holland. In Scheveningen at the Kurhaus set and props, including the mime tape, were burnt to ashes. Last Thursday and Friday they played for the cold Venetians.[6]

It is very good of you to offer to put me up. Perhaps some day I shall avail myself of your kindness. At the moment I feel I am only fit for something like the Regent Palace.[7]

I hope you will be over in August, with Donald and Magee. I don't know where I'll go from Belgrade or how long I'll stay there and am not having my mail forwarded. So I can't have news of you before the end of the month.

Affectionately

s/ Sam

TLS; 1 leaf, 1 side; *env to* Mrs Barbara Bray, 121 Brighton Road, Purley, Surrey, Angleterre; *pm* 7-7-58, Paris; TCD, MS 10948/1/7.

1 SB had requested that the tapes of the BBC Third Programme broadcast of readings by Patrick Magee from *Malone Dies* be sent to the BBC Paris office at 59 Avenue Hoche.

2 *Waiting for Godot* had been translated into Serbo-Croat as *Čekajući Godoa* by Andreja Milicevic in 1953, although it was not published until 1964 (Beograd: Srpska književna zadruga, 1964). The play was rehearsed and performed in clandestine circumstances in 1954, produced for the first time in the Eastern Bloc in 1955 by the Belgrade Drama Theatre, where it was banned; the play was given its first public performance from 17 December 1956 at the Atelier 212 in Belgrade. See Octavian Saiu, "Samuel Beckett Behind the Iron Curtain: The Reception in Eastern Europe," in Matthew Feldman and Mark Nixon, eds., *The International Reception of Samuel Beckett* (London: Continuum International Publishing, 2009) 254; and Predrag Todorović, "Godot in Belgrade," *The Beckett Circle*, 34.2 [Fall 2011] 8–10.

The dinar was not convertible with other European currencies until 1966.

3 "Restes accommodés" (tarted-up leftovers).

4 Barbara Bray had been meeting playwrights Arthur Adamov, Eugène Ionesco, and Robert Pinget in Paris and London to commission work from them for the BBC Third Programme (Bray to the editors, 6 December 2007).

5 On 4 July, George Devine held a reading of *Endgame* at the Royal Court Theatre for Sir St. Vincent Troubridge (1895–1963) who was representing the Lord Chamberlain's Office (George Devine to Sir Norman Gwatkin, Lord Chamberlain's Office, 30 June 1958; TxU, English Stage Company, 1.2). Troubridge wrote to Sir Norman Gwatkin on 5 July: "I saw nothing truly objectionable except the specific line about God" (Lord Chamberlain's Office, British Library 58/578). Devine wrote to SB on 5 July: "I still feel desperately that to be forced to do it under Club conditions is from my point of view a capitulation to the attitudes of the Lord Chamberlain's Office and all that it implies" (TxU, English Stage Company, 1.2).

6 The *Fin de partie* tour in Holland and in Venice: 2 June 1958 to Ethna MacCarthy-Leventhal, n. 9. The fire on the night of 23 June at the Kurhaus-cabaret, Scheveningen, destroyed the sets of *Fin de partie* and *Acte sans paroles I*; however, Blin's company was able to perform *Fin de partie* as scheduled at the De La Mar-theater in Amsterdam on 24 and 25 June. The soundtrack for *Acte sans paroles I* could not be replaced in time, therefore it was omitted ("Kurhaus-cabaret door brand vrijwel verwoest," *Utrechts Nieuwsblad*, 24 June 1958: 1).

7 The Regent Palace Hotel, Piccadilly, London.

GEORGE DEVINE
ROYAL COURT THEATRE, LONDON

July 7th 1958

6 Rue des Favorites
Paris 15me

Dear George

Thanks for your letter to which I hasten to reply before leaving Paris.

It is quite impossible for me to consent to a weakening of this passage.

If the position is that the Lord Chamberlain, having taken his stand against "bastard", is now committed to its removal, but would accept a different term of more or less equal force, then a compromise is still possible.[1]

I could accept, for example, "The swine, he doesn't exist".

If on the other hand, as I suppose, his demand is for a change of term that will render the line quite inoffensive, i.e. kill it, then I have nothing to offer him.

As I do not know where I shall be in Jugoslavia I can't leave instructions for the forwarding of my mail, so there's no chance of my hearing from you now before the end of the month, when I shall be back in Paris.

Yours ever
s/ Sam

TLS; 1 leaf, 1 side; TxU, English Stage Company, 1.2.

1 Following the reading of *Endgame* on 4 July, Devine reported to SB that St. Vincent Troubridge's unofficial word was that the issue "now boiled down to one word [. . .] 'bastard'." He added: "I am therefore writing once again to ask if you would be ready to consider submitting a couple of alternatives for this word" (5 July 1958; TxU, English Stage Company, 1.2).

JACOBA VAN VELDE
AMSTERDAM

15.7.58

Hotel Beograd
LOVRAN
Yougoslavie

Chère Tonny

Merci de votre lettre. Ça n'a pas l'air folichon là où vous êtes. Vous devriez venir dans ce pays dépenser vos dinars. C'est ce que je fais en ce moment, avec Suzanne et Jean Martin. Nous avons été à Belgrade et vu Madame Kaka et son mari. Elle débloque plus que jamais mais a été formidablement gentille, Konstantinovic aussi. J'ai eu du mal à me faire payer mes droits (opérations bancaires très compliquées), ce qui nous a obligés à rester à Belgrade un peu trop longtemps.[1] Mais si on prévient un peu à l'avance on n'a même pas besoin d'aller jusqu'à Belgrade, on peut les faire virer sur une ville de la côté [*for* côte]. Ici c'est un petit port près de Fiume (Rijeca). Mer et soleil magnifiques, je suis dans la mer toute la journée, vous adoreriez ça. Kaka nous a proposé sa maison à Rovin[j] bien sûr, et à vous aussi elle la donnerait certainement. Là avec 150.000 dinars vous pourriez vivre trois mois facilement. Ce serait toujours ça de pris à l'ennemi. Nous restons ici jusqu'au 27, puis regagnons la merde via Zagreb. Jean rentre par Venise où ils ont donné Fin de Partie il y a 10 jours.[2] Nous avons retrouvé Roger et Nicole ici, ils sont partis à Paris ce matin. J'ai été à Berne avec Bram, Jacques, Andrée et Cie. Belle exposition, accueil formidable. J'ai écrit un petit monologue qui sera donné à Londres avec Fin de Partie à la place du mime. A part ça rien, sauf achèvement de la traduction de L'Innommable (déjà placards corrigés).

Affectueusement

Sam

ALS; 1 leaf, 1 side; BNF, 19794/54.

15.7.58

Hotel Beograd
LOVRAN
Yugoslavia

Dear Tonny

Thank you for your letter. Where you are does not sound like much fun. You ought to come and spend your dinars in this country. That is what I am doing at the moment, with Suzanne and Jean Martin. We have been to Belgrade and seen Madame Kaća and her husband. She is crazier than ever, but was tremendously nice. Konstantinovic too. I had trouble getting my rights paid (very complicated banking operations), which forced us to stay on in Belgrade rather too long.[1] But if one gives a little notice, one does not even have to go all the way to Belgrade: one can have them transferred to a coastal town. Here it is a little port near Fiume (Rijeca). Magnificent sea and sun. I am in the sea all day, you would adore it. Kaća offered us her house in Rovinj of course, and she would certainly give it to you too. There, on 150.000 dinars, you could easily live for three months. That much more the enemy wouldn't get their hands on. We are staying here till the 27th, then back to the dungheap via Zagreb. Jean is going back by way of Venice where they put on *Endgame* 10 days ago.[2] We caught up with Roger and Nicole here. They left for Paris this morning. I have been to Berne with Bram, Jacques, Andrée & co. Fine exhibition, wonderful welcome for us. I have written a little monologue which will be put on in London along with *Endgame* instead of the mime.

That apart, nothing, except finishing off the translation of *L'Innommable* (galleys already corrected).

Love

Sam

1 SB's trip to Yugoslavia was motivated not least by the wish to spend his royalties which could not be transferred internationally. An extract from *Molloy* had been published by the Kosmos publishing house at which Kaća Samardžić (d. 1996), wife of the philosopher Radomir Konstantinović (1928–2011), was a reader. Writing the "ć" (pronounced "ch") "k", SB plays here on Kaća's name.

2 Jean Martin and Roger Blin had played in two performances of *Fin de partie* at the Venice Biennale on 3 and 4 July (1958, Festival international du Théâtre, Biennale; Archivio Storico).

RADOMIR KONSTANTINOVIĆ AND KAĆA SAMARDŽIĆ BELGRADE, YUGOSLAVIA

20.7.58 HOTEL MAJESTIC, BEOGRAD

Lovran

Chers amis

On m'a remis hier soir vos deux lettres, arrivées en même temps. Merci de la photo. Mon passage à Belgrade semble vous avoir créé pas mal d'ennuis à tous les deux, et j'en suis navré. Je suis prêt à vous signer un certificat comme quoi vous n'y êtes pour rien et que tout est la faute de mon sale caractère.[1] Nous sommes très touchés par l'empressement que vous mettez à nous inviter dans votre maison de Rovinj et nous regrettons vivement de ne pas pouvoir vous y retrouver. Il m'est absolument impossible de m'absenter plus longtemps de Paris et nous avons pris toutes nos dispositions pour y retourner le 28, partant d'ici le 27. J'espère que ce n'est que partie remise et qu'une autre fois nous pourrons profiter de votre hospitalité. Moi aussi j'ai beaucoup regretté de ne pouvoir parler avec Rade. J'ai lu l'extrait de la Souricière avec le plus vif intérêt. La traduction est de toute évidence très insuffisante.[2] Je lis en ce moment le texte radiophonique et en suis très pris. Je vous en reparlerai quand je l'aurai terminé.[3] Vous êtes tout à fait gentils d'avoir fait le nécessaire pour que je puisse toucher ici les quelques dinars que me vaut la publication d'un extrait de Molloy.[4] Je ne les ai pas encore reçus. Pour ce qui est de ma biographie je ne vois vraiment pas ce que je pourrai ajouter aux éléments que vous possédez déjà. Enfin je vous indique sur la feuille ci-jointe, et à toutes fins utiles, les têtes de chapitres de cette regrettable histoire, mais j'ai l'impression que là il n'y a rien que vous ne connaissiez déjà. Si vous avez des précisions d'ordre biographique à me demander, je serai heureux de vous les fournir.[5]

Nous nous plaisons bien ici et nous garderons un très bon souvenir de notre bref séjour en Yougoslavie, et surtout de Beograd et des heures passées avec vous deux.

Bien amicalement

Votre Sam. Beckett

Chers Kaća et Rade,

Encore une fois mille mercis pour votre accueil. Sam vous dit d'autre part le plaisir que nous aurions eu à aller à Rovinj. Malheureusement c'est impossible.

Nous pensons plus particulièrement à vous (bien que nous parlions de vous chaque jour) à l'heure des confitures!

Elles sont délicieuses.

Bien à vous, avec l'amitié de

Jean Martin

Chers vous deux,

Malheureusement je ne sais pas écrire
Malheureusement je ne sais pas parler
Malheureusement je ne sais pas nager
C'est triste.
Mais je peux vous dire que vous êtes tout à fait gentils tous les deux.

Votre

Suzanne

ALS (facsimile and transcription); 2 leaves, 2 sides; *letterhead*; previous publication Radomir Konstantinović, *Beket prijatelj* (Beograd: Otkrovenje, 2000) 17–22; transcribed here with variants.

20.7.58 HOTEL MAJESTIC, BEOGRAD
Lovran

My dear friends

Your two letters were delivered yesterday at the same time. Thank you for the photo. My stay in Belgrade seems to have made quite a lot of trouble for you both, and I am really sorry. I am ready to sign a certificate to the effect that none of it is your fault and that it is all the fault of my foul character.[1] We are greatly touched by the eagerness with which you invite us to your house in Rovinj, and regret keenly that we can't join you there. It is quite impossible for me to stay away from Paris any longer, and we have made all the arrangements for getting back on the 28th, leaving here on the 27th. I hope that it is only a postponement, and that another time we shall be able to take advantage of your hospitality. I too am very sorry that I wasn't able to have a talk with Rade. I have read the excerpt from *La Souricière* with great interest. The translation is manifestly very unsatisfactory.[2] At the moment I am reading the text for radio, and am greatly taken with it. I'll say more about it when I've finished it.[3] It is very kind of you to have done the needful for me to be paid the few dinars that an excerpt from *Molloy* has earned me here.[4] I have not yet received them. As for my biography, I really don't see what I could add to the material that you have already. Anyhow, on the enclosed sheet I am setting down, for whatever use it may have, the chapter headings of this sorry history, but I have the feeling that there is nothing that you don't already know. If you need more detailed biographical information, I would be happy to supply it.[5]

We are enjoying being here, and will have very good memories of our short stay in Yugoslavia, and above all of Beograd and the time spent with you two.

Warmest wishes

Your Sam. Beckett

Dear Kaća and Rade

Once again a thousand thanks for your welcome. Sam is telling you too how much we would have enjoyed going to Rovinj. Unfortunately it is not possible.

We think of you specially (although we talk about you every day) at jam time!

They are delicious.

Fondly, and with the good wishes of

Jean Martin

Dear both of you

Unfortunately I cannot write

Unfortunately I cannot speak

Unfortunately I cannot swim

It is sad.

But I can tell you that you are both very nice.

Your

Suzanne

1 On 27 April, SB had written to Kaća Samardžić: "Cela m'a fait grand plaisir de vous rencontrer, vous et votre mari, chez Jacoba van Velde" (Konstantinović, *Beket prijatelj*, 7–8) (It was a great pleasure to meet you and your husband, at Jacoba van Velde's).

The photograph, which depicted Beckett with Samardžić walking outside the building of the Kosmos publishing house (reproduced in *Beket prijatelj*, 23), had been taken by an uninvited press photographer on 12 July and published in *Politika* with the heading "Samuel Beckett in Yugoslavia." The couple were acutely aware that SB did not want it to be public knowledge that he was in Yugoslavia; also that he loathed all publicity.

2 Konstantinović's novel *Mišolovka* (The Mouse-Trap) had been published by Kosmos in Belgrade in 1956, and translated into French as *La Souricière*.

3 SB has read Konstantinović's radio play, *Saobraćajna nesreća* (1958; Traffic Accident), in a German translation by Milo Dor (pseud. of Milutin Doroslovac), *Der Zeuge* (*The Columbia Guide to the Literatures of Eastern Europe Since 1945* [New York: Columbia University Press, 2003] 298).

4 In his account of his meeting with Beckett, Konstantinović reports being unable to recollect which passages from *Molloy* had been published, or where (*Beket prijatelj*, 29).

5 This last sentence is inserted in the top margin with an arrow leading to it. SB does attach to this letter a list of his major works in English and French (*Beket prijatelj*, 32).

RADOMIR KONSTANTINOVIĆ AND KAĆA SAMARDŽIĆ BELGRADE, YUGOSLAVIA

25.7.58 LOVRAN

Chers amis

Comme promis je vous renvoie ci-joint les deux extraits de La Souricière. Ils m'ont fait une forte impression. Il faudrait revoir sérieusement la traduction française.

Der Zeuge m'a également beaucoup plu. Ça devrait très bien marcher à la radio. J'ai l'impression que le traducteur a un peu simplifié par endroits. Il n'en reste pas moins que même en allemand c'est un texte très fort et très émouvant et dont la lecture me fait vivement regretter de ne pas mieux connaître le travail de Rade.

Nous quittons Lovran demain pour regagner Paris, Jean par Venise, nous par Zagreb où nous prendrons l'avion lundi le 28.

Je n'ai pas reçu l'argent de l'extrait de Molloy. Ça ne fait rien.

Notre séjour ici s'est très bien passé, malgré les orages, et nous garderons un très bon souvenir de notre premier voyage en Yougoslavie. J'espère qu'il y en aura d'autres.

Nous vous remercions encore une fois pour tout ce que vous avez fait pour nous et vous envoyons nos meilleures amitiés.

Sam. Beckett

ALS (facsimile and transcription); 1 leaf, 1 side; previous publication Konstantinović, *Beket prijatelj*, 33–35; transcribed here with variants.

25.7.58 LOVRAN

My dear friends

As promised I am sending back the two excerpts from *La Souricière*. I was greatly impressed by them. There would have to be a serious revision of the French translation.

I also greatly liked *Der Zeuge*. It should work very well on radio. I get the impression that the translator has simplified a little here and there. Nevertheless, even in German it is a very powerful and very moving text, and reading it makes me regret not knowing Rade's work better.

We leave Lovran tomorrow to go back to Paris, Jean via Venice, us via Zagreb where we will take the plane on Monday 28th.

I didn't get the money for the *Molloy* excerpt. It doesn't matter.

Our stay here has gone off very well, in spite of the storms, and we shall have very good memories of our first trip to Yugoslavia. I hope that there will be others.

Our thanks once again to you for all that you have done for us, and we send our warmest wishes.

Sam. Beckett

GEORGE DEVINE
ROYAL COURT THEATRE, LONDON

July 28th 1958

6 Rue des Favorites
Paris 15me

Dear George

Thanks for your note of July 21st awaiting me here on my return yesterday from Titonia.[1]

To be quite frank with you I am very tired, and you must be even more so, of all this buggering around with guardsmen, riflemen and hussars. There are no alternatives to "bastard" agreeable to me. Nevertheless I have offered them "swine" in its place. This is definitely and finally as far as I'll go. What is the point of my submitting two other terms of equal "virulence", as they would necessarily be? Even if I could think of them, and I can't. If "swine" is not acceptable, then there is nothing left but to have a club production or else call the whole thing off. I simply refuse to play along any further with these licensing grocers.

I should like to assure you, whatever course you adopt, and to mark in a small way my gratitude to you personally and to the Royal Court theatre, that I undertake here and now to offer you the first option on UK rights of my next play, in the unlikely event of my ever writing another.

Yours ever
s/ Sam

TLS; 1 leaf, 1 side; *letter typed without indentation, paragraphs separated by line spaces*; TxU, English Stage Company, 1.2.

1 Devine had requested three replacements for "bastard [. . .] obviously leaving out such words as 'bugger' which will not be passed!" (Devine to SB, 21 July 1958; TxU, English Stage Company, 1.2).

SB refers to Marshal Josip Broz Tito, who ruled Yugoslavia from 1945 to 1980.

ROBERT PINGET
PARIS

3.9.58 Ussy

Cher Robert - Merci de votre mot. C'était bien l'autre soir. Ça m'a fait du bien de vous écouter et de vous parler. Un peu des semblables, non?[1] Je pense depuis à votre travail. J'espère qu'il marche mieux que le mien. J'en suis au gag des lampes. Envie de le pousser jusqu' à la frénésie. Mais n'en ferai rien. Et j'ai trouvé un oiseau chanteur, dans un coin. Je ne l'avais pas vu, rapport à l'obscurité. Tout d'un coup il chante. Dix secondes. Et un deuxième, mort, dans la même cage, sur le plancher. La femme? Le mari? Discussion ornitho. Plumage, ramage. Etc.[2]

Affectueusement de nous 2 et à bientôt
Sam

APCS; 1 leaf, 1 side; "Jouarre: Ancienne Abbaye Notre-Dame, Crypte Saint-Paul. Tombeau de l'évêque Agilbert"; *to* Monsieur Robert Pinget, 4 Rue de l'Université, Paris 7me; *pm* 4-9-58, La Ferté-sous-Jouarre; Burns Library, Samuel Beckett Collection, SB-RP.

3.9.58 Ussy

Dear Robert - Thanks for your letter. It was really nice, the other evening. It did me good to listen to you and talk to you. We're not all that unlike, wouldn't you say?[1] I've been thinking since then about your work. I hope it's going better than mine. I've got to the lamp gag. Feel like pushing it all the way to frenzy. But I'll do no such thing. And I've found a songbird, in a corner. I hadn't seen it, because of the dark. Suddenly it sings. Ten seconds. And a second one, dead, in the same cage, on the floor. The wife? The husband? Bandying of bird-lore. Plumage, song. Etc.[2]

Affectionately from the 2 of us, and till soon.

Sam

1 In an unpublished and undated typescript in the Bibliothèque littéraire Jacques Doucet entitled "Journal Pinget sur Beckett," Robert Pinget noted differences as well as similarities: "Pour moi je ne peux pas parler comme Beckett, parce qu'il a la voix même de l'impuissance acceptée (impuissance vis-à-vis de lui-même, vis-à-vis des autres; il se sent impuissant à rien changer), de la souffrance, de la maladie, du désespoir fondamental" (Doucet, unclassified, Pinget Collection, 1) (For myself, I cannot talk like Beckett, because his is the very voice of impotence accepted (impotence in respect of himself, in respect of others; he feels impotent to change anything), in respect of suffering, illness, fundamental despair).

2 To judge from what he wrote in his journal and memoir, Pinget appears to have discussed at length with SB the work in progress that will become *Fragment de théâtre II* (where the "lamp gag" is to be found) (CSP, 84). In his "Journal Pinget sur Beckett," he writes of SB's hopes for the play: "Le drame se dénoue par un accident, un événement imprévu, qui donne sa liberté au prévenu. Beckett veut faire quelque chose de grave, de racinien. N'y arrive pas. Dit que tout ce qu'il trouve est affreusement comique." (Doucet, unclassified, Pinget Collection, 1.) (The drama is resolved by an accident, an unforeseen event, which sets free the defendant. Beckett wants to do something of high seriousness, something Racinian. Can't manage it. Says that everything he comes up with is appallingly comical.) In "Notre ami Samuel Beckett," Pinget elaborates:

> Il m'a expliqué que ça le dégoûtait de tomber dans le dialogue amusant, facile. Il m'a souvent parlé avec amertume de la putainerie ou putasserie comme on voudra dont il faut faire preuve en écrivant une pièce de théâtre. S'occuper des réactions du public. Il ajoute qu'il a peut-être tort d'être aussi traditionnel mais qu'il n'envisage pas autrement le travail du dramaturge. D'où son dégoût à un moment donné pour le théâtre où on ne dit pas ce qu'on veut, comme dans le roman ou le poème, et sa volonté d'y renoncer définitivement. (Doucet, unclassified, Pinget Collection, "Notre ami Samuel Beckett," 15–16.) (He explained to me that he hated slipping into light amusing dialogue. He has often spoken bitterly about the ugly come-ons or wheedlings, take your pick, that you have to go in for when writing a play for performance. Bothering about the reactions of the public. He adds that maybe he is wrong to be so traditional, but that he can't envisage the dramatist's work any other way. Hence his disgust at one point for the theatre, where one doesn't say what one wants to, as in novels or poems, and his strong wish to give it up for good.)

BARBARA BRAY
PURLEY, SURREY

[19/20 September 1958] [Paris]

The Dome

Life goes on. Time passes. But much more agreeably in the company of my disreputable acquaintances, S.B. and P.M. Bonne soirée hier. Aujourd'hui bonne soirée. Bonne demain soirée. Dommage que vous n'en soyez pas – Sam. *The next time you call me Alice-in-Wonderland, you-are-dead! Pat Magee.*[1]

APCS; 1 leaf, 1 side; "Paris, La Place du Tertre"; *to* Mrs. B. Bray, 121, Brighton Road, Purley, ANGLETERRE; *pm* 21-9-58, Paris; TCD, MS 10948/1/711. *Dating*: from pm and from SB to H. O. White, 17 September 1958 (TCD, MS 3777/17). SB's note suggests that the evening began on 19 September and continued into the early hours of 20 September.

1 Postcard written jointly by Donald McWhinnie, SB, and Patrick Magee.

"Bonne soirée hier. Aujourd'hui bonne soirée. Bonne demain soirée. Dommage que vous n'en soyez pas – " (Nice evening yesterday. Today nice evening. Tomorrow – nice evening. Pity there's no you in it all –).

SB wrote to A. J. Leventhal: "McWhinnie is directing Krapp (i.e. Pat Magee) which is great security for me. They were both in Paris and we went into the script very carefully." (20 October 1958; TxU, Beckett Collection.)

CHRISTIAN LUDVIGSEN
HELLERUP, DENMARK

23.9.58 6 Rue des Favorites
Paris 15me

Dear Mr Ludvigsen

Thank you for your letter of September 20th.

In your translation of Fin de Partie I think you should stick as closely as possible to the original French and not pay too much heed to the English version, which is often unsatisfactory. When rehearsing the French production we cut the boy scene because we found it dragged and that all that really matters is that the possible existence of this boy should be registered. But in another production it might be possible to give the full scene as written. The song does not figure in the English text simply because I could not find any satisfactory equivalent. I should prefer it in.[1]

I agree more or less with what Nadeau says. The clue to the whole thing is perhaps in Nell's speech: "Rien n'est plus drôle que le malheur... Nous la trouvons toujours bonne, mais nous ne rions plus." Endgame is not Godot, and any clowning or playing for a laugh would I think be quite wrong. It doesn't matter whether the audience laughs or not.[2]

If you cannot secure the services either of Mendel or of John Beckett, I am now prepared to let you do the mime in your own way and with your own music – or without music. The score or tape of John's music is of no help to you unless you know how it is coordinated with the argument. The worst solution would be an application of this music in a way that was not intended.[3]

There is only one other mime. It has not been performed and no music has yet been written for it. Herewith.[4]

Yours sincerely

s/ Sam. Beckett

TLS; 1 leaf, 1 side; T *env to* Chr. Ludvigsen, C.V.E. Knutsvej 18a, Hellerup, Danemark; *pm* 24-9-58, Paris; Ludvigsen Collection.

1 Clov reports seeing a figure outside, through the window, which does indeed instigate a "complication." In the French original, this begins with the exclamation "Aïeaïeaïe!" and continues up to Clov's "Je vais y aller" (Beckett, *Fin de partie*, 103–105). The Grove edition of *Endgame* reflects this cut (78). S. E. Gontarski's note in The Theatrical Notebooks of Samuel Beckett summarizes the change (II, *Endgame, with a Revised Text*, 180).

The song in the French edition: 21 November 1957 to Alan Schneider, n. 21.

2 Maurice Nadeau (1911–2013; Profile, II) wrote: "L'originalité de Beckett . . . réside dans sa capacité à transformer quelques interrogations métaphysiques en situations amèrement cocasses, à donner à la tragédie le vêtement de la farce" ("'Fin de partie' de Samuel Beckett," *France Observateur* 28 February 1957: 15) (Beckett's originality . . . lies in his ability to transform certain metaphysical lines of questioning into bitterly uproarious situations: to dress tragedy in the clothes of farce).

"Rien n'est plus drôle que le malheur . . . Oui, c'est comme la bonne histoire qu'on nous raconte trop souvent, nous la trouvons toujours bonne, mais nous ne rions plus." (*Fin de partie*, 33-34.) ("Nothing is funnier than unhappiness . . . Yes, it's like the funny story we have heard too often, we still find it funny, but we don't laugh any more.") (*Endgame*, 18–19.)

When Ludvigsen was concerned about the acting style of *En attendant Godot*, SB had assured him: "let people laugh by all means, and then be reminded it is no laughing matter" (1 May 1956).

3 In his letter to Ludvigsen of 2 March 1957, SB had written: "I am afraid you must abandon the idea of doing the mime for the moment. The music has not yet been completed." On 6 March 1957, SB reiterated: "I am afraid the mime without the music is out of the question" (Ludvigsen Collection).

Deryk Mendel, John Beckett, and the music for *Acte sans paroles I*: 14 January 1957 to Alan Simpson.

4 SB enclosed *Acte sans paroles II*.

BARBARA BRAY
PURLEY, SURREY

10.10.58 [*for* 10 November 1958] Paris

Dear Barbara

Thanks for your letter. Glad your production is well over and hope you'll like it when you hear it.[1] I have been laid up since I got back, first in bed, then merely indoors. Beginning to crawl out again now. I read Heppenstall's ignoble and indelicate balderdash yesterday and bitterly regret I ever opened my mouth to him.[2] I don't think I'll be back in London in the near future. I'll have to go to Dublin end of this month or beginning of next, for a week I suppose, and after that be fit only to come straight back here and go to bed again. Every thing has got too much for me and everything beyond me and the strange vision assails me of a hole in the pines and the dunes of the Landes, that perishing area, wherein to bury the head and the rest of the beast.[3] Some day I hope there'll be a play in English at the Court with Donald directing, but there never will be if I don't get away and stay away from all the fuss. Nerves in such ribbons that soon the neighbours will be complaining of my howls. It was great being with you all and I won't forget all your goodness to me, especially yours. I haven't yet read your two radio scripts, but shall soon.[4] Give my love to Francesca and Julia and my respects to Miss Richards and my love to Donald.[5] The French party were enthusiastic over Krapp. I think he's meeting them this evening.[6]

Forgive all my sadness & foolishness and try and find some happiness somewhere.

Love

Sam

ALS; 1 leaf, 1 side; *env to* M$^{\underline{rs}}$ Barbara Bray, 121 Brighton Road, Purley, Surrey, Angleterre; *pm* 11–11–58, Paris. *Dating*: internal evidence confirms November as the month; TCD, MS 10948/1/11.

1 Bray had just completed production of Arthur Adamov's *En Fiacre*, which would be broadcast on the BBC Third Programme on 10 December. Describing the play about three elderly women who "isolate themselves from society by living in cabs," Bray wrote that it was "a psychological sociological fable, presenting a moving study of the isolation of individuals in the midst of society, with occasional macabre qualities" ("Adamov's Play about Isolation," *The Times* 26 November 1959: 6).

2 Rayner Heppenstall (1911–1981) wrote a piece for *The Observer* that described SB's demeanor in rehearsals of *Endgame* and *Krapp's Last Tape* at the Royal Court Theatre, as well as at lunch in a pub nearby:

> He was in London and spent a good deal of time at rehearsals, but it was understood that he did not give interviews and would not be photographed. There he sat in the darkened auditorium, saying very little but ready to do all he could when appealed to. If he ventured to make a point of his own, it would be of a technical nature, the direction, for instance in which an actor should turn while moving from a table to a door. The cast insisted that he had been most helpful. They clearly viewed him with affection.
>
> At midday, he sat in the pub nearby, not precisely holding court but somewhat frequented. He smoked French cigarettes and drank stout . . . The voice was light and not without edge, but friendly, recognisably Irish. He would talk about anything else, not his work. ("Messenger of Gloom," 9 November 1958: 13.)

Heppenstall presents many personal details, some of which SB may have given to him, but SB is not quoted. There are four photos of SB.

3 Of the many features of this département, the one of significance here is its many stretches of pine forest, beaches, and sand dunes.

4 It is not known which scripts Bray may have given to SB. Earlier in the year, when she was translating and adapting *Le Square* and *Moderato Cantabile*, SB had written to Bray: "I am glad to hear you are doing Moderato Cantabile. I do not know Marguerite Duras personally, but I understand she is 'très bien', St. Germain des Prés and of a retiring nature, if that adds up to anything." (26 April 1958; TCD, MS 10948/1/5.)

5 Francesca (known as Checchina, b. 1948) and Julia (b. 1952), Bray's daughters. Miss Richards was Bray's "elderly Kentish housekeeper at Purley, with whom Sam used to have long conversations about cricket" (Bray to the editors, 6 December 2007; Francesca Bray to the editors, 31 May 2012).

6 Suzanne Deschevaux-Dumesnil, Roger Blin, Jean Martin, and the Lindons planned to see the production in London, with Patrick Magee as Krapp (SB to Ethna MacCarthy-Leventhal, 18 November 1958; TxU, Beckett Collection. SB to Thomas MacGreevy, 19 October 1958; TCD, MS 10402/217).

GEORGE REAVEY
NEW YORK

15.11.58 Paris

Dear George

Thanks for your letter. I am horribly sorry to disappoint you, but I can't provide anything on Pasternak. I don't know his work well enough to speak of it and I can feel little sympathy for him in his present "trouble". Is it because of the mighty word "Nobel" that we are suddenly to cry out against that ancient ignominy? And be sorry for the "artist" who condones it with his stipend? You know more about it all than I do and I may be quite wrong. But I simply can't work up a squeak of indignation.[1]

Indeed I wish you would come over soon and I'd be glad to help you with finances here. I never see Geer (prosperous I am told) and but seldom Bram (prosperous I know). Tonny is in Holland in poor and I fear unhappy circumstances. Bram has some new gouaches just varnished at the Galerie Warren which I have not yet seen. Hayter has a British Cou[n]cil exhibition coming off with two others, never see him either.[2] Am just back from London and working on Krapp. Marvellous performance by Pat Magee marvellously directed by Donald McWhinnie.[3] Going to Dublin for a week early in December (first time since my brother's death in 54). Tom had pretty bad heart trouble and has to take things very quietly and my old friend Ethna MacCarthy (Mrs. Levent[h]al) is mortally ill. Hate the thought of going, but must. Quite snowed under now with silly things. If I don't get right away very soon it's the end of all the stringy beans.[4] Sorry to hear Rosset has not been correct with you, he has always been good to me. I hope your reading and lecture will have been a big success.[5] Forgive my blankness and believe me, dear George, always your affectionate friend

Sam

TLS; 1 leaf, 1 side; T *env to* George Reavey Esq, 158 East 88th Street, New York, N.Y., USA; *upper left corner* Air; *pm* 15-11-58, Paris; TxU, Reavey Collection, recip., 45.6.

1 Boris Pasternak was awarded the Nobel Prize in Literature on 23 October, and responded positively ("Telegram from Prizewinner," *The Times* 25 October 1958: 6). However, on 29 October, he declined it ("Mr. Pasternak's Refusal of Nobel Award," *The Times* 30 October 1958: 10). According to *The Times*, other Soviet writers had suggested that if he left the country to receive the award, he might not "be allowed to return"; Soviet attacks on Pasternak and the Nobel award, as well as his expulsion from the Writers' Union as an "internal émigré," incited protest by British writers, International PEN, and the Society of Authors ("Writers' concern for Fate of Mr. Pasternak," 30 October 1958: 8). His novel *Dr. Zhivago* had been rejected as counter-revolutionary in the Soviet Union ("Mr. Pasternak Denounced in Moscow: Award a 'Hostile Act'," *The Times* 25 October 1958: 6).

George Reavey was a friend of Pasternak and a translator of his work: *Last Summer* (London: P. Owen, 1959) and *The Poetry of Boris Pasternak 1917–1959* (New York: G. P. Putnam's Sons, 1959).

2 Paintings and engravings by Stanley William Hayter (1901–1988) were shown in an exhibition organized by the British Council at the Musée d'Art Moderne (22 November - 22 December), with oils by William Scott (1913–1989) and sculptures by Kenneth Armitage (1916–2002); all had represented Britain at the 1958 Venice Biennale ("Hayter," *Le Monde* 12 December 1958: 7).

3 *Krapp's Last Tape*, the curtain-raiser for *Endgame* at the Royal Court Theatre, opened on 28 October. The premiere of *Krapp's Last Tape* was very well received: "Magee's miming and speaking of the solo part is a brilliant *tour de force*, as strong in imagination as in execution" ("End-Game Revived: Conflict of Man and Master," *The Times* 29 October 1958: 3). On 6 August, the substitution of "swine" had been accepted by the Lord Chamberlain's office and it was announced to Devine that the license for the Royal Court Theatre could be drawn up.

4 The French colloquial expression "la fin des haricots" (literally, "the end of the beans") is used to mean something like "the last straw," "the absolute end." SB makes play with the beans, running them down even further.

5 SB uses "correct" in the French sense, suggesting that Rosset had not behaved as he should towards Reavey.

George Reavey had published his own poetry (*The Colours of Memory*, 1955) and translations from Russian (Aleksey Tolstoy, *A Week in Turenevo and Other Stories*, 1958) with Grove Press; his translation of Andrey Bely's *St. Petersburg* would be published in 1959. On 15 November, he was interviewed by Professor Warren Bower for a program entitled "The Pasternak Story," broadcast on WNYC Radio in New York; on 16 November, Reavey read from his own writings and those of Boris Pasternak at the Kaufman Concert Hall, New York; on 23 November, he appeared in a report on Pasternak, "The Case of Dr. Zhivago," on WRCA-TV, New York.

BARBARA BRAY
PURLEY, SURREY

17.11.58 Ussy-sur-Marne

Dear Barbara

Thanks for your letter. I'm sorry you are having all this trouble on my account. I spend my life explaining to earnest Scandinavians that neither the score nor the recording of John's music for the mime indicates the coordination between the music and the action and that unless this coordination is known the music cannot be used. I then go on to say that the only solution, in the absence of an annotated score that makes the thing clear, is the collaboration of either John or Deryk Mendel. I then proceed further to remark that if this cannot be secured they are free to provide their own music, in function of their own interpretation, or to present the mime without music of any kind. But as these elucidations are clearly all in vain the simplest thing is to give them what they ask for and let them do what they like, both with the mime music and with Clov's song. All my thanks for looking after all this, without which God knows you have enough on your hands.[1]

I have no ideas positive or negative of any kind on the U extracts and leave it entirely to you and Donald.[2]

Many thanks too for the trouble you have taken over Daiken script. I think it would be a very good idea for you to see him. He is very anxious to have this done in some form or other and I am sure would lend himself to any transformations you see fit to propose.[3]

I got here a few hours ago and was hardly inside the door when the telephone went as a result of which I have to return to Paris on Saturday, but I hope for only a few hours. I am informed by France-Observateur that Blin is to give a reading of Krapp at the Vieux Colombier on December 12th or 16th I forget, in a new series of "lectures à une voix" organized by Duvignaud and Claude Sarraute. Rehearsals and recording of Tous Ceux qui Dégringolent any day now, director Trutat, Blin playing Rooney and God knows who the Blur, perhaps Françoise Rosay or Christine Tsingos (the original Nell) and Martin Tommy.[4] I listened to your production the other day (played it for Trutat) and enjoyed Pat's performance more than ever before.[5]

Hoping for some calm from the mild desolation peculiar to this place at this time. Already the mouth opens to howl and closes as often as not without having done so, though none to hear. A personage for next time – says nothing, just howls from time to time.

Hamm and Clov were I thought unnecessarily severe on George's <u>Endgame</u> and disinclined to benefit by any of it, though admitting they haven't got it right either. Very anxious to work on it again, but I don't think they can change much.[6]

Any news of the recording of Krapp with Stage Sound?[7]

Bon courage, bon travail, portez-vous mieux, affectueusement à tous.[8]

s/ Sam

TLS; 1 leaf, 2 sides; *env to* Mrs Barbara Bray, 121 Brighton Road, Purley, Surrey, Angleterre; *pm* date illeg, La Ferté-sous-Jouarre; TCD, MS 10948/1/12.

1 How Bray acted on behalf of SB's work is not known. SB's explanations to Christian Ludvigsen about music for *Acte sans paroles I* and *Fin de partie*: 23 September 1958, and n. 1, n. 3.

2 The BBC Third Programme planned to present a reading of extracts from *The Unnamable*.

3 On 27 September, SB acknowledged receipt of Leslie Daiken's *The Circular Road*, and on 12 November he informed Daiken that he had sent the manuscript to Donald McWhinnie and Barbara Bray at the BBC Third Programme, "with sincere recommendation." On 21 November, SB told him that Bray had suggestions: "If you come with her to an agreement about the changes to be made there would emerge a play for radio with performance assured" (TxU, Daiken Collection, 1.1). The radio play was eventually broadcast on 21 September 1960.

4 "Lectures à une voix" (readings for one voice).

Jean Duvignaud (1921–2007), writer and sociologist of art; in 1956, Blin had directed his *Marée basse*. Claude Sarraute (b. 1927), daughter of Nathalie Sarraute (1919–1998), was a journalist with *Le Monde*. The Théâtre du Vieux-Colombier, 21 rue du Vieux-Colombier, Paris 6.

Alain Trutat (1922–2006) directed a production of *Tous ceux qui tombent* for the Chaîne Nationale with Roger Blin as Mr. Rooney, Jean Martin as Tommy, and Maryse Paillet as Mrs. Rooney (whom SB calls "the Blur"); it was recorded on 28 December (Clas Zilliacus, *Beckett and Broadcasting: A Study of the Works of Samuel Beckett for and in Radio and Television*, Acta Academiae Aboensis, series A humaniora, 51.2 [Aabo, Sweden: Aabo Akademi, 1976] 69). Françoise Rosay (1891–1974), a film and television star. Christine Tsingos (1920–1973; Profile, II) had played Nell in the London production of *Fin de partie*. "Dégringolent" (tumble).

5 In the original BBC Third Programme production of *All That Fall*, Patrick Magee played Mr. Slocum.

6 SB refers to the critique made by Roger Blin and Jean Martin (the original Hamm and Clov) of how they had seen Hamm played at the Royal Court Theatre (where George Devine played the role and also directed).

7 Stage Sound, a London recording company.

8 "Bon courage, bon travail, portez-vous mieux, affectueusement à tous" (Keep your spirits up, work well, and get better, love to all). This sentence is handwritten.

BARNEY ROSSET
GROVE PRESS, NEW YORK

20.11.58 Ussy

Dear Barney

I arrived in London a week before the opening and 5 days before the 1st dress rehearsal. My intention was to concern myself only with Krapp, but on arrival I found Endgame in such a state that I had to take it on too. Impossible however to do much in so short a time. But Krapp made up for everything. Unerringly directed by McWhinnie Magee gave a very fine performance, for me by far the most satisfactory experience in the theatre up to date. I wish to goodness Alan could have seen it, I can't see it being done any other way. During rehearsal we found various pieces of business not indicated in the script and which now seem to me indispensable. If you ever publish the work in book form I should like to incorporate them in the text. A possible solution in the meantime would be for me to see Alan again (hardly feasible) or to write him at length on the subject and prepare for him a set of more explicit stage directions. Blin and Martin saw it in London and were impressed and bowled over by Magee.[1] The French translation is now more or less right. I know nothing so far of any plans for its performance here, but it is to be read by Blin on December 12th in a new series of "lectures à une voix" at the Vieux Colombier organised by Duvignaud and Claude Sarraute. It might be given with Fin de Partie which Blin would like to revive for a month before going on tour with it in January to Switzerland and Italy.[2] The English press on the whole was very sour. Hobson was ill and could not come to the opening, a big loss. He is better now and is to do an article before the end of the run. But it comes too late to make much difference.[3] McWhinnie promised me to do a complete studio recording of Krapp with Stage Sound and have the tape sent to you, but I do not know if he has done so. I stayed on in London for a week after the opening and got back to Paris tired and poorly, but am better now. I have to go to Dublin for a week at least at the beginning of December to see an old friend who is very ill, the usual Irish errand. Then I hope straight back here for a long spell, but I'm always hoping that and it never comes off. The BBC are doing extracts from the Unnamable, read by Magee, in January, with learned discourse by Cronin who did the TLS article and whom I met in London (Wexford man).[4] The Lindon also came over for the opening and I lunched the next day with them and Calder who then announced the 3 in 1 for end of January, but I understand now it is postponed to March.[5] The Evergreen was on sale in the theatre. When I get back from London, if I can't get on with any new work I'll start on the translation of Textes pour Rien. I made a balls of the new act in French I was telling you about. I'll try it again, but am not even sure it's viable in the present setup.[6] I feel I'm getting more and more entangled in professionalism and self-exploitation and that it would be really better to stop altogether than to go on with that. What I need is to get back into the state of mind of 1945 when it was write or perish. But I suppose no chance of that. I ran into Joan and Riopelle one Saturday evening late in the Dôme Bar, in good form and contemplating boar hunting in Sologne on the morrow. I want to go with them to the circus some evening, perhaps there's a future for me there. Thanks for Chelsea Review of which I received another copy from Ursule Molinari together with a number of her plays for appreciation, God help me. I dislike all this personal stuff, but was much touched by Alan's great friendliness. But why frame under-the-table-talk?[7] I hope you are in better form than when you left and that you are having happy meetings with Peter. I feel I should have left you alone more when you were over, but – as my West Meath Nanny used to tell me – I have no conduction.[8]

Greetings to Link. Scribble me a line some time.

Ever

s/ Sam

TLS; 1 leaf, 2 sides; Burns Library, Samuel Beckett Collection, SB-BR.

1 Some of the new business added to *Krapp's Last Tape* in rehearsal for the London premiere is given in SB's letter of 21 November to Alan Schneider:

> All the things we talked about together here were used and worked (with the exception of the banana peel into the pit which had to be cut because of

> proximity of front stall seats!) He simply boots it out of his way towards the wings. The most interesting discovery was the kind of personal relationship that developed between Krapp and the machine. This arose quite naturally and was extraordinarily effective and of great help in the early stages whenever the immobility of the listening attitude tended to be tedious [. . .] At the very end, when "I lay down across her etc." comes for the third time, the head goes down on the table and remains down until "Here I end etc", on which it comes up and the eyes staring front till the end. At this point too he has his arm round the machine. Because of the apron at Royal Court the table with the recorder and boxes is visible before the curtain from the outset. Lights out, Krapp slips into place from behind the curtain, then the sudden full blaze on him. At the end on the contrary we had a fade-out and the quite unexpected and marvellous effect of recorder's red light burning up as the dark gathered, this unfortunately visible only to half the house because of the position of the machine at the edge of the table to Krapp's left. Krapp's route from table to shadows was the roundabout one I foresaw. (Beckett and Schneider, *No Author Better Served*, 50–51.)

The play had been published in Grove's *Evergreen Review* in summer 1958; when published by Grove in book form in 1960, there was no change in the text and stage directions.

2 Pierre Leyris (1907–2001) prepared a draft French translation, *La dernière bande*, and collaborated with SB on its revision. SB wrote to Thomas MacGreevy on 19 October: "I have been struggling with the French translation of Krapp's Last Tape and have now got it more or less acceptable and can show it to Blin. Great mistake giving such work to another and a great bore having to do it oneself." (TCD, MS 10402/217.) To Alan Clodd, SB wrote: "Re La Dernière Bande my recollection is that Leyris, in view of small part he had in the translation, preferred to withdraw his name" (25 June 1971; NLI, Clodd MS 35,293/4).

Blin's tour did not take place.

3 W. A. Darlington announced a "Boring Lack of Humanity in 'End-Game'," (*Daily Telegraph* 29 October 1958: 10). J. W. Lambert wrote that SB was a "poet whose unwearied theme is fallen man"; he added, "all this must be disagreeable, a squalid exercise in self-pity, if it does not find the right interpreters" ("Pawns in an Old Game," *The Sunday Times* 2 November 1958: [Magazine] 21). Kenneth Tynan's contribution in *The Observer*, "Slamm's Last Knock," parodied the play (2 November 1958: 19).

Harold Hobson's reviews for the *Sunday Times* had been pivotal in the success of *Waiting for Godot* in London; at the end of J. W. Lambert's review was the note: "Harold Hobson is indisposed."

4 Anthony Cronin (b. 1928), who was born in Co. Wexford, reviewed *Malone Dies* and *Watt*: "Paradise of Indignity," *The Times Literary Supplement* 28 March 1958: 168. With Donald McWhinnie, he had discussed *Krapp* in a Royal Court Symposium on 16 November ("Things to Come," *The Observer* 16 November 1958: 19).

5 Jérôme and Annette Lindon (b. 1927).

6 Probably the fragment that later became *Rough for Theatre II* (UoR, BIF MS 1396/4/41–42).

7 Le Dôme, 108 Boulevard du Montparnasse, Paris 14.

Alan Schneider published a memoir about working with SB, "Waiting for Beckett: A Personal Chronicle," *Chelsea Review*, 2 (Autumn 1958) 3–20. SB wrote to Schneider on 21 November: "I have just read your article in the Chelsea Review and am deeply touched by its great warmth of attachment for my dismal person and devotion to my grisly work. Thanks from my heart." (Beckett and Schneider, *No Author Better Served*, 50.) Novelist and playwright Ursule Molinaro (1916–2000) was co-founder and Co-Editor of the journal. SB writes "Molinari" for "Molinaro."

8 Rosset's son Peter (b. 1956), from his marriage to Hannelore Eckert (b. 1923).
Bridget Bray (1881–?), SB's nanny, known familiarly as "Bibby" (Knowlson, *Damned to Fame*, 35–36).

MARY MANNING HOWE
CAMBRIDGE, MASSACHUSETTS

21.11.58 Paris

Dear Mary

Thanks for yours of 20th ult. I hear on all hands great accounts of Questors production. Wish I had seen it. Very ingenious adaptation. Thanks for sending it. Spoilt tenor my rump. Soft! Jesus! O'Connor gives me the bloody flux.[1] Powerful week in London rehearsing Krapp. Terrific performance by Magee, pitilessly directed by McWhinnie. Best experience in the theatre ever. Endgame not good, though McGowran could have been. No production. Press sour. Hobson laid up with bladder trouble, couldn't come. Article later, nimis sero.[2] Boozed round for a few days after the opening, in the murk, living with Magee in a boarding-house West Cromwell Road, need you to describe it, then collapsed back here coughing up everything. Have to go to Dublin for all sins and omissions beginning of next month for a week to see Ethna MacCarthy-Leventhal very ill. That should about finish me. Everything in flitters in any case. Don't want to see anyone there, but Susan of course. What can you do in a week, living decent in Killiney and screaming in Lr Baggot Street?[3] Con was in London, like silk. Either he doesn't realise or the old mask is in great fettle. The latter probably. No more now. Greetings to Fanny.[4] Love always.

s/ Sam

TLS; 1 leaf, 1 side; T *env to* Mrs Howe, 58 Highland Street, Cambridge, Mass., U.S.A.; *pm* 22–11–58, Paris; TxU, Beckett Collection, 8.10.

1 In September, Questors Theatre in Ealing performed *The Voice of Shem*, the adaptation by Mary Manning (as she continued to call herself when writing) of Joyce's *Finnegans Wake*; she had sent SB the adaptation which had been published by Faber and Faber (1957). The play was "enlivened" with ballads from the novel *Finnegans Wake* and Irish airs (Austin Clarke reviewed it positively in "Dear, Dirty Dublin," *The Irish Times* 7 June 1958: 8).

Mary Manning Howe's reference to O'Connor's comments has not been traced.

2 Harold Hobson's brief mention of *Endgame* did not appear until 30 November ("But where is Swinburne?" *The Sunday Times* [Magazine] 17). "Nimis sero" (Lat., too late).

3 Susan Manning (1874–1960), mother of Mary Manning Howe. SB stayed in Killiney with his sister-in-law Jean Wright Beckett. Later, he wrote to Mary Manning Howe: "I stayed with Jean and went home every evening from the Leventhals by the last train from Westland Row, not having hired a car for fear of driving when drunk. I had only a brief and unsatisfactory meeting with Susan at the end." (2 January 1959; TxU, Beckett Collection, 8.10.) Ethna and Con Leventhal lived at 36 Lower Baggot Street. Leventhal had come to London to see *Endgame* and *Krapp's Last Tape* at SB's invitation.

4 Mary Manning Howe's daughter, the American poet and novelist Fanny Howe (b. 1940).

BARNEY ROSSET
GROVE PRESS, NEW YORK

23.11.58 Paris

Dear Barney

Good to hear from you after so long. I am sorry RC has your heckles up. All she suggested to me in London was the possibility of Magee's being invited to the States with Krapp and some readings, to which I had no objection, and her passing on the idea to some butty in NY, to which I seemed to have none either. No shadow of infringement of your rights seemed to be involved thereby.[1] It is true this hurried conversation was held on a street corner after an overwhelmingly oppressive and depressive lunch with Monteith and de Sautoy [sic], in the course of which Krapp was hailed as "frightfully funny", and while I was calculating with anguish the chances of my bladder's holding out to the only public lavatory known to me in the West End, viz. in the Piccadilly Underground (it did almost).[2] But I am coming at last to see that the only sensible course is for me not to open my mouth to man or beast on any matter remotely concerning me.

Who, for example, owns the European rights of Krapp? The question was sprung on me yesterday by Stefani Hunzinger (Fischer) who wants the performance rights. I told her I didn't know and to ask you. I met her briefly, in the hotel where I first met Alan, with Frau Fischer (not her real name, I know) who spoke of you and Grove Press with real enthusiasm.[3] They were on their way to London where they can see Krapp if they wish and if it is still running, which I don't know. I take it from your letter – though you don't say so in so many words – that you have received the Krapp recording. I am so glad you and Alan like it. I have suggested to Alan that I might send him, if he approves, an annotated (in the light of what arose in London) text of Krapp, but I have no copy left, so would you send me a few. Joan also clamors [sic] for her copy subtilised from her by you at the last moment in the Pont Royal bar.[4] Thanks to both of you for all the trouble you have taken over the Endgame recording, I look forward greatly to hearing it.[5] I realise now that what greatly damaged both Paris and London productions is Noël's set and I am determined, if there ever is a revival here, to get rid of it. This is my mistake as much as Noël's, or more.[6] Thanks for Evergreen 6 with excellent Mandiargues story.[7] With regard to More Pricks I should prefer them never again to see the light of day, either together in a book or severally in periodicals. Indeed after Watt I should prefer no old work to be republished with the exception of some poems, of which I have no news from Limes Verlag.[8] The only chance for me now as a writer is to go into retreat and put a stop to all this fucking élan acquis and get back down to the bottom of all the hills again, grimmer hills that [*for* than] in 45 of cherished memory and far less than then to climb with, i.e. nice proportions.[9] It's not going to be easy, but it's definitely the only last gasp worth trying to pant as far as I'm concerned. So if all goes well no new work for a long time now, if ever. I gave an aborted radio script to McWhinnie, unbroadcastable as it stands, a kind of attempt to write for radio and not merely exploit its technical possibilities, of which I'll sent [sic] you a copy if I can find one. It was written a couple of years ago, then thrown away, then recovered, but with a page missing of which I could remember nothing and which personally I don't miss.[10] Congratulations on the 5000 Unnamables, a bloody miracle. Talking of which pray to Jude for me next week in Dublin - and at all times.[11]

Ever

s/ Sam

TLS; 1 leaf, 2 sides; NSyU, Grove Press Records; Burns Library, Samuel Beckett Collection, SB-BR.

1 Rosica Colin's communication with Rosset has not been found. As the first publisher of *Krapp's Last Tape*, Rosset held the rights and wished to manage its US premiere.

2 Charles Monteith (1921–1995; Profile, II) was then an editor at Faber and Faber; Peter du Sautoy CBE (1912–1995) joined Faber and Faber in 1946 as general manager.

3 Stefani Hunzinger (1913–2006; Profile, II) was in Paris with Brigitte Fischer (1905–1991); Gottfried Bermann Fischer (1897–1995) added his wife's family name to his own. Brigitte Fischer's father, Samuel Fischer (1859–1934), had founded S. Fischer Verlag in 1886.

SB and Alan Schneider first met in the lobby of the Hôtel Lancaster, 7 Rue de Berri, Paris 8 (Schneider, *Entrances*, 223).

4 An annotated copy of *Krapp's Last Tape* in the *Evergreen Review* edition is in the Alan Schneider Collection, CUSD, MSS 103/13/23.

The Hôtel Pont Royal, 7 rue Montalembert, Paris 7.

"Subtilised from her by you": Gallicism for "made off with by you."

5 The recording of the *Endgame* production at the Cherry Lane Theatre was not released commercially by Evergreen Records until 1968 (EVR-002STER). SB wrote to Rosset on 21 August: "With regard to music for Endgame recording I am prepared to admit it may help the record and only ask that it be as scant and unharmonious as possible" (NSyU, Grove Press Record).

6 Jacques Noël's set: 7 April 1958, n. 2.

7 André Pieyre de Mandiargues, "The Diamond," tr. Brian Howard, *Evergreen Review* 6.22 (January–February 1962) 61–80.

8 *More Pricks Than Kicks* (1934) had long been out of print; stories from this collection had been reprinted: "The Smeraldina's Billet-doux," in Themistocles Hoetis, ed., *Zero Anthology* no. 8 ([New York: Zero Press, 1956] 56–61); "Yellow," *New World Writing* 5.10 (November 1956), 108–119; "Dante and the Lobster," *Evergreen Review* 1.1 (December 1957), 24–36. Grove Press published *Watt* in 1959 as an Evergreen Book. Limes Verlag published *Gedichte*, a German edition of Beckett's poems with the French and English originals (Wiesbaden, 1959).

9 "Elan acquis" (momentum).

10 The radio script was an early draft of what would become *Embers*.

11 Grove Press had published *The Unnamable* in New York in September 1958 as an Evergreen Book. SB invokes Saint Jude as his patron saint of lost causes.

BARBARA BRAY
PURLEY, SURREY

29.11.58 Paris

Dear Barbara

Many thanks for your letter and all trouble over U extracts (but please always write Rue des Favorites, whence forwarding assured, whereas it doesn't work the other way). If you decide to do it that way they seem to me well chosen. But even these will add up to something little intelligible and my feeling now is that we plump for the whole hog and give the bastards a single long unbroken extract ending at the end (say from "Help help" p. 157 to end or from "Yes, in my life" p. 153 to end) and ask Cronin to do his best in his introduction to make its way straight. I think this would be much more effective than the dribs and drabs and would certainly give Magee a better chance to crown his readings with something really unbearable. I shd of course have spoken of this before and tried to save you all the headaches, but speech (as distinct from yelps) is only beginning to return. In any case I now leave the decision to Donald and you. If you continue to prefer your way, the extracts you indicate are all right with me. But I think it's punch-pulling.[1]

Many thanks to Donald and Pat for the Krapp recording. It has arrived and is much appreciated. I asked for the bill to be sent to me, but if it has been sent to Rosset I know he will cheerfully pay it. I have no news of any kind (but yours) from London and do not know if the show is on or off.[2] Blin will not do the reading after all and there is no talk yet of his giving it a normal stage performance. His latest idea is that when they go on tour with Fin de Partie in Jan (Switzerland, Italy and perhaps elsewhere, probable a dozen performances) Pat should join them and do Krapp in English. Not a bad idea, but I doubt if it can be made financially interesting for Pat.

I am very touched by what you say of the U. I wish I could think it is important as you say, but of course I can't. I am in acute crisis about my work (on the lines familiar to you by now) and have decided that I not merely can't but won't go on as I have been going more or less ever since the Textes pour Rien and must either get back to nothing again and the bottom of all the hills again like before Molloy or else call it a day. This seems to involve retreat from Paris to a place remoter than Ussy, so I hope if you are coming you will come soon. I don't thing [*for* think] I can do anything with He and She (not the title whatever it may be) beyond change a few words and try to rewrite the Addie lessons. It was really less much less for the Drama Department than for you and Donald personally to have your opinion on the Bolton-Holloway experiment. It is a very aborted and unsatisfactory text and I'd be just as glad if you never did it. But you may if you wish.[3] I have translated about half a page of the first Texte with the usual calamitous loss of tension and precision at every turn, if I ever finish it I'll send it along to you.[4] I still prefer not to record my Beaujolais Gauloise pantgasp, forgive me. I listened to Dylan Thomas reading his fat poems and being witty on poetry, poets and himself and didn't like any of it, the pulpit voice and hyperarticulation and sibilation, but I'm lousy public.

I'm due to fly to Haemorrhaldia day after tomorrow. Hope not to exceed a week. No light in the sky for the past 10 days, and little on earth, but I'm told air traffic is as usual. So Monday night shall probably be hearing the little waves on the pillows of sand like four and a half years ago mutatis mutandis.[5]

Love to the children and to yourself.

s/ Sam

TLS; 1 leaf, 2 sides; *Tenv to* Mrs Barbara Bray, 121 Brighton Road, Purley, Surrey, Angleterre; *pm* 30-11-58, Paris; TCD, MS 10948/1/13.

1 The BBC Third Programme intended to present a reading from *The Unnamable* with Patrick Magee, in connection with publication of the novel by John Calder. Passages had been proposed by Bray to which SB offers alternatives: "Help help, if I could only describe this place . . ." or "Yes, in my life, since we must call it so, there were three things, the inability to speak, the inability to be silent, and solitude, that's what I've had to make the best of" (SB's references are to the Grove Press edition).

Anthony Cronin provided an introduction to the BBC reading, followed by a six-minute interval of music, and then the hour-long reading – of snippets, not of a single extended extract – on 19 January 1959.

2 SB refers to the long-awaited recording of *Krapp's Last Tape* by Sound Stage of the Royal Court Theatre performance with Patrick Magee.

The final performances of the Royal Court Theatre productions took place on Saturday 29 November ("Concerts," *The Times*: 2).

3 Addie, Bolton, and Holloway are characters in what becomes the radio play *Embers*. The Bolton–Holloway experiment is a story within the narrative that opens the play.

4 SB refers to *Textes pour rien*.

5 "Haemorrhaldia" is SB's portmanteau word: "haemorrhoid" and "emerald," as in "the Emerald Isle," i.e. Ireland.

SB recalls time spent in Dublin in 1954 as his brother Frank was dying.

CHRISTIAN LUDVIGSEN
HELLERUP, DENMARK

December 15th 1958

6 Rue des Favorites
Paris

Dear Mr Ludvigsen

The coït-coite-coïte pun is untranslatable. My attempt to transfer it to English is feeble, though it sometimes produced a titter.

The expression "se tenir coi" (feminine "se tenir coite") is common in French and means to "lie low". Clov uses it speaking of the flea, but mispronounces "coite" as if there were a diaeresis on the i ("coïte"), thereby producing the same sound as the other French word "coït" (also quite common) meaning "sexual union". But of course the expression "se tenir coït" does not exist. If it did it could only mean "fuck oneself". Hence Hamm's alarm, for if the flea were fucking itself more fleas might be expected. You should also note that "baiser" is the slang for "fuck."[1]

In English "to lie doggo" is common and means "to lie low, to stay quiet". This is the expression Clov wishes to use speaking of the flea, but instead of "lying" he says "laying" ("to lay" = "pondre"). "To lay doggo" does not exist, but if it did it might be taken to mean "to lay eggs on the quiet". Hence Hamm's alarm, for if the flea were laying eggs more fleas might be expected.

I hope this is now as clear as semen.

Pierre levée: cromlech, menhir. No confusion with the boy. You're inclined to over-interpret. The boy, if it is a real boy and not one of Clov's visions, simply appears to be sitting with his back against the cromlech.[2]

I am quite prepared to accept a small fee for ALL THAT FALL. But here again you must get the consent of Grove Press.

Thanks for KRAPP articles and photos. I like the photos very much. Congratulations on your success.[3]

ENDGAME was not good in London, but KRAPP was excellently played and directed and I was very pleased with it indeed.

I'm afraid there is not much chance of my going to Denmark for the opening. But thanks for suggesting it.

Yours sincerely
s/ Samuel Beckett

TLS; 1 leaf, 1 side; T *env to* Chr. Ludvigsen, C. V. E. Knuthsvej 18a, Hellerup, Danemark; *pm* [illeg], La Ferté-sous-Jouarre; Ludvigsen Collection.

1 Ludvigsen's questions pertain to his Danish translation of *Endgame* (Samuel Beckett, *Slutspil; og, Scene uden ord*, tr. Christian Ludvigsen [Fredensborg, Arena, 1959]). *Fin de partie* (51); *Slutspil* (44); *Endgame* (34):

HAMM: Laying! Lying you mean. Unless he's *lying* doggo.
CLOV: Ah? One says lying? One doesn't say laying?
HAMM: Use your head, can't you. If he was laying we'd be bitched.

2 "La pierre levée" (*Fin de partie*, 104); "Den store sten" (*Slutspil*, 87). The line was cut in *Endgame*.

3 The production of Ludvigsen's translation, *Krapps sidste bånd*, had taken place in November in the Studentascene at Aarhus, directed by Jørgen Andersen.

JOHN CALDER
JOHN CALDER (PUBLISHER) LTD., LONDON

19th December 1958 Ussy-sur-Marne

Dear John

Thanks for your letter.

I'm afraid I can't undertake a preface for THE SQUARE. I'm quite incapable of criticism or comment of any kind. Please forgive me.[1]

I'm glad to have confirmation of your decision to publish the three in one. I can think of no general title. TRINITY would not do. It seems to me the three separate titles should be enough. If anything better occurs to me I'll let you know.[2]

I'm not well and don't expect to be back in Paris before the New Year. You can get me on the phone (18 at Ussy-sur-Marne, Seine-et-Marne) any evening.

Sorry to be so unsatisfactory.

With best wishes,

Yours ever

s/ Sam

TLS; 1 leaf, 1 side; *datestamped* 23.DEC.1958; InU, C&B, Beckett; AL draft *on* John Barber 15 December 1958 to SB (TLS; 1 leaf, 1 side); GEU, MS 1221.

1 John Calder* (b. 1927) had asked SB to write an introduction of three or four pages to the English edition of Marguerite Duras's *Le Square* which he would soon be publishing in an English translation by Sonia Pitt-Rivers and Irina Morduch (17 December 1958; InU, C&B).

2 "Three in one": *Molloy*, *Malone Dies*, *The Unnamable*.

CHRONOLOGY 1959

1959	1 January	Overthrow of the government of Cuban President Fulgencio Batista, who resigns and flees the country; Fidel Castro assumes power on 16 February. Opening of the European Common Market.
	19 January	The BBC Third Programme broadcasts extracts from *The Unnamable*, read by Patrick Magee, with music by John Beckett.
	February	André Malraux appointed by De Gaulle as France's first Ministre de la Culture.
	12 February – 7 March	Henri Hayden exhibition, Waddington Galleries, London; catalogue includes SB text "Henri Hayden."
	4 March	*Les Lettres Nouvelles* publish "La dernière bande."
	20 March	SB reports that he has given permission to Marcel Mihalovici to make a chamber opera of *La dernière bande*.
	30 March	Death of Peter Suhrkamp, SB's German publisher.
	4 April	SB attends France–Wales rugby match at Colombes Stadium, with Claude Simon.
	19 April	Meets Jean-Louis Barrault, Roger Blin, and Jean Martin to discuss new production of *En attendant Godot* in the next season as well as *Fin de partie* revival with *La dernière bande*.
	24 May	Death of Ethna MacCarthy-Leventhal.

24 June	The BBC Third Programme broadcasts *Embers*.
26 June	Limes Verlag, Wiesbaden, publish poems as *Gedichte*. SB grants German publication and performance rights of his work to Suhrkamp Verlag; Fischer Verlag retain performance rights for the plays they had already published in German.
2 July	Receives honorary D. Litt. from Trinity College Dublin. Suzanne Deschevaux-Dumesnil attends and spends a few days in Dublin.
14 July	SB returns to France via London, where he hears a playback of *Embers* at the BBC.
21 August	Death of Denis Devlin, in Dublin.
13–17 September	SB is in Sorrento where Radiotelevisione Italia awards *Embers* the Italia Prize on 15 September.
16 September	De Gaulle recognizes Algeria's right to self-determination.
October	Olympia Press publish *Molloy*, *Malone Dies*, and *The Unnamable* as a single volume for European market; Grove Press publish the "three in one" in November.
before 14 October	SB buys a Citroën 2CV.
20 November	Writes letters of introduction for Robert Pinget to acquaintances in the United States.
21 December – 1 February 1960	Bram van Velde exhibition, Stedelijk Museum, Amsterdam.
18 December	Faber and Faber publish *Krapp's Last Tape* with *Embers*.

JOHN CALDER
JOHN CALDER (PUBLISHER) LTD., LONDON

January 6th 1958 [for 1959]

6 Rue des Favorites
Paris 15me

Dear John

Not "Trilogy", I beseech you, just the three titles and nothing else.[1]

Yours ever

s/ Sam

TLS; 1 leaf, 1 side; *datestamped* 7.JAN.59; InU, C&B, Beckett. *Dating*: Calder to SB, 29 December 1958.

1 Concerning publication of *Molloy*, *Malone Dies*, and *The Unnamable* in a single volume, John Calder had written to SB: "May we just use a general title 'Trilogy' on the jacket with the three books listed underneath?" (29 December 1958; InU, C&B, Beckett).

BARBARA BRAY
PURLEY, SURREY

23.1.59

Ussy sur Marne

Dear Barbara

Re radio script:

"He" should be replaced by "Henry" and "She" by "Ada" throughout.

The following titles have occurred to me:

"The Water's Edge."

"Why life, Henry?"

"Not a Soul."

"All day all night"

Let me know what you think.[1]

I got back here on the Friday. I have written a few lines. I have written to Donald and Pat and John.[2] I have begun Zhivago. The names got me down, among other things. But I'll persevere. You were very good to give it to me.[3]

An old man who helped build this little house is dead. He fell down dead as he was shaving. His name was Auguste.[4]

I hope you had a good flight back and that Bath wasn't too tiring.[5] I shall remember our evenings together. Forgive my being such a lifeless corse.

Love

Sam

ALS; 1 leaf, 1 side; *env to* Mrs Barbara Bray, 121 Brighton Road, Purley, Surrey, Angleterre; *pm* 27–1–59, La Ferté-sous-Jouarre; TCD, MS 10948/1/16.

1 SB's radio script was a draft of *Embers*. This list is part of the typed manuscript that contains "Addie's Music Lesson" and "Addie's Riding Lesson" (TCD, MS 4664, 22r).

2 Donald McWhinnie, Patrick Magee, and John Beckett had been involved in recording extracts from *The Unnamable* that had been broadcast on the BBC Third Programme on 19 January.

3 *Doctor Zhivago* by Boris Pasternak, tr. Max Hayward and Manya Harari (London: Collins and Harvill Press, 1958).

4 Raymond Lucas, a mason from the village of Ussy-sur-Marne, assisted in the construction of SB's cottage at Ussy; the worker named Auguste has not been further identified (Paule Savane, *Samuel Beckett à Ussy sur Marne* [Ussy-sur-Marne: Association pour la sauvegarde d'Ussy-sur-Marne, 2001] 12).

5 Bray had informed SB of her plans to be in Paris during January, and he had responded: "Of course I would drop my bucket and spade and hasten up to town to see you, what a question, what an answer. Let me only know a little in advance if you can, as I am very slow, even when making haste." (1 January 1959; TCD, MS 10948/1/15.) Bray's parents Henry Jacobs (1899–1975) and Violet Jacobs (1902–2003) lived in Bath.

NANCY CUNARD
PARIS

26.1.59 Ussy-sur-Marne

Bien chère Nancy

Thanks for your letter and the nice things you say about that jolly evening in Sloane Square.[1]

Whoroscope was indeed entered for your competition and the prize of I think 1000 francs. I knew nothing about it till afternoon of last day of entry, wrote first half before dinner, had a guzzle of salad and Chambertin at the Cochon de Lait, went back to the Ecole and finished it about three in the morning. Then walked down to the Rue Guénégaud and put it in your box. That's how it was and them were the days.[2]

I was very disappointed we did not meet in London. I had a brief and exhausting time there trying to get things the way I wanted, right or wrong. I was very pleased with Krapp, but not with Endgame, which needed another week's rehearsal.[3]

You wouldn't know where to live these days, or why. Here is the best I have, not a sound and the Ile de France bowing itself out. I don't find solitude agonising, on the contrary. Holes in paper open and take me fathoms from anywhere.

Much love and vivement les retrouvailles.[4]

s/ Sam

TLS; 1 leaf, 1 side; TxU, bound into copy no. 7 of *Whoroscope* inscribed to Nancy Cunard by SB. Previous publication: Carlton Lake, *No Symbols Where None Intended*, 13.

1 Nancy Cunard (1896–1965; Profile, I) had been to see *Krapp's Last Tape* and *Endgame*, playing between 28 October and 29 November 1958 at the Royal Court Theatre, on Sloane Square.

2 The Cochon de Lait, 7 Rue Corneille, Paris 5. The original edition of SB's 1930 poem "Whoroscope" had a wrap-round band explaining: "This poem was awarded the £10 prize for the best poem on Time in the competition judged by Richard Aldington (1892–1962; Profile, I) and Nancy Cunard at the Hours Press, and is published in an edition of 100 signed copies at 5 s. and 200 unsigned at 1 s. This is also Mr. Samuel Beckett's first separately published work." See also Thursday [? 17 July 1930], n. 5.

3 On 18 November 1958, SB wrote to Ethna MacCarthy-Leventhal: "London was not for nothing, very pleased with performance of Krapp and something saved thanks to McGowran – of Endgame. Very exciting working with Magee and McWhinnie, I want no other director henceforward." (TxU, Leventhal Collection, 1.7.)

4 "Vivement les retrouvailles" (Here's to the next time – may it be soon).

A. J. LEVENTHAL
DUBLIN

3.2.59 Ussy

Dear Con

Thanks for your letter. I haven't written to Ethna since my first letter to her in hospital, not knowing if it were advisable or not. I shall do so now. I don't know what to say to her, or to you, but it doesn't matter, you both know, and as you say even the silly words will be a little event for her lying there.[1]

At the same time as yours a letter from Ho with the flabbergasting news. The first movement is to decline as usual, but I finally realize this is hardly possible and I have written to Ho that I shall accept the honour if it is offered to me. I don't underestimate it, nor pretend I am not greatly moved, but I have a holy horror of such things and it is not easy for me. If I were a scholar or a man of letters it might be different. But what in God's name have doctoracy and literature to do with work like mine? However there it is, right or wrong I'll go throught [sic] with it if they ask me. Of course my letter to Ho is not like this, as I assume he will have to cite it to the Provost. Scatter this to the blessed winds, it is for you only.[2]

I think Arrabal is more than a disciple of mine. Of course he is already labelled as such here. He is a very young man and with luck, and given a little span (his health is poor), I am sure he will do important work. His first novel – Baal Babylone – is due very shortly from Julliard.[3]

I spend all the time I can cloistered here. I go in to lunch with Harold Hobson day after tomorrow, but straight back in the evening I hope. I have given up all thought of theatre and radio and am struggling to struggle on from where the Unnamable left me off, that is with the next next to nothing. A few lines a day is an achievement. Brilliant bitter days. I have given, after long hesitation, a rather aborted radio text, written in English a few years ago, to the BBC. The 3rd will do it in June.

Write soon again. Affectionately.
s/ Sam

TLS; 1 leaf, 1 side; TxU, Leventhal Collection, 1.4.

1 On 9 December 1958, SB had written to his cousin Robina Sheila Page (née Roe, known as Sheila, also Eli, 1905–1993): "Ethna is now in hospital in East Ham and I fear there is nothing more to be done for her" (Babcock Collection). On 10 January, he had written from Ussy to Ethna MacCarthy in East Ham Memorial Hospital, London:

> Though we said little in Dublin I think all was said there and nothing to add for the moment. My silly old body is here alone with the snow and the crows and the exercise-book that opens like a door and lets me far down into the now friendly dark. I don't think, dearest Ethna, I can be of any use just now, either to you or Con. But if you want me all you have to do is send for me. I send you again all that was always and will always be in my heart for you. (TxU, Leventhal Collection, 1.7.)

2 SB wrote on the same day to H. O. White:

> I am knocked all of a heap by the news that the Board contemplated giving me a D.Litt. to which I honestly feel I have no title. I think you know and understand my need of personal obscurity and dread of public notice such as this. But there is no question of my declining such an honour from my own University and I shall accept it, if it is offered to me, with emotion and gratitude. (TCD, MS 3777/18.)

3 SB had been in touch with the Spanish artist, playwright, dramatist, and polymath, Fernando Arrabal* (b. 1932) since 1957 when Arrabal and his wife Luce Moreau (b. 1933) requested permission to stage *Fin de partie* in Spain. Arrabal's autobiographical novel *Baal Babylone* (1959) told of a nightmarish upbringing in Franco's Spain; it became the basis for Arrabal's 1971 film *Viva la muerte* (*Long Live Death*).

BARBARA BRAY
PURLEY, SURREY

4.2.59 Ussy

Dear Barbara

Thanks for your letters and to Checchina for hers so beautifully written, worded, spelt and punctuated. That must have been a memorable Tuesday when she did 98 sums out of 100. Give them both my love.

The point you make about "20 years earlier" is good. I suppose Henry could be made at this point to take the gentle listener into his confidence. But that wouldn't do. The complete and sudden change of voices and sea sound should be just enough, I think, to make it just clear enough.

I can't see what offence can possibly be given by the nice healthy honest-to-God out-of-door life-loving deflowering that follows. I can't change it in any case and I hope it won't be managed discreetly. Do radio "plays" come in for more preliminary scrutiny than readings? I suppose they must.[1]

Re title no other ideas for the moment.

It is good news that you will be doing All That Fall again in June.[2]

It is very good of you to take such trouble with my work, I mean Penguin Murphy and mime music. I don't see how the latter, unless annotated to the teeth, is going to help them. The world rights of Murphy belong now to Grove Press and their permission would have to be got. They were having not so long ago a bit of a skirmish with Penguin publications, so I feel rather dubious.[3]

I should be very glad to have the Wells pamphlet. Many thanks too for remembering this.[4]

The work drags on at snail's pace, the heart or whatever it is not seeming in it and the difficulties too great. I neither let light in nor keep it out, I only try to say as little more than I find as possible, that doesn't sound right somehow, and as little less.

The weather continues bright and bitter cold and through one or other of the four windows of the two rooms the sun floods all day long. I wish I could rot here always. Tomorrow I have to be in Paris all day, but back here in the evening I hope. Then all next week probably in Paris.

I have finished Pasternak with mixed feelings, which is more than I hoped for.

Love
s/ Sam

TLS; 1 leaf, 1 side; *env to* Mrs Barbara Bray, 121 Brighton Road, Purley, Surrey, Angleterre; *pm* 4-2-59, La Ferté-sous-Jouarre; TCD, MS 10948/1/17.

1 Abrupt shifts of time and setting occur in *Embers*, and Bray had suggested adding transitional markers; SB took her suggestion of inserting "20 years earlier":

HENRY: Don't don't . . ..
[*Sea suddenly rough.*]
ADA: [*Twenty years earlier, imploring.*] Don't! Don't! (*CSP*, 100).

This hint at deflowering is immediately interrupted by the sound of the sea. The subsequent dialogue between Henry and Ada is situated in present time, on the same shingle beach: "Where we did it at last for the first time" (101).

2 *All That Fall* would be re-broadcast on the BBC Third Programme on 18 June.

3 Bray's attempt to interest Penguin Books in a paperback edition of *Murphy* was unsuccessful. Grove Press had published *Murphy* in an Evergreen paperback edition in June 1957; John Calder distributed it in the UK. John Beckett's music for *Act Without Words I* was not recorded.

4 SB mentioned H. G. Wells's *Mind at the End of its Tether* (1945) to Patrick Bowles when they met on 17 February. Bowles recalls that SB said of it: "Complete abandonment of all the early work. As if determined to prove its ruin." (Patrick Bowles, "How to Fail: Notes on Talks with Samuel Beckett," *PN Review* 20.4 [March–April 1994] 38.)

ETHNA MACCARTHY-LEVENTHAL
LONDON

4.2.59 Ussy

Dearest Ethna

I keep wondering and wondering. Con was vague in his letter from Dublin. This does not mean I expect you to write, absolutely not, I know how difficult it is lying in bed. Perhaps Claude would be kind enough to drop me just a very brief line now and then.[1]

I am here nearly all the time now, st[r]uggling feebly to "go on". Ce n'est pas une vie, but it's the nearest I ever got to one.[2] Brilliant bright bitter cold days, the sun flooding in through one or other of the 4 windows all day long. Losing battle with the moles, la pelouse n'est plus qu'une plaie.[3] I have to get up tomorrow in the dark at 6 and go to town to have lunch with Harold Hobson, but I'll get back here in the evening, to the stillness. I have given a rather ragged radio text, written a couple of years ago, to the BBC, the 3rd will do it in June and <u>All That Fall</u> again. You'd find me a title for it, but I can't. Hayden's exhibition opens at the Waddington Galleries Feb 12th I think, with an ancient foolish text of mine in the catalogue, in French, since I couldn't

5 Henri Hayden, "Self-Portrait 1955"

translate it.[4] He won't go over with the cold and his groggy knee. Avigdor is having his in London in April with Matthiessen [sic] and talks of going to Israel between now and then to recuperate his fiancée.[5]

Enough for now. Don't dream of writing, just a scribble from Claude if you think it's not too much to ask.

Je t'embrasse tout doucement tout tendrement.[6]

s/ SAM

TLS; 1 leaf, 1 side; TxU, Leventhal Collection, 1.7.

1 A. C. M. Elman (known as Claude, 1901–1978) was consulting physician to Queen Mary's Hospital and to East Ham Memorial Hospital; he was a friend and colleague of Ethna MacCarthy-Leventhal ("Obituaries: A. C. M. Elman," *The British Medical Journal* [26 August 1978] 643).

2 "Ce n'est pas une vie" (It's no kind of life).

3 "La pelouse n'est plus qu'une plaie" (The lawn is nothing more than an open sore now). SB had tried for some time to fend off the invasion of moles at Ussy. Barney Rosset sent SB "a drum of Chlordane," and wrote that he hoped that "duty and shipping in France do not cost you more than a flock of mole killing cats" (11 December 1957; NSyU). SB responded: "Again all my thanks for the molebane. I have told them about it and they are holding meetings." (26 December 1957; NSyU.)

4 Hayden's exhibition at the Waddington Galleries, London, opened on 12 February. SB's essay "Henri Hayden, homme peintre" was written in January 1952, "'commissioned by a private collector of Hayden's work who was compiling an illustrated catalogue of the works in his collection'" (Jean Tormey to the editors, 19 April 2001, quoting Josette Hayden). As SB later explained in a letter to the London book dealer Alan Clodd (1918–2002):

> I return herewith Hayden catalogue inscribed. This text was written many years ago, in the early fifties I think, at my friend Hayden's request, not for a gallery, but for a private collector in Cherbourg (a wealthy ironmonger) who felt he would like to have texts, (MS) by various writers, on the painters collected by him. The understanding was that none of these texts were for publication, as it was this that induced me to oblige. I have no qualifications to write about painting and greatly dislike doing so. Then, at Hayden's request again, and with the ironmonger's consent, I agreed, reluctantly, to this publication in Waddington's catalogue. That is the little story. (21 November 1961; NLI, Clodd, MS 35,293/1.)

The piece was first published in *Les Cahiers d'Art – Documents* [Geneva] 22 (November 1955) [2]; it was reprinted in *Henri Hayden: Recent Paintings, 12th February – 7th March 1959* (London: The Waddington Galleries, 1959) [2]. A facsimile of the original corrected typescript appears in *Henri Hayden: 1883–1970* (Cherbourg: Musée Thomas-Henry, 1997) 12–15.

5 Arikha would have a show of his work at the Matthiesen Gallery, London, in April 1959. Arikha had met Hagit Meiry (transcribed as Haguit in French, b. 1935, Tel Aviv, later married to historian Saul Friedlander) after she came to Paris in 1956 to study music at the Ecole Normale de Musique; he subsequently introduced her to SB. She left for Tel Aviv in summer 1958, promising to return after giving a series of recitals (Hagit Friedlander to the editors, 8 February 2012).

6 "Je t'embrasse tout doucement tout tendrement" (A gentle, tender kiss).

MOLLY ROE
PRINCETON, NEW JERSEY

6.2.59 Ussy

Dearest Molly

Many thanks for your letters and for the beautiful scarf. It arrived yesterday while I was in Paris. It was very cold and I was going out for lunch, so I used it without delay. It is very warm and comfortable. Thank you also very much for Suzanne's handkerchief which gave her great pleasure. If she were here with me in the country she would add a line to this, but she is in Paris at present. She was very touched by your kind remembrance of her.

It is great news that you are so well and happy and that there is a chance of our meeting this summer. I think I may have to go to Dublin at the beginning of July and perhaps that will fit in with your trip there.[1]

I had a week in Dublin at the beginning of December. Poor Ethna MacCarthy was and still is very ill. At present she is in hospital in London and I'm afraid there is nothing more to be done. She is a very old friend and had been married only a couple of years to another old friend, Con Leventhal, now working in TCD. I spent most of the week with them and it was a sad time. I stayed out in Killiney of course, except for one night in town. Jean is well and has her financial situation now well in hand. Caroline will be finishing her Froebel course this year and then should command at once a good salary. She works and plays very hard and has strings of young men attending her.[2] Edward is a fine young lad, as tall as I am now and very like Frank, I enjoyed seeing him again and being with him very much. I was up at Columba's a number of times. He is already, after only a little over a year's study, a quite impressive flautist. I was talking to his teacher, a Frenchman, who told me he is the most gifted subject he has come across since he has been in Ireland. If he sticks to it he should turn out a first class amateur and have great times playing chamber music and in orchestra. He seems to be in love with the instrument and works at it as hard as he can considering all the other things he has to do.[3] The only other friend I saw at all in Dublin was Tom MacGreevy who had a rather severe heart attack about the middle of last year and was two months in a nursing home. He seems pretty well over it now, but has to take things very quietly, no stairs, that kind of thing. I only saw Susan once, and briefly, and felt she was hurt at my lack of assiduity, but I simply couldn't manage it. I found her changed, rather querulous and wandering in her conversation and unhappy in the place where she is living, as she always ends up by being no matter where she is.[4] I also saw Howard and Jim and Peggy and Ann. Howard is 70 and weathering the storm well. Jim has also had heart trouble, but is still practising in a small way, dental work only I think. Peggy (Gerald's) had a very painful hip bone condition, and had been told that only an operation could relieve it. I don't know if she has had it.[5] Jean took me driving over some of the dear old roads, including the Ballyogan, which is just the same, including its tinkers, except for a big rather handsome ESB construction on the right going towards Carrickmines.[6] On the same day we had a gawk into Cooldrinagh now occupied by Dr Wheeler, the nephew I think of the Wheeler that lived in the Goods' old house. The old place had I believe gone more or less to rack and ruin with the people who bought it from the Martins, but is now in good shape again.[7] We called on the Stuarts (or Stewarts?) and found Queenie racked with rheumatism grubbing in the garden in the bitter cold and May poking about the house. I think they were pleased we went.[8] Christie is still working at New Place, Mrs Bewley is very poorly I forget with what, Winnie Ormsby is still going strong, the Hamiltons are all dead now and the place up for sale, they didn't leave a stivver to poor Eddy, in fact I think he was owed a lot of wages![9]

I spent [sic] most the time here in the country now. I try to go on writing, but with little success at present. I keep well enough, but am tired. Suzanne is well and very active. The little house is behaving well and very easy to run. I have got attached to the place and the great peace and quiet and find Paris and being with friends more and more upsetting and exhausting. My books are selling fairly well and my plays are being played here and there, which brings me in enough to continue this independent and rather indolent way of living. But the cost of living and taxation are now so high that I think I shall have to realise some of the Dublin capital and have it transferred here soon. Fortunately this is much easier now than it was a few years ago and the occasion of far less red tape and formalities. I am putting it off as long as possible, in the hope of fat cheques from New York!

Sheila's trip seems to have tired her, but she writes apart from that in good form. I'm sorry I missed Jack and felt envious of his golf at Miami. Perhaps we'll have a game yet, before the great bunker whence no recovery.[10]

Much love, dearest Moll, from us both, long may you be prosperous and happy.

s/ SAM

Forgive this flimsy paper – it's all I have at the moment.

TLS, with APS; 1 leaf, 2 sides; Babcock Collection.

(To prepare the notes below, the editors consulted the IGPArchives website for Kilternan Cemetery, and www.census.nationalarchives.ie)

1 At this time, SB's cousin Maria Belis Roe (known as Molly, 1903–1986) was an "executive housekeeper" for an unrelated family also named Roe in Princeton, New Jersey.

2 SB had stayed with Jean Beckett at Shottery in Killiney. His niece Caroline Beckett (b. 1938) was studying in the Froebel Education course at Alexandra College, Dublin, to become a primary school teacher.

3 SB's nephew Edward Beckett was a pupil at St. Columba's. His flute teacher was André Prieur (see 2 June 1958 to MacGreevy, n. 6).

4 SB's visit to Susan Manning: 21 November 1958. SB wrote to her on 28 December 1958: "But for Howard and his car I don't think I'd ever have got to your door," and to Mary Manning Howe on 2 January 1959: "I had only a brief and unsatisfactory meeting with Susan toward the end, Howard with me pawing to be off before he was well inside the door [. . .] I feel guilty that I didn't do more about her, but there it is, what I was there for was already too much for me." (TxU, Beckett Collection, 9.4, 8.10.)

5 SB speaks of his paternal uncles: Howard Beckett (1888–1965) and James Beckett (1884–1971) whose wife was Peggy (née O'Connell, d. 1978). The widow of Gerald Beckett (1886–1950) was also named Peggy (d. 1968); their children were the twins John and Ann Beckett (1927–2002).

6 The Ballyogan Road leads from Leopardstown to Carrickmines, Co. Dublin. ESB: Electrical Supply Board.

7 Cooldrinagh, Brighton Road (formerly 14 Kerrymount), was purchased from May Beckett (1871–1950) by Herbert H. Martin, who sold the house in 1955 to John Paul Kennedy (1909–1991), an architect. Kennedy sold it to Dr. Desmond de Courcy Wheeler, who owned it until 1976. Lt. Col. S. Gerald de Courcy Wheeler, The Barn, Torquay Road, Foxrock, was an uncle of Dr. Wheeler (Dr. Wheeler to Caroline Murphy; Edel Morgan, "Location, location, location … proves its worth in Beckett's Foxrock family home," *The Irish Times* 2 December 1999: 52). The William Good family lived at what was formerly 28 Kerrymount; they had a son the same age as SB and a daughter a year younger than Frank Beckett (1902–1954; Profile, I).

8 Neighbors in Foxrock included the daughters of Mrs. Harriet E. Stewart, Hatley, Brighton Road (formerly 11 Kerrymount): Agnes Grace (Queenie,

1877–1950), Harriet Amy (Harpie, 1879–1965), and Mary (May, 1875–1969). Queenie had died in 1950, so it may be that SB mistook Harpie for her (*The Irish Times* 8 September 1950: 8).

9 Christy was the Beckett family's gardener, who, after Cooldrinagh was sold, continued to work for May Beckett at New Place, Brighton Road, Foxrock. Charlotte Clibborn Bewley (1880–1965) was the widow of Louis Bewley, Blencarn, Kerrymount Avenue (formerly 6 Kerrymount) (Caroline Murphy to editors, 20 June 2012); Mrs. R. G. Ormsby (Winnie) lived in Tullycot, Brennanstown Road, Carrickmines. The Arthur Hamilton family had lived in Hollybrook, Brighton Road (formerly 31 Kerrymount); Eddy has not been identified. (*Thom's Directory of Ireland for the Year 1934* [Dublin: Alex Thom, 1934] 1667, 1975.)

10 Molly Roe's sister Sheila Page had been visiting in Canada. Their brother John Roe (known as Jack, 1907–1982) had emigrated to Canada in the late 1920s; he had worked in lithography there. During World War II, he served in the Canadian Army and was later posted to the Middle East. He eventually retired to the Toronto area.

BARBARA BRAY
PURLEY, SURREY

Tuesday 17.2.59 [Paris]

Dear Barbara

Still drunk this morning after sudden hopeless useless midnight bucket of brandy and sitting in special ever since 37 pub and have yours to hand and in head grinding old poem in vain by Hölderlin influenced entitled Dieppe circa 37 also, viz

Encore le dernier reflux
le galet mort
le demi-tour puis les pas Hölderlin
vers les vieilles lumières

suggesting for title of Bolton-Holloway first The Last Ebb and next some hours later because enough of lasts that are never EBB simply without more which please for Christ's sake approve, adopt, enterine & announce, though last night before dip occurred to me or was it again The Water's Edge but no, The Elder Statesman and The Potting Shed, no, EBB for God's sake, On the Strand is utterly impossible, why not Baile's.[1] Of all days to have appointment with dentist, grudgingly accorded & uncancellable, unshaved and breath old fine and fresh beer, I'm terrified, teeth rotting under bridges, head full of fibrous tumours. This evening Arrabal reading at the Poche, Les 2 Bourreaux[,] Guernica and another, Friday Ionesco's Tueur at the Récamier, putain de vie.[2] Thanks for cuttings, Jesus how I hate them. You shd. have gone to Lansdowne Road, charming venue, full of memories, cricket unexpectedly with brother's huge bat, hardly lift it, loss of railway ticket, fear of whiskered porter, walk home devious ways 10 miles, huge bag, father rampaging on Mrs Rooney's road, mother in furious swoon, police alerted in vain, midnight, foodless to bed, charming ground – Dicky Lloyd, Wakefield, Jaurreguy, ape-armed uncle beating down umbrella's [sic] with short stick, part of boyhood, heroic days.[3] Work no good, hammer hammer adamantine words, house inedible, hollow bricks, small old slates from demolished castle, second hand, couvreur fell off backward leaning scaffolding and burst, fat old man, instantaneous the things one has seen and not looked away. RTF studio for recording of a passage of All That, complete confusion, not good, but can one tell, Trutat worried, Blin trying to howl Oui![4] Enough for today, close now, Wells crazy, liquefied again, thanks for all, love to the girls, and up and go to hell, no future here, no present, no Johnson, well rid, head on table, wind, little quick clouds, light, dark, etc.[5]

Love

Sam

ALS; 1 leaf, 2 sides; *env to* Mrs Barbara Bray, 121 Brighton Road, Purley, Surrey, Angleterre; *pm* 17-2-59, Paris; TCD, MS 10908/1/19.

1 SB quotes his poem "Dieppe" (Samuel Beckett, *Collected Poems 1930–1978* [London: John Calder, 1984] 50–51). He circles both "puis" and, in the right margin, "Hölderlin," connecting them with a line. Lawrence Harvey discusses Hölderlin's "Der Spaziergang" as the "starting point" of "Dieppe" (*Samuel Beckett: Poet and Critic* [Princeton, NJ: Princeton University Press, 1970] 218–219). In addition to the titles SB had already offered Bray for his new radio play in his letter of 23 January, SB now adds a phrase taken from the first line of "Dieppe": "again the last ebb." Dismissed as titles are T. S. Eliot's *The Elder Statesman* (1958), Graham Greene's *The Potting Shed* (1957), and W. B. Yeats's *On Baile's Strand* (1904).

"Enterine," adapted from the French "entérine" (confirm).

2 "Old fine" (old brandy). The reading of Fernando Arrabal's *Les deux bourreaux* (1958) and *Oraison* (1958) at the Théâtre de Poche was announced in "Arrabal Théâtre et Baal-Babylone," *Arts* 714, 18–24 March 1959: 3. José Quaglio (1923–2007) directed Eugène Ionesco's *Tueur sans gages* which was to open two days later at the Théâtre Récamier; SB may have attended a rehearsal."Putain de vie" (bloody awful life).

3 Lansdowne Road was a rugby stadium, Dublin 4; it was demolished in 2007 and replaced in 2010 by the Aviva Stadium. SB refers to the loss of a railway ticket which led to a long walk home when he was twelve: see Knowlson, *Damned to Fame*, 51. In *All That Fall*, Mrs. Rooney walks along the Brighton Road to the Foxrock Station.

Richard Averill Lloyd (Dicky, 1891–1950) had been at Portora Royal School and played for Ireland while still a pupil there, in 1910. Wavell Wakefield, 1st Baron Wakefield of Kendal, played rugby for England, and was a Member of Parliament from 1935 to 1963. Adolphe Jauréguy (sometimes written Jaurréguy, 1898–1977), French rugby player from the 1920s and later an officer of the French Rugby Union. (Frédéric Humbert to the editors, 17 August 2012).

4 "Couvreur" (roofer). Alain Trutat directed *Tous ceux qui tombent* for Radio Télévision Française: 17 November 1958, n. 4. SB wrote to Ethna MacCarthy-Leventhal on 15 February: "I was in a RTF studio yesterday for the recording of a bit of All That Fall, Roger Blin in the rôle of old Rooney. Not good I thought." (TxU, Leventhal Collection, 1.7.)

5 Bray had sent SB *Mind at the End of its Tether* by H. G. Wells. Mary Manning Howe had sent SB a book on Dr. Johnson for Christmas (SB to Mary Manning Howe, 2 January 1959; TxU, Beckett Collection, 8.10).

AVIGDOR ARIKHA
JERUSALEM

25.2.59 Paris

Cher Avigdor

Merci de votre lettre. Content de vous savoir bien rendu et avec Haguit.[1] Ci-joint le poème. Je ne trouve pas la formule de dédicace. Le plus simple c'est de le présenter sans date.[2]

Ici c'est toujours la même vie stupide et assassine. Je reste encore quelques jours pour pouvoir assister au vernissage de Lipsi chez Denise René, samedi je serai à Ussy.[3] Vu Tueur sans gages l'autre soir, pas de sa meilleure encre. Ce soir Les Possédés rapport aux copains.[4] Aujourd'hui ou demain je retourne chez Castelucha reprendre votre aquarelle, c'est une bien belle chose.[5]

Et voilà. Amitiés à Haguit. Portez-vous bien tous les deux et revenez bientôt ensemble.

Amitiés

Sam

ALS; 1 leaf, 1 side; InU, Arikha.

25.2.59 Paris

Dear Avigdor

Thank you for your letter. Glad to know you're back safely, and with Haguit.[1] Enclosed the poem. I can't find the right dedicatory phrase. The simplest thing is to present it undated.[2]

Here still the same stupid, murderous life. I'm staying on a few days so as to be able to go to the Lipsi private view chez Denise René.[3] On Saturday I shall be in Ussy. Saw *Tueur sans gages* the other evening, not him at his best. This evening *Les Possédés*, on account of our friends.[4] Today or tomorrow I'm going to Castelucha's to retrieve your watercolour. It's a really fine thing.[5]

And that's it. All best to Haguit. Keep well, the two of you, and come back soon together.

Your friend

Sam

1 Arikha's fiancée Hagit Meiry: 4 February 1959 to MacCarthy-Leventhal, n. 5.

2 Arikha himself chose SB's poem "Accul" to appear in the catalogue of his exhibition (*Paintings, Gouaches and Drawings* [London: Matthiesen Gallery, 1959] [2]). The exhibition was to take place at the Matthiesen Gallery, between 8 April and 2 May.

3 Two months earlier, on 28 December, SB had written to Arikha: "J'essaie de travailler, mais c'est toujours la même chose. J'espère pouvoir continuer – c'est le cas de le dire – quand même. Ça donne comme un tout petit goût au torrent qui s'écoule." (I am trying to work, but it's always the same thing. I hope I can go on – now there's a phrase – for all that. It's giving a sort of little taste to the torrent that's flowing.) (InU, Arikha.)

The exhibition, Sculptures by Morice Lipsi (1898–1986), was held at the Galerie Denise René, from 27 February to 21 March; see also 11 August 1948, n. 1.

4 *Les Possédés*, written and directed by Albert Camus, opened on 29 January at the Théâtre Antoine, Paris 10; Jean Martin played the role of Chigalev and Roger Blin played Tikhone.

5 Arikha had given SB an untitled abstract watercolour (28 × 37.5 cm, private collection), which he was having framed.

JOHN ASHBERY
PARIS

25.2.59

6 Rue des Favorites
Paris 15$^{\underline{me}}$

Dear M$^{\underline{r}}$ Ashbery

I am not familiar with Roussel and fear I cannot be of much help to you. Joyce took whatever could be made to serve his purpose wherever he happened to find it. I never heard him mention Roussel and find it hard to believe there was any influence there worth speaking of.[1]

Sorry to be of so little use.

Yours sincerely
Sam. Beckett

ALS; 1 leaf, 1 side; *env to* Monsieur John Ashbery, 14 Rue Alfred Durand-Claye, Paris 14$^{\underline{me}}$; *pm* 25-2-59, Paris; Ashbery Collection.

1 In 1958–1959, American poet and art critic John Ashbery was in Paris to do research for a doctoral dissertation on Raymond Roussel; he had met SB through the American painter Joan Mitchell (1925–1992) (John Ashbery to the editors, 26 August 2012). Although Ashbery did not complete the doctorate, he later published extensively on Roussel's writings.

BARBARA BRAY
PURLEY, SURREY

25.2.59

Paris

Dear Barbara

Thanks for your letter. Glad you like EBB.[1]

I sent you the Ionesco programme. Not his best play by any means. No, I've never read Ivy C. B.[2] I should be sorry to think we are not to meet again and such a possibility had never occurred to me. It's I should drink less, not you. The stupid life here goes on. I have a vernissage on Friday, then back to Ussy and head versus wall again. I don't know why time isn't helping you, it has all my old troubles churned into emulsion till tears are about nothing & everything.

Forgive this terrible scribble, I can't do better at the moment.

Love

Sam

ALS; 1 leaf, 1 side; *env to* M[rs] Barbara Bray, 121 Brighton Road, Purley, Surrey, Angleterre; *pm* 25–2–59, Paris; TCD, MS 10948/1/20.

1 SB's provisional title for the radio play eventually entitled *Embers*.

2 Ivy Compton-Burnett's writing and SB's work are mentioned together in an article by Alan Pryce-Jones, "The Anti-Novel in France" (*Times Literary Supplement* 2972 [13 February 1959]: 82). This may have prompted Bray's question. Between 1911 and 1958, Compton-Burnett had published seventeen novels. Bray must have sent one of her novels to SB, as he would write to her on 19 March: "No, many thanks, but no more Ivy" (TCD, MS 10948/1/23).

BARBARA BRAY
PURLEY, SURREY

2.3.59 Ussy sur Marne

Dear Barbara

Retyping the radio text for N. Y. and elsewhere I have made a few small changes. Herewith the script I should like you to use. I have changed the title to Embers of which I hope you will not disapprove too highly. If EBB has already been announced I'm afraid this may inconvenience you. I hope not too much.[1]

I enclose also the translation of the first Texte pr. Rien. It is to appear – of all places – in Esquire! It is the only one I have done so far and does not encourage me to do the others.[2] I have now to revise Seaver's translation of La Fin.[3] Lovely time I'm having. Lovely weather without, first crocuses – very small and pale. Slow walks in the gloaming with a crooked old stick.

Love

Sam

ALS; 1 leaf, 1 side; *env to* Mrs Barbara Bray, 121 Brighton Road, Purley, Surrey, Angleterre; *pm* 4–3–59, La Ferté-sous-Jouarre; TCD, MS 10948/1/21.

1 The radio play had not yet been announced by the BBC Third Programme.

2 David Solomon (1925–2009), then Assistant Editor of *Esquire Magazine*, had asked SB for a contribution to the publication's anniversary issue. SB offered to send his translation of one of the *Textes pour rien* (SB to David Solomon, 28 November 1958; GEU, MS 1221).

3 Richard Seaver had sent "The End" to SB on 1 February, as well as a few questions about "L'Expulsé," which he was translating as "The Expelled." SB returned "The End" with his corrections on 6 March and wrote to Seaver: "Your translation is excellent and they are for the most part just fussiness and contrariness and author's license [sic]. If there are any you disagree with let me have a note of them and we'll find something else or revert to your text." (TxU, Seaver, R 16501.)

ALAN SCHNEIDER
NEW YORK

3.3.59 Ussy

Dear Alan

Glad to have news of you. All wishes for a happy new pa and ma ternity. You don't say how your father is. Much better I hope.[1]

With regard to Krapp I don't much like the night club idea, I think it could only be bungled in such an atmosphere. The Monday performance, though not exhilarating, would I think be preferable. It is a delicate and technically rather ticklish production and needs at least quiet. Another possibility is just to leave it for the moment, until there is or I have something to go with it. It is not because it is there written that you must feel it must be done at once, I was never in a hurry about such things.[2] There will be no theatre or radio from me now until I have done something that goes on from The Unnamable and Texts for Nothing or decided there is no going on from there for me, either of which operations will take a long time probably. I have send [sic] the other radio text (two years ago) to Grove, but apart from the air it can only be done as a reading, no question of a stage performance. It is not of any great interest in any case. It will be broadcats [sic] by the 3rd I think in June.[3] As typing shows tired tonight after slogging all day for nothing, it seems to produce metatheses, I've often noticed it.[4] Have been in Paris lately and saw the

Camus Dostoevsky and the new Ionesco both depressing to me and a reading of Arrabal at the Montparnasse Poche, a good evening that. Back here now until some convivial pal pops up in Montparnasse, always irresistible. Have to be in Dublin early July, otherwise no plans. Hope you'll have a production in Europe this summer. In the meantime goodluck [sic] to all ypur [sic] projects Broadway, off and road and affectionately to you all.[5]

s/ SAM

TLS; 1 leaf, 1 side; Burns Library, Samuel Beckett Collection, SB-AS. Previous publication: Beckett and Schneider, *No Author Better Served*, 55.

1 The Schneiders were expecting their first child in April. Alan Schneider's father Leopold Victorovich Schneider (1891–1963) had suffered a heart attack in 1958 (Schneider, *Entrances*, 262, 339).

2 Schneider's letter to SB of 22 February had reported that there were two immediate options available for staging *Krapp's Last Tape* in New York: The Five Spot Cafe on Third Avenue and St. Marks Place ("a rather well-known bohemian-cabaret" which featured "jazz combos" but also hosted readings of poetry), or Monday evenings at one of the smaller Greenwich Village theatres (where the play could be run several times in an evening). Rosset favored the former, whereas Schneider worried about "getting a proper performance in a night-club atmosphere"; still, Schneider allowed that it could be "just the right off-beat situation" (Beckett and Schneider, *No Author Better Served*, 54).

3 *All That Fall* had been sent to Grove in December 1956 (SB to Rosset, 5 December 1956; NSyU).

4 SB's typing in this letter exhibits metatheses, as demonstrated by his correction of "leats" to "least," and "aprat" to "apart."

5 Schneider directed *Kataki* by Shimon Wincelberg (1924–2004) (which opened on Broadway on 9 April, following previews in Philadelphia); he then directed *Epitaph for George Dillon* by John Osborne and Anthony Creighton, which opened at the Arena Stage, Washington, DC, on 5 May ("2-Role War Play 'Kataki,' to Open," *New York Times* 14 March 1959: 26; Schneider, *Entrances*, 263, 393).

BARBARA BRAY
PURLEY, SURREY

11.3.59 Ussy

Dear Barbara

Thanks for your letter and comments on the text. I have not yet gone through it with them. But I know they will be a great help. All my thanks. That kind of thing is really not possible for me in English. I began the second and gave it up.[1]

The omission of "Vega in the Lyre . . ." is a mistake. Will you please restore it in your script, I have hastened to do so in mine.[2]

It was good to hear your voice again. It is hard to deal with such matters on the phone. The reason for Embers has really nothing to do with religious considerations. I did not realise my changes had made this element more apparent, for me in this text it is quite unimportant. This does not mean that the fasting overtone is not worth having. I decided on Embers because for one thing it receives light in the course of the piece and for another because embers are a better ebb than the sea's, because followed by no flow. The real title is the first line of the little poem, Again the Last Ebb, which I would accept, and Embers says that more or less in one word. I do not feel the old fashionedness of the word as you do and anyway what the hell. The sea and shore are so unreal, compared to Bolton's room and the dying fire etc., that I feel the reference should rather be to the latter. But again if you and Donald decide you prefer Ebb, keep it, and if you think Again the Last Ebb is acceptable, adopt it. The Last Ebb alone would not do.[3]

I'm struggling along with the new moan, trying to find the rhythm and syntax of extreme weakness, penury perhaps I should say. Sometimes I think I'm getting on, then realise how far I am from it still. This is the fifth or sixth version of the opening.

I got the bicycle out of its winter dereliction and went for a violent ride in the sun and wind. Legs not quite gone, but going. I uprooted 20 wild broom in the wood and planted them in a crescent round the garbage heap. Unfortunately no bush is more transparent even at its densest. Brief moving bloom. Soon mowing will begin again.

I shall be happy to meet the new controller. A little in advance please the day, place and hour of his choice. Perhaps I should know something of his novels beforehand. No?[4]

I think Dublin in July will be straight to and fro. But I have a sister-cousin coming from Princeton this summer and must see her. She will go to Dublin, but perhaps not while I am there. In which case

I would probably see her in Surrey at her sister's place in or near Godalming. Is that near Purley?[5]

I am sorry you are so tired and down. I who had hoped to help you seem to have made things even worse for you. If you come over you know what a welcome to you will be mine and what an unsatisfactory mess you will have to put up with. Write whenever you like, I look forward to your letters. There are periods when I can, others when I find it very difficult.

If Donald produces whatever the thing is called we should really try and meet beforehand.

Love

s/ Sam

TLS; 1 leaf, 2 sides; *env to* Mrs Barbara Bray, 121 Brighton Road, Purley, Surrey, Angleterre; *pm* 11-3-59, La Ferté-sous-Jouarre; TCD, MS 10948/1/22.

1 Bray's comments were on SB's English translation of the first text of *Textes pour rien*.

2 "Vega in the lyre very green. [*Pause*.] Vega in the Lyre very green. [*Pause*]" is a line in *Embers* (*CSP*, 95).

3 The first line of "Dieppe" is "again the last ebb" (see 17 February 1959, n. 1).

4 P. H. (Howard) Newby (1918–1997) was Controller of the Third Programme from 1958 to 1971. By 1959, Newby had written ten novels; Bray would send SB *Picnic at Sakkara* (1955) (SB to Barbara Bray, 7 April 1959; TCD, MS 10948/1/26).

5 After the death of their mother, SB's cousins Molly, Sheila, and Jack Roe had attended schools in Dublin and lived with the Beckett family in Foxrock during school holidays (Knowlson, *Damned to Fame*, 44–45). Sheila and Donald Page (1901–1989) lived in Wormley, near Godalming (4 miles south of Guildford). Bray lived in Purley in the London borough of Croydon.

AVIGDOR ARIKHA
JERUSALEM

12.3.59 Ussy

Cher Avigdor

Merci de votre lettre. Amitiés à Haguit. Pas d'histoire[s], qu'elle rapplique ici avec vous. Bien sûr que ça doit s'arranger. J'espère que le récital du 10 s'est bien passé.[1]

Une carte d'Ethna. Con est venu passer deux jours auprès d'elle. Il revient le 19. Je ne sais pas où ça en est médicalement. Tout le monde est gentil pour elle, elle est certainement très bien soignée. Télévision dans sa chambre et alimentation enfin. Très droguée aussi probablement.

Je suis à Ussy, seul, depuis bientôt 15 jours. Côté travail je fais ce que je peux, ce n'est pas brillant. Le rythme et la syntaxe de la faiblesse et de la pénurie, pas commode à attraper.[2] J'y arrive quand même peut-être un peu – 6<u>me</u> version du début. Je vous montrerai ça à votre retour, à moins que je ne me torche avec d'ici là. A part ça, ballades [*for* balades] en vélo et petit jardinage. Lamentable vie mais qui dit mieux?

Bonne randonnée. Salut à Jérusalem.

Amitiés

Sam

ALS; 1 leaf, 1 side; InU, Arikha.

12.3.59 Ussy

Dear Avigdor

Thank you for your letter.

All best to Haguit. Let's hear no more about it: she's to get back here with you. Of course it must be possible to arrange it. I hope the recital on the 10th went off well.[1]

A card from Ethna. Con came over to spend a couple of days with her. He is coming back on the 19th. I don't know how things stand medically. Everyone is being nice to her. She is certainly being looked after very well. Television in her room and food, anyhow. Very drugged too, probably.

I've been alone in Ussy for what will soon be a fortnight. On the work front, I do what I can. It's not brilliant. The rhythm and the syntax of weakness and penury: not easy to catch.[2] All the same, I am getting a little closer – 6th version of the beginning. I'll show it to you when you get back, unless I use it to wipe myself between now and then. Apart from that, bike rides and gentle gardening. Lamentable life, but is there any better?

Have a good trip. Say hello to Jerusalem for me.

All best

Sam

1 SB was aware of Arikha's plan to return to Paris to marry his fiancée Hagit Meiry, and Arikha had presumably made him aware of her (in the end overwhelming) hesitations. Arikha accompanied her on her piano recital tour which included, on 10 February, a concert at the Mishmar Ha-Emek kibbutz.

2 On the same day, 12 March, SB wrote to Leslie Daiken "Struggling to get on with new work, but with scant success. Like trying to make a shape with dust & not much of it." (TxU, Daiken Collection, 1.1.)

BARNEY ROSSET
GROVE PRESS, NEW YORK

20.3.59 Ussy

Dear Barney

Good to hear from you after this long time. Forgive my not having written. I've been rather overpowered with one thing and another. I'm delighted to hear of your acquisitions and plans for the future. The negro shrine seems just the place for Krapp.[1] I haven't yet been able to play the tape of Endgame. The record is perhaps waiting for me in Paris. As soon as I hear it I'll let you know frankly what I think.[2] I wonder why the radio script never arrived, I sent it by airmail some time ago. Here it is again, with a few changes as compared with the text I sent you, notably the title. If you use it use this second version. It's not very satisfactory, but I think just worth doing. The 3rd will do it end of June. They are also going to broadcast All That Fall again. I don't know to whom you should write for permission to use their broadcasts. I suggest you write to Barbara Bray (Mrs), Drama Department, BBC, and tell her your problem. She is a good friend of mine and I'll prepare her when I next write.[3] They are very cagey about their tapes and you'll probably have difficulty. I'll be meeting the new Controller in Paris soon (John Morris's successor). Magee did the Unnamable reading, I actually have the tape, but I'm not supposed to have it. There were mistakes in rhythm and interpretation, but on the whole it was excellent, John's "music" also, though not always in the right place.[4] I am so glad you like the first Text for Nothing, I am very touched by what you say about it. I can't see it in Esquire. I began the second, then left it in disgust. I'll do them all in the end.[5] I went through Seaver's translation of La Fin, made some suggestions and returned it to him. I think it comes off quite well. It is nice to think of Seaver at Grove and I hope it comes off. I didn't see very much of Howard, he was very busy. I should have liked to give him dinner one evening, but it was towards the end of his stay when I was in Paris and he hadn't a spare moment.[6] Marcel Mihalovici, French Roumanian musician, wants to make a chamber opera out of Krapp, for the RTF and for a theatre in Germany. I gave him permission and suppose you have no objection. He is a fine musician and a good friend, husband of the pianist Monique Haas.[7] There has been a successful revival of Godot in the Düsseldorf municipal theatre, directed by Stroux who made such a balls of it in Berlin six or seven years ago, he replaced Gründgens at Düsseldorf.[8] I have been in Ussy over a fortnight now, struggling with the new work (in French). It is devilishly difficult and I can't do much at a stretch. After months of false starts and rewriting I have about ten very approximate pages. I don't know if I'll ever make it, I certainly won't try anything else until I either do or decide it's hopeless, though the call of the theatre is strong. One of those queer compulsions. I have to be in Paris at the beginning of April, for the purpose among other things of seeing the France-Wales rugby match at Colombes, invited by Claude Simon.[9] I have to be in Dublin at the beginning of July, TCD having taken the strange notion to give me a Litt.D., that will be jolly. I nearly said the usual no, then decided I couldn't. I saw something of Joan and Riopelle about a month ago, billiards in the little café near her place, dinner and Dôme Bar. I have great friendship for Joan and admire her work enormously. They are very occupied with her new studio in the 15th arrondissement, it sounds fine, but won't be ready for a while yet.[10] Fall was I am told delighted with his reception by you and I am very glad to hear you are to bring out the little book on Bram. My main text was written in English, so no problem there, I simply have to try and translate the other fragment, no easy matter as I remember it.[11] Arikha, who did the drawings for Nouvelles et Textes, gave me a very beautiful water-colour, he is having a big exhibition in London next month, with an old French poem of mine by way of introduction![12] Cronin delivered his discourse before the Unnamable broadcast, I had the text, but God knows what I've done with it, it was all right, not very exciting, Barbara Bray would let you have a copy.[13] Inferno, the Girodias super-review, fell to the ground and I gave French Krapp to Nadeau; it appeared in the first number of the weekly Lettres Nouvelles.[14] God knows when Blin will put it on here, at the moment he is playing in Camus' adaptation of Dostoevsky's Possédés, Jean Martin too in a very minor role, it is doing well and will probably run to the summer. Tueur sans Gages was rather diffuse, he is now being staged in three Paris theatres, Huchette still, Studio des Champs Elysées and Récamier, they call him the Roussin of the advance-guard![15] Pinget's new book is receiving a lot of notice, I liked it very much, also the play, though I think the 2nd act needs revision.[16] I went to an Arrabal reading at the Montparnasse Poche and enjoyed it, very well presented by Serr[e]au and others, extracts, nothing from the Cimetière which I think is probably the best, though Les 2 Bourreaux should play very well.[17] I've started pottering about the place in the afternoon, got the old bike out of its winter cobwebs and had a few spins with what's left of puff and legs. It's a dull lonely life, but I see nothing else for it. You'll have had your bellyful of my blather by now so here ends for today. I hope Peter is quite well again and no return of the trouble. Let's keep in better touch from now on. Warm greetings to LinK. [sic].

Affectionately

s/ SAM

EMBERS enclosed.[18]

TLS, with APS; 1 leaf, 2 sides; NSyU.

1 No record of Rosset's further suggestion has been found (see 3 March 1959, n. 2).

2 The New York production of *Endgame* with Lester Rawlins and Gerald Hiken had been recorded (see 23 November 1958, n. 5).

3 SB had sent a typescript of *Embers* to Grove Press before 3 March 1959.

4 Patrick Magee's reading from *The Unnamable*, with music composed by John Beckett, had been broadcast on 19 January 1959 on the BBC Third Programme.

5 SB sent "Text 1" to Grove Press on 1 March, but, as Judith Schmidt told him in her letter of 23 March: "Esquire (after all of their bothering) decided not to use TEXT FOR NOTHING I. We heard from them last week and sent it on to Mademoiselle" (NSyU).

6 Richard Seaver joined Grove Press on 2 February (Richard Seaver, *The Tender Hour of Twilight* [New York: Farrar, Straus and Giroux, 2012] 248).

The poet, critic, and translator Richard Howard (b. 1929) had translated Alain Robbe-Grillet's novels as well as work by Arthur Adamov, Fernando Arrabal, André Breton, E. M. Cioran, Edgar Morin, Robert Pinget, and Jules Roy, for Grove Press.

7 Marcel Mihalovici, Monique Haas, and the proposal to compose an opera of *Krapp's Last Tape*: 10 April 1958 and n. 5.

8 Karl-Heinz Stroux (1908–1985; Profile, II) was Generalintendant of the Düsseldorfer Schauspielhaus from 1955 to 1972; his revival of *Warten auf Godot* opened there on 7 March. Alions Neukirchen wrote "Die Inzenierung von Karl Heinz Stroux kommt der Pariser Uraufführung in der Grazie des Komödianten nahe, übertrifft sie jedoch in der Wucht und dem Nachdruck, womit Sinn und Widersinn gegeneinandergeführt werden" ("Poesie am Rande des Abgrunds," *Düsseldorfer Nachrichten* 9 March 1959: 2) (Karl-Heinz Stroux's production comes close to the Paris premiere's comic grace, but it surpasses it in the force and emphasis with which sense and nonsense are juxtaposed). Stroux had directed the Berlin production at the Schlossparktheater in September 1953 (SB to Stroux, 13 September 1953). Gustaf Gründgens (1899–1963) had been Generalintendant of the Düsseldorfer Schauspielhaus (1951–1955); he then became Generalintendant of the Deutsche Schauspielhaus in Hamburg (1955–1963) (Thomas Blubacher, *Gustaf Gründgens* [Hamburg: Ellert and Richter, 2011] 153).

9 Claude Simon's novels were published by Editions de Minuit. The France–Wales rugby match was held on 4 April at the Stade Colombes; France would win the match 11–3.

10 The Canadian artist Jean-Paul Riopelle (1923–2002), then lover of Joan Mitchell (Rosset's former wife). Their new studio at 10 Rue Frémicourt, Paris 15, was a "top-floor warehouse" which needed complete renovation (Patricia Albers, *Joan Mitchell, Lady Painter: A Life* [New York: Alfred A. Knopf, 2011] 273).

11 Georges Fall (b. 1920) established the Musée de Poche, a series of books on contemporary painters; *Bram van Velde* (1958) was published in this series, with essays by SB, Georges Duthuit, and Jacques Putman. SB's contribution is a passage from Samuel Beckett and Georges Duthuit's "Three Dialogues" ("The realisation that art has always been bourgeois . . . It seems to have nothing to do with art, in any case, if my memories of art are correct," 9–15; this was originally published in *Transition Forty-Nine* no. 5, 102–103, and is reprinted in Beckett, *Disjecta*, 144–145). A further short passage by SB from "Peintres de l'empêchement" appeared on page [7]: "Parmi les masses . . . art d'incarcération" (*Derrière le miroir* 11–12 [June 1948] 7; rpt. Beckett, *Disjecta*, 136–137).

The Grove Press edition of *Bram van Velde*, tr. Samuel Beckett and Olive Classe (1960), includes the selection from "Three Dialogues" (9–10, 13), but not the passage from "Peintres de l'empêchement."

12 Beckett's poem "Accul": 25 February 1959 to Arikha, n. 2. Frederick Laws would write of Arikha's exhibition at the Matthiesen Gallery:

> From Israel with a supporting poem by Samuel Beckett in French with puns, sublimities and no capital letters or punctuation, comes an impressive show of Avigdor Arikha, at the Matthiesen Gallery, 142 New Bond Street. Stormy colours and tortured form are organized into good pictures which hardly need titles like "The Threat" or "Anguish" to suggest that the end of the world is near and could be beautiful. ("Painters of the English Scene," *The Manchester Guardian* 23 April 1959: 6).

13 Anthony Cronin's talk "The Unsayable" was presented on the BBC Third Programme just prior to the readings from *The Unnamable* on 19 January (WAC, Radio Talks 101 [microfilm partially illegible]; Jeff Walden to the editors, 13 June 2012).

14 The journal proposed by Maurice Girodias, publisher of Olympia Press, did not materialize. "La dernière bande," *Les Lettres Nouvelles*, nouvelle série (2) 1 (March 1959) 5–13.

15 Eugène Ionesco's current plays in Paris were *Tueur sans gages* at the Théâtre Récamier, *La Cantatrice chauve* and *La Leçon* at the Théâtre de la Huchette, and *Victimes du devoir* at the Studio des Champs-Elysées. SB compares the currently very successful Ionesco with the most popular and frequently performed French playwright of the period, André Roussin (1911–1987).

16 Robert Pinget's novel *Le Fiston* and his play *Lettre morte* were published in 1959 by Editions de Minuit.

17 Serreau directed the evening of readings from Arrabal's work, including *Le cimetière des voitures* (see 17 February 1959, n. 2).

18 The PS is circled.

AIDAN HIGGINS
JOHANNESBURG

24.3.59 Paris – Ussy

Dear Aidan

Thanks for all your letters. Forgive my not having written. No reason, no excuse, killed with fatuous mail and struggles to write. Delighted to hear your stories are coming out with Grove and Calder. Warmest congratulations. I wish I could undertake to write a preface for it, since you ask me to, but I can't. I can't do that kind of thing and never try.[1] The Hayden preface was written in 52, bilge, not for publication, for a private collector, now they've dragged it out, Waddington, but I refused to translate it. I'm sorry to disappoint you. Anyway you're better without me.[2] The Mexican anthology, not chosen but translated by me for UNESCO, is not worthy your attention. Pot boiler, 52. Nine tenths of the poems are shit.[3] The Unnamable should be out soon with Calder I suppose, in one vol with the other two, unless he's changed his mind, I have no news. If I had a Grove copy here I'd send it, but I haven't. I don't even know if I have one in Paris. If I haven't I'll ask Grove to send you one. Queer idea to be saving up to return to Dublin, however perhaps you're right. Perhaps New York would be an idea for you, I can understand you can't face London again.[4] I have no news only the old song. Endgame and Krapp were a great flop in S.W. something, the latter magnificently played by Magee, couldn't wish for anything better, directed by McWhinney [sic]. Endgame not good, poor Jackie McGowran sadly wasted, now Joxering in NY O'Casey musical murder.[5] I have a new radio play, not very satisfactory, with the 3rd in June, written in English. I won't do anything more now for theatre or radio until I finish what I'm on now (French), an attempt to go on from where the Texts for Nothing left me off, or decide it's hopeless, no doubt the latter, I should know in a year or two. No news of John, I hear he was harpsichording in Dublin in the Matthew Passion. He did some good screeches for the Unnamable reading.[6] I was there for a week in December and was down in Greystones. Saw practically no one. Yes, sidled into the Arts Club with Con one evening for dinner, corn beef and cabbage I believe. Poor Ethna is dying in the East Ham Memorial Hospital, cancer of the mouth, a few weeks to "go". Fucking fucking earth.[7] I have to go back to Dublin in July, another week. I spend most of my time in the country at Ussy, pottering and bulloxing around, paper and grass, battling with moles, dull sad life and nothing else for it, riding a bicycle and refusing to give in on the hills, puff and legs in Golden Shred.[8] I'll try and see Arland in July if he'll have me, want to see does he still wear the piss stain on his fly and stand his cigarette end up on the counter.[9] Glad you are prosperous. Don't let the ads get you know [*for* ? now], back to work back to work, write all the starch out of it.[10] No more for this once. All the best to one and all.

Yours ever

s/ Sam

TLS; 1 leaf, 1 side; T *env to* Aidan Higgins, 36 Mount Willmar, 36 Isipingo Street, Bellevue, Johannesburg, Afrique du Sud; *pm* 24-3-59, La Ferté-sous-Jouarre; TxU, Beckett Collection, 8.9.

1 John Calder published six stories by Aidan Higgins as *Felo de Se* (1960); Grove Press later published the same stories under the title *Killachter Meadow* (1961). SB wrote to Leslie Daiken of Higgins: "to be published will do him a lot of good and I think he is capable of fine work" (25 February 1959; TxU, Daiken Collection, 1.1).

2 SB writes "bilge" by hand in upper margin, with a line to the place of insertion. SB's essay "Henri Hayden, homme peintre": 4 February 1959, n. 4.

3 Octavio Paz, ed., *Anthology of Mexican Poetry*, tr. Samuel Beckett (London: Thames and Hudson, 1958; UNESCO Collection of Representative Works: Latin American Series, Bloomington: University of Indiana Press, 1958); see 27 [February 1950], n. 5 and n. 6. SB did the translation in 1950, not 1952.

4 Higgins was living in South Africa, having gone there to tour with the John Wright Marionette Company in 1957 (Aidan Higgins, *Donkey's Years: Memories of a Life as Story Told* [London: Secker and Warburg, 1995] 263–273; Aidan Higgins, *The Whole Hog* [London: Secker and Warburg, 2000] 136–137).

5 *Endgame* and *Krapp's Last Tape* ran for thirty-eight performances at the Royal Court Theatre from 28 October 1958 (Richard Findlater, ed., *At the Royal Court: 25 Years of the English Stage Company* [New York: Grove Press, 1981] Appendix 2, Financial Tables, np). Jack MacGowran had played Clov to George Devine's Hamm. MacGowran was currently in the role of Joxer in *Juno*, a musical adaptation of Sean O'Casey's *Juno and the Paycock* by Joseph Stein and Marc Blitzstein, which had opened on 9 March at the Winter Garden Theatre in New York (Brooks Atkinson, "Theatre: A Musical 'Juno' Arrives," *The New York Times* 10 March 1959: 41).

6 John Beckett played the harpsichord for Bach's *St. Matthew Passion* on 15 March with the St. James's Gate Musical Society at St. Francis Xavier Hall, Dublin (C. C., "Impressive Performance," *Irish Times* 16 March 1959: 7). John Beckett composed the music for the BBC Third Programme reading from *The Unnamable*.

7 SB had visited Ethna MacCarthy-Leventhal in Dublin in December; as her condition worsened, she was hospitalized in London. SB wrote to her on 24 March: "This is just my heart to you and my hand in yours and a few wood violets I'd take from their haunt for no one else" (Leventhal Collection, 1.7). The United Arts Club is at 3 Upper Fitzwilliam Street, Dublin.

8 "Golden Shred," made by Robertson's, was and still is a popular type of marmalade. SB often speaks of hard exercise turning his legs and feet into "marmalade," a French idiom, "en marmelade" (a soggy mess).

9 Arland Ussher had complained to Aidan Higgins on 12 January: "Sam, I am informed, was in Dublin recently. Naturally he kept aloof from me, Godot-like." (TCD, MS 9031-9041/1528.)

10 Higgins was working in an advertising agency in Johannesburg (Higgins to the editors).

BARBARA BRAY
PURLEY, SURREY

26.3.59 Ussy

Dear Barbara

Thanks for your letter. I am so pleased you will be doing Lettre Morte. I rang up Pinget with the good news and his gladness is touching. You must meet him when you are next over, or when he is next in London (he goes regularly to friends there), whichever first. I am glad you are translating it yourself. Will you do it as it stands or do you think it needs adapting for the air? The rights are certainly free, application to Editions de Minuit.[1] Very glad also to hear from Daiken that his script has been received for the Home, he is in bad need of a little good fortune.[2]

It was good of you and Naughton (wonderful name for a character, why did I never think of it) to send me his book. I wrote him c/o you after having read only a few pages. I have now finished it. Great authenticity, easy and enjoyable reading.[3] I accept with gratitude the Yale Johnson if it's not too expensive, I find it hard to resist anything to do with that old blusterer, especially his last years. I received a card from Foyle stating that one book is not available (I forget the title).[4] I haven't yet received the 3rd Lettres Nouvelles, it must have got stuck in Paris, I'll send it in due course. Unbelievably stupid article on Le Fiston by Coiplet in the Monde, but should probably sell some copies.[5] I think Rosset and Penguin have had a bit of a dustup, and Rosset has world rights on Murphy, so not much prospect there. Grove will no doubt do a pocket some time, perhaps they have already. No news from Calder, but I was told the 3 in 1 was imminent. Please God he doesn't call it a trilogy.[6]

I battle on here, average of half a page daily, in a year or so I might have a rough draft. The thing makes itself as it goes, but that's not the point alas.

We seem to be doing some of the same things. I drove Hayden's new 2nd-hand Dauphine yesterday, first drive for a long time, and am reading seriously for the 1st time La Jalousie. Good idea to have Brain on him, but I'm afraid hallucination won't wash, here, except in so far as scrutiny at this intensity partakes of it. It is systematic Sachlichkeit, which of course has nothing to do with realism. What worries me is all his own theorising, but the result belies it and is I think very imp[o]rtant and remarkable.[7]

Two little peasant girls, sisters, age of yours, visit me both mounted on an old donkey know[n] locally as Le Ministre, no doubt because of his ministrations to cows (work that out). I give them a recipient and they bring me farm cream the next day.[8] The blasted Parisians are there for Easter with their screaming brats. I potter about the garden from after lunch to dark. Back to Paris towards end of next week, but not for long.

Love

s/ Sam

P.S. I am arranging for you to receive from now forth the Evergreen Review commencing with No. 7 just out, a fat magnificent Mexican number, with Blanchot's article on me (mainly) translated by Howard & perhaps ce qu'on a fait de mieux on that gruesome subject, so don't be going buying it from Calder.[9] Enc. best so far on Pinget.[10]

TLS, with APS inserted in a box; 1 leaf, 1 side; enclosure Jean-René Huguenin, "Le Nouveau Roman se demande s'il a une signification"; *env to* Mrs Barbara Bray, 121 Brighton Road, Purley, Surrey, Angleterre; *pm* 27–3–59, La Ferté-sous-Jouarre; TCD, MS 10948/1/24.

1 SB had requested that Editions de Minuit send *Lettre morte* to Bray (SB to Bray, 12 February 1959; TCD, MS 10948/1/18).

2 Leslie Daiken's *The Circular Road*: 17 November 1958, n. 3. The BBC Home Service was a national radio station from 1939 to 1967.

3 William Naughton (Bill, 1910–1992) was born to an Irish family in Bolton, Lancashire. Naughton's most recent novel was *One Small Boy* (1957); SB wrote to thank him on 21 March: "It is very strong and moving and I am reading it with great enjoyment" (Naughton Archive, Bolton, 2NA/4/214/2).

4 Samuel Johnson, *Diaries, Prayers, Annals*, ed. E. L. McAdam, Jr., with Donald and Mary Hyde, The Yale Edition of the Work of Samuel Johnson, I (New Haven: Yale University Press, 1958). SB may have ordered other books about Johnson from Foyle's, a bookstore in London.

5 Robert Coiplet, "*Le Fiston* – Lettre Morte de M. Robert Pinget," *Le Monde* 21 March 1959: 9.

6 Grove Press published *Murphy* as an Evergreen book in 1957 and had world rights because the original publisher, Routledge and Kegan Paul, had allowed the book to go out of print.

7 Henri Hayden's Renault Dauphine was an economy car with a rear-mounted engine.

Alain Robbe-Grillet's *La Jalousie* (1958) is a novel in which the narrating consciousness, everywhere present, is never given an identity, and the "story" is the detailed record of what that consciousness *sees* (seeing is the driving force of the narration): sometimes through a Venetian blind (une jalousie), but also through the visions and inventions that can be prompted by jealousy. Bray was seeking a way to stimulate discussion of Robbe-Grillet's novel in England; she may have considered the BBC television program *The Brains Trust*. On the program, a panel of intellectuals responded to viewers' questions on live television.

"Sachlichkeit" (matter-of-factness).

8 "Recipient": Gallicism, from "récipient" (container).

9 *Evergreen Review* 2.7 (Winter 1959) featured a collection by Mexican writers entitled "The Eye of Mexico" and an essay on SB's three novels by Maurice Blanchot, translated by Richard Howard as "Where Now? Who Now?" (222–229; "Où maintenant? Qui maintenant?" *Nouvelle Revue Française* 2.10 [October 1953] 678–686). "Ce qu'on a fait de mieux" (the best anyone's done). John Calder distributed *Evergreen Review* in England.

10 Jean-René Huguenin wrote about a discussion of the "nouveau roman" in "Le Nouveau Roman se demande s'il a une signification" (*Arts* 714, 18–24 March 1959: 3). The only mention of Pinget occurs in his final paragraph:

> On se lève, les photographes se précipitent, et tandis que Claude Simon, Robbe-Grillet et Pinget illustrent pour la caméra l'aile marchante des Editions de Minuit, chacun se console en songeant que, si l'histoire n'entre pas dans la littérature, voilà du moins une soirée littéraire digne d'entrer dans l'Histoire. (All stand up, the photographers rush forward, and while Claude Simon Robbe-Grillet and Pinget illustrate, for the press camera, the First Eleven of the Editions de Minuit, everyone comforts himself with the thought that, if history has no place in literature, here at least is a literary evening worthy of a place in History.)

BARNEY ROSSET
GROVE PRESS, NEW YORK

8.4.59 Paris

Dear Barney

Alain Bosquet as you probably know is doing a seminar at Brandeis University. His students are studying, inter alia, Nouvelles et Textes pour Rien. On leaving here Bosquet asked me for an inédit to have polycopied and used in his class. I gave him an old unpublished story, Premier Amour, contemporary with the 3 Nouvelles and scrapped long ago.[1] Bosquet now appears to be the victim of a hoax. He tells me that at the request of one Guy Davenport of Harvard he has sent this text somewhere (he doesn't say) "for publication", Davenport having told Bosquet I knew him (I don't) and that he was making this request "de ma part" (he wasn't).[2]

This little piracy is unimportant, but it upsets me. I am absolutely opposed to the publication of this text or to its circulation in any form outside Bosquet's class. I have written in haste to Bosquet asking him to try and retrieve the situation and the text. I want you to know, if you suddenly see it in print God knows where and translated God knows how, that it is entirely in spite of me.

Yours ever
s/ SAM

More heartening news. When the organisers of the Dublin Dramatic Festival 1958 knuckled under to their Archbishop Quaid and accepted his veto on Joyce and O'Casey I withdrew Endgame and the Mime which the Pike Theatre was to have done and decided I didn't want my plays to be performed in Eire in the future. Now I learn that some group I never heard of, having announced in an evening paper they had succeeded in "talking me round" (never had sight or sound of any of them), are doing Endgame AND Krapp in a Dublin theatre, Curtis Brown having gaily given them the rights without consulting me, though they should have known from their ex-employee Kitty Black what the situation was. Result: a letter from the Pike wounded to the heart (naturally). I tried to stop the production. Impossible. Lovely life the literary.[3]

TLS; 1 leaf, 1 side; NSyU.

1 Alain Bosquet* (1919–1998) was, by this time, a trusted friend (Bosquet describes his first meeting with SB in *Les Fruits de l'an dernier* [Paris: Grasset, 1996] 219; see also 4 September 1956, n. 1).

In November 1958, Bosquet asked SB, Eugène Ionesco, E. M. Cioran, and René de Obaldia for an unpublished manuscript to use in his Brandeis University course on the avant-garde in France since 1945.

2 Hugh Kenner (1923–2003) had asked SB about the unpublished manuscript of "Premier amour"; SB replied that Alain Bosquet had the manuscript somewhere "in America." Kenner enlisted Guy Davenport (1927–2005), then a doctoral student at Harvard, to contact Bosquet. Bosquet sent him the manuscript and Davenport "read it, and sent it on to Kenner in Santa Barbara" (Guy Davenport to the editors, 30 November 1991). SB wrote to Alain Bosquet on the same day he wrote to Rosset:

> J'ai beau chercher, je ne vois pas du tout qui est Guy Davenport. Je n'ai dit à personne de vous écrire de ma part. Je ne veux absolument pas que ce texte soit publié ou qu'il circule en dehors de votre cours. (Doucet MS. série-Ms 47.200/7.) (Try as I may I cannot make out who Guy Davenport is. I have told no one to write to you on my behalf. I am absolutely determined that this text should not be published or circulated outside your course.)

3 On 19 March, Alan Simpson told SB that Art Theatre Productions, Dublin, a company founded by Louis Lentin and Robert Somerset, had announced their forthcoming production of *Endgame* and *Krapp's Last Tape* at The Players' Theatre, Trinity College Dublin (TCD, MS 10731/72). Lentin claimed that he had "encountered no difficulty when he got in touch with Beckett's agent about staging these two new plays" ("New Group to Stage New Beckett Plays," *The Irish Times* 26 March 1959: 6). On 24 March, having received another letter from Alan Simpson that day (TCD, MSS 10731/73), SB wrote to Margaret McLaren at Curtis Brown:

> I knew nothing whatever about it and never met any of these people or received the least communication from them. I have not changed my mind about not wishing my plays to be performed in Eire and if I had it would have been in favour of the Pike Theatre (I had already given them the rights when the 1958 Festival row took place and I was obliged to withdraw) [. . .] It is scandalously unfair to the Pike Theatre and places me vis-à-vis them in a position of acute embarrassment. And I repeat, <u>I do not wish my plays to be performed in Eire</u> whether by amateurs or by professionals. (Curtis Brown Collection.)

A. J. LEVENTHAL
DUBLIN

21.4.59 Ussy sur Marne

Dear Con

It was good being with you again.[1] I am writing to Ethna this evening. I drove out here this afternoon with the Hayden in their new car. I hope to stay a fortnight at least and get a few more pages down. I saw Barrault on Sunday at the Palais-Royal Theatre with Blin and Martin. The meeting went pleasantly and we are all in agreement about Godot at the Odeon next season. He opens with Claudel's Tête d'Or in October and we go on in November, Blin playing Estragon to Raimbourg's Vladimir and Martin of course Lucky, the Pozzo remaining to be found. Formal signature later, but the engagement seems quite definite.[2] The prospect of Godot on a really big stage pleases me greatly. His "little theatre" plans still vague, but he said he wants to play Krapp with an Endgame revival, sometime next year I hope.[3]

A note from young Gregory thanking for the free drinks, me and my "Dublin friend of almost uncanny personal charm".[4]

I can't find my copy of Embers and shall ask Barbara to send a script to Ethna. She writes that she was out at East Ham during your absence. Donald's television production seems to have been very successful.[5]

A note from Arland with his Hone obituary and a groan under burdin [sic] of stepmother annuity![6]

When you don't feel it too much of an effort drop me a line to tell of your safe arrival and how you found Ethna on the way.

Yours ever

Sam

ALS; 1 leaf, 2 sides; TxU, Leventhal Collection, 1.4.

1 Leventhal has visited SB in Paris from 16 to 19 April, a respite that SB had encouraged, writing to his friend on 2 April: "It would be great if you could make a trip to Paris even for 24 hours" (TxU, Leventhal, 1.4). SB wrote to Barbara Bray: "We were together every evening. He is very brave and calm outwardly. Up with him till morning and no sleep." (19 April 1959; TCD, MS 10948/1/28.)

2 Paul Claudel's *Tête d'or* would become the first play to be put on by Jean-Louis Barrault in his role as director of the Théâtre de l'Odéon (renamed the Odéon-Théâtre de France), a role he officially assumed in October and kept until 1968; the play opened on 21 October.

Lucien Pierre Raimbourg (1903–1973).

3 By the "little theatre," SB is referring to Barrault's plan to screen off portions of the upper balconies to create a more intimate space; although not accomplished immediately, Barrault clearly had it in mind:

> Grâce à un velum en tissu de verre, nous nous arrangeâmes pour changer par des moyens rapides le volume de la salle de l'Odéon. Il n'en restait plus que l'orchestre et la corbeille: 650 places. Un véritable théâtre "royal." L'atmosphère y était extraordinaire. Pour certaines œuvres que j'appelle "de chevalet," c'était l'idéal. C'est dans ce format que fut créé le chef-d'œuvre de

Beckett: *Oh! les beaux jours*. (Jean-Louis Barrault, *Souvenirs pour demain* [Paris: Editions du Seuil, 1972] 323.) By means of a muslin canopy we found a way of altering the volume of the Odéon auditorium quite quickly: all that was left of it was the stalls and the first circle – six hundred and fifty seats. A true "royal" theatre. Its atmosphere was extraordinary. For certain plays that I call "easel plays" it was ideal. It was in that format that Beckett's masterpiece, *Oh! Les Beaux Jours*, had its first performance. (Jean-Louis Barrault, *Memories for Tomorrow: The Memoirs of Jean-Louis Barrault*, tr. Jonathan Griffin [New York: E. P. Dutton, 1974] 289.)

4 The poet, critic, and translator Horace Gregory (1898–1982) taught at Sarah Lawrence College; he had written an early review of SB's work (Horace Gregory, "Beckett's Dying Gladiators," *Commonweal* 65.4 [26 October 1956] 88–92). His son, Patrick Bolton Gregory (b. 1932), who first met SB in 1957, recollects this meeting on the terrace of the Dôme: "Beckett was very solicitous of his old Dublin friend, and clearly took deep satisfaction in having transported him to the tumultuous midst of bohemian Paris" (letter to the editors, 5 November 2010).

5 Donald McWhinnie directed a television production of D. H. Lawrence's short story "Samson and Delilah," with Kathleen Michael and Patrick Allen, for BBC TV, which aired on 16 April (BBCWAC, Michael, Kathleen, TVART 1, 23/03/59; BBCWAC, Allen Patrick, TVART 1, 31/03/59).

6 Joseph Hone had been a friend of SB's father, William Beckett (1871–1933; Profile, I), before getting to know SB. Ussher's obituary ended: "So long as his friends live, they will continue to talk of him, to quote him, to tell quaint anecdotes about him – and always bitterly to feel what they have lost in him" (*The Irish Times* 30 March 1959: 7). The second marriage of Ussher's father Beverley Grant Ussher (1867–1956), to Sophia Ellen Lucie Marie Hales (known as Moira, d. 1968), took place on 29 September 1938 (thepeerage.com/p33427.htm, accessed 11 October 2012). Arland Ussher's share of the family estate was diminished by the claim on the estate by his father's widow.

JACQUES PUTMAN
PARIS

28.4.59 Ussy

cher Jacques

Ravi pour Bram.[1]

D'accord pour textes et tableaux.[2]

J'aimerais beaucoup aller à Amsterdam avec vous. Je ferai mon possible.

Ci-joint traduction de ce paragraphe imbécile.[3]

Amitiés

Sam

ALS; 1 leaf, 1 side; Stedelijk.

28.4.59 Ussy

Dear Jacques

Delighted for Bram.[1]

Texts and pictures: fine by me.[2]

I would really like to go to Amsterdam with you. I'll do everything I can.

Attached translation of that idiotic paragraph.[3]

All best

Sam

1 Jacques Putman, Bram van Velde's agent/dealer, had just that day received word that the Stedelijk Museum in Amsterdam proposed an exhibition of his work (notes of the Director of the Museum Wilhelm Sandberg [1897–1984], Director; Bibliothek, Stedelijk Museum).

2 Three pieces written by SB would be republished in the catalogue of the Exhibition (*Bram Van Velde: Stedelijk Museum, Amsterdam, December 1959 – Januari 1960* [Amsterdam: Stedelijk Museum, 1959] [4–6]: an extract from "Peintres de l'empêchement," 3–4, 7; an extract from Beckett and Georges Duthuit, "Three Dialogues," as published, in French, in Samuel Beckett, Georges Duthuit, Jacques Putman, and Bram van Velde, *Bram van Velde*, Musée de Poche (see 20 March 1959, n. 11); and SB's text for the invitation to Van Velde's exhibition at the Galerie Maeght, 1952 (see [before February 1952]). SB lent his two paintings by Van Velde, the same works that SB later donated to the Musée National d'Art Moderne (an oil, *Sans titre* 1937 [AM1982-244] and a gouache, *Sans titre* ("Grande gouache bleue") 1939–1940 [AM1982-243], reproduced in Mason and Ramond, eds., *Bram et Geer van Velde*, 326 and 327).

3 All of the writings of SB on Bram van Velde had been published previously in French.

BARNEY ROSSET
GROVE PRESS, NEW YORK

5.5.59 Ussy

Dear Barney

Good to have your good letter. Thanks for all the rest, cheques, statements, Watts and limited edition jacket (fine), splendid Casement book in which I am plunged.[1]

First re enclosure. RC sent me Faber contract which for some unknown reason having read I saw it covered Canadian rights. I won't sign it unless you agree. I should like to have a ruling from you re Canadian rights, for example that you want them for Grove always or that you will let Faber have them (for what they are worth!) when their contract is prior to yours. I shall abide by whatever you say.[2]

In reply to Julia's note I should be glad if you would send Watt Ltd 3 and 4 to Dr A. J. Leventhal, 35 Lower Baggot Street, Dublin and to Mr Jake Schwartz, 14 Chichester Terrace, Brighton, Sussex, England.[3]

Great relief to know PREMIER AMOUR in Kenner's safe keeping. Rosset [*for* Bosquet] replied saying he had lost Davenport's letter, did not know where he had sent MS and that Davenport had presented himself not only as my friend but also more or less as from Grove Press. Strange affair. Well out of that, Jesus yes.

Pike Theatre wrote a nice letter understanding situation. No news whatever of production.[4]

I played the Endgame record and liked it. Clov's feet, trailing ladder, ticking at end, excellent. Of the four I preferred Nell. Hamm was inclined to declaim, Clov a bit wooden though he improved as it went. Music all right. On the whole fine job. Thanks to you all.[5]

You'll be glad to hear that Barrault wants GODOT for the Odéon (Théâtre de France), opening in November. I saw him with Blin and Martin and we are all in agreement. Nothing signed yet, as he hasn't yet taken over the theatre. Blin producing and playing probably Clov, Martin of course Lucky, the original Raimbourg Didi and Pozzo to be found. Barrault also wants to play Krapp to which I also agree as Roger, if it was created as it would be with revival of Endgame, could not play Hamm and Krapp same evening. I'm lepping to see Godot on a really bieg [sic] stage like the Odéon's. What a dinner we'd have at the Cochon de Lait across the way if you were over then!

So glad you like EMBERS. I think it just gets by for radio. McWhinnie should do a good job, talk of McGowran for the man.[6] I wrote to Dick Seaver in reply to some queries and await La Fin final version. Haven't got on at all with Textes pour Rien.[7] Struggling on with new work which as you rightly surmise has nothing to do with theatre or radio. I hear their siren voices and tell them to stick it up. It is in French, an attempt to go from where the Textes left me off, horribly difficult I needn't say. It will be in three parts of which before I leave for Dublin end of June I hope to have completed rough very rough draft of first. Shortish I imagine, 100 pages approx. I see fairly well what I have to do but so far can't get very near it, only near enough to keep me from giving up in disgust. I rely a lot on demolishing process to come later and content myself more or less with getting down elements and rhythms to be knocked hell out of when I'm ready. It all "takes place" in the pitch dark and the mud, first part "man" alone, second with another, third alone again. All a problem of rhythm and syntax and weakening of form, nothing more difficult.

Delighted to hear you are doing the 3 in 1 soon. Simply can't think, as I told Calder, of a general title and can't bear the thought of word trilogy appearing anywhere, what a hopeless unsatisfactory bastard I am. If it's possible to present the thing without either I'd be grateful. If not I'll cudgel my fused synopses [sic] for a word or two to cover it all.

I enjoyed being out with Joan till Riopelle started being silly and felt it was too much for me. She must be having a frightful time. Remember me to her affectionately.

Herewith poor translation but best I can do of that silly paragraph on Bram. I have sent it also to Putman (Jacques).[8] Great news, Bram is to have a big retrospective in Amsterdam in December. I hope to go.

Internationaux de France on at Roland Garros but haven't been, nearly all the time here in the mud. Saw the France-Wales Rugby match at Colombes, great enjoyment, French a great team, wish I had been in Dublin to see them undeservedly beaten by Ireland.[9]

Shall probably be leaving Rue des Favorites for Boulevard St-Jacques next Spring, after 21 years. Nothing definite yet, shall let you know when it is.

I know I can count on you for proof of Text 1, there are a few changes I have to make.

All good things, and to Link.

Yours ever

s/ Sam

TLS; 1 leaf, 2 sides; NSyU.

1 On 23 April, Judith Schmidt had sent SB copies of *Watt* and the jacket for the limited edition of *Watt* with photo of SB by Brassaï on the back, as well as number 1 of four copies of the limited (hors commerce) edition of *Watt* (Raymond Federman and John Fletcher, *Samuel Beckett: His Works and His Critics* [Berkeley: University of California Press, 1970] 26). Peter Singleton-Gates and Maurice Girodias, *The Black Diaries: An Account of Roger Casement's Life and Times with a Collection of His Diaries and Public Writings* (New York: Grove Press, 1959).

2 Rosica Colin. Normally, Grove Press contracts included North American rights and, thereby, Canadian rights.

3 In her letter of 23 April, Judith Schmidt (not Julia) had asked SB to designate recipients of the hors commerce special editions numbered 3 and 4.

4 Alan Simpson wrote to SB on 20 April of the Lentin and Somerset production of *Endgame* in Dublin: "we realise it was no-one's fault" (TCD, MS 10731/75).

5 In the recording of *Endgame* produced by Evergreen Records, a subsidiary of Grove Press, the few lines of music were composed by David Amram (b. 1930). The recording was with the original cast of the production (see 29 December 1957, n. 2).

6 Donald McWhinnie would direct *Embers* for the BBC Third Programme, and Jack MacGowran would play the role of Henry.

7 SB had given Richard Seaver a few suggestions for his translation of "La Fin": "If it is possible to use 'cabman' I prefer it to 'driver'. Just 'steps' or 'front steps' should be enough for 'perron' if 'flight of steps' proves cumbersome." (11 January 1960; TxU, Seaver, R16501.) SB had returned Seaver's translation, "The End," with his letter of 6 March (TxU, Seaver, R 16501).

8 SB's paragraph on Bram, published in the French edition of *Bram van Velde*, was not used in the Grove Press edition (see 20 March 1959, n. 10).

9 The tennis matches of the Internationaux de France (now called the French Open) were held from 19 to 31 May at the Roland-Garros Stadium, Paris 16. SB attended the France-Wales rugby match at the Colombes Stadium on 4 April; Ireland beat France on 18 April when they played at Lansdowne Road in Dublin.

BARBARA BRAY
PURLEY, SURREY

27.5.59 Ussy

Dear Barbara

Thanks for yr. letter here this morning.

Miss Reeves's secretary rang up about Unnamable tape. I told her I wd. manage to have it left round Av. Hoche by the end of this week. I won't bother asking T. P. for a copy, I can't profit by it.[1]

I rang up Pinget and he said he could go to London in a fortnight or three weeks. As soon as he knows exact date, he will write to you. I have sent you review with extract from what he is now working on. I hope you will agree with me that it is remarkable.[2]

I have laid aside Part I and wrote 1st paragraph of Part II this morning. Part I is longer than I thought. It was in great danger of the bonfire via the paper-basket but has been reprieved.

A note from Con this morning with the bad news of Ethna's death last Sunday and her cremation yesterday. She will not have received my last letter too long delayed. I am glad she is dead.[3]

Suzanne is better but still coughing & temperature.

I thought Con had spoken very freely.

Did I tell you we shall be leaving Rue des Favorites for Bd St. Jacques! Probably next April. I shall keep on Rue des Favorites if I can.

I am stuck rather in Johnson's Welsh Journey. All this seems familiar to me and the comment is without interest.[4]

The sparrows failing with their nest even worse than usual I nailed a box for them to a beam under the eaves. After a few days suspiciousness they have adopted it.

I go out to look for something to do in the garden. Yesterday I mowed the grass which did not need to be mown. Perhaps to day with rain threatening I shall water it. I sowed parsley which has come up, marigolds which have not yet come up, we steep their heads in alcohol to make a lotion.

Rosset gave me Mrs Chatterley's Lover which he has just published (60.000 sold in 3 weeks) and is being sued by the P.O. for singularly unexciting work.[5]

Love

Sam

Pinget's address in case you have it not & wd. like to write to him: 4 Rue de l'Université, 7e.[6]

ALS; with APS; 1 leaf, 2 sides; *env to* Mrs Barbara Bray, 121 Brighton Rd., Purley, Surrey, Angleterre; *pm* 28–5–59, La Ferté-sous-Jouarre; TCD, MS 10948/1/34.

1 SB had asked to listen to a tape of the 19 January broadcast of Patrick Magee reading from *The Unnamable* on the BBC Third Programme. The Paris office of the BBC was at 59 Avenue Hoche, Paris.

2 In SB's letter to Bray of 2 April, he had written: "It wd. be a good thing too for you to talk with Pinget before setting about L. M."; Bray planned to translate *Lettre morte* into English for the BBC (TCD, MS 10948/1/25). SB had sent to Bray *Les Lettres Nouvelles* with Pinget's "Simultanément," an excerpt from his forthcoming novel *Clope au dossier* (12 [May 1959] 16–20).

3 Ethna MacCarthy-Leventhal died on 24 May. SB had written to Bray on 22 May: "I am incapable of writing to Ethna, some insuperable empêchement, I hope she doesn't think too badly of my silence, it's the kind of thing she used to understand." (TCD, MS 10948/1/32). "Empêchement" (preventedness). Before he learned of Ethna's death, SB had written to Con Leventhal:

> I had a few lines from Ethna making it clear she did not wish me to come over. I agree there is no good now and I feel too we said goodbye in Dublin. All these last weeks I have found it impossible to write to her. I got off a short note at last two days ago. [. . .] These are dreadful days for you and my heart goes out to you. I can think of nothing I can do to help you. If you can please tell me. (26 May 1959; TxU, Leventhal Collection, 1.4.)

4 Samuel Johnson's *Diaries, Prayers, Annals*: 26 March 1959, n. 4. This volume included the diaries from Johnson's tour of North Wales, from 5 July to 9 September 1774 (163–214).

5 Grove Press published an unexpurgated edition of D. H. Lawrence's novel *Lady Chatterley's Lover*, deliberately challenging censorship of the book by the United States Post Office which had declared that it was obscene and, therefore, "unmailable." As Richard Seaver reports: "books began shipping to the stores in early April." Later in April copies had been confiscated from bookstores, and on 6 May the Postmaster of New York had seized cartons of the novel that were in the mail. (Seaver, *The Tender Hour of Twilight*, 262; "Lawrence Novel is Seized in Test," *New York Times* 7 May 1959: 34.)

6 The postscript is written vertically in left margin of side 1.

MARY HUTCHINSON
LONDON

2.6.59 Ussy sur Marne

Dear Mary

Thank you for your letter this morning and also for your previous one with text by Lequier. It reads like a prize composition to me and I find it of no interest but for God's sake don't mind what I say I can read nothing any more and have no judgement.[1]

I am glad to hear X on its way at last. I of course shall give you any help I can but you must realize I cannot give very much, I do not know what is being written in France and haven't a gramme of energy or enthusiasm available. I hope you have all thought seriously about the advisability of publishing a text in French in your first number, I am convinced that commercially it is bad for the review such odour of bilinguism, I shall of course give you the few pages as promised but think about it again.[2]

I do not think I shall be in France June 25th. My idea is to go to Dublin about a week before Commencements (July 2nd) and leave immediately after. At the moment I am not well and if I do not feel better between now & then shall just go in time to get the damn thing and leave immediately after. I am sorry I accepted it but know if I hadn't I would have felt a goujat, and should of course have that little courage. So you see I simply can't make an appointment in Paris for June 25th. On the other hand I may stop off for a few days in England on the way back, I have cousins I have promised to see in Surrey, in which case we might have a few hours in London. Sorry to be so confused, I seem to have reached the point where I can't count on my old carcass from one day to the next[.][3]

Re Lettre Morte Barbara Bray of the BBC has made the translation which I have not seen and to use it you would need of course her permission undoubtedly forthcoming. The rights however are another matter and you would have to apply for them to the Editions de Minuit where you wd. certainly have no difficulty either. I am glad you are giving some notice to Pinget. Of the younger writers whose work I know he seems to me by far the most interesting. There was a most remarkable fragment from his new work in I think the 2nd last no. of Les Lettres Nouvelles [–] you must have seen it – "Simultanément".[4]

Perhaps in a week or so I shall see things more clearly and be able to let you know more or less definitely what my plans. Any introductions you may want and I am able to give you – for example to Pinget, Editions de Minuit, Nadeau etc. – don't hesitate to ask for them.

Yours ever

Sam

ALS; 1 leaf, 2 sides; TxU, Hutchinson, 2.4.

1 Pierre Leyris had recommended for inclusion in *X* a text by the French philosopher Jules Lequier (1814–1862) that had formed part of an introduction to "La Feuille de Charmille," *La Recherche d'une première vérité* (1865). It was not published in *X*.

2 Mary Hutchinson was an advisor to *X, A Quarterly Review**, published from November 1959 through 1962, founded and edited by Irish painter Patrick Swift (1927–1983) and South Africa-born poet David Wright (1920–1994).

3 SB planned to be in Dublin to receive an honorary degree from Trinity College in July. He had written to A. J. Leventhal on 2 April: "I dread the commencement farce. I have no clothes but an old brown suit, if that's not good enough they can stick their Litt.D. up among their piles. If one has to dress up for this thing there's no point in my going over, I can't." (TxU, Leventhal Collection, 1.4.)

"Goujat" (mannerless clod).

Robert Pinget would have an appointment with SB on the morning of the latter's departure for Dublin, in order to finalize his translation of *Embers* into French; he wrote in his memoir of this meeting: "le pauvre Sam était plus nerveux et déprimé que jamais. Il croyait avoir de mauvais pressentiments sur son voyage et me l'a avoué comme un enfant, commençant sa phrase par: Vous allez me trouver ridicule mais il faut que je vous dise. Il avait peur de mourir et avait fait son testament." (Doucet, unclassified Pinget Collection, "Notre ami Samuel Beckett," 19.) (poor Sam was more uneasy and depressed than ever. He thought he was having bad premonitions about his journey, and admitted as much to me, like a child, beginning his sentence with: You're going to think me ridiculous, but I must tell you. He was afraid of dying, and had made his will.)

4 Pinget's "Simultanément" had appeared in *Les Lettres Nouvelles* nouvelle série 7.12 (May 1959) 16–20.

HUGH KENNER
SANTA BARBARA, CALIFORNIA

27.6.59

6 Rue des Favorites
Paris 15me

Dear Mr Kenner

Your letter today. I don't know much about racing cycling. Godeau (can't think of Christian name) is a veteran still going strong. He is a "stayer" and I think specialist of "poursuite" (derrière Derny). He did well in the recent national championships. I don't think he has distinguished himself in the Tour de France, if he was ever selected for it, but he has had some success in town to town races, Bordeaux-Paris for example. I think he is a 6 Jours man too. I have the feeling he is bald.[1] I'll try and find out more about him for you when I get back from Ireland where for my sins I have to go tomorrow.

Godot was written either between Molloy and Malone or bteween [sic] Malone and L'Innommable, I can't remember. Round about 1948 in any case.[2]

I saw a chainless bike in Dublin when I was a boy, transmission by a rod apparently.

I am sending you today the Limes edition of the poems. There are 3 or 4 I don't regret. Eva Hesse's translation is very incorrect, the other all right.[3]

All the best.

Yours

s/ Sam Beckett

TLS with handwritten salutation; 1 leaf, 1 side; T *env to* Mr. Hugh Kenner, 1415 Bluff Drive, Santa Barbara, California, USA; *pm* 27-6-59, Paris; TxU, Kenner, 41.2.

1 Kenner was working on "The Cartesian Centaur," his essay on the importance of bicycles in SB's work; the essay would be published in *Perspective: A Quarterly of Literature and the Arts* 11.3 (Autumn 1959) 132–141. Kenner incorporates SB's letter, writing: "it is right that there should ride about France as these words are written, subject to a Mr Beckett's intermittent attention, a veteran racing cyclist, bald, a 'stayer,' recurrent placeman in town-to-town and national championships, Christian name elusive, surname Godeau, pronounced, of course, no differently from Godot" (136).

Roger Godeau (1920–2000) turned professional as a cyclist in 1942 and had an illustrious career until his retirement in 1961, most notably as a "stayer" (in the "demi-fond" or middle distance), achieving his most noted and numerous victories at the Vélodrome d'Hiver de Paris – on 17 April 1959, he won at the Vél d'Hiv (which had become infamous, since its use in the War as an internment camp for Jews), in the last race to be held there, as part of the stadium's Closing Gala. His most recent national victory had taken place in 1957, when he was Champion de France de demi-fond; he came fifth, not first, in the Bordeaux–Paris Grand Prix in 1947; the most notable of his successes in 6-Days events came in 1954 when he was first in both Paris and Aarhus; he was indeed, if not bald, then noted from a young age for his lack of hair (see "Palmarès de Roger Godeau," Mémoire du cyclisme. www.memoire-du-cyclisme.net/palmares/godeau_roger.php, accessed 11 January 2010). On the Derny (pacing motorcycle), see Thursday [? 30 March or 6 April 1950], n. 9.

2 *En attendant Godot* was written between October 1948 and January 1949, after *Malone meurt* and before *L'Innommable*.

3 *Gedichte*, the German edition of SB's poems, incorporated Eva Hesse's translations from the English (Wiesbaden: Limes Verlag, 1959); see further SB to Eva Hesse, 14 February 1957.

BARBARA BRAY
PURLEY, SURREY

7.8.59 Ussy

Dear Barbara

Thanks for your two letters the second here this morning together with Huxley for which also many thanks.[1] When I get through the morning struggle can't face any more pen and paper so taking this morning off, first hours at least, hoping converse not true. Back here a week today praying for a few weeks uninterruption. Morning average up from half a page to one, but very rough stuff. Great trouble with sudden inburst of hypothetical dynasty of witnesses and scribes, [illeg 1 word] I think, denied of course with its usual too usual "and yet". Have long since given up giving thought to the problems of your last letter, just hunch down deep like a hare in its form all affright and melancholy and [illeg 1 word], not at all to be recommended. About halfway through second part anyway, Pim hasn't much to say in the end. Can't talk about it. Read the Freud with great enjoyment, incredible suffering and fortitude of last fifteen years. Amusing story, his strictures on Céline's Voyage which Marie Bonaparte sent him and he tried to read to please her.[2] When I'm next in Paris I'll send you Blanchot's Le Livre à Venir, I think he's on to something very important which he probably over-systematizes. I won't read it now, it would only get in my way.[3] Fell mildly off the bike and cut foot through espadrille, healing slowly. Marvellous weather again. Hope family invasion repulsed. Still putting up shelves and mucking about with paint, making the den, watering in the evening the arbores vitae. Forgive this stupid letter, head keeps going down on the wood. Love to the children. And to yourself. Not to Miss Richards, just thanks for the compliment.[4]

Ever

Sam

ALS; 1 leaf, 1 side; *env to* Mrs Barbara Bray, 121 Brighton Road, Purley, Surrey, Angleterre; *pm* 8-_-_, La Ferté-sous-Jouarre; TCD, MS 10948/1/41.

1 Aldous Huxley's *The Doors of Perception* and *Heaven and Hell* had been published by Chatto and Windus in 1954 and 1956, respectively; they were republished in one volume by Penguin Books in 1959.

2 SB was reading volume III of Ernest Jones's *Sigmund Freud: The Life and Work* entitled *The Last Phase, 1919–1939* (London: Hogarth Press, 1957). Freud had written to French writer and psychoanalyst Princess Marie Bonaparte (1882–1962), who had given him a copy of Louis-Ferdinand Céline's *Voyage au bout de la nuit* (1932; *Journey to the End of the Night*): "I have no taste for this depicting of misery, for the description of the senselessness and emptiness of our present-day life, without any artistic or philosophical background. I demand something other from art than realism. I am reading it because you wished me to." (176.)

3 Maurice Blanchot, *Le Livre à venir* (1959; *The Book to Come*).

4 Francesca Bray has explained to the editors that Miss Richards "prepared a Sunday lunch and ate it with us, so if my mother had a guest . . . Miss Richards met the guest too. My mother says Miss Richards adored Sam." (Francesca Bray to the editors, 20 June 2012.)

BARBARA BRAY
PURLEY, SURREY

27.8.59 Ussy sur Marne

Dear Barbara

Thanks for your letter. I didn't think I had the catalogue you asked for, but rummaged round and found one. Herewith.[1] Donald kindly sent me the I.P. Embers. I have corrected Faber's distressing proofs and made a few more changes. Pinget said Donald wd. be going to Baden-Baden which means I hope that I shall see him in Paris.[2] I have been unfaithful to Pim these last days, just tinkering about in the sun, hope to resume tomorrow. Suhrkamp Verlag keep pestering me to go to Frankfurt, first to read my work, then to listen to someone else doing so, tired of saying no.[3] Have to go to Paris next week Sept. 2nd for 2–3 days, not longer I hope. Shall send you then the Blanchot. Enclosed "literary" page of Combat, thought the Yugoslavia article might interest you, no mention of Konstantinovič whose radio script ("Der Zeuge" in translation) I came across in Paris and shall keep for you or send to you, rather good I thought but according to him badly translated.[4] Marvel at all the reading you go through, the green tea is a help I realise. Started an Oedipus Rex in queer literal German translation but haven't got far.[5] Read the Huxley without much pleasure. Mind-at-large and the Divine not-self of Flannel Bags too much for me.[6] The swallows have finished school and are making ready to depart. Another funeral of an old woman I knew here. She was queer in the head, her bones went as brittle as pipe clay, she fell and broke everything.

Love

Sam.

ALS; 1 leaf, 1 side; *enclosure* Alain Bosquet, "Littérature yougoslave d'aujourd'hui," *Combat*, 27 August 1959: 7; *env to* Mrs Barbara Bray, 121 Brighton Road, Purley, Surrey, Angleterre; *pm* 28-8-59, La Ferté-sous-Jouarre; TCD, MS 10948/1/43.

1 The catalogue sent to Bray has not been identified.

2 Submissions for the Italia Prize were presented in two languages; the BBC had commissioned Robert Pinget to translate *Embers* (*Cendres*) (BBCWAC, RCONT7, Robert Pinget, copyright Misc 1959). The Faber and Faber proofs were *Krapp's Last Tape* and *Embers*. SB described the small changes he had made to the text of *Embers* to the Tophovens:

> Dans "Embers" quelques petits repentirs de dernière heure: "Venezuela" devient "the Argentine", "Tibet" "the Pampas", histoire de rapprocher un peu + père et fils, "bring her into the world" "drag her". (In *Embers* a few last-minute pentimenti: "Venezuela" becomes "the Argentine", "Tibet" "the Pampas", the idea to bring father and son a bit closer together, "bring her into the mood" "drag her". (24 August 1959; Tophoven Collection.)

Donald McWhinnie had been invited to direct *Embers* in German (translated as *Aschenglut*) for Südwestrundfunk (SWR) in Baden-Baden in September. On 17 July, SB had written to McWhinnie: "The translation is excellent, very close to the original. It is by my usual German translator, Elmar Tophoven, and we have gone over it together." (BBCWAC, RCONT1, Samuel Beckett, Screenwriter I.)

3 On 7 August, Siegfried Unseld* (1924–2002) had invited SB to participate in an evening series sponsored by Suhrkamp Verlag. SB replied on 16 August: "Lire en public des extraits de mon travail, j'en serais tout simplement incapable. Rien qu'à y penser j'ai les jambes qui flageolent, et pas que les jambes." (Giving a public reading of

extracts from my work is something of which I would be simply incapable. The mere thought sets my legs trembling, and not just my legs.) Unseld persisted, writing again on 24 August; he received a firmer no from SB on 30 August (DLA, Suhrkamp VL, Samuel Beckett: 1954–1959).

4 Alain Bosquet's article in *Combat*: see bibliographical note above. Radomir Konstantinović's radio play translated into German as *Der Zeuge*: 25 July 1958.

5 Sophocles, *König Ödipus*, tr. Wolfgang Schadewaldt (Frankfurt: Suhrkamp, 1955).

6 In *The Doors of Perception*, Huxley examines the potential of the conscious mind, what he calls the "Mind at Large," which psychedelic drugs can release. He writes: "'This is how one ought to see' . . . Just looking, just being the divine Not-self of flower, of book, of chair, of flannel" (30).

ROBERT PINGET
PARIS

14.9.59 Sorrento

Terra inclita ove Torquato nacque.[1]

Sam

et Amitiés de Donald.

APCS; 1 leaf, 1 side; "Sorrento Panorama"; *to* Monsieur Robert Pinget, 4 Rue de l'Université, Paris 7me, FRANCIA; *pm* 14-9-59, Napoli; Burns Library, Samuel Beckett Collection, SB-RP.

14.9.59 Sorrento

Terra inclita ove Torquato nacque.[1]

Sam

and best wishes from Donald.

1 (Lat., Illlustrious land where Torquato was born). SB quotes from the biographical poem *Il Torquato Tasso* (canto 1, octave 3, line 3) by Jacopo Cabianca (1809–1878). Tasso was born in Sorrento in 1544. SB had traveled to Italy the previous day to receive, with Donald McWhinnie, the Italia Prize, awarded by Radiotelevisione Italia to the BBC for *Embers*, which Pinget had translated into French. The minutes of the General Assembly of the Prize recapped the prize's purpose: "The three Juries, in awarding the Prizes, kept in mind Article 3 of the Statute, which reads as follows: 'The entries submitted must have been especially created for broadcasting and must be in a form best suited to be presented through the medium of radio. The entries submitted must present high

aesthetic qualities and must also include elements which enrich broadcasting experience." (General Assembly, Sorrento, 12–14 September 1959; Prix Italia Archive.)

Of this postcard Pinget writes:

> Je lui demande bêtement si la citation qu'il m'avait écrite de Sorrento était de Dante. Il me répond qu'évidemment non puisque Le Tasse est du 16e. J'aurais pu réfléchir, me dire qu'il a horreur des gens qui ne savent pas. Tant pis. Il croit que le vers en question est d'un poète inconnu. (Doucet, unclassified Pinget Collection, "Notre ami Samuel Beckett," 41.) (I stupidly asked him if the quotation he had written to me from Sorrento was from Dante. He answers that of course not, since Tasso is 16th century. I should have taken thought, told myself that he can't bear people who don't know. Ah well. He thinks the line in question is by an unknown poet.)

ALAN SCHNEIDER
NEW YORK

21.9.59 Ussy

Dear Alan

Many thanks for your interesting letter. So glad you are pleased with production and reception[.] Can't see it in the round but my fault.[1]

Back in the country working after a quick trip to Italy. Have an idea for 2 variants on the Krapp theme but can't do anything about it till I finish what I'm doing. One would be situation if instead of sacrificing the girl in the boat for the opus.. magnum he had done the reverse. You see the idea, triptych, three doors closed instead of one, the one we have already no. 3.

1 Krapp, Mrs Krapp, child. }
2 " " children } ?
3 " alone. }

Nice thing to offer the public.[2]

Looking forward to Barney next week. Best to you and I hope Jean next spring. Good luck with Summer. What a worker you are![3]

Affectionately to you all

Sam

ALS; 1 leaf, 1 side; Burns Library, Samuel Beckett Collection, SB-AS. Previous publication: Beckett and Schneider, *No Author Better Served*, 57.

1 Schneider's production of *Waiting for Godot* at the Alley Theatre, Houston, opened on 9 September; at this time, the theatre had only one stage with seating in the round (Lauren Fischer to the editors, 20 June 2012). "The applause at the curtain calls was deafening" (Jim Hilburn, "Alley Theater 'Waiting for Godot,'" KTRK-TV, 10 September 1959; CUSD, MSS 103/16/6).

2 SB told Dougald McMillan: "'I thought of writing a play . . . with Mrs. Krapp, the girl in the punt, nagging away behind him, in which case his failure and his solitude would be exactly the same'" (Dougald McMillan and Martha Fehsenfeld, *Beckett in the Theatre: The Author as Practical Playwright and Director* [London: John Calder; New York: Riverrun Press, 1988] 288–289).

3 Schneider's production of *Summer of the Seventeenth Doll* by Australian dramatist Ray Lawler (b. 1921) had opened at the Arena Stage in Washington DC on 28 April 1958; it opened in New York at the Players Theatre on 13 October 1959. Schneider felt that this production was crucial to his career: "If *Doll* didn't make it, there was no way I could continue to work in the New York theatre" (Schneider, *Entrances*, 265).

MARY HUTCHINSON
LONDON

21.9.59 Ussy

Dear Mary

Thanks for your letters.

I received the proofs and returned them to Wright with a few author's corrections. The proofs were excellent, not a mistake as far as I remember.[1]

Glad you found the books you wanted. I am advising a young Irish writer living in South Africa to submit a story to X. I think he is very promising and should be encouraged. Calder is doing his first book soon. His name AIDAN HIGGINS.[2]

The last number of L.N. will interest you. Reverzy is interesting, especially last works.[3]

Was foolish enough to let myself be coaxed to Sorrento to get Italian radio prize. Nearly killed me. Never be the same again.

Glad St. Denis liked Endgame.[4] Have an idea for a Krapp triptych. But can't do anything about it now.

Take care of yourself.
Yrs. ever
Sam

ALS; 1 leaf, 1 side; *env to* Mrs Hutchinson, 21 Hyde Park Square, London W.2, Angleterre; *pm* 22–9–59, La Ferté-sous-Jouarre; TxU, Hutchinson, 2.4.

1 SB was returning to editor David Wright the proofs of his contribution to the first issue of *X*, "L'Image" (November 1959) 35–37.

2 No story by Aidan Higgins was published in *X*.

3 Born in 1914 of a French father and an Irish mother, the novelist Jean Reverzy, who had worked as a general practitioner in Lyon, had died in July the previous year; *Les Lettres Nouvelles* devoted much of its 16 September 1959 issue (7.21) to a commemoration of him. In his editorial, Maurice Nadeau compared Reverzy's cursus to that of Beckett ("Jean Reverzy," 3); Charles Juliet published "Visites à Jean Reverzy" (16–19); and the journal printed two of Reverzy's texts, "Un jour…" (10–15) and "La Conversation" (20–40). The last work published by Reverzy during his lifetime was *Le Corridor* (Paris: Julliard, 1958).

4 The French actor and director Michel Saint-Denis (1897–1971) had worked with his uncle Jacques Copeau at the Vieux-Colombier in Paris. In 1934, he established the London Theatre Studio (LTS), and in 1946 the Old Vic Centre; George Devine worked closely with Saint-Denis, indeed became his "right-hand man" at the LTS (Irving Wardle, *The Theatres of George Devine* [London: Jonathan Cape, 1978] 48–58). Later, Saint-Denis helped to create and was a consultant-director of the Julliard Drama Division of Lincoln Center, New York (1960–1969), and Co-Director (1962–1965) of the Royal Shakespeare Company with Peter Brook.

THOMAS MACGREEVY
DUBLIN

21.9.59 Ussy

Dear Tom

Many thanks for yr. letter and photo of drawing, it is very fine. I was distressed by what you say about your tether's end and veux croire it was only a moment of exhaustion. It really is time you stopped prostrating yourself for that damn gallery. You were so much better on your way back from Aix.[1]

A young Irishman working in Rome, O'Grady, called on me and told me of Dennis's death, it really knocked me all of a heap.[2] Italian misdiagnosis, he said, and how kind he had been to young Irishmen living in Rome and trying to write. I had not seen him for many years and had much fondness for him.

I was foolish enough to let myself be persuaded to go to Sorrento to receive the Italia prize surprisingly awarded to Embers. It was a grim jamboree with organised excursions to Capri etc. and the few days nearly finished me. Robert Fadden and his wife were there, insufficient consolation.[3] Back in the quiet now with what relief I can't say but Paris and people again next week. They'll have me in a monastery in the end.[4]

What is the French for "Rest on the Flight", can't for the life of me think of it.[5]

Forgive more now, dear Tom, and do please spare yourself. Much love from us both.

Ever Sam

ALS; 1 leaf, 1 side; TCD, MS 10402/223.

1 "Veux croire" (I have to hope).

MacGreevy had been Director of the National Gallery of Ireland since June 1950 (see 9 May 1950). He had visited SB on his way to and from Aix-en-Provence (19 September 1959; TCD, MS 10402/222).

2 Irish poet and translator Desmond O'Grady (b. 1935) had known Denis Devlin (1908–1959; Profile, I) in Rome, where Devlin was Ambassador to Italy. O'Grady had first met SB in Paris as a young writer in 1954, and when they saw each other in early summer of 1959, O'Grady brought a salutation from Devlin – unaware that the greeting would become a valediction (Desmond O'Grady, "Desmond O'Grady Recalls Beckett in Paris," *Poetry Ireland Review* 37 [Winter 1992–1993] 126–132). Devlin died in Dublin on 21 August 1959. SB here misspells his name as 'Dennis." SB wrote of Devlin to Niall Montgomery (1914–1987; Profile, II) on 28 September: "I had not seen him for years. Great fondness for him and esteem." (NLI, Acc 6471, Lot 5 personal correspondence.)

3 Robert Farren (1909–1984) joined Radio Éireann in 1939, and by 1953 he had been promoted to Controller of Radio Programs; he had married Maureen Smyth. SB here misspells Farren's name as "Fadden."

4 Two days previously, on 19 September, SB had written to MacGreevy: "I struggle along at the new work, very dissatisfied and today so discouraged that I just left it. I know the great thing is not to be in a hurry and I'm not, having decided to give it another year at least. But the average of half a page, and very provisional – a day gets me down sometimes."

5 More than twenty years before, SB had enthused to MacGreevy about two paintings of the *Rest on the Flight* in London's National Gallery by the "School of

Patinir" (see 14 February 1935). However, given that in a letter written two days before he had written to MacGreevy about his friend's attempts to publish a book on Nicolas Poussin, it is likely that the context here is one of Poussin's two drawings or three paintings of the subject, works to which MacGreevy refers in his study (*Nicolas Poussin*, 22 and 35). The standard French title of *Rest on the Flight* is *Repos pendant la fuite en Egypte*.

EDWARD BECKETT
DUBLIN

29.9.59 Paris

Dear Edward

Thanks for your letter and congratulations. The award was a great surprise to me. The money will be useful.[1] I went to Sorrento for the "giving", expenses paid, and stayed a few days. Awful jamboree, I was glad to get back. Have been in the country ever since working. Back in Paris now for a week or so, people to see. Decided to buy a little 2 H.P. Citroen, ugly little brute of a car but "increvable" (look that one up).[2] One has normally to order it a year in advance but through friends I hope to have it soon. Useful for getting up and down between Paris and Ussy, tired of that same old train journey.

Shall be writing to Jean soon.[3] Have a good term and good music and keep your valuable hands out of the scrums.[4]

Much love

Sam

ALS; 1 leaf, 1 side; *env to* Edward Beckett, St. Columba's College, Rathfarnham, Co. Dublin, IRLANDE; *pm* 29-9-59, Paris; Edward Beckett Collection.

1 The jury awarding the Italia Prize comprised six members involved with radio in six different countries (the United States, Austria, Ireland, Luxembourg, Switzerland, Yugoslavia); it chose SB's play from the twenty entries submitted. The prize money was 1,125,000 lire. (Italia Prize General Assembly, Sorrento, 12–14 September 1959; Prix Italia archive). SB accepted the award with a few words: "It is a great honour for me to have been awarded the Italia Prize for my radio play *Embers*. I do not ordinarily write for radio, but I think that it is a medium which has not been fully exploited, and that there are great possibilities for writers in this form of expression." (www.ubumexico.centro.org.mx/sound/

beckett_samuel/various/Beckett-Samuel_Acceptance-Speech-Italy-Prize_ Sorrento_1959.mp3, accessed 14 September 2012.)

2 The Citroën 2CV (the "deux-chevaux") had been in production since 1948; it had proved so popular that delays of several years were not uncommon between order and delivery. "Increvable" (tough as old boots).

3 On 19 September, SB had written to Thomas MacGreevy of Jean Beckett: "A letter at last from Jean. No reason for her silence. All well with them all." (TCD, MS 10402/222.)

4 Edward Beckett was attending St. Columba's College in Rathfarnham, Ireland, where rugby was part of the weekly sporting activity.

JOHN MANNING
DUBLIN

15.10.59 Paris

Dear John – Thanks for your letter. I know of no general study on the young cinéastes you mention, only seen the usual foolish articles here & there. I am quite out of touch with cinema. However I shall consult friends in the swim and try and dig up something for you. I have met Resnais, the most gifted of the lot probably, though his Hiroshima was not very satisfactory. Nuit et Brouillard was very fine.[1]

Hope Susan is keeping as well as possible. Shall be writing to her soon.[2]

All the best.

Yrs. ever

Sam

APCS; 1 leaf, 2 sides; John Manning Esq, 35 Wellington Place, Dublin, IRLANDE; *pm* 15-10-59, Paris; MoSW, Samuel Beckett Papers, MSS 008, 1.4.

1 John Manning (1908–1997), brother of Mary Manning Howe, was interested in the work of Nouvelle Vague (New Wave) film directors, among them Alain Resnais (1922–2014) who had been proposed as director for a film of *Tous ceux qui tombent* in 1958. Resnais made the film of Marguerite Duras's screenplay *Hiroshima mon amour* (1959). His *Nuit et Brouillard* (1955) is a documentary about the Holocaust.

2 Susan Manning, John Manning's mother.

BARBARA BRAY
PURLEY, SURREY

17.10.59 Ussy sur Marne

Dear Barbara

Thanks for your letter. Pinget told me of his lunch with you and Donald.[1] It was good of C. & J. to write and send pictures. I liked the chevalier very much.[2] At this point of my letter my eyes begin to go, an old trouble. It means a couple of hours mild migraine and semi-blindness. Never know why it comes on. I continue none the less, don't need a clear view of what I'm writing. Got back here this afternoon, pleasant drive, but the wind buffeting the little car so light unpleasantly. Just put down a little pine brought from near St. Tropez. Don't think it has much future. Usual tiring days in Paris since Wednesday, Rosset again on his way back, and yesterday for my sins but unavoidable a group photo before the Eds. de Minuit for Illustrazione with all the bright boys of the class - Robbe-G., Ollier, Simon, Pinget, Sarraute (!), Claude Mauriac. Horrible but couldn't refuse Lindon.[3] Began reading the Donne, shall never be a Donne fiend - but brazen here and there. By all means do Godot whenever you like. I mentioned it to Lindon who has no objection and you need not bother applying for his authorisation.[4] In an interview in the Figaro a few days ago Barrault committed himself publicly on the subject for as far I know the first time, next February directed by "mon ami Roger Blin".[5] Have launched idea of Krapp & Lettre Morte same time at the Lutèce, hasn't got beyond the pinhead yet.[6] Wind howling round the house, expect all the lights to go out any minute. Clambered up stairs & ladders to 7th floor Bd. St. Jacques yesterday afternoon and looked at what I'll be looking at - Observatoire, Val de Grâce, Panthéon, a tower of Notre-Dame, Sacré-Coeur when clear hélas, Rocher de Vincennes, Gare de Lyon, a height which I suppose is Belleville or/and Buttes-Chaumont, the Santé prison, gardens of convents & hospitals, cool north light, quiet, perhaps I'll be able to work in Paris again.[7] No further trouble with car except a summons for non-unilateral parking in my own street! Some

6 Authors of Editions de Minuit: Alain Robbe-Grillet, Claude Simon, Claude Mauriac, Jérôme Lindon, Robert Pinget, Samuel Beckett, Nathalie Sarraute, Claude Ollier

zealous bastard. And the Rue Racine taken against the one-way with no ill results. The police-station in the Rue de la Gaieté [sic] had been transferred, I was told, the day before we threaded it à rebrousse-poil.[8] On other things as usual speechless, except perhaps that the non-causing of pain is only a small part of the story. To go some of the old places again in January wd. be good, but it's a poor season to be travelling in Eastern Europe. Do you know Günther Eich? He was very taken with Krapp, Tophoven told me.[9] Saw one vague non-committal article on Embers, the attitude in Germany now seems to be "at his old pranks and croaks again, will he never change his tune".[10] How I wish he could.

Basta. Eyes nearly out.

Love

Sam

ALS; 2 leaves, 2 sides; *env to* M$^{\underline{rs}}$ Barbara Bray, 121 Brighton Road, Purley, Surrey, Angleterre; *pm* 19-[10]-59, La Ferté-sous-Jouarre; TCD, MS 10948/1/53.

1 Following Pinget's lunch with McWhinnie and Bray, Bray requested that Pinget's radio play *La Manivelle* be undertaken by the BBC Third Programme (Barbara Bray to Heather Dean, 26 October 1959; BBCWAC, RCONT7, Robert Pinget, Copyright Misc: 1959).

2 Checchina or Julia Bray, one of whom drew a picture of a chevalier.

3 Barney Rosset was in Paris before and after the Frankfurt Book Fair.
Mario Dondero took the photo of the Editions de Minuit's authors with Jérôme Lindon; from left to right: Alain Robbe-Grillet, Claude Simon, Claude Mauriac, Jérôme Lindon, Robert Pinget, SB, Nathalie Sarraute (with whom SB was not on friendly terms), Claude Ollier.

4 Bray proposed that *Waiting for Godot* be presented on the Third Programme.

5 Jean-Louis Barrault announced the forthcoming season which would include *En attendant Godot* in the last trimester ("L'Odéon sera le théâtre des audaces et des combats," *Le Figaro* 15 October 1959: 18).

6 SB's suggestion that the Théâtre de Lutèce might take the plays did not develop; later in the year, when the opportunity arose to produce them at the Théâtre Récamier, SB mentioned to Pinget that Lindon would need to recover the rights to the play (21 December 1959; Burns Library, Samuel Beckett Collection, SB-RP).

7 SB's new flat was at 38 Boulevard Saint-Jacques, Paris 14.

8 "Threaded," a Gallicism from "enfiler" (to thread, coll. go through). A rebrousse-poil (the wrong way).

9 The German poet and radio dramatist Günter Eich (1907–1972) was also published by Suhrkamp Verlag; his radio plays had been produced by the BBC Third Programme in the 1950s (F. M. Fowler, "Günter Eich," in *Essays on Contemporary German Literature*, ed. Brian Keith-Smith, German Men of Letters [London: Oswald Wolff, 1966] 89).

10 McWhinnie's production of *Aschenglut*, co-directed with Lothar Timm, had been broadcast on 6 October by SWR, Baden-Baden.

BARBARA BRAY
PURLEY, SURREY

5.11.59 Ussy

Dear Barbara

Many thanks for your letter and card. It is very kind of you to order for me the Joyce book, I haven't a copy and shall be glad to have one.[1]

Wouldn't open More Pricks for a king's ransom. I remember Yellow vaguely, and Dante the Lobster [sic], the others not at all, not a clue. Glad you got something from them, don't know how you do it.

You will no doubt have heard from Robert that I have undertaken translation of La Manivelle. It is a charming and amusing piece, on the light side as he wants it. The rhythms are interesting and amusing trying to get them in English. I have done about 6 pages and hope to have it ready in about a fortnight, but have so much work (including Embers in French) and so many interruptions that it may take longer.[2] Robert has got his travelling scholarship in the States after all and hopes to leave soon. I think he will go to London first so you will probably be seeing him.[3]

The 3 in 1 is just out from Grove and I have asked them to send you a copy so don't be going ordering it. There will be one for Donald too. It is a handsome volume once you get rid of the jacket and I am pleased to have the 3 between 2 boards at last.[4]

Went in to Paris last night to see the Nègres. Better impression than at rehearsal, but 2nd half very long and slow. Great success theatre booked out for a week. Delighted for Roger. Ionesco walked out in the middle – perhaps just a pain.[5] Lindon got a bad pain in a theatre 2 days ago and they whipped out his appendix same evening. No complications. I found myself in Paris without any papers of any kind, car or personal, having left them here, where I chanced driving back this morning without them. Have to go back Paris tomorrow to see MacGreevy.[6] Very hard to get on with anything. Have written about 6 pages of Part III, can't see how I'll ever do the 25 or 30 I need. Dark as 5th Canto of Hell – "d'ogni luce muto" – and no one in any one's arms.[7]

Tête d'or has flopped and talk of putting on that old battle-horse Hamlet in a hurry.[8] Was talking to Blin about Godot in February. Didn't sound too keen. Neither am I.

Mist all day, just enough visibility to get out of the valley. No mellow fruitfulness than [*for* that] I can observe.[9] Have now to rush into La Ferté to interview a chimney sweeper. Then back with the last light and down into the hole again.

Love

Sam

ALS; 2 leaves, 2 sides; *env to* Mrs Bray, 121 Brighton Rd., Purley, Surrey, Angleterre; *pm* 5–11–59, La Ferté-sous-Jouarre; TCD, MS 10948/1/56.

1 Bray sent SB Richard Ellmann's biography *James Joyce* (London: Oxford University Press, 1959).

2 SB received a copy of *La Manivelle* from Pinget on 29 October (SB to Barbara Bray, TCD, MS 10948/1/55). SB and Pinget were revising Pinget's French translation of *Embers* (*Cendres*) done "in haste" for submission for the Italia Prize (SB to Margaret McLaren, Curtis Brown [after 28 October]; GEU, MS 1221; *Cendres*, as submitted for the Italia Prize: TxU, Beckett Collection, 3.4).

3 SB had been asked by novelist and playwright Mateo Lettunich, Head of the Arts Division of the Institute of International Education in New York, to serve as a consultant to their Young Artists Project and to nominate three French writers for the program; on 18 June 1959, SB wrote to Lettunich that he was "recommending a young Swiss writer of whom I have a high opinion and who is in great need of help and encouragement. I do not propose to make any other recommendation."

> Of the younger generation of writers in French I regard Robert Pinget as one of the most gifted and most promising.
>
> His published achievement already considerable (5 or 6 novels and one play) reveals an unremitting tension and progression towards a personal expression of high originality. With his latest novel LE FISTON, published early this year, he has reached in my opinion the threshold of something very important indeed.
>
> [. . .] I feel he is now at a critical moment when help, moral and material, such as the Young Artists Project Grant would supply, is of vital importance for the furtherance of his work and the realisation of his exceptional possibilities.
>
> His personal characteristics are those of a man of great goodness, simplicity and integrity. His interests and culture are wide and if he has much to receive in America he has also much to give. (Burns Library, Samuel Beckett Collection, SB-RP.)

Earlier, SB had written to Bray that Pinget's "American application was unsuccessful" (19 August 1959; TCD, MS 10948/1/42).

4 The dust jacket on the Grove Press edition of the *Three Novels: Molloy, Malone Dies, The Unnamable* (1959) featured a Brassaï photograph of SB. The book was bound in dark blue cloth stamped in gold on the spine.

5 Bertrand Poirot-Delpech wrote of Blin's production of *Les Nègres*: "La mise en scène de Roger Blin est en tout cas la plus intéressante de toutes celles qui ont été présentées cette année" ("'Les Nègres,' de Jean Genet," *Le Monde* 4 November 1959: 13) (Roger Blin's production is in any case the most interesting of all those staged this year).

6 SB had encouraged MacGreevy to take his planned trip to Italy, offering to help with expenses. When MacGreevy thanked SB for making the trip possible, SB replied: "You mustn't be thanking me like that, it was all for me easy and from the heart. I am sorry I am such a dull silent dog, I've gone all dark and empty." (SB to MacGreevy, 30 November 1959; TCD, MS 10402/226.)

7 SB cites "Io venni in luogo d'ogni luce muto" ("I came to a place where all light was mute") (Dante, *Inferno*, V.28). In Canto 5, the carnal sinners are punished.

8 Jean-Louis Barrault did not stage *Hamlet*, but rather *La Petite Molière* by Jean Anouilh, which opened on 11 November.

9 The opening line of "To Autumn" by John Keats: "Season of mists and mellow fruitfulness" (John Keats, *Complete Poems*, ed. Jack Stillinger [Cambridge, MA: Belknap Press of Harvard University Press, 1982] 360).

JACOB SCHWARTZ
BRIGHTON

5.11.59 Paris

Dear Jake

Many thanks for Murphy (I had not seen the edition), Tyndall and your letter.[1]

I remember Hayman. His thesis is learned and ingenious but doesn't quite convince me. I think you can prove anything with Finnegan – like statistics.[2]

The 3 in 1, Molloy to Unnamable, is just out from Grove. I have written asking them to send you a copy so don't be buying it. It is a very handsome volume – once you get rid of the jacket – and I am very pleased to have the 3 between the same boards at last.

I shall of course do the transcript you ask for, but not immediately. I'm killed with work – horribly difficult new work in French 6 months still to go at least, French translation of EMBERS and English of a new radio play by Robert Pinget commissioned by BBC. But you may count on the transcript in due course – of the printed text I presume, and in French, it wd be impossible to copy the original MS.[3]

I have read the Tyndall with pleasure, it is written with great charm and liveliness. He seems like so many American professors rather Joyce-drunk and I can't follow him in those parallels, though there may be more in them than meets my eye.[4] There is nothing I particularly want changed in his text and in any case I refuse to interfere in another man's writing, better he should go wrong in his own way than perhaps slightly less so in mine. I also find it quite impossible now to speak or even think of my own work, the hole I have got myself into now is as "dumb of all light" as the 5th canto of

HELL and by God no love. So by all means as far as I am concerned do a printing of the Tyndall as it stands. Do you want the pages back?

I have also for you a copy of the German trilingual edition of the Poems (Limes Verlag). Remind me to give it to you when we meet. Or I can send it if you prefer.[5]

A très bientôt j'espère. Hommages à Madame Schwar[t]z[6]

Yours ever

s/ Sam

TLS; 1 leaf, 1 side; T *env to* Jake Schwartz Esq, 14 Chichester Terrace, Brighton, Sussex, Angleterre; *pm* 5-11-59, La Ferté-sous-Jouarre; OSU, Spec.rare.133; AL draft; 1 leaf, 1 side *on verso* Jake Schwartz to SB, 31 October 1959; GEU, MS 1221.

1 *Murphy: Roman*, translated into German by Elmar Tophoven, was published by Rowohlt Verlag (Hamburg, 1959).

William York Tindall (1903–1981), whose name SB misspells as "Tyndall," taught at Columbia University in New York from 1931 to 1971. Schwartz had sent SB the manuscript of Tindall's essay *Beckett's Bums*, later privately printed in a limited edition by the Shenvel Press (London: 1960). In his essay, Tindall examines SB's novels in light of *The Unnamable*, and draws comparisons between Joyce and Beckett. Schwartz had written to SB on 31 October:

> I told him I would like to print 70 copies or so for private circulation to Librarians and teachers [. . .] but before I do so I want you to read the stuff and if it is HOPELESS let me know and I will drop the matter. But if it has any merit and you care to correct any gross errors, etc – please stick a piece of paper on the margins and add any emendations or any deletions and I shall be pleased to print it. (GEU, MS 1221.)

2 SB's letter to David Hayman (b. 1927) about his thesis on Joyce and Mallarmé discussed Hayman's assertion that there were "Mallarmean elements" in *Finnegans Wake* (see 22 July 1955).

3 Schwartz had requested that SB make a fair copy of *En attendant Godot*; this is now at the Harry Ransom Center, University of Texas in Austin (Lake, *No Symbols Where None Intended*, 66). Schwartz wrote to SB on 31 October: "I know you are sentimental about the French version of GODOT and want to hold it. But can you MAKE A TRANSCRIPT of it please as you did for the English version and shall pay you 50 POUNDS for your trouble" (GEU, MS 1221). Of this fair copy, SB would later write to Rosemary Pountney: "The Godot MS at Austin is of no interest [. . .] being merely a fair copy made in a foul moment for the sake of a few quid" (22 March 1974; Pountney Collection).

4 In *Beckett's Bums*, Tindall wrote: "My guess is that *Molloy* and the subsequent novels owe something to Joyce in theme, structure, and meaning; that Beckett's trilogy, in one sense, is a kind of portrait of the artist – as an old man; and that *Molloy* is a parody of *Ulysses*" (10).

5 Beckett, *Gedichte*.

6 "A très bientôt j'espère. Hommages à Madame Schwar[t]z" (Till very soon, I hope. My respects to Mrs Schwartz).

BARBARA BRAY
PURLEY, SURREY

13.11.59 Ussy

Dear Barbara

Thanks for your letters. A bibliography. Time enough if ever. When it can be final. Not long now. Many thanks for Joyce. Reading it with interest. References to me – unimportant.[1] Drunk and 3/4 dead already. Nothing changed except the fraction. Have finished rough version of La Manivelle (THE OLD TUNE) and shall be sending it to you probably Monday. A bit too free and Irish. But couldn't get the rhythms any other way. Should be grateful for your suggestions. Shall indicate doubtful passages when sending.[2] You will be seeing Robert. Off to USA in 10 days. A few days in Paris and work extinguished for a week. Here now I hope till Thursday and back double quick. Car still on the road. Dull little brute to drive. Pim – on the point of abandoning. First part in any case quite impossible. Nothing to relate. Hand on desk, head on hand, pen forgotten in other. Shall write again with ms.

Love

Sam

ALS; 1 leaf, 1 side; *env to* Mrs Barbara Bray, 121 Brighton Rd., Purley, Surrey, Angleterre; *pm* 14–11–59, La Ferté-sous-Jouarre; TCD, MS 10948/1/57.

1 Richard Ellmann's biography *James Joyce*.

2 SB's marked translation, *The Old Tune*, has not been found.

BARBARA BRAY
PURLEY, SURREY

Saturday [14 November 1959] Ussy

Dear Barbara

Finished La Manivelle earlier than I expected. Herewith. I hope I can improve it later, but for the moment I can't do more. The names could be improved. A go[o]d tune that was on the barrel-organ that came to the house when I was a child is The Bluebells of Scotland, hence bluebells in text on assumption of its availability. The doubtful passages are the military and legal. Foot, gunners, Chatham, Caterham, Chesham, Assizes, Common Pleas - if anything here too wrong or invraisemblable for English listeners please point out, though accuracy obviously secondary consideration.[1] I tried to keep down Irishism but it kept breaking through. Couldn't get his rhythms and loose syntax any other way. Roar of engine simply à titre indicatif.[2] They are on a corner where cars slow down to turn, change down and then blaze on. The noise could be varied and its points of incidence changed, though we feel it is perhaps better to leave it monotonous and keep such noises as pneumatic drill, fire engine etc. as elements in the background noise. Any comments you may have to offer will be most welcome.

Have written ten shaky lines of Pim since Wednesday. Hope now to get down to it better though heart not in it much and on with Embers translation. Danish translator to call on me this afternoon. Could have done without that. Shall give him this to post in Paris this evening.[3] Here till Thursday I hope. Then Paris as briefly as possible. Received "X". Pinget well translated to judge by cursory reading without comparison of texts.[4]

Love
s/Sam

TLS; 1 leaf, 1 side; T *env to* Mrs Barbara Bray, 121 Brighton Road, Purley, Surrey, Angleterre; *pm* 16-11-59, La Ferté-sous-Jouarre; TCD, MS 10948/1/58. *Dating:* Saturday prior to postmark.

1 "Bluebells of Scotland" is a traditional Scottish folk song.

Details about the British regiments and their garrison towns concern the characters Cream and Gorman, who contradict each other. Some of the doubtful passages were also queried by Howard Newby in an inter-office memo to Barbara Bray, dated 7 and 9 March:

> One point. Beckett has translated it into an Irish idiom. Will you "place" it in Dublin? If so, what about the references to English garrison towns?
>
> It occurs to me, incidentally, that Gorman couldn't talk of "the Foot." Didn't the Foot-Regiments disappear long before his time. Wouldn't he say that the Artillery were at Woolwich (not Chatham, a naval town) and the Hussars (say) at Aldershot (not Caterham which is the Guards depot)?

Bray's notes on the memo indicate "All these points already settled between Mr. Beckett & myself. BB 9/3 [60]" (BBCWAC, RCONT1, Samuel Beckett, Scriptwriter I).

Until abolished in 1972, the Courts of Assize were temporary courts set up in seven circuit districts in England and Wales. Justices of the Court of King's Bench travelled to hold local courts, generally in quarterly sessions, to try serious criminal cases. Justices of the Court of Common Pleas heard cases brought by one citizen against another.

"Invraisemblable" (improbable).

2 "A titre indicatif" (by way of indication).

3 Christian Ludvigsen visited SB in Ussy with his friend the Danish journalist and writer Leif Blædel (b. 1923). SB mailed the manuscript of *The Old Tune* and this letter to Bray from La Ferté-sous-Jouarre on the following Monday.

4 Robert Pinget, "Simultaneously," tr. Wayland Dobson, *X, A Quarterly Review* 1.1 (November 1959) 37–41.

ROBERT PINGET
NEW YORK

30.11.59 Ussy sur Marne

Cher Robert

Ta lettre ce matin.[1] On te sent cafardeux. Ne te décourage pas, ça passera. Il te faudrait un autre logement et voir des gens qui te soient un peu sympathiques.[2] Je pense qu'avec Albee ça pourrait marcher. Et avec Rosset. As-tu été le voir? Dick Seaver qui travaille pour lui est un garçon très gentil, j'aurais dû te donner un mot pour lui. Sa femme est française. Il a traduit mes Nouvelles. Mais tu le rencontreras forcément.[3]

J'ai été voir Nadeau. Je lui [ai] donné CENDRES dont je viens de terminer la révision. Ils m'ont demandé de voir La MANIVELLE. J'ai dit que je leur passerai mon texte quand je n'en aurai plus besoin (pas encore le cas). D'accord? Je voudrais l'envoyer aussi à Copenhague, à mon traducteur danois, probable qu'il pourra le placer à la radio danoise.[4] Je le donnerai également à Tophoven bien sûr. J'ai vu Jérôme et il a reparlé de faire une édition des deux textes, français et anglais, ensemble. Je lui ai dit que j'étais d'accord. Une lettre de Barbara où elle dit que THE OLD TUNE leur plaît beaucoup, mais que ma transposition a entraîné certaines anomalies. Je ne vois pas lesquelles ni très bien ce qu'elle veut dire et attends des précisions. Je te tiendrai au courant. La mère Hutchinson est venue et m'a fait plutôt suer. Je lui ai dit de garder pour toi à Londres le cachet qui te revient pour ton texte dans X. C'est entendu.[5]

Je travaille avec beaucoup de mal – de plus en plus. J'ai vu tout d'un coup la "chose" très clairement pour la première fois, c'est plutôt gênant qu'autre chose, et ça fout en l'air une grande partie de ce que j'avais fait déjà. Il faudrait pouvoir se dire, ça ne presse pas, j'en ai jusqu'à ce que je crève, et ne donner le bon à tirer qu'avec le dernier soupir.

Madame Zeist a téléphoné très gentiment pour nous annoncer ta bonne arrivée et tes aventures au départ.[6] Une heure après ton télégramme. Merci de nous l'avoir envoyé.

Bon courage, tiens le coup et écris-nous bientôt,

Affectueusement

Sam

ALS; 1 leaf, 2 sides; Burns Library, Samuel Beckett Collection, SB-RP.

30.11.59 Ussy sur Marne

Dear Robert

Your letter this morning.[1] You're feeling low, by the sound of it. Don't lose heart: it will pass. What you'd need is somewhere else to live, and to see people you can like.[2] I think it might work out well with Albee. And Rosset. Have you been to see him? Dick Seaver who works for him is a very nice lad; I ought to have given you a note for him. His wife is French. He translated my *Stories*. But you're bound to meet him.[3]

I've been to see Nadeau. I gave him *Cendres*, which I have just finished revising. They asked to see *La Manivelle*. I told them that I'll pass the text over to them as soon as I no longer need it (not yet the case). Is that all right? I would like to send it to Copenhagen too, to my Danish translator; good chance that he'll be able to get it on Danish radio.[4] I'll give it to Tophoven too, of course. I've seen Jérôme, and he has again talked of making an edition of the two French and English texts together. I told him that I agreed. A letter from Barbara in which she says that they really like *The Old Tune*, but that my transposition has given rise to certain anomalies. I can't see which, nor really what she means, and I await details. I'll keep you informed. The Hutchinson woman came round, and made a nuisance of herself. I told her to keep in London the fee you're owed for your text in *X*. That's settled.[5]

I'm having trouble, more and more trouble working. I saw "it", very clearly, for the first time, it's embarrassing rather than anything else, it wrecks a large part of what I'd already done. I've got to learn to tell myself there's no hurry, it'll be there with me till I kick the bucket, and not to say "passed for press" before my last gasp.

Madame Zeist very sweetly telephoned to tell us of your safe arrival, and your adventures at the start.[6] An hour later, your telegram. Thanks for sending us it.

Keep your spirits up, stick to it, and write to us soon.

Affectionately

Sam

1 In his memoir, Pinget writes of meeting SB in July to discuss SB's translation of *La Manivelle*: "J'ajoute qu'à l'occasion de cette nouvelle gentillesse il m'en proposait une autre, celle de nous tutoyer. C'était au St Claude, à St-Germain des Prés, en buvant un verre." (Doucet, unclassified Pinget Collection, "Notre ami Samuel Beckett," 22.) (Let me add that, in the course of this latest demonstration of niceness, he was proposing yet another: our moving to "tu" terms. It was in the Café St Claude, in St-Germain-des-Prés, over a glass.)

2 Pinget had left Paris on 23 November to take up his grant from the International Cultural Exchange Program, funded by the Ford Foundation, and run by the Institute of International Education which had just launched a Young Artists' Project. Pinget was initially rejected, then belatedly selected, which explains his late departure for New York. The Institute's "Program Statement" outlined:

> The Young Artists' Project is designed to make it possible for young professionals in various fields of the creative arts to visit the United States for six months of observation and study. The program seeks to contribute to the professional growth of the young foreign artists and the American colleagues whom he will meet, and thus to strengthen cultural ties between the United States and other nations [. . .]. The first year's program will be devoted to six young writers, to be chosen among critics, essayists, novelists, poets, playwrights, and translators. They will be invited to arrive here in November 1959, and to remain through April 1960. (Doucet, PNG.C.349.3/14.)

The first group in fact comprised seven writers: Fernando Arrabal (Spain), Italo Calvino (Italy), Hugo Claus (Belgium), Matti Megged (Israel), Claude Ollier (France), Charles Tomlinson (England), and Pinget (Switzerland).

Pinget was then residing at the Hotel van Rensselaer, 15 East 11th Street; it had been built at the start of the century and was now in serious decline.

3 SB had made the acquaintance of Edward Albee earlier the same month in Paris and had asked him to send a copy of the script of *The Zoo Story*. SB wrote to Albee in New York on 20 November:

> Many thanks for the play. I like it very much. I want to read it again a couple of times. Then I'll write you again. This chiefly to introduce my friend Robert Pinget whose work I think has great importance. The chief object of his visit to the States is to study theatre conditions & production. I'd be very grateful for any help you can give him. (Albee Collection.)

SB wrote similarly, on the same day, to introduce Pinget to Herbert Berghof, Mary Manning Howe, George Reavey, Kenneth Rexroth, and Alan Schneider (Reavey Collection, recip, 45.5; Burns Library, Samuel Beckett Collection, SB-AS [Berghof, Manning, Rexroth, Schneider]).

Richard Seaver and Jeannette Medina married on 18 July 1953 in Paris (Seaver, *The Tender Hour of Twilight*, 173–177).

4 SB's Danish translator was Christian Ludvigsen, who wrote: "the Danish State-Radio thought it was too ... much Beckett-like and refused" the play (Ludvigsen to the editors, 21 October 2012).

5 Pinget's short story "Simultaneously" followed Beckett's untranslated prose "L'Image" in *X, A Quarterly Review* 1.1 (November 1959) 35–37.

6 Madame Zeist has not been identified.

BARBARA BRAY
PURLEY, SURREY

1.12.59 Ussy

Dear Barbara

Thanks for your letter of november 25th and the following received this morning with script and annotations. Thanks for all the trouble you have taken.[1]

I feel I can't go into it all now, so tired and dizzy with Pim. I don't feel this need to explain things or to make quite sure that the dear listener will not be left with the hideous feeling that the two old chaps are slightly unlikely. But no doubt you're right and these things are important.

He is not playing the organ for his pleasure but for his living and zwar on a street corner with the cars roaring under his nose, I thought this at least was clear. No doubt he was playing sitting on a box for example (surely verisimilar in spite of his freedom from rheumatism which with less self control I had called rheumatics) and got up to give Cream his seat or if you prefer had got up in order to mend the works from off his seat which thus was free for Cream to occupy.[2]

The two old chaps have a displaced persons quality which is perhaps not without significance and Toupin in particular is strongly Savoyard and uses at least two expressions which no normal Frenchman understands. In any case I can't put them in Ireland. I can't do it either without the help of Irish rhythms and inversions. I am inclined to feel that perhaps the best solution would be to have put into decent English by someone more in sympathy with English listeners and more alive to their needs than I am.[3]

I suppose you will feel now I am annoyed, but believe it or not I am not, only immensely tired and lost in my work. At the next glimmer of euphoria I'll try and think it all over and write to you again.

I have to go to Paris tomorrow for three or four days. Relief to fly from this Pim hell and I won't have driven ten miles before I'll be fidgeting to get back to it.

Letter from Robert from NY seemingly in the lowest spirits. Plane seven hours late and lice in his hotel room.

Often play chess alone in the evening with the bottle beside me and know of few less unpleasant occupations.

May struggle to Amsterdam in the car end of this month if weather not too appalling for van Velde's big exhibitions. Am lending my two. Saw his latest work the other day. Incomparable.[4]

Discovered the other day there was no oil in the engine. Put some in and all seems well. Unlovable little bastard of a yoke. Cut out for me.

French text of Embers finished at last. Giving it to Nadeau rather than an extract. Hate the sight of it in both languages. Understand it better.[5]

Sorry to sound grumpy. Can't help it. Should be in Mount Melleray.[6]

Love

s/ Sam

TLS; 1 leaf, 2 sides; T *env to* Mrs Barbara Bray, 121 Brighton Road, Purley, Surrey, Angleterre; *pm* 2-12-59, Paris; TCD MS 10948/1/60.

1 *The Old Tune.*

2 In *The Old Tune*, Gorman plays the barrel organ on a street corner. Cream, an acquaintance, comes along, and Gorman offers him a seat. "Zwar" (Ger., more precisely).

3 Responding to SB's request to point out difficulties that might exist for English listeners, Bray suggested that the use of Irish rhythms without an Irish setting might pose a problem.

4 Bram van Velde's retrospective at the Stedelijk Museum was held from 21 December 1959 through January 1960. SB lent his painting and a gouache: 28 April 1959, n. 2.

5 SB's revision of Pinget's French translation of *Embers*, *Cendres*, was sent to Maurice Nadeau to be published in *Les Lettres Nouvelles*: nouvelle série (2) 36 (December 1959) 3-14.

6 SB refers to the Cistercian monastery of Mount Melleray in the Knockmealdown Mountains near Cappoquin, Co. Waterford; known as a peaceful retreat, the Abbey was established in 1832 by monks from the monastery of Melleray in Brittany.

BARBARA BRAY
PURLEY, SURREY

8.12.59 Ussy

Dear Barbara

Thanks for yours of 4th.

Back here yesterday in usual state of post-Paris debility. Yesterday drove a friend out to 20 miles beyond DREUX in Normandy in the morning, then back to Paris alone, then out here in the afternoon, all in the rain.

Can't understand why you didn't get the book same time as Donald. You were on same list. If by yr. next letter it hasn't arrived I'll get after them.[1]

Quite liked look and feel of Faber book. From a quick look inside some mistakes in text. Shall be sending copies in due course to Donald, Pat, Jackie, you of course.[2]

Quite lost in Pim. Shall either

1 bungle it

2 give it up

3 keep writing it for years

no doubt as always the first

Another gloomy letter from Robert. Haven't yet gone over the traduction with your notes. No great hurry I take it. Sorry to have sounded cross. If I have I wasn't. Something quite different.[3]

Never read a line of Mill or de Chardin. Don't understand a word of Wittgenstein. Had boots brushed once in Zagreb with no feeling but mounting dislike of bootblack.[4]

Simply must have a long stay here now. May go to Paris for an afternoon and evening to correct proofs of CENDRES for Nadeau and go to a reading at the Alliance Française of Arrabal's unpublished TRICYCLE.[5] But not sure. Back next day in any case. Don't think I shall go to Amsterdam for vernissage after all, too mondain. Ambassadors, Veeps, etc. Perhaps later to see the work all together. My two pictures left a few days ago.[6]

Spent an evening, or the second part, with John Calder and saw the musician Marc Wilkinson who has done a setting of a passage from Godot (VOICES) to be performed in London I think in February.[7]

Love

Sam

Offer of a film of Godot by Bergman. Prefer not.[8]

ALS; 1 leaf, 2 sides; *env to* Mrs Barbara Bray, 121 Brighton Rd., Purley, Surrey, Angleterre; *pm* 8-12-59, La Ferté-sous-Jouarre; TCD, MS 10948/1/61.

1 SB had promised a copy of the Grove edition of *Molloy*, *Malone Dies*, and *The Unnamable* to Bray and McWhinnie (see 5 November 1959 to Bray).

2 The Faber and Faber edition of *Krapp's Last Tape and Embers* published together in a small volume (1959) had just arrived (*Krapp's Last Tape* had been published separately in *Evergreen Review* in 1958).

3 In his letter of 1 December, SB had responded to Bray's suggestions for adjusting his translation of *The Old Tune* for English audiences. Bray replied that he sounded irritated.

4 On 3 December, the centenary of John Stuart Mill's essay *On Liberty* was heralded ("Centenary of a Great Essay," *The Times*: 17). *The Phenomenon of Man* (*Le Phénomène Humain*, 1955) by Pierre Teilhard de Chardin, translated by Bernard Wall, had been recently reviewed ("Evolution May Not Have Done with the Old Adam," *The Times* 26 November 1959: 15; Ivor Thomas, "The Chain of Evolution," *The Times Literary Supplement* 3013 [27 November 1959] 685–686). The BBC Third Programme planned a broadcast of "The Life and Work of Ludwig Wittgenstein" for 13 January 1960.

5 Jean-Marie Serreau was to present a reading of Fernando Arrabal's play *Tricycle* at the Alliance Française on 14 December, but, as SB would write to Arrabal on 15 December: "Je croyais que c'était à 21h, mais c'était à 17h. Je l'ai donc ratée. Je regrette beaucoup." (Arrabal Collection.) (I thought it was at 9 o'clock, but it was at 5 o'clock. I therefore missed it. I am so sorry.)

6 "Veeps" (colloq., Very Important Persons).

7 Composer Marc Wilkinson had requested permission to set to music a passage of Lucky's speech from *Waiting for Godot*. His composition for soprano and chamber orchestra, *Voices*, was to be performed in the Festival Hall, London, on 14 March 1960, as part of the "Music Today" series organized by John Calder.

8 Judith Schmidt had written to SB on 3 December:

> I know that you've already told us that you do not wish to have GODOT made into a film. However, we've just had an inquiry which we thought we should tell you about.
>
> The plan is to have a film produced by Tyrone Guthrie and Leonid Kipnis. (Kipnis produced the Yeats version of OEDIPUS REX, which I saw and liked very much.) The film would be made in Europe by Ingmar Bergman. We think Bergman is pretty great, and that this, therefore, is not the usual request for movie rights. Of course, if you're not interested, we'll just drop the matter.

SB replied: "Continue not to want GODOT 'turned' into a film, even by Bergman. Sorry" (SB to Judith Schmidt, 8 December 1959; NSyU).

ROBERT PINGET
NEW YORK

13.12.59 Ussy

Cher Robert

Content d'avoir de tes nouvelles. Elles ne sont pas resplendissantes. J'espère qu'avec Schneider ça a marché et qu'il te sera utile. Ce n'est pas un aigle mais il a très bon coeur. Peut-être seras-tu demain à la causerie de Mayoux.[1] Je crois qu'il rentre bientôt. Rosset arrive mardi. Toujours du passage. Plus moyen de travailler plus de 4 ou 5 jours d'affilée. J'ai avancé pas mal la 3me partie, aux dépens évidemment des 2 premières qu'il va falloir refaire aux dépens n'en doutons pas du [sic] troisième et ainsi de suite.

A propos de THE OLD TUNE j'ai été un peu agacé par les chinoiseries de Londres mais ça va s'arranger. On me demande: Où sont les bonshommes? En Irlande? En Angleterre? Si en Angleterre d'où ce langage? Si en Irlande pourquoi ces noms d'endroit? Etc. Ce genre de petite bête. Ils sont en Angleterre et ils parlent comme ça. Je vais tout reprendre en essayant de me mettre à la place de ces chers auditeurs. Je les comprends si mal! Puis voir Barbara pour les fignolages.[2] Ça ne presse pas mais m'empêche d'envoyer les 2 textes à Copenhague et de donner le français à Nadeau.

La radio nous achète CENDRES (une transmission) 6000 fr. belges soit dans les 55.000 français. J'ai demandé à Curtis Brown qu'on te garde la moitié à Londres jusqu'à ce que tu puisses la toucher là-bas. Ai-je bien fait?[3]

J'ai donné CENDRES à Nadeau. Ça passera dans le 1er no. de l'année prochaine paraît-il.[4]

Jérôme est en plein dans ses histoires de juge d'instruction. Il a été inculpé et prépare les dossiers. Il n'a pas l'air de s'en faire.[5]

Je n'irai pas après tout à Amsterdam pour l'exposition de Bram. Trop de mondanités. Peut-être plus tard pour voir le travail. Mes 2 tableaux sont partis.

Je rentre à Paris demain. Demain soir à l'Alliance lecture (Serreau) d'une pièce d'Arrabal que je ne connais pas – TRICYCLE.[6] LES NEGRES marchent toujours du tonnerre.[7] Plus rien sur GODOT à l'Odéon. Transmission enfin de CEUX QUI TOMBENT samedi prochain. Impression que c'est complètement raté.

Te fais pas trop chier et mets quelques fafiots à gauche – au moins ça. Il me semble que tu devrais te plonger dans des histoires de théâtre.[8]

Pardonne cette lettre stupide. Il faut l'être tellement pour Pim. Peut-on t'envoyer des livres, des journaux?

Affectueusement

Sam

ALS; 1 leaf, 2 sides; Burns Library, Samuel Beckett Collection, SB-RP.

13.12.1959 Ussy

Dear Robert

Glad to get your news. It doesn't sound brilliant. I hope that it went off well with Schneider, and that he will be useful to you. He's no genius, but he's very kind-hearted. Perhaps you'll be at Mayoux's talk tomorrow.[1] I think he's coming back soon. Rosset is coming on Tuesday. Always comings and goings. No way of working more than four or five days in a row. I've pushed the third part on a fair bit, at the expense, of course, of the first two, which I will have to redo, at the expense no doubt of the third, and so on.

About *The Old Tune*: I was a bit annoyed by all the London logic-chopping, but it's going to be all right. They are asking me: where are these men? In Ireland? In England? If in England, whence this language? If in Ireland, why these place names? That's the piddling sort of thing. They are in England and they talk like that. I'm going to go through it all again, trying to put myself in the place of these dear members of the audience. I am so bad at understanding them! Then see Barbara for the polishing up.[2] There is no urgency, but it's stopping me from sending the two texts to Copenhagen and giving the French to Nadeau.

The radio is buying *Cendres* (one broadcast) for 6,000 Belgian francs, or about 55,000 French francs. I have asked Curtis Brown to keep half of it in London for you until you can pick it up there. Did I do the right thing?[3]

I've given *Cendres* to Nadeau. It will come out in the first issue next year, apparently.[4]

Jérôme is caught up in his business with the examining magistrate. He has been charged, and is preparing his brief. He seems unworried by it all.[5]

I shan't go to Amsterdam after all for the Bram exhibition. Too many society people and things. Maybe later to see the works. My two pictures have gone.

I'm going back to Paris tomorrow. Tomorrow evening at the Alliance a reading (Serreau) of a play by Arrabal that I don't know: *Tricycle*.[6] *Les Nègres* is still going great guns.[7] Nothing more about *Godot* at the Odéon. Broadcast at last of *Tous ceux qui tombent* next Saturday. Impression that it's been totally botched.

Don't let it all get you down, and put a few greenbacks aside: at least there'll be that. Seems to me that you should really get involved in theatre.[8]

Forgive this stupid letter. I have to be like that so much for Pim. Can we send you any books, newpapers?

Affectionately

Sam

1 Jean-Jacques Mayoux's "causerie" (talk) in New York has not been identified.

2 In his memoir of this period Pinget writes:

> Avant mon départ, en septembre sans doute, Barbara Bray m'avait demandé de lui refaire quelque chose pour la BBC. Je transcrivis en dialogue une scène de mon nouveau roman L'OIE où deux vieux parlent du temps passé, et le montrai à Sam avant de l'envoyer. Il lui a plu tellement qu'il m'offert spontanément de le traduire en anglais. Le titre français est LA MANIVELLE. Celui trouvé par Sam THE OLD TUNE. Inutile de dire les qualités de cette traduction. Sam a transposé l'atmosphère française en atmosphère anglo-irlandaise. Mes deux croulants bien de chez nous sont devenus deux Irlandais installés à Londres. Sam m'a demandé l'autorisation de faire cette transposition et de changer même les noms. (Doucet, unclassified Pinget Collection, "Notre ami Samuel Beckett," 21–22.) (Before I left, in September it must have been, Barbara Bray had asked me to rejig something for the BBC. I transcribed, in dialogue, a scene from my new novel *L'Oie*, where two old men are talking about times past, and showed it to Sam before sending it off. He liked it so much that he offered unprompted to translate it into English. The French title is *La Manivelle*. Sam came up with *The Old Tune*. No need to speak of the qualities of this translation. Sam has transposed the French atmosphere into an Anglo-Irish one. My two old codgers, French of the French, have become two Irishmen living in London. Sam asked my permission to do this transposing and to change even the names.)

3 Margaret McLaren had written to SB on 3 December, reporting that Mr. Wallenborn of the Belgian Radio planned to produce *Embers* as soon as Pinget's translation was received; she had mentioned that she had asked them to increase their fee, which they had agreed to do (GEU, MSS 1221).

4 SB had given his play for publication in Maurice Nadeau's journal, *Les Lettres Nouvelles*.

5 Not for the last time, Jérôme Lindon was, in December 1959, prosecuted for harming military morale, incitement to disobedience, and defamation of the police. Lindon had taken a long and principled stance against French military intervention in Algeria, and particularly against the military's systematic and widespread use of torture (see Knowlson, *Damned to Fame*, 492–495). In early 1958, he had published Henri Alleg's *La Question*, in which the author recounted his own experience of being tortured; in June 1959, copies of Minuit's publication *La Gangrène*, reporting the experience of torture undergone by five Algerians in Paris, were seized by the authorities. Nine books in the Minuit series "Documents" were seized and forbidden.

6 *Mon Programme Radio-Télé* later announced broadcast of *Le Tricycle* by Fernando Arrabal on National France 3 (17 January 1960) in the following terms: "Représentée 'dans le cadre' des lectures-spectacles du banc d'essai de la R.T.F., sur la petite scène de l'Alliance Française, la pièce a été enregistrée en public sous la direction artistique de J.-M. Serreau" (1081 [16 January 1960] 6, 8) (Put on as part of the RTF's test programme of staged readings, the play was given a public recording, on the little stage of the Alliance Française, under the artistic direction of J.-M. Serreau). The cast included actors who had played SB's *Tous ceux qui tombent* on the radio: Nicole Courcel, Pierre Vernier, Georges Adet, Roger Blin, Jacques Gripel, and Max Amyl. In the event, SB missed the reading, having mistaken its time, as he explained to Arrabal in his letter of 15 December (Arrabal Collection).

7 Jean Genet's *Les Nègres*, directed by Roger Blin with the African Compagnie des Griots, had its premiere on 28 October at the Théâtre de Lutèce, Paris 5. Writing in *Le Monde*, Claude Sarraute cited Blin on Genet: "'Il l'a fait … sans s'attendrir. Aucun rapport entre ces nègres et ceux de la Case de l'oncle Tom. La pièce est courageuse, insolente'." ("'Qu'est-ce que c'est donc un noir?' demande Jean Genet dans sa nouvelle pièce," 30 October 1959: 13.) (He did it … without appeal to sentiment. Nothing in common between these Blacks and those of *Uncle Tom's Cabin*. The play is courageous, insolent.)

8 In his memoir, Pinget writes, commenting on SB's remark in this letter: "Je me suis effectivement plongé dans des histoires de théâtre en faisant donner en lecture mes deux pièces Dead Letter et The Old Tune par le Theatre Workshop de Louis Beachner qui était emballé par ces textes" (Doucet, unclassified Pinget Collection, "Notre ami Samuel Beckett," 25) (I did indeed get involved in theatre business, setting up a reading of my two plays *Dead Letter* and *The Old Tune* by the Louis Beachner Theatre Workshop. He was really keen on these texts). In the report he completed at the end of his stay in America, Pinget gave details: "J'ai réussi en janvier 1960 à faire donner au Gate Theatre (Studio Luther James) par le Workshop de Louis Beachner (303 W 11 Street) une lecture de ma pièce Dead Letter dont j'ai été extrêmement satisfait. L'esprit ouvert de ce petit groupe et de son directeur m'a été précieux et je leur en suis reconnaissant." (Doucet PNG.C.349.13/14.) (In January 1960 I managed to get put on at the Gate Theatre (Luther James Studio) by the Louis Beachner Workshop (303 W 11th Street) a reading of my play *Dead Letter* that I thought went extremely well. The open-mindedness of this little group and its director was a delight for me, and I am grateful to them.)

ROBERT PINGET
NEW YORK

21.12.59 Ussy

Cher Robert

Merci pour le programme avec ton mot. Arrabal me l'envoie en même temps avec la mention: "J'ai passé une mauvaise soirée."[1] TCQT est passé à la radio hier. Mauvais.[2] Je suis en train de corriger pour Jérôme les épreuves de KRAPP et CENDRES. Celui-là pue la traduction, l'autre moins. CENDRES passe dans les LN le 31 décembre. Je verrai Barbara vers le 6 janvier et mettrai avec elle The O.T. au point. Copenhague me le réclame. Je serai peut-être obligé d'ajuster certains détails dans l'original (les temps par exemple). Comme Jérôme veut publier les deux ensemble il y a peu de chance qu'il autorise Les LN à publier le texte français. Mais je lui demanderai. Quand je donnerai le MS à Jérôme (vers la mi-janvier probablement) je te l'enverrai pour que tu me fasses part de tes suggestions. Pour la correction des épreuves je peux m'en occuper tout seul, si tu es d'accord.

Les revues qui paient - connais pas. Match me semble tout indiqué. Tu as bien fait de t'adresser à Belmont.[3]

Rosset m'a parlé vaguement d'un projet de lecture du O.T. à NY. Il serait préférable d'attendre le texte définitif. Mais à la rigueur ça peut se donner, du moment qu'on ne l'imprime pas encore, tel quel.

Très content que tu te sentes mieux et aies de la sympathie pour Schneider. C'est un bien brave type. Qui est Blee? Tu ne confonds pas avec Albee? Si tu vois ce dernier dis-lui que je m'excuse de ne pas lui avoir encore écrit au sujet de sa pièce qui me plaît beaucoup et que je le ferai bientôt.[4] On annonce pour la saison prochaine du Théâtre des Nations une mise en scène allemande (j'ignore laquelle) de Krapp sans doute avec Zoo Geschichte.[5]

Jean attend le nouvel an pour se mettre en branle pour Lettre Morte en en faisant reprendre les droits par Jérôme.

Je passerai les fêtes ici avec Pim. La voix va bientôt se taire (tout à fait) qui lui parle par petites bribes d'une vie qu'il aurait eue, a et aura.

J'en ai encore pour six mois ou pour tout mon petit toujours, pas encore fixé.

En ce moment le vernissage Bram à Amsterdam. J'ai pu seulement envoyer un télégramme.

Mes amitiés à George Reavey.

Bonne continuation, bonne fin d'année et bonne année début milieu et fin.

Bien affectueusement de nous deux.

s/ Sam

TLS; 1 leaf, 1 side; Burns Library, Samuel Beckett Collection, SB-RP.

21.12.1959 Ussy

Dear Robert

Thank you for the programme, with your note. Arrabal sends me it at the same time with the comment: "I spent a bad evening."[1] *TCQT* went out on the radio yesterday. Bad.[2] I am in the middle of correcting for Jérôme the proofs of *Krapp* and *Cendres*. The former stinks of translation, the other less. *Cendres* is coming out in the *Lettres Nouvelles* on the 31st of December. I shall be seeing Barbara on the 6th of January or thereabouts, and will put the finishing touches to *The O.T.* with her. Copenhagen is pressing me for it. I may have to adjust certain details in the original (the tenses for instance). As Jérôme wants to publish the two together, there is not much chance that he will allow the *LN* to publish the French text. But I'll ask him. When I give the MS to Jérôme (about half-way through January, probably), I'll send it to you so that you can let me have your suggestions. The proof correcting I can do on my own, if you agree.

Magazines that pay – don't know any. *Match* seems just right. You did well to approach Belmont.[3]

Rosset talked vaguely about a projected reading of *O.T.* in NY. It would be preferable to wait for the definitive text. But it could just about be done as it stands, as long as we're not yet publishing it as it is.

Very glad that you are feeling better, and that you like Schneider. He's a really nice fellow. Who is Blee? Aren't you mixing him up with

Albee? If you see the latter, tell him that I'm sorry not to have written to him yet about his play, which I greatly like, and that I will write soon.[4] There is talk, for the next Théâtre des Nations season, of a German production (I don't know which one) of *Krapp*, along with *Zoo Geschichte* no doubt.[5]

Jean is waiting for the New Year to make a start on *Lettre morte* by asking Jérôme to get back the rights.

I shall be spending the festive season with Pim. The voice will soon fall (totally) silent that speaks to him in little gobbets of a life that he might have had, has, will have. It will take me another six months, or the little that's left to me: which not settled.

At this very moment Bram's private view in Amsterdam. All I could manage was a telegram.

My regards to George Reavey.

Hope things keep going well. Happy end of year and beginning, middle and end of new year.

Love from us both

s/ Sam

1 Pinget comments: "Arrabal se trouvait à NY en même temps que moi, invité par la même fondation. Nous avions assisté ensemble à une représentation de Krapp à NY et avions des réactions différentes. J'avais aimé." (Doucet, unclassified Pinget Collection, "Notre ami Samuel Beckett," 27.) (Arrabal was in New York at the same time as me, invited by the same Foundation. We had gone together to a performance of *Krapp* in New York, and had different reactions. I had liked it.) *Krapp's Last Tape*, in a double bill with *The Zoo Story*, would open on 14 January 1960 at the Provincetown Playhouse, 133 MacDougal Street, New York.

2 *Tous ceux qui tombent* was broadcast on 19 December on France III. The cast comprised Roger Blin, Raymone (Raymonde Duchateau), Léonce Corne, Georges Adet, Albert Rémy, Jean Martin, Pierre Latour, Patrick Maurin, Patrice Maufras, Jacqueline Harpet, Marise Paillet, and Arielle Semenoff (*Mon Programme Radio-Télé* 1076 [12 December 1959] 49–50).

3 In his memoir, Pinget comments on his request of SB: "Je lui demandais dans ma lettre de m'indiquer à Paris une revue qui serait intéressée par une traduction que je venais de faire à NY avec George Reavey d'un texte de Pasternak" (Doucet, unclassified Pinget Collection, "Notre ami Samuel Beckett," 27) (I was asking him in my letter to point me to a Paris review that might be interested in a translation I had just done in New York with George Reavey of a Pasternak text). Georges Belmont, the person originally responsible for introducing Pinget to SB, had worked at *Paris-Match* in 1953–1954, and was currently working at *Marie-Claire*.

4 SB had in fact written to Albee to tell him he had enjoyed *The Zoo Story* (see 30 November 1959, n. 3).

5 From 1957, the Théâtre Sarah-Bernhardt (now Théâtre de la Ville) was a location for the Théâtre des Nations, with international troupes playing in their native languages; a German production of the double-bill did not occur in 1960.

CHRONOLOGY 1960

1960	4 January	Death of Albert Camus.
	After 5 January	Publication of *La dernière bande, suivi de Cendres* by Editions de Minuit.
	14 January	*Krapp's Last Tape* opens at the Provincetown Playhouse, New York, directed by Alan Schneider.
	24 January – 1 February	Insurrection in Algiers, known as "La semaine des barricades."
	2–3 February	The French government takes on emergency powers to deal with the worsening situation in Algeria.
	27 March	Générale of *La dernière bande*, directed by Roger Blin, and *Lettre morte*, directed by Jean Martin, Théâtre Récamier.
	29 March	SB refuses a commission by R. B. D. French to write a play to benefit the Library, Trinity College Dublin.
	30 March	SB's tribute to Sean O'Casey published in *The Irish Times.*
	31 March	*Molloy, Malone Dies*, and *The Unnamable* published by John Calder in a single volume as *Three Novels.*
	27 April	The BBC Third Programme broadcasts *Waiting For Godot.*
	7 May	SB lifts his embargo on production of his work in Ireland.

8 June	Attends Berliner Ensemble production of Brecht's *Die Mutter*, Sarah Bernhardt Theatre, Paris; leaves at first opportunity.
before 15 June	Calder's edition of *Three Novels* is seized from Fred Hanna's bookshop in Dublin, under Irish government order.
17 June	SB attends, with Alan Schneider in Paris, the Berliner Ensemble production of Brecht's *Galileo*.
6 July	Attends a run-through of Cyril Cusack's production of *Krapp's Last Tape* for the Théâtre des Nations, Paris.
2 August	Completes revision and typing of his new work, which becomes *Comment c'est*.
8 August	Dates a draft of what becomes *Happy Days*.
18 August	Writes his first letter to Harold Pinter.
23 August	The BBC Third Programme broadcasts *The Old Tune*, produced by Barbara Bray, with Jack MacGowran and Patrick Magee.
6 September	*Vérité-Liberté* publishes a *Déclaration sur le Droit à l'Insoumission dans la Guerre d'Algérie* signed by 121 writers and artists; it becomes known as the Manifeste des 121.
After 19 September	Pinget's *La Manivelle* and SB's English text, *The Old Tune*, published by Editions de Minuit.
20 September and 28 September	SB works on translation of "L'Expulsé" with Richard Seaver, in Paris.
30 September	Jérôme Lindon arrested.

7 October	A letter condemning the "apologists of desertion and disobedience" and defending the Army appears in *Le Figaro* with 185 signatories.
by 19 October	SB has begun to move into his new apartment at 38 Boulevard Saint-Jacques, Paris 14.
4 November	De Gaulle outlines his conception of the "Algerian Republic."
7 November	John F. Kennedy is elected President of the United States.
16 November	SB goes to see *On the Bowery* directed by Lionel Rogosin.

ALAN SCHNEIDER
NEW YORK

4.1.60 Ussy

Dear Alan

Thanks for your two letters, second today. I hasten to reply. First your specific points:

1. Spool instead of reel if you wish.
2. Post Mortems by all means.
3. Instead of weir suggest sluice or lock.
4. Should prefer you to keep stem.
5. If dell is clearer than dingle by all means. Same thing.[1]

Now the rest.

Know nothing whatever about "extra speaker to tape recorder" in Berlin and am not sure what this means. If it does what I fear it is plain murder and unpardonable.[2] I dream sometimes of all German directors of plays with perhaps one exception united in one with his back to the wall and me shooting a bullet into his balls every five minutes till he loses his taste for improving authors. Krapp has nothing to talk to but his dying self and nothing to talk to him but his dead one. I think we discussed the technical problems raised by the machine. The text recorded should be spoken obviously in a much younger and stronger voice than Krapp's for his last tape (though as McWhinnie remarked voices don't always age abreast of the rest), but unmistakably his. The visible machine on the table should obviously be a dummy (too risky otherwise with all the violent manipulations), by which I mean of course a real machine visibly working and stopping when switched on and off but the tape silent. The machine heard has to be worked off stage which involves very delicate cue work from the wings but there seems no other way of doing it.[3] By the way for God's sake make sure in your script that there are no omissions or variations in the repeated passages.

What helps for the cue is for Krapp to have a very special gesture for switching on and off which though it has to be abrupt may be prepared by a change of posture (straightening a little out of his crouch for example), the same each time. Hard to explain these things in writing. When writing the piece if I had been more familiar with tape recordings I might have had Krapp wind back and forward without switching off for the sake of the extraordinary sound that can be had apparently in this way (Blin dixit), but it would certainly complicate things technically and better not try it. I told you about the beautiful and quite accidental effect in London of the luminous eye burning up as the machine runs on in silence and the light goes down. It is not visible from all parts of the house unless you can manage two eyes, one on each side, or the eye in front in the middle![4] This requires of course a slow fade out at the end which I think is good in any case, but not a fade on at the beginning. It is better the curtain should go up on a dark stage and then suddenly full blaze on Krapp seated at his table. He should be in a pool of light and of course near the front (just enough room between table and edge of stage for banana gag and walk backstage[)]. All backstage as black as possible, he can disappear through black drapes for his drinks and dictionary.[5] Nothing whatever on stage but table. We also I think discussed his itinerary from table backstage. The one I recommend and which we used in London is quite unnatural but correct dramatically, it is

and has the great advantage of lengthening the walk (to compensate immobility) and of allowing Krapp to be inspected in motion as he would not be if he took the normal route in a straight line from behind table backstage. I think this is important. With regard to costume it should be sufficiently clear from text (don[']t be afraid of exaggerating with boots). Black and white (both dirty), the whole piece being built up in one sense on this simple antithesis of which you will find echoes throughout text (black ball, white nurse, black pram, Bianca, Kedar – anagram of "dark" – Street, black storm, light of understanding, etc.)[.][6] Black dictionary if you can and ledger. Similarly black and white set. Table should be small (plain kitchen table) cluttered up with tapes and boxes until he sweeps them to the ground (maximum of violence). In the light everything as visible as possible, hence unnatural opening of drawers towards audience, i.e. when he extracts spool from left drawer he holds it up so that it can be seen before he puts it back, similarly with bananas as soon as taken from drawer, similarly with envelope and keys and whenever else possible, almost (only almost!) like a conjuror exhibiting his innocent material. Another good effect is for the transition from repose to motion to be made as abrupt as possible. He is motionless at table then suddenly (shock) in laborious motion, not fast because he can't go fast, but looking fast because of sudden start and effort entailed. Similarly when having eaten first banana he broods. What next? Suddenly back to table. Similarly when after second banana he "has an idea". Sudden turn and as fast as he can backstage. At the end, towards close of third repeat of boat passage, he can steal his arm round machine and sink his head on table. Then slowly up and staring front on "past midnight etc" to end.[7] Throughout when listening to tape even if crouched down over machine he should have his face up and full front maximally visible, staring eyes etc. Lot to be done with eyes. They can close for example for boat passage. Pity Davis is tall. I saw Krapp small and wizened.[8] What else? Can't think. Bit late in day anyhow. Hope you have the right old tune for "Now the day etc." Herewith in case not.

Hope these hurried notes may be of some service. Let me know how it goes.

Affectionately to you all.

s/ SAM

Now the day is ov - er night is draw-ing nigh-igh shad-ows of the ev' ning steal a-cross the sky -

TLS; 1 leaf, 2 sides; Burns Library, Samuel Beckett Collection, SB-AS. Previous publication: Beckett and Schneider, *No Author Better Served*, 59–61.

1 The term "reel" is used only in Krapp's final speech, and in the stage directions of *Krapp's Last Tape* ([New York: Grove Press, 1958] 28). Schneider wished to substitute "Post Mortems" for "P.M.s" (16), and to replace "weir" (19), "stem" (23), and "dingle" (26) with terms more familiar to an American audience. In performance, Schneider's only substitution was "lock" for "weir" (Schneider to SB, 16 January 1960; Burns Library, Samuel Beckett Collection, AS-SB; Beckett and Schneider, *No Author Better Served*, 61–62. All citations below are to this letter).

2 Edward Albee had told Schneider about the Berlin performance of *Das letzte Band* directed by Walter Henn on a double bill with his own *The Zoo Story* that had opened at the Schiller-Theater-Werkstatt on 28 September 1959. Schneider wrote: "I was delighted by your comments regarding that extra speaker because I had had a big argument with Ed Albee about it. He said it had worked well in the Berlin production and gave me the impression you had approved, which is why I asked."

3 Schneider wrote: "we actually have Davis manipulate the tape [. . .] and Davis has never missed a cue!" The Canadian actor Donald Davis (1928–1998) played Krapp.

4 Schneider added an "eye" to the tape-recorder (a light indicating that the machine was on), since the machine they used for the production lacked one.

5 Schneider added an overhead lamp "which helps to create the pool, light Krapp's face, make him stoop more, and in general give the feeling of a work table [. . .] to see his eyes we need a light source closer and more directly overhead than was possible in this particular theatre."

6 "The black ball" (13); not the "white nurse," but "the dark nurse" (13); "black hooded perambulator, most funereal thing" (19); "Bianca in Kedar Street" (16).

7 The third repeat of the boat passage (27–28): "Past midnight. Never knew such silence" (28).

8 Schneider assured SB that Donald Davis "does wonderful things with his eyes [. . .] In spite of his height I think you would have liked him."

ROBERT FARREN
RADIO EIREANN, DUBLIN

January 9th 1959 [*for* 1960]

6 Rue des Favorites
Paris 15me

Dear Mr Farren

Thank you for your letter of January 4th.

I wish most heartily I could agree with you about EMBERS. My own feeling is that it would have to be entirely reshaped and practically rewritten before it could face stage conditions.[1]

I have perhaps an exaggerated sense of what separates the two media, but there it is. It has prevented me already from taking advantage of the many offers made to me to present ALL THAT FALL in the theatre. And I think EMBERS is a more specifically radio play than ALL THAT FALL. At least I tried to make it so.

Will you please express to the Board of the Abbey Theatre how greatly I feel honoured by their proposal and with what regret I find myself obliged to decline it.[2]

It was very pleasant meeting you in Sorrento and I am sorry we did not have more time together. If you are ever in Paris I hope you will not fail to look me up.

My kind regards to Mrs Farren.

Yours sincerely

Samuel Beckett

TLcc; 1 leaf, 1 side; GEU, MS 1221. *Dating*: Farren's letter to SB is from 4 January 1960.

1 Robert Farren and SB met when they were both in Sorrento for the Italia Prize (see 21 September 1959). On 4 January, Farren had written to SB about adapting *Embers* as a one-act play for the stage (GEU, MS 1221).

2 Farren was a director of the Abbey Theatre from 1940 to 1973, and, on its behalf, proposed that the theatre produce the stage premiere of *Embers*.

BARBARA BRAY
PURLEY, SURREY

22.1.60 Ussy

Dear Barbara

Thanks for your letter here today.

Since I got here the day after your departure I have not been well. I should be in Paris this evening at Rhinoceros and had made appointments for tomorrow but have called everything off and stay here. Nothing serious but bad cough and cold and very down. Have not been able to do much work and unanswered mail piling up. Have hardly moved outside the 5 walls except once to buy food and tobacco at La Ferté.[1]

I have never seen things so dark for myself both physically and writing, never I think also with such indifference.

Pim: trying to break up into short units the continuum contrived with such difficulty. Apart from that nothing. You are far too indulgent about my work. I don't think you see it much better than you see me.

Wilkinson sends me the programme of the "Music Today" Feb. concert at the Festival Hall Recital Room announcing as literary titbit "reading from a new 'novel' by S.B." and tells me Pat Magee is the reader. I had said I wd. do my best but promised nothing as far as I can remember. I translated thus stimulated the beginning of Part III but feel it is impossible. Have told Wilkinson to lay on a step in.[2]

News from New York of Krapp at the Provincetown Playhouse with Zoo Story. Seems to have gone well and Davis to have been good. Schneider did everything I asked. He says the actor was able to work the machine on the table and no complicated wiring necessary.

Shall send book to Ada and Zoo Story to Barbara if I can lay my trembling hands on them.[3]

Nice note from Jackie thanking me for book, saying he is to spend the year at Stratford.[4]

Reading more Benn. Often insufferable, often moving and convincing. A beautiful essay – one of the last – a lecture I think – on the Aging Artist.[5]

My companions are the ladybirds, as every year at this time and other times I forget, suddenly on the paper I'm writing on, or typing on, then a little flight, then back. Hatch out in the house I suppose. Or hibernate here, come out with the warmth.

Have signed you on for Arts beginning with this week[']s issue. Please tell me if you don't receive it regularly. Lousy rag.[6]

Live on eggs, rice and gruyère. And Nicolas's table wine.[7]

Robert seems better. Busy in some actors' workshop and making friends.

I know this is not the letter you want. Off it goes nevertheless. Love to your two flowers.[8]

Love

Sam

ALS; 1 leaf, 2 sides; *env to* Mrs Barbara Bray, 121 Brighton Rd, Purley, Surrey, Angleterre; *unstamped*; TCD, MS 10948/1/66.

1 SB had driven to Ussy on 12 January. When he wrote to Bray the next day to say, "Hope you got home all right and found the children well," he added: "Came out here yesterday after all, roads pretty bad, but got through in the end. Just as well I didn't wait till today, the conditions are worse, snow everywhere." (TCD, MS 10948/1/65.)

Eugène Ionesco's play *Rhinocéros* directed by Jean-Louis Barrault opened on 20 January at the Odéon-Théâtre de France; the Générale took place on 22 January. SB cancelled his appointment with Rosica Colin and Peter du Sautoy in Paris (SB to Rosica Colin, [after 18 January 1960]; GEU, MS 1221).

2 Marc Wilkinson sent SB the announcement in *The Times* for the program in the "Music Today" series of 8 February, which stated that Patrick Magee would read from "a new and as yet unfinished 'novel' by Mr. Samuel Beckett" ("Reading from New Work by Samuel Beckett," *The Times* 1 February 1960: 3).

3 SB made this note to send a copy of Albee's play to Bray as well as a copy of *Embers* to Kathleen Michael (pseud. of Kathleen Smith, b. 1917), who would play the role of Ada in the BBC Third Programme production.

4 Jack MacGowran had been invited to join the Royal Shakespeare Company, Stratford, to play some of Shakespeare's clowns (Jordan R. Young, *The Beckett Actor: Jack MacGowran, Beginning to End* [Beverly Hills, CA: Moonstone Press, 1987] 70–72).

5 SB may have read "Altern als problem für Künstler" by Gottfried Benn (1886–1956) in the Limes Verlag four-volume edition of the *Gesammelte Werke* (I, *Essays, Reden, Vorträge*, ed. Dieter Wellershoff [Wiesbaden, 1959] 552–582); the essay can be found in *Primal Vision: Selected Writings of Gottfried Benn*, ed. E. B. Ashton [New York: New Directions, 1960] 183–208).

6 *Arts, lettres, spectacles, musique: l'hebdomadaire de l'intelligence française*, a weekly arts publication (the title of this publication varies).

7 Nicolas, a chain of wine shops.

8 Bray's daughters Francesca and Julia.

BARBARA BRAY
PURLEY, SURREY

29.1.60 Ussy sur Marne

Dear Barbara

I had to go to Paris yesterday after (came back here today) and found your Etoile card and letter waiting for me. Glad to hear you have the Turgenev script off your hands, you work far too hard. Sorry about disintegration of envelope, it seemed a remarkably stout one to me. It won't happen again. There were just the 3 items you mention.[1] Sorry you don't like Zoo Story, I think there is something. I wish all the same you would apply your intelligence to eliciting from the script what happened at the Zoo. Was a keeper eaten? Strangely concerned with this. The news of the N.Y. production is good. Stupid article[s] mostly, but mostly favourable for once. Looks as if it might have a bit of a run. Alan Schneider seems to have done a very careful mise en s. and all I suggested he might do. The line of the reviews: "The author Godot. Human after all!"[2] I finished revising Pim III early in week and was fastening myself together for an assault on the O.T. when a brick arrived in the form of an American translation of Texte pour Rien III by one Anthony Bonner – American edition of some collection of French "short stories" by one Germaine Brée (!) of which I knew nothing. The translation was appalling, to point of unrevisability. Publication imminent etc. So of course I had to do it myself in a rush and get it off. I think it goes better into English than n° I. Shall send it along sometime if you'd like to see it.[3] Expect to spend all tomorrow catching up on mail and – unless more bricks – to get going on the O.T. day after. Lindon told me today that he wants to publish the two texts, French and mine, as soon as possible. Rather embarrassing but I suppose it doesn't matter – can hardly call it a translation.[4]

I think the set up of part III is an improvement – opens the whole thing up and makes future insertions and adjustments much easier. Have next to see can I do the same thing with I – II. The extracts you have read – break it all up into brief packets, anything from seven lines to one, with space between them, not easy because of all the conjunctival elements to be got rid of. Some of the writing in III still very stiff, plenty of work to be done.[5] Wish I had The Old Tune off and something else begun in English to work on along with Pim. Not an idea and a half to jangle together. But I know if I stare at a sheet of paper long enough something will arise.

I must have said step-in to Wilkinson. Hope it amuses him. Translated beginning of III, but not satisfactory. Shall try and have something for them by March. Poor Pat, get up on his hind legs and read that![6]

Had the car greased, washed and vidangée this morning. Beginning to go a bit better.[7]

There's nothing to be done for me, except to try and see me as I am, and be patient with the result. You speak of the happiness one gives and gets. The situation I see is one where no matter what I do pain will ensue somewhere for someone.

Love Sam

ALS; 1 leaf, 2 sides; *env to* Mrs Barbara Bray, 121 Brighton Road, Purley, Surrey, Angleterre; *pm* 30–1–60, La Ferté-sous-Jouarre; TCD, MS 10498/1/68.

1 Bray had adapted *Rudin* (1856), Ivan Turgenev's first novel; it would be broadcast on the BBC Third Programme on 5 July.

2 SB's question about Edward Albee's *The Zoo Story* is oddly literal; he may be teasing Bray.

"Mise en s[cène]" (production).

Judith Schmidt had sent all the notices in the morning papers following the opening (SB to Alan Schneider, 23 January 1960; Beckett and Schneider, *No Author Better Served*, 63). According to Louis Calta, the plays "scored a hit Off Broadway" winning "the unanimous support of the six reviewers who appraised it yesterday" ("Double Bill Praised," *New York Times* 16 January 1960: 15).

3 Richard B. Fisher, Managing Editor at Dell Publishing, had asked Anthony Bonner (b. 1928) to translate several of the stories, including "Text for Nothing, III," in *Great French Short Stories*, ed. Germaine Brée (New York: Dell, 1960) 311–317. Bonner indicated to the editors that he had been surprised "that part of the package involved translating Beckett whose English was undoubtedly better than mine"; he also noted that SB's "corrections involved mostly decolloquializing" (5 January 2011).

4 *The Old Tune*, SB's translation of *La Manivelle* by Robert Pinget.

5 SB refers to his work in progress, which would become *Comment c'est*.

6 Rather than the expected "stand-in," SB had written to Marc Wilkinson: "Surely I didn't promise a text for Feb. 8th? It's not at all sure I'll have one. [. . .] I'll do my best, but you had better lay on a step-in in case." (19 January 1960; Wilkinson Collection.)

7 "Vidangée" (oil changed).

RICHARD SEAVER
GROVE PRESS, NEW YORK

30.1.60 Ussy

Dear Seaver

Thanks for your letter. Trocchi MS received. I'm reading it. I like his work. But I prefer my appreciations to remain private. I'm not a critic, unless possibly the world's worst, and have no public comment to make on other writers. I've had to take a stand about this as about interviews, otherwise there's no end to it. It places me in an unenviable situation in the case of someone like Trocchi whom I know and like and I know I must appear very unfriendly. I'm extremely sorry, but there's nothing I can do about it.[1]

Bless you for having Fisher send me translation of Text 111. It was grim, unrevisable. I had to do it myself in a rush. Result far from satisfactory. But at least possible. I have written to Fisher explaining-apologizing and suggesting that my text appear as "translated by A. Bonner and the author".[2]

I've been too absorbed in this cursed French book to do any more work on the Texts. I had a shot at the second and gave it up, couldn't do it. I could do them all in a month if necessary, but shd prefer to leave them for the moment. I don't suppose there's any great hurry. If I'm right take your time with the nouvelles.[3]

All the best.

Yours

s/ Sam. Beckett

TLS; 1 leaf, 1 side; TxU, Seaver, R 16501.

1 Seaver had sent SB Alexander Trocchi's novel *Cain's Book*, due to be published by Grove Press in April. When SB had finished reading the book, he wrote to Judith Schmidt: "Very good indeed I think. Shall be writing to Trocchi next semi-lucid intermission." (12 February 1960; NSyU.)

2 SB's letter to Richard B. Fisher at Dell Publishing about "Text III" has not been found, but evidence that it was received is clear from Fisher's letter to Anthony Bonner of 4 April 1960: "You will be interested to know that Beckett, although he was complimentary about your translation, made some further revisions in it; the story will now appear with yours and Samuel Beckett's name as joint translators" (Bonner Collection).

3 SB had agreed to translate *Textes pour rien* while Seaver translated three of the *Nouvelles* for a Grove edition.

JOHN MAWSON
THE INTERNATIONAL SCHOOL, GENEVA

January 30th 1960

6 Rue des Favorites
Paris 15me

Dear Mr Mawson

Thank you for your letter.

When rehearsing FIN DE PARTIE with Roger Blin for the Royal Court production I was obliged to reduce the scene of the boy "seen" from the window to its simplest expression. They [*for* the] play had already been published by the Editions de Minuit, which explains why this cut does not figure in the French text.[1]

The cut was therefore primarily technical in function of this particular production which in spite of our efforts dragged badly at this point and simply would not take the full passage. I thought then and am still prepared to think that with a different Clov and a different rhythm of production this reduction might not be necessary. Nevertheless, when translating the play into English, I decided to carry it over into my text. It seemed to me that nothing more is required here than the baldest possible statement, as explosive as you like, of the possibility of existence without and that to enlarge on it was a mistake technically and dramatically. For one thing there has been more than enough business already with peering out of window and telescope and for another it delays and weaken's [sic]

Clov's reaction which is panic and haste to go and deal with the matter.

I think it likely that you may have the same experience in rehearsal. If not and if you prefer to play the passage as it stands in the French edition, by all means do so. My own feeling now is that the play gains by its suppression and that brief, violent, horrified and unqualified boy is all that is needed at this late hour.

If there is anything else you wish to know, do not hesitate to ask me.

With best wishes to you all for your production,

Yours sincerely

Samuel Beckett

TLcc; 1 leaf, 1 side; GEU, MS 1221.

1 John Mawson (1929–1995), who taught at the Ecole Internationale de Genève from 1958 to 1962, had seen *Fin de partie* at the Royal Court Theatre, London, in April 1957. He was preparing to direct students in a production of *Endgame* when he wrote to SB to inquire about cuts to the boy passage in the English edition: "it seems valid in French, theatrically, to emphasise the small boy here. The English text tends to let the audience ignore him." (John Mawson to SB, 18 January 1960; GEU, MS 1221; *Fin de partie* [Minuit] 103–105; *Endgame* [Faber and Faber] 46.)

SB later wrote in similar terms to Robert S. Cohen (b. 1938), Professor of Theatre, University of California, Irvine: "The other passage you mention was cut during Paris rehearsals because the scene dragged. I simplified English version accordingly. The scene of the boy [. . .] was similarly reduced in English translation. I think these lines merely labour the point, but you are free to put them back if you wish." (5 October 1960; Cohen Collection.)

BARBARA BRAY
PURLEY, SURREY

4.2.60 Ussy

Dear Barbara

Thanks for your letter of Jan 31st today with enclosures.

Herewith the O.T. I hope it'll do. I can't do more with it. I'm very tired of it. I'm sorry I haven't been able to make a better job of it. Make whatever changes you like. I shd. prefer if possible to avoid the word "translation". Perhaps "English text" or just "English" by SB. For Lindon's edition I'll put "version anglaise" or "texte anglais", not "traduit par".

7. Donald McWhinnie

So glad to hear of Donald's production at the Arts.[1] I shd. like some time to read a play by Pinter. But not just now. I read Passage to India a long time, vague recollection like swallowing fine sand. Won't undertake it again just at the moment. Read the Amis without much difficulty, more trouble with the Red Badge but got to the end. Have not yet read the scripts.[2]

Went to Paris today, only stayed a few minutes, left at 2, back at 6. Car a bit more lively which means $\frac{\text{car + driver}}{2}$ no loss of liveliness. I haven't looked at Pim for a week. Might have a quick peep tomorrow. Wish I had something in English going - in the light. Can't think of anything in the light. Have a good stare at a white sheet (of paper) tomorrow maybe. Ear glued to Europe No 1 up to a few days ago - news. We seem to have squeezed through for the moment.[3]

Won't be Bd. St. Jacques till April, if then. Demands for large sums of income tax pouring in. Seem to have bitten off more than etc., a bit more than. However Krapp seems off to a good start at the Provincetown, even grudging recommendations from the Kerrs & Atkinsons and Watts Juniors. Davis must be really good il faut croire.[4] I didn't go to Rhinocéros, felt lousy and [? slouched] on here. What I have heard doesn't encourage me to go. He seems to be lapping up the whole silly business and talks in interviews of his "cher ami Gauthier"![5] Practically no chance now I think of Godot at the Théâtre de France, Barrault refusing to guarantee the minimum no. of performances demanded by Blin. Rather relieved than otherwise. Not for the likes of us all that.[6] Martin trying to arrange for double-bill Krapp – Lettre Morte. Afraid Blin not very keen. No further news from Robert. Arrabal writes and sends cuttings.[7] N.Y. Herald Tribune cabled for an interview. Prefer not. So it goes. Shall be here I hope till middle of next week. Then I fear a rather unpleasant spell in Paris. Wilkinson writes I'm excused for the 1st concert, they want something for Pat for the 3rd (concert) in April. Do my best I suppose.[8]

Forgive again usual letter.

Love Sam

ALS; 2 leaves, 2 sides; *env to* Mrs Barbara Bray, 121 Brighton Road, Purley, Surrey, Angleterre; *pm* 5-2-60, La Ferté-sous-Jouarre; TCD, MS 10948/1/69.

1 Donald McWhinnie would direct Harold Pinter's play *The Caretaker*, opening at the Arts Theatre on 27 April.

2 E.M. Forster's novel *A Passage to India* (1924) was adapted for the theatre by Santha Rama Rau (1923–2009) and presented at the Oxford Playhouse from 19 January; it transferred to the Comedy Theatre, London, from 21 April. Bray may have mentioned this adaptation, and may have offered to send it or the novel to SB.

Bray had sent SB scripts of Kingsley Amis's *Lucky Jim* (1954) and Stephen Crane's *The Red Badge of Courage* (1895), adapted by H. A. L. Craig (1921–1978) for the BBC Third Programme for broadcast on 16 March. Although when SB acknowledges receipt on 23 January, he only mentions scripts, Bray may have also sent the novels (TCD, MS 10649/1/67).

3 On 29 January, the provisional government of Algeria exhorted sympathetic followers and French soldiers who had "a problem of conscience" to "join or support the rebel national liberation army" ("Rebels Call on Conscripts to Desert," *The Times* 30 January 1960: 8). A stand-off between France and Algerian rebels was narrowly averted by Charles de Gaulle's address later that night in which he affirmed that "self-determination" for Algeria was the "only policy worthy of France" while cautioning that this would be a lengthy process; De Gaulle refused "to countenance disobedience in the Army or among the insurgents in Algeria." His speech concluded with a call for French unity ("Gen. de Gaulle Orders His Army to Obey, No Going Back on Decisions on Algeria," *The Times* 30 January 1960: 8; the full text of the speech was published in "Le Discours du Général de Gaulle," *Le Figaro* 30–31 January 1960: 5, and "Gen. de Gaulle's Reminder to Algeria Settlers," *The Times* 30 January 1960: 7).

4 Brooks Atkinson admired the Canadian actor playing Krapp: "Donald Davis makes every movement significant and every line caustic . . . Mr. Beckett has a terrifying sense of the mystery of life" ("Theatre: A Double Bill Off Broadway," *New York Times* 15 January 1960: 37). Richard Watts Jr. wrote: "'Krapp's Last Tape' turns out to be the most human of [Beckett's] works for the stage" ("An Absorbing Off-Broadway Evening," *New York Post* 15 January 1960: 52). Walter Kerr concluded: "This is the same Beckett who let the world turn icy cold in 'Waiting for Godot' and then dumped it into the two nearest ashcans in 'Endgame.' Mr. Beckett has not, I hasten to say, entirely changed the spots before his eyes . . . what has been added, in short, is feeling." ("Two One-Act Plays Given at Provincetown Playhouse," *Herald Tribune* 15 January 1960: 8.) "Il faut croire" (or so we're told).

5 Jean-Jacques Gautier, drama critic of *Le Figaro*, felt the play was overwritten, but praised its effectiveness: "La découverte que le héros fait de sa solitude au centre de la montée des périls est émouvante" ("A l'Odéon: 'Rhinocéros' d'Eugène Ionesco," 26 January 1960: 14) (The discovery that the hero makes of his solitude in the midst of mounting perils is moving). Bérenger was played by Jean-Louis Barrault.

6 As the Director of the Odéon-Théâtre de France, Barrault had faced a series of challenges. The official opening of the theatre on 21 October 1959 exemplified the pressures that would be brought to bear by his constituencies: "Le Tout-Paris est là, celui des arts, de la littérature, de la politique et du gouvernement" (Catherine Levasseur, *Dans l'intimité des Renaud-Barrault*, ed. Jean Desailly and Simone Valère [Paris: Pygmalion, 2003] 107) (Everyone who's anyone in Paris was there, those in the arts, literature, politics and government). See also Barrault, *Souvenirs pour demain*, 318–319; Barrault, *Memories for Tomorrow*, 269–270.

7 Jean Martin wanted to direct Robert Pinget's play *Lettre morte* with *La dernière bande*. Pinget and Fernando Arrabal were both in New York on fellowships (see 30 November 1959, n. 2).

8 Patrick Magee's reading from SB's newest work was rescheduled for 5 April (Music Today, Minutes of meeting, 18 February 1960; InU, C&B, Beckett).

ROBERT PINGET
NEW YORK

6.2.60 Ussy

Cher Robert

Ci-joint ton texte et mon impertinente traduction dernier état. J'envoie tout ça aujourd'hui à Jérôme qui se dit pressé de sortir le livre. Egalement à Tophoven et à Ludvigsen mon traducteur danois qui m'a relancé et qui j'espère pourra le faire jouer à la radio danoise. On ne peut pas dire "traduit par", c'est vraiment trop libre. Es-tu d'accord avec "texte anglais"? Suzanne aimerait mieux "version anglaise", ça a un petit remugle scolaire qui me déplaît. Inutile de te dire que ma traduction ne me satisfait pas. Mais je n'arrive plus à l'améliorer. Encore plus abruti que d'habitude tous ces temps-ci. Peut-être au moment des épreuves quelques lueurs encore. Jérôme t'enverra des épreuves bien sûr.[1]

J'ai reçu des Lettres Nouvelles 180 NF pour CENDRES. Ta part est comprise dedans. Fais-moi penser de te la donner si je n'y pense pas.

Barbara me dit qu'elle veut passer ça le plus rapidement possible.

Jean multiplie ses démarches. Il aura la réponse de Vilar dans quelques jours. Personnellement j'ai l'impression que ça pourrait marcher de ce côté-là. Jean pense que non. Il a déjà vu Mme Geiger (aide à la première pièce). Elle l'a reçu très gentiment mais pas de décision immédiate évidemment. Si Vilar marche plus de problème côté fric.[2]

Je vais tâcher maintenant de redescendre dans ma boue. Elle s'est un peu éloignée. J'aimerais avoir un autre travail en train, pour le théâtre et en anglais, mais je ne vois rien.

Je suis ici presque tout le temps. J'ai ramené Suzanne à Paris avant-hier. Départ d'ici à 2 heures, retour à 6. J'aimerais pouvoir ne plus bouger d'ici, mais ce n'est pas encore possible. La petite voiture commence à marcher un peu mieux. Elle a maintenant 5000 km dans le coco.

Marthe est invitée aux E.-U. pour une quinzaine de jours ou 3 semaines, une histoire de chromosomes, départ d'ici un mois je crois. Ca a l'air de la tenter.[3]

8 jours abominables, collés toutes les heures à Europe No 1. Ca se calme un peu.[4]

Voilà mon cher Robert, rien à dire, pas couic. Raconte-nous un peu comment ça s'est passé le spectacle-lecture et si ça se dessine un théâtre pour plus tard et comment tu vas, toutes tes nouvelles quoi.[5]

Bien affectueusement de nous deux.

s/ Sam

Un coup de fil de Suzanne à l'instant. Paraît que tu es à Frisco. Préférable donc que je t'envoie ça c/o Lettunich.

TLS, with APS; 1 leaf, 1 side; Burns Library, Samuel Beckett Collection, SB-RP.

6.2.60 Ussy

Dear Robert,

Herewith your text and my impertinent translation, final version. I'm sending it all today to Jérôme who apparently is keen to get the book out quickly. Also to Tophoven and Ludvigsen, my Danish translator, who has been nudging me, and who, I hope, will be able to get it put out on Danish radio. We can't say "translated by": it's really too free. Can you agree to "English text"? Suzanne would prefer "English version", but that has a fusty schoolroom air that I dislike. No need to tell you that my translation doesn't satisfy me. But I can find no way of improving it. Even more mindless than usual these days. Maybe a few glimmerings again when the proofs come. Jérôme will send you proofs of course.[1]

I have received from *Les Lettres Nouvelles* 180 new francs for *Cendres*. Your share is included. Remind me to give it to you if I don't think of it.

Barbara tells me that she wants to get it through as quickly as possible.

Jean is following up all sorts of lines. He will have Vilar's reply in a few days. Personally I have the impression that we might get somewhere with him. Jean thinks not. He has already seen Mme Geiger (First Play Grant). She received him very kindly, but no immediate decision of course. If Vilar jumps, no more cash worries.[2]

I'm going to try to get back down into my mud. It has moved away a little. I would like to have some other work in hand, for the theatre and in English, but I can see nothing.

I am here almost all the time. I brought Suzanne back to Paris the day before yesterday. Left here at 2 o'clock, back at 6. I would love it if I never had to leave here, but that's not possible yet. The little car is beginning to run rather better. Now it has 5,000 kilometres on the clock.

Marthe is invited over to the States for two or three weeks, something to do with chromosomes, leaving here in a month's time, I think. It seems to tempt her.[3]

Dreadful week, the two of us with our ears glued to Europe No. 1 every hour. Things a little quieter now.[4]

There it is, dear Robert, nothing to say, not a squeak. Do let us know how the reading / performance went off, and if there are signs of a possible theatre for later, and how you are – well, all your news.[5]

Love from us both

Sam

Phone call from Suzanne this very minute. Appears you're in Frisco. Better, then, if I send it c/o Lettunich.

1 SB's translation of Pinget's *La Manivelle* (*The Old Tune*): 13 December 1959, n. 2. The Danish response: 30 November 1959, n. 4. "Texte anglais de Samuel Beckett" was indeed the formula used when *La Manivelle* was printed (with SB's English "version" following) in September 1960.

2 In his letter of 14 January, SB had explained to Pinget the steps Jean Martin was taking to try to get Pinget's play *Lettre morte* staged in Paris: "Je sais seulement que Vitaly perd l'option et que Jean s'en occupe. Blin, paraît-il, disposé à jouer Levert." (Burns Library, Samuel Beckett Collection, SB-RP.) (I only know that Vitaly is losing the option and that Jean is taking care of it. Blin, it appears, ready to play Levert.)

Madame Geiger, involved in administration of the "aide à la première pièce," has not been further identified.

3 Marthe Gautier* (b. 1925) was a friend of Jean Martin who had become a close friend of Suzanne Deschevaux-Dumesnil. Having earned her doctorate in Medicine in 1955, and after a stint at Harvard, she carried out innovative research under Professor Turpin at the Hôpital Trousseau, "to verify the number of chromosomes in infants with Down's syndrome" (S. Gilgenkrantz and E.M. Rivera, "A History of Cytogenetics: Portraits of Some Pioneers," *Annales de Génétique* 46.4 [October–December 2003] 433–442).

4 In this period, the bewildering succession of events and reactions at all levels meant that nobody was certain of the current state of Franco-Algerian relations.

5 On the public reading of Pinget's *Lettre morte* in New York, see 13 December 1959, n. 8. In his memoir, Pinget elaborates: "La date du 17 (janvier) est celle de la lecture de LM au Workshop de Louis Beachner. J'avais demandé à Sam qui y inviter de riche qui puisse s'intéresser à financer une production théâtrale." (Doucet, unclassified Pinget Collection, "Notre ami Samuel Beckett," 29.) (The 17th of January is the date for the reading of *LM* at the Louis Beachner Workshop. I had asked Sam which moneybags I could invite that might be interested in putting up money for a theatre production.)

EDWARD BECKETT
DUBLIN

7.2.60 Ussy /s/ Marne

Dear Edward

Glad to have your letter. You're very wise not to burn your boats at this stage. After a year or so of Trinity you'll be in a much better position to judge. And you're young enough to postpone the decision till then. Don't worry if in the meantime you feel you are not devoting to your music the time you should. Just keep it going and the moment will come when it will simply claim your life or be content with only a part of it.[1]

It's a relief to know you are rid of rugby, no game for a flautist. If there's anything you want in the way of an out of the way score don't hesitate to ask me.

I don't suppose you met John when he was over. I wish you could and have a good talk and play with him. I think he could advise you very usefully.[2]

With us everything much as usual. I spend most of my time here in the country, great quiet and solitude. The little car is going as well as it knows how. There's a new 7 H.P. Peugeot just out which tempts me, but I think I'll hang on to what I have for this year anyway.

We are leaving Rue des Favorites probably in April and moving into a more spacious place in a more pleasant district. In spite of the advantages it will be a bit of a wrench moving, 20 years and more in the same place puts roots down.

As busy as I can, but not much to show for it. A short play on in New York at the moment and doing well to judge by the notices. It is a play that has been made into an opera by a Rumanian composer living in Paris and which will probably be performed in Paris and Germany some time this year.[3]

I wonder when you will come to Paris. Some day soon I hope, before I'm too old to keep up with you!

Much love

Sam

ALS; 1 leaf, 2 sides; *env to* Edward Beckett, St. Columba's College, Rathfarnham, Co. Dublin, IRLANDE; *pm* 8–2–60, La Ferté-Sous-Jouarre; Edward Beckett Collection.

1 Edward Beckett had just been accepted by the School of Engineering at Trinity College Dublin.

2 John Beckett lived in London; indeed Edward Beckett did not see him during his visit to Dublin.

3 SB refers to *Krapp's Last Tape*, and to the chamber opera of it being composed by Marcel Mihalovici.

AIDAN HIGGINS
JOHANNESBURG

7.2.60 Ussy sur Marne

Dear Aidan

Forgive scribble, can't stand any more typewriter.

Thanks for your letters and greetings. Also for Perspective. I like your story and look forward to Felo. Calder is very slow and I wouldn't count it for the spring.[1] I had lunch with him or was it dinner the other day in Paris, very nice but in rather a mess. If I was sitting with you over some kind of a bottle or even on a bench out of the wind somewhere I could talk to you about Nightfall but I can't write about writing. It's a fine start that's all I can say and some day perhaps many years hence from the terrible urgency of weakness, being and utterance all gone to the dogs, you'll come across it and say how the hell did I ever have the strength to do that.

I had an illegible letter from John from Greystones after a very long silence. I hear from friends in London he is getting on well. Commissioned I know at the moment to compose music for a BBC production of UBU.[2] He says he'll be over in France soon.

Arland sent me his Spanish book which I enjoyed, the vitality that man has. I saw him briefly in Dublin in July, with Con Leventhal in Jammet's, not much contact, my fault.[3]

No news of Ralph this long time. I'm told he's in better health. Roy married a local girl. Some misery there I fear.[4]

I spend most of my time here in the country. Struggling with very difficult and loathsome work in French this past year. End not in sight. Hope to start some thing in English for the theatre soon. No idea what.

Seychelles sound fine.[5] Hope you will make Paris on yr. way home. Have a 2 H.P. Citroen now. No fun to drive. Great help.

Saw a good film on your dear Union "Come back Africa." Certainly hasn't been shown with you. Shot more or less clandestinely. Wonderful end. Forget the man's name. Rogosin? Forget.[6]

I have the Ellmann book. Good job of work. Mistakes here and there. Needless things. I thought.[7]

Greetings to Jill. And to Carl if that's possible.[8]

yours ever

Sam

ALS; 2 leaves, 3 sides; *env to* Mr Aidan Higgins, 36 Mount Willmar, 36 Isipingo Street, Bellevue, Johannesburg, Afrique du Sud; *pm* 8-2-60, La Ferté-sous-Jouarre; TxU, Beckett Collection, 8.9.

1 Higgins had sent SB "Nightfall on Cape Piscator," published not in *Perspective* but in *Prospect* [Cambridge, UK] 2 (Winter 1959) 10–19. The story was from Higgins's forthcoming collection *Felo de Se* (London: Calder, 1960; rpt. as *Asylum, and Other Stories* by Calder, 1978; published as *Killachter Meadow*).

2 The BBC Third Programmme production of Alfred Jarry's *Ubu Roi* would air on 23 February. Barbara Wright (1915–2009) translated the text, Barbara Bray was the producer, and John Beckett composed the music ("First Surrealist Manifesto," *The Times* 24 February 1960: 15).

3 Arland Ussher had recently published *Spanish Mercy* (London, Gollancz, 1959); in it he recounts his five-month tour of Spain.

4 Ralph Cusack and SB's cousin Nancy Sinclair lived in Spéracèdes, near Grasse. The eldest son from Cusack's first marriage to Kira von Heiseler (1912–1990) was Roy Cusack (b. 1937); he and Paulette Pellegrin (n.d.) from Le Plan de Grasse married in 1959 (www.thepeerage.com/p37747.htm#i377463, accessed 15 October 2012; Igor Cusack to the editors, 15–16 October 2012).

5 Higgins wrote in his autobiography, *The Whole Hog*: "We toy with the idea of living in the Seychelles, a windy French possession away from the beaten track; or St. Helena, a thousand miles into the North Atlantic . . . We decided to return to Dublin." ([London: Secker & Warburg, 2000] 137.)

6 *Come Back, Africa*, directed by documentary film-maker Lionel Rogosin (1924–2000), "which takes its title from an African National Congress slogan, focuses on the plight of a single Zulu family driven from their village by famine" (John Wakeman, ed., *World Film Directors II: 1945–1985* [New York: H. W. Wilson, 1988] 914).

The film, an exposure of South African apartheid, had the singer Miriam Makeba in a small role; it won the 1960 Venice Critics Award.

7 Richard Ellmann's biography, *James Joyce* (1959).

8 Carl Nicolas, the first son of Aidan and Jill Higgins, had been born on 6 August 1959 in Johannesburg.

THOMAS MACGREEVY
DUBLIN

7.2.60 Ussy sur Marne

Dear Tom

I should have written long ago. Forgive me. No excuse except the widening gap between all there is to be done and the power to do.

I liked the poem very much. For a time I had trouble with the last verse, but it came straight with rereading. I think it was the word "bound" that disturbed me. Your quality and spirit, so uniquely yours and so difficulty [sic] to say exactly in what consisting, are there from beginning to end. There is inclination sometimes to ask for more labour towards that level of phrase and rhythm where magic necessity hides, then the thought that this might be the loss of something more precious and beyond the reach of form, sorrow and wisdom of spirit murmuring unwitnessed together. If you have changed it I shd. like very much to see the result and if you have written others I hope you will send them.[1]

As you are probably in Morehampton Road now I am addressing this to the Gallery.[2] We shall not get in to Bd. St. Jacques till April at the earliest, the keys having been promised for January. It will be a more pleasant season for the move, but Suzanne is pawing the ground to get out of Rue des Favorites. I spend nearly all my time here – with not much work to show for it. I have finished "a" version of this horrible business in French, but there is probably another year's work on it and I hope to be able to get going on something in English concurrently without having the least idea what except that it would be theatre again. Blin and Barrault can't come to an agreement about Godot and I think that's off. I'm really just as glad – from all I hear about the set-up there. Krapp has got off to a very good start in New York off Broadway needless to say, I have never had such good notices, even the Atkinsons, Kerrs and Watts Juniors. The action [*for* actor], a Canadian, sounds very remarkable and the metteur en scène seems to have done all I asked him to do.[3]

Jean and the children wrote after a longish silence, all well. Edward is being very reasonable about his music and burning no boats at the moment, going docilely into the Engineering School for a start anyway.

Perhaps it will be possible to work again in Paris and have a life a little less solitary when we move into the new place, though the view of the Santé Prison from the den I'll have is beginning to upset me in prospect! I'll learn to raise the eyes to Val de Grâce, Panthéon and the glimpse of Notre-Dame.

Write very soon dear Tom and tell me how all is going.

Much love from us both and my remembrance as always to your sister and nieces.[4]

Sam

ALS; 2 leaves, 2 sides; *env to* Thomas MacGreevy Esq, Director, National Gallery, Merrion Square, Dublin, IRLANDE, *marked* Personal; *pm* 8-2-60, La Ferté-sous-Jouarre; TCD, MS 10402/227.

1 The final stanza of MacGreevy's poem "Moments Musicaux," which SB has been reading, runs:

> Divided by half of a world,
> Sundered by half of a lifetime,
> Yet you are bound;
> And, together, you take them to her,
> While, together, you leave them
> To others,
> Of hers.

The poem would receive its first publication in *Poetry* 99.2 (November 1961) 85; rpt. MacGreevy, *Collected Poems of Thomas MacGreevy: an Annotated Edition*, ed. Susan Schreibman (Dublin: Anna Livia Press; Washington: The Catholic University of America Press, 1991).

2 MacGreevy's move to 49 Morehampton Road was due to his need to live in an apartment without stairs (Margaret Farrington, 4 October 2012). It is possible that SB did not recall the street number.

3 Jerry Tallmer wrote in his article "Theatre: The Tape & the Zoo," in *The Village Voice*: "the performance by Donald Davis as Krapp and the staging in every minute

particular by Alan Schneider – not least the phenomenal synchronization of living actor and dead voice – is inspired, inspirited, perfect" (20 January 1960: 9–10).

4 Margaret Phelan and her daughters: 18 February 1958, n. 4.

ROBERT PINGET
SAN FRANCISCO

16.2.60 Paris

Cher Robert

Ce mot en vitesse pour te confirmer notre télégramme de ce matin. Ça y est. Jean et Blin ont vu Vilar hier et c'est fait.[1] Carte blanche pour tout, techniciens du Chaillot à notre disposition. Répétitions dès qu'on pourra. Quel que soit le succès du spectacle Vilar s'engage à le continuer pendant 60 représentations minimum. Blin joue et met en scène <u>Krapp</u>. Jean joue le barman et met en scène <u>Lettre Morte</u>. Il n'a pas encore choisi les autres acteurs. Il est ravi, nous tous, Lindon et Annette fous de joie. J'ai vu Lindon hier. Il fait tout le nécessaire pour toi auprès de la Société des auteurs. Tu recevras probablement des papiers à signer. Première le 22 mars. Vu Matias et Jean hier soir. Ils travaillent ferme sur le décor déjà.[2] Avec Suzanne j'ai vu hier soir la pièce de Vian. Le théâtre est vraiment très bien, plus de 500 places, et le quartier parfait.[3] Quel dommage que tu ne sois pas là. On collera le plus possible à tes indications mais il y aura forcément des décisions à prendre avec lesquelles tu ne serais peut-être pas d'accord. Tel que ça se présente il est au moins sûr que le spectacle sera encore là à ton retour.[4]

<u>Manivelle Old Tune</u> en fabrication. Je crois que Jérôme va proposer à Rosset de faire l'édition avec lui, c'est à dire même livre à N.Y.

Tophoven l'a donné au Südwestfunk (Baden-Baden). Très bon espoir de ce côté-là.[5] Pas de nouvelles de Copenhague. Barbara très contente de la "traduction" révisée. Date de transmission pas encore retenue.

Affectueusement, cher Robert, et bravo bravo.

Sam

Cher Robert – Je suis dans le ravissement. On est tous dans un état d'excitation incroyable. Il ne manque que vous. Il y a beaucoup de vrai, croyez-le bien, dans ces exagérations.

Pour ça, on ne vous oublie pas! Mais si on vous écrit moins c'est qu'on pense que vous êtes "bien" maintenant. Et on se laisse aller à penser surtout à soi.

Vous embrasse. On vous tiendra soit l'un soit les autres au courant de vos "choses".

Suzanne

ALS; 1 leaf, 2 sides, with ANS Suzanne Deschevaux-Dumesnil; Burns Library, Samuel Beckett Collection, SB-RP.

16.2.60 Paris

Dear Robert

This in haste to confirm our telegram of yesterday. It's all on. Jean and Blin saw Vilar this morning and it's settled.[1] Carte blanche for everything, Chaillot technical staff at our disposal. Rehearsals as soon as we can. However the show goes, Vilar has undertaken to keep it on for a minimum of 60 performances. Blin will act and direct *Krapp*. Jean will play the barman and direct *Lettre morte*. He has not yet chosen the other actors. He is delighted, we all are, Lindon and Annette are thrilled out of their wits. I saw Lindon yesterday. He is doing the necessary for you with the Société des Auteurs. You will probably be receiving papers to sign. Premiere on the 22nd of March. Saw Matias and Jean yesterday evening. They're hard at work on the set already.[2] Saw Vian's play yesterday evening with Suzanne. The theatre is really very good: more than 500 seats, and the perfect part of Paris.[3] What a pity you're not here. We'll stick to your instructions as far as possible, but there are bound to be decisions to take that you might not agree with. As things stand, it is at least certain that the show will still be running when you get back.[4]

Manivelle/Old Tune at the printer's. I think that Jérôme is going to propose to Rosset to publish it with him, that is, same book in New York.

Tophoven has given it to Südwestfunk (Baden-Baden). Very good prospects there.[5] No news from Copenhagen. Barbara very pleased with the revised "translation". Date of broadcast not yet settled.

With all affection, dear Robert, and bravo bravo.

Sam

Dear Robert – I'm in ecstasies. We're all in a state of unbelievable excitement. All that's missing is you. There's a great deal of truth, believe me, in this exaggerated talk.

For all that, we're not forgetting you! But if we write less often, it's because we think you're "all right" now. And we let ourselves slip into thinking most of all of ourselves.

Big hugs. We'll keep you (either the one or the others) up to date with what is happening to your "things".

Suzanne

1 Jean Martin had been endeavoring to have Jean Vilar and the Théâtre National Populaire help to get Pinget's *Lettre morte* staged (see 6 February 1960, n. 2), and SB has learned that it is to be put on at the Théâtre Récamier.

2 Matias (né Charles Henrioud, 1926–2006), who worked both as an illustrator of children's books and for the press as a drawer and draftsman, had been introduced to SB by Pinget. He went on to become a stage designer who often worked with SB, designing his first set for Pinget's play *Lettre morte*.

3 *Les Bâtisseurs d'empire ou Le Schmürz* (*The Empire Builders*) by Boris Vian (1920–1959) had opened on 22 December at the Théâtre Récamier, directed by Jean Negroni. Henri Virlogeux (1924–1995) played the father in this play and Levert in *Lettre morte*. Constructed in 1908, the theatre was situated at 3 Rue Récamier, Paris 7; between 1959 and 1961 it was the TNP's second venue, after the Chaillot.

4 In his memoir, Pinget wrote:

> Bien beau souvenir pour moi qu'évoque cette lettre. Ma première pièce au théâtre. Le télégramme je ne l'avais pas reçu, étant parti de San Francisco pour le Mexique [. . .]. Je combinais, dans mon excitation, un retour à Paris pour assister à la première, mais la chose n'a pas pu se faire. J'avais tellement confiance en mes amis que j'étais absolument tranquille quant au succès de l'affaire. En écrivant ça, moins d'une année après, je me trouve bien privilégié d'avoir tant de sollicitude autour de moi. (Doucet, unclassified Pinget Collection, "Notre ami Samuel Beckett," 33.) (Really lovely memory for me this letter evokes. My first play, in a theatre. The telegram I hadn't received, having left San Francisco for Mexico [. . .]. In my excitement I was planning a return to Paris, to be there for the premiere. But it didn't work out. I had such confidence in my friends that I was absolutely unworried about the success of

it. Writing this, less than a year later, I see myself as greatly privileged to have such eager care round me.)

5 Südwestdeutscher Rundfunk, SWF (now merged with Süddeutscher Rundfunk, SDR), would broadcast *Die alte Leier*, the German translation of *The Old Tune*, on 7 March 1961. The play was not broadcast in Copenhagen.

BARBARA BRAY
PURLEY, SURREY

18.2.60 Paris

Dear Barbara

Thanks for your letter.

"Country" is not deliberate, but a mistake for "county". Sorry. Yes, Cream would have it right.[1]

John's music sounds like what's needed. Hope the recording successful and all well.[2]

Yes, your Zoo Story exegesis did interest me and no doubt you are right.[3]

I have not yet begun the Johnson and probably won't till I get back to Ussy. The Moore sounds interesting and I'd be glad to have it. But you spend too much on books for me.[4]

We are beginning rehearsals of Lettre Morte & Krapp next Monday at the Récamier. Générale I think March 27th. Blin is playing Krapp. Jean Martin is directing Lettre Morte and playing the barman and P.O. employee. It was all decided rather suddenly over the week-end. Vilar does not want the news released for a week or so and has asked us not to mention it. So under your hat please for the moment. Pity Robert is not here. We are guaranteed a minimum of 60 performances so it will still be on when he comes back. This evening I am having a reading with Blin of Krapp. Reading over the text this afternoon I thought it stank of translation. No doubt shall make some changes.

This means no Ussy for a week or so at least, then perhaps a few days before the last rehearsals. The Vilar set-up is very efficient, no technical or financial worries. The theatre holds about 560 and is pleasant. I went the other evening to see Boris Vian's Bâtisseurs d'Empire. Very good things. I can't remember if you saw it. The actor who plays the father will probably play Levert.

I of course wrote Jedermann instead of Biedermann. I get every thing wrong.[5]

According to latest news Robert is in Hollywood – after S. Francisco. I think he is to go to Mexico before returning to N.Y. unless he curtails his stay and comes back in time for the opening.

Pim also suspended as a result of all this. Can't do any serious work here.

Got another contravention today, forgot to stick up the disc de stationnement. Another 1000 francs.[6]

Hope you have better news of your father. I forgot to ask you in my last letter.[7]

Climbed up again to 7th floor Bd. St. Jacques. Doesn't seem much further on than the last time. But keys promised for April. What difference will that make? Vide-ordures and change of view.[8]

Love

Sam

ALS; 1 leaf, 2 sides; *env to* Mrs Barbara Bray, 121 Brighton Road, Purley, Surrey, Angleterre; *pm* 19-2-60, Paris; TCD, MS 10948/1/71.

1 Since Gorman and Cream correct each other constantly, Bray queries whether the error was SB's intention; the change is made in the final BBC script and in all editions (Minuit, 35).

2 John Beckett composed incidental music for Alfred Jarry's play *Ubu Roi*, which Bray adapted and produced for radio; it would be broadcast on the BBC Third Programme on 23 February. John Beckett "provided music of unusual but appropriately grotesque ugliness" ("First Surrealist Manifesto," *The Times* 24 February 1960: 15).

3 Bray's exegesis of Edward Albee's *The Zoo Story* has not been found.

4 Bray had sent SB a reprint of Walter Raleigh's 1908 edition of *Samuel Johnson on Shakespeare* (London: Oxford University Press, 1959). He would write in his next letter: "Have started the Johnson. Read the Proposals and now the Preface. [. . .] Pretentious moralising. Looking forward to the notes." (22 March [*for* 22 February] 1960; TCD, MS 10948/1/76.) Bray also had offered to send a book by the philosopher G. E. Moore (1873–1958).

5 On 12 February, SB had written to Bray: "I have been re reading Frisch's Homo Faber, more to read German than to read Frisch. Blin has thoughts of producing his Jedermann which I don't know." (TCD, MS 10948/70.) Frisch's novel *Homo Faber* was published in 1957 by Suhrkamp Verlag. Roger Blin was interested in directing a

production of *Biedermann und die Brandstifter* (1958; *Biedermann et les incendiaires*; variously translated into English as *Biedermann and the Firebugs*, *Firebugs*, and *The Arsonist*) which was first written by Frisch as a radio drama, and then adapted for the stage. SB had confused *Biedermann* with Hugo von Hofmannsthal's play *Jedermann* (1911).

6 "Contravention" (parking ticket); "disque de stationnement" (spelled "disc" by SB; disc allowing temporary parking).

7 Bray's father had been ill.

8 "Vide-ordures" (rubbish chute).

PATRICK MAGEE
LONDON

26.2.60 Paris

Dear Pat

It was good to have your letter and your news.

I jog on the same old way, i.e. intermittent banging of head against literary (?) walls. I hear from Barbara there is a chance of your doing Lucky in the BBC Godot. I do hope you will. I think you would do it excellently well. I'm afraid there is little chance of my getting over.[1] French Krapp (Blin directing Blin) is billed to open end of March at the Récamier (Vilar's second theatre since the reorganisation). It is a fine little theatre (580 seats) in the Saint-Germain quarter. Originally a theatre, then for many years a cinema, it is now for the past two years a theatre again. The sorely needed support will be supplied by Robert Pinget's Lettre Morte which Barbara produced I think last summer for the Third, a play I like very much and which will be directed by Jean Martin.[2]

The New York Krapp seems to have been well received. Even the bonzes like Atkinson and Watts Jr., conscientiously hostile up to now, had a kind word to say. The actor, Donald Davis, a Canadian, is most remarkable by all accounts. And Alan Schneider, assisted by my imperishable memories of our London rehearsals, must have done a very good job.[3]

I hear you are prepared to read some more gasps from my pen, if it can emit them in time, at this literary-musical do in the Recital

Room of the Festival Hall, April I believe. To this end I am trying to translate the opening pages (ten minutes worth) of the French work I have been struggling with for the past year. What will meet your disgusted eye is a series of short paragraphs (average of 4 or 5 lines) separated by pauses during which panting cordially invited and without as much punctuation as a comma to break the monotony or promote the understanding. The uttered voice, fragments of an inner voice ill heard, is that of a man (?) lying on his face in the mud in the dark. I have made the writing as clear as such dreadful circumstances permit, but I intend also to have the goodness to point the copy I shall be sending you in a fortnight or three weeks from now. It is I think a microphone text, to be murmured, and if you agree with me I hope it will be possible for you to use one, notwithstanding the liveness of the occasion. I have never committed anything – I trust – so exhausted and unpalatable and shall not be in the least offended if you refuse to have anything to do with it.[4]

I'd give a gret [sic] deal to be able to get to London and see you all again. I'll manage it somehow before the year is out, but God knows when. April will be consumed in moving to a new apartment the other side of Montparnasse after 22 years in the cage you know.

Remember me very kindly to Mrs Bird.[5]

Yours ever

s/ Sam

TLS; 1 leaf, 1 side; TCD, MS 11313/3.

1 Patrick Magee would play Vladimir in the BBC radio production of *Waiting for Godot*, in which the role of Lucky would be played by Donal Donnelly (1931–2010) ("Waiting for Godot on Sound Radio," *The Times* 28 April 1960: 6).

2 Bray's translation and production of Pinget's *Lettre morte* (*Dead Letter*) was broadcast on the BBC Third Programme on 21 July 1959.

3 "Bonzes" (bigwigs). The reviews by Brooks Atkinson and Richard Watts Jr.: 7 February 1960 to MacGreevy, n. 3.

4 SB describes the opening pages of *Comment c'est* which he translated for Magee to read in the Music Today program. SB inserts as a handwritten note in the left margin: "or promote the understanding."

5 Mrs. Bird owned the house in which Magee lived (Caroline McGee, daughter of Patrick Magee, to the editors, 7 December 2010).

JACOBA VAN VELDE
AMSTERDAM

2.3.60 Paris

Chère Tonny

1) Nicht? ou Nein? je m'en fous. Simple expression d'un très léger doute.[1]

2) Viduity = Witwerstand. Il faut trouver un mot rare ou vieux, sinon le gag du dictionnaire n'a pas de sens. Chercher dans un grand dictionnaire. A la rigueur le mot latin viduitas (Cicéron!). Mais ce serait dommage.[2]

3) Scène de la mort de la mère. Elle est dans une clinique située près du canal. Il est assis sur le bord du canal d'où il peut voir sa fenêtre. Le store se baisse, indiquant qu'elle vient de crever enfin. Wier = barrage: dont la fonction est de régulariser le débit des voies d'eau. Mais il s'agit d'un petit canal et barrage fait un peu grand. Je propose donc "écluse", bassin où les péniches changent de niveau.[3]

4) Jetty etc. Changement de scène, autre incident tout à fait. Il a fait avancer la bande, sautant un tas de conneries. Il est au bord de la mer, sur le môle, la nuit, dans la tempête. Là je le vois debout, pour une fois. Il a une sorte de révélation, comme quoi le noir et l'orage sont ses vrais éléments. Il a eu tort de vouloir les exclure de son "oeuvre". Vision de ce qu'il lui reste à faire.[4]

"Now the day etc." Cantique protestant très connu, chanté souvent à l'office du soir. J'ai remplace [*for* remplacé] en français par un cantique protestant français. Ce n'est sûrement pas ça qui manque dans votre chère patrie.[5]

Voilà. Vous embrasse.

s/ Sam

TLS; 1 leaf, 1 side; BNF, 19794/66.

2.3.60 Paris

Dear Tonny

1) Nicht? or Nein? I don't mind. Mere expression of a very faint doubt.[1]

2) Viduity = Witwen*stand*. You must find a rare or old word, otherwise the gag about the dictionary is meaningless. Look in a big dictionary. If all else fails, the Latin word *viduitas* (Cicero!). But that would be a pity.[2]

3) Scene of the mother's death. She is in a clinic near the canal. He is sitting on a canal-side bench, from which he can see her window. The blind is drawn down, indicating that she has at last popped off. Weir = "barrage"; function that of regulating the release of the bodies of water. But what we have is a little canal, and *barrage* sounds a bit grand. I therefore propose "écluse", a gate controlling a stretch of water in which barges change level.[3]

4) Jetty etc. Change of scene, quite different incident. He has wound the tape on, skipping over a whole lot of nonsense. He is at the seaside, on the jetty, at night, in a storm. There I see him, for once, standing up. He has a sort of revelation, that somehow the darkness and the storm are his true elements. He has been wrong to want to keep them out of his "work". Vision of what work lies ahead for him.[4]

"Now the day etc." Very well known Protestant hymn, often sung at Evensong. I have replaced it in French by a French Protestant hymn. Surely no shortage of those in your dear motherland.[5]

There. Fondly

Sam

1 In assisting Van Velde in her translation into Dutch of *Krapp's Last Tape*, SB is almost certainly referring to the moment when Krapp utters, "What remains of all that misery? A girl in a shabby green coat, on a railway-station platform? No?" (*Krapp's Last Tape*, 17). The "No?" becomes "Niet?" in Van Velde's translation (Samuel Beckett, "Krapp's laatste band," tr. Jacoba van Velde, *Randstad* 1 [Autumn 1961]) 8–18; rpt. Samuel Beckett, *Wachten op Godot; Eindspel; Krapp's laatste band; Gelukkige dagen; Spel* [Amsterdam: Uitgeverij de Bezige Bij, 1965] 146).

2 SB refers to the moment when Krapp says: "where mother lay a-dying, in the late autumn, after her long viduity" (18). Van Velde translates "viduity" by "viduïteit"

(*Wachten op Godot*. . . 147). SB writes "Witwerstand" (widowerhood) for the feminine "Witwenstand" (widowhood).

3 SB misspells "weir" when referring to the moment when Krapp says, " – bench by the weir from where I could see her window" (19). In the French translation which Beckett did with Pierre Leyris, the term is "bief" (*La dernière bande* [Paris: Editions de Minuit, 1959] 20). Van Velde uses the term "sluis" (*Wachten op Godot*. . . 147).

4 The scene of Krapp on the jetty: 20–21.

5 "Now the Day is Over" by Sabine Baring-Gould (1834–1924) was replaced by SB in his French translation by lines from "L'ombre descend de nos montagnes" by J. W. Lelièvre (d. 1919) (*Louange et prière: psaumes, chorals, cantiques, chants liturgiques* [Paris: Editions Delachaux et Niestlé, 1939] 492–494; *La dernière bande*, 18). (Further on his hesitations about the song, see Samuel Beckett, *Krapp's Last Tape with a Revised Text*, ed. James Knowlson, The Theatrical Notebooks of Samuel Beckett, III [London: Faber and Faber; New York: Grove Press, 1992] 28.) Van Velde chose a line from the first verse of a popular Dutch folk song, "'t Zonnetje gaat van ons scheiden" (Beckett, "Krapp's laatste band," 17).

BARBARA BRAY
PURLEY, SURREY

4.3.60 Ussy /s/ Marne

Dear Barbara

Thanks for your two letters and ms. No sign of Moore so far. I have asked Lindon to see [*for* send] you his Hüsserl [sic] (Wahl, Levinas and others). I have not yet read it myself but think you will be interested.[1]

I was in Paris for 24 hours and got back here yesterday, back and forth in sheets of rain and the screenwiper not wiping. Congratulations on passing your test. Also on success of UBU.[2]

I have not been to any rehearsals. The thing is quite public & official now, I shd. have told you in my last letter. Sorry. I hear L.M. is coming along and that Levert (Virlogeux) will be good. Strictly between you and me my relations with Blin are a little strained at the moment and I'm leaving him to it unless he expressly asks for me. I don't think he has appeared on the set so far, fiddling round with recorders in TNP studios probably. He can do it all right, being who he is and having seen Donald's production.[3]

A letter at last from Robert from Mexico City. He never received my telegram, but did the confirming letter, so he now knows and is of course delighted.

A nice – unexpected letter from Pat. I have written to him about the text he is to read poor devil at Music Today next month I think. It is the latest beginning of Pim about 6 pages. I shall send copies in a few days to Calder, Wilkinson & Pat. If I can manage 5 on my machine I'll do one for you too. It is unsatisfactory, but all I can do at the moment. I am having great difficulty with the re-writing of Part I, stuck now at page 10.[4] A lot of the material & writing is atrociously bad and quite irrecuperable. I'll send you Text III also as soon as I can [get] round to retyping it. Not a word from the people I sent it to in America.[5]

I don't know Moses and Aron.[6]

I'm not prescribing anything for anyone, I'm just being my lousy self.[7] You know what I'd give to know you happier or less unhappy, but I can't escape from myself and my conditions any further than I do and have. I think you do understand that, but sometimes you write as if you didn't. You make me nervous even writing to you when you speak of the panic my letters cause you and ask for something you can understand. There is no question of my permitting or forbidding you anything whatever. We go round in the same old circles always, it is tiring. If it is a trickle of sad phrases it is because I am sad and tired and coming to an end, don't talk to me for God's sake about the duty of happiness, do you want me to put on a black moustache and pad out my cheeks with cotton wool, I'll be very glad if you come over and do all I can and enjoy doing it to give you at least a little of what you want. But it's not much I can do and there's not much I can say. What's the good of writing like this. Forgive and understand – these so different things – I'll never be any better than I am – don't be wanting me to change.[8]

Love

Sam

ALS; 1 leaf, 2 sides; *env to* Mrs Barbara Bray, 121 Brighton Road, Purley, Surrey, Angleterre; *pm* 5-3-60, La Ferté-sous-Jouarre; TCD, MS 10948/1/72.

1 Bray may have sent the final typescript of *The Old Tune* to SB.
Husserl was a collection of papers presented at the Troisième Colloque Philosophique de Royaumont (1957); it included contributions by Jean Wahl, Emmanuel Levinas, and others (Paris: Editions de Minuit, 1959). SB regularly writes the name of the philosopher with an unwarranted umlaut.

2 Bray had passed her driving test.
The BBC production of Jarry's *Ubu Roi* was the third in the series "Art – Anti-Art." Critical response was positive: "The Third Programme deserves our gratitude for . . . the opportunity to go behind criticism and commentary . . . In purely theatrical terms the play is obviously effective . . . we cannot doubt its quality as an original and entertaining work." ("First Surrealist Manifesto," *The Times* 24 February 1960: 15.)

3 The TNP production of *La dernière bande* and *Lettre morte* at the Théâtre Récamier had been announced on 23 February ("Le T.N.P. va monter Salle Récamier 'La Dernière Bande' de Samuel Beckett," *Le Monde*, 13). Roger Blin had seen the production of *Krapp's Last Tape* at the Royal Court Theatre in 1958.

4 SB is limited in the number of carbon copies he can prepare at one time on his typewriter.

5 SB refers to his revision of the English translation of "Text 3" prepared for publication in *Great French Short Stories* (see 29 January 1960, n. 3).

6 Arnold Schoenberg's opera *Moses und Aron* (*Moses and Aaron*).

7 SB had closed his letter to Bray of 22 February 1960: "Take better care of yourself. Sleep eat and be not unmerry for it's not for tomorrow one feels the regrets I mean I suppose." (TCD, MS 10948/1/76.)

8 SB had written earlier:

> The only alternative is between calling it a day and just stumbling on from meeting to meeting, let us then stumble on if you will. I am in tatters and all I can offer you is a few tatters. You say you see me pretty clearly but if you did you would see through to the other side. Just over by your head where it probably is not that things can ever be better or easier, they cannot bar a very extraordinary accident or series of accidents. But you know the whole thing and there is no point in the pain of writing it. Not the wisest certainly but perhaps the best is to go on as we were with that which is added neither excluded nor taken for granted. Since I knew of your trouble I wished to help you and that you say I have is a happiness for me. But don't wish happiness on me, I'm not fitted for it. Let's leave it at that and write and talk easy again. (21 July 1959; TCD, MS 10948/1/39.)

BARBARA BRAY
PURLEY, SURREY

10.3.60 Paris

Dear Barbara

Thanks for your letter. So glad to hear of your success with UBU. I don't remember what you told me about Rudin. Please refresh my memory.[1] I'll be glad to see Newby next month. As I shall be mostly in the country then I hope – unless the move has me here – I'll be glad to know a little in advance when he expects to be here.

I corrected the Minuit proofs of L. M. and O. T. yesterday and enclosed are the change[s] I made. It occurred to me, but I let it stand as it is – that "Oak Saloon" might be better than "Oak Lounge". I don't know if they had "lounge" in the old chaps' day. I leave that question to you.[2]

Things at the Récamier are pretty disastrous – for me. I despaired of getting down to work with Blin and went away to the country. It was naturally understood that he was to play the rôle. Last Monday he telephoned to say he had decided to direct only and had given the rôle to Chauffard (very good in Le Square). I saw Chauffard with Blin day before yesterday and went through the text and a few movements. Yesterday and today he was not available, playing Victim[e]s du Devoir at Poitiers. In other words we have literally not begun, 10 days before the couturière! Suicide. I don't know what has come over Blin. If I didn't feel a duty towards the work – and towards Robert whose "spectacle" it is a[s] much as mine, I'd simply wash my hands of it and leave them to it. I don't think – but may be wrong that Chauffard is the man for it. Certainly not in the time at our disposal. It's a sorry outcome of my association with Blin which I thought indissoluble. Very saddening and upsetting & incomprehensible. All this strictly confidential. L. M. is well advanced. Virlogeux (Levert) very good indeed, Martin adequate, the two actors unsatisfactory. It should just come off, thanks to Levert.[3]

All afternoon in the beautiful 18th century premises of the music editors Heugel discussing contract for Mihalovici's Krapp opera.[4] They are to publish the reduction for piano with triple text (French, English, German). M. is now beginning his orchestration. I shall have to modify slightly here and there the English to adapt it to music written to French text.

Marvellous spring day here. Lunched with Mihalovici at St. Germain then on foot over the river through the Tuileries and Palais Royal to Rue Vivienne where Heugel's offices are and back idem.

Dread the coming ten days, French actors' and directors' incalculable susceptibilities. Have not yet typed the text for Pat. Meant to do it this evening but don't feel equal to it.

No sign of the Moore. Hope you received the Hüsserl. Asked Lindon today if he had sent it - yes.

Dined last night at the Iles with Ludvigsen (Danish translator) and his young Swedish wife. Nice couple. On their way in a 2-chevaux to Malaga.[5] Oysters, duck I couldn't swallow, Sancerre and Beaujolais I could. No Marc, deep restraint. Ah for a real bust.

Voilà, dear Barbara.

Love and to the children and long may their [*for* they] wake up singing -

Sam

Enclosure:

Page	Line[6]	
3	34	Replace "done with that" by "done to that"
5	21	" "and the square." by "do you think I don't know Harrison's Oak Lounge there on the corner of dammit I'll forget my own name next and the square it'll come back to me."
5	28	Replace "confused" by "mucked up"
6	25	" "all one" by "all Six of one"
6	32	Do.
9	20	" "fine" by "fine and grand"

ALS; 2 leaves, 2 sides; T *enclosure*, 1 leaf, 1 side; *env to* M$^{\underline{rs}}$ Barbara Bray, 121 Brighton Road, Purley, Surrey, Angleterre; *pm* 10-3-60, Paris; TCD, MS 10948/1/74.

1 Bray's adaptation of Turgenev's novel *Rudin* for radio: 29 January 1960, n. 1.

2 *Lettre morte* and *La Manivelle* and *The Old Tune* were published together in one volume by Editions de Minuit.

3 Jean Martin indicated that Roger Blin did not wish to play the role of Krapp because the character was "too old and too depressing" (21 November 1977 to Martha Fehsenfeld). René-Jacques Chauffard had played the role of Choubert in Ionesco's *Victimes du devoir* in both the 1953 premiere and a 1960 reprise. Jean Martin played two roles in *Lettre morte* (Le garçon and L'employé), as well as directing the play; Paul Gau (n.d.) played Fred and the comic actress Laurence Badie (b. 1928) played Lili.

SB had written to Bray: "I was hoping to work with Blin as I did in London with Donald and Pat, as closely, but it isn't going to happen that way." SB added: "I feel more and more ill at easy [sic] in the theatre, full or empty. All the hanging round and fumbling and arguing." (22 March [*for* 22 February] 1960; TCD, MS 10948/1/76.)

4 The offices of music publisher Editions Heugel were just north of the Palais Royal at 2 bis Rue Vivienne, Paris 2. Mihalovici's score of *Krapp, ou la dernière bande*, op. 81 (Paris: Heugel, 1961).

5 Christian and Silvia Hagberg Ludvigsen were travelling to Marbella, Spain. SB ordered a grand meal for the Ludvigsens and a simple omelet for himself; when they asked why, he replied "I have tasted it" (Silvia and Christian Ludvigsen to the editors, 23 September 2012).

6 The pagination and line numbers refer to the preliminary BBC typescript of *The Old Tune*. In the Minuit bilingual edition: "done to that" (21); "do you think I don't know Harrison's Oak Lounge there on the corner of dammit I'll forget my own name next and the square it'll come back to me" (29); "mucked up" (31); "all six of one" (35); "fine and grand" (47).

CONNOLLY COLE
THE IRISH TIMES, DUBLIN

March 18th 1960

6 Rue des Favorites
Paris 15me

Dear Mr. Cole

My contribution to your O'Casey tribute is as follows:

"To my great compatriot Sean O'Casey, from France where he is honoured, I send my enduring gratitude and homage."[1]

Yours sincerely
s/
Samuel Beckett

TLS; 1 leaf, 1 side; NyPL, Berg Collection, MSS O'Casey. Previous publication: *The Irish Times* 30 March 1960: 8.

1 Connolly Cole (1931–2002) was a literary reviewer for *The Irish Times*. Asked by Cole for a tribute to Sean O'Casey on the occasion of the playwright's eightieth birthday, SB replied on 15 March: "I am up to my eyes in rehearsals here and shall not be able to write the article you suggest. But I should like very much to be associated with your tribute to Sean O'Casey and shall send you a few lines of homage in the course of this week." (NyPL, Berg Collection, MSS O'Casey.)

BARBARA BRAY
PURLEY, SURREY

19.3.60 Paris

Dear Barbara

Glad to have your letter and your news. You seem very tired and down. You have too much on your shoulders. Re Godot, Pat is all right for me in any rôle, the other I don't know. Perhaps it would have been better to postpone it. I should not have minded in the least.[1] I sent Pat his Pim script, with marks to facilitate understanding. I think it is for the April concert. I think he will make something of it – if not a silk purse.[2] Mihalovici is in Germany at the moment. When I see him I'll tell him of your suggestion. I should think he'd be pleased. He has still months of toil with his orchestration. He aims vaguely at the coming Berlin Festival. Both Tophoven and I will have to adjust our texts here and there, he more than I it appears. I have not much idea what the music will be like. None of what Wilkinson's was.[3]

The rehearsals are unpleasant and laborious. I have lost contact with Blin and hardly expect to renew it. Chauffard is doing his best and has good things. The recorded text is not satisfactory – we did it at Chaillot on Wednesday. Lack of preparation & understanding. I fear Martin is making rather a hash of Lettre Morte. Lack of understanding again. He seems nervously exhausted and we are all apprehensive.

Couturière on Monday, abonnés and public Tuesday & Wednesday, press Friday. I'll stay as long as it is possible to work on the play, then hasten to Ussy. Perhaps Monday, certainly not later than Wednesday. Very tired and depressed of the whole thing.[4]

An exhausted card from Robert on his way to Yucatan and Cuba. Wish to God he were here.

Wrote two lines of a tribute to O'Casey for a special number of the Irish Times, March 30th I think. They asked for 700 words.

Declined grovellingly an invitation from your University to deliver the next Judith E. Wilson Lecture.[5]

Received 1st number of 2-monthly Lettres Nouvelles. Shall send it on when I've had time to glance through it.[6]

Many thanks for Moore. I can follow some of it but haven't got very far. Nor with the Hüsserl. A long spell at Ussy is indicated. But with the move probably next month is hardly possible.

Congratulations on your driving exploits. Mine continue. Another contredanse for abusive stationing.[7]

Went to the Préfecture to renew my identity card. 10 years now before the next. Felt, not without relief, it was the last time I'd call on them.

Have to be up tomorrow at 6 to drive Suzanne to Orly to meet her mother.[8] Then all day nothing. Rehearsal at 9 p.m.

Love, dear Barbara.

Sam

ALS; 2 leaves, 2 sides; *env to* Mrs Barbara Bray, 121 Brighton Road, Purley, Surrey, Angleterre; *pm* __-3-60, Paris; TCD, MS 10948/1/75.

1 Patrick Magee played Vladimir, and Wilfrid Brambell (1912–1985), who had acted at the Abbey and Gate theatres in Dublin, played Estragon. The recording of the Third Programme production of *Godot* was completed before 31 March, for broadcast on 27 April.

2 On 17 March, SB had sent Magee the typescript of his translation of the first eight pages of *Comment c'est*, later published as "From an Unabandoned Work" in *Evergreen Review* 4.14 (September–October 1960) 58–65. SB had pointed the text for Magee; he wrote: "I have marked the places where you may pause for a quick prayer" (TCD, MS 11313/4). Magee's reading would take place on 5 April.

3 Bray may have proposed that the Mihalovici opera be recorded for broadcast on the BBC. The Berlin Festival was generally held in September. The version that was published by Heugel was trilingual and would reflect changes to the German text necessitated by the music. Marc Wilkinson's composition *Voices*: 28 June 1958, n. 2.

4 The Théâtre National Populaire studios were at the Palais de Chaillot, Paris 16. The Couturière (costume rehearsal) would be on Monday 21 March, the performance for "abonnés" (subscribers) and public on 22 and 23 March, and for the press on 25 March.

5 John Stevens, the Secretary of the Faculty Board of English, University of Cambridge, wrote to SB on 12 March to invite him to present the annual Judith E. Wilson Lecture on Poetry or Drama; previous lecturers had been Tyrone Guthrie, Louis MacNeice, and Peter Hall (GEU, MS 1221). Judith E. Wilson (d. 1960) was born in Co. Limerick; a lecture series at Cambridge University had been endowed by Wilson in 1956.

6 The new series of *Les Lettres Nouvelles* was published every two months, first issue March–April 1960.

7 "Contredanse" (slang for parking ticket).

8 Jeanne Deschevaux-Dumesnil (1876–1967) was Suzanne's mother.

BARBARA BRAY
PURLEY, SURREY

24.3.60 Ussy

Dear Barbara

Thanks for yr. letter with cutting.

I crawled back here yesterday, having washed my hands of Krapp. The couturière Monday was disastrous. I worked out simplifications that night, not of text (except suppression of hymn) but of stage business, hoping to reduce deadly slowness of the whole thing, and brought them along to rehearsal Tuesday afternoon. They practically refused to listen to me so I lost my temper, said "démerdez-vous" & swept out. I'm finished with Blin.[1] Chauffard is quite unfitted for the part. No voice, no face, no eyes, no presence, no dexterity, no weight, no violence, no madness. He may have a success, though I can't imagine. For me it's a fiasco.[2] After 10 days rehearsal! L. M. is more or less au point, Virlogeux good, Martin adequate, but it doesn't come over.[3] Was talking to Vilar on Monday. He asked me to do something for them. If there's ever another I suppose I might as well offer it to him.

Midday, all these big windows and the desk lamp on the sky is so dark or is it my eyes. Arrived yesterday to find the house cold and the heating broken down. Got it going again.

Suppose now I must go back to Pim. Lost touch, faith, interest. Patch up something. La Ferté this afternoon. Carrots and such like. Lie on the bed in the evening and peck at Moore & Hüsserl, peck, brood on nothing, peck, brood on nothing, peck, doze. House St. Jacques in same state apparently. Went up to 7th and looked out of north windows. Silly flowers here in wildly precocious blossom as usual, palest pink. Have to be in Paris Saturday fortnight, hope to stay here till then.[4] Mow the first grass, trim the edges, plow, go the little tracks over the plain and learn where the corn is this year. After Monday row walked all afternoon, over the river, Tuileries, Champs-E., Etoile, Av. Foch, Porte Dauphine, great game of boules at the edge of the wood, tea in the pavilion where we once had drinks out of doors, then through the wood trying to spot a wood pecker, then back tired in a decrepit Russian taxi and dinner with the Hayden at the old Dôme where once you and Donald and Donald's little act.[5] So it goes and no doubt some day if not quite gone from mind it will be a kind of good old day.

Love

Sam

ALS; 1 leaf, 2 sides; *env to* Mrs Barbara Bray, 121 Brighton Road, Purley, Surrey, Angleterre; *pm* __-3-60, La Ferté-sous-Jouarre; TCD, MS 10948/1/77.

1 A handwritten page with SB's suggestions for changes in the Théâtre Récamier production of *La dernière bande* was inserted in a copy of the play (InU; Beckett, *Krapp's Last Tape, with a Revised Text*, 283). SB's page of notes:

1. Bande enregistrée. Rien à faire.
2. Synchronisation.
3. Animer l'écoute.
4. Intensifier enregistrement.
5. Simplifier jeu de l'acteur:
   a. montre seule 8–11
      pas de clefs
      rien dans 1er tiroir
      simplifier et accélérer
      bananes. Première dans
      l'avidité. 2me empochée
      pour être épluchée.
   b. Un seul bouchon. Pas de chanson. Tout seul. 18
   c. Montre seule. Pas de verre. Un seul bouchon. 26
      Il revient avec bande vierge, va droit à la table.
   d. supprimer débranchements (2) 27/8
      et rebranchements (2)
   e. supprimer chanson. 30
      brusque passage de l'immobilité au mouvement.
      Démarche plus rapide: trottinement

(1. Tape recorded. Nothing needing to be done.
2. Synchronisation
3. Make more of the business of listening.
4. Play recording louder
5. Simplify the actor's movements and gestures:
   a) watch only 8–11
      no keys
      nothing in the 1st drawer
      simplify and accelerate
      bananas: first greedily. 2nd pocketed
      to be peeled later.
   b) One cork only. No song. All alone. 18
   c) Watch only. No glass. One cork only. 26
      He returns with fresh tape, goes straight to the table.
   d) Suppress unpluggings (2) and repluggings (2) 27/8
   e) Suppress song. 30
      Quick changeover from motionlessness to movement.
      Quicker step, almost a trot.)

"Démerdez-vous" (You can bloody well sort it out yourselves). SB wrote later to A. J. Leventhal: "I have practically broken with Blin, very distressing, I thought that wd. never happen. At the last moment he dropped the rôle and put in Chauffard. We had only 10 days rehearsal! No explanation." (8 May 1960; TxU, Leventhal Collection, 1.4.)

2 Chauffard was a slight man; a photo of him as Krapp appeared with the review by Robert Kanters, "'La Dernière Bande', 'Lettre Morte': deux héros à bout de souffle," *L'Express* 31 March 1960: 36.

3 *Lettre morte* was "au point" (ready).

4 SB had been asked if he could be free to meet Siegfried Unseld in Paris; he confirmed that he would save Sunday 10 April for that purpose (SB to Frau Schnenk, Suhrkamp Verlag, 25 March 1960; DLA, Suhrkamp, VL, Samuel Beckett: 1960–1961).

5 SB's long walk took him to the Bois de Boulogne. Le Dôme, the oldest of the great cafés in Montparnasse.

AVIGDOR ARIKHA
PARIS

31.3.60 Ussy

Cher Avigdor

Merci de votre lettre.

J'ai demandé à Lindon de vous faire avoir une autre invitation. J'espère que vous l'avez bien recue.[1]

Suzanne est retournée voir le spectacle dimanche et hier. Chauffard est toujours aussi mauvais et le sera toujours. C'est foutu, il n'y a qu'à tirer une croix dessus. Ces cons de critiques ne comprennent rien. Plus je remâche tout ça, plus je suis désolé. Je ne travaillerai jamais plus avec Blin.

Je n'ai pas la tête à Pim et n'ai rien fait. Ça ne m'intéresse plus et je n'y crois plus. Ça reviendra peut-être. Je passe le plus clair (!) de mon temps à regarder par la fenêtre, tantôt l'une, tantôt l'autre. On ne peut même pas dire rêvasser. Je bricole un peu dehors, tire le lourd rouleau pendant des heures, sur les mauvaises herbes. J'apprends par coeur Matthias Claudius! "Freund Hain."[2] En être arrivé là! Pense beaucoup à la mer.

Voilà, mon pauvre vieux. C'est ce qu'il me faut en ce moment. Tombé sur des vers de Goethe:

"Die Welt geht auseinander wie ein fauler Fisch,
Wir wollen sie nicht balsamieren"[3]
Je rentre le 9 ou le 10 je ne sais pas.
Bien amicalement
Sam

ALS; 1 leaf, 2 sides; InU, Arikha. Previous publication: Anne Atik, *How It Was*, 63–64.

31.3.60 Ussy

Dear Avigdor

Thank you for your letter.

I asked Lindon to get you another invitation. I hope you've received it.[1]

Suzanne went to see the show again on Sunday and yesterday. Chauffard is as bad as ever, and always will be. It's hopeless, nothing left but to put a cross on it. These bloody stupid critics have no idea. The more I go over it all, the more dismal I feel. I shall never work with Blin again.

My mind isn't on Pim at all, and I've done nothing. It doesn't interest me any more, and I don't believe in it any more. Maybe it will come back. I spend the best (!) part of my time looking out through the window, sometimes this one, sometimes the other. Can't even be called daydreaming. I do odd bits of work outside, pull the heavy roller for hours through the weeds. Am learning Mathias Claudius by heart! "Freund Hain"[2] To have come to this! Think about the sea a lot.

That's it, my poor old friend. It's what I need just now. Stumbled on some lines of Goethe:

"Die Welt geht auseinander wie ein fauler Fisch
Wir wollen sie nicht balsamieren"[3]
I'm coming back on the 9th or 10th, I don't know.
All the best
Sam

1 Roger Blin's production of *La dernière bande* had opened at the Théâtre Récamier on 22 March.

SB omits the cedilla in "reçue."

2 By "Freund Hain" (or "Freund Hein"), a personification of death, SB is almost certainly alluding to the verse by Matthias Claudius first published in 1797, "Der Tod":

> Ach, es ist so dunkel in des Todes Kammer,
> Tönt so traurig, wenn er sich bewegt
> Und nun aufhebt seinen schweren Hammer
> Und die Stunde schlägt.
> (Oh, the darkness of Death's chamber,
> Sounds so dismal when he starts his rounds,
> Then uplifts his heavy, fateful hammer
> And the hour resounds.)
> (Robert M. Browning, ed., *German Poetry from 1750 to 1900* [New York: Continuum, 1984] 12–13.)

Anne Atik* (b. 1932) recounts of SB and Arikha: "A stanza from Claudius which they recited often and which never failed to make our spines tingle came from Claudius's 'Der Tod' . . . Sam presented A. with his old, small, three-volume edition of Claudius – bought during his travels in Germany – which they read out of" (*How it Was*, 66).

3 SB cites Goethe's verse, one in a series entitled "Annonce": "Die Welt geht auseinander wie ein fauler Fisch / Wir wollen sie nicht balsamieren" ("The world is disintegrating like rotten fish. Let's not embalm it." (Goethe, *Goethe: With Plain Prose Translations of Each Poem*, 290.)

JACOBA VAN VELDE
AMSTERDAM

1.4.60 Ussy

Chère Tonny

"Laisser filer ça." Comment dire ça plus simplement? La fille, les yeux, tout ce qu'il y trouvait ("la lumière, l'obscurité, etc."), l'amour, la femme, laisser partir tout ça, perdre tout ça, renoncer à tout ça, au profit soi-disant de l'oeuvre à faire.[1]

Bram est rentré à Paris, paraît-il, et installé dans le nouvel appartement des Putman.[2] Je lui avais écrit en Suisse en lui demandant de me faire signe quand il serait de retour à Paris. Aucun signe. J'ai envie de le revoir seul, pas envie de passer par

Jacques. Il travaille paraît-il. Arikha l'a vu plusieurs fois (le peintre israélien).

Krapp se joue au Récamier avec Lettre Morte mal joué par Chauffard qu'on trouve "prodigieux", dans une mise en scène bâclée de Blin qu'on trouve au poil. Bonne presse dans l'ensemble pour les 2 pièces, même le Colonel Gauthier![3] Comme j'en ai marre des critiques, des acteurs, des metteurs en scène et des spectateurs.

Me berce avec les vers de Goethe:

Die Welt geht auseinander
wie ein fauler Fisch,
Wir wollen sie nicht
balsalmieren.

Amitiés à Fritz.

Je vous embrasse.

Sam

ALS; 2 leaves, 2 sides; BNF, 19794/67.

1.4.60 Ussy

Dear Tonny

"Laisser filer ça." How to say that more simply? The girl, the eyes, all that he found there ("the light, the dark, etc."), the love, the woman: *let go of* all that, lose all that, give up all that, for the so-called benefit of the work to be written.[1]

Bram has gone back to Paris, it appears, and moved into the Putmans' new flat.[2] I had written to him in Switzerland, asking him to let me know when he would be back in Paris. Not a squeak. I feel like seeing him on his own. No wish to go through Jacques. He is working, apparently. Arikha has seen him several times (the Israeli painter).

Krapp is playing at the Récamier with *Lettre morte*, badly acted by Chauffard, who is being spoken of as "outstanding", in a rather slapdash production by Blin that is being being spoken of as sensational. A good press on the whole for both plays – even

Colonel Gauthier![3] How sick I am of critics, actors, directors, and spectators.

Comforting myself with Goethe's lines:

Die Welt geht aus einander
wie ein fauler Fisch
Wir wollen sie nicht
balsamieren.

Regards to Fritz.

Fondly

Sam

1 The English original of the expression which SB is helping Van Velde put into Dutch is "Leave it at that" (*Krapp's Last Tape*, 26). Van Velde translates it as "Laat het hierbij" (Beckett, "Krapp's laaste band," 10).

2 Jacques and Andrée Putman had recently moved into a spacious apartment at 5 Rue des Grands-Augustins, Paris 6.

3 In *L'Express*, Robert Kanters enthused more about Beckett's play than about Pinget's, saying of its director: "M. Roger Blin a parfaitement minuté la mise en scène" ("'La Dernière Bande', 'Lettre Morte': deux héros à bout de souffle," 31 March 1960: 36) (In Mr Roger Blin's production, the timing is perfect). In *Le Monde*, Bertrand Poirot-Delpech expressed some reservations about Pinget's play while praising Beckett's unreservedly ("'Lettre morte' de Robert Pinget, 'La Dernière Bande' de Samuel Beckett," 27–28 March 1960: 15). Jean Paget praised Chauffard's performance as "prodigieux" ("'Lettre morte' de Robert Pinget et 'La dernière bande' de Samuel Beckett," *Combat* 28 March 1960: 2). In *Le Figaro*, Jean-Jacques Gautier wrote positively of both plays ("'Lettre morte' et 'La dernière bande,'" 28 March 1960: 21). Of *Lettre morte*:

> Cette pièce a deux actes. Un premier acte merveilleusement composé qui satisfait notre sensibilité et, psychologiquement, affectivement, dramatiquement inattaquable. Et puis un second acte qui se veut plus démonstratif et sent son procédé. Mais le premier acte, à lui seul, vaut que l'on se rende au théâtre Récamier. (This play is in two acts. A first act marvellously composed, which satisfies our sensibility: psychologically, affectively, dramatically beyond criticism. And then a second act that makes a point of being more demonstrative, and rather self-consciously is so. But a visit to the Théâtre Récamier is worth it for the first act alone.)

Of *La dernière bande*, Gautier continued: "Ce monologue est d'une écriture admirable. Samuel Beckett a su y faire passer une beauté mélancolique aux portes du désespoir. Il a créé une espèce de grandeur en marge du sordide." (The writing in this monologue is admirable. Samuel Beckett has managed to bring to it a melancholy beauty that verges on despair. He has created a sort of grandeur in and beyond the sordid.)

ROBERT PINGET
NEW YORK

2.4.60 Ussy

Cher Robert

Suzanne, restée à Paris, m'a lu ta lettre au téléphone hier. Content de vous savoir rentré à NY à peu près entier.[1]

Le spectacle a bien démarré. Je n'ai pas lu beaucoup de critiques, mais il paraît qu'elles sont bonnes dans l'ensemble, pour les deux pièces. Tu en auras sans doute déjà reçu. Je ne suis pas du tout d'accord avec Chauffard et la mise en scène de Blin et m'en suis bruyamment lavé les mains le lendemain de la couturière, devant l'impossibilité de me faire entendre, très pénible et trop long à raconter. Je te dirai tout ça plus tard. L. M. est très proprement monté, mais le climat n'y est pas à mon avis. Mais c'est du bon boulot. Je crois que tu en seras assez content. Paraît que Vilar est très content. Ce qui est bien, c'est que pour toi c'est une bonne chose qui t'amènera beaucoup de lecteurs et de sympathies. On attend déjà une autre pièce de toi.

Je suis parti le lendemain de la couturière et suis ici depuis. Ce qui fait que je n'ai pas eu le plaisir de voir tes parents et ta soeur. Suzanne a déjeuné avec eux et ça a très bien marché. Je crois qu'ils étaient très heureux.

J'espère que tu ne seras pas trop mécontent des épreuves de La Manivelle. J'ai fait encore quelques petits changements dans le texte anglais. A la BBC c'est prévu pour le "3me trimestre", c'est vague.

Je n'ai pas vu une seule allusion au décor de Matias qui est très bon. Quels cons ces critiques, vraiment sourds et aveugles. Il nous a envoyé une carte de Suisse où il boit des milks glacés. Nous l'aimons beaucoup. Comme tu le sais sans doute il change de canard: moins de travail et plus de fric.[2]

Mon travail est au point mort. Je n'y crois plus et ça ne m'intéresse plus. Vouloir trop étreindre! ou trop peu.

Sois tranquille pour le spectacle, sois content même. C'est très bien parti et doit marcher.

Quand rentres-tu? Fin du mois, n'est-ce pas?

Pardonne ce petit mot fatigué.

Bien affectueusement de nous 2. Sam

ALS; 1 leaf, 2 sides; Burns Library, Samuel Beckett Collection, SB-RP.

2.4.60 Ussy

Dear Robert

Suzanne, who is staying on in Paris, read me your letter on the telephone yesterday. Glad to know you're back in NY more or less in one piece.[1]

The show had a good start. I haven't read many reviews, but it seems that they're good on the whole, for both plays. You will probably have had some already. I don't agree at all with Chauffard or with Blin's production, and noisily washed my hands of it the day after the first dress rehearsal, faced with the impossibility of putting my view over, very painful, too long to go into. I'll tell you all about it later. *Lettre morte* is very decently staged, but the climate is not right in my opinion. But they've done a good job. I think you will be quite pleased with it. Apparently Vilar is very pleased. What is nice is that, for you, it is a good thing that will bring you a great many readers and good opinions. People are already waiting for another play from you.

I left the day after the first dress rehearsal, and have been here since. Which means that I did not have the pleasure of seeing your parents and your sister. Suzanne had lunch with them and it went off very well. I think they were very happy.

I hope that you won't be too dissatisfied with the proofs of *La Manivelle*. I have made some more changes in the English text. At the BBC it is slated for "the third term": vague.

I have not seen a single reference to Matias's set, which is very good. What clods, these critics: really deaf and blind. He sent us a card from Switzerland where he is drinking iced milk-shakes. We are very fond of him. As you no doubt know, he's moving to another rag: less work and more money.[2]

My work has come to a halt. I don't believe in it any more, and it no longer interests me. Wanting to take on too much! Or too little.

Have no worries about the show; be pleased even. It has made a very good start and should do well.

When are you coming back? End of the month, isn't it?

Forgive this tired little note.

Love from us both. Sam

1 This letter is the first in which SB addresses Pinget by the familiar "tu."
In his memoir, Pinget wrote of his travels: "Après le Mexique et Cuba, je suis rentré à NY. Sam m'y écrivit." (Doucet, unclassified Pinget Collection, "Notre ami Samuel Beckett," 33.) (After Mexico and Cuba I went back to New York. Sam wrote to me there.) In his report on his stay in America Pinget wrote:

> J'y ai récolté des impressions multiples et belles qui me semblent en contradiction avec celles que nous suggère la publicité américaine en Europe. Les profondes qualités humaines de la population m'ont touché au point de me faire désirer de m'établir aux USA si l'occasion un jour se présente. (Doucet, PNG.C.349.13/14.) (I have picked up a great many lovely impressions which seem to me very much at variance with those suggested by American publicity in Europe. The profound human qualities of the people touched me to the point where I felt a desire to settle in the USA, should the chance present itself one day.)

2 A large deposit of maquettes, both two- and three-dimensional, of Matias's stage sets exists at the Bibliothèque Nationale de France (DON: DDD-ASP-2007-18), but the collection does not include Matias's design for *Lettre Morte*.

DONALD McWHINNIE
LONDON

April 6th 1960 Ussy

Dear Donald

Glad to have your letter and good news of GODOT. I look forward to hearing the tape. But don't bother to send it over. Listening Avenue Hoche gives me the willies. Next time I'm in London.[1]

All the best with THE CARETAKER He's a lucky man to have you.[2]

I understand Pat's trepidation. To read that in private is asking too much of anyone, let alone in public. I simply had nothing else to offer them. Too long to explain what it's all about, not much help if I did. A "man" is lying panting in the mud and dark murmuring his "life" as he hears it obscurely uttered by a voice inside him. This utterance is described throughout the work as the fragmentary recollection of an extraneous voice once heard "quaqua on all sides". In the last pages he is obliged to take the onus of it on himself and of the lamentable tale of things it tells. The noise of his panting fills his ears and it is only when this abates that he can catch and murmur forth a fragment of what is being stated within. The work is in three parts, the first a solitary journey in the dark and mud terminating with discovery of a similar creature known as Pim, the second life with Pim both motionless in the dark and mud terminating with departure of Pim, the third solitude motionless in the dark and mud. It is in the third part that occur the so-called voice "quaqua", its interiorisation and murmuring forth when the ranting stops. That is to say the "I" is from the outset in the third part and the first and second, though stated as heard in the present, already over. The extract is the beginning pf [*for* of] Part 1. I'm afraid this will be of little help to Pat. All he can do is gasp it out very short of breath, into a microphone if possible, and hope for the best. I have marked the rhythms on his copy. The "unabandoned" is possibly optimistic. I have only a rough (though 4th or 5th) version in French and am not at all sure I can bring it any further. If I can't I'll throw it away.[3]

Very disappointed by French KRAPP. Slovenly production (ten days rehearsals, final tape three days before couturière) and very unsatisfactory performance by Chauffard simply unfitted, vocally and every other way, for the part. I only say this to my friends. Not in the same parish as your production and Pat's marvellous performance. LETTRE MORTE is a conscientious job by Martin with an excellent actor – Virlogeux – playing Levert.[4] The press seems to have been favourable on the whole, but even more foolish than usual. I am told there are good houses. Wild horses wouldn't drag me into the theatre. But I'd give a lot to have seen the NY production now about its 100th.[5]

I do hope you'll be over after THE CARETAKER. It would be good to see you again.

Affectionately s/ Sam

TLS; 1 leaf, 1 side; OSU, Spec.rare.124, McWhinnie.

1 McWhinnie had written to SB on 31 March: "Just a line to let you know that 'Godot' is now on tape and the first transmission will be in the Third Programme on 27 April, I was very pleased with the result." McWhinnie's intention was, essentially, to present the play as a reading:

> We treated the stage directions quite formally, beginning with the words 'Act One' and ending with the words 'Curtain', and linking the descriptions of the action tightly to the dialogue. It seemed to work. Indeed, at many moments it positively enhanced it. We used no sound effects at all except the whip. (BBCWAC, RCONT1, Samuel Beckett, Scriptwriter I.)

2 McWhinnie also mentioned in this letter: "I am just about to start rehearsals for the Arts Theatre production of Harold Pinter's new play, 'The Caretaker'. This will keep me pretty fully occupied until April 25th, which is our opening date."

3 "From an unabandoned work" was read by Patrick Magee on 5 April as part of the Music Today series presented in the Recital Room of the Royal Festival Hall.

4 Henri Virlogeux had trained in Charles Dullin's school and had joined the Compagnie Grenier-Hussenot in the mid-1950s.

5 *Krapp's Last Tape* had been performed seven or eight times per week since it opened at the Provincetown Playhouse, New York, on 14 January 1960, and thus would reach nearly 100 perfomances by the time it temporarily shifted to the Players Theatre from 19 April through 29 May ("due to previous bookings at the Provincetown Playhouse"). Schneider had written: "we are going strong, the show holding up and business good"; indeed, the play would return to the Provincetown Playhouse from 31 May through 30 October (Schneider to SB, 9 April 1960; Burns Library, Samuel Beckett Collection, AS-SB; Beckett and Schneider, *No Author Better Served*, 67; Advertisement, *New York Times* 17 April 1960: 2X).

BARBARA BRAY
PURLEY, SURREY

8.4.60 Ussy

Dear Barbara

Thanks for card & poem and brief letter.

After over a fortnight solitary here I return to Paris this afternoon. Lot of tiresome things to do before I leave, so as not to leave the place too filthy and disordered behind me. Have done hardly any work, a few hours technical on Part I these last few days. Le coeur n'y est plus, ni la tête, ni rien.[1] Unfathomably tired of Life and letters. First swallows yesterday in the twilight and tomtit as usually trying to build in letter-box. Listen for cuckoo in vain. Taken to driving into La Ferté about 7 just to sit in the square and watch. Don't even take a

8. Barbara Bray

drink. Letter from Donald from which I gather he may come over when he's through with The Caretaker. Nice to see him again far from Capri.[2] I look forward to seeing you this month, next month or any month. I again don't know why you ask my "permission". You know how things are and that I may not be able to be with you as much as I'd like. And that whenever you come over I'll see as much of you as I can and try and make things a bit happy for you. I think a flying visit would perhaps upset you more than anything else, but that's your affair. Just let me know a little in advance. I'll probably be in Paris now all next week, lot of things to do and people to see. Perhaps even beyond Easter. No sign of the move yet, the house is far from finished. I'm in no hurry but I'd like to have it over and all paid up God knows how. No plans for going anywhere. I'd like to spend a week with my cousin again this summer but don't know if it will be possible.[3]

Suzanne is not well and I'm worried. Nothing serious I hope but she'll have to be careful and quiet for a bit. The play unpleasantnesses upset her a lot.

Donald says Pat is truly nervous about the Pim text. Perhaps you could calm him down a bit. It's unfriendly to ask anyone to read that in public, but I had nothing else to give them. Calder arrives 18th. He says the 3 in 1 are out but hasn't sent me a copy. Not that I want one.[4]

I asked Schwartz to send me the page of O'Casey tribute in Irish Times of March 30th. Have a queer feeling they did not include my brief contribution, or modified it. They asked for 700 words which of course I preferred not. Perhaps you'd ask Craig. I'd be upset vis à vis O'Casey if my homage wasn't in. So he's a ram too. Ça ne m'étonne pas.[5]

Have to start now and clean up. No wish to go. Could latitate here, dreaming and muttering, till being found wouldn't matter.

Love

Sam

ALS; 2 leaves, 4 sides; *env to* Mrs Barbara Bray, 121 Brighton Rd., Purley, Surrey, Angleterre; *pm illeg*, Paris; TCD, MS 10948/1/79.

1 "Le coeur n'y est plus, ni la tête, ni rien" (The heart is no longer in it, nor the head, nor anything).

2 SB and McWhinnie had last seen each other in Sorrento, at the awarding of the Italia Prize, in September 1959.

3 SB's cousin Sheila Page lived near Godalming, Surrey.

4 John Calder had written to SB on 5 April that "The Three Novels" had been reviewed by V. S. Pritchett in the *New Statesman* ("An Irish Oblomov," 59 [2 April 1960] 489) and that he had encouraged Pritchett to attend the reading by Patrick Magee in the Music Today program (InU, C&B, Beckett).

5 SB's tribute for Sean O'Casey's 80th birthday was published in facsimile in *The Irish Times* ("From Samuel Beckett: 'Gratitude and Homage,'" 30 March 1960: 8). O'Casey was born on 30 March, making him an Aries, like SB. "Ça ne m'étonne pas" (No surprise there).

H. A. L. Craig was a scriptwriter for the BBC and drama critic of the *New Statesman*; he was a graduate of Trinity College Dublin and had been an Assistant Editor of *The Bell* in the 1940s.

ROBERT MALLET
GALLIMARD, PARIS

le 23 avril 1960 — 6 Rue des Favorites
Paris 15me

Cher Monsieur

Je vous remercie de votre lettre du 21 avril.

Je vous donne bien volontiers mon accord sur le principe d'un ouvrage sur mon travail à paraître dans votre collection la Bibliothèque Idéale.[1]

Si Maurice Blanchot voulait se charger de cette étude j'en serais fort heureux.[2]

Je vous prie d'exprimer à Monsieur Gaston Gallimard combien je suis sensible à l'honneur qui m'est ainsi fait.[3]

Croyez, cher Monsieur, à mes sentiments très cordiaux.

Samuel Beckett

TLcc; 1 leaf, 1 side; an AL draft written on Robert Mallet's letter of 21 April 1960 to SB; GEU, MS 1221.

23rd April 1960 — 6 Rue des Favorites
Paris 15me

Dear Monsieur Mallet

Thank you for your letter of 21st April.

I gladly give my consent on the principle of a study of my work, to appear in your Bibliothèque Idéale series.[1]

If Maurice Blanchot were willing to take on this study I would be delighted.[2]

Please convey to M. Gaston Gallimard how conscious I am of the honour being done to me.[3]

Very cordially yours

Samuel Beckett

1 Robert Mallet (1915–2002), poet, novelist, worked with the editorial team at Gallimard from 1949 until the late 1950s, after which he became an important academic administrator. While at Gallimard he was in charge of two series, Jeune Poésie and La Bibliothèque Idéale; the latter he continued to direct even after ceasing to work at Gallimard. Between 1958 and 1967, thirty-seven critical studies were published in the Bibliothèque Idéale collection, including, by the time Mallet approached SB, ones on Claudel, Saint-Exupéry, Jouhandeau, Camus, Michaux, and Supervielle. On 21 April, Mallet wrote to SB for his permission to commission a volume on him, adding "Auriez-vous l'obligeance, en me répondant, de me dire quel serait le critique que vous pourriez nous conseiller (ou les critiques)?" (GEU, MS 1221.) (Would you be kind enough, when replying, to tell me which critic (or critics) you would recommend?)

2 Mallet later explains why the volume was never written: "Monsieur Blanchot pressenti refuse parce qu'il a trop de travaux en cours. Mais il me dit l'intérêt qu'il prend au projet, sur le plan de la critique." (Robert Mallet to Gaston Gallimard, 18 September 1961; Gallimard archives, Bibliothèque Idéale collection.) (Maurice Blanchot, who has been approached, declines because he has too much work in hand. But he speaks of the interest he feels in the project, to him as a critic.)

3 Gaston Gallimard (1881–1975) was the co-founder of the *Nouvelle Revue Française*, and the founder and director of Editions Gallimard.

ALAN SIMPSON
PIKE THEATRE, DUBLIN

May 7th 1960

6 Rue des Favorites
Paris 15me

Dear Alan

Thanks for your letter and for not standing in the way of Cusack's KRAPP.[1]

I have decided it is now time I fell off my high Eire moke and have written to John Barber of Curtis Brown Ltd. to tell him so. I made it clear in my letter that we now revert to the situation that obtained before the the [sic] Dublin Festival hullabaloo and that you have the first option on all my work in Eire. He will authorize any production you may have in mind and of course the reading of ALL THAT FALL and will handle contracts with you. I suggest you do ENDGAME, but it is as you wish. There is no other play in sight and will not be probably for a long time if ever.[2]

I am glad to be able to write this to you and apologize again for the inconvenience I have caused you.

Greetings to Carolyn.

Yours
s/ Sam
Samuel Beckett

TLS; 1 leaf, 1 side; TCD, MS 10731/80, Simpson; TLcc; GEU, MS 1221.

1 Cyril Cusack planned to perform in *Krapp's Last Tape* at the Abbey Theatre, Dublin, from 20 to 25 June, prior to his performance in the Théâtre des Nations Festival in Paris in July. Cusack's telephone call to Simpson had prompted Simpson to write to SB on 2 May: "Does this mean that you have revoked 'the ban' on performances of your works in Dublin, or is it merely that you feel it would be unreasonable to object to a few performances here, since the production is really intended for Paris?" (TCD, MS 10731/77; copy GEU, MS 1221).

2 SB wrote to John Barber, Curtis Brown, on the same day: "I have decided to authorize henceforward production of my plays in Eire. I have authorized Cyril Cusack Productions to give a few performances of KRAPP'S LAST TAPE in Dublin next month and then present it in July, with ARMS AND THE MAN, at the Paris Théâtre des Nations." (GEU, MS 1221.)

JACOBA VAN VELDE
AMSTERDAM

9.5.60 Ussy

Chère Tonny

Bien reçu votre triste lettre. Ça me fait de la peine de vous savoir dans cet état. Il vous faudrait un petit séjour à Paris. Peut-être le mois prochain. Je paierais l'hôtel. Vous pourriez voir les frangins et tirer tout ça au clair. Moi non plus je n'y comprends rien. C'est de l'inconscience sûrement, pas autre chose. Je ne les vois jamais ni l'un ni l'autre. J'aimerais bien voir Bram, mais seul. Ça ne semble pas facile. Je lui avais demandé de me faire signe. Bernique.[1] J'entends mon nom dans la rue, à côté de Sèvres-Babylone, me retourne, c'est une femme que je n'avais jamais vue. Eva. Elle ne [*for* me] l'a dit elle-même. Elle promenait une petite fille. Comme elle a vieilli. Je lui ai demandé des nouvelles de Geer et Lisl. Elle n'a pas l'air de les voir souvent. Elle m'a dit, Ils voyagent beaucoup. Pauvre femme. Je l'ai quittée en me disant – Elle m'a reconnu![2] Je suis seul à Ussy. Moi aussi, des journées sans parler à personne. Ça ne me gêne pas. Je ne parle même plus tout seul. De temps en temps je pousse un rugissement. Le voisin doit me prendre pour un fou – inoffensif. Il jardine toute la journée, en sifflant sans arrêt. Je ne lui ai jamais parlé. J'ignore son nom. De loin je lui fais de grands signes d'amitié en agitant la main. Il répond de même. Je ne peux pas me concentrer non plus. Le travail est en panne. Je l'ai repris aujourd'hui – première fois depuis 3 semaines. Je casse, casse. Durs comme fer les mots. Je les voudrais en poussière. Comme l'âme. The rotten little car va mieux. Nous sortons la nuit quand il fait beau. Petits villages endormis. Que faire maintenant? Ce soir. Il est 8 heures. Faire cuire un chou et boire mon demi-litre. Jouer aux échecs tout seul. Je pourrais vous envoyer un chèque. En francs ou en sterling. Mais pourriez-vous le négocier? Ce serait avec joie. Faites-moi savoir. Pour votre travail: forcez-vous, une heure par jour pour commencer, une demi-heure. C'est le seul remède. Chessman l'avait compris.[3] Je vous embrasse bien affectueusement. Dites-moi ce que je peux faire. En dehors de ces conneries de mots.

Sam

ALS; 2 leaves, 2 sides; BNF, 19794/68.

9.5.60 Ussy

Dear Tonny

Got your sad letter. I feel bad, knowing that you are in this state. You could do with a little stay in Paris. Maybe next month. I would pay for your hotel room. You could see the bros, and clear the whole thing up. I don't understand any of it either. They're just not thinking, I'm sure of it. I never see either of them. I would like to see Bram, but on his own. That doesn't seem easy. I had asked him to get in touch. Nothing doing.[1] I hear my name in the street, by Sèvres-Babylone, I turn round: it's a woman I'd never seen. Eva. She told me herself. She was walking a little girl. How she's aged. I asked her for news of Geer and Lisl. She doesn't seem to see them much. She told me they travel a lot. Poor woman. I left her, telling myself: she recognized me![2] I'm on my own in Ussy. Me too, whole days without speaking to anyone. It doesn't bother me. I don't even talk to myself any more. From time to time I let out a howl. The neighbour must take me for a (harmless) lunatic. He gardens all day, whistling endlessly. I've never spoken to him. I don't know his name. From a distance I wave energetically, in a friendly way. He answers the same way. I can't concentrate either. The writing is stuck. I went back to it today – first time for 3 weeks. I hammer and hammer. Hard as iron, the words. I'd like them in dust. Like the spirit. The rotten little car is running better. We go out at night, when the weather is good. Little sleeping villages. What to do now? This evening. It's 8 o'clock. Cook a cabbage and drink my half-litre. Play chess on my own. I could send you a cheque. In francs or in sterling. But could you cash it? I'd be really pleased to do it. Let me know. For your work: force yourself, an hour a day to start with, or half an hour. It's the only remedy. Chessman had seen that.[3] A loving kiss and hug. Tell me what I can do. Apart from these bloody silly words.

Sam

1 On 29 February, SB had written to Jacoba van Velde, about her brother whose partner Marthe Arnaud had died in August the previous year after being knocked down by a car: "Il y a huit jours j'ai reçu, à ma grande surprise, une carte de Bram de Genève, en me disant qu'il se reposait chez des amis et essayait de retrouver le goût de travailler et demandant de me revoir" (BNF, 19794/65) (A week ago, to my great surprise, I had a card from Bram from Geneva, telling me that he was taking a break, staying with some friends, and was trying to get back a taste for work, and wanted to see me again).

2 Eva has not been identified.

3 Also on 29 February, SB had encouraged Van Velde with her work:

> Comment vous aider avec votre livre? Il me faudrait savoir plus exactement ce qui ne va pas et ce qui vous arrête. C'est difficile par lettre. J'ai un mal fou avec le mien dont je suis en train de refaire la première partie. Il faut s'acharner, t'acharner. Des fois je me dis que ça ne peut marcher qu'à condition que tout le reste soit foutu. Ce serait plutôt mon cas j'ai l'impression. Essayez de m'expliquer un peu mieux en quoi consiste la difficulté. (How to help you with your book? I'd need to know more precisely what is going wrong and stopping you. It's not easy in a letter. I'm having terrible trouble with my own and am in the process of reworking the first part. One has to keep at it, you have to keep at it. Sometimes I tell myself that that will only work if it's goodbye to everything else. That could well be the case for me, I have the impression. Try to explain to me a little better what the difficulty is.)

It is probable that Van Velde was working on her novel *Een blad in de wind* which was published the following year (Amsterdam: Querido, 1961).

Caryl Chessman (1921–1960), a prolific writer during his twelve years on death row, had been put to death (after numerous well-publicized stays of execution) in San Quentin Prison on 2 May. After the publication of his very popular *Cell 2455, Death Row* in 1954, the legal authorities and prison guards attempted to prevent Chessman from writing, which obliged him to exploit legal loopholes and resort to subterfuge. Joseph E. Longstreth (Chessman's literary agent) wrote:

> Chessman went "underground" – writing in secret, writing in code, even during one stretch in an isolation cell, writing on toilet paper and smuggling his efforts out of the prison to an eagerly waiting outside world. (Joseph E. Longstreth and Alan Bisbort, "Introduction" to *Cell 2455, Death Row* [New York: Carroll and Graf, 1954] xxi.)

ROBERT PINGET
PARIS

20.5.60 Ussy-sur-Marne

Cher Robert

Merci de ton gentil mort [*for* mot]. Très touché que tu penses un peu à moi.[1]

Je ne vais pas très bien. C'est ici que je suis le moins mal.

Le travail avance à pas d'escargot. Trois spasmes en avant, deux en arrière. Je ne suis pas pressé. J'ai bon espoir que cette fois c'est le dernier et qu'il pourra se prolonger le temps nécessaire.[2]

Ne sois pas déprimé pour le tien. Tu peux en être fier.[3]

Bien affectueusement

Sam

ALS; 1 leaf, 1 side; Burns Library, Samuel Beckett Collection, SB-RP.

20.5.60 Ussy-sur-Marne

Dear Robert

Thank you for your kind note. Very touched that you should be thinking of me a little.[1]

I am not very well. This is where I am least ill.

The work is advancing at snail's pace. Three spasms forward and two back. I am in no hurry. I am in hopes that this time it is the last, and that it will stretch itself out as long as needed.[2]

Don't be depressed about yours. You can be proud of it.[3]

Affectionately

Sam

1 Pinget had returned from his six-month stay in the United States on 16 May.

2 In his memoir entry for 25 July, Pinget wrote:

> Il me parle ensuite de son travail. Dit qu'il en est dégoûté. Aurait tellement voulu que ça dure toujours. Impossible. Toujours ce complexe vis-à-vis de Joyce, Dante etc. Je lui dis que cela prouve que le fruit est mûr puisqu'il tombe. Il me dit en riant qu'il l'écrase. Ne veut plus du titre "Thalic par pitié", trouvé après Cher fruit cher vert, qu'il ne veut pas reprendre. Trouvera autre chose. Suzanne propose Selon Pim, pour emmerder tout le monde si ça paraît après Selon Clope. Sam est en train de taper son texte définitif. Papiers sur son bureau. Me dit qu'il a besoin d'un avis, il n'y voit plus clair. Je lui demande de me faire le plaisir de me le faire lire. Le donnera à lire à Lindon, Suzanne et moi. Je lui dis que je ne pourrai que le trouver beau. Me dit qu'il me faudra être objectif [. . .] (je l'ai hélas été par la suite [. . .]) (Doucet, unclassified Pinget Collection, "Notre ami Samuel Beckett," 39–40.) (Then he talks to me about his work. Says he is sick of it. Would so much have wanted it to go on for ever. Impossible. Always this complex, about Joyce, about Dante etc. I tell him that proves that the fruit is ripe, since it's falling. He says, laughing, that he squashes it. No longer wants the title "Thalie par pitié", found after "Cher fruit cher vert", which he doesn't want to go back to. Will find something else. Suzanne proposes "Selon Pim", to get under everyone's skin if it comes out after "Selon Clope". Sam is busy typing out his definitive text. Papers on his desk. Tells me he needs an opinion, he can't see straight any more. I ask him to be so kind as to let me read it. Will give it to Lindon, Suzanne and me. I tell him I can't fail to find it fine. Tells me I must be objective [. . .] (alas, I was, later [. . .])

3 SB had recently read a draft of Pinget's as yet unpublished novel, later entitled *Clope*.

BARBARA BRAY
PURLEY, SURREY

4.6.60 Ussy

Dear Barbara

Just a line to thank you for your letters and essay to all of which I shall reply more seemingly in a day or two.[1]

Back here yesterday after a few wildish days in Paris (Riopelle & Hayden exhibitions) during which I lost all my papers and found them again.[2]

Another present of a painting by/from Joan Mitchell whose work I like very much.[3]

Here now till Tuesday or Wednesday when Berliner Ensemble at Bernhardt. Reading with loathing Die Mutter. Shall finish revision of Part II these next few days.[4]

I told "X" they shd. present Cioran and ask Bosquet for a text on him and still think this is well worth doing. He has just published a 4th book – collection of essays already published in NRF & elsewhere. A choice of passages from the Petit Traité and Tentation d'Exister wd. seem to me most indicated. The aphorismes are I think less interesting. I enclose cutting from last Thursday's Combat.[5]

Saw Geneviève Serreau yesterday. They are doing a special number on Malcolm Cowley [*for* Lowry] which I'll send you in due course.[6]

The mad idea for a play I inflicted on you in the Iles has taken root and the day I lost my papers I cd. think of nothing else. Quite unrealisable but shall have to have a shot at it when Pim is out of the way.

Tired tired and nerves alcoholized to rags and strange wish to work. To La Ferté now for usual bread cheese and carrots. Shall write again Monday at latest. Take care of yourself.

Love

Sam

ALS; 1 leaf, 2 sides; enclosure: Alain Bosquet, "Un prophète cynique: E. M. Cioran," *Combat*, 2 June 1960: 9; *env* to Mrs Barbara Bray, 121 Brighton Rd., Purley, Surrey, Angleterre; *pm* _-6-60, La Ferté-sous-Jouarre; TCD, MS 10948/1/88.

1 Two days later, SB responded:

> I have read again your essay and return it herewith. I like it very much but don't feel qualified to comment. Art is certainly the best there is for some of us and the nearest we ever get to anything. That's a long way from hypostatisation and I wouldn't venture any further myself. I'm too stupid to talk about and too far from any need of light or reality. You write out of some kind of nobility that I lack. The sentence beginning "To anyone who knows pain . . ." is absolutely true for me, and what do we do? (SB to Bray, 6 June 1960; TCD, MS 10948/1/89.)

Bray's essay to which SB refers has not been found.

2 The exhibition of works by Jean-Paul Riopelle at the Galerie Jacques Dubourg from 31 May to 21 June included recent paintings and sculptures. Henri Hayden's exhibition of gouaches was held at the Galerie Suillerot in June–July (*Arts, Spectacles* 1–7 June 1960: 9).

3 Joan Mitchell's painting did not have a title (20 in. × 24 in.); its current owner is not known (Edward Beckett to the editors, 24 and 25 July 2012).

4 Beginning on 7 June, the Berliner Ensemble performed Bertolt Brecht's *Der aufhaltsame Aufstieg des Arturo Ui* (*The Resistible Rise of Arturo Ui*), *Die Mutter* (*The Mother*), *Leben des Galilei* (*Life of Galileo*), and *Mutter Courage und ihre Kinder* (*Mother Courage*) in the Théâtre des Nations Festival. "Decided I couldn't face Berliner Ensemble consecutive evenings so shall go Wednesday only" (SB to Bray, 6 June 1960; TCD, MS 10948/1/89).

5 SB had last met Mary Hutchinson on 13 April 1960; she had asked him to suggest texts for *X, A Quarterly Review*. Although SB mentions E. M. Cioran's *Petit Traité*, Nicolas Cavaillès (editor of E. M. Cioran, *Œuvres*, Bibliothèque de la Pléiade [Paris: Gallimard, 2011]) suggests that SB probably intended *Précis de décomposition* (1949; *A Short History of Decay*). SB may have conflated "Traité" (treatise) with "Précis" (short treatise); "Cioran lui-même a parfois fait l'erreur" (Cioran himself sometimes made the mistake) (Nicolas Cavaillès to the editors, 14 August 2012).

Cioran's other works included *La Tentation d'exister* (1956; *The Temptation to Exist*) and a book of aphorisms: *Syllogismes de l'amertume* (1952; *All Gall is Divided: Gnomes and Apothegms*).

6 The special issue of *Les Lettres Nouvelles* on Malcolm Lowry would be no. 3, new series (July–August 1960).

BARBARA BRAY
PURLEY, SURREY

13.6.60 Paris

Dear Barbara

Thanks for your letter. I hasten to reply as God knows when next I shall get the chance. This is a terrible week here with people and it continues last. With people and Bd. St. Jacques. I got the keys today, the carpenter is at work and the painter will be soon. Alan Schneider is over and many another. I like him and am very glad to see him but it[']s all too much. He saw Pinter in London who sent nice messages to me. I wish I could nip over but see no chance of it.[1] I went to Die Mutter and left at the 1st opportunity. Unendurable. Even the Weigel. Am going again with Alan on Friday to Galileo. Didn't go to Arturo Ai (?), Suzanne walked one for me.[2] Haven't seen much of Pinget but hear he is working. Was getting on with nth revision before coming in to Paris. It will be the last in any case till free of stage. Unless I throw it all away. Think I'm kidding myself about the play. One long act possible, but not two, unless perhaps in disproportion of 75 and 15 minutes respectively. Have to try it I suppose. Looking over prison, hospitals and gardens to where the great are grinning up at the lid.[3] Delighted with Donald's success and prospects. I heard from Curtis Brown re television Godot. They now talk of 90 minutes and my request that Donald be invited to direct seems accepted.[4] Got an offer from Hollins University, Virginia (young ladies) of 10000 dollars for eight months 61–62. Wavered 24 hours, then preferred not.[5] KRAPP back at the Provincetown and still going strong[.] Nice for TCD.[6] Saw Wilkinson and received score of VOICES, very ponctuel. I think the word is – beyond me.[7] Shall be working this week with Mihalovici a[d]justing KRAPP where required – "Jesus Christ" instead of "Jesus" I suppose that kind of thing – or perhaps merely "Jaysus".[8] No further news of Cyril Cusack, but I believe it's announced July 1–4. Rather dread it.[9] Aim to get to Ussy this day week for a week but God knows. I agree the Cioran aphorisms are not up to much, but there are very good things in the Petit Traité and Tentation. – Wonder how you got on with Mary Hutchinson.

Love

Sam

ALS; 1 leaf, 2 sides; *env to* Mrs Barbara Bray, 121 Brighton Road, Purley, SURREY, Angleterre; *pm* 14–6–60, Paris; TCD, MS 10948/1/90.

1 Alan Schneider had seen Harold Pinter* (1930–2008) in London on 9 June; he had come to Paris on 12 June and would return to London on 18 June (WHS, Alan Schneider Collection, series 8, box 3).

2 Advertisements for the plays of Brecht gave their French titles, but the performances were in the language of the company (in this case in German), following the convention of the international festival until 1962 (Daniela Peslin, *Le Théâtre des Nations: Une aventure théâtrale à redécouvrir* [Paris: L'Harmattan, 2009] 28, 30–31, 73, 94). Brecht's wife Helene Weigel had acted the role of Pelagea Vlassova in *Die Mutter* in 1932. SB attended the performance on Wednesday, 8 June. He would attend *Galileo* on 17 June with Alan Schneider.

3 SB outlines the view looking north from the room that will be his study in the new apartment towards the Panthéon, where the great of France lie.

4 The BBC had requested television rights for presentation of *Waiting for Godot* in the *Clubs Theatre Play* series (60 minutes). SB responded to this request: "GODOT cannot be played in 60 minutes"; he added, "If we reach an agreement I should like Donald McWhinnie to be invited to direct" (SB to Margaret McLaren, Curtis Brown, 23 May 1960; GEU, MS 1221).

5 Professor Louis Rubin (1924–2013) of Hollins University in Roanoke, Virginia, had made the offer to SB in his letter of 2 June. SB declined: "I am greatly honoured by your generous proposal [. . .] I am quite unfitted for the position you have in mind" (SB to Rubin, 10 June 1960; NcU, Louis Decimus Rubin Papers, #3899).

6 The production of *Krapp's Last Tape* in New York: 6 April 1960, n. 5. Trinity College Dublin was the beneficiary of SB's royalties from this production.

7 Marc Wilkinson had brought the score of *Voices* with him when he met SB for lunch; SB wrote to Wilkinson on 12 June that the score, which had been forgotten, would be left for him with the concierge. William Colleran, Universal Edition London, had sent the score of *Voices* to SB on 2 June (SB to William Colleran, 8 June 1960; GEU, MS 1221).

8 In the final trilingual score of Mihalovici's *Krapp*, the word "Jésus" is preserved in the French, and "Jesus" in the English. In the German, "Cette voix! Jésus" becomes "Diese Stimme nein" (measures 226–227), and, where it occurs later, "Jésus" becomes "Mein Gott! " (measure 685) (Samuel Beckett and Marcel Mihalovici, *Krapp ou la dernière bande* [Paris: Heugel, 1961] 38, 109).

9 Cyril Cusack's *Krapp's Last Tape* was performed from 7 to 10 July as part of the Théâtre des Nations.

BARBARA BRAY
PURLEY, SURREY

4.7.60 Ussy

Dear Barbara

Thanks for your letter. You ask such difficult questions. I'm at the end of my explanations if they could ever be called that. You know what my position is and what my imperatives are - or do you really? You know also how fond I am of you and therefore how glad I wd. be to see you more often. All the answers are there - if you can find them. There's no good your looking to me for permissions or forbiddances - you won't get any. You can only be sure that whatever you decide to do I'll try and help you and that my ability to do so is necessarily and so far as I can see permanently restricted. Your living in Paris might improve matters or worsen them - I simply can't tell. If you simply arrange to come over more frequently it is unlikely that at each visit I shall be able to see as much of you as the last time. You can't ORGANIZE such things, just try and make the best of each situation as it arises. I can't write any more in this way.

I return to Paris tomorrow with this damn Irish presentation of KRAPP - hate the thought of it.[1] I can't revise the book much further. I'll type it out clean and give it to Lindon - or put it away in a drawer for the rainy day. I am reading Pinget's CLOPE in MS - very good. Last week continued work with Mihalovici on KRAPP. Like his music - what the piano can tell me - more and more. Should finish in a couple of séances. Vega is to make a record.[2] Hope to be back here this day week and for a good stretch to finish the work and work over the place now invaded by vegetation - autumn and summer. Feel myself going completely off the rails not that I was ever on any I suppose. Should like to see Rudin.[3] Forgive more now. Full of blood and screams, better go for a walk or dig a hole.

Love

Sam

ALS; 1 leaf, 2 sides; *env to* Mrs Barbara Bray, 121 Brighton Rd., Purley, Surrey, Angleterre; *pm* 5-7-60, Paris; TCD MS 10948/1/95.

1 Cyril Cusack's performance in *Krapp's Last Tape*: 13 June 1960, n. 9.

2 The proposed Vega recording seems not to have been made (Edward Beckett, William Dooley, and James Knowlson to the editors).

3 Bray's adaptation of Turgenev's *Rudin*: 29 January 1960, n. 1.

BARBARA BRAY
PURLEY, SURREY

Monday [11 July 1960] Ussy

Dear Barbara

Thanks for your note and letter. I got here yesterday in state of chassis.[1] Heavy week in Paris beginning with reception given for Cusack & Co. by Irish Ambassador who the next day sent me three bottles of 12 yr. old J. J.! Cusack is a good actor but his Krapp was quite unsatisfactory - no feeling for text, no direction to it. And only just saved by some queer presence and compulsion this kind of good actor has on the stage - but not saved. They have it after 3 acts of Shaw which further diminished its chances. I at least understand better than ever before which is saying something when and why its weakness, here and in my other plays, and made the new one seem quite impossible as planned, awful English this. I saw quite a lot of the company and found them pleasant in that forgotten Irish way that leaves you so dubious. At least better than Chauffard - in a way.[2] Another cousin musician hitherto unmet by name Walter also turned up from Venice and we had some time together - having a hard time.[3] Here now for usual week of which first days simply recuperating. Shall finish revision and start typing it out - then decide whether to give or withhold. Finished work with Mihalovici. Opening announced for Bielefeld in Feb. Vega want to make a record, music seems fine to me - but my text had to get it in the neck here and there.[4] Spoke to Robert on the phone this morning. He is very touched by your suggestion he might stay with you but says he has decided not to go over for the rehearsals. I read his new work again and think it the best thing he has done.[5] High coldish wind here today, rose as from the dead not unrefreshed at 11 a.m. but couldn't remain standing any length of time. New flat: two rooms finished and main carpentry done. Lift working with marvellous silence. Shall give notice soon now. We should be able to move in August. This day week driving S. to

Troyes to see her mother – infuriating old lady with all her teeth. Here I end this reel. Sorry I couldn't write before leaving Paris. I got up, went out, drove drank blattered and home at 2 a.m.

Love and to the children

Sam

Shall see about Equarrissage when I get back to Paris.[6]

ALS; 1 leaf, 2 sides; *env to* Mrs Barbara Bray, 121 Brighton Rd., Purley, Surrey, Angleterre; *pm* [12]–7–60, La Ferté-sous-Jouarre; TCD, MS 10948/1/96. *Dating*: postmark written by Barbara Bray on letter; 11 July was a Monday in 1960.

1 SB adopts the phrase from Sean O'Casey's *Juno and the Paycock*: "the whole worl's in a state of chassis!" ([London and New York: Samuel French, 1932] 16).

2 J. J. is John Jameson, an Irish whiskey. SB attended a party at the Irish Embassy on 5 July in honor of the Cyril Cusack productions of *La dernière bande* and George Bernard Shaw's *Le Héros et le soldat* (*Arms and the Man*). The Irish Ambassador to France from 1954 to 1960 was William Fay (1909–1969); his wife was the pianist Lillian Conolly.

Cyril Cusack's stage presence was acknowledged by Bertrand Poirot-Delpech ("L'Irlande au Théâtre des Nations," *Le Monde* 9 July 1960: 13). He received high praise from French critics who compared his performance to Chauffard's as Krapp. Morvan Lebesque wrote in *Carrefour*: "la mise en scène de M. Cusack est de loin supérieure à celle de M. Roger Blin ... parce que M. Cusack a compris cette chose élémentaire: qu'il fallait *deux voix* et non pas une seule" ("Des soirées qui se suivent ... et ne se ressemblent pas," 13 July 1960: 28). (the production of M. Cusack is far better than that of M. Roger Blin ... because M. Cusack captured this elementary thing: that there must be two voices and not just one). The Cusack Company, which produced the two plays, included Shelagh Richards (1903–1985), Maureen Cusack (1945–1977), Ann O'Dwyer, Godfrey Quigley (1923–1994), P. G. Stephens, Paul Farren, and Shamus Locke.

3 Walter Beckett (1914–1996) was teaching English at the Scuola Navale in Venice while composing vocal and orchestral adaptations of Irish music for Radio Éireann; he had published *Liszt* (1956) and worked with Humphrey Searle on *Ballet Music: An Introduction* (1958). In October 1960, Walter Beckett would present his proposal for a book, *The Music of Ireland*, to John Calder for his consideration.

4 The operatic premiere of Mihalovici's *Krapp ou La dernière bande* would take place at the Städtische Bühnen in Bielefeld, Germany, on 25 February 1961.

5 Bray produced SB's translation, *The Old Tune*, of Pinget's *La Manivelle*, for the BBC Third Programme; the play was to be rehearsed and recorded on 24 and 25 July. SB has been reading Pinget's *Clope au dossier* (SB to Barbara Bray, 4 July 1960; TCD, MS 10948/1/95).

6 Boris Vian's play *L'Equarrissage pour tous* (Paris: Toutain, 1950) (see 18 February 1960, n. 5). SB's note is added to the back of the envelope.

JOHN CALDER
JOHN CALDER (PUBLISHER) LTD., LONDON

July 24th 1960 | 6 Rue des Favorites
Paris 15me

Dear John

Thanks for your letter of July 15th.[1]

I think it is preferable to exclude French poems from your edition and confine it to those written in English and the few - without original text - translated from the French. Apart from my preferring it that way there is the question of Minuit. I have always said to Jérôme Lindon that I did not want an edition of the French poems and he would not understand my letting them appear with you and not with him. Already he did not much relish their being published by Limes. But there my hand was forced more or less, I'll tell you in what circumstances when next we meet. I hope you will not be too disappointed about this. There will be no further translations of French poems, so you can carry on with the texts you have. I shall need proofs needless to say.[2]

Sorry to hear about the latest Dublin bosthoonery. Perhaps MOLLOY was banned at some stage - or MALONE, I don't remember.[3]

The new work should be finished next month - ended rather. Not sure yet whether I'll give it to Minuit or put it away in a drawer.

Looking forward to seeing you in September, if not before.

Yours
s/ Sam

TLS; 1 leaf, 1 side; *datestamped* 27.JUL.1960; TxU, Beckett Collection, 8.1.

1 John Calder had proposed "an edition of the collected poems, giving the French poems that are translated in the original and English on facing pages, with the untranslated poems given in a special section" (John Calder to SB, 15 July 1960; InU, C&B, Beckett).

2 SB's French poems had been published in *Gedichte*, in a trilingual edition by Limes Verlag. SB's letter to Calder of 7 July enclosed "4 poems translated from the French and one written in English (St-Lô) which does not figure in the Limes edition" (InU, C&B, Beckett). The four translations were "Dieppe," "my way is in the sand flowing," "what would I do without this world faceless incurious," and "I would like my love to die"; these were published as "Quatre Poèmes" in both French and English

in *Poems in English* (London: John Calder, 1961) 45–53. The three poems following "Dieppe" had been published in both languages when they first appeared in *Transition Forty-Eight* no. 2 (June 1948) 96–97.

3 Calder had written: "I am sorry to tell you that 6 copies of the Trilogy have just been seized from Hanna's Bookshop by the Police. I shall lodge a protest in the appropriate quarter." *More Pricks Than Kicks*, *Watt*, *Molloy*, and *Malone Dies* had been banned previously in Ireland (see 7 May 1936, n. 3; SB to Alan Simpson, 17 November 1953, n. 1; 2 February 1956, n. 4).

As Robert Pinget recorded in his journal entry of 25 July 1960, SB was far from indifferent to this further act of censorship:

> Me parle longuement à propos de la saisie récente des 3 romans à Dublin, de l'erreur qu'il a faite en renouant des relations d'amitié avec le théâtre dublinois qui lui demandait l'option sur toutes ses pièces. Parlons de la duplicité des Irlandais, aimables par devant et ennemis par derrière. Sam souffre beaucoup de tout ça. Se laisse toujours prendre par les sentiments. Suzanne lui dit de faire une croix définitive sur son pays. (Doucet, unclassified Pinget Collection, "Notre ami Samuel Beckett," 42.) (Talks at some length to me about the recent confiscation of the 3 novels in Dublin, the mistake he made in going back to friendly dealings with the Dublin theatre that was asking for an option on all his plays. We talk about the duplicity of the Irish, all niceness on the outside and enemies within. Sam takes all this very badly. Always gets caught by his feelings. Suzanne tells him to give up on his country for good.)

JACOBA VAN VELDE
AMSTERDAM

2.8.60 Paris

Chère Tonny

Merci de votre lettre et du livre bien arrivé cette fois. J'espère qu'il marche bien à N.Y.[1]

Je viens de terminer le mien – de l'arrêter plutôt. Il n'est pas beau.

Déjeuné avec Bram tout seul. Quoi qu'il ait pu faire je l'aimerai toujours beaucoup.[2]

Je suis creux comme un vieux radis. J'aimerais passer 2 mois à creuser des trous à la campagne en remplissant chacun au fur et à mesure avec la terre obtenue du suivant.

Deux cafards se rencontrent. Le premier: Ça ne va pas? Le deuxième: J'ai l'homme.[3]

A bientôt j'espère. Amitiés à Fritz.
Affectueusement
Sam

ALS; 1 leaf, 1 side; BNF, 19794/70.

2.8.60 Paris

Dear Tonny

Thank you for your letter and for the book, which did get here this time. I hope it's doing well in NY.[1]

I have just finished mine. Stopped it, rather. It is no beauty.

Had lunch with Bram on his own. Whatever he may have done, I shall always be fond of him.[2]

I am as hollow as an old radish. I would like to spend two months in the country digging holes, filling up each one as I go with the earth from the next one.

One louse meets another louse. The first says: "Anything wrong?" The second: "I'm feeling man-y."[3]

Till soon I hope. Best to Fritz.
Love
Sam

1 SB had written to Van Velde: "Je n'ai pas reçu l'édition américaine de votre livre. J'aimerais l'avoir." (7 July 1960; BNF, 19794/69.) (I haven't received the American edition of your book. I'd like to have it.) Simon and Schuster had published the American edition of Van Velde's novel *De grote zaal*, *The Big Ward* (translator unacknowledged); it was not the same as the earlier English edition, translated by Ellen and Roy Hulbert, which had been published in London by Neville Spearman in 1955.

2 Also in his letter of 7 July, SB had written to Jacoba van Velde about her brother:

> Il a l'air bien - un peu perdu et irréel. J'ai vu le nouvel appartement (de Jacques) - superbe. Il m'a dit qu'il avait reçu votre lettre mais qu'il ne peut pas écrire. Je ne sais pas qui vous a envoyé l'argent. Bram n'a pas beaucoup travaillé. Jacques dit qu'il ne s'est pas remis de la mort de Marthe, qu'il erre sans but. Je vais essayer de le voir davantage. (BNF, 19794/69.) (He seems all right: a bit lost, unreal. I've seen the superb new flat (Jacques's). He told me that he had received your letter, but he can't write. I don't know who sent you the money. Bram has not been doing much work. Jacques says that he hasn't got over Marthe's death, that he's drifting aimlessly. I'm going to try to see more of him.)

3 SB employs an almost untranslatable joke: "un cafard" is a "cockroach"; colloquially, "avoir le cafard" means "to feel low, depressed." A man (un homme) might say "J'ai le cafard"; SB's joke inverts this, with a "cafard" saying "j'ai l'homme."

BARBARA BRAY
PURLEY, SURREY

4.8.60 Ussy

Dear Barbara

A line before I get involved again in the Paris confusion – that is this afternoon. I have been here for about a week working like mad and finished the book (revision and typing) yesterday. I don't know what to think of it and hope to think of it no more. It could be pushed much further – but mechanically only. I don't think I can write at it any more. Thanks for LISTENER. The physicists didn't help me – most of it I couldn't follow.[1] It is good new[s] that the Montmartre studio is in the bag. Perhaps you wd. bring a tape of O. T. I have another I want to hear – N.Y. Davis KRAPP.[2] Went to S[t]-J. not exactly coming to a boil but in that direction. Suzanne working on it like mad in Paris – stimulating wilting painters plumbers etc. Shall start moving books soon.[3] What I shd. like now is a couple of months of nothing but pottering in the open air, cleaning up the grass etc., digging holes for winter plantation. Hope to get there somehow. Sorry to inflict another possible title on you: POUSSE TIRE. The full phrase repeated ad nauseam throughout is: "Demi-flanc gauche jambe droite bras droit pousse tire plat ventre éjaculations muettes demi-flanc droit jambe gauche bras gauche pousse tire plat ventre éjaculations muettes dix mètres quinze mètres halte" or similar. Grateful for a view.[4]

Marvellous day at last when I have to go. Went for a walk in the amica silentia of her chastehood with I think Jupiter in attendance – last night or this morning 1 a.m. Sat on a bench and gaped across the plain to the faint Paris glow.[5] Lawn after the rain covered with young woodpeckers grazing like mad – lovely gay birds with a dead straight beak about 3" long and a tuft. Or are they hoopoes? Woodpeckers, I saw the mother having a brief eye on them "L'histoire que j'avais la naturelle."[6]

Delighted at prospect of seeing you so soon. Till then take care of yourself.

Love
Sam

ALS; 1 leaf, 2 sides; *env to* Mrs Barbara Bray, 121 Brighton Road, Purley, Surrey, Angleterre; *pm* 4–8–60, Paris; TCD, MS 10948/1/101.

1 In celebration of the tercentenary of The Royal Society, *The Listener* published several presentations on the history of the society and a series of talks entitled "Prospects of Science." The first four were by physicists: A. B. Pippard, "The Quantum World," and Denys H. Wilkinson, "Matter and Sub-Matter" (64.1634 [21 July 1960] 92–96); A. R. Ubbelohde, "The Solid State," and R. Hanbury Brown, "The New Astronomy" (64.1635 [28 July 1960] 152–156).

2 SB asked Bray to bring the tape recording of *The Old Tune* which she had directed for the BBC Third Programme. Richard Barr, a producer of *Krapp's Last Tape* with Donald Davis in New York, had sent SB a tape recording of that production (SB to Barr, 30 July 1960; NyPL, Billy Rose, Barr–Wilder Collection Box 36, F. 15).

3 SB's new apartment at 38 Boulevard Saint-Jacques.

4 SB proposes to use "pousse tire" (push pull) as a title. The phrase is used twenty-nine times in *Comment c'est*. From the time of this letter, SB would continue to make changes to the text. The passage on p. 63 of the 1961 Minuit edition comes closest to SB's quotation (Grove, 1964, 40).

5 SB alludes to W. B. Yeats's prose work "Per Amica Silentia Lunae" in the eponymous collection (1918). Jupiter was visible in the midnight sky at this date.

6 The phrase "l'histoire que j'avais la naturelle" occurs in *Comment c'est* (Minuit, 1961, 20); in *How It Is*, this phrase becomes "the history I knew my God the natural" (Grove, 1964, 15).

ALAN SCHNEIDER
NEW YORK

4.8.60 Ussy

Dear Alan

The Bartok record is superb and we are delighted to have it. All our thanks. As you will see from enclosed Suzanne wrote at once, but I held it up hoping to hear from you.[1] I suppose you have been up to your eyes with M FOR M. I hope all went well.[2] Cusack's KRAPP was very disappointing, no feeling for the thing or the wrong feeling, under-acted out of existence, recording inaudible, synchronisation unspeakable, direction execrable when there was any. All the more disappointing as he is a remarkable actor with great presence and properly handled could have been excellent. The Mihalovici opera is finished and as far as I can judge a very fine job. Barr very kindly send [sic] me a tape (entire play recorded live). I have not yet had a chance of hearing it.[3] I had lunch with Driver, very pleasant and understanding.[4] Fed up as you can imagine with all this NTA botheration. Won't sign anything till things are clarified and notably Myerberg's obstructions. Unless you can do it exactly as you wish we'll drop it altogether. The Big Banana film was obviously out of the question, even with controls and guarantees it would have been a disaster. I have told Curtis Brown, who urged me to accept, that I shall never allow such a film to be made and asked him to send me a copy of Myerberg's GODOT contract which I have never seen and which takes on a more and more mythical air.[5] I finished my still titleless book last night (revision and typing) at last and think now I can send it forth. I have not been able to give much thought or none to give to the play we talked about. I shall start stalking it soon. I should like to know what exactly he has in those pockets – what he had.[6]

It was good seeing so much of you when you were here and may it not be too long before you are over again.[7]

Bd St-Jacques not yet ready to enshrine us. Defaulting carpenters painters plumbers and like moguls.

Love to Jean and the children.

Yours ever

s/ SAM

TLS; 1 leaf, 1 side; no enclosure from Suzanne Dumesnil-Deschevaux is with this letter; Burns Library, Samuel Beckett Collection, SB-AS.

1 The recording of music composed by Béla Bartók is not known.

2 Alan Schneider directed *Measure for Measure*, New York Shakespeare Festival, Central Park, which had opened on 25 July.

3 Richard Barr had sent SB a tape of *Krapp's Last Tape* directed by Schneider.

4 Tom Faw Driver (b. 1925) taught Theatre, Poetry, and Theology at Union Theological Seminary; Driver wrote about the meeting, where SB is reported to have said: "To find a form that accommodates the mess, that is the task of the artist now" ("Beckett at the Madeleine," *Columbia University Forum* 4.3 [Summer 1961] 23).

5 National Telefilm Associates (NTA) proposed to film and televise *Waiting for Godot* in their *Play of the Week* series; SB agreed "on condition that A Schneider direct the production and be given general responsibility for it" (SB to Margaret McLaren, Curtis Brown, 29 January 1960; GEU, MS 1221). Michael Myerberg, who held American production and film rights, objected to the NTA contract, not least because he had received an offer from Bert Lahr to star in a film of *Godot* with Paramount Pictures. Although Curtis Brown advised SB to accept the far more lucrative film contract, SB declined, explaining that the decision was "imposed on me by the necessity of protecting my work." (15 July 1960; Curtis Brown. SB to Curtis Brown, 23 July 1960; TLcc, GEU, MS 1221, and CUSD, MSS 130/2/3.)

6 SB here uses a masculine pronoun and speaks of "pockets" because his original thought was that the main figure in the play was male.

7 Schneider had been in Paris in June (see 13 June 1960, n. 2).

ELLISEVA SAYERS
NEW YORK

7.8.60 Paris

Dear Elliseva

Thanks for your letters. Glad to know you are safe home and pleased with your jaunt.[1]

Cusack's KRAPP was very disappointing. He received the Festival award for the best actor. This must have referred to his performance in Arms & The Man. I gave him your greetings and he lit up all over.[2]

I have just finished my book after 18 months of intermittent struggle and feel relieved and lost as a result. I should like to spend 2 months digging deep holes in the ground filling each one as the work proceeds with the earth provided by the next.[3]

I'm a poor fist at letter writing too and shall therefore now close saying how much I enjoyed seeing you again far from 38 and in the city of cities.[4]

If you see Mr Palmer give him my kind regards.[5]

All the best.

Yours

Sam. Beckett

ALS; 1 leaf, 1 side; Sayers Collection; photocopy, TCD, MS 11331/2/5.

1 Elliseva Sayers (1912–2007) had been one of SB's students and an honors graduate of Trinity College Dublin (1934). As she wrote: "I had been an awed pupil at TCD trying to fathom his diffuse analysis of Marcel Proust. He was handsome, distant, a reluctant teacher trying to find himself." She admitted to SB that "I did not understand a word" of his lectures. SB's response, "delivered with a grin":

> Neither did I . . . I had read up on the subject the night before. I was terrified . . . That, and having to go on talking for half an hour or longer. I was hoping nobody would understand so I continued non-stop to ward off questions. I couldn't wait to bolt. ("The Irish Mavericks," *The World of Hibernia* 1.2 [Autumn 1995] 124–125.)

Sayers wrote for Irish and British papers (*The Irish Times*, the *Dublin Evening Mail*, the *Manchester Daily Express*, and *The Daily Mail*) until after the War; she then moved to New York, where her writing appeared in *The Saturday Evening Post*, *Connoisseur*, and *The New York Times Magazine*, and where she established a public relations firm.

Sayers described her first meeting in Paris with SB as the "highlight of a dazzling wine-tasting trip" to France and Switzerland. "He introduced me to a Blanc de Blancs champagne and excellent food at the Closerie des Lilas. Then we went – he drove his 'deux-chevaux' – to an outdoor café on the Champs-Elysées and had a cognac and coffee." (Elliseva Sayers to the editors, 27 August 1992.)

2 Cyril Cusack was awarded Best Actor for *Arms and the Man* in the Théâtre des Nations ("Le challenge 1960 au Berliner Ensemble," *Les Lettres Françaises*, 834 [21–27 July 1960] 6).

3 Sayers responded to SB's letter: "I thought it difficult to write to you. But it was much more difficult to read your letter to me. I tried everything to decipher it, using mirrors, reading it upside down. Here and there a sentence stood out. The rest is a blur." (Sayers, "The Irish Mavericks," 125.)

4 SB refers to his rooms at Trinity College Dublin, in 39 New Square, but writes "38," the number of his new apartment, then under construction, on Boulevard Saint-Jacques.

5 Possibly James Edward Palmer (b. 1935), then Fiction Editor of *Cosmopolitan* in New York (Elliseva Sayers to the editors, 25 January 1999).

ROBERT PINGET
PARIS

11.8.60 Ussy

Cher Robert

Merci de ta gentille lettre. J'ai bien compris ta réaction. C'est celle que je craignais, ce qui m'a un peu abattu sur le moment. Je te suis reconnaissant d'avoir été si franc. C'est ça l'amitié.[1] Ton titre est bien, je vais y réfléchir.[2] Je crois que cette fois je me suis à peu près coupé la gorge enfin. J'hésite encore à le rendre public. Je serai à Paris à partir de mardi prochain, le coeur demeurant ici. A très bientôt donc, cher Robert, et encore merci.

Amitiés

Sam

ALS; 1 leaf, 1 side; Burns Library, Samuel Beckett Collection, SB-RP.

11.8.60 Ussy

Dear Robert

Thank you for your nice letter. I did understand your reaction. It is the one that I feared, which was a bit of a blow on the moment. I am grateful to you for being so frank. That is friendship.[1] Your title is good; I'll think some more about it.[2] I believe that this time I have finally just about cut my throat. I still hesitate about making it public. I shall be in Paris from Tuesday next, my heart still here.

Till very soon, Robert, old friend, and thank you again.

All best

Sam

1 SB is responding to Pinget's written reaction to the as yet untitled *Comment c'est* (see 20 May 1960, n. 2). In his memoir, Pinget describes his response, and SB's reaction to his response, at some length. First he describes visiting SB (on 6 August) to give him back the manuscript:

> Suis allé hier rendre à Sam le ms qu'il m'avait passé trois jours avant pour le lire. J'appréhendais beaucoup de devoir donner mon avis. Le texte est si difficile qu'il demande à être relu plusieurs fois. Je n'avais pas le droit d'être violemment contre puisqu'il s'agit sûrement d'une chose de la plus haute importance. Il m'a reçu avec un curieux air angoissé. Attendait probablement mon jugement. Je n'ai fait ni une ni deux et lui ai dit que c'était trop difficile à juger après une première lecture. Il paraissait surpris que ce soit si difficile car dit-il il a fait son possible pour être compris. La lumière ne peut venir que par petites trouées dans tout ce noir et cette boue. Suzanne était d'accord avec moi et m'a d'ailleurs, ensuite, félicité de lui avoir parlé sur ce ton plutôt que de lui dire d'emblée c'est extraordinaire. Je lui indiquai quelques fautes de frappe, tout ce que je pouvais faire. Je lui rappelle que lui-même lorsqu'il y travaillait m'avait dit que ce serait illisible. Il me reprend disant j'ai dit imbuvable. Toute la différence est là! Il m'offre un whisky, puis un second. Je lui dis qu'il me doit bien ça après m'avoir mis à une telle épreuve avec son texte. J'avais chialé en le lisant, de rage et de dépit. Dans la troisième partie un certain lyrisme se dégage de ces nombres. Me dit que selon lui c'est la partie la plus faible. Je suis d'accord, mais on y respire mieux. Le halètement des deux premières est insupportable. Sam dit

> qu'il a rêvé la nuit d'avant que je lui disais lui parlant de son livre que c'était une énormité japonaise! Appréhendait donc en quelque sorte mon jugement. Cela est bien troublant pour moi. (Doucet, unclassified Pinget Collection, "Notre ami Samuel Beckett," 43–44.) (Yesterday went to hand back to Sam the ms. he'd given me three days before to read. I was dreading having to give my opinion. The text is so difficult that it requires several re-readings. I had no right to be violently against, since what is at issue is something of the highest importance. He greeted me with an odd, deeply troubled look. Was probably waiting for my judgement. I made no bones about it and told him that it was too difficult for me to judge after a first reading. He seemed surprised that it should be difficult for, he said, he had done everything he could to be understood. Light can only come in through tiny cracks in all this darkness and this mud. Suzanne agreed with me, and indeed later on congratulated me on having taken this tone rather than blurting out it's extraordinary. I pointed out a few typos, all I could do. I remind him that he himself, when he was working on it, had told me that it would be unreadable. He takes me up on this, saying "I said unpalatable". There's a world of difference! He offers me a whisky, then another. I tell him he owes me nothing less after putting me through such a test with his text. I had blubbed as I read, from fury and pique. In the third part a certain lyrical quality emanates from these rhythmic fragments. Tells me that for him this is the weakest part. I agree, but one breathes more easily in it. The gasping in the first two parts is unbearable. Sam said that he had dreamt the night before that I was saying, as I talked to him about his book, that it was a "Japanese enormity"! So was rather dreading my judgement. This is very disturbing to me.)

In his entry for 10 August Pinget writes:

> Après-midi avec Suzanne. Me dit la réaction de Sam à mon verdict. Dans sa fureur et sa déception a dit que j'avais un jugement de concierge. Un jugement moral. J'aurais dû juger le texte en spécialiste, techniquement. Je ne reviens pas de cette réaction. Comment s'attacher à la technique avant de s'attacher au fond? Non je n'en reviens pas. Suzanne se croit obligée de me faire tout un développement sur les faiblesses de Sam, que je l'aime trop, qu'il ne faut pas s'attacher à lui qui ne s'attache à personne etc. De retour chez moi j'écris une lettre à Sam à Ussy, une sorte d'excuse de n'avoir pas compris. (Doucet, unclassified Pinget Collection, "Notre ami Samuel Beckett," 45.) (Afternoon with Suzanne. Tells me Sam's reaction to my verdict. In his fury and disappointment said I had the judgement of a concierge. A moral judgement. I should have been judging the text as a specialist, technically. I can't get over this reaction. How can you get involved in the technical before you've got involved in the main matter? No, I can't get over it. Suzanne feels she has to do a whole number on Sam's weaknesses, that I'm too fond of him, that I shouldn't get attached to this man who doesn't get attached to anyone, etc. Back home I write a letter to Sam in Ussy, a sort of apology for not having understood.)

It is to this letter from Pinget that SB is responding.

2 In his memoir Pinget elaborates: "Je lui propose en outre un titre puisqu'il en cherche un. I II III" (Doucet, unclassified Pinget Collection, "Notre ami Samuel Beckett," 45) (I also propose a title since he's looking for one. I II III).

HAROLD PINTER
LONDON

August 18th 1960

6 Rue des Favorites
Paris 15me

Dear Harold Pinter

Many thanks for your letter and for THE CARETAKER which I have read with much pleasure and am now reading again. I am so glad to know of its great success in London and wish I could have seen it.[1] In French its chances will be lessened a little, but I think it should do well nevertheless. I am very touched by what you say of my work and look forward to meeting you when you are here. If in the meantime I can be of any service to you do not hesitate to call on me.

Yours sincerely
s/ Sam. Beckett

TLS; 1 leaf, 1 side; BL, Add MS 88880/7/2/2.

9. Harold Pinter

1 Donald McWhinnie's production of *The Caretaker* had received accolades: "McWhinnie has calculated every pause, every inflexion to the last degree, and is finely served by his cast" ("A Slight Play that Pleases and Dazes," *The Times* 28 April 1960: 6).

KAY BOYLE
ROWAYTON, CONNECTICUT

August 29th 1960

6 Rue des Favorites
Paris 15me

Dear Kay

Thanks for your letter. You must decide for yourself whether to lecture on me or not. All this exegesis in terms of Joyce seems to me beside the point and indeed misleading, but if that's how you see it that's how you must do it, it is no business of mine.[1] Belacqua for me is no more than a kind of fetish. In the work I have just finished he appears "basculé sur le côté, las d'attendre, oublié des coeurs où vit la grâce" (cor che in grazia vive), and I hope that's the end of him.[2] I have no unpublished essays or other material that could be of any help to you. Go ahead and do it your own way, if you do it at all, whether I agree or disagree with what you say is of no importance. Sorry to be of so little use.

All the best always.

Yours ever

s/ Sam

TLS; 1 leaf, 1 side; T *env to* Kay Boyle, Greycote, 98 Wilson Avenue, Rowayton, Conn., USA; *pm* 29-8-60, Paris; TxU, Beckett Collection, 8.3.

1 Boyle had given a lecture at the University of Delaware, "Samuel Beckett and the Tradition of Loneliness," which was predicated on a resemblance between SB and Belacqua (see 12 July 1957, n. 1). A later essay, "All Mankind is Us," presents her memory of meeting SB in 1930, and his mention then of Virgil in Dante's *Inferno* (not Belacqua) (Ruby Cohn, ed., *Samuel Beckett: A Collection of Criticism*, [New York: McGraw-Hill, 1975] 15–19).

2 In a letter of 12 April 1958, SB had reminded Boyle of his abiding interest in Dante, evoking the opening of his story "Dante and the Lobster" as he informed her: "Have been in the moon canto again with no better success than 30 (odd) years ago. Piccoletta barca." (TxU, Beckett.) In *Comment c'est*, SB writes: "la tête minuscule près des

genoux enroulé autour du sac Belacqua basculé sur le côté las d'attendre oublié des cœurs où vit la grâce endormi" ([Paris: Editions de Minuit, 1961] 37). In SB's translation this becomes: "the tiny head near the knees curled round the sack Belacqua fallen over on his side tired of waiting forgotten of the hearts where grace abides asleep" (*How It Is* [Grove Press, 1961] 24). For a different assessment of the importance to SB of Dante's figure of Belacqua (whom SB cites here from Dante's *Purgatorio*, IV.134), see 21 April 1958 to A. J. Leventhal. Further on Belacqua, see C. J. Ackerley and S. E. Gontarski, ed., *The Grove Companion to Samuel Beckett: A Reader's Guide to His Works, Life, and Thought* (New York: Grove Press, 2004) 46–48.

BARBARA BRAY
PURLEY, SURREY

Wednesday [21 September 1960] Paris

Dear Barbara

Stopping in Paris on my way back to Ussy to write to you and get the letter off in the city. Last days here have been full and it is the usual upwing flight back to a few of quiet. Rosset has been here on his way to Frankfurt Fair and will be back next week. Dick Seaver also with whom I worked a few hours yesterday afternoon on his translation of L'Expulsé.[1] Your old friend Jake Schwartz announces himself for end of month, clamouring for Mss. I gave book to Lindon and he is warm about it, brief and warm. I shall probably call it TOUT BAS DES BRIBES or TOUT BAS tout court. Will probably be "out" early December.[2] Writing worse than usual because on glass top of café table with which I am more familiar in other ways. Bd. St. Jacques not yet finished painted, awful English. But hot water on tap already. Shall probably go to Cluny (300 km.) for a couple of days end of next week.[3] Grand to hear of Donald's TV success, wish to God I had something to offer him.[4] Schneider wrote from London, he sounded weary after his NTA TV production of Godot and his battle with Burgess Meredith and Zero Mostel.[5] Money still pouring in to TCD from KRAPP. Faced now with choice of translating (Textes pr. 0. and Pseudo-Pim) or setting about play in which language. Had dinner with TCD chair of English on verge of retirement and shaky, but enjoying his Brouilly and marc chez Marius. He had news of Con who wd. have come over but for his sundry obligations in Dublin (theatre & cinema).[6] Hear that Alan Simpson is getting out and going to London. Rather a relief to me, won't need now to let my plays be done there.[7] To pin any kind of flag to this rotten old mast seems to me grand folly – but I know there's no good saying that again. Adorno sent me his Mahler and Mayoux his Vivants Piliers in which he lends sympathetic ear to my confuses paroles.[8] From one Martin Esslin today his chapter on my plays from his book on the "Theatre of the Absurd" in which he deals also with Ionesco, Adamov, Genet, Pinter, Simpson and others. Have not read it yet apart from usual liminal reference to my right hand bowling, left hand batting and scrum halfing – the popular oaf. This I know makes all clear and Pim mud = Portora playing fields.[9] No more now.

Love
Sam

ALS; 1 leaf, 2 sides; *env to* M$^{\underline{rs}}$ Barbara Bray, 121 Brighton Rd., Purley, Surrey, Angleterre; *pm* 21–9–60, Paris; TCD, MS 10948/1/111. *Dating*: from pm.

1 SB worked with Richard Seaver on the English translation of "L'Expulsé" (SB to Barbara Bray, [14 September 1960]; TCD, MS 10948/1/109.

2 In his memoir entry for 17 August, Robert Pinget wrote about his conversation with SB concerning the title:

> Ensuite me parle de mon titre pour son livre. I II III. Le trouve trop intellectuel. Il faut mettre l'accent sur la désarticulation du langage. Ce sont des bribes. Lindon aime beaucoup du reste ce terme de bribes et voudrait le mettre en sous-titre (comme on met nouvelles ou roman), le titre choisi par lui, d'accord avec Sam étant Tout bas. Je dis que je n'aime pas, ou plutôt je le répète. Je voudrais qu'il change. (Doucet, unclassified Pinget Collection, "Notre ami Samuel Beckett," 46.) (Then talks to me about my title for his book. I II III. Finds it too intellectual. The emphasis must be on the disconnectedness of the language. These are bits and pieces. Lindon, actually, greatly likes the term "bits and pieces", and would like to put it in as sub-title (as one puts "short stories", or "novel"), the title chosen by him, in agreement with Sam, being *Tout bas*. I tell him, or rather I repeat that I don't like it. I would want him to change.)

3 SB and Suzanne had been invited by Marthe Gautier to join her in Cluny (Saône-et-Loire, Burgundy) where she was on holiday (SB to Barbara Bray, 27 September 1960; TCD, MS 10904/1/112).

4 Donald McWhinnie had directed the television production *Without the Grail* by Giles Cooper (1918–1966). The reviewer praised McWhinnie's "always inventive use of sound to create atmosphere and suspense," and noted that McWhinnie's television

production exhibited "a finely judged control of tempo and a clever exploitation of the visual symbolism" ("Effective Transfer from Sound to Vision," *The Times* 14 September 1960: 13).

5 Burgess Meredith (1907–1997) and Zero Mostel (1915–1977) played Vladimir and Estragon in the NTA television production of *Waiting for Godot*. Before they were cast, Schneider had to struggle with the NTA producers who had proposed Gene Rayburn (1908–1999) and Dee Finch (1918–1983), a pair of "early-morning radio personalities," and then film and television stars "Bob Hope and Jack Benny, Laurel and Hardy, Sid Caesar, Milton Berle" (Schneider, *Entrances*, 281–282; Beckett and Schneider, *No Author Better Served*, 73). For the first time, Schneider was his own cameraman.

6 SB had invited H. O. White to dine with him on 15 September at Le Petit Marius, 6 Avenue George V, Paris 8 (SB to H. O. White, 9 September 1960; TCD, MS 3777/20). Brouilly is one of the Beaujolais crus. From 22 June to 21 December, Con Leventhal presented a weekly review radio program on RTE (Dublin), *Plays of Stage and Radio*.

7 Alan Simpson left Dublin to direct at the Theatre Royal, Stratford East, London.

8 Theodor Adorno, *Mahler: Eine musikalische Physiognomik* (1960). Jean-Jacques Mayoux's *Vivants piliers: le roman anglo-saxon et les symboles* includes the chapter "Samuel Beckett et l'univers parodique" (Paris: Les Lettres Nouvelles, 1960, 271–291). SB cites "confuses paroles" (confused words) from Baudelaire's poem "Correspondances" in *Les Fleurs du Mal*: "La nature est un temple où de vivants piliers / Laissent parfois sortir de confuses paroles" ("The pillars of Nature's temple are alive / and sometimes yield perplexing messages") (*Œuvres complètes*, I, ed. Claude Pichois and Jean Ziegler, Bibliothèque de la Pléiade [Paris: Gallimard, 1975–1976] 11; *Les Fleurs du Mal: The Complete Text of The Flowers of Evil*, tr. Richard Howard [Boston: David R. Godine, 1982] 15).

9 With his letter of 18 September, Martin Esslin* (1918–2002) had sent a draft of his chapter on SB (Private Collection). Here Esslin describes SB as: "a popular and brilliant scholar [who] also excelled at games, batting left-handed and bowling right at cricket, and playing scrum half at Rugger" (*The Theatre of the Absurd* [London: Eyre and Spottiswoode, 1961; rpt. Garden City, NY: Anchor Books, Doubleday, 1961] 1–2).

BARBARA BRAY
PURLEY, SURREY

1.10.60 Paris

Dear Barbara

Thanks for your letter which I found waiting for me here. This will be just another of my usual, written in tiredness and depression or is it dejection and wishing I were back in Ussy. Rosset and Seaver have gone back, saw something of them.[1] Had an evening with Schwartz and his Irish wife and of course promised him the latest MS. already promised to Fletcher.[2] Had lunch today with Robert off to marry his sister in

Geneva tomorrow. He doesn't much like TOUT BAS. Moi non plus.[3] No talk of anything here but the Jeanson trial and the Manifesto of the 121. If I weren't a foreigner I suppose I'd be in it.[4] Claude Simon's new book just out, but haven't begun it. Terrifyingly abundant.[5] Finished (very roughly) L'Expulsé with Seaver, but of course will have to go through it all again. Lunched with Christopher Logue on his way to Ghent to see his friend Claus and talking about his Antigone due soon at the Royal Court.[6] Painters out of St. Jacques at last tomorrow or the next, then cleaning and carpets. Hope nevertheless to get back to Ussy about Wed. for a few days. Perhaps try and get down some of the play but probably nothing. Mow some more grass, lie on the bed and read German, Fontane & Claudius. Read the former's IRRUNGEN WIRRUNGEN, not as good as Effie, but good, marvellous things.[7] Almost daily now demands for musical rights latest from a friend of Albee wanting to operatize KRAPP and from another American to set for string quartet and voice from "picking gooseberries" to end of speech.[8] Read Robert's new play. Very good, full of 1st rate theatre, 3 acts, entitled La Gare de l'Aube, but I shd. think he'll find something better. Manivelle-Old Tune due out next week, if the Editions don't go sky high before.[9] Saw Bram van Velde and his Amsterdam sister last night, he has a 2 years contract with Knoedler, big show here next May, then N.Y. following October. Big thing financially. He paid for dinner for 5 upstairs chez Marius, lashings of Brouilly and pancakes.[10] Dining this evening with the Hayden.[11] Despairing conviviality. Drink to get through the evening. Always went to the dogs, but never quite like this.

Love

S

ALI; 1 leaf, 2 sides; *env to* Mrs Barbara Bray, 121 Brighton Rd., Purley, Surrey, Angleterre; *pm* 3-10-60, Paris; TCD, MS 10948/1/113.

1 Seaver returned to Paris from Frankfurt on 30 September (SB to Barbara Bray, 27 September 1960; TCD, MS 10948/1/112).

2 SB had offered London book dealer and theatre bibliographer Ifan Kyrle Fletcher (1905–1969) the manuscripts of *Comment c'est*: "The book I am at present writing – in French – will have accumulated a considerable body of material, both holograph and typescript. It should be available in about six months from now." (SB to Fletcher, 5

March 1960; NYCU.) SB would later inform Fletcher that he had sold this material to "my usual buyer," explaining "I could not bring myself to pass him over" (13 January 1961; NYCU). Schwartz sold them to the Harry Ransom Center, University of Texas in Austin (TxU, Beckett Collection, Boxes 1 and 2).

3 Robert Pinget's sister Blanche-Marie was to marry Andreas Léo Schnyder. "Moi non plus" (Nor do I).

4 French philosopher Francis Jeanson (1922–2009) met Albert Camus and Jean-Paul Sartre in Algiers in 1945; from 1951 to 1956, he worked at Sartre's *Les Temps Modernes*. Jeanson established what became known as the Jeanson Network (also "Porteurs de valises" [Case bearers]) in support of Algerian independence from France; it raised and transferred funds, made available false identity papers, housed Algerian militants, and undertook other resistance activities on behalf of the Front de Libération Nationale (FLN). In September 1958, Jeanson founded a clandestine bulletin *Vérités Pour* to disseminate information about the conflict as well as present the organization's positions (Marie-Pierre Ulloa, *Francis Jeanson: A Dissident Intellectual from the French Resistance to the Algerian War*, tr. Jane Marie Todd [Stanford, CA: Stanford University Press, 2007] 165).

Accused of "breaching the security of the state," twenty-four defendants were brought to trial before "the permanent Armed Forces tribunal"; Jeanson himself was absent. The presiding judge "imposed censorship from the start, proscribing use of the expression 'Algerian War'" (Ulloa, 206–207).

On 5 September, a day before the Jeanson trial began, the *Déclaration sur le droit à l'insoumission dans la guerre d'Algérie* (Declaration on the right to resist the draft in the Algerian War), known as the Manifeste des 121, was broadly released (Ulloa, 209). Maurice Blanchot and Dionys Mascolo (1916–1997) composed the document, which was signed by writers associated with Sartre and *Les Temps Modernes*, Nadeau and *Les Lettres Nouvelles*, Lindon and Editions de Minuit, and others: among them Arthur Adamov, Simone de Beauvoir, Maurice Blanchot, Roger Blin, Pierre Boulez, André Breton, Michel Butor, Marguerite Duras, Monique Lange, Michel Leiris, Jérôme Lindon, Dionys Mascolo, Jean Martin, André Masson, Jean-Jacques Mayoux, Maurice Nadeau, Claude Ollier, Denise René, Alain Resnais, Alain Robbe-Grillet, Nathalie Sarraute, Jean-Paul Sartre, Geneviève Serreau, Claude Simon, François Truffaut, Tristan Tzara, and Vercors.

SB cancelled "sign" and replaced it with "be in": "If I weren't a foreigner I suppose I'd be in it."

5 Claude Simon's latest book, *La Route des Flandres* (1960; *The Flanders Road*), was 314 pages long.

6 SB was in Paris on 26–27 September (Georges Wildemeersch, Hugo Claus archive, to the editors, 4 September 2012). Christopher Logue's plays *Antigone* and *The Trial of Cob and Leach* were performed at the Royal Court Theatre under the title of *Trials by Logue* from 23 November, directed by Lindsay Anderson (1923–1994). Hugo Claus (1929–2008) translated *Antigone* into Dutch for production in March 1961 in Ghent and also in Rotterdam (www/ua/ac/be/main. aspx?c=*CLAUS&n=24734, accessed 2 August 2012).

7 Theodor Fontane's *Irrungen Wirrungen* (1888; *Delusions, Confusions and the Poggenpuhl Family*) is compared to Fontane's *Effi Briest* (1894), which SB persists in spelling "Effie." SB was reading the poetry of Matthias Claudius and memorizing some of the poems (see 31 March 1960, 1 April 1960).

8 Albee had written on behalf of his lover, the composer William Flanagan (1923–1969); SB replied on 1 October that the rights to *Krapp's Last Tape* were no longer available because Mihalovici had the world rights (Albee Collection). SB had turned down a request from the Munich music publisher Hans Wewerka on behalf of Austrian composer Hanns Jelinek (1901–1969) for a musical adapation of *En attendant Godot* (SB to Ude Bruhns, S. Fischer Verlag, 27 September 1960; DLA, Hunzinger, MS 2000.16.27/2; SB to Barbara Bray, 27 September 1960; TCD, MS10904/1/112). SB also spurned a request to set the text of "From an Unabandoned Work" by composer Peter Tod Lewis (1932–1982), writing to Judith Schmidt at Grove Press: "No, no music please. Sorry." (1 October 1960; NSyU.)

9 Robert Pinget's new play would be published as *Ici ou ailleurs* (1961).

10 SB wrote to Françoise Porte, the first wife of Jacques Putman, about his dinner with Bram and Jacoba van Velde, Jacques and Andrée Putman (1 October 1960; Porte Collection).

11 SB had just helped the Haydens move from the country back to Paris; he gave them "a hand with transport of canvasses and baggage and then up the 7 flights to their studio" (SB to Bray, 27 September 1960; MS 10948/1/112).

BARBARA BRAY
PURLEY, SURREY

4.10.60 Paris

Dear Barbara

This hurried line to thank you for letter, card and Hopkins which if I ever succeed in reading anything again I look forward to reading. Very good of you to send me your copy.[1] Lindon as you will have seen was not detained long, but if the cat jumps the wrong way it's the end of Minuit.[2] I continue with my stupid drunken Paris life. I've decided to take flight to Ussy tomorrow for a few days only, longer impossible with St. Jacques etc. Just time to quiet down a little, I quivering for all my sins and stupidities. Notwithstanding all[,] see every day or every second something for the play and today I think solved itself as I drove in the Paris rain the problem of how to get her to speak without speaking to herself or to the public or to the merely imaginary interlocutor. And yes alone on the stage, riddle me that our Cambridge scholar.[3] Perhaps get down a few words in Ussy, but hardly. Logue sent me his Antigone, have not yet read.[4] I hope there will be enough money left somehow or coming in to pay for a private ward. I rang up the Société des Auteurs en désespoir de cause expecting a telephonic spit in the gob and was told I had over 2000 N.F.[5] The painters finish today and the carpets down by the end of the week if one is to believe what one is told. Can't think of a title for the dog, unless perhaps PIM.[6] Out now again to drive about in the rain simply. Goodbye then now for the present and may gods and men be good to you.

Love

Sam

ALS; 1 leaf, 2 sides; *env to* Mrs Barbara Bray, 121 Brighton Rd, Purley, Surrey, Angleterre; *pm* 5-10-60, Paris; TCD, MS 10948/1/114.

1 The edition of the poems of Gerard Manley Hopkins sent by Bray has not been identified.

2 On 30 September, Jérôme Lindon was arrested with four other persons for his participation in the diffusion of the Manifeste des 121. As Lindon wrote to his colleagues in a letter dated 7 October: "Grâce à la réaction immédiate de l'opinion française, quatre d'entre nous ont été relâchés, sans explication après vingt-trois heures passées sans interrogatoire dans les locaux de la police." (Thanks to the immediate reaction of French public opinion, four of us were released, without explanation, after twenty-three hours in police custody *without being questioned*.)

Lindon states the case and calls for solidarity:

> Comme le disait, samedi, le journal Le Monde, "la hâte mise à procéder à cette véritable 'rafle dans les milieux intellectuels' est malheureusement révélatrice d'une méfiance, voire d'une hostilité systématique à l'égard de ceux-là même que le président de la République, au dernier conseil des ministres, appelait 'les penseurs', en demandant qu'on les laisse s'exprimer".
>
> Il est à craindre que, dans ce domaine, la situation ne s'aggrave rapidement en France. Comme éditeur, je fais aujourd'hui appel à votre solidarité professionnelle et intellectuelle, en vous demandant de rester prêt, le cas échéant, à apporter un concours précieux à ceux d'entre nous qui, luttant contre la guerre d'Algérie, risquent de payer de leur liberté personnelle leur attachement aux droits de l'homme.
>
> (As was pointed out on Saturday in the newspaper *Le Monde*, "the haste displayed in proceeding to what amounts to a 'raid on intellectuals' is unfortunately indicative of a distrust, even hostility towards the very people whom the President of the Republic, at the last Cabinet meeting, called 'the thinkers', asking that they should have freedom of expression".
>
> There are grounds for fearing that, in this domain, the situation in France may worsen. As a publisher, I appeal today to your professional and intellectual solidarity, asking you to be ready, should the occasion arise, to offer precious support to those of us who, in the struggle against the Algerian War, risk having to pay with their personal liberty for their devotion to the rights of man.) (Konstantinović, *Beckett: prijatelj*, 68.)

3 "And yes alone . . . Cambridge scholar." This is inserted in the left margin.

4 SB later said of Christopher Logue's *Antigone*: "Brechtian and strong in his disputatious way" (SB to Richard Seaver, 11 October 1960; TxU, Seaver, R 16501).

5 "En désespoir de cause" (as a last resort).

6 Julia Bray was given a dog in 1960.

BARBARA BRAY
PURLEY, SURREY

10.10.60 Ussy

Dear Barbara

Thanks for letter here this morning and for nice photo which I am very glad to have. I have been here since I think last Wednesday, in bed all the time with grippe, but better today, temperature down and me up in dressing gown. I had appointments in Paris Saturday, Sunday and tomorrow, but have cancelled them all. Suzanne is alone in Paris dealing with St. Jacques problems. I understand the place has been cleaned, the carpets down but not adjusted and some new furniture due in this afternoon. It is unnecessary for me to say how glad I shd. be to see you, but I could not see you now. I see I must be careful not to write too sadly, since it upsets you so. I wd. be disturbed more than I am about the new life you are preparing if I did not know it is largely at least a professional necessity.[1] You have never understood what a rag I am and how little to be relied on and how little I can do for anyone and in brief how little there remains now of the being and the writer, how little of the little there ever was. It is like being in a wheel chair rolling slowly down and putting on the brakes every now and then to have a look round or just out of pusillanimity and then letting them off and waiting for the descent to resume, which it does not immediately the slope is still so gentle, and all the things one may say to oneself then, while waiting. I write all this without any particular sadness and indeed without any at all as far as I am concerned. But a creature so committed already to the lying back & folded hands and closed eyes and gathering speed – no place for that in solutions. I know I might as well be saying this to the wind and the leaves and so I suppose I am, like everything I ever said, having never grasped the nature of human conversation. I put the tip of my little finger into the imbedded female solo machine, to the extent of writing a few stage directions and a scrap of dialogue

She (loud)	Can you hear me?
He (off, loud)	Yes.
She (less loud)	And now?
He (" ")	Yes.
She (soft)	And now?
He (")	Yes.
She (very soft)	And now?
He (" ")	Yes.
She (very soft)	Fear no more the heat of the sun. (Pause. Do.) Did you hear that?
He (very soft)	Yes.
She (" ")	What?
He (" ")	Fear no more the heat of the sun.

Mais le coeur n'y est pas, seul le bout du petit doigt.[2]

Love

Sam

ALS; 1 leaf, 2 sides; *env to* M$^{\underline{rs}}$ Barbara Bray, 121 Brighton Road, Purley, Surrey, Angleterre; *pm* 10–10–60, La Ferté-sous-Jouarre; TCD, MS 10948/1/115.

1 On 18 September, Bray wrote to Joseph Weltman (1910–2004), who produced radio talks and features, as well as *The Critics* for the BBC Third Programme, indicating that she planned to leave the BBC and inquiring about freelance work; in a further memo to Weltman on 1 December, Bray gave the date of her resignation as 31 December and said that she would be in Paris from April 1961 (BBCWAC, RCONT1, Barbara Bray, Talks).

2 The situation of the new play was of a woman embedded in a mound; it was begun on 8 October and the initial notes are headed "Play Female Solo" (UoR, MS 1227/7/7/1). The dialogue here is similar to one of the exchanges between Willie and Winnie in *Happy Days* ([New York: Grove Press, 1961] 25–26). "Fear no more the heat o' the sun" (Shakespeare, *Cymbeline*, IV.ii.258).

"Mais le coeur n'y est pas, seul le bout du petit doigt." (But the heart is not in it, only the tip of my little finger.)

BARBARA BRAY
PURLEY, SURREY

16.10.60 Ussy

Dear Barbara

Thanks for your letter. I am so sorry to hear about all this office unpleasantness and hope by now you are feeling less upset. I suppose he is in a hurry to impose his taste on 3rd Drama, which will be unpleasant for Michael and others. However as you have decided to get out, the sooner the better, so long as you receive your salary up to June. What do you expect of a man who was obviously always against what you & Donald were doing? Expressions of appreciation?[1]

You say I shd. know better than that. Well, I just don't. Anyway I have said all I can say and shall say no more.

The solution is to have a real interlocutor at the outset (just enough to establish his reality, in the event the back of his head) and then get rid of him for the rest of the play. In this way she is alone on stage talking neither to herself nor to the audience nor to an imaginary character. I have got on a little way and "he" is proving more difficult to dismiss than desirable. However I hope tomorrow (4th page) he'll be gone for keeps, except occasionally his voice - and unsolicited ejaculations. Most is stage directions so far and they are proving unusually difficult. So many objects (from bag), whole thing has to be watched very carefully. Suddenly realise she has her spectacles on when they need to be off & so on or has forgotten to put down the mirror. It's inclined as always in English to shit and pullulate - but there's a play there all right I think - if I can restrain my native vulgarity.

Going back alas to Paris day after tomorrow - get on with new flat, sign Krapp opera contract and so on. Mihalovici and Tophoven came out the other day to work with me on the German which had gone all haywire under pressure of musical exigencies. Got it more or less right. Concert performance at Chaillot with de Falla's Retable [sic] early in February, then Bielefeld Erstaufführung towards end of month. Vega record almost certain and best of all Fischer-Dieskau interested for Music Festival.[2]

Wish to god I could stay here and work a few hours a day and potter and prowl and lie about the rest of the time. Feel so much better. A week in Paris and all the people and I'm corpsed.

Decided to buy a small picture from a young Spanish painter having 1st exhibition now, promising, confused and in dire need of encouragement. That this week too.[3] Back here I hope early next week. Know I won't be able to do any work on play in Paris.

Reading Fontane with avidity.

Cheerful letter from Yod.[4]

Love to children and Donald.

Love

Sam

ALS; 1 leaf, 2 sides; *env to* Mrs Barbara Bray, 121 Brighton Rd, Purley, Surrey, Angleterre; *pm* 18–10–60, La Ferté-sous-Jouarre; TCD, MS 10948/1/116.

1 When Donald McWhinnie resigned as Assistant Head of Drama (Sound) of the BBC, on 11 August, effective 14 October, to pursue stage and television direction, Martin Esslin replaced him; at the same time, Michael Bakewell (b. 1931) was named as Script Editor, Drama (Sound), effective 1 January 1960 (Trish Hayes, BBC Written Archives to the editors, 30 August 2012 and 3 September 2012; *The Times* 1 November 1960: 16). In 1960, Val Gielgud (1900–1981) was Head of Drama. Bray had found it increasingly difficult to work with him, especially without McWhinnie as a buffer (Michael Bakewell to the editors, 7 August 2012). BBC radio producer Philip French (b. 1933) observed that when Esslin succeeded Gielgud in 1963, he was "able to build on the work that had been done by McWhinnie and Bakewell, to which Gielgud hadn't been particularly sympathetic" (Humphrey Carpenter, *The Envy of the World: Fifty Years of the BBC Third Programme and Radio 3: 1946–1996* [London: Weidenfeld and Nicolson, 1996] 239–240). Bray reflected on her situation at this time in a letter written to *The Times*: "From 1953 to 1960 I was Script Editor, Drama (Sound) in the B.B.C. Even in those days it was clear that the Corporation's machinery for decision and policy-making was outgrown, not to mention 'undemocratic'. There was no effective contact or open consultation between production and management." ("Administrator v. Producer," 21 February 1970: 7.)

2 Elmar Tophoven's German translation had to be adjusted to fit Mihalovici's score for *Krapp, ou la dernière bande* in the trilingual edition of this setting of the text (see 13 June 1960 and 4 July 1960). The oratorio presentation at the Palais de Chaillot would be on the program with the opera *El Retablo de Maese Pedro* by Manuel de Falla (1876–1946). The Erstaufführung (premiere) of the opera would take place at the Bielefeld Opera, Westphalia. Dietrich Fischer-Dieskau did not sing the role of Krapp.

3 SB purchased a painting by Manuel Martí Fandos (b. 1928, known as Manolo Fandos) who had studied at the Ecole des Beaux-Arts in Paris (1957–1959). Fandos had

met SB through Jean Martin (José Francisco Fernández, "Surrounding the Void: Samuel Beckett and Spain," *Estudios Irlandeses* 9 [2014] 50–51).

4 SB had received a letter from Leslie Daiken before 30 September indicating that he was out of the hospital (SB to Daiken, 30 September 1960; Cuming Collection).

BARBARA BRAY
PURLEY, SURREY

28.10.60 Ussy

Dear Barbara

Thanks for your 2 letters secured this morning.

I don't see why you should not take money from me if you need it and I think you should allow yourself to be reassured by the knowledge that it is at your disposal at any time. What of course you need to know is whether your salary will be paid up to June as in one of your letters you seemed to think.

As I think I told you Martin Esslin sent me his essay on me to appear in his book The Theatre of the Absurd. It was all right, biographically and bibliographically accurate for once at least.

There is no reason that I can see why you should not write about my work. The only objection wd. be that you set it – as far as I know – too high, but that as Blin wd. say is not rédhibitoire.[1]

The Manivelle is only just out. I'll send you a copy next week when I get back to Paris. By then you will probably have received a copy from Robert. I have not yet seen the book.[2]

I was very worried about Lindon last evening after hearing the reportage on the students' manifestation by Europe I at 7.30. I rang him up and his wife said he had not come in. Then an hour later and he had – unscathed. He said the police were unprecedentedly brutal, batoning the women as readily as the men.[3]

I can't make any headway with the play, sit at the table for hours unable to write a line. I suppose some work is done during this time, but nothing to show for it, not even a note. See a number of things already in first few pages that will have to be removed. The hat and head are still there – bent at the moment on an obscene postcard – but he will now be sent back into his hole. He should be as close to a mere ear as possible – and dubious as the divine. Perhaps a yes or no now and then to help things along. Perhaps a Christ! or Jesus! now and then. I don't know. I don't really know what it is about – but nothing new there. Keep the help down to a minimum is the principle. Even the bag must not be too rich. Never [over-]do it, that's the size of it.[4] Wish I could renounce writing once and for all and just potter about for the rest of the . . . time. Perhaps start reading a little again.

Enclosed line to thank Julia for her own imaginary lake.

Love

Sam

Enclosure:

28.10.60 Ussy sur Marne

Dear Julia

Many thanks for your lake. It is very prettily drawn and coloured. I imagined one too once, but I much prefer yours.

I hope you are having a happy term and not working too hard.

Much love to Checchina and yourself.

Sam

ALS; 1 leaf, 2 sides; *enclosure*, ALS to Julia Bray, 1 leaf, 1 side; *env to* Mrs Barbara Bray, 121 Brighton Road, Purley, Surrey, Angleterre; *pm* 29–10–60, La Ferté-sous-Jouarre; TCD, MS 19048/1/118.

1 "Is not rédhibitoire" (is no reason not to).

2 Robert Pinget's *La Manivelle* was published with SB's English text *The Old Tune* by Editions de Minuit; the imprint date was 19 September 1960.

3 Between 7 and 8.30 p.m. on 27 October, a rally of some 3,000 students advocating a "negotiated peace in Algeria" in a hall on Place Maubert erupted in violence when "Rightist advocates of French Algeria" threw smoke bombs inside, while thousands of persons milled around outside the hall; meanwhile rightist groups began a counter-demonstration at the intersection of Boulevard Saint-Michel and Boulevard Saint-Germain. Police and riot troops attempted to keep the two groups apart and "sought to restore order by swinging clubs and lead-weighted capes at the heads and backs of the demonstrators" ("Parisian Rioters Clash on Algeria: Thousands of Leftists

and Rightists Battle and Fight Police – 485 Arrested," *New York Times* 28 October 1960: 1, 7; "Paris Police in Clash with Crowds; Many Injured, Baton Charges to Clear Streets," *The Times* 28 October 1960: 12.) In *Le Monde*:

> Tous les témoignages concordent pour souligner la violence de certains incidents ... même la visible délectation avec laquelle certains policiers attaquaient quelques groupes de journalistes ou d'hommes politiques. "Inadmissibles brutalités", écrit *Le Figaro*, déplorant qu'une quinzaine de reporters et de photographes aient été blessés. ("Après les manifestations pour une paix négociée en Algérie: climat d'attente inquiète à l'approche du sixième anniversaire de la rébellion," 29 October 1960: 1.) (All reports agree in emphasising the violence of certain incidents ... even the visible pleasure with which some policemen were attacking certain groups of journalists or politicians. "Unacceptable acts of brutality", writes *Le Figaro*, deploring that some fifteen reporters and photographers had been injured.)

4 In the completed play, Willie's "hand reappears with a postcard which he examines close to his eyes." When Winnie turns, she sees the card, asks for it, and examines it: "this is just genuine pure filth! (Examines card.) Make any nice-minded person want to vomit." (Beckett, *Happy Days*, 18–19.)

BARBARA BRAY
PURLEY, SURREY

Saturday [5 November 1960] Paris

Dear Barbara

Thanks for your letter. I hope you are feeling better. I'm glad you are prepared to take money from me if necessary. I am writing this in a café Bd. St. Jacques opposite the house, waiting for a sandwich – ordered half an hour ago – to arrive and a beer. All the books and pictures are now moved – and the 2 Brams on the study wall.[1] No furniture yet and don't expect residence to begin before next month. Have done nothing all this week but rush madly in 2 CV in all directions.[2] Quite stuck with play – now that he has gone into his hole. No matter what she says and what the quality of the text just talking can't do it for an hour and a half and the bag can obviously only be used sparingly. It seems another insoluble. Going to Ussy in any case tomorrow for 4 or 5 days to bang my skull against it again.

Hayden was very pleased with the Telegraph clipping, he had quite forgotten the picture and wonders who can have sold it to York. Waddington is to see him today and talks of an exhibition in January. Hayden a beaucoup baissé (physiquement) il aura 77 ans je crois le 24 décembre.[3] You'll have a letter for your birthday, at least I'll post you one the 23rd.[4] I had lunch believe it or not with Cyril Connolly and his wife, introduced by your friend Schwartz! It went all right – at the Iles. He said he had written against the 3 in I. I said I hadn't read the article and that in any case it was of no . . . then wriggled out of it somehow! He had memories of Paris late 20s early 30s and that helped. They left me to [? salute] the Gilbert. He produced three works for me to sign! Invited me to stay with them in Suzzex! Tout ça – qui l'eût cru?[5] Spent an evening with Unseld (Suhrkamp Verlag) & Tophoven. Have now two German engagements in Feb, Bielefeld 25th and Frankfurt 27th for a Beckett-Abend with Adorno discoursing – drank too much whiskey and agreed to be present, now don't see how to get out of it.[6] What the hell anyway. Charming notion – by me incontinent accept – from Sunset Boulevard of an animated cartoon of Act Without Words I. They sent drawings – quite amusing – a future in animated cartoons – ça me sourirait.[7] Recuperated in my ? the half forgotten Mallarmé line -

Calme bloc ici-bas chu d'un
désastre obscur.[8]

Extraordinary exhibition parait-il at the Musée d'Art Moderne – "Les sources de l'art moderne" – on or and [illeg. 2 words]. Pierre Schneider was all worked up about it.[9] Martin back from Finland today.[10] Frisch was here for Serreau's production of his Biedermann, trying to stop it, couldn't, postpone it, non plus, swept out back to Zurich without seeing the première.[11] Chose and paid for the Manolo Fandos – he shd. do something some day. Swapped a small Hayden oil for a much smaller gouache.[12] Car covered with wounds inflicted anonymous en stationnement. No more now. Sac vidé.[13] Go back across the road and wait for delivery of table and chairs. Then back Rue des Favorites to pack more stuff.

Love

Sam

ALS; 2 leaves, 3 sides; *env to* Mrs Barbara Bray, 121 Brighton Rd., Purley, Surrey, Angleterre; *pm* 5-11-60, Paris; TCD, MS 10948/1/119.

1 Beckett's two works by Bram van Velde: 21 April 1958 to Thomas MacGreevy, n. 6.

2 SB's Citroën 2CV (deux-chevaux): 29 September 1959.

3 Bray had sent a cutting from the *Daily Telegraph and Morning Post* which noted that the York Museum of Art had recently "made several excellent purchases. Notable among them is a painting by Henri Hayden entitled *Old Town by the Sea*." (Terence Mullaly, "London to See Feininger Art; Stimulating Art in the Provinces," 3 November 1960: 17.) The painting was purchased in October 1960 from the London art dealers Roland, Browse and Delbanco, with the help of the Calouste Gulbenkian Foundation; it is now entitled *Saint Lunaire* (1914; YORAG: 965; Victoria Adams, York Museums Trust, York Art Gallery, to the editors, 5 January 2011).

Victor Waddington was Hayden's gallery agent in London. "Hayden a beaucoup baissé (physiquement) il aura 77 ans je crois le 24 décembre." (Hayden has gone downhill (physically). He will be 77, I think, on 24 December.)

4 Barbara Bray's birthday was 23 November.

5 Cyril Connolly (1903–1974), literary critic and Editor of *Horizon* from 1940 to 1949, was a bibliophile whom Jake Schwartz had advised for several years (Jeremy Lewis, *Cyril Connolly: A Life* [London: Jonathan Cape, 1997] 507–508). Connolly married Deirdre Craven, his third wife, in 1959; they lived in Firle, East Sussex. SB reports on lunch with the couple: "Only news of moment Cyril Connolly's expression as on my recommendation he ate two oursins. I told him to eat them with a spoon [. . .] He left to have tea with Gilbert which I hope restored his palate." (SB to Herbert Myron, 13 November 1960; MBU, Myron.)

Connolly's review of SB's *Watt*, *Molloy*, and *Malone Dies* was entitled "Surrealist Shandygaff," *The Sunday Times* 9 March 1958: 7. "Tout ça - qui l'eût cru?" (All that - who'd have thought it?)

6 Siegfried Unseld, Elmar Tophoven, and SB had met on 30 October at the Closerie des Lilas, where they discussed the Beckett-Abend (Beckett-Evening) in Frankfurt. Adorno planned to read from his essay "Versuch, das Endspiel zu verstehen" ("Trying to Understand *Endgame*") as part of the Beckett-Abend (Knowlson, *Damned to Fame*, 428, 709; Stefan Müller-Doohm, *Adorno: A Biography*, tr. Rodney Livingstone [Cambridge: Polity Press, 2005] 356–357, 575).

7 The proposal for an animated cartoon of *Act Without Words I* by William Scott was sent to Grove Press by Jay Ward Productions, Hollywood, a firm that had created animated films such as *Bugs Bunny*, *Gerald McBoing-Boing*, and *Mr. Magoo*. Judith Schmidt forwarded some of the drawings to SB which he liked; he asked to see more of them to check them against the scenario (Judith Schmidt to SB, 19 October 1960; Schmidt to Jay Ward, 4 November, conveying SB's acceptance; NSyU). SB wrote to Judith Schmidt on 7 November: "Decidedly I like the cartoon very much. It follows the scenario faithfully.

The few deviations are perhaps improvements. Herewith a few notes nevertheless. The only obvious mistake is when he sees tree before whistle calls his attention to it." (NSyU.) SB's notes are presented by Clas Zilliacus in "'Act Without Words I' as Cartoon and Codicil," *Samuel Beckett Today / Aujourd'hui* 2 (1993) 295–304; Scott's letter to Zilliacus, reprinted in this essay, indicates that the cartoon was never completed.

"Ça me sourirait" (I'd rather like that).

8 SB quotes a line from Stéphane Mallarmé's poem, "Le Tombeau d'Edgar Poe": "Calme bloc ici-bas chu d'un désastre obscur" ("Calm block fallen down here from some dark disaster") (*Œuvres complètes*, II, ed. Bertrand Marchal, Bibliothèque de la Pléiade [Paris: Gallimard, 2003] 727; "The Tomb of Edgar Poe," in *Stéphane Mallarmé: Poems*, tr. Roger Fry [New York: New Directions Books, 1951] 109).

9 Les sources du XXe siècle: les arts en Europe de 1884 à 1914 (The Sources of the XXth Century: The Arts in Europe 1884–1919) took place at the Musée National d'Art Moderne from 4 November 1960 to 23 January 1961. It was the sixth in a series of annual international exhibitions exploring modern European art movements. Pierre Schneider (b. 1925), an art historian, critic, and collaborator with Georges Duthuit on *Transition*, is an authority on the work of Henri Matisse.

10 Jean Martin had directed Boris Vian's play *Les Bâtisseurs d'Empire* (*En trapp a upp*) at the Lilla Teatern, Helsinki, which had opened on 29 October (Clas Zilliacus to the editors, 19 January 2013; Hanna Helavuori, Theatre Info Finland).

11 Max Frisch was in Paris for the production of his play *Biedermann und die Brandstifter* (*Biedermann et les incendiaires*; *Biedermann and the Firebugs*), directed by Jean-Marie Serreau at the Théâtre de Lutèce from 26 October. SB originally had planned to meet him with Siegfried Unseld on 30 October. "Non plus" (here: couldn't either). SB inserts "crumbs" in right margin with a line drawn to a scratched-out word before "swept" – a reminder that he was eating a sandwich while he wrote.

12 The Manolo Fandos painting purchased by SB has not been identified. The new gouache by Henri Hayden has not been identified.

13 "En stationnement" (while parked). "Sac vidé" (bag emptied).

BARBARA BRAY
PURLEY, SURREY

17.11.60 Paris

Dear Barbara

Thanks for your card Tuesday and letter this morning with Craig's article. I wish I could agree with the quarter of it. Thanks for what you wrote and to him for what he did – and signed.[1] She is stuck now again with parasol aloft in left hand after having been aloft in right. Can't think how she can ever move or speak again – and 75 minutes at least to go! I am particularly stupid and shaky after 2 evenings stupid drinking. However relatively reasonable last night and saw a superb film – On the Bowery ("Come Back Africa" man with Russian name), shall go again this evening if I can keep out of pubs.[2] Saw Robert. We are both – he naturally more than I – very remorseful and crestfallen at having omitted mention of you and BBC in Manivelle. He was very upset indeed and was to try and get Lindon to insert rectifying slip – I imagine he'll refuse.[3]

Have been able to arrange matters with bank and herewith second hundred. I wouldn't want them back with the ashes in me now.[4]

Glad you liked the two specimens. You'd reassure a French horn on a winter Sunday.[5]

Glad John likes idea of music text with me and that there is no hurry. Perhaps the rough idea might be re envisaged.[6]

Tophoven has begun translation of Comment C'est and we work together this afternoon, at his place at Rueil of all places, only the vaguest notion how to get there. Terrified in advance of Bielefeld & Frankfurt. Get drunk and be a worse fool than sober.[7]

Love to the children and to Donald when you write and don't forget to thank Craig or should I write myself?

Love

Sam

ALS; 1 leaf, 2 sides; *env to* M[rs] Barbara Bray, 121 Brighton Rd., Purley, Surrey, Angleterre; *pm* 17-11-60, Paris; TCD, MS 10948/1/121.

1 H. A. L. Craig wrote: "Beckett has brought more to the theatre than anyone else in his generation," and, comparing SB to Pinter, added, "Beckett alone has the language, invention and unremitting discipline to sustain poetry for the length of the play" ("Poetry in the Theatre," *The New Statesman* 60.1548 [12 November 1960] 734, 736).

2 The feature documentary *On the Bowery* (1956) and the anti-apartheid film *Come Back, Africa* (1960) were directed by Lionel Rogosin.

3 In the Minuit edition of *La Manivelle*, with the English version by SB, there was no mention of the play's English premiere on the BBC Third Programme. SB wrote to Bray on 23 November: "I saw Lindon. He is printing an erratum slip for The Old Tune and a copy thus rectified will be sent to Newby" (TCD, MS 10948/1/122).

4 SB had offered to help Bray with money in his letter of 12 November:

> If you want another 100 immediately please write at once and you'll have it before end of next week. Don't please send me a post-dated cheque, I shd. be

> upset if you did. It's of no importance to me when you repay me or if you never repay, so don't think of it until you are affluent. Apart from the other 100 I suggest for the end of next week you may count on 100 or 150 end of January. I don't need this money, get that into your head. You know me well enough to know I wouldn't offer to anyone anything I needed myself! (TCD, MS 10948/1/120.)

SB plays upon Krapp's line "I wouldn't want them back. Not with the fire in me now." (Beckett, *Krapp's Last Tape and Other Dramatic Pieces*, 28.)

5 SB had sent Bray a sample from the play he was writing with his letter of 12 November: "She (idly turning open parasol). Yes, there is so little to do, so little to say, and the fear so great, certain days, of finding oneself high and dry, with nothing left to do, nothing more to say, and the days go by, certain days go by, and little or nothing done, little or nothing said."

6 Bray had initially suggested to SB that he collaborate with John Beckett on a work for radio, to which SB replied: "In principle, yes, for something with John – if he is interested" (SB to Bray, 12 November 1960).

7 SB wrote to Mary Hutchinson on 2 November that he had "decided to call the book Comment C'est" (TxU, Hutchinson, 2.4). In his memoir entry for 25 November, Robert Pinget recollects discussing the title with SB:

> Sam revenait de chez Jérôme avec la suite des épreuves de son livre. A déjà corrigé la moitié. Je lui demande en riant s'il a trouvé des fautes de ponctuation, étant donné qu'il n'y a pas de ponctuation. Me répond sur le même ton qu'il a trouvé quelques points, avec horreur! M'a dit aussi qu'il venait de signer le contrat. Jérôme a accepté de renoncer au titre Tout bas, Des bribes qu'il désirait mais a fait remarquer que Comment c'est prêtait à un jeu de mot et il a proposé Comment c'était comment c'est, que Sam a momentanément accepté. (Doucet, unclassified Pinget Collection, "Notre ami Samuel Beckett," 57.) (Sam was coming back from Jérôme's place with the remainder of the proofs of his book. Has already corrected half. I ask him, laughing, if he has found any wrong punctuation, given that there is no punctuation. Answers me in the same tone that, to his horror, he has found several full stops! Told me also that he had just signed the contract. Jérôme has agreed to give up the title *Tout bas, Des bribes* that he wanted, but pointed out that *Comment c'est* set up a possible pun, and suggested *Comment c'était comment c'est*, which Sam provisionally accepted.)

The Tophovens lived in Rueil-Malmaison, Seine-et-Oise, west of Paris.

MATTI MEGGED
KIRYAT-TIVON, ISRAEL

21.11.60

Paris
New address:
38 Bd. St. Jacques,
Paris 14me

10. Matti Megged

Dear M. M.

Forgive delay in writing to thank you for your letters. I have great difficulty with correspondence and am sorely tried with stupid mail that simply has to be dealt with daily.

All you say is very familiar to me. But if I set out to write to you about it at length, as I have done more than once, I know I shall never finish the letter, any more than I finished the others. We must wait until we can meet again, with the Goddess Bottle between us, and have it all out in the give and take of talk.[1] As far as helping you is concerned, it all boils down to two suggestions that I think are worth making.

The first is that you should succeed at all costs in writing and publishing in English – as well as Hebrew.

The second is more difficult to formulate and has to do with the view you seem to hold of the relationship between living and writing. It seems to me that this is probably your chief difficulty. Your view seems to be that what you can't live you should at least be able to state – and then you complain that your statement has devitalized its object. But the material of experience is not the material of expression and I think the distress you feel, as a writer, comes from a tendency on your part to assimilate the two. The issue is roug[h]ly that raised by Proust in his campaign against naturalism and the distinction he makes between the "real" of the human predicament and the artist's "ideal real" remains certainly valid for me and indeed badly in need of revival.[2] I understand – I think no one better – the flight from experience to expression and I understand the necessary failure of both. But it is the flight from one order or disorder to an order or disorder of a different nature and the two failures are essentially dissimilar in kind. Thus life in failure can hardly be anything but dismal at the best, whereas there is nothing more exciting for the writer, or richer in unexploited expressive possibilities, than the failure to express. It was some realization of all this and what it involves that enabled me to go on (about 15 years ago) in a situation probably very different from yours, but certainly no less critical. This is perhaps quite beside the point in your case, but I don't think so. Forgive me if it seems to you irrelevant or impertinent.

Write soon and tell me how you are getting on.

All the best

Yours

Sam. Beckett

ALS; 1 leaf, 2 sides; GEU, Aston, MSS 1068 (also with T transcription, 1 leaf, 1 side).

1 SB had been introduced to Israeli author Matti Megged* (1923–2003) by Judith Schmidt, who was then Megged's lover (SB to Schmidt, 22 April 1960; GEU, Aston, MSS 1068). SB plays here upon Rabelais' expression "la dive bouteille." Megged described, to the editors, meeting SB in Paris in May: "We'd spent the whole night talking (drinking too. . .), mostly about writing in a foreign language" (Megged to the editors, 24 March 1999).

2 As far back as 1931, in his study *Proust*, SB had written:

> The identification of immediate with past experience, the recurrence of past action or reaction in the present, amounts to a participation between the ideal and the real, imagination and direct apprehension, symbol and substance. Such participation frees the essential reality that is denied to the contemplative as to the active life. What is common to present and past is more essential than either taken separately. Reality, whether approached imaginatively or empirically, remains a surface, hermetic. Imagination, applied – a priori – to what is

> absent, is exercised in vacuo and cannot tolerate the limits of the real. Nor is any direct and purely experimental contact possible between subject and object, because they are automatically separated by the subject's consciousness of perception, and the object loses its purity and becomes a mere intellectual pretext or motive. But, thanks to this reduplication, the experience is at once imaginative and empirical, at once an evocation and a direct perception, real without being merely actual, ideal without being merely abstract, the ideal real, the essential, the extratemporal. ([New York: Grove Press, 1957] 55–56.)

BARBARA BRAY
PURLEY, SURREY

1.12.60 Paris
St. J.

Dear Barbara

Thanks for letter of 26th, and for Listener, and to Checchina for card.

I saw Martin one evening. He is very grateful for your help with Pinter. But for you I do not think he could have arranged things. He is having trouble with his casting, but is pleased with his Toupin (Adet – Nagg) & Pommard.[1]

I was out drinking weeping & blathering all night in Montparnasse and am very hazy today. I have a dinner with Stuart Gilbert tomorrow, otherwise would be in Ussy. Shall drive there tomorrow night. Back here Tuesday.

Done no work. Mildred still speechless under immovable parasol. Think of her sometimes, lui cherche un mouvement de l'âme.[2]

John wrote, having been with his sister in All That Fall disaffected station and attenant line. Seems pleased at idea of collaborating. No ideas.[3]

Here all day. Far from well yet. Jumpy as cat. Have corrected proofs of book – one reading. 4 more necessary. Found a mistake (author's). Avec Pim instead of avant Pim. Prime importance.[4]

Glad to read of you in Listener & to know people are being kind. I think you wd. hate Unesco. Hope you will soon [illeg. 2 words].[5]

Robert very pleased.

Hayden[']s two gouaches on the floor fornenst me. One acid, one warm. Dying light. Pas qu'elle. A la fenêtre flèches, tours, domes [sic], une sorte [de] cheminée, Hôpital Cochin.[6]

Found my morphine during move. Enough to kill a poet. Present from Ethna. Unless it goes stale and loses vitriol. Still drunk.

Broke key in switch again. Left bit in. Switch on with stub. Hard to believe.

She says, holding up parasol, "I used to perspire freely". (Long pause.) Now hardly at all. (LP) The heat is much greater. (LP) The perspiration much less. (LP.) That is what I find so wonderful. (LP) The way man adapts himself. (LP) To new conditions. (LP. Transfers parasol to other hand.) Holding up wearies the arm. (LP.) Not if one is going along. (LP.) Only if one is at rest. (LP) That is a curious observation. (LP) I hope you heard that, Edward. (LP) I should be sorry to think you had not heard that.[7]

Love

Sam

ALS; 1 leaf, 2 sides; *env to* Mrs Barbara Bray, 121 Brighton Rd., Purley, Surrey, Angleterre; *pm* 2-12-60, Paris; TCD, MS 10948/1/124.

1 Jean Martin planned to direct Harold Pinter's *The Caretaker* (*Le Gardien*) with Robert Pinget's *La Manivelle* at the Théâtre de Lutèce. On 23 November, SB had written to Bray: "Martin is or has just been in London to try & straighten out some rights complications with The Caretaker. The agent is difficult by all accounts [...] Apparently they won't hear of The Caretaker being done with another play. But the quota regulations here oblige them to present a French work with the foreign one." Georges Adet, who had played Nagg in *Fin de partie*, was cast as Toupin the organ grinder in *La Manivelle*; Henri de Livry (1884–1979) was cast as Pommard.

2 Mildred was an early name given to Winnie in *Happy Days*. "Lui cherche un mouvement de l'âme" (I'm after a characteristic reaction for her).

3 "Attenant" (here: associated).

John Beckett and his twin sister Ann Beckett had visited the Foxrock station which features in *All That Fall*. In his memoir, Pinget records that SB:

> Me dit en outre que son cousin vient de lui envoyer une si gentille lettre lui disant qu'il avait enfin réalisé un vieux projet: refaire à pied le trajet de la petite ligne de chemin de fer dont il est parlé dans TCQT. La fait avec sa sœur qui a un pied en moins, jambe articulée. La ligne est maintenant désaffectée. (Doucet, unclassified Pinget Collection, "Notre ami Samuel Beckett," 56.) (Tells me too that his cousin has just sent him such a nice letter telling him that he has finally carried out an old plan: to walk the whole length of the little railway that's

mentioned in ATF. Does it with his sister who has only one foot, artificial leg. The line is no longer in service.)

Bray had suggested that SB and John Beckett collaborate on a work for radio.

4 *Comment c'est* is structured in three parts: Avant Pim, Avec Pim, Après Pim, and the full phrase "avant Pim avec Pim après Pim," as well as portions of it, are repeated throughout the text.

5 In *The Listener*, Frederick Laws wrote:

> It is bad news for the radio drama enthusiasts that Donald McWhinnie has left the B.B.C. to concentrate on his work in the theatre, and that Barbara Bray is leaving at the end of the year. Producers of their quality and enterprise are rare and they will be missed . . . [Producers] hunt for new writers and drag new plays from established ones. Their handling of the scripts of beginners is the chief means by which understanding of the techniques of radio is spread and the medium has its chance to become an art form serious in content. ("Drama, Producers," 65.1652 [24 November 1960] 953.)

6 SB had written to Barbara Bray on 23 November: "Have 2 new Hayden gouaches exchanged for a gouache & a painting – the latter snapped up by Waddington" (TCD, MS 10948/1/122). The new gouaches have not been identified. "Pas qu'elle. A la fenêtre flèches, tours, domes, une sorte [de] cheminée, Hôpital Cochin" (Not the only thing (that's dying). From the window, steeples, towers, domes, a sort of chimney, the Hôpital Cochin).

7 This passage is a draft, only slightly altered in *Happy Days* (Grove, 35–36).

BARBARA BRAY
PURLEY, SURREY

8.12.60 Paris

Dear Barbara

Thanks for cards and cuttings. So glad Pinter[']s Dwarfs well received.[1]

I won't manage much in the way of a letter today and I wonder how I'll get through to day – and be sage.[2] I'm drowning in my inch of old ditchwater – hate myself as perhaps never before – though it is difficult to say.

I saw Robert yesterday very pleased with every thing and en effet ça a l'air de se présenter très bien. Martin telephoned this morning. He also on top of world – Blin now [illeg. 1 word] playing the Caretaker or as it arises playing and staging.[3]

Shall give corrected proofs to Lindon next week. Book due now in Jan. Title Comment c'est. Hé oui.[4]

I don't know what Mildred dream you refer to. I only knew one – when a boy – a fat bespectacled girl surname Coote with a sister Dolly and a small brother Hubert who used to go to the old Eye and Ear Hospital (pronounce Iondeer) every few days to have his eyes – as he said – "scraped".[5] I remember the blue place and was in the café fornenst it with the billiard tables again the other day.[6]

I can't succeed in liking St. Jacques. Hammering and perforating all day. No water today, can't make myself a cup of tea nor wash my shirt. Should be dining with the Hayden this evening, but shall try and put it off. The two gouaches are still on the floor before me. Acide douceur.[7]

No headway with play. Have hardly given it a thought. See her sometimes – and he invisible in burrow. Faudrait un miracle.[8]

? vieillesse à tout asservie
par ? j'ai perdu ma vie.[9]
No more no more.

Love
Sam

ALS; 1 leaf, 2 sides; *env to* Mrs Barbara Bray, 121 Brighton Road, Purley, Surrey, Angleterre; *pm* 8-12-60, Paris; TCD, MS 10948/1/125.

1 Barbara Bray produced Harold Pinter's radio play adapted from an unpublished novel, *The Dwarfs*, on 2 December; the review Bray sent SB called it "some of the most subtly effective writing he has ever produced" ("Mr. Pinter at his Most Subtle," *The Times* 3 December 1960: 10; Humphrey Carpenter, *The Envy of the World*, 210–212).

2 "Be sage" (behave myself).

3 "Et en effet ça a l'air de se présenter très bien" (and things do indeed seem to be shaping up very well). Roger Blin was to play the tramp (Davies) in the French production of Pinter's *The Caretaker* directed by Jean Martin.

4 "Hé oui" (Afraid so).

5 In *Happy Days*, Winnie begins the story of Mildred scolding and undressing her new doll under a table in the nursery, when "Suddenly a mouse – (*Long Pause*)" (55). After a long interruption, Winnie completes the story: "Suddenly a mouse . . . (*Pause.*) Suddenly a mouse ran up her little thigh and Mildred, dropping Dolly in her fright, began to scream" (59).

The Cootes had been neighbors of the Becketts in Foxrock; the younger children were Dorothy (b. 1896, called Dolly, m. Dudgeon), Mildred (b. after 1911), and Hubert (b. 1899) (www.census.nationalarchives.ie/pages1911/Dublin/Ballybrack/Kerrymount/966630). Dorothy Dudgeon's sister Mildred said that "'a mouse did run up her leg at Beckett's house'" (Colin Duckworth, "Beckett's Early Background: A New Zealand Biographical Appendix," *New Zealand Journal of French Studies* 1.2 [October 1970] 67). Hubert Coote's eye treatment may have been corneal debridement.

6 SB refers to one of the apartments that Bray was considering in Paris.

7 "Acide douceur" (Acid sweetness).

8 "Faudrait un miracle" (It would take a miracle).

9 SB alters the lines of the opening verse of Arthur Rimbaud's poem "Chanson de la plus haute tour"; indicating the missing words he cannot recall with question marks and substituting "vieillesse" (age) for "jeunesse" (youth):

Oisive jeunesse
A tout asservie,
Par délicatesse
J'ai perdu ma vie.

(Arthur Rimbaud, *Œuvres complètes*, ed. André Guyaux and Aurélia Cervoni, Bibliothèque de la Pléiade [Paris: Gallimard, 2009] 210–213).

Idle youth
A prey to everything,
By undue refinement
I wasted my life.

ALAN SCHNEIDER
NEW YORK

9.12.60 Paris

Dear Alan

Thanks for your letter. You sound rather low and I hope things are better. Washington would probably be depressing at the beginning, but it might work out all right if you could make provision for a certain period of absence.[1] Pleased to hear that Krapp has been extended in extremis, looks as if the old ruffian might pant on to 1961. I hear there were four of them at the party and wish I had been with you.[2] I am badly stuck in the new play after about half an hour and haven't yet found out whether the thing is possible or not. An hour and a half necessary, exclusive of interval. Two acts, the second considerably shorter than the first. Same set for both. The first problem was how to have her speak alone on the stage all that time without speaking to herself or to the audience. Solved that after a fashion. No movement possible in first act except of Oberleib, no movement of any kind possible in the second.[3] No help from anywhere once the situation has been established except from bag (pockets if it had been a man as was originally the case). Bag obviously better dramatically and of more helpful content. In first act she is imbedded up to waist in a mound, in second up to neck. Empty plain, burning sun (she wonders mildly if the earth has lost its atmosphere). Scene extended to maximum by painted backcloth in trompe-l'oeil as pompier as possible. This to give you some idea. Too difficult and depressing to write about. Bag of no help except visually in 2 as she has no longer access to it, but the memory of the help it was a great help I hope, in fact I am counting a lot on memory of I for 2, which is stupidly said, I mean a kind of physical post image of 1 all through 2. Opulent blonde, fiftyish, all glowing shoulders and décolleté. Enough, Gott hilfe [sic] mir, amen.[4]

Time very much taken by move to Bd St.-Jacques, where I am now most of the day (and at the moment), but still sleeping Rue des Favorites. Not at all used to the new place and very uneasy. Hammering and grinding and boring going on all day overhead, a doctor I think fitting up his torture chambers. Finishing correcting proofs of new book for Editions de Minuit, title COMMENT C'EST, due out early January. Glad you liked THE END, apart from a few poems it was my very first work in French.[5] THE CARETAKER (LE GARDIEN) in rehearsal at the Lutèce with Pinget's MANIVELLE, both directed by Martin, Blin playing the tramp in the Pinter, Adet (Nagg) the organ-grinder in the MANIVELLE. Things are going well and Pinget and Martin very pleased, have not yet seen a rehearsal. Opening Jan 17th. Pinter due over beginning of Jan, I look forward to meeting him. Have seen nothing but Rogosin's marvellous ON THE BOWERY, went two nights running and want to go again. Have promised to go to Germany (Bielefeld) late Feb for opening of Mihalovici's KRAPP opera, hope you will see it in NY some day. All I know of the music is what he could show me on his piano, I was impressed. We had to go over the script together (English) and modify a few things, as he composed his music on the French text.

Voilà. Affectionately to you all and premature wishes for a happy Xmas and New Year.

s/ Sam

Read an article by Blau in some theatre magazine – a letter to his company. Very intelligent, rather superior about European theatre.[6]

TLS, with APS; 1 leaf, 2 sides; Burns Library, Samuel Beckett Collection, SB-AS. Previous publication: Beckett and Schneider, *No Author Better Served*, 77–78.

1 Schneider's letter to SB of 26 November mentioned that he had been offered "permanent artistic directorship of Washington's Arena Theatre." Schneider added, "Am tempted but unsure about leaving New York, free-lancing, off-Broadway potentialities" (Burns Library, Samuel Beckett Collection, AS-SB; Beckett and Schneider, *No Author Better Served*, 75–76).

2 Schneider's production of *Krapp's Last Tape* was to have closed on Sunday 20 November, but it was extended. Judith Schmidt wrote to SB that there was a party that evening with four actors who had played the role of Krapp: Donald Davis, Henderson Forsythe, and two unnamed understudies (Judith Schmidt to SB, 21 November 1960; NSyU).

3 "Oberleib" (upper body).

4 "Gott helfe mir, amen" (God help me, amen).

5 Richard Seaver and SB had translated "La Fin" as "The End"; it was published in *Evergreen Review* 4.15 (November–December 1960) 22–41.

6 Herbert Blau, "'Meanwhile, Follow the Bright Angels,'" *Tulane Drama Review* 5 (September 1960) 89–101. Blau wrote this article as a letter to the company of the Actor's Workshop in San Francisco.

CHRONOLOGY 1961

1961	1 January	With A. J. Leventhal, SB attends Max Frisch's *Biedermann et les incendiaires*, Théâtre de Lutèce, directed by Jean-Marie Serreau.
	before 7 January	Meeting with Sylvia Beach and other authors who contributed to *Our Exagmination* (1929) to receive lettered copies and limited first edition.
	8 January	The French proposal for Algerian self-determination receives 75 percent of the votes in a referendum.
	after 8 January	*Comment c'est* published by Editions de Minuit.
	9 January	Opening of Henri Hayden's exhibition at Waddington Galleries, London.
	11 January	SB's first meeting with Harold Pinter.
	16 January	SB dates completion of a draft of *Happy Days*. Begins revision (dated 16 January – 2 February).
	29 January	Attends Pinter's *Le Gardien*.
	13 February	Attends concert performance of Mihalovici's opera *Krapp* at the Théâtre de Chaillot.
	25 February	Attends dress rehearsal of Mihalovici's opera *Krapp* in Bielefeld, Germany.
	28 February	Attends Suhrkamp evening in Frankfurt.
	4 March	Returns to Paris, driving with the Tophovens, having visited Amsterdam, Delft, and Haarlem.
	8–25 March	Resident in Folkestone prior to his marriage to Suzanne Deschevaux-Dumesnil.
	25 March	SB and Suzanne marry in the Folkestone Register Office, and return to Paris.

3 April	WNTA TV (New York) broadcasts *Waiting for Godot* directed by Alan Schneider.
10 April–5 May	SB manages rehearsals of *En attendant Godot* in Blin's absence in London.
11 April	Trial of Adolf Eichmann begins in Jerusalem.
12 April	Yuri Gagarin, aboard the Soviet satellite *Vostok 1*, becomes the first human in outer space.
17–20 April	Bay of Pigs "invasion" of Cuba by US.
21 April	Attempted coup, in Algiers, by Generals Challe, Salan, Jouhaud, and Zeller, against De Gaulle's policy of self-determination for Algeria.
1 May	Cuba declares itself a Democratic Socialist Republic.
3 May	Opening of *En attendant Godot*, Théâtre de l'Odéon.
4 May	SB awarded the first Prix International des Editeurs (also known later as the Prix Formentor, and the Prix International de Littérature), shared with Jorge Luis Borges; SB does not attend the ceremony.
by 28 May	Barbara Bray and her daughters have moved to Paris.
16–30 June	SB in Surrey with Sheila and Donald Page until 22 or 23 June, then in London.
23 June	Attends an England vs. Australia Test Match at Lord's, London, with Donald Page and cousin Molly Roe.
26 June	BBC TV broadcasts *Waiting for Godot* directed by Donald McWhinnie.
28 June	SB attends Glyndebourne performance of Donizetti's *L'Elisir d'amore*.
3–4 July	The Bielefeld production of Mihalovici's opera of *Krapp* performed as part of the Théâtre des Nations, Paris.
5 July	SB attends John Osborne's *Luther* performed as part of the Théâtre des Nations, Paris.
7 July	Finds his Ussy cottage has been broken into during his absence.

15 July	Begins English translation of *Comment c'est.*
11–22 August	Increasingly frequent OAS attacks in many areas of France.
13 August	The German Democratic Republic (GDR) begins construction of the Berlin Wall.
20–23 August	SB in Etretat.
1–11 September	SB in England.
8 September	Failed attempt on the life of General de Gaulle.
17 September	World premiere of *Happy Days* at the Cherry Lane Theatre, New York, directed by Alan Schneider.
24 October	Opening of Bram van Velde's retrospective, Knoedler Gallery, Paris.
20–22 November	SB writes a draft of *Words and Music*, planned for music by John Beckett and presentation on the BBC.
by 10 December	SB's *Poems in English* published by John Calder.
13 December	SB sends petition to John Calder and Harold Hobson for signatures to protest against the trial of Jérôme Lindon for his publication of *Le Déserteur* and for his anti-torture position on Algeria.

BARBARA BRAY
PURLEY, SURREY

7.1.61

38 Bd. St. Jacques
Paris 14me

Dear Barbara

Thanks for your morning letter.

Please write in future to above address.

Con left on Wednesday. No sign of Gibson. Con in good form in spite of tightly bandaged leg. Late nights and too much to drink, great consequent fatigue.[1]

Reading Darwin book with much pleasure.[2]

Difficult page proofs of Comment C'est last week, book out tomorrow. The printer had a problem with his page endings but did what I asked and there should not be many mistakes though the correcting was rushed by the Editions God knows why. Total indifference to its coming into world and reception, never look at it again.

Strange reunion chez Sylvia Beach 12 rue de l'Odéon to discuss re-publication of Our Exagmination dropped apparently by Faber and Laughlin. Present Gilbert, Brion, Sage, all contributors, Mrs Jolas. Sylvia presented us all with special and ordinary copies of original edition (1929). Lot of blablablather about old times, when Shakespeare bookshop was on 3rd floor including sign. S.B. (guess which) very old and shaky. Drove the Gilberts home to their island.[3]

Nice cold sunny day for referendum and another shot at Mildred.[4] Sleeping St. Jacques, rose unexpectedly at 8.45 (1st time for years) to find all radiators cold. Fortunately Bd. rooms inundated with sun, so shall move to other side when I begin to shiver (oh not before!). Neighbours infernally audible, don't know what to do about it. Nothing I suppose.

No sign from Pinget, suppose he is back for rehearsals. No news how they are going.[5] Saw Biedermann with Con and liked it. Superb performance by Serreau and lively too lively production, understand why Frisch disapproved and also how stupid and narrow authors can be.[6]

Don't count to get to Ussy at all. Concert Tuesday with Mihalovici's Phèdre (Goll). Tomorrow cousin Sally. Perhaps you will be at Hayden opening Tuesday. Think it will be his best London show.[7]

Looking forward immensely to seeing you.[8]

Love

Sam

ALS; 1 leaf, 1 side; *env to* Mrs Barbara Bray, 121 Brighton Rd., Purley, Surrey, Angleterre; *pm* 9-1-61, Paris; TCD, MS 10948/1/131.

1 Con Leventhal had arrived in Paris on 27 December and returned to Dublin on 4 January (SB to Bray, 24 December 1960 and 2 January 1961; TCD, MS 10948/1/128 and /129).

2 Although SB had not mentioned receiving a book on or by Darwin, the 1959 centennial of *On The Origin of the Species* stimulated re-editions of Darwin's work as well as books related to Darwin.

3 The meeting of Sylvia Beach (1887–1962; Profile I) with contributors to *Our Exagmination Round His Factification for Incamination of Work in Progress* (1929) included SB, Stuart Gilbert (1883–1969), Marcel Brion (1895–1984), and Robert Sage (1899–1962), as well as Maria Jolas. Despite initial hesitation, Faber and Faber would reissue the collection in 1961; James Laughlin (1914–1997), founder of New Directions, agreed to publish it in the United States in 1962 (SB to Sylvia Beach, 27 March 1961; NjP, Sylvia Beach).

In 1941, Beach had refused to sell her own copy of Joyce's *Finnegans Wake* to a German officer, who then threatened to confiscate everything. Stock and sign were moved to the third floor of 12 rue de l'Odéon: "Within two hours, not a single thing was to be seen in the shop" (Sylvia Beach, *Shakespeare and Company* [New York: Harcourt Brace, 1959] 216). Stuart and Moune Gilbert lived on the Ile Saint-Louis, Paris 4.

4 On Sunday 7 January, there was a referendum on Charles de Gaulle's proposals for self-determination in Algeria; reorganization of public authorities in Algeria was a pre-condition in De Gaulle's proposal.

5 SB wrote to Bray on 24 December 1960: "Robert disappeared into Switzerland without as much as a word or a drink" (TCD, MS 10948/1/128). His play *La Manivelle* was in rehearsal at the Théâtre de Lutèce.

6 Jean-Marie Serreau acted the title role of Biedermann as well as directing the production of *Biedermann et les incendiaires* by Max Frisch at the Théâtre de Lutèce. Frisch left Paris before the opening (see 5 November 1960, and n. 11).

7 The concert performance of Mihalovici's *Phèdre*, op. 58 (composed in 1948), an opera in five scenes, with a libretto by Yvan Goll (1891–1950), took place at the Théâtre

des Champs-Elysées on 9 January (Andreas Kramer and Robert Vilain, *Yvan Goll: A Bibliography of the Primary Works* [Oxford: Peter Lang, 2006] 335).

SB's cousin Sally Sinclair Armstrong. Henri Hayden's exhibition of paintings would open on 9 January at the Waddington Galleries, London.

"Count to get to" is a Gallicism for "count on getting to."

8 SB had suggested that Bray come to Paris in the second part of January (2 January 1961; TCD, MS 10948/1/129).

THOMAS MACGREEVY
DUBLIN

9.1.61

38 Bd. St. Jacques
Paris 14me

Dear Tom

Thanks for your letter. Monique's address is 15 Rue du Dragon, 6me. I think she is away at the moment. Tonight at Théâtre des Champs-Elysées concert performance of Mihalovici's Phèdre (libretto Ivan Goll). An old work. Suzanne and I are going. Comment C'est is just out and you will receive your copy soon. The proofs were difficult. I gave your Poussin to Gilbert and the next time I saw him he spoke very warmly of it.[1] In a few days we'll be gone from Favorites for good. I have slept here for the last few days. I am troubled by the strangeness and unfamiliar noises and it will take some getting used to. Leventhal was over for a week and I saw a lot of him. Also Sally Armstrong (Cissie's daughter) on her way to and from Geneva to spend the festivities with Sonny.[2] Something always turns up to prevent me from getting to Ussy which I have not seen now for over a month. I badly need a rest there but don't know when I'll get it, Hayden's vernissage at Waddington's today, it should be a fine show. Thanks for what you say about re-reading me. I never felt more sceptical about my work. But I couldn't have done any thing else, or otherwise. Have been reading a lot in W.B.'s Collected Poems, with intense absorption.[3] Am trying to get on, in the odd moments of quiet, with the play in English. Same strange feeling of wrongness, but necessary wrongness. I embark on this year with great misgiving.

It will be good to see you so soon. Chip's piano and voice score with the 3 languages is just out. He has not been too well and I hope this evening to find him in better form. Haskill's death was a great distress for them both.[4]

Much love from us both

Sam

ALS; 1 leaf, 2 sides; TCD, MS 10402/235.

1 SB writes "Ivan" for "Yvan" Goll.

SB had given MacGreevy's *Nicolas Poussin* to Stuart Gilbert. In his memoir, Robert Pinget reports SB's mention of Poussin (November 1960): "Me parle aussi de Poussin, un critique de ses amis venant de faire un ouvrage sur ce peintre. Il me demande si je comprends qu'après toute une vie de critique avertie et très à la page on puisse se rabattre en définitive sur Poussin. Je dis que oui, sans bien savoir pourquoi." (Doucet, unclassified Pinget Collection, "Notre ami Samuel Beckett," 50.) (Talks to me about Poussin too, a friend of his having just produced a work on this painter. He asks me if I can understand how after a lifetime of informed and up-to-date criticism, anyone should finally fall back on Poussin. I say I can, without really knowing why.)

2 SB's cousin had spent the holidays with her brother Morris Sinclair and his family in Geneva. Sally and Morris Sinclair were children of Frances Beckett Sinclair (known as Cissie, 1880–1951; Profile, I), SB's paternal aunt.

3 SB was reading W. B. Yeats's *Collected Poems* in the 1955 second edition (London: Macmillan).

4 MacGreevy planned to be in Paris in February, in part to hear Mihalovici's chamber opera *Krapp, ou la dernière bande*; it was to be performed as an oratorio on 13 February at the Palais de Chaillot. The Romanian pianist Clara Haskil (1895–1960) had been a pupil of Lazare-Lévy (1882–1964) at the Paris Conservatoire, as had Monique Haas.

BARBARA BRAY
PURLEY, SURREY

28.1.61 Paris

Dear Barbara

Thanks for your letters.

Not a good week here. Robert had to withdraw La Manivelle from the Lutèce programme, the abominable Germain having telephoned him the very day of the générale (Thursday) to say the spectacle was too long and that he should withdraw in the interests of Pinter and Martin![1] Poor Robert – very noble about it all, but a bad shock. Never heard of such a thing and of course Martin should have refused such a transaction. All indemnified of course, Robert and the two actors, and good chance of finding a home for it elsewhere, perhaps at the Poche with Arrabal's Tricycle or at Studio des C. E. with Les Chaises revived by Mauclair.[2] So outraged did not go to générale on Thursday but shall go tomorrow night. Bad press for Le Gardien. Unbelievably gross and stupid. Have kept a few notices for you, but forgot them at the Hayden last night. Shall send them on as soon as recovered. Paget in Combat is quite good. Don't fancy the play will have a long career after this orchestrated onslaught, but apparently last night it went quite well to a small house. Wednesday with the critics was apparently terrible. I'm dragged into copiously as you'll see in the Monde article.[3] This is their chance to get some of their own back. Whole thing very upsetting, and the Thursday affair made me feel physically ill. Spent the evening with Robert.

Just seen Serreau & his associates and it seems likely that Godot will come off at Odéon in May & June with Les Bonnes-Amédée directed by Blin who won't be able to play, at least before mid-June, because of Les Nègres at Royal Court.[4]

Revising first act of Winnie & Willie – needed it badly – before attacking second – a mere (!) question of writing.

Dining this evening with Bosquet and Arikha. Kind article by Nadeau in L'Express – some bad mistakes, but friendly. A stupidity in Arts which you will have seen.[5]

Writing separately to children to thank them for their nice letters – Checchina's quite extraordinary for her age.[6]

Thinking of going to Ussy Monday for a week – but not sure that I'll make it.

Thanks for all the trouble over Boswell. I'll think about it and let you know. Unless you have the courage to ask at Foyle's some day you're in the neighbourhood.[7]

Love

Sam

ALS; 1 leaf, 2 sides; *env to* Mrs Barbara Bray, 121 Brighton Rd., Purley, Surrey, Angleterre; *pm* _-1-61, Paris; TCD, MS 10948/1/133.

1 Lucie Germain was the manager of the Théâtre de Lutèce, which she established "as a rudimentary theatre" of 200 seats in 1956 (Odette Aslan, *Roger Blin and Twentieth-Century Playwrights*, tr. Ruby Cohn [Cambridge: Cambridge University Press, 1988] 60). The Générale for the double bill of Pinter's *Le Gardien* and Pinget's *La Manivelle* was scheduled for Thursday 26 January. Jean Martin was to have directed both plays, while also acting in *Le Gardien*. "Spectacle" is a Gallicism for "show" or "performance."

2 Pinget, Georges Adet, and Henri de Livry were "indemnified" (guaranteed compensation for rehearsals). SB's speculation that Pinget's play might be done elsewhere proved empty: Fernando Arrabal's *Le Tricycle* had been given a reading at the Théâtre de Poche, but it would not be produced until April 1964 at the Théâtre de Lutèce. Jacques Mauclair (1919–2001) had directed Eugène Ionesco's *Les Chaises* at the Studio des Champs-Elysées, but there was no indication that *Les Chaises* would be revived in 1961.

3 Jean Paget reviewed the play in "Le Gardien," *Combat*, 27 January 1961: 8. But most reviews were unfavorable from the start. Bertrand Poirot-Delpech wrote in *Le Monde*:

> Il est vrai que Roger Blin et Jean Martin, par ailleurs remarquables de conviction dans les deux rôles principaux, ont peut-être exagéré le caractère pitoyable et morbide du texte, obsédés qu'ils sont par la vision de Beckett d'une humanité en pleine putréfaction.
>
> Auprès de tant de rengaines, le spectacle mérite un succès de curiosité. ("'Le Gardien', de Harold Pinter," 28 January 1961: 9.)
>
> (Admittedly, Roger Blin and Jean Martin, incidentally splendidly convincing in the two main parts, perhaps stressed unduly the pitiful, morbid nature of the text, obsessed as they are by Beckett's vision of a humanity far gone in putrefaction.
>
> Compared with so many tired old pieces, this show deserves a certain success, as a curiosity.)

4 Jean-Marie Serreau and Aldo Bruzzicchelli proposed two productions by their newly formed company, Le Théâtre Nouveau, at the Odéon-Théâtre de France while the company of Jean-Louis Barrault was touring abroad in May and June. Serreau would direct the reprise of *En attendant Godot* and Ionesco's *Amédée, ou comment s'en débarrasser* (*Amédée, or How to Get Rid of It*), and Blin would direct the production of Genet's *Les Bonnes* (*The Maids*). Blin's prior commitment to direct Genet's *The Blacks* at the Royal Court Theatre, London (opening 24 May), made it impossible for him to play the role of Pozzo. SB inserts "with Les Bonnes-Amédée" in the left margin.

5 Nadeau wrote in his review of *Comment c'est*:

> Est-il possible de progresser dans le néant? Il faut le croire puisque, partant toujours d'un point situé plus bas que ses bases de départ antérieures, il aboutit à un "no man's land" encore plus désert . . . Mais cet "à peu près rien" possède une telle force de déflagration qu'on peut y voir, comme dans les ouvrages précédents de Beckett, l'image entière et désespérée de notre condition . . . "Le génie impérieux" de Beckett . . . le mène toujours plus près du silence . . . Silence, solitude, écrasement, souffrance et ce, pour des siècles,

pour l'éternité. Beckett veut-il dire que c'est cela notre condition, que c'est cela le "comment c'est" où nous vivons. Qui en douterait? (Maurice Nadeau, "'Comment C'est' par Samuel Beckett," *L'Express* 26 January 1961: 25–26.) (Is it possible to progress in a state of nothingness? We have to believe it is since, starting from a point lower than his last starting-point, he ends up in an even more deserted no-man's-land . . . But this "almost nothing" possesses such a force of combustion that we can see in it, as in Beckett's preceding works, the entire and desperate image of our condition . . . Beckett's "imperious genius" . . . always leads him closer to silence . . . Silence, solitude, defeat, suffering, lasting for centuries, for eternity. Does Beckett mean that this is our human condition, that this is "how it is" where we live. Who would doubt it?) (Nadeau, "Express," tr. Larysa Mykyta and Mark Schumacher, in Lawrence Graver and Raymond Federman, eds., *Samuel Beckett: The Critical Heritage* [London: Routledge and Kegan Paul, 1979] 224–229.)

In his review of *Comment c'est*, Matthieu Galey wrote: "Il faudrait précisément inventer un qualificatif nouveau, et une esthétique, un vocabulaire différents pour en parler" ("Des limbes et des rêves," *Arts, Lettres, Spectacles* 806 [25–31 January 1961] 4). (Precisely what would be needed, in order to talk about it, is to invent a new qualifier, a different aesthetic, a different vocabulary).

6 SB would write to Francesca and Julia Bray on 1 February: "Thank you for your nice letters and card. Jan sounds a very fine dog – like D[r] Johnson's cat Hodge. I hope you will be able to bring him when you come to live in France. But I am not sure he would like French ways." (TCD, MS 10948/1/135.)

7 SB was interested in finding an early edition of Boswell's *Life of Johnson*. Foyle's bookstore in London, then the largest in the world, once stocked used and new books alongside each other. "Si tu as le courage" (if you can face it).

HAROLD PINTER
LONDON

30.1.61

38 Bd. St.-Jacques
Paris 14me

Dear Harold

Jean Martin is too upset to write to you, so I'm doing it for him.[1] The daily press was bad. We are all thunderst[r]uck by the stupidity and vulgarity of the critics. Paget's article in Combat was the only one I saw with any understanding. He wrote about the play again today.[2] I am sending Barbara four or five cuttings which she can show you if you have not seen them already. The better weeklies may provide something worth having (Express,

France-Observateur) but the production has been greatly damaged by the daily bastards. On the Wednesday (press night) the reception was icy. The next day (générale) Mme Germain drove Pinget into a situation where he had simply to withdraw his play and Thursday Le Gardien was given alone. She also rang up the critics who had seen the two plays Wednesday and instructed them to make no reference to La Manivelle in their notices. To protest against these infamies we did not go to the générale. We went last Sunday. There was a small but enthusiastic house and we enjoyed the production very much. Both Blin and Martin are excellent in my opinion and Mick more than adequate.[3] The more I know and see the play the more I like it. We are all very upset and ashamed for French criticism. Spoken criticism will certainly be warm and possibly just sufficient to save the situation. I am so sorry to have to write you this and hope it will not prevent your coming over again soon as you planned. I have read The Birthday Party and The Room with much admiration, The Dumb Waiter not yet. Congratulations on success at the Arts.[4]

All good wishes.

Yours

s/ Sam

TLS; 1 leaf, 1 side; BL, Add MS 88880/7/2/3.

1 SB and Pinter had met for the first time on 11 January, in Paris. Pinter describes the meeting:

> When we did *The Caretaker* in Paris in 1961, Roger Blin was in it, and one day he said, "Would you like to meet Beckett?" It was almost too much for me – the thought of such a thing. I had written to him . . . I came into this hotel and he was very vigorous and chatty and extremely affable and extremely friendly and we spent the whole *night* together. (Mel Gussow, *Conversations with Pinter* [New York; Grove Press, 1994] 32.)

2 The second review by Jean Paget discusses dramaturgy inspired by the tape recording, drawing on *Le Gardien* as an example (Jean Paget, "Le Magnétophone," *Combat* 31 January 1961: 8).

3 The role of Mick was being played by José Varela (b. 1933).

4 Pinter's 1958 play *A Slight Ache*, first presented on radio in 1959, had opened at the Arts Theatre on 18 January, directed by Donald McWhinnie, in a triple bill with John Mortimer's *Lunch Hour* and N. F. Simpson's *The Form* – under the collective title *Three* ("Entertaining Triple Bill," *The Times* 19 January 1961: 16).

BARBARA BRAY
PURLEY, SURREY

3.2.61 Paris

Dear Barbara

Thanks for letter and script. I like it very much - quite sincerely. You have "understood" the book as no one so far. You of course greatly overrate it and me, but we won't go into that again. What you say of its being not about something, but something, is exactly what I wrote of Finnegans in the Exagmination. It must have been very difficult to state the thing so briefly & clearly. I don't know how you do it. Congratulations, dear Barbara, and all my thanks.[1]

No further reactions here (that I know) except just now a phone call from Cioran - very warm and understanding.

Very tired this evening and avalanches of letters to answer and other obligations. Also great inner urgency (Wucht) to get on with play of which 2nd act under way. Enclosed some more, - what wd. you call you? Sirreverence? Sarraute takes the pan. Lemarchand is nice as usual. Very poor houses. But warm. Hope Harold will come over nonetheless.[2]

Don't bother any more about Boswell. Only if you happen to be near Foyles, they might have the 6 vol. Hill (1890?) 2nd hand or the old illustrated Croker. But don't go to any further trouble. Unimportant.[3]

Revival of Godot with Bonnes - Amédée seems now pretty certain May-June at Théâtre de France. Genet sent me his Paravents. Not for me I fear from quick look.[4] Have to write a few lines for T. de France programme, a few more for Bielefeld programme.[5] What will be left of me after this year?

Love
Sam

ALS; 1 leaf, 2 sides; enclosures: Claude Sarraute, "Le Gardien: Quel est le sens caché?" *France-Observateur* 2 February 1961: 20; J.[acques] L.[emarchand], "'Le Gardien' de Harold Pinter au Théâtre de Lutèce," *Figaro Littéraire* 4 February 1961: 34; Robert Kanters, "Théâtre: 'Le Gardien': Un mélange d'ennui et de curiosité," *L'Express* 2 February 1961: 34–35; *env to* Mrs Barbara Bray, 121 Brighton Rd., Purley, Surrey, Angleterre; *pm* 4-2-61, Paris; TCD, MS 10948/1/136.

1 In her review of *Comment c'est* which was presented on the BBC Third Programme on 2 February 1961, Bray writes: "COMMENT C'EST isn't about anything. It is something." Although it is described by its publisher as a novel, Bray continues:

> It is a novel if the DIVINE COMEDY is a novel. Otherwise it's poetry, pure if not simple. The book is divided into three sections and it's set out in short passages resembling stanzas rather than paragraphs. There's no punctuation – the words punctuate themselves. The object is to represent with as few artificial distractions as possible a broken, continually self-contradicting utterance.
>
> The speaker is the vehicle of a voice which he seems to hear first without and then within, and which he relays as best he can, given the imperfection of his hearing, of his understanding, and of the voice itself, by muttering it inaudibly into the mud in which, or so the voice tells him, he lies. All his information comes through the voice; he has no utterance of his own. Or so the voice tells him [. . .]
>
> This is a piece of "total writing", in which all the apparently contradictory powers, rational and irrational, of a uniquely rich and delicate sensibility and a uniquely piercing intelligence are brought together to give as pure a rendering of modern consciousness as words have yet been made to convey. The Idols of the Tribe, and of the Theatre, and of the Market-place are shattered. The Idols of the Cave or Den, that Murphy so delighted in, are still there all right. But the years, and the "art of known and feeling sorrow", have changed them from idiosyncrasy to poetry. (BBCWAC, T85, *Comment*, 2 February 1961, 1–4.)

SB refers to his essay on Joyce's *Finnegans Wake*, explicitly to his statement: "His writing is not about something; *it is that* something itself" (Samuel Beckett, "Dante. . . Bruno. Vico.. Joyce," *Our Exagmination Round His Factification for Incamination of Work in Progress* [Paris: Shakespeare and Company, 1929], 14).

2 "Wucht" (force).

Reviews enclosed of Pinter's *Le Gardien*: see the bibliographical note to the present letter, above. SB later reports that he did see Pinter in Paris, with Roger Blin and Jean Martin, on 11 February: "He was very nice to them all about Le Gardien and I think genuinely liked the production" (SB to Bray, 12 February 1961; TCD, MS 10948/1/137).

3 SB refers to the George Birkbeck Hill edition of Boswell's *Life of Johnson* (Oxford: Clarendon Press, 1887), extra-illustrated with hundreds of portraits and views, and the John Wilson Croker edition of the same title in its second edition, revised by John Wright (London: John Murray, 1835), which was extra-illustrated with over 100 engraved plates.

4 Jean Genet's play *Les Paravents* (1961, *The Screens*).

5 SB did not write a note for the program of *En attendant Godot* produced by the Théâtre Nouveau at the Odéon-Théâtre de France in May. In the program of the Bielefeld premiere of Mihalovici's opera, SB supplied and signed a line from "Texte pour Rien V," although in the program the first two clauses are inverted to read: "Ich führe die Feder, ich führe das Protokoll, bei den Verhandlungen ich weiß nicht welcher Sache, warum wollen, daß es meine sei, mir liegt nichts daran" [2] (cf. Samuel Beckett, *Erzählungen und Texte um Nichts*, tr. Elmar Tophoven [Frankfurt: Suhrkamp Verlag, 1997] 122). ("I'm the clerk, I'm the scribe, at the hearings of what cause I know not. Why want it to be mine, I don't want it.") (Samuel Beckett, "Text for Nothing 5," *Stories and Texts for Nothing* [New York: Grove Press, 1967] 95.)

BARBARA BRAY
PURLEY, SURREY

17.2.61 Paris

Dear Barbara

Thanks for your letters, the second today. Enclosed another cry of alarm. You may be amused to hear that the first edition is sold out, unprecedented in my annals.[1]

Don't bother at all about the Boswell and thanks for the trouble you have taken already.

Sorry to hear of the Observer complication. I don't think it should affect matters much.[2] You say to be careful what I say, yes, I must be more & more careful about that. I say then with care that it would be very foolish of you to refuse any shall we say pleasure that comes your way. You have a way of asking questions to which you know the answers. You know it grieves me to think of you lonely and abstinent. So if you want me to be less grieved try and be a little less of both.

I should like very much to show you the play - and to Donald, but shall not till I have revised it. I showed it to Alan because I wanted to be thinking of it. One of his comments was very much to the point[3] - I have written to John about the words music idea and await his reaction. I told him he could go ahead and get us commissioned if he wished. I have not been able to think about it much, but a little, and have written a page.[4]

Alan Simpson turned up. He is writing a book on Behan and me. A line from Harold Hobson after a long silence. Lunch with him at the Closerie tomorrow.[5]

My telephone number - PORt-Royal 96.60.

Leaving for Germany 24th and back here I hope 29th. Dreading it. Heard concert performance of Krapp at Chaillot a few days. Music very fine, well played, well sung, no attempt at mise en scene, text rather obliterated. At Bielefeld more will remain.[6]

Love and be a little good to yourself.

Sam

ALS; 1 leaf, 2 sides; enclosure: Luc Estang, "Comment C'est de Samuel Beckett," *Le Figaro Littéraire* 18 February 1961: 15; *env to* Mrs Barbara Bray, 121 Brighton Rd., Purley, Surrey, Angleterre; *pm* 18-2-61, Paris; TCD, MS 10948/1/138.

1 After quoting three passages from *Comment c'est*, Luc Estang wrote:

> Et comme ça cent soixante-quinze pages durant. Mais cette absence de ponctuation dans la logorrhée constitue la moindre menace de céphalée! ... Ce flux de paroles qui déborde la formulation consciente exige d'être "dit" et non pas seulement "lu" ... Cela n'est pas de la littérature; cela ne peut pas en être. ("Comment C'est de Samuel Beckett," *Le Figaro Littéraire* 18 February 1961: 15.) (And on and on like this for another one hundred and seventy-five pages. But the lack of punctuation in the logorrhoea is the least of the impending headaches! ... This flood of words which outruns conscious formulation demands to be "spoken" and not just "read" ... This isn't literature: it can't be.)

The initial print run of *Comment c'est* was 3,000 copies; a second edition of 3,000 copies was printed on 9 March 1961 (Federman and Fletcher, *Samuel Beckett*, 68).

2 The complication with *The Observer* is not known; it may have been related to Bray's column, "Paris Perspective," which would begin on 28 May.

3 On 1 February, in advance of Alan Schneider's visit to Paris, SB wrote to him about the manuscript of *Happy Days*:

> I'll be able to show you first act of play which I'm now revising (first act). I'll be very glad of the chance to talk to you about it and hear what you think. Beyond a few notes have done nothing on impossible second act ... Terrible role, all evening alone on stage and for last 20 minutes without a gesture to help voice. Perhaps it[']s just madness. You'll tell me. (Burns Library, Samuel Beckett Collection, SB-AS.)

Schneider gives a detailed account of reading and discussing the typescript with SB in his autobiography *Entrances* (293–295): "Sam asked me for my opinion on two questions he had not yet settled" – namely, the choice between "When Irish Eyes are Smiling" and "The Merry Widow" for the music box, and the title. Schneider adds, of "The Merry Widow": "Perhaps it was overly sentimental. But in the context of Winnie's unusual circumstances, perhaps the sentiment would seem justified or, at least, suitably ironic. Sam agreed. 'The Merry Widow Waltz' it would be, for eternity." The possibilities for the title were: *Many Mercies* or *Tender Mercies* or *Happy Days*. "Again, it was the ironic significance of the latter title, its double or even triple overtones, that made me tell Sam he had to call the new play *Happy Days*" (Schneider, *Entrances*, 294).

4 SB and John Beckett had been asked to collaborate on a radio play for the BBC, which would eventuate as *Words and Music*. SB's initial notes, dated 16 February 1961, are in the "Eté '56" notebook [p. 45] (UoR, BIF, MS 1227/7/7/1; MoSW). Richard Admussen has cast doubt on the year, writing that SB "may have intended 1962"; however, this letter confirms that SB had begun the radio play in 1961 (Richard L. Admussen, *The Samuel Beckett Manuscripts: A Study*, ed. Jackson Bryer, A Reference Publication in Literature [Boston: G. K. Hall, 1979] 94).

5 Alan Simpson and SB met on Wednesday 15 February; Simpson's book included an account of the Pike Theatre's role as producer of the works of both

playwrights (*Beckett and Behan, and a Theatre in Dublin* [London: Routledge and Kegan Paul, 1962]).

6 The opening of the Festival at the Städtische Bühnen Bielefeld was planned for 24 February, with a discussion of Modernes Musiktheater; the program announced that this would be presented by SB, Mihalovici, Winfried Zillig, the General Music Director Bernhard Conz, and the Director of the Bielefeld Opera Dr. Joachim Klaber (TCD, MS 10948/1/130a). SB had reluctantly agreed to attend this discussion. When asked to make a few remarks, he stood, hesitated, and then said: "'Actually I don't want to say anything at all about my work'" (Knowlson, *Damned to Fame*, 427). The first staged performance of *Krapp, oder Das letzte Band* followed the next evening, sung by American baritone William Dooley (b. 1932). Derik Olsen (b. 1923), whom SB called "a good Swiss baritone," had sung the role in the concert performance on 13 February in Paris (SB to Judith Schmidt, 12 February 1961; NSyU).

BARBARA BRAY
PURLEY, SURREY

Wednesday [1 March 1961] Frankfurt

Dear Barbara

All over thank God and on to Cologne in an hour by train and thence tomorrow by road with the Tophoven home. All has gone as well as such things can I suppose, no comparison anyway with the Sorrento inferno. The opera at Bielefeld with Mihalovici and many friends of us both was a success, wonderfully sung by a young American who'll be a big name in not so long.[1] Drove with Unseld here next day and last night the hommage with profundities from Adorno and a good reading by Tophoven of his translation of From an A. W. I'm sorry you weren't there to see me - and of course for other reasons - stagger up on the platform and return thanks in German (?) to all the mice and men I could think of. Met all the Suhrkamp Verlag crowd - very nice indeed. Eich came on the way from his Bavarian retreat. I liked him greatly.[2] But so tired, so tired, to the point almost of inability to do anything for myself. This is the only letter I have written all the time here. People, people, signatures, smiles, confusion of names. I suppose another mistake, but what the hell - all I have missed is my solitude - i.e. for the work's sake – and must go on missing. My box Bd. St. Jacques must be groaning with letters – and alerady [sic] 50 unanswered. Ça devient tout à fait impossible. Shall try and wind up Happy Days and get on with John job.[3] Then begin translating. I speak as if I were sure I had the time – and am not. No more now. Shall write again if and when I get to Paris.

Love

Sam

ALS; 1 leaf, 2 sides; *env to* Mrs Barbara Bray, 121 Brighton Rd., Purley, Surrey, England; *pm* 1–3–61, Frankfurt; TCD, MS 10948/1/140.

1 SB took the train from Frankfurt to Cologne to meet the Tophovens, who, having just purchased their first car in Germany, planned to drive back to Paris via Amsterdam overnight, with a stop in Delft. SB did some of the driving (Erika Tophoven to the editors, 13 December 2012). Friends present for the premiere: Suzanne Deschevaux-Dumesnil, Marthe Gautier, Matias, Siegfried Unseld, Elmar and Erika Tophoven.

William Dooley was the soloist in *Krapp oder Das letzte Band* (sung in German) in Bielefeld; Dooley became a leading performer at the Deutsche Oper Berlin (1962–1964), and went on to sing with the New York Metropolitan Opera (1964–1977) and the Vienna State Opera (1977–1982).

2 The Suhrkamp evening on 27 February is described in detail by Knowlson (*Damned to Fame*, 428); it was one of several similar occasions held during the year, in which Suhrkamp presented their authors to other writers of the house. Those present included Günter Eich, Karl Krolow (1915–1999), Hans Magnus Enzensberger (b. 1929), as well as professors, publishers, bookdealers, editors, translators, journalists, readers, and students (K. K., "Beckett in Frankfurt: Suhrkamp Verlagsabend," *Frankfurter Allgemeine Zeitung* 1 March 1961: 20). The event took place in the Cantata Hall, Frankfurt. Adorno presented extracts from his study of SB, "Versuch, das Endspiel zu verstehen" (*Noten zur Literatur II*, Bibliothek Suhrkamp [Frankfurt: Suhrkamp Verlag, 1961] 281–321; translated in English as "Trying to Understand *Endgame*," in Theodor W. Adorno, *Can One Live After Auschwitz? A Philosophical Reader*, tr. Rodney Livingstone *et al.*, ed. Rolf Tiedemann [Stanford, CA: Stanford University Press, 2003] 259–294.)

Of SB's few words of thanks in German, the *Frankfurter Allgemeine Zeitung* reported: "Das sehr schmalr [sic], ein wenig geistesabwesende, asketische Gesicht belebte sich freundlich. Der Mann gewinnt durch schlichte Natürlichkeit. Der meint es ehrlich." (1 March 1961: 20.) (The face, narrow, ascetic, and somewhat absent-minded, came alive in a friendly manner. His simple unassuming ways make him winsome. He means what he says.)

3 "Ça devient tout à fait impossible" (It's getting to be altogether impossible).

SB's collaboration with John Beckett on a radio play for the BBC Third Programme.

THEODOR ADORNO
? FRANKFURT

9.3.61 Folkestone (Kent)

Dear Professor Adorno

I am reading your essay on Endspiel and shall write to you again when I have finished it and thought about it.[1]

I shall be in England till the end of the month, which means that I cannot have the pleasure of seeing you in Paris. I regret this extremely. I was looking forward so keenly to such another evening as we spent together when you were lecturing at the Sorbonne.[2]

Thank you again, dear Professor Adorno, for your friendship and for your belief in my work.[3]

With kindest regards to your wife.[4] I am

yours very cordially

Sam. Beckett

ALS; 1 leaf, 1 side; Adorno Archiv.

1 SB was reading a typescript of Adorno's talk delivered in Frankfurt, "Versuch, das Endspiel zu verstehen" ("Trying to Understand *Endgame*"); SB's copy was inscribed with a note dated on the day of the presentation: "Für S.B. [. . .] eine Entschuldigung [. . .] und als kleines Zeichen herzlicher Verehrung." ("for S.B. [. . .] an apology [. . .] and as a small token of heartfelt esteem.") (Facsimile, Sotheby's catalogue, *English Literature, History, Children's Books, Illustrations and Photographs*, 8 July 2004, item 131.) As later published, the essay bears a dedication to Beckett, "to S.B. in memory of Paris, Fall 1958" (Adorno, *Noten zur Literatur*, 281; Adorno, *Can One Live After Auschwitz? A Philosophical Reader*, 259).

2 Adorno gave three lectures at the Sorbonne in November 1958: one on the experiential contents of Hegel's philosophy, another on the sociology of music, and a third on the relation between sociological theory and social research. His first meeting with SB occurred on 28 November at the Hotel Lutetia. According to Adorno's diary, his conversation with Beckett lasted well into the night at the Coupole and Aux Iles Marquises. This meeting prompted Adorno to begin making notes for his essay on *Endgame* (notes documented by Rolf Tiedemann in his essay "Gegen den Trug der Frage nach dem Sinn" (Müller-Doohm, *Adorno*, 357).

3 On 6 November 1960, SB had written to Siegfried Unseld: "Je vous prie de faire mes amitiés au Professeur Adorno et de lui dire combien je me félicite de l'avoir comme exégète" (Suhrkamp Verlag Leitung Autorekorr, SB: 1960–1961) (I would ask you to pass on my greetings to Professor Adorno, and tell him how glad I am to have him as exegete).

4 Adorno's wife was Margarete ("Gretel") Karplus (1902–1993, m. 1936). She was part of the intellectual circle that included Walter Benjamin, Bertolt Brecht, and Ernst Bloch (Detlev Claussen, *Theodor W. Adorno: One Last Genius* [Cambridge, MA: Harvard University Press, 2008] 276).

AVIGDOR ARIKHA
PARIS

9.3.61 Folkestone

Sang tourne
plus calme
dans la ville
de Harvey[1]
prière

S.[2]

APCI; 1 leaf, 1 side; "Folkestone Harbour"; *to* Monsieur A. Arikha, 10 Villa d'Alésia, Paris 14, FRANCE; *pm* 9-3-61, Folkestone; InU, Arikha.

9.3.61 Folkestone

Blood goes round
calmer
in the town
of Harvey[1]
prayer

S.[2]

1 Folkestone was the birthplace of William Harvey (1578–1657), author of *De Motu Cordis* (1628) which gave the first systematic account of the circulation of the blood pumped by the heart.

2 Arikha reported to the editors that SB had joked to him, some months before: "If you marry Anne, I'll marry Suzanne." (Arikha married Anne Atik on 3 May 1961.)

On 10 March, SB wrote to Thomas MacGreevy, alluding indirectly to his reason for being in Folkestone, which was to make the arrangements for his marriage to Suzanne Deschevaux-Dumesnil:

> Here now with car (le Touquet-Lydd "hop") to deal with the little matter I mentioned to you. Have seen the registrar and all is arranged. Suzanne will arrive about 22nd and we shd. be back in France by the 25th. I need not stay here all the time, so long as I keep on my room, so shall probably run up to see Sheila next week and perhaps one or two friends near by. Glad to sit quiet here for the moment, unknown and undisturbable. The days pass dealing with accumulation of unanswered mail and walking by the sea. The place is very pleasant – if the damn mist would only lift and let through a bit of sun and warmth. (TCD, MS 10402/237.)

Further on SB's marriage, see Knowlson, *Damned to Fame*, 429–432.

BARBARA BRAY
PURLEY, SURREY

2.4.61 Paris

Dear Barbara

Thanks for your letters. Ne parlons + de ça.[1]

I'm in poor form with flu and can't lie up because of Godot rehearsals. Usual complications, chief of which departure of Blin for London April 20th leaving onus of direction chiefly on me practically till opening May 3rd.[2] Means I have to try and get his mise en scène into my head again. Difficulties with Raimbourg too who is not coming to rehearsals because of some film in the provinces. Appointment with him to-day to make it clear he must rehearse assiduously from now on or relinquish the role. He seems to think a fortnight's rehearsal at the end will be enough for him – for him, yes, but not for the play, with the new Pozzo (very good I think) and new Estragon.[3] Means the Etretat trip is off. And Happy Days held up again. And if Raimbourg goes, by whom replace him? So it goes.

A letter from John's sister. He is much more comfortable but has to face another operation this week, X-ray having shown that union is not satisfactory and will not give perfect movement. Appears he has taken it very well. They have rigged up some gadget enabling him to read.[4]

Love

Sam

ALS; 1 leaf, 1 side; *env to* Mrs Barbara Bray, 121 Brighton Rd., Purley, Surrey, Angleterre; *pm* 2-4-61, Paris; TCD, MS 10948/1/144.

1 "Ne parlons + de ça" (Let's have no more talk of this).

2 Roger Blin would be in London for rehearsals of the English production of Genet's *The Blacks* at the Royal Court Theatre; it would open on 24 May, ten days before the opening of *En attendant Godot* in Paris.

3 Lucien Raimbourg played Vladimir, as he had done in the original production. Raimbourg was acting in *Dynamite Jack*, a French Western directed by Jean Bastia (n.d.) and filmed in the south of France. In the new production of *En attendant Godot*, Jean-Jacques Bourgeois (1922–2001) played Pozzo and Etienne Bierry (b. 1918) played Estragon.

4 While he was in Folkestone, SB learned that John Beckett had had a serious automobile accident. SB wrote to Goddard Lieberson (1911–1977; profile, II) on 16 March: "everything bust except the vital part" (CtY, Gilmore, MSS 69); he told Barney Rosset that his cousin was "all bust up to hell, arms and legs, but life not in danger. Went to sleep at the wheel driving home from a concert and ran into a wall. 6 months in hospital probably." (17 March 1961; NSyU.) John Beckett's twin sister Ann was staying in contact with SB.

BARBARA BRAY
PURLEY, SURREY

6.4.61 Paris

Dear Barbara

Thanks for your letter from Bath and the other. Glad your foot is better.

Banish from your mind any thought that I am particularly in need of money. Am in no hurry whatsoever to be repaid, please forget about it[.] I'll probably sell Ussy because it's too much for me now, I can't be there to look after the place, and I've lost interest. I could get along quite well without the money it will yield (not a great deal I expect). I may go Saturday afternoon to pick up some things I need.

Not much to tell of rehearsals. We'll muddle through somehow as usual. I've no illusions about my directorial powers – but find I can get things better now & then. Giacometti was invited to provide the tree, but declined (too busy). I'm pretty limp, with dregs of flue [sic], and occasional dry whoops to bust the belly's skin. Done practically nothing with H.D. A line from Gibson announcing arrival next week and need to discuss a "project" with me. Je connais ça. Glad to read Hobson's article. Robert says he will not go to England for the opening.[1] Dined last night with Hayden – as usual. Very low myself, till very end of evening, walked home careless. No more news of John, expect a letter from Ann any day. Invited to Guerre & Poésie (Barrault-Pichette) this evening, but not there. Won't be at Searle & others matinée Sunday either – rehearsal on stage, last with Blin.[2] Don't know the French essayist you mention. Lot of people to see and things to do apart from rehearsals next week & ça durera ce que ça durera.[3] Reading Suhrkamp's letters and A. Monnier's Gazettes, without relish either.[4] Only 10.30 but good for nothing but bed where I won't sleep. Marvellous summer day to-day, walked down Luxembourg to theatre about noon, light footed, crawled back up the hill at 4. Heat lightning in the sky tonight & rain wd. be welcome. Two very hostile notices of N.Y. television Godot – transmitted at last.[5] Chestnuts superb B$^{\underline{d}}$ Arago.

Can't go on.

Love

Sam

ALS; 1 leaf, 2 sides; *env to* M$^{\underline{rs}}$ Barbara Bray, 121 Brighton Rd., Purley, Surrey, Angleterre; *pm* 7-4-61, Paris; TCD, MS 10948/1/145.

1 John Gibson's proposal has not been identified. "Je connais ça" (I know what *that* means). Later, on 29 June, Stephen Hearst proposed to John Gibson that SB be asked to contribute "a personal reminiscence of Joyce in Paris," as a basis for a film on Joyce; SB's words were to be spoken by an actor (BBCWAC, RCONT1, Samuel Beckett, Scriptwriter I). The proposal was not realized.

Harold Hobson mentioned the opening of Robert Pinget's *Dead Letter* and Marguerite Duras's *The Square* on 11 April at the Little Theatre in Bromley, saying of Pinget that he "has a talent that only squares will ignore" ("Little Ones Not Lost," *The Sunday Times*, 2 April 1961: 35).

2 *Guerre et Poésie* presented a selection of poems on the theme of war, from the Middle Ages to the present, selected by Henri Pichette (1924–2000); it was performed by the Compagnie Renaud-Barrault, accompanied by projections by cinema artist Carlos Viladebo (b. 1926) and music by Maurice Roche (1924–1997) (Henri Pichette, *Guerre et Poésie*, *Cahiers Renaud-Barrault* 35 [April 1961]). On Sunday 9 April, the matinée program at the Théâtre Sarah-Bernhardt, as part of the Théâtre des Nations, would feature four short operas: Boris Blacher's *Abstract opera Number 1*, Erik Satie's cantata *Socrate*, Paul Hindemith's *Hin und zurück*, and Humphrey Searle's *Diary of a Madman* (adapted from a short story by Nikolai Gogol), presented by the Berlin Opera Studio (Genêt [Janet Flanner], "Letter from Paris," *The New Yorker* 37.11 [29 April 1961] 139–140).

3 SB had plans to see Jack and Jean Page and their family, as well as photographer Lüfti Özkök and two other persons on the following Tuesday; then John Gibson on Wednesday, Bray on Thursday, Pamela Mitchell (c. 1922–2002; Profile, II) on Friday. (SB to Sheila Page, 17 April 1961; Babcock Collection. SB to Barbara Bray, [10 April 1961]; TCD, MS 10948/1/146. SB to Pamela Mitchell, 26 March 1961; UoR, BIF MS 5060.)

"Ça durera ce que ça durera" (It will take as long as it takes).

4 Peter Suhrkamp and Siegfried Unseld, *Brief an die Autoren* (Frankfurt: Suhrkamp, 1961). Adrienne Monnier, *Gazette: 1925–1945* (Paris: Julliard, 1953).

5 The television production of *Waiting for Godot* directed by Alan Schneider was broadcast on *Play of the Week* on WNTA-TV in New York, from April 3 through April 5. Jack Gould criticized the transition to television: the "fragile rapport between the company on the stage and the audience never seems realized in the TV show" ("TV: 'Waiting for Godot,'" *The New York Times* 4 April 1961: 75). Sid Bakal wrote that in his months of reviewing *Play of the Week*, he had "yet to see the producers rack up this big and fat a zero" ("TV Review: 'Play of the Week,'" *New York Herald Tribune* 4 April 1961: 32).

BARBARA BRAY
PURLEY, SURREY

26.4.61 [Paris]

Dear Barbara

In haste, before dashing (!) off to rehearsal, to thank you for your letters.

Here apparently all quiet again. Tanks etc. gone. Great sigh of relief on coming back late from Odéon last night and hearing news on radio.[1]

Raimbourg was here for 2 rehearsals, disappeared again last Sunday & has not been seen since.[2] Giacometti's tree now on stage. Very fine. Plan of 6 leaves now decided.[3] New Estragon & Pozzo working with great heart. But what can they do without their Vladimir? May be necessary for Serreau to play the part.[4] Boy will be just adequate. Hand full of trumps played like a fool.[5]

No time for anything but Odéon to and fro and trying to keep up with letters and people. Lunch with Ellmann tomorrow. Letter from Daiken touchingly concerned for me. They will probably be coming over. John was to have an arm pinned on Monday.[6] No news yet how it went.

Note address & tel. number

Love, à bientôt

Sam

ALS; 1 leaf, 1 side; *env to* Mrs Barbara Bray, 121 Brighton Road, Purley, Surrey, Angleterre; *pm* 26-4-61, Paris; TCD, MS 10948/1/149.

1 The revolt in Algiers of four French generals (Maurice Challe, Raoul Salan, Edmond Jouhaud, and André Zeller), who had threatened an attack on Paris, was ended on 25 April. On 22 April, the retired generals had taken control of Algiers. At midnight on 23 April, the French government broadcast a "warning that the insurgents might be on the point of landing aircraft or parachutists at various air fields in metropolitan France . . . in an attempt to seize power." Charles de Gaulle invoked emergency powers, and citizens were called upon to assemble at regional airports when a siren sounded ("Rebels Plot to Seize Power in Paris; Sirens to Warn Citizens of Algeria Parachutists; General De Gaulle Assumes Dictatorial Powers," *The Times* 24 April 1961: 14). Trade unions called a general strike in support of de Gaulle on 24 April. On 25 April, an atomic bomb was exploded in the Sahara to prevent it from falling into rebel hands. Tanks and roadblocks had been set up in response to the threat in Paris. By early on 26 April, General Challe had surrendered.

2 Lucien Raimbourg was unavailable for rehearsals; an exasperated SB had written to Bray on 21 April: "Raimbourg promised to be here yesterday and will not be here till next Tuesday when I suppose with luck not till following Saturday, i.e. a few days before we open!" (TCD, MS 10948/1/148).

3 To Bray on 21 April, SB reported on the tree Alberto Giacometti had made: "Superb. The one bright spot in this so far dreary exhumation" (TCD, MS 10948/1/148). According to James Knowlson, SB and Giacometti "stood for hours on either side of the tree contemplating how the plaster leaves that Giacometti had also sculpted could best be fixed on for the beginning of the second act" (*Damned to Fame*, 711).

4 Etienne Bierry (Estragon) and Jean-Jacques Bourgeois (Pozzo). Jean-Marie Serreau was producing the play. Knowlson reports that SB even played Vladimir in rehearsal "when Serreau, too, was not free" (*Damned to Fame*, 433).

5 The first actor who played the boy had moved from Paris; he was replaced by Jean Lévy.

6 SB encouraged Leslie and Lilyan Daiken to come to Paris over the Whitsun holiday as his guests (SB to Leslie Daiken, 27 April 1961; Cuming Collection).

John Beckett's surgery was to reset his arm: "John is getting on as well as can be expected. Other operations will be necessary, pinning, resetting and such horrors. He seems to be taking it all very calmly." (SB to Donald and Sheila Page, 28 April 1961; Babcock Collection.)

MARGARET MCLAREN
LONDON

May 19th 1961

38 Boulevard St.-Jacques
Paris 14me

Dear Mrs McLaren

Thank you for your letter of May 17th.[1]

I suppose we should authorize this new production of GODOT by the BBC, though I feel the play is being done to death and would much prefer to be represented in this series by ENDGAME which has never had a satisfactory production in England. I should like Donald McWhinnie to direct, if he is available and willing. He is at present rehearsing TV GODOT. Transmission June 26th.[2]

Many thanks for suggesting and congratulations on obtaining increased fee.

With best wishes,
Yours sincerely
Samuel Beckett

I hear that Richard de la Mare of BBC TV Monitor Arts Programme wishes to present a TV production of my <u>Act Without Words II</u>. I am writing to give him permission and saying that the contract will be handled by you. The U.K. rights of this mime belong to me.[3]

TLcc, with APS; 1 leaf, 1 side; GEU, MSS 1221.

1 Margaret McLaren's letter of 17 May had requested permission for a new production of *Waiting for Godot* in the BBC's new series *From the Fifties*.

2 Michael Bakewell wrote to Margaret McLaren in response to SB's suggestion of *Endgame*: "We particularly wanted to do 'WAITING FOR GODOT' in this context,

since we felt that it marked the turning-point of drama in the 'fifties, and should be included for that reason" (26 May 1961; BBCWAC, RCONT1, Samuel Beckett, Scriptwriter I). He promised to raise the suggestion of an independent production of *Endgame*.

3 Richard de la Mare's proposal to produce *Act Without Words II* on BBC TV's *Monitor* did not eventuate; it was replaced by the general *Monitor* programme on *Waiting for Godot*, broadcast on 4 June, with excerpts from the British and French productions and a discussion of the play by Peter Hall, Alan Simpson, and Donald McWhinnie.

ALAN SCHNEIDER
NEW YORK

20.5.61

38 Bd St. Jacques
Paris 14me

Dear Alan

Thanks for your letter. I hope the children are quite well again now and all apple-pie order in H-o-H.[1]

Had a hard time here with Godot rehearsals in absence of Blin and Serreau rehearsing Raimbourg's part till a week before opening. But we made out and it is now doing very well at Odéon. I could do nothing else while it lasted, but since beginning of May have been working on the new play and hope to start typing definitive text next week and to send it out towards end of month. You could go on labouring for ever on these things, but the time comes, and I think it has come here, when you have to let them go. You won't find much difference from the script you read – got in the hubby in both acts and think the song will be the Valse duet (I love you so) from the Merry Widow

"Though I say not what I may not
Let you hear,
Yet the swaying dance is saying
Love me dear. ."
etc

Perhaps a bit late (1905) for a music-box popularisation, but there is a Regina recording (same quality of sound) – I'll let you have details and reference in due course.[2] Willie's costume is changed for appearance at end and Winnie has on her hat through 2nd act. Other odds and ends, but essentially unchanged.[3] I saw Bessler (Schlosspark) and he wants it for Berlin Festival Sept. – October. I have written to Grove about this. I don't know if you attach importance to a N.Y. world première or if you would authorize eventually prior productions in London (McWhinnie Royal Court) & Berlin. Though if Cherry Lane is available in Fall you will almost certainly be the first. I'll be going to England late June and look forward to talking to McWhinnie – who will have read the script by then.[4] There's a bad Simpson revival of *Godot* at Stratford E. which was sprung on me & which I tried to stop, but couldn't. All Irish and uproarious. Very upsetting, the more so as McW. now rehearsing TV *Godot* for release June 26th.[5]

New flat is working out all right. Have decided to sell Ussy. Don't seem to be able to get there any more to look after it, or to want to. Better get rid of it.

Affectionately to you all

Sam

ALS; 1 leaf, 2 sides; Burns Library, Samuel Beckett Collection, SB-AS. Previous publication, Beckett and Schneider, *No Author Better Served*, 81–83.

1 The Schneiders lived in Hastings-on-Hudson, New York.

2 Schneider had read a draft of *Happy Days* when he was in Paris (see 17 February 1961, n. 3). SB adapted the words from "For I Love You, So" (popularly known as "The Merry Widow Waltz"); he retained the tune of Franz Lehár's operetta *Die lustige Witwe* (1905; *The Merry Widow*) (*Gems from The Merry Widow* [Chicago, New York: The May Company, n.d.]); *Happy Days* ([Grove] 64; hereafter, all citations of this play are to this edition). SB refers to the sound typical of the Regina Music Box.

3 In Act I, Willie is naked (SB to Alan Schneider, 3 September 1961; Burns Library, Samuel Beckett Collection, SB-AS; Beckett and Schneider, *No Author Better Served*, 101). In Act II, Willie appears "dressed to kill – top hat, morning coat, striped trousers, etc., white gloves in hand" (61).

4 SB wrote to Judith Schmidt on the matter on 18 May (NSyU).

Albert Bessler (1905–1975) was chief dramaturg of the Schlosspark Theater from 1947, and of the Schiller-Theater from 1951; SB writes "Schlosspark" for "Schiller-

Theater-Werkstatt" here. SB first met Bessler in connection with the production of *Warten auf Godot* at the Schlosspark Theater in 1953.

5 SB wrote to John Barber, Curtis Brown, on 29 April: "I know nothing of this revival of Godot by Alan Simpson at Stratford E. and do not authorize it. Please tell Mr Simpson to stop his production." (GEU, MSS 1221.) SB ultimately relented, but limited the run to four weeks without transfer to the West End, and stipulated: "No change to be made in text of play without consultation with me" (SB to Barber, 2 May; GEU, MSS 1221). The production featured an Irish company and was billed as an "uproariously funny" comedy. Irving Wardle noted: "The language runs naturally into Irish cadences, but the trouble is that a good deal of it starts sounding like blarney" ("Americans under the Skin," *The Observer* 21 May 1961: 22).

JACOBA VAN VELDE
AMSTERDAM

20.5.61 Paris

Chère Tonny

Merci de votre lettre. Content que vous vous acharniez sur votre livre.[1] Moi ça va – malgré toutes mes conneries. Difficiles répétitions malgré l'absence de Blin (à Londres avec Les Nègres) et de Raimbourg qui est arrivé 8 jours avant la première! On s'en est tiré tant bien que mal et ça marche maintenant très bien à l'Odéon. L'Opéra Krapp (Bielefeld) vient au Théâtre des Nations (3 et 4 juillet), c'est enfin définitif. J'ai repris Happy Days et ce sera bientôt terminé. Je ne sais pas ce que ça vaut, je devais le faire, c'est tout. J'aurais pu le faire mieux mais je n'ai pas pu. Faut maintenant que je me fasse chier avec la traduction de Comment c'est et Textes pr. Rien. J'en aurai pour jusqu'à la fin de l'année au moins. Puis? Puis puis ou [sic] va-t-on de puis en puis? Je serai en Angleterre à partir du 16 juin jusqu'à la fin du mois. Je verrai notamment mes cousines, un match de cricket et McWhinnie rapport à la pièce. Je voyagerai sans doute avec la rotten little comme la dernière fois, on est + libre. Sonny vient me voir cet après-midi, en route pour Rotterdam et New York. Des années que je l'ai pas vu.[2] Beaucoup d'amis et de connaissances de passage, mais je refuse de bouger avant 19h. Puis je me rattrape hélas, et c'est en général le coup de 3 h. du matin.

Je devrais être à l'hôpital, patience ça viendra.

Le nouvel appartement marche pas mal, malgré les bruits. Je vais vendre Ussy, + envie de le voir. Vu les Tophoven au Sarah-Bernhardt avec Bessler (Schillertheater) qui demande Happy Days pr. le Festival de Berlin. Meinetwegen . . .[3] Top vient de temps en temps voir avec moi sa traduction de Comment c'est. Suhrkamp va le sortir en édition bilingue, riche idée. Voilà. Le pauvre John toujours plâtré dans tous les coins, il en a encore pour longtemps. J'avais dans l'idée d'aller le voir avant l'Angleterre, mais finalement non, + tard peut-être. J'aimerais bien revoir Amsterdam + longuement + tranquillement, ça viendra peut-être aussi. Aucune nouvelle de Geer et de Bram ni de l'exposition de celui-ci chez Knoedler, c'est peut-être remis.[4] Que vous veniez en juin ou en septembre comptez sur moi côté fric, je suis pas mal argenté en ce moment et le percepteur m'a oublié jusqu'à présent. Mais finir le livre avant tout.

Amitiés à Fritz. Je vous embrasse bien affectueusement

Sam

ALS; 1 leaf, 2 sides; BNF, MSS 19794/76.

20.5.61 Paris

Dear Tonny

Thank you for your letter. Glad you are keeping working away at your book.[1] I'm all right – in spite of all my silly bloody nonsense. Rehearsals difficult in spite of the absence of Blin (in London with *Les Nègres*) and Raimbourg who arrived a week before the first night! We got through somehow or other, and things are going very well now at the Odéon. The *Krapp* opera (Bielefeld) is coming to the Théâtre des Nations (3 and 4 July). This is settled, at last. I've gone back to *Happy Days*, and it will soon be finished. I'm not sure if it's any good; I had to do it, that's all. I could have done it better, but couldn't manage to. Now I've got to put myself through it with the translation of *Comment c'est* and *Textes pour rien*. That will take me till the end of the year at least. And then? Then where do we go from then to then? I shall be in England from the 16 of June till the end of the month. I'll be seeing mainly my female cousins, a cricket match, and McWhinnie, about the play. I'll probably travel in the rotten little, like last time. That way you're freer. Sonny is coming to see me this afternoon, on his way to Rotterdam and New York. Haven't seen him for years.[2] Lots of friends and acquaintances, people on their way through, but I refuse to go anywhere before 7 p.m. Then, alas, I make up for it, and it's usually back to the 3 in the morning business.

I should be in hospital. Patience, that will come.

The new flat is working out quite well, in spite of the noises. I'm going to sell Ussy. Don't want to see it any more. Have seen the Tophovens at the Sarah-Bernhardt with Bessler (Schillertheater) who is asking for *Happy Days* for the Berlin Festival. Meinetwegen ...[3] Top comes round from time to time to go over his translation of *Comment c'est* with me. Suhrkamp is going to bring it out in a bilingual edition – now *there's* an idea. That's it. Poor John is still up to his neck in plaster, and will be for a long time yet. I had had an idea of going to see him before England, but in the end no. Later maybe. I would like to see Amsterdam again, quietly and for longer. Maybe that too will happen. No news of Geer and Bram, or of the latter's exhibition at Knoedler's; perhaps it's been put off.[4] Whether you come in June or September, count on me for the money side: I'm pretty flush just now, and the taxman has forgotten me so far. But above all finish the book.

Best to Fritz. Much love to you.

Sam

1 SB had written to Jacoba van Velde on 1 February: "Comment va le livre? Suez sang et eau, c'est le seul moyen." (BNF, 19794/74.) ("How is the book going? Sweat blood and tears, that's the only way.") Van Velde was working on what would become her novel *Een blad in de wind* (Amsterdam: Querido, 1961).

2 SB had written to A. J. Leventhal on 18 May: "Sonny expected this weekend. Brief visit on his way to New York via Rotterdam, paying his passage with lectures" (TxU, Leventhal Collection, 1.4). SB's "rotten little" is his 2CV car.

3 The Théâtre Sarah-Bernhardt (now Théâtre de la Ville) and the Café Sarah-Bernhardt are situated on the Place du Châtelet, Paris 4.

"Meinetwegen" (All right by me).

4 Bram van Velde's exhibition had been projected for May 1961 (see 1 October 1960).

BARBARA BRAY
PARIS

26.6.61 [London]

Dear Barbara

Thanks for your card today. Got the Gleem & TCP. Asked for TNP.[1] Party at Donald's last night. Pat & Mme, Jackie & do., Eric, jinks of feeble elevation. Jackie rapidly & tiresomely drunk. He's going to Paris Tuesday mainly he says to see Godot & Amédée. Eric I don't know how drunk, head bowed, few words, no contact.[2] Donald acutely nervous about TV Godot this evening, dissatisfied with productions – Jackie also with his performance. Not much looking forward to seeing it this evening at Woodthorpe's in Chelsea, with Donald & the Calders.[3] Pat still limping with stick, lunch with him tomorrow.[4] Great – no – moderate uneasiness in me all evening. Lunch in half an hour at Calders' with Hobson. Drinks with Barrys tomorrow. Dined with Daikens & Duff, only had to listen – wish I were back in Surrey on the croquet lawn with no fingers no spoilt etc.[5] Jackie on the Manahan. Think she's out. Gave Donald 2nd script for Devine.[6] Won't forget Molesworth. Meant to look for it this morning, then went to see a psychoanalyst instead, old school & TCD butty. You're well out of all this.[7] Of course your article is only next Sunday.[8] Can't conceive possibility of ever doing any work again. Telephoned John Gibson. Dinner with him alone tomorrow, shall hear about Klope. He said on phone he thought yr. adaptation superb.[9] Glyndebourne Wed. in flannel bags for Donizetti's Elixir. Picnic at entr'acte, what a people.[10]

Love to you all

Sam

ALS; 1 leaf, 1 side; *to* Madame Bray, 14 Rue Le Sueur, Paris 16$^{\underline{me}}$, FRANCE; *pm* 26-6-61, London; TCD, MS 10948/1/154.

1 Gleem is a brand of toothpaste. TCP is a brand of liquid antiseptic; in the chemist's shop, SB may have had a slip of the tongue, requesting TNP (Théâtre National Populaire) rather than TCP.

2 With SB at Donald McWhinnie's party were Patrick and Belle Magee, Jack and Gloria MacGowran, and Eric Ewens. Ewens (1917-1998), who had a Ph.D. from Trinity College Dublin, worked in the Radio Drama Department of the BBC from 1950 to 1951, and from 1954 to 1963. Jack MacGowran planned to see the production of *Godot* and Ionesco's *Amédée, ou Comment s'en débarrasser* directed by Jean-Marie Serreau; both were produced by the Théâtre Nouveau at the Odéon-Théâtre de France.

3 SB planned to view the broadcast of McWhinnie's TV production at the home of Peter Woodthorpe, 7 Wellington Square, Chelsea.

4 The nature of Patrick Magee's injury is not known.

5 John and Bettina Calder hosted the lunch for SB and Harold Hobson.

Actor, director, and producer Michael Barry (1910–1988) was Head of BBC television drama (1951–1961); his wife was Rosemary Corbett Barry (d. 1968, stage name Rosemary Lomax). At the time of SB's visit, the Barrys were packing up for a move to Dublin (Michael Barry had been "loaned" by the BBC to Telefís Éireann as a programme controller from 1961 to 1963).

Leslie and Lilyan Daiken hosted SB and Charles Duff (1894–1966), linguist and educator, whose essay "Dr. O'Cassidy's Neutrality Mixture" was included in *They Go, The Irish* (1944), edited by Daiken. SB refers to his visit beginning 16 June at the home of his cousin Sheila and her husband Donald Page in Wormley, Surrey. "No fingers, no spoilt" is from a line in "Sanies I": "ah to be back in the caul now with no trusts / no fingers no spoilt love" (Beckett, *Echo's Bones and Other Precipitates*, [20]).

6 Irish actress Anna Manahan (1924–2009), who worked with Hilton Edwards and Micheál MacLíammóir at the Gate Theatre, had been mentioned as a possible choice to play Winnie in *Happy Days*. George Devine required a script in order to consider the play for production at the Royal Court Theatre.

7 Geoffrey Willans (1911–1958) wrote a series of books set in a prep school; the series was based on his column for *Punch* and it was illustrated with cartoons by Ronald Searle. *The Compleet Molesworth* was published in 1958; *Back in the Jug Agane* was published posthumously in 1959.

SB went to see Arthur Geoffrey Thompson (known as Geoffrey, 1905–1976; Profile, I).

8 Bray's article "Britain Misses an Opening" was published in her column "Paris Perspective" (*The Observer* 9 July 1961: 21). It discussed the relative lack of government support for the British submissions to the Théâtre des Nations, especially in comparison with the support for the German offerings.

9 John Gibson produced Robert Pinget's play *Clope* for broadcast on the BBC Third Programme on 12 July; it was adapted for radio and translated by Bray. The play was published by Editions de Minuit as *Ici ou ailleurs*. Under the title *Here or Elsewhere*, Bray submitted the script to John Calder along with Pinget's play *Dead Letter*, having converted them "from radio back to stage scripts" (Barbara Bray to John Calder, 12 December 1961; InU, C&B, Pinget). SB's spelling "Klope" is whimsical; Pinget's play is *Clope*.

10 With John and Bettina Calder, SB attended a performance of Gaetano Donizetti's opera *L'Elisir d'amore* (1832; *The Elixir of Love*) conducted by Carlo Felice Cilario (1915–2007); it was produced and designed by Franco Zeffirelli. Glyndebourne is an opera concert venue in Sussex, where the custom in "the season" (May–September) is that the audience, formally dressed, has a picnic supper in the long (hour and a half) interval.

DONALD PAGE
WORMLEY, SURREY

8.7.61 Ussy sur Marne

Dear Donald

Many thanks for your letter. The week I spent at Sweetwater was the happiest for many a long day and I am deeply moved by the goodness and affection you all lavished on me. Blessings on the three of you.[1]

The opera on Monday and Tuesday was a success and very well received. The young American baritone who sang the role of Krapp has been awarded the prize of best singer in the Festival and on the strength of his performance received an offer from the Milan Scala.[2]

The journey back to Paris went without hitch till I lost my way in the boulevards extérieurs!

Came here yesterday for a few days breather. The place has been burgled, the iron shutters forced, a window broken and the whole place turned upside down. A number of things stolen, but nothing of value. A picture by Hayden overlooked and my books and papers merely scattered about the floor. Spent the day today cleaning up the mess. The gendarmes told me there was an average of 12 such burglaries per week![3]

Had lunch with Devine, director of Royal Court Theatre. He had read the new play and wants it for his theatre. We shall try to get Joan Plowright. With McWhinnie going to America in August and Devine's own plans, (& J.P.'s baby!) production can hardly be before November. It will be done at Berlin Festival end of September and in New York about the same time.[4]

11. Sheila Page, Samuel Beckett, Molly Roe, July 1961 at Sweetwater cottage

Don't know yet when I'll be able to go to Ireland. Hope also to get down to Etretat and have a bang with the clubs you gave me. Should have my nose to the old grindstone already, a few more days here and they'll be together.

Greetings to Jack, Jean, Mick & Madge, and Mrs Winter.[5]

Much love to you all.

SAM

ALS; 1 leaf, 2 sides; Babcock Collection.

1 SB stayed at Sweetwater Cottage from 16 to 23 June with his cousins Sheila and Donald Page, and Molly Roe. SB left his car there, while staying with the Calders in London from 24 to 29 June; he returned to Sweetwater Cottage before travelling back to Paris on 30 June. SB wrote to his school friend John F. Lawrence (1904–1984):

> I went to Lords on the Friday with Donald Page and brought Molly Roe on your ticket. Beautiful day but alas poor cricket. However I greatly enjoyed being at Lords again and hope another year we shall be there together. Frank Woolley was in the bar escorting blind Rhodes wearing an ear transistor. Met Harold Hobson later who is a member of the MCC and he offered to put me up for membership. (7 July 1961; Joynt Collection; transcription, UoR, JEK A/2/159.)

Frank Woolley (1887–1978) was Wisden Cricketer of the Year in 1911; Wilfred Rhodes (1877–1973) was Wisden Cricketer of the Year in 1899 (Wisden Almanack, 1899, 1911: www.espncricinfo.com/wisdenalmanack, accessed 2 July 2013).

2 William Dooley sang the role of Krapp in Mihalovici's opera on 3 and 4 July at the Théâtre Sarah-Bernhardt. SB later wrote to Thomas MacGreevy, who had been in Paris for the performances, that he had run into Dooley, who announced that "he had been awarded the prize of best singer in the Festival, bracketed with Zagreb opera bass. He was very pleased. He has also been offered, I think by Scherchen, on the strength of his Krapp, an engagement at the Scala in I forget what modern opera." (17 July 1961; TCD, MS 10402/241.)

3 SB added to MacGreevy: " A lot of small trivial stuff removed, including all my old underwear! They enjoyed on the premises all the food and drink they could find." (17 July 1961; TCD, MS 10402/241.)

4 SB had lunch in Paris with George Devine on 6 July. SB and Devine discussed a production of *Happy Days* at the Royal Court. SB's preferred director was Donald McWhinnie, who planned to be in New York in August with his production of Pinter's *The Caretaker*. Actress Joan Plowright had been mentioned for the role of Winnie.

5 Jack and Jean Page were the twin brother and sister-in-law of Donald Page. Mick and Madge Bendon were neighbors of Donald and Sheila Page. Mrs. Winter was a daily housekeeper with the Page family at Sweetwater Cottage. (Caroline Murphy, Jill Babcock, to the editors, 22 September 2012.)

ALAN SCHNEIDER
NEW YORK

13.7.61 Ussy

Dear Alan

Thanks for your letter with photos of children they're a bonny pair and the boy a great chip of old you.[1]

It's the first time I won't have been able to collaborate in the first production of a stage-play of mine, and naturally I'm sorry. No question I'm afraid of my getting to N.Y. It looks as though you will be the first to do it. At Berlin Festival it is scheduled to open September 30th - though German text not yet available! In London (now definitely Royal Court, direction McWhinnie) rehearsals as far as I can see can hardly begin before mid-October at earliest. We shall try to get Plowright (in spite of imminent baby). Don't rush it in any case, without adequate actress it hasn't a hope in hell. I'm not keen on repertory set-up, wd. rather have the issue clearer, but if it helps you won't hold out against it.[2] Enclosed a few sketches which may help you, though of course the proportions are all wrong. I think in Act I she should be sitting on a high stool (standing, unless a very small woman, will make it too high), and in Act II on a low one. I can't see why, if the mound properly constructed, there should be any difficulty with Willie's concealment. He should never have to move except (1) when he is required to sit up with head and hands visible and (2) when he appears at end of play.[3] The "abrupter fall" can actually if necessary overhang as (seen from side)[4]

If he is invisible no problem obviously with hole, his "movement" towards it being simply expressed by Winnie's text and play. And if he cannot be completely hidden, then no problem either, he has merely to crawl off-stage to hole.

Wish we could meet and go over it all in detail. Since we can't we must just do the best we can by letter. It's a much more difficult job

I've given you here than any so far – all poised on a razor-edge and no breathers anywhere.

Affectionately from us both to you all.

Sam

Enclosures:

ALS; 1 leaf, 2 sides; *enclosures* 3 leaves, 3 sides; Burns Library, Samuel Beckett Collection, SB-AS. Previous publication, Beckett and Schneider, *No Author Better Served*, 85–89.

1 Schneider's two children, Vicky and David (b. 1959).

2 Ruth Patricia White (1914–1969) was selected for the role of Winnie. Theatre 61, the production company of Richard Barr (1917–1989) and Clinton Wilder (1920–1986), had proposed "introducing HAPPY DAYS in repertory with Albee, starting it at four times a week" at the Cherry Lane Theatre, 38 Commerce Street (Alan Schneider to SB, 6 July 1961; Burns Library, Samuel Beckett Collection, AS-SB; Beckett and Schneider, *No Author Better Served*, 83–85).

3 In his letter, Schneider had expressed concern about the "exact geography of Willie's position in and out of his hole," as well as about "how to do this exactly and in the particular theatre?"

4 The stage direction in *Happy Days*: "Back an abrupter fall to stage level" (7). SB's sketch in the letter locates Willie's "hole," and how it should be created as part of the set design.

HILTON EDWARDS
RADIO TELEVISION ÉIREANN, DUBLIN

27.7.61 [Paris]

Dear Hilton Edwards

Thanks for your letter.

I am very unfamiliar with TV and its possibilities and so hesitate to write for this medium. And if I did I'm afraid the result would be unacceptable in Ireland. Nevertheless I am grateful to you for your suggestion and shall keep it in mind. To be agreeable to you personally would give me much pleasure.[1]

With best wishes,

AL draft; 1 leaf, 1 side; *verso* Hilton Edwards to SB, 18 July 1961; GEU, MSS 1221.

1 Edwards, who had taken over the Drama Department for Radio Telefís Éireann, had written to SB to ask him to "consider writing us something for an early programme [. . .] I would consider it an enormous feather in my cap if we could persuade you to write something for us." (18 July 1961; GEU, MSS 1221.) On 30 July, SB wrote to Elliseva Sayers: "Saw Godot on TV and that cured me – of my bright idea. Hilton Edwards – directing Irish TV drama wrote asking for a script. It's a medium for fleas." (Sayers Collection; photocopy TCD, MS 13331/2/2.)

HENRI LEFEBVRE
BRUSSELS

1.8.61

38 Bd. St. Jacques
Paris 14me

Cher Henri Lefeb[v]re

Merci de votre beau dessin et de vos nombreuses lettres qu'à ma confusion j'ai dû laissées [*for* laisser] sans réponse, ayant perdu votre adresse jusqu'à l'enveloppe de votre dernier envoi.[1]

Je suis très touché par tout ce que vous me dites et répétez. Il me faudrait, pour vous répondre, des mots du même sang que les vôtres. Mais ce serait par là les avant-derniers.

Je vous dirai donc simplement merci, c'est en fidèle, d'être passé, comme lorsqu'on ose ouvrir à quelqu'un venu de très loin, à pied, l'hiver.

J'aimerais néanmoins vous sentir moins préoccupé de moi et de mon travail. Je vous parle là en ami – et en connaissance de cause.

Même ces pauvres lignes me donnent beaucoup de mal. Je ne pourrai pas vous écrire souvent. Mais de loin en loin si vous le voulez. En tout cas je ne perdrai plus votre adresse.

Une bonne poignée de main
bien amicalement
Sam. Beckett

ALS; 1 leaf, 1 side; *env to* Monsieur Henri Lefeb[v]re; 20 Place Annees[s]ens, Bruxelles, Belgique; *pm torn off*; De Staël Collection.

1.8.61

38 Bd. St. Jacques
Paris 14me

Dear Henri Lefebvre

Thank you for your lovely drawing and your many letters which, to my embarrassment, I must have left unanswered, having lost your address until the envelope of your last missive.[1]

I am greatly touched by all that you say and repeat. To answer you I would need words of the same blood as yours. But then they would be my penultimates.

So I shall say simply thank you, faithfully, for having come my way, as when one dares to open the door to someone who has come a long way, on foot, in winter.

Nonetheless I would like it if you were less concerned about me and my work. There I speak as a friend – and one who knows what he is talking about.

Even these poor lines are costing me a lot. I shall not be able to write often. But very occasionally, if you like. In any case, I will not lose your address again.

A warm handshake, and every good wish

Sam Beckett

1 On 18 April, SB had written to the Belgian artist Henri Lefebvre* (?1925–?1972) for the first time to say: "Merci de vos signes. J'en suis vraiment très touché. J'aimerais pouvoir vous écrire une vraie lettre. Je ne peux pas. Merci de la main que vous me tendez. Je la serre avec amitié et reconnaissance." (De Staël Collection.) (Thank you for your signs. I am much touched by them. I should like to write you a proper letter. I cannot. Thank you for the hand you reach out to me. I shake it in friendship and gratitude.)

BARBARA BRAY
LONDON

16.8.61 Ussy

Dear Barbara

Thanks for your good Bath letter here this morning. Hope you got mine in London though I wonder, not having name care of whom.[1] Had a letter from Harold asking for a copy of H.D. but have no spare left, suggested he ask Donald to send him his or get a proof from Grove in N.Y. Silly letter from Schiller asking me 1) to assist at opening (no) 2) to write a note on the play for programme (no) 3) to say whether in second act the "colline" (sic) comes up or Winnie goes down – and adding that people will think they are mad to present such a work as theatre.[2] Why do it? All very promising. Tophoven points out that Willie may benefit by Brandt, particularly after the elections ("You've exposed yourself enough now, Willie, go back into your hole.").[3] No news from Schneider. Wretched weather, wind & rain, last few days, but beautiful this morning. Read all books here and have been reduced to En. Brit. and an old issue of the Neue Rundschau, but got some Série Noire from the Hayden last night.[4] New arrêts à bascule fiasco again, wrong kind of gate dawned on me at last, tore all up and filled in holes, back to the old boulders.[5] Mow today. Have been battering away at How it is, part II leaving only first and first, third and last, leaving gaps for such things as si l'on veut & à la bonne heure.[6] Back to Paris iron in soul Saturday, then Etretat Sunday & back to Paris and Edward Thursday, then to England Sept. 1st or 3rd, undecided. Wish as usual after a week here that I could stay for the duration, thought of Paris hurly-burly makes me feel sick. Shan't hear you again next Sunday because of trip to Etretat.[7] Cup of old black boiled coffee now and to work. Shall post this in La Ferté this afternoon. Write henceforward to Paris. Can't imagine anyone feasting on Roget. Haven't got a tip from it yet. Get me a copy, will you, to bring back with you, and the Penguin dic. of quotations, to supplement my dear old family Bartlett.[8]

Love

S.

ALI; 1 leaf, 1 side; *env to* Mrs Barbara Bray, 6 Duncan Terrace, London N. 1, Angleterre; *pm* 16–8–61, La Ferté-sous-Jouarre; TCD, MS 10948/1/158.

1 Bray was in London to take part in the BBC programme *The Critics*.

2 Albert Bessler had written to SB on 9 August, on behalf of the Schiller-Theater, Berlin; SB responded on 13 August: "Je suis tout à fait incapable d'écrire sur mon travail. Ça fait + de 10 ans que je le dis et redis à ceux qui me font l'honneur de m'y inviter. Ça aussi je le regrette infiniment et vous prie de ne pas m'en vouloir." (I am wholly incapable of writing about my work. For more than 10 years now I have been saying and repeating this to those who do me the honour of asking me to do so. That too I deeply regret, and ask that it should not be held against me.) SB added that the mound was the same in both acts: "C'est le personnage, au-dessus, qui s'est enfoncé" (GEU, MSS 1221) (It is the character up on top who has sunk farther down).

3 SB wrote to Bray on 14 August about working on the translation of *Happy Days* with Elmar Tophoven: "I had 7 hours with Tophoven on his Glückliche Tage" (TCD, MS 10948/1/157). Winnie says to Willie, "Go back into your hole now, Willie, you've exposed yourself enough" (25). In 1961, Willy Brandt, Mayor of Berlin, was the Social Democratic candidate, running against Konrad Adenauer, who had held the office of Chancellor since 1949. The campaigns leading to the elections on 17 September were marked by acrimony. Shortly before this letter was written, on 13 August, the German Democratic Republic had begun to put up the Berlin Wall that would divide East from West. Tophoven found the conjunction of names worth comment.

4 SB owned the 11th edition of the *Encyclopædia Britannica* (see 15 March and 12 April 1958). *Die Neue Rundschau* is a literary journal published by S. Fischer Verlag since 1890. The Série Noire detective fiction was published by Gallimard.

5 SB had installed an "arrêt à bascule" (self-latching gate) at the road entrance to his cottage at Ussy. Admitting afterwards that it was the wrong kind of gate, SB then put back into place the boulders he had used previously to block unwanted vehicles.

6 *Comment c'est* uses many phrases repetitively; in the end SB did not translate each occurrence of the phrase in the same way, but variously (in each instance, the first page number refers to the 1961 Minuit edition, and the second number refers to the 1964 Grove English edition): "si l'on veut" is translated as "if you want" (51, 42), "at a pinch" (84, 68), "manner of speaking" (118, 96), "no objection" (129, 106), "if you prefer" (150, 123), "if it be kindly" (158, 131), "if you like" (162, 134); "à la bonne heure" is translated as "cheers" (52, 43), "God be praised" (87, 71), "bravo" (127, 105).

7 SB planned a golfing weekend in Etretat, where Jérôme Lindon had a holiday home. Edward Beckett was arriving in Paris, as SB wrote to Mary Hutchinson, "to work at his flute, he is going to have a shot at the Paris Conservatoire in October, and I shall be busy at the beginning of his stay looking after him and showing him round" (3 August 1961; TxU, Hutchinson, 2.5).

8 SB possessed his family's copy of John Bartlett, *Familiar Quotations* (Boston: Little Brown, 1885) (UoR, JEK A/3/2). SB asked Bray to bring J. M. Cohen and M. J. Cohen, eds., *The Penguin Dictionary of Quotations* (Harmondsworth and New York: Penguin Books, 1960). *Roget's Thesaurus* (first published in 1852) had been reprinted in various formats and editions by several publishers in the years 1960 and 1961.

ALAN SCHNEIDER
NEW YORK

17.8.61 Ussy

Dear Alan

Thanks for yours of Aug. 13 here today.

Mound: I see it extending across entire opening, sloping down to a few inches above stage level at either side

i.e. less hump than undulation. Texture: perhaps a kind of brown canvas with something to suggest scorched grass – but smooth, i.e. no stones sticking up or such like, nothing to break monotony of symmetry. What should characterize whole scene, sky and earth, is a pathetic unsuccessful realism, the kind of tawdriness you get in 3rd rate musical or pantomime, that quality of pompier, laughably earnest bad imitation. A curved drop is all right with me. Colour: that which best conveys heat and dessication [sic]. But this will be more a question of lighting than of painting. Hot blue sky (if blue can be hot, which I doubt) and yellow-brown scorched earth. Suggest striped parasol, echoing striped ribbon of Willie's boater, say blue and yellow again. The bag must be a marketing bag (bottom of p. 21). I see it like the big black capacious French "cabas".[1] The bell as shrill and wounding as possible. In case I didn't give you musical-box reference, there is an American recording of a Regina (big box) playing this tune: Old Music Box Melodies, RCD4, information from Bornard Music Box Co., 139 Fourth Avenue, Pelham, N.Y. If this box too big for bag or not a "winder", it can be played off and Winnie have a small dummy of kind we need.

1. Willie invisible need not move at all, except to sit up etc., till end of play. It's only if he cannot be hidden completely that he wd. need to crawl offstage.[2]

2. I think it must be obvious from outset (p. 2, "hoo-oo" . . . "poor Willie") that someone is there behind mound. She leans well back & down to her right and apostrophizes him, then when she comes back front comments on his capacity for sleep. May mention here that all this leaning and turning and motion of arms and bust in Act I should be as ample and graceful (memorable) as possible, in order that its absence Act II may have maximum effect. Hope your girl has desirable fleshiness. Audience thoughout Act II should miss this gleaming opulent flesh – gone.[3]

3. No, just say lines, same tone throughout, polishing mechanically, no emotion on "blaze of hellish . . .". What tone? This of course is the problem. I can find no better word for it than "mild". That is the basic tone throughout and should only be deviated from as indicated (voice breaks, murmur, scream). In a word I am asking here for vocal monotony and relying on speech rhythms and speech-gesture complexes, eyes, switching on and off of smile, etc., to do the work, all these in their turn requiring, if they are to operate fully, vocal tranquillity & transparency.[4]

4. Yes, what you think.[5]

5. "Ensign crimson . . . pale flag", Juliet's lips, Act III I think, I'll let you have exact reference when I get back to Paris and other quotation references. No irony. Mild blank tone.[6]

6. If you have to explain this passage you may describe Winnie's "reasoning" as follows: when no further pains are possible (in pursuit of information) one has only to sit tight and lost knowledge will come back into the mind, the examples given (duration of lunar night & degree of heat at which flesh melts) being obviously prompted by her situation.[7]

7. Above all no "in". "Never bear to do such wilderness" straight through, imperturbable, ex. of vocal normality – speech abnormality mentioned in 3.[8]

8. No one will get this reference, tant pis. It is to a line of Browning "I say confusedly what comes uppermost".[9]

9. Willie feels "fucked up", not "sucked up". His surprise is at the s.[10]

10. She simply can't move, that's all. Times when she can't speak, times when she can't move. Her problem is how to eke out, each "day", and organise economy of these two orders of resources, body and speech (the 2 lamps). Act of God required when both burn down together.[11]

11. Shower (rain). Shower & Cooker are derived from German "schauen" & "Kuchen" (to look). They represent the onlooker (audience) wanting to know meaning of things. That's why (p. 17) she stops filing, raises head & lets 'em have it ("And you, she says. . .).[12]

12. Snot from his nose.[13]

13. "Thing" is right, meaning this Shower-Cooker episode.[14]

14. "Beechen green": Keats's "beechen green and shadows numberless", and of course referring back to "horse-beech" (p. 5) under which she sat on Charlie Hunter's knees.[15]

15. "Them": all these objects she can see[.][16]

16. "Bumper": brimming glass. Drink a bumper, toss off a brimming glass. It's the "happy days" toast.[17]

17. "Bast". Fibrous twine used by gardeners. Also called "bass". Always gets into a tangle. Same thing as "raphia" by which if more familiar replace it.[18]

P. 17 line 17, between ".. put on my glasses" and "(Finishes left hand, etc . . .)", insert "(Pause.) Too late now."[19]

Frustrating to have to deal with all this by letter, everything cries out for nuance & enlargement. Better than nothing I suppose, hope you agree.

Berlin confirmed for Sept. 30th in the very small "Werkstatt" theatre, with Gerta [*for* Berta] Drews (good it appears, & well-know[n], but rings no bell in me). No news from Devine or Plowright. I think Donald McWhinnie leaves in about a week. Pinter also going over.[20] It's as well you should know my plans: back to Paris day after tomorrow Aug. 19th. Aug. 20th – 23rd Etretat. Paris then till Sept. 1st. England then till Sept. 11th. Then Paris and Ussy.

At your entire disposal for any help I can give.

Affectionately to you all

SAM

ALS; 2 leaves, 3 sides; Burns Library, Samuel Beckett Collection, SB-AS. Previous publication, Beckett and Schneider, *No Author Better Served*, 94–96.

(SB's page numbers refer to the script; in the notes that follow, quotations from the play refer to the Grove Press text of *Happy Days*.)

1 "Cabas" (capacious shopping bag).

Schneider's letter to SB of 13 August (Burns Library, Samuel Beckett Collection, SB-AS; Beckett and Schneider, *No Author Better Served*, 90–93) is referred to throughout the present notes; in it, Schneider reports on decisions, and poses many questions: "The mound is going to be exactly as you pictured it, . . . about 12 feet wide from end to end and about 3 to 5 feet in depth." "Would you object to a curved drop, painted as you indicate, but which went off on each side into infinity? Have you any preferences for color of the backcloth? Of the mound? How about the texture of the mound?" Schneider questioned SB's preference about the color of the parasol, and he wondered whether a shopping bag were preferable to a handbag: "Would not the latter be logical in view of what it contains" (*Happy Days*, 7). Direct quotations in the subsequent notes cite Schneider's queries, unless otherwise indicated.

2 "Gather you don't want us to see Willie in entirety at all until the end of the play; until then, we see only an arm, a hand, the paper, the back of his head, etc."

3 "Hoo-oo" (*Happy Days*, 9, 11).

4 "Is there anything special you could or would say about sequence of 'holy light' through 'blaze of hellish light'? In terms of tone you want[?]" (*Happy Days*, 11.)

5 "I assume that 'Now the other' . . . refers to what I think it does" (*Happy Days*, 14).

6 Schneider had asked what SB meant by "Pale flag" (*Happy Days*, 15). SB enclosed notes to the quotations with his letter to Schneider of 25 August; SB indicated the source as Shakespeare, *Romeo and Juliet*, V.iii.94–96: "Beauty's ensign yet / Is crimson in thy lips and in thy cheeks, / And death's pale flag is not advanced there."

7 Schneider had asked about the line: "the happy day to come when flesh melts at so many degrees and the night of the moon has so many hundred hours" (*Happy Days*, 18). Schneider justified the question: "The actor will ask."

8 Schneider had asked if a word had been left out in the script: "when I must learn to talk to myself a thing I could never bear to do (in) such wilderness" (*Happy Days*, 27).

9 "Does Brownie refer to Browning? Or to the gun? Or to both? (Are you making a pun here?)" In the text, the reference is, "Ever uppermost, like Browning" (*Happy Days*, 33). In Robert Browning's *Paracelsus*, III, the line is "I say confusedly what comes uppermost" (*The Poetical Works of Robert Browning*, I, *Paracelsus*, ed. Ian Jack and Margaret Smith [Oxford: Clarendon Press, 1983] 301). "Tant pis" (too bad). In his letter to Schneider of 3 September, SB elaborates: "The revolver is called 'Browning – Brownie', not because there is a weapon of that name – but because it is always uppermost. If the line was by another poet the revolver wd. be called by the name of that other poet." (Burns Library, Samuel Beckett Collection, SB-AS; Beckett and Schneider, *No Author Better Served*, 101–104.)

10 Referring to Winnie's line: "Don't you ever have that feeling, Willie, of being sucked up?" Willie replies "Sucked up?" (*Happy Days*, 33–34).

11 Winnie tries various ways of holding the parasol once she unfurls it, because she is unable to put it down – until, that is, it catches fire and she tosses it behind the mound (*Happy Days*, 35–37). Schneider had asked, "Why cannot Winnie put down the parasol?" Winnie refers to her "two lamps" (*Happy Days*, 36–37).

12 Schneider had asked how "to pronounce Shower?" (*Happy Days*, 41–42). SB's response refers to Winnie's line: "And you, she says, what's the idea of you, she says, what are you meant to mean" (*Happy Days*, 43).

13 "Am I correct in assuming what Willie is eating [?]" with reference to Winnie's line: "Oh really! (Pause.) . . . Have you no delicacy. (Pause.) Oh, Willie, you're not eating it!" (*Happy Days*, 42).

14 Schneider had questioned whether it should be "Strange things" or "Strange thing" in the line "Strange thing, time like this, drift up into the mind" (*Happy Days*, 44).

15 Schneider had queried the reference to "beechen green" (*Happy Days*, 51). SB quotes the line from John Keats's "Ode to a Nightingale" (line 9), and he notes the previous reference to Charlie Hunter (*Happy Days*, 15–16).

16 Schneider had asked about the referent of "them" in the lines "What would I do without them? (*Pause.*) What would I do without them, when words fail?" (*Happy Days*, 53.)

17 "The last bumper with the bodies nearly touching" (*Happy Days*, 60).

18 "The tangles of bast" (*Happy Days*, 16).

19 SB now adds a change to the text to read ". . . put on my glasses. (*Pause.*) Too late now. (*Finishes left hand, inspects it.*)" (*Happy Days*, 42.)

20 Berta Drews (1901–1987) performed the role of Winnie in Berlin; she had been a member of the company of the Schiller-Theater since 1951. McWhinnie was going to New York to direct Harold Pinter's *The Caretaker*.

BARBARA BRAY
LONDON

29.8.61 Ussy

Dear Barbara

Thanks for your letter. Here with Edward for the day, marvellous weather. Been busy with him since his arrival last week. He's very sympa and it's not difficult. Satisfactory audition with his new flute professor who says he is well up to Conservatoire standard and should get in. If he does it means certainly two & probably 3 years in Paris. At the moment he's a bit dazed and lost, but he'll settle down and be all right.[1] Didn't hear last Critics but probably shall the next, at Sheila's.[2] Got the Editors' Prize at last without having had to ask for it, a fat cheque from Gallimard. It comes at a good time.[3] It's very good of you to offer to help with HOW IT IS, but I'm afraid I must either do it myself or – as I'm more and more tempted – leave it untranslated. I haven't a ghost of new work in me in any case. I shd. be working for John, but simply can't face the thought. No news from any H.D. front. I simply prefer its lst appearance to be in English, since it was English written. You seem to be having a lovely time, tant mieux. I find on the outer window sill a sparrow & mouse dead side by side. I supposed an owl had left them there uneaten or to be eaten later, but Mme Cochard says they'd been sucked by a stoat.[4] Shall probably go over to the Hayden after tea and spend the evening with them. Then back in the cool of the night.[5] Shall ring you from Surrey some morning earliest and perhaps we can arrange something.

Love

S.

ALI; 1 leaf, 2 sides; *env to* M$^{\underline{rs}}$ Bray, 6 Duncan Terrace, London N. 1, Angleterre; *pm* 30–8–61, Paris; TCD, MS 10948/1/161.

1 SB had written to Sheila Page on 21 August to confirm his plans to arrive at her home on 1 September; he also mentioned that Edward and Caroline Beckett would arrive in Paris on 24 August (Babcock Collection). Edward Beckett's flute teacher in Dublin, André Prieur, had studied at the Paris Conservatoire (see SB to Thomas MacGreevy, 2 June 1958, n. 6). "Sympa" (colloq. for sympathique: kind, nice).

2 From 27 August through 17 September, Bray was contracted to appear on *The Critics*, a weekly discussion of the arts, on the BBC Home Service. SB thought he might be able to hear the program on 3 September, while he was staying with Sheila and Donald Page in Wormley.

3 Richard Seaver writes about the evolution of the Prix Formentor and the Prix International and recounts the debates over the first awards in *The Tender Hour of Twilight* (306–308, 312–314).

In May 1961, SB and Jorge Luis Borges shared the first Prix International des Editeurs to honor the body of work of an author. At the same time, the Prix Formentor was awarded for the best unpublished manuscript submitted by one of the six international publishers who sponsored the awards: Gallimard, Einaudi Editori, Rowohlt Verlag, Weidenfeld and Nicolson, Editorial Seix Barral, and Grove Press (Lewis Nichols, "In and Out of Books," *The New York Times* 21 May 1961: BR8; Barbara Bray, "Drama, Trophies and Digestion," *The Observer* 28 May 1961: 28).

4 "Tant mieux" (all the better). Mme Cochard was a neighbor in Ussy.

5 Henri and Josette Hayden spent summers in nearby Reuil.

ALAN SCHNEIDER
NEW YORK

12.9.61 Paris

Dear Alan

Back from England last night. Your letter today. I feel the great effort you are all making and am very grateful. No, I am not nervous, just curious about the work's viability.[1] On re-reading I realise Act I more vulnerable than II. I too thought reverse when writing. Better so I suppose. Congratulations on musical-box, neckpiece, parasol flames, set, etc. Try and accentuate eyes in II.[2] It's a tremendous job for an actress. Please tell R. W. how much I am with her in thought and admire her courage. Had a letter from Herbert Myron who crashed a rehearsal and was much moved.[3]

1. Narrative tone only for this particular day's instalment. "She is now 4 or 5 etc" to be regarded as synopsis of previous instalments. All this has already been told in narrative tone on countless preceding days.[4]

2. "But no etc" refers only to "Let go of me... Drop dead." On the contrary they continue hand in hand.[5]

3. Willie's behaviour never tied up with Winnie's. He is not reacting to her. It is not even certain that he hears her. Coincidence therefore. German translator asked today if his "collapse" (P. 9) depended on his hearing word "blessing". No.

Coincidence. Sorry.[6]

Affectionately to you all.

s/ Sam

TLS; 1 leaf, 1 side; Burns Library, Samuel Beckett Collection, SB-AS. Previous publication: Beckett and Schneider, *No Author Better Served*, 107–108.

1 SB responds to Schneider's letter of 6 September; quotations and questions in the notes below are from this letter (Burns Library, Samuel Beckett Collection, AS-SB; Beckett and Schneider, *No Author Better Served*, 104–106).

2 Schneider had mentioned to SB that a "neck piece" had helped the actress sit "absolutely still for the second act without developing cramps and aches."

3 "R. W." refers to Ruth White. SB responded to Herbert Myron's comments about the production, saying: "Very shaky in mind about this work and relieved to have your reactions (first to date)" (12 September 1961; MBU, Myron).

4 "Why don't you start Narrative tone at start of her story?" This in reference to the stage direction in the middle of Winnie's story about Milly: "(*Pause. Narrative.*) "The sun was not well up when Milly rose . . ." (*Happy Days*, 55).

5 "Is her 'But no. No, no.' in relation to 'Drop dead!' The whole event? Not entirely clear." The phrase occurs in two circumstances (*Happy Days*, 54, 58); in relation to "Drop dead!" it refers to the narrative of Mr. Shower – or Cooker (*Happy Days*, 58).

6 "Why does Willie wait until this point to come out? Has he been waiting for proper opportunity? Is he just ready now? Is it coincidence?" (*Happy Days*, 61.) Elmar and Erika Tophoven translated *Happy Days* into German. Willie collapses behind slope, his head disappears, just after Winnie says "not a day goes by – (*smile*) – to speak in the old style – (*smile off*) – without some blessing" (*Happy Days*, 24). SB's page reference is to the script.

ALAN SCHNEIDER
NEW YORK

Friday 15th [September 1961] Paris

Dear Alan

This scribble in haste to thank you for your letter of last Sunday arrived only today. Naturally very pleased by all you tell me and appreciate very much your finding time to write at such a busy & anxious time for you. I think myself that a commercial success is very unlikely and don't anticipate much mercy from the critics. So I am interested in the "professional" reaction in the sense that it will help me to decide whether this is really a dramatic text or a complete aberration and whether there is justification for trying to push further this kind of theatre. I am surprised by length of running time. Probably I have made I a bit too long. My heart goes out to Ruth White, it must be a big ordeal for her. Thank you all again for your devotion. I'm not sure when you open so can't send you a cable. Think of me as right with you whenever it is - and no matter how it goes.[1]

Ever

Sam

ALS; 1 leaf, 1 side; Burns Library, Samuel Beckett Collection, SB-AS. Previous publication: Beckett and Schneider, *No Author Better Served*, 109–110. Dating: prior to opening of *Happy Days*, Cherry Lane Theatre, New York (17 September 1961); 15 September fell on a Friday in 1961.

1 On 10 September 1961, Schneider had written after "one and a half audiences," which included Herbert Myron on Saturday and Donald McWhinnie on Sunday: "General reaction is one of being intensely moved, shattered. They say they have rarely if ever felt this way in a theatre." Schneider reported a running time of one hour for Act I and just over 30 minutes for Act II. (Burns Library, Samuel Beckett Collection, AS-SB; Beckett and Schneider, *No Author Better Served*, 106–107.)

KAY BOYLE
ROWAYTON, CONNECTICUT

7.10.61 [*for* 6 October 1961] Paris

Dear Kay

Thanks for your letter of Sept. 30th. I have not seen the V.V. article to which you refer. They have been friendly to my work up to now - & fairly understanding. Very good of you to write in any case.[1] The question as to what Willie is "after" - Winnie or the revolver - is like the question in All That Fall as to whether Mr Rooney threw the little girl out of the railway carriage or not. And the answer is the same in both cases - we don't know, at least I don't. All that is necessary as far as I'm concerned - technically & otherwise - less too little, more too much - is the ambiguity of motive, established clearly

I hope by Winnie's "Is it me you're after, Willie, or is it something else? . . . Is it a kiss you're after, Willie, or is it something else?" and by the conspicuousness of revolver requested in stage-directions at beginning of Act II.[2] To cast the doubt was dramatically a chance not to be missed, not to be bungled either by resolving it. That's what I felt in any case. I know creatures are supposed to have no secrets from their authors, but I'm afraid mine for me have little else.

Yours ever

Sam

ALS; 1 leaf, 1 side; *env to* Mrs Kay Boyle, Greycote, 98 Wilson Avenue, Rowayton, Conn., U.S.A.; *pm* 6-10-61; TxU, Beckett Collection, 8.3. Dating: pm precedes date in the letter.

1 Jerry Tallmer's review "Theatre: Happy Days" (*Village Voice* 6.48 [21 September 1961] 9–10). Boyle wrote a letter in response; it was published as: "'Happy Days,'" *Village Voice* 6.49, 28 September 1961: 4).

2 *Happy Days*, 63.

STEFANI HUNZINGER
S. FISCHER VERLAG, FRANKFURT

le 14 octobre 1961

38 Bld. St.-Jacques
Paris 14me

Chère Stefani

Merci de votre lettre du 10 octobre. Je ne tiens pas à ce que Fin de Par[t]ie soit donné à la TV.[1] Il me faudrait l'adapter profondément, ce dont je n'ai ni le temps, ni le désir. D'une façon générale, je vais être obligé de m'opposer à l'avenir à toute adaptation de de [*for* ce] genre, afin que ne soient plus présentées qu'au théâtre les pièces conçues pour le théâtre, plus qu'à la radio celles conçues pour la radio.

A bientôt j'espère.

Amicalement.

s/ Sam

Samuel Beckett

TLS; 1 leaf, 1 side; S. Fischer Verlag Archive.

14th October 1961

38 Bld. St.-Jacques
Paris 14me

Dear Stefani

Thank you for your letter of 10th October. I have no wish to see *Fin de partie* done on TV.[1] I would have to adapt it profoundly, something for which I have neither the time nor the desire. More generally, I am going to be obliged from now on to hold out against any adaptations of this kind, so that only in the theatre will there be performances of plays for theatre, only on radio of those for radio.

Till soon I hope
Yours in friendship
s/ Sam
Samuel Beckett

1 Hunzinger had written that a German production company was interested in the TV rights for *Endspiel*, and had asked if SB approved (Fischer Verlag Archive).

THOMAS MACGREEVY
DUBLIN

23.10.61

38 Boulevard St. Jacques
Paris 14me

Dear Tom

Your good letter this morning. It does me good to feel you are in better form. So sorry to hear about Delia. Remember me to her very kindly with my vows of prompt reestablishment.[1]

Edward sailed through his first exam. last Wednesday & we phoned the good news to Jean that evening. His teacher here (Crunelle, prof. of flute at Conservatoire) says he is sure to get through the final test early next month, so Edward is radiant.[2] Working very hard too and very good all around. Wed. night we had dinner with Chip & Monique, the three of us, & Chip inscribed and gave to Edward t[w]o compositions of his own for flute.[3] Jean's Spanish painter friend Manolo also on top of world, having just got a foot in Maeght Gallery (two paintings sold & promise of a group show, first interest from a real gallery so far).[4] Party to celebrate event tonight at Lindon's - Suzanne, Marthe, Jean, Manolo, Pinget and self. I bought a very beautiful gouache at the Arikha show last week and am impatient to have it on my wall.[5] Tomorrow Bram van Velde's rétrospective at Knoedler's new gallery, with banquet to follow Place de la Bastille! I lent my painting.[6] So great goings on, but I'd give it all for a little peace at Ussy where I could only manage 48 hours last week, but hope to return for a fortnight this week. Went with Edward last night to the Richter Schubert recital at Chaillot - very impressive, but something wrong something [sic]. Too interior was as near as I could get, though this sounds queer for Schubert, when the interior is as genuinely poetic as Richter's. He played notably the rather long-winded unfinished sonata and the great last sonata of 1828 - heart-breakingly beautiful till he seems to throw his poor hat at it in the final rondo.[7]

Very pleased to hear of American publication of your poems. I wish you had enough for another little volume. But perhaps you have and are just indifferent.[8]

A card from Sylvia Beach to tell me that Miss Weaver had died - and a letter from Kay Boyle asking what I thought of the Eichmann trial![9]

Have just read Kenneth Clark's Landscape into Art - I confess not without pleasure.[10]

Very pleased with good news of John. He was to marry Vera today I believe.[11] I don't know when I'll be over. No date from Royal Court. There are so many people I would like to see, and who are hurt if I don't, and whom perhaps I won't be able to, in London & Dublin, that sometimes I feel the only thing to do is not to stir.

Much love from us both.

Sam

ALS; 1 leaf, 2 sides; TCD, MS 10402/243.

1 MacGreevy's sister Bridget McGreevy (1896–1977) was known as Delia; she had recently retired as a schoolteacher in Bristol, was suffering from severe arthritis, and

had broken her hip (Margaret Farrington to the editors, 15 October 2012). SB deliberately employs a Gallicism: the contrast between the inflated "prompt reestablishment" (prompt rétablissement) and the expectable "quick recovery."

2 The entrance examination to the Conservatoire National Supérieur de Musique consisted at this time of two parts: the first required performance of a piece of the applicant's choice; the second, if the applicant was successful with the first, required performance of a set piece which the applicant was given three weeks to learn. Edward Beckett's first exam was on 17 October, and his final one was on 6 November (SB to Thomas MacGreevy, 15 October 1961; TCD, MS 10402/242). Edward Beckett's teacher of flute at the Conservatoire was Gaston Crunelle (1898–1990); Crunelle taught there from 1941 to 1969.

3 By "the three of us" SB intends himself, Suzanne Beckett, and Edward Beckett. Mihalovici's two compositions were *Mélodie* and *Pastourelle Triste*, both for flute and piano, both composed in 1959.

4 Fandos had been invited to bring his work to the Galerie Maeght for inspection. "Beckett offered to take him and his paintings to the *Galerie Maeght* ... When the gallery director, Aimé Maeght, saw the famous playwright going up the stairs with his burden he was 'paralized [sic] with astonishment'." (Fernández, "Surrounding the Void," 51.) Maeght bought all the paintings, but Fandos did not have an exhibition at the Galerie Maeght.

5 Avigdor Arikha's solo exhibition at the Galerie Karl Flinker, Paris 7, had opened on 11 October and was to run until 4 November. SB's purchase is untitled (Private Collection).

6 SB's painting by Bram van Velde: SB to Thomas MacGreevy, 21 April 1958, n. 5.

7 Sviatoslav Richter (1915–1997) was playing in France for the first time: his recitals at the Palais du Chaillot were originally scheduled for 3, 6, and 9 October, but then had been rescheduled. The Schubert recital that SB attended had been set for 9 October, but was postponed to 22 October (*Le Monde* 8–9 September 1961: 15; 10 September 1961: 13; 12 October 1961: 13).

8 Two poems by Thomas MacGreevy, "Moments Musicaux" and "Breton Oracle," were published by *Poetry Magazine* 99.2 (November 1961) 85–89.

9 The previous day, 22 October, SB had written to Sylvia Beach, the founder of Shakespeare and Company: "I had not heard of Miss Weaver's death. I met her I think only twice. I bow again to what she did and shall think of her when I think of goodness." (NjP, Sylvia Beach Papers, CO 108.) Born in 1876, Harriet Shaw Weaver died on 14 October; she had been the patron of James Joyce, among others (Lidderdale and Nicholson, *Dear Miss Weaver*, 455).

The trial of Adolf Eichmann began in Jerusalem on 11 May and ended on 14 August; at the time of Kay Boyle's question to SB, the judges were deliberating their verdict.

10 *Landscape into Art* (1949) by Kenneth Clark (1903–1983) was based on lectures he had delivered as Slade Professor of Art at Oxford University.

11 John Beckett and Vera Nielson Slocombe (1913–?) were married from 1961 to 1969; her first husband was the cinematographer Douglas Slocombe (b. 1913) (Douglas Slocombe to the editors, 12 May 2010).

KAY BOYLE
PETERBOROUGH, NEW HAMPSHIRE

30.10.61 Ussy sur Marne
Seine et Marne

Dear Kay

Thanks for your two letters. I am here till next week and shall not fail to look up your friend Arthur Deshaies when I get back to Paris.[1]

Can't think of anything worth saying to say about Eichmann. Jewish friends here speak of him with indulgence. Just the I suppose flippant vision of his being sentenced to be treated kindly and shown in a comfortable cage on the fairgrounds of the world.[2]

Best always
Sam

ALS; 1 leaf, 1 side; *env to* Kay Boyle, The MacDowell Colony, Peterborough - N.H., U.S.A.; *pm* 30-10-61, La Ferté-sous-Jouarre; TxU, Beckett Collection, 8.3.

1 Arthur Emillien Deshaies (1920–2011) was an American painter and printmaker, born to French parents; he taught at Indiana University, the Pratt School of Design in New York, the Ogunquit School of Painting and Sculpture in Maine, and, for the last twenty-five years of his career, at Florida State University, Tallahassee. Boyle met him in 1959, and "declared herself 'in love'" with him; he assumed "the role of her companion" and he "virtually moved in" with her. Boyle "offered access to people who might help him" (Joan Mellen, *Kay Boyle: Author of Herself* [New York: Farrar, Straus and Giroux, 1994] 410–414).

2 Almost the entire trial of Adolf Eichmann was widely broadcast on television, showing the defendant inside a bulletproof glass booth.

HERBERT MYRON
CAMBRIDGE, MASSACHUSETTS

8.11.61 Paris

Dear Herbert

Many thanks for cards & letters and forgive inadequacy of response. Glad you liked text of H.D. I hear it's off in N.Y. So much piss as my old French professor at T.C.D. used to say.[1]

Very pleasant evening yesterday with your friend Larry Harvey, at the Closerie Bar to get up a little steam, then Iles Marquises (fruits de mer) Rue de la Gaité. Soupe de poisson, grillades, Sancerre and marc. Found Harvey very sympa and hope to see more of him. Shall be very glad to help him in any way I can, i.e. short of talking of my opera.[2]

Nothing much to tell you. Struggling to translate Comment C'est, hopeless and afflicting undertaking. Ussy as often as possible, not often enough. Back there I hope next week for a longish spell.[3]

H.D. in French. Not on visible horizon. Shall have to do it myself and don't feel equal to it. Perhaps never.

Best as always

Sam

ALS; 1 leaf, 1 side; *env to* Mr Herbert Myron, 8 Plympton St., Cambridge, Mass., U.S.A.; *pm* 8-11-61, Paris; MBU, Myron.

1 The repertory production of *Happy Days* at the Cherry Lane Theatre completed its run on 3 November ("Goings on About Town," *The New Yorker* 37.38 [4 November 1961] 4; Judith Schmidt to SB, 23 October 1961; NSyU). SB quotes Professor Thomas Rudmose-Brown (1878–1942; Profile, I), his French professor at Trinity College Dublin. "So much piss" is a pretend translation of the French "tant pis" (so much the worse).

2 Lawrence Harvey (1925–1988), then Associate Professor of French and Italian at Dartmouth College, had been introduced to SB by Herbert Myron; Harvey was writing a critical study of SB's poetry and criticism, and, with it, a biography. After their evening together, SB wrote to Harvey: "Let me say again that I am more than willing to help you in any way I can. It won't amount to much, because of my inarticulateness and, I'm afraid, great tiredness which obliges me to be a lot alone, away from Paris." (20 November 1961; NhD, Beckett Collection MS 122/1.6.)

3 On 31 October, SB wrote to Barbara Bray of his work on the English translation of *Comment c'est*: "I've been working hard for me, 287 'stanzas' in 3 days, and finished part 3. Type it now and then start on second half of part 1." In this letter SB also said of working at Ussy:

> The more I think of it all the more self-banishment seems the only way, with just a day or two off on, and off. A little longer here and I'd be driven to an attempt at new work – or go quite mad, it's not so far. Paris seems quite impossible henceforward without a new inside to skull or reformation of character or both and much too late for either. Dismal prospect. (TCD, MS 10948/1/165.)

GEORGE REAVEY
NEW YORK

9.11.61

8 Bld. St. Jacques
Paris 14me

Dear George

Many thanks for your letter.

Have only a very confused picture of Happy Days in N.Y. Not surprised to hear its little day is over, in spite of Alan Schneider's & Ruth White's noble efforts.[1] No word from Alan since the opening.

I have not yet been able to read Jean's play. I am going to the country next Monday and shall be writing to her towards the end of the week.[2] I am very sorry to be so slow about it, but Paris has become impossible, and the country is the only chance.

The Calder poems are composed of Whoroscope, Echo's Bones (with due acknowledgments to you & Europa) and odds and ends, some translated from the French.[3] They should have been out long ago. He is very slow and I know about his reputation. We have always been good friends and I have no complaints.

The Mexican Anthology was just an alimentary chore for UNESCO in 1950. I just got paid for the job and no further interest. No royalties. It should have been published by UNESCO here, but came out finally, much later, with Indiana University Press. Grove has no interest in this work. It is besides quite unimportant. The original poems, chosen by Paz, are execrable for the most part. My only excuse, which I know is not one, is that I was very broke at the time.[4]

Wonderful Bram rétrospective at Knoedlers. It opens at their N.Y. gallery mid-February – with a few new works. I think he will go over.[5] Not seen Geer & Lisl, but hear they are well and prosperous. Tonny came from Amsterdam and stayed a few weeks.

Tom writes poorly and depressed, very fed up with the Gallery.[6]

A line from Brian Coffey after years of silence. Look forward to renewing contact if I go to London. H.D. is to be done at Royal Court, probably with Joan Plowright, but I don't know when, perhaps not before the Spring[.][7]

Struggling to translate <u>Comment C'est</u>. Hopeless & depressing undertaking. Tempted to drop it.

Do hope you'll both be over next year. Depuis le temps . . .[8]

Affectionately to you both

Sam

ALS; 1 leaf, 2 sides; *env to* Mr George Reavey, 221 East 85th Street, New York 28, N.Y., U.S.A.; *pm* 9–11–61, Paris; TxU, Reavey Collection, recip, 45.6.

1 George Reavey had written to SB with his reactions to *Happy Days* on 16 September; this may have included Reavey's three-page essay on the play (NSyU; InU, C&B, Reavey). SB had responded to Reavey on 22 September:

> I am very interested by your reactions. I did not write with such things in mind – far too preoccupied with seeing and hearing it in its mere particularity – but they may well be there. I appreciate very much in any case your being moved to putting them down. I'm afraid for me it is no more than another dramatic object. I am aware vaguely of course of the hidden impetuses that are behind its making, but concern with their elucidation would prevent the making. (TxU, Reavey Collection, 45.5.)

2 George Reavey sent SB *Poised for Violence*, the first full-length play by Jean Reavey (1917–1987). Although written for the stage, it was broadcast on WBAI, New York, on 2 July ("WBAI's 'Poised for Violence' Throwback to Plays Written Especially for Medium," *New York Times* 3 July 1961: 31).

3 SB's *Poems in English* republished the poems of *Echo's Bones and Other Precipitates* with acknowledgment of the original publication of this collection by George Reavey's Europa Press in 1935. A limited edition of 100 copies, on handmade paper and signed by the author, had been published by John Calder in late August 1961, "in advance of the first edition" (Federman and Fletcher, *Samuel Beckett*, 33).

4 SB's translations of poems in the *Anthology of Mexican Poetry*: 27 February 1950, n. 5; 20 October 1956; 21 June 1958; 24 March 1959.

5 The Bram van Velde Rétrospective, at the Galerie Knoedler, 85 bis Rue du Faubourg Saint-Honoré, Paris 8, was held from 24 October to 18 November.

6 Thomas MacGreevy continued as Director of the National Gallery of Ireland, despite having suffered two heart attacks.

7 For an article on *Murphy*, Brian Coffey (1905–1995; Profile, I) had written on 11 October to ask SB about a review of the novel and about a poem SB had written in 1938. Coffey also asked about something that he recalled SB saying: "that writing is an act of revenge [. . .] I wondered how relevant you might think the statement now." SB replied: "I remember when I was young and perhaps a little less foolish than I am having some theory of art as escape and revenge (Monte Christo [sic]), but I am quite in the dark now." SB closed his reply with the wish that, when he was in London for rehearsals of *Happy Days*, they "might touch foreheads again" (Coffey to SB, 11 October 1961, and SB to Coffey [after 11 October 1961]; GEU, MSS 1221).

Coffey's essay "Memory's Murphy Maker" was published in *Threshold* 17.20 (1962) 28–36. In an undated letter to MacGreevy, Coffey explained: "I finished a long article on Sam and sent it off – it's to appear in Threshold [. . .] I tried to say a few things that no one mentions when talking of Sam here. Knocked a couple of clichés on the head and got as far, I hope, as his compassion. I could write a book on Sam alone. I hope he'll like it." (TCD, MS 8220/49.) Coffey closes his essay: "Far beyond . . . words, there is the man who, because of those sources in him of compassion . . . has himself been loved greatly and by many" (36).

8 "Depuis le temps" (after all this time).

THOMAS MACGREEVY
DUBLIN

4.12.61 Paris

Dear Tom

Glad to have your letter.

I'm not at all in agreement with Devine's plans as announced in Times. It was always understood that McWhinnie would direct. Apparently Joan Plowright wants Devine. I have written to him and await his reply. I may have to withdraw the play. He has not been well and is away resting.[1]

We are all very pleased about Edward. It was good of you to write and by now you will have heard from him. He is to be home for about 10 days over Xmas.

We went in a party of eight yesterday to concert of Lamoureux Orchestra at Pleyel. Monique played a Mozart concerto and on the programme was Chip's Esercizio per Archi (1959), very fine. Orchestra a bit perfunctory and sloppy and poorly directed by I forget whom. Monique not quite at her best, or because we were too close to piano, but much applauded, as also Esercizio. A rollicking Fifth about finished me.[2]

To please Chip have produced a laborious radio scenario (to be filled in by us first) for words and music, commissioned by RTF. Also a more finished affair for John & the BBC.[3] Otherwise still struggling on and off with translation of Comment c'est.

Suzanne is thinking of going with Marthe and another friend middle of this month to Cologne & Düsseldorf to see the productions there of Happy Days. I hear the Cologne actress is good and great things expected from Düsseldorf production.[4]

I get to the country as often as possible and am happiest there in the quiet. I won't be over to Dublin this year.

I am no longer tied to Simpson – since the march he laid on me for his East London production of Godot.[5] But I'm afraid no prospects for my work at the Gaiety.

Pinget is a good friend of ours, I think you must have met him. Novelist and dramatist, very talented, not yet sorti as he deserves. From Geneva. He was with us at the concert yesterday.[6]

Forgive such a poor scratch. More tired and stupid than I want to admit. And tired above all of dodging people – unsuccessfully.

Much love from us both.

Ever

Sam

ALS; 2 leaves, 2 sides; TCD, MS 10402/244.

1 An unsigned article in *The Times* announced: "September will bring the production of Mr. Samuel Beckett's new play *Happy Days* which will be directed by Mr. George Devine. Miss Joan Plowright will return to the Royal Court to play one of the parts in this two-character play." ("Court Theatre Chooses Its Plays for a Year," 17 November 1961: 17.)

2 At the Salle Pleyel, Rudolf Albert (1918–1992) conducted the Orchestre des Concerts Lamoureux, with Monique Haas as piano soloist; the program consisted of the Overture to Mozart's *Impresario*, K. 486; Mozart's *Concerto for piano in A Major*, no. 23, K. 488; as well as Mihalovici's *Esercizio per archi*; Debussy's *Prélude à l'après-midi d'un faune*; and Beethoven's Symphony No. 5 in C Minor, Op. 67 (*Officiel des Spectacles* 785 [29 November – 5 December 1961] 52–53).

3 *Cascando* was written for Mihalovici; *Words and Music* was written for John Beckett. With his letter of 29 November to Barbara Bray, SB sent an untitled six-page typed manuscript in French which appears to have been an initial scenario for *Cascando*. SB wrote: "Keep enclosed till I see you. I won't send it to John till I have your impression" (TCD, MS 10948/1/167); this precedes the manuscript of *Cascando* identified by Richard Admussen as the first draft (*The Samuel Beckett Manuscripts*, 26).

John Beckett wrote to Michael Bakewell on 14 December: "Sam sent me the finished script of a radio work provisionally entitled WORDS AND MUSIC. Most most beautiful. Most moving. I have told him that I will of course be honoured to compose the music for it." (BBCWAC, RCONT1, John Beckett, Composer I.)

4 *Glückliche Tage* had opened on 5 November in Cologne, where Grete Mosheim (1905–1986) played Winnie, and it would open in Düsseldorf on 17 December, directed by Karl Heinz Stroux, with Maria Wimmer (1911–1996) playing Winnie. Suzanne Beckett saw these productions, and SB later reported on her impressions: "Neither of them right, but good acting (Wimmer and Mosheim) and good conscientiousness and care" (SB to Alan Schneider, 21 December 1961; Burns Library, Samuel Beckett Collection, SB-AS; previous publication Beckett and Schneider, *No Author Better Served*, 116).

5 After the Pike Theatre closed, Simpson began work at Stratford East, London; his production there of *Waiting for Godot* was staged without SB's approval (see 20 May 1961 to Alan Schneider, n. 5).

6 "Sorti" (in the public eye).

URSULA BALZER
SUHRKAMP VERLAG, FRANKFURT

le 7 décembre 1961

38 Boulevard Saint-Jacques
Paris 14me

Chère Madame

Merci de votre lettre du 4 décembre.

Je préfère de beaucoup la mise en page de Happy Days dans l'édition américaine à celle de la brochure Fischer.[1]

Cette disposition est celle que j'ai adoptée pour toutes mes pièces et vous l'avez suivie vous-mêmes dans Spectaculum II (Endspiel).[2]

Elle me paraît pour ainsi dire indispensable ici où, encore plus que dans les autres pièces, texte et geste sont étroitement liés, se prolongent, se soutiennent et s'éclairent l'un l'autre. Dans la mise en page de Fischer cette continuité est complètement disloquée.

Croyez, chère Madame, à mes sentiments très cordialement dévoués.

Samuel Beckett

TLcc; 1 leaf, 1 side; AL draft on Ursula Balzer to SB, Suhrkamp Verlag, 12 April 1961; GEU, MSS 1221.

7 December 1961

38 Boulevard Saint-Jacques
Paris 14th

Dear Frau Balzer

Thank you for your letter of 4th December.

I much prefer the page layout of *Happy Days* in the American edition to the Fischer one.[1]

This is the pattern that I have adopted for all my plays, and you yourselves have followed it in *Spectaculum II* (*Endspiel*).[2]

It seems to me so to speak indispensable here where, even more than in the other plays, text and movement are closely linked, each continuing, supporting, and illuminating the other. In the Fischer layout this continuity is completely dislocated.

Cordially yours

Samuel Beckett

1 Fischer Verlag had published the acting edition of *Glückliche Tage*, translated by Elmar and Erika Tophoven. Its page layout separated the stage directions from the spoken text, printing them on a separate line. Ursula Balzer, who was charged with the composition of the text, advised adopting this format for the Suhrkamp edition. In the Grove Press edition of *Happy Days*, the stage directions were interwoven with the spoken text.

2 *Endspiel* had appeared in *Spectaculum* 2 (1959) 7–42; *Spectaculum*, a periodical of Suhrkamp Verlag, published plays.

JUDITH SCHMIDT
GROVE PRESS, NEW YORK

9.12.61 Paris

Dear Judith

Thanks for your letter of December 7.

You may authorize Canadian TV to do Godot. It has been so battered by now that a little more or less can't make much difference. We'll just try and keep the others clean.[1]

Best

Sam

ALS; 1 leaf, 1 side; NSyU.

1 On 6 September, Judith Schmidt had informed SB that the Canadian Broadcasting Company had written to Richard Barr, producer of *Happy Days*, to request television rights for the play. In her letter of 7 December, Schmidt conveyed the CBC's interest in securing television rights for Godot: "I know you refused to allow these people to do HAPPY DAYS. But I'm sending you a copy of this letter in case you've changed your mind about television programs." (NSyU.)

SB had been unhappy that Curtis Brown had granted television rights for *Waiting for Godot* to Danish Television without consulting him (Margaret McLaren to SB, 1 August

1961; GEU, MSS 1221). As SB wrote to Christian Ludvigsen: "The play does not lend itself to this medium. [. . .] I think the problem is how to give the space on the small screen. Roughly speaking I think the solution is in a counterpoint of long shots and close-ups." (SB to Ludvigsen, 30 August 1961; Ludvigsen Collection.)

JOHN BARBER
CURTIS BROWN, LONDON

December 10th 1961 | 38 Boulevard Saint-Jacques
Paris 14me

Dear Mr Barber

Thank you for your letter of December 6th.

I am very sorry to hear of this coincidence of title and have given much thought, with the desire to be agreeable to Mr Greenwood, to the possibility of calling my play by another name.[1]

I have come to the conclusion that I cannot do this.

The play has already been published in America, Germany and Italy, and played in America and Germany, under the title Happy Days (Glückliche Tage, Giorni Felici), and could not therefore be retitled without damage and embarrassment to the publishers, agents and theatre managements concerned.[2]

Moreover the title is to such a degree function of the text and its loss would entail a damage to the work itself which I simply have not the right to accept.

Please express to Mr Greenwood and to Samuel French Ltd. with what care I have considered their request and with what regret I find myself unable to comply with it.

Yours sincerely
Samuel Beckett

TLcc; 1 leaf, 1 side; AL draft, *on* John Barber, Curtis Brown, to SB, 6 December 1961; GEU, MSS 1221; photocopy, TLS, 1 leaf, 1 side; V and A, THM/273/4/1/18 Production Files.

1 On 6 December, John Barber forwarded to SB a letter from Walter Greenwood (1903–1974) that had been received by the Royal Court Theatre. Greenwood, who had written a play entitled *Happy Days* that was produced in 1958, requested that SB change

the title of his play. The Samuel French agency in New York, which handled amateur rights of Beckett's work in the United States, had made a similar request of Beckett. Barber added: "There is of course no copyright in titles and the decision is entirely yours" (GEU, MSS 1221).

2 *Glückliche Tage: ein Stück in zwei Akten*, tr. Elmar and Erika Tophoven (Frankfurt: Fischer Verlag, 1961). *Giorni felici*, tr. Carlo Fruttero (Turin: Einaudi, 1961).

MARY HUTCHINSON
LONDON

10.12.61 Paris

Dear Mary

Thanks for your letters.

When I saw Times announcement of Royal Court programme I wrote to George at the theatre. I suppose he did not get the letter. Richardson replied rather confusedly, apologising for incorrect announcement, but saying Joan Plowright wished to be directed by George.[1] Of course there can be no question of taking the play away from McWhinnie. Then George wrote from the country, thanks to you I think, saying there was never any question of his directing. It is all very confused & confusing. I don't want to bother George till he is better and some clarification can be had from him.

I enclose two poems by a young Englishman I met here. I think they are good and wd. be very pleased if "X" would publish them. Rawson is an interesting young man in rather desperate circumstances materially and capable I think of doing important work if he were encouraged and helped. He has not produced much so far. Will you please ask Cremin [sic], Swift & Co. to consider the poems and show a little interest in the man. I am also giving him a letter to John Calder. He has been working in Germany & France on building sites and is in great need of sympathy & help.[2]

I have done a radio script for John & am doing another for Mihalovici. Apart from that "How it is" advancing slowly.

I hope to spend Xmas & the N.Y. in the country, far from the christifying.

Yours ever

Sam

ALS; 1 leaf, 2 sides; *env to* Mrs Hutchinson, 21 Hyde Park Square, London W.2, Angleterre; *pm* 11-12-61, Paris. TxU, Hutchinson, 2.5.

1 Devine was on leave from the Royal Court because of illness. Director Tony Richardson (1928–1991) responded as Devine's associate at the Royal Court and in his absence.

2 SB had become acquainted with the Welsh-born poet Nicholas Rawson (b. 1934) in Paris. SB mistakenly writes "Cremin" for David Wright, one of the editors of *X*. The two poems by Rawson that SB sent to Mary Hutchinson have not been identified; *X* published nothing by Rawson.

SB wrote to John Calder, also on 10 December: "He is a writer of very great promise indeed, in my opinion. I have just submitted two of his poems to "X". He will tell you about himself and his difficult situation. I should be very grateful indeed if you would give him whatever help and encouragement you can and perhaps a few introductions to likely people." (InU, C&B, Beckett.)

JOHN CALDER
JOHN CALDER (PUBLISHER) LTD., LONDON

Wednesday [13 December 1961] Paris

Dear John

Herewith text of Lindon manifesto. Thought you might like to sign it & have it signed en attendant yours. Have sent another to Hobson. Lindon knows I am sending you this and approves.[1]

Good to hear your voice to day and looking forward to Monday 1 p.m. Closerie.

Best to Bettina.

Yrs. ever

Sam

Manifesto needn't be back before end of next week.

ALS; 1 leaf, 1 side; *datestamped* 18.DEC.1961; InU, C&B, Beckett. *Dating:* 13 December 1961 was the Wednesday prior to 18 December.

1 On 6 December, Jérôme Lindon had appeared before the Tribunal de Première Instance de la Seine, accused of "provocation à la désobéissance" (encouraging the

disobedience of orders). The ostensible cause was his publication of *Le Déserteur*, by Jean-Louis Hurst under the pseudonym Maurienne (Paris: Editions de Minuit, 1960). That night near midnight, his apartment at 7 Boulevard Arago was bombed ('Nombreux attentats au plastic," *Le Monde* 8 December 1961: 4). On 9 December, a firebomb was thrown through a window of Editions de Minuit ("Les Attentats Activistes," *Le Monde* 10–11 December 1961: 5). A manifesto in support of Jérôme Lindon was circulated and signed by artists, editors, and intellectuals, among them, SB.

> Un certain nombre d'éditeurs, écrivains et artistes "conscients de tout ce que les Editions de Minuit ont fait pour le rayonnement dans le monde de la culture", dénoncent "les méthodes criminelles des hommes de main de l'O.A.S. qui, le soir même du jour où, pour la première fois en France, un éditeur, Jérôme Lindon, était traduit en justice en raison d'opinions émises par les personnages d'un roman, détruisaient en pleine nuit, au moyen d'une charge d'explosif, une partie de l'appartement qu'il occupe avec sa femme et ses trois jeunes enfants". ("Cent-vingt écrivains, artistes et éditeurs expriment à M. J. Lindon 'leur entière solidarité'," *Le Monde* 19 December 1961: 8). (A certain number of publishers, writers and artists, "having in mind all that the Editions de Minuit have done to further culture worldwide", denounce "the criminal methods of the OAS thugs who, the very evening of the day in which, for the first time in France, a publisher, Jérôme Lindon, was facing trial because of opinions expressed by characters in a novel, were destroying, under cover of darkness, by means of an explosive device, part of the apartment where he lives with his wife and his three young children".)

A similar manifesto of solidarity was circulated by SB to Calder, Harold Hobson, Avigdor Arikha, and Fernando Arrabal; it was published as "Deux cent trente intellectuels assurent J. Lindon de leur solidarité," by *Les Lettres Françaises* (906 [21–27 December 1961] 4).

AIDAN HIGGINS
DUBLIN

18.12.61 Paris

Dear Aidan

Thanks for your letter.

I am so glad you like Happy Days.

There is a contract for Italian Murphy with I think Einaudi.[1]

Was to have lunched with Calder today, but Bettina rang to put it off. Some legal trouble with ex-wife and daughter.[2]

Mrs Hutchinson wrote to say how much she liked the extract you sent her. Says "X" is having difficulties.[3]

Haven't seen last issue of Evergreen.[4]

I thought I might get over before Xmas for a week but finally can't. Glad to have such good news of John.

Edith Fournier is an intelligent young woman who is trying to extricate herself, through translation and literary journalism, from a teaching career. In spite of excellent English she has failed twice at her agrégation (viva nervousness). I have not seen her lately, but she must by now have finished her translation of Felo. She wrote a good article on Comment c'est in Critique.[5] The director of Editions de Minuit, Jérôme Lindon, has been having a bad time on account of his anti-torture Documents and was dragged before the courts the other day for his publication The Deserter. Same night at midnight he was "plasticated" – his private apartment. No one hurt but much damage to premises. Verdict day after tomorrow. Fine probably. And he goes in permanent personal danger.

Was hoping to get to the country for the christifying, but impossible. Con Leventhal arrives 27th for a week. It's just a year since I saw him last.

Hope you'll come through Paris on your way to Spain and that we may see us other then [sic].

Best to you all

Sam

ALS; 2 leaves, 2 sides; *env to* Aidan Higgins Esq, Garden Flat, 47 Charleston Road, Ranelagh, Dublin 6. IRLANDE; *pm* 18-12-61, Paris; TxU, Beckett Collection, 8.9.

1 On 19 May, SB had written to Giulio Einaudi, Director of Edizioni Einaudi: "Je suis heureux que Murphy, Nouvelles et Textes pour Rien et Comment C'est paraissent chez vous" (GEU, MSS 1221). (I am glad that *Murphy*, *Nouvelles et Textes pour rien*, and *Comment c'est* will be coming out under your imprint). Giulio Einaudi (1912–1999), a doctor and publisher, founded in 1933 the publishing house that bears his name in Turin.

2 John Calder's first wife was Mary Ann Simonds (the actress Christya Myling); they divorced in 1961. Their daughter Jamie was born in 1954. (John Calder, *Pursuit: The Uncensored Memoirs of John Calder* [London: Calder Publications, 2001] 52–57, 78, 83–84.)

3 The extract sent by Higgins to Hutchinson was taken from *Langrishe, Go Down*; it was published in the final number of *X* 2.3 (July 1962) 226–234. In revised form it would become chapter 10 of *Langrishe, Go Down* (London: John Calder, 1966, 85–96; New York: Grove Press, 1966, 81–92).

4 *Evergreen Review* 5.21 (November–December 1961) was the current issue; Higgins had written to Arland Ussher on 16 November that he expected to publish a radio play

there. "Sign and Ground" was published in *Evergreen Review* 7.30 (May–June 1963) 85–92 (TCD, MSS 9031–41/1495).

5 Edith Fournier's article on the themes and poetic structure of *Comment c'est*, "Pour que la boue me soit contée … ," appeared in *Critique* 17.168 (May 1961) 412–418. SB knew Edith Fournier as a friend and "former pupil" of Mania Péron (Knowlson, *Damned to Fame*, 433).

CHRONOLOGY 1962

1962	12 January	SB in Ussy to complete draft translation of *Comment c'est* (*How It Is*).
	8 February	Demonstration against the OAS at the Charonne Métro Station provokes police response that ends in death of nine persons; this triggers a general strike in Paris on 13 February.
	11 February	Jean-Jacques Mayoux's home is bombed.
	20 February	Bram van Velde's first New York exhibition opens, Knoedler Gallery.
	18 March	With the signing of the Evian Accords, a ceasefire takes effect in Algeria on 19 March.
	3 April	With Roger Blin, SB attends Mary Manning's play *The Voice of Shem* in the Gate Theatre production as part of the Théâtre des Nations, Paris.
	5 May	Attends Henri Hayden vernissage, Galerie Suillerot.
	8 May	Attends vernissage of Joan Mitchell double show, Galerie Jacques Dubourg and Galerie Lawrence, Paris.
	before 15 May	Has begun work on a play for three faces and lights (ultimately, *Play*).
	16 May	Lunches with the Stravinskys in Paris.
	22 May	The BBC Third Programme broadcasts *Endgame*, directed by Alan Gibson.
	15 June	Faber and Faber publish *Happy Days*.
	17 June	Agreement signed between the Algerian FLN (National Liberation Front) and the OAS effectively ends the Algerian war.

3 July	After the approval of the Evian Accords by the electorate of Algeria, De Gaulle pronounces Algeria an independent country.
19 July	SB finishes draft of new play (*Play*).
5 August	Attends Pinget double bill of *La Manivelle* and *Architruc* at the Comédie de Paris.
7–25 August	Holidays with Suzanne in Kitzbühel. Returns to Paris on 25 August.
22 August	Second attempt on the life of General de Gaulle.
5 September	De Gaulle dissolves the French National Assembly, now allowing the President to be directly elected by the people.
21 September	SB sends complete manuscripts of *Cascando* to Herbert Myron for deposit in the Harvard University Theatre Collection.
7 October	Arrives in London to begin rehearsals of *Happy Days* on 8 October.
13 October	Attends Jack MacGowran's run-through of his one-man Beckett show, *End of the Day*. The BBC Third Programme broadcasts *Words and Music.*
15 October	Start of the Cuban missile crisis.
26 October	SB attends recital by Dietrich Fischer-Dieskau singing Hugo Wolf songs, Royal Festival Hall.
26–29 October	Spends the weekend at Sheila and Donald Page's home in Surrey.
1 November	London opening of *Happy Days* at the Royal Court Theatre. SB returns to Paris. SB grants George Devine and the Royal Court Theatre first option on production of his future work in London.
3 November	Consults an eye specialist in Berne.
13 November	The BBC Third Programme broadcasts *Words and Music.*
19 November	Henri Hayden taken ill and hospitalized in London.

before 27 December	SB attends Ionesco's *Le Roi se meurt* with George Devine, Jocelyn Herbert, and her daughter Jenny.
27 December	Attends, with Robert Pinget, Roland Dubillard's *La Maison d'os.*

JEAN REAVEY
NEW YORK

16.1.62 Ussy

Dear Jean

Please forgive my not having written to you before now.[1] Things have been too much for me lately – or I suppose I should say I have been too little for them.

I have read your play with great interest. It has remarkable originality and inventiveness. It is perhaps a little too long, over-explicit and under-written. Could you not by some means make your "canvas" postulate a little less sweeping. It is difficult to reduce stage space systematically to such dimensions and in fact the play transgresses them continually, as it must. As constructed, in alternations of "canvas" being and apparent suspension of same, it sometimes gives the impression not only of diverging from its premises, but of being embarrassed and hindered by awareness of this divergence. That is why it occurs to me that a less total commitment at the outset to the "canvas" conception, and less explicit reference to it in the course of the play might be worth considering. But by "canvas" you must mean something very different from the flat and silent finity it suggests to me. Otherwise you would not write that "the action of the entire play takes place on a canvas." So what I have said will probably seem to you quite irrelevant. If so forgive me[.] I see everything blurred my own undispersable mists and no one is less competent or inclined than I to comment on another's work.[2]

Please thank George for his letter and tell him I'll be writing soon.

Am I to return MS?

Affectionately to you both

Sam

ALS; 1 leaf, 1 side; *env to* Mrs George Reavey, 221 East 85th Street, New York 28, N.Y., U.S.A.; *pm* 17-1-62, La Ferté-sous-Jouarre; TxU, Reavey Collection, Misc.

1 When George Reavey had asked SB to read his wife's play, SB wrote: "I am a bad reader and worse counsellor but shall of course be very glad to read Jean's play & stammer back its effect on me" (22 September 1961; TxU, Reavey). SB acknowledged receipt of Jean Reavey's play *Poised for Violence* on 14 October 1961, but wrote then that he had "not yet had time for more than a look through" (TxU, Reavey).

2 Although Jean Reavey's play had been written for the stage, its initial production had been on WBAI Radio in New York, on 2 July 1961. Jack Gould's review suggests the difficulties of the play:

> The play's device is to explore society's obsession with disaster and violence through the eyes of a group of artist's models who remain part of someone else's painting . . . Somewhere in Mrs. Reavey's play there is both protest and aspiration of merit. But its relentless discursiveness and determined complexity are . . . overwhelming. ("WBAI's 'Poised for Violence' Throwback to Plays Written Especially for Medium," *New York Times* 3 July 1961: 31.)

Jean Reavey wrote appreciatively about SB's letter in an unpublished memoir: "He wrote me a long critique pointing out I'd mixed a stage metaphor. Sam's care and concern about this shocked me into a better recognition of what I was trying to do." ("How it is with Sam," ©1972; TxU, Reavey.)

BARBARA BRAY
PARIS

7.2.62 Ussy

Dear Barbara

Susse Delikatessen from you this morning. All I can say is bless your heart and please don't. I'm still nibbling away at the previous and am not much of a fist at sweet things. Ceci dit, merci de tout coeur.[1]

I feel a bit better this morning for the first time, but wouldn't bet on its lasting till evening - or afternoon. Have just succeeded - without having to lie down [on] it immediately afterwards - in making the bed with fresh sheets (and pillow slips!), not because the old were too soiled for my taste, but because they were perished.

Why suddenly in my memory a phrase from Swift's Journal to Stella: "My cold hand starves my thigh" and the old wondering what that means? Couldn't say - why or what.[2]

Still have about 10 pages to type of my gruesome translation. Manage on an average a page a day.

Made myself a large ragoût de veau yesterday which will do me to the end of the week if it doesn't go bad with the warm weather.[3]

My Harvey from Dartmouth, New Hampshire, brought me a bottle of fine Spanish Sack to remind me of the Tavern behind Liberty's and what an overstatement it was the not a soul there.[4]

Raining again this morning. The Hayden may turn up tomorrow. He is on the point of buying a house near La Ferté (Firmitas).[5] They want me to see it with them.

Disappointed by Scherchen's Schubert (Stuttgart orchestra probably).[6] The Beethoven with the French nerves was superb.

Arikha phoned, said he had seen Bram on the eve of his leaving for his show in N.Y. – on Le France! My painting has gone too, without as much as by your leave. Poor Arikha is having a hard time with his stained glass.[7]

A sad line from Kay Boyle saying she had to have a "rather major operation" and enclosing a photo in case she didn't come through. And after more than 20 years a letter from Lucia Joyce from her bin in Northhampton. Something wrong with that cupboard.[8]

Checked Murphy's game of chess and made a small change. Mr Endon's 42nd move: K-Q2 instead of K-K2. Pretty feeble joke the whole thing. Could do it a little better now – but not much.[9]

Take care of yourself,

Love

Sam

ALS; 1 leaf, 2 sides; *env to* Mrs Barbara Bray, 14 Rue Le Sueur, Paris 16me; *pm* 7-2-62, La Ferté-sous-Jouarre; TCD, MS 10948/1/170.

1 "Süsse Delikatessen" (sweet delicacies). SB writes "Susse." "Ceci dit, merci de tout cœur" (That said, heartfelt thanks).

2 Jonathan Swift's *Journal to Stella* is composed of his letters to Esther Johnson (Stella, 1681–1728) and her companion Rebecca Dingley (c. 1665–1743). In "Letter 15" Swift writes: "I wish my cold hand was in the warmest place about you, young women, I'd give ten guineas upon that account with all my heart, faith; oh, it starves my thigh" (Jonathan Swift, *Journal to Stella*, I, ed. Harold Williams [Oxford: Clarendon Press, 1948] 181). A letter from Pamela Mitchell to SB refers to these lines (see 12 January 1954, n. 3).

3 "Ragoût de veau" (veal stew).

4 There are two pubs behind Liberty (a department store located on Regent Street, London): The Clachan, 34 Kingly Street, which was once owned by Liberty, and the Shakespeare's Head, 29 Great Marlborough Street. SB invokes Krapp: "Celebrated the awful occasion, as in recent years, quietly at the Winehouse. Not a soul." (*Krapp's Last Tape*, [Grove] 14).

5 La Ferté-sous-Jouarre had been known earlier as Firmitas Ansculfi.

6 SB had probably heard a recording or a radio concert directed by Hermann Scherchen (1891–1966).

7 Bram van Velde sailed on the maiden voyage of the SS *France* (then the largest ocean liner) from Le Havre to New York on 3 February, in the company of Jacques Putman and Pierre Alechinsky, to be present for a retrospective of his work at the Knoedler Gallery, 14 East 57th Street, which would open on 13 February (Stoullig and Schoeller, eds., *Bram van Velde*, 202–203). Avigdor Arikha had been commissioned to create thirty stained-glass windows for the B'nai Israel Synagogue, Woonsocket, Rhode Island (Duncan Thomson, *Arikha* [London: Phaidon Press, 1994] 35, 142, 146).

8 SB had replied to Boyle's letter on 6 February (TxU, Beckett Collection, 8.3). Lucia Joyce (1907–1982; Profile, I) was living in St. Andrew's Hospital, Northampton.

9 The moves in Mr. Endon's chess game with Murphy are given in detail (*Murphy* [Grove] 243–245).

JEAN-JACQUES MAYOUX
PARIS

15.2.62 Ussy sur Marne

Cher Jean Jacques

Deux heures de grand contentement hier, grâce à vous et à Constable. Maintenant j'apprends par la radio que ces salauds sont passés chez vous. Je pense bien fort à vous tous et vous envoie ma très affectueuse sympathie. D'après le speaker, Sophie a été commotionnée, j'espère que ce n'est pas grave et qu'elle s'en est bien remise. Embrassez-la bien pour moi. Une grande poignée de main, cher Jean-Jacques, bon courage, et bien amicalement à vous tous.[1]

Sam

ALS; 1 leaf, 1 side; Mayoux Collection.

15.2.62 Ussy sur Marne

Dear Jean-Jacques

Two hours of deep content yesterday, thanks to you and to Constable. Now I learn from the radio that those bastards moved in on you. My best thoughts are with you all, and I send my warmest sympathy. According to the announcer, Sophie was badly shaken. I hope it isn't too serious and that she has fully recovered. Give her a big hug from me. And to you, dear Jean-Jacques, my hand. With fond wishes to you all.[1]

Sam

1 Jean-Jacques Mayoux's lectures were broadcast on Radio-Sorbonne which aired during term time. Every Wednesday at 2 p.m. that academic year, it broadcast Mayoux on "La Peinture anglaise de 1600 à 1900" (English painting from 1600 to 1900). His most recent lecture had been on the work of John Constable.

As a signatory of the Manifeste des 121, Mayoux was liable to reprisals from the far-right OAS. In columns devoted to a "Nouvelle Série d'Attentats à Paris" (New Series of Bomb Attacks in Paris), *Le Monde* reported: "Une charge de plastic a explosé au 1, rue Monticelli, au deuxième étage, devant l'appartement de M. Jean-Jacques Mayoux, professeur de littérature anglaise à la Sorbonne. Sa fille a été commotionnée par la déflagration, qui a provoqué des dégâts très importants." (17 February 1962: 3.) (A plastic explosive device was detonated in 1 rue Monticelli, on the second floor, in front of the apartment of M. Jean-Jacques Mayoux, Professor of English Literature at the Sorbonne. His daughter was badly shaken by the explosion, which caused considerable damage.)

Sophie Mayoux reports:

> In February 62, I was thirteen – a teenager, aware of the Algerian fight for independence, very much aware that my intellectual family had taken sides. This does not mean that I understood clearly what was at stake, what was happening on either side of the sea. People were struggling for justice, people were being killed – that much I knew. So I don't think I was much surprised when the bomb burst. Shocked, certainly – the sheer noise and destructiveness of it had an inescapable physical effect, even if the place where I was sitting inside the flat was remote enough from the explosive charge for me to suffer no injury. The main door to the flat was blown up, the doormat was blown into tiny hairy shreds which we found everywhere afterwards, the marble top console and the chandelier in the entrance hall were shattered. In the farthermost part of the fairly large flat the charlady was hoovering, and I believe that she thought the vacuum cleaner had exploded. At that time, only the two of us were in the flat. I rushed to the telephone and called my best friend, whose family had taken sides, too – the same as us. "Ils nous ont eus", I said. And she answered: "Viens à la maison". I can't remember if I left a note explaining where I was – I suppose so, I hope so! I wanted to leave the scene, to be sure. But I was quite surprised when the papers said that I had been "commotionnée",

unless it was a way of stating the obvious. (Sophie Mayoux to the editors, 8 March 2013.)

"Ils nous ont eus" (They did us over). "Viens à la maison" (Come over here to us).

BARBARA BRAY
PARIS

Jeudi [Friday 16 February 1962] Ussy

Dear Barbara

Thanks for your letters. I note week-end beginning April 20th and will keep that evening free. I'm so sorry you are sleeping so badly and your shoulder giving you pain. You should try and get hold of a good doctor. Mine is impossible, so won't suggest him. You wouldn't get through one day of his prescription. Probably massage a couple of times a week would do you good, for the insomnia too. I don't expect to be back much before the end of the month, when I'll have to see my witch again. I feel a bit better physically, but completely bet in spirit. Tried twice to get going in French again, but threw it away in loathing. How It Is is quite dreadful and I haven't the heart to start revision.[1] Perhaps I should begin looking for a job. New York rang again yesterday for another petty TV authorisation. Endgame Sunday not so good apparently.[2] Another letter from Kay Boyle, op. postponed. She says she had a photo of me in her guest chamber and that a man using it one night filed out the eyes! The wind blows & blows and the tits come every fifteen minutes or so for their butter. I listened to Mayoux on Constable for 2 hours on Wednesday (Sorbonne broadcast), then next day heard he had been bombed. Not a word from Devine needless to say. Another request from Dublin Festival, same answer.[3] Reading the Wassermann with scant gust, but plodding on.[4] Don't know what I'm going to do with Edward till Sunday, but suppose it will work out somehow. Teach him to drive the car perhaps.[5] Hope he brings his flute and plans some work. Cook large carnous meals. Have trouble with heating, but was able to fix it myself. Last time had merely let the tank run dry of fuel. Enough of this blather. Love to the children.

Love

Sam

ALS; 1 leaf, 2 sides; *env to* M<u>rs</u> Bray, 14 Rue Le Sueur, Paris 16<u>me</u>; *pm* 16–2–62, La Ferté-sous-Jouarre; TCD, MS 10948/1/171. *Dating*: from pm.

1 SB completed a draft of his translation, *How It Is*, on 31 January 1962 (OSU, Spec. rare.MS.ENG.30; Admussen, *The Samuel Beckett Manuscripts*, 57).

2 On behalf of The San Francisco Actor's Workshop, Jules Irving had asked Grove Press for permission to televise a section from *Krapp's Last Tape*, directed by Herbert Blau. They planned to tape on 25 February, which made the request urgent. (Judith Schmidt to Jules Irving, 12 February 1962; NSyU.)

The revival of *Endgame* had opened in repertory at the Cherry Lane Theatre on Sunday 11 February with new actors in the roles of Hamm (Vincent Gardenia), Clov (Ben Piazza), and Nell (Sudie Bond) (Beckett and Schneider, *No Author Better Served*, 121).

3 Brendan Smith had written from Paris, on the weekend of 20–21 January, and again on 26 January, asking SB to encourage the Royal Court Theatre to open its production of *Happy Days* at the Dublin Theatre Festival. On 15 February, SB had replied that he did not wish to ask the Royal Court to forgo its priority, failing to understand (as Smith would write on 20 February) that the Festival invitation was for Devine's production of *Happy Days*. (V and A, THM/2374/4/1/18 Production File.)

4 SB may have been reading a book by the German writer Jakob Wassermann (1873–1934).

5 Edward Beckett has reported that SB "did let him drive his 2CV locally, but was a nervous passenger" (to the editors, 17 September 2007).

RUBY COHN
SAN FRANCISCO

16.2.62 | 38 Bld. St. Jacques
Paris 14<u>me</u>

Dear Miss Cohn

Thank you for your letter of Feb. 4<u>th</u>.

Yes, I had read Celine before the war.[1]

The quotation is from Gray's "On a Distant Prospect of Eton College."[2]

I chose the poems. I thought of including Ooftish and decided not. It did not occur to me to include the Textes pour Rien which I have not yet translated.[3]

I have finished first draft of HOW IT IS. Very unsatisfactory.

Yours sincerely

Sam. Beckett

ALS; 1 leaf, 1 side; UoR, BIF, MS 5100/4.

1 Ruby Cohn* (1922–2011) may have been aware that there was once a possibility of SB's writing a study of the work of Louis-Ferdinand Céline (see 7 March 1937, and n. 20). SB writes "Celine" rather than "Céline."

2 In *Happy Days*, Winnie utters "what is that wonderful line . . . laughing wild . . . something something laughing wild amid severest woe" (Beckett, *Happy Days*, 31), echoing lines 79–80 from Thomas Gray's 1742 poem "Ode on a Distant Prospect of Eton College": "And moody Madness laughing wild, / Amid severest woe" (Thomas Gray, *The Complete Poems of Thomas Gray*, ed. H. W. Starr and J. R. Henrickson [Oxford: Clarendon Press, 1966] 9).

3 SB refers to his selection made for *Poems in English*. "Ooftish" (*transition* 27 [April–May 1938] 33) is not included in *Gedichte* (1959) or in the John Calder and subsequent Grove Press reprint (1963) editions of the poems; see 6 April 1957.

AVIGDOR ARIKHA AND ANNE ATIK
PARIS

17.2.62 Ussy

Chers amis

Merci beaucoup de vous être donné tant de mal. Fort intéressant et je suis content d'avoir pu le lire. Je lui [*for* vais] lui écrire. Merci encore de tout cœur.[1]

C'est bien que les vitraux redémarrent.[2] Dites-moi surtout si avez vous besoin de fric en attendant les dollars. Je pense rester ici toute la semaine prochaine. La guenille va un peu mieux, mais la tête pas du tout. J'ai fini le premier jet de How It Is, mais n'ai pas le courage d'en commencer la révision. J'ai essayer [sic] de repartir en français, mais ai tout foutu en l'air. Du mauvais Molloy. C'est comme une muraille à quelques millimètres. Il faut les franchir, eux aussi, mais comment.

John a promis sa musique.[3]

Mercredi j'avais écouté Mayoux pendant deux heures, sur Constable. Très bien. Puis le lendemain cette infamie.

Appelez-moi sans faute si vous êtes fauchés.

Bien amicalement

Sam

ALS; 1 leaf, 1 side; InU, Arikha.

17.2.62 Ussy

Dear Both

Thank you very much for taking so much trouble. Most interesting, and I'm glad to have read it. I'll write. Heartfelt thanks again.[1]

It's good that the stained glass windows are getting going again.[2] Above all let me know if you need any cash while you're waiting for the dollars to come through. I'm thinking of staying on here all next week. The old carcass is a little better, but definitely not the head. I've finished the first draft of *How It Is*, but don't feel up to making a start on the revision. I tried restarting in French, but threw it away. Bad *Molloy*. It's like a great wall, a few millimetres away. I have to get over these too, but how.

John has promised his music.[3]

On Wednesday I had listened to Mayoux for two hours, on Constable. Very good. Then the next day, this unspeakable thing.

You must definitely ring me up if you're broke.

All the best

Sam

1 It is not known what Arikha had sent SB to read.

2 Arikha had stalled on his commission of thirty stained glass windows for B'nai Israel Synagogue, partly because of their size: twelve were to be seven meters high, in thick glass, and several contained black glass (which SB told him met with his approval).

3 John Beckett's music for what would become *Words & Music*.

12. Aidan Higgins

MARY HUTCHINSON
LONDON

22.2.62 Ussy

Dear Mary

Thanks for your letter. I am very grateful for your kindness to Rawson. His best chance to break through is a radio play - un texte quelconque. I have suggested this to him. The Third Programme people are good with young writers and open to them. I am writing to him today to suggest this again & that he should see Michael Bakewell. I am so glad he is to appear in X, with Aidan.[1] The trouble is he has so little to show - very understandable with the life he has had. If he can stick it out for a couple of years, with whatever help we and others can give him, and with luck, he should get through.

Your X number sounds fine. The only chance for me is a few pages from How It Is. They are all so unsatisfactory and have so little meaning isolated that I really think better not. I have literally nothing else. I tried to get going again, but failed completely. Not many shots left I'm afraid in my old locker, if any.

You may have seen that Mayoux had a visit from the dynamiters. All out but the youngest daughter Sophie who was "merely" shocked. Jean-Jacques writes cheerfully. I listened to him lecture on Constable last week, two hours, Sorbonne broadcast, very good.

I have been here some weeks and am feeling a bit better than when I arrived. Back to Paris next week.

Bram had his first New York show opening last Tuesday at Knoedlers, N.Y. He went over on the France! Don't know why that tickles me, but it does. Had no echo[e]s so far. Riopelle's sculpture show opens to day at Dubourg's Gallery. I'm sorry to miss it.[2]

Take care of yourself and thanks again for your goodness.

Yrs. ever

Sam

As I find I haven't Rawson's address here I'm writing c/o you, if you would be kind enough to forward.

ALS; 1 leaf, 2 sides; *env to* Mrs Hutchinson, 21 Hyde Park Square, London W.2, Angleterre; *pm* 23-2-62, La Ferté-sous-Jouarre; TxU, Hutchinson, 2.5.

1 "Un texte quelconque" (some text or other). Rawson had not yet written a radio script (SB to John Calder, 26 January 1962; InU, C&B, Beckett). Barbara Bray wrote to Michael Bakewell, Script Editor of Sound Drama, introducing Rawson: "Sam has suggested that he might get in touch with you and try something for radio" (Thursday [before 28 February 1962]; BBCWAC, RCONT1, Central, Bray, Scriptwriter).

Aidan Higgins's story "Langrishe, Go Down" would be published in *X, A Quarterly Review* 2.3 (July 1962) 226–234. Rawson later informed John Calder: "Mrs. Hutchinson bought one prose fragment and three poems from me during February last. These were to be shown to the editors of 'X'. They have refused them." The prose fragment may have been "Prudd & the Up-men" (13 February 1963; 9 July 1962; InU, C&B, Rawson).

2 Jean-Paul Riopelle's bronze sculptures were exhibited at the Jacques Dubourg Gallery, Paris, from 22 February to 22 March (Pierre Schneider and Jean-Paul Riopelle, *Bronzes de Riopelle: la sculpture de peintre* [Paris: Jacques Dubourg, 1962]).

JACOBA VAN VELDE
AMSTERDAM

9.3.62 Paris

Chère Tonny

ah is at points![1]

Burrough Green etc. B.G. est un village dans le Surrey. Tu peux le remplacer par un endroit en Angleterre familier aux Hollandais (Dover, par example [sic], ou Harwich). Pas une grande ville. Il faut garder le climat anglais - ou bien tout transposer. Ce qui n'est pas à conseiller. Elle se rappelle être assise sur les genoux de l'ecclésiastique à l'ombre du horse-beech, espèce de hêtre. Horse se met devant certains noms d'arbre. Le cas le plus connu est celui de horse-chestnut. Beech ici est important, à cause de beechen shade plus loin. Il faut que l'écho y soit.[2]

Toolshed, remise à outils, à cause de la signification de tool (pénis) en anglais argotique. Mais cette petite obscénité n'est pas indispensable. La longueur et la rareté du mot hollandais ne me gênent pas du tout, au contraire, trois fois de suite ça serait peut-être presque drôle.[3]

Bumper: un verre débordant. Restés seuls tous les deux (fiancés? jeunes mariés?) après le départ des invités, ils se rapprochent l'un de l'autre jusqu'à ce que les deux corps se touchent presque et se portent un dernier toast (happy days!) avec des verres flûtes remplis jusqu'aux bords de champagne rose.[4]

Reynolds' News: infâme torchon populaire. Pas à remplacer par l'équivalent hollandais à moins de tout transposer partout (voir plus haut). Je te propose "gutter press" ou "courrier du coeur" oder so was.[5]

Suis en train de lire le dernier roman de Geneviève (Ressac) qui vient de sortir dans la collection Nadeau.[6] J'irai les voir bientôt et les relancerai pour toi.

Amitiés à Fritz.

Je t'embrasse

Sam

ALS; 1 leaf, 1 side; BNF, 19794/85.

9.3.62 Paris

Dear Tonny

ah is at points![1]

Burrough Green etc.: B.G. is a village in Surrey. You may replace it by a place in England that the Dutch are familiar with (Dover, for example, or Harwich). Not a large town. You must keep the feel of England – or else transpose *everything*. Which is not to be recommended. She remembers sitting on the parson's knees in the shade of the *horse-beech* (a type of beech). *Horse* is put in front of certain names of trees. The best known case is that of *horse-chestnut*. *Beech* is important here because of *beechen shade* farther on. The echo must be there.[2]

Toolshed, shed for storing tools, because of the meaning of *tool* (penis) in English slang. But this mild obscenity is not indispensable. The length and the rarity of the Dutch word do not bother me at all. On the contrary, three times in a row and it might almost be funny.[3]

Bumper: a glass that is overflowing. When the two (engaged couple? newly-weds?) are finally alone, after the guests have gone, they draw closer to each other until their bodies are almost touching and drink a final toast (Happy days!) from flutes brimming over with pink champagne.[4]

Reynold's News: nasty popular rag. Not to be replaced by the Dutch equivalent unless you are transposing *everything* throughout (see above). I suggest "gutter press" or "agony column" oder so was.[5]

Am reading the latest novel by Geneviève (*Ressac*) which has just come out in the Nadeau collection.[6] I shall call in on them soon and give them a nudge on your behalf.

Regards to Fritz.

Fondly

Sam

1 Winnie utters the interjection, "Ah," twenty-two times (either alone or in combination as "ah well," "ah yes," "ah that's better") in the course of *Happy Days*.

2 Winnie recollects: "Charlie Hunter! I close my eyes – and am sitting on his knees again, in the back garden at Borough Green, under the horse-beech" (*Happy*

Days, 15–16). Despite SB's advice, Van Velde transposes "Burrough / Borough Green," turning it into "Broek in Waterland," a small town north of Amsterdam (*Wachten op Godot* ... (collection) 159; Samuel Beckett, *Gelukkige dagen: een toneelstuk in twee bedrijven*, tr. Jacoba van Velde [Amsterdam: Uitgeverij de Bezige Bij, 1962] 18). (Burrough Green is a village in Cambridgeshire; Borough Green, spelled as it appears in the published text, is in Kent.) For "horse-beech," Van Velde chooses "wilde beuk" (wild beech); for "beechen green" (which SB cites here as "beechen shade") she chooses "beukegroen" (Beckett, *Happy Days*, 16; *Wachten op Godot* ... 180; *Gelukkige dagen*, 18).

3 Winnie recollects her first kiss: "Within a toolshed, though whose I cannot conceive. We had no toolshed and he most certainly had no toolshed." (Beckett, *Happy Days*, 16.) Van Velde translates "toolshed" by "gereedschapsschuur," employing the cumbersome word three times, but by its use not retaining the mild obscenity (*Gelukkige dagen*, 19).

4 Close to the end of *Happy Days*, Winnie recalls: "That day. The pink fizz. The flute glasses. The last guest gone. The last bumper with the bodies nearly touching" (Beckett, *Happy Days*, 60). Van Velde translates: "Die dag. (Pause) De roze champagne. (Pause) De slanke kelken. (Pause) De laatste gast weggegaan. (Pause) Het laatste volle glas terwijl de lichamen elkaar bijna beroerden. (Pause)." (Beckett, *Wachten op Godot* ... 185; *Gelukkige dagen*, 73).

5 Winnie says to Willie: "Oh I know you were never one to talk, I worship you Winnie be mine and then nothing from that day forth only titbits from *Reynolds' News*" (*Happy Days*, 62). *Reynolds's Weekly Newspaper* was founded by George W. M. Reynolds in 1850, and by early 1962 was being published under the title *Reynolds News and Sunday Citizen*, its fortunes having been in serious decline since the 1950s (Dennis Griffiths, ed., *The Encyclopedia of the British Press: 1422–1992* [London: Macmillan Press; New York: St. Martin's Press, 1992] 484–485). Van Velde chooses again to transpose, invoking *Piccolo*, a popular weekly published in the Netherlands during the 1950s: "O, ik weet dat je nooit spraakzaam was: Ik aanbid je, Winnie, wees de mijne en verder niets van die dag af, alleen pikante stukjes uit Piccolo" (Beckett, *Wachten op Godot* ... 186; *Gelukkige dagen*, 75).

"Oder so was" (Ger., or something like that).

6 Geneviève Serreau's novel *Ressac* (Paris: Julliard, 1962) was no. 23 in Maurice Nadeau's Les Lettres Nouvelles series.

HERBERT MYRON
CAMBRIDGE, MASSACHUSETTS

26.3.62 Ussy sur Marne

Dear Herbert

Many thanks for cards and letters and two good stories, can't cap either.

I suppose I must rebound too, but very slow and very low, which reduces next crash.

Had a good session with Larry at Closerie & environs. If only he'd leave his tablets behind and not make me blather about me & my work. Scampi fritti & fried parsley.[1]

He has written a remarkable study (80 pages) on Whoroscope which in my opinion doesn't deserve five lines. However I thought a little better of it having read him and memories of old Baillet came pleasantly back and my old turne at Normale when the fucking old world was young.[2] Twas then my aunt Cissie said she envied me "young and in Paris and the ball at your feet". Answer (a fortnight later). "What a ball. What feet."

Tried & failed to write you a Bacon (Roger) limerick, but don't despair.

"There once was a fifth offendiculum . . ."[3]

Back here for the bol d'air, the daily prick o'er the plain.[4] Lashings of green cabbage cooked in a flash & lacking only the floury spud.

Read in the Mill on the Floss (Chap. VIII) "Mrs Glegg had doubtless the glossiest and crispest brown curls in her drawers, as well as curls in various degrees of fuzzy laxness."[5]

Best

Sam

ALS; 1 leaf, 1 side; *env to* Mr Herbert Myron, 8 Plympton Street, Cambridge, Mass., U.S.A.; *pm* 26-3-62, La Ferté-sous-Jouarre; MBU, Myron.

1 Lawrence Harvey was preparing his study of SB's poetry while spending the year in Limeil-Brévannes, Seine-et-Oise, near Paris.

2 Harvey would publish his analysis of SB's *Whoroscope* as the first chapter in *Samuel Beckett: Poet and Critic*, 1–66. Adrien Baillet's two-volume biography *La Vie de Monsieur Descartes* (Paris: Daniel Horthemels, 1691) was a source common to SB in writing *Whoroscope* and to Harvey in writing about the poem (*passim* 8–66).

"Turne" (student slang: room). "Normale" (Ecole Normale Supérieure). Cissie Beckett.

3 The philosopher and educator Roger Bacon (c. 1220–1292) wrote about four kinds of errors "which he called . . . *offendicula*: impediments or obstacles to truth" (Kathryn Schulz, *Being Wrong: Adventures in the Margin of Error* [New York: HarperCollins, 2013] 137).

4 "Bol d'air" (lungful of fresh air).

5 George Eliot, *The Mill on the Floss*, ed. Carol T. Christ (New York: Norton, 1994) 46.

ROBERT PINGET
NICE

8.4.62 Paris

Bien cher Robert

Ton livre m'a énormément impressionné et ému.[1] Je suis en train de le relire, l'ayant fait trop rapidement avant le dernier départ pour Ussy (d'où je t'avais écrit) et voulant le laisser à Suzanne. Sans parler de l'écriture inouïe de souplesse et de transparence, ce qui m'a frappé le plus est cette sorte d'éclairage de l'âme qui enrobe tout et apaise tout, comme l'air de l'Ombrie caressant une mise au tombeau. C'est une étreinte de l'être dont toi seul es capable. C'est là dans presque tout ce que tu as fait, mais jamais à un tel degré de rayonnement qu'ici. C'est d'un grand écrivain et d'un grand coeur.

Très affectueusement
à toi
Sam

P.S. Que tu sois d'accord avec toi pour titre et virgules, c'est tout ce qui compte.

Pour le reste, relaxe-toi bien et bon courage. Si je peux t'être utile en quoi que ce soit, je compte sur toi.

S

ALS; with API; 1 leaf, 1 side; *env to* Monsieur Robert Pinget, Résidence Négresco, Nice, A.M.; *pm* 8–4–62, Paris; Burns Library, Samuel Beckett Collection, SB-RP.

8.4.62 Paris

My dear Robert

Your book impressed and moved me tremendously.[1] I am now re-reading it, having read it too quickly before the last departure for Ussy (where I had written to you from), and wanting to leave it for Suzanne. Without talking about the writing, matchless in ease of flow and transparency, what struck me most is this sort of lighting of the spirit from within that enfolds all things and brings peace to all things, like the air of Umbria caressing an entombment. It is an embracing of being that you alone are capable of. It is there in almost everything you have done, but never to such a degree of radiance as here. It is the work of a great writer and a great heart.

Love

Sam

P.S. That you should agree with yourself on title and commas is all that matters.

For the rest, just relax – and bon courage. If I can be of use to you in any way whatever, I'm counting on you (to let me know).

S

1 SB is almost certainly re-reading the typescript of Pinget's novel *L'Inquisitoire* (*The Inquisitory*), which would go to press later in the year, on 11 September.

JUDITH SCHMIDT
NEW YORK

13.4.62 Paris

Dear Judith

Very touched by your card and remembrance. I was born on Good Friday 13th, so can't share your high opinion of the conjunction. And yet when I have the courage to take a quick look back I can see that the miracles haven't been wanting and that but for them it's in the better place I'd be this long time. I hope it'll be a happy day for you and the beginning of happier times. Here it looks a little like Spring at last and from my window I can see the frail green of the chestnut-trees Bld. Arago. The big hulk of the Santé prison too alas, which Jouhaud must be just leaving now for the last day of his trial.[1] It's noon here and you must be just preparing to struggle out of bed. Have a good day and all my thanks again for your good thought.

Best always

Sam

ALS; 1 leaf, 1 side; Burns Library, Samuel Beckett Collection, SB-JD.

1 Former General of the Air Force Edmond Jouhaud (1905–1995) had participated in the Algiers coup (21 to 25 April 1961) and deserted. On 25 March 1962, Jouhaud had been arrested in Oran, Algeria, where he had led OAS actions. On the evening of 13 April, "le Haut Tribunal Militaire" condemned him to death. Jouhaud would not request clemency from President de Gaulle, but his counsel did; on 28 November his sentence would be commuted to life imprisonment ("Reprieve Sought for Jouhaud," *The Times* 16 April 1962: 10; "A Reprieve for Jouhaud: Gen. De Gaulle's Clemency," *The Times* 28 November 1962: 12).

BARBARA BRAY
LONDON

26.4.62 Paris

Dear Barbara

Many thanks for Latin anthology from which I look forward to dulce utile & decorum.[1] I was hoping to get away to the country tomorrow for long weekend, but further torrent of passages (including Rosset) prevents. Last night very late and rather drunk, no clear memory of driving home. In afternoon to Troyes and back which perhaps diminished resistances.[2] Tonight Mihalovici symphony. Tomorrow lunch Quinn & Byrne (inédits) at Closerie.[3] False start with 3 white boxes, but so false, hardly dare try again.[4] Wonderful warm days, wish there was tennis at Roland-Garros, perhaps there is.[5] Edward back to-day but don't know what flight so can't meet. Very dim and hazy still so forgive more. At first return of strength shall go out and drift. How I shall have deserved all the great trouble in store – hope it will help to endure.

Love

Sam

ALS; 1 leaf, 1 side; *env to* Mrs Bray, c/o Miss Ramsay, 33 Elizabeth Street, London SW1, Angleterre; *pm* 26–4–62, Paris; TCD, MS 10948/1/179.

1 Bray may have sent SB *The Penguin Book of Latin Verse*, ed. Frederick Brittain (London: Penguin, 1962) which had been mentioned in *The Times* on 19 April ("This Ageless Language," 13). "Dulce utile & decorum" (Sweet, useful, right). This is SB's variant on a line, originally by Horace (*Odes*, III.2.13), "Dulce et decorum est pro patria mori," revived in the poem by Wilfred Owen (1893–1918), "Dulce et decorum est."

2 SB had driven Suzanne Beckett to visit her mother in Troyes on 23 April (Easter Monday); he repeated the journey on 25 April, when he fetched her and returned to Paris (SB to Thomas MacGreevy, 19 April 1962; TCD, MS 10402/250).

3 Marcel Mihalovici's *Sinfonia Variata* (1960) had its first performance conducted by Manuel Rosenthal with the Orchestre National de France at the Théâtre des Champs-Elysées on 26 April (Jacques Lonchampt, "La 'Sinfonia variata' de Marcel Mihalovici," *Le Monde* 28 April 1962: 18). Quinn and Byrne have not been identified. "Inédits" (unpublished authors).

4 Early drafts of SB's *Play* described the set with three white boxes which later became urns; the undated first draft depicted two men (Syke, a chicken farmer, "Bald, florid, plump, very long (18″) absolutely horizontal blond moustache," and Conk, "sleek black hair... drooping moustache") and a woman (Nickie, "that carrot-haired slut") (Admussen, *The Samuel Beckett Manuscripts*, 78–79; Mary Bryden, Julian Garforth, and Peter Mills, eds., *Beckett at Reading: Catalogue of The Beckett Manuscript Collection at The University of Reading* [Reading: Whiteknights Press and the Beckett International Foundation, 1998] 75–76); UoR, BIF, MS 1227/7/16/6, "Before Play," 1.

5 The qualifiers for the Championnats de Paris were determined by play at Roland-Garros Stadium on Thursday, 26 April ("Les Championnats de Paris," *Le Monde* 27 April 1962: 11).

BARBARA BRAY
LONDON

Monday [7 May 1962] Paris

Dear Barbara

You will like to hear about our afternoon yesterday. I called for them at noon, met Jill who seems very nice, and took them (yours only) to Quasimodo on St. Louis where they struggled bravely with canard à l'orange but enjoyed the Profiteroles. Then on to Jardin des Plantes which was beautiful. Julia had a ride on a pony but wouldn't try the camel. Then all round the Zoo and back Rue Le Sueur at 4. They were very good and charming and I think enjoyed themselves.[1] I told Checchina I'd ring from the country on Thursday in case they may need something. If I were staying in Paris I'd bring them out again, but I'll hardly be back from Ussy before 16th.

Pleasant party last night at the Waldbergs' with Arletty, Ernst, Marcel Duhamel, Yves Bonnefoy, Roland Penrose (whose opinion I obtained on Coldstream) & others.[2] Managed to remain sober & slip away before the close, so feeling a bit better today & the pit of stomach less infernal than these last days. Hayden vernissage big success. Party afterwards at Iles Marquises. Home long after dawn. Joan Mitchell tomorrow.[3] Hope to behave and get away Wednesday to Ussy in fair order.

Love

Sam

ALS; 1 leaf, 1 side; *env to* M[rs] Barbara Bray, c/o Glen Doepel, 6 Duncan Terrace, London N.1, Angleterre; *pm* 7-5-62, Paris; TCD, MS 10948/1/181.

1 Barbara Bray had hired an au pair named Jill to look after her daughters while she was in London working on *The Critics* for the BBC. Quasimodo, a restaurant on the Ile St-Louis, Paris 4. The zoo in the Jardin des Plantes, Paris 5.

2 Guests at the party given by critic Patrick Waldberg (1913–1985) and his wife, the sculptor Isabelle Farner Waldberg (known as Line, 1911–1990): the actress Arletty (1898–1992); Max Ernst; critic and translator Marcel Duhamel (1900–1977); poet, essayist, and translator Yves Bonnefoy (b. 1923); English writer and art critic Roland Penrose (1900–1984).

British painter Sir William Coldstream (1908–1987) was a founder of the Euston Road School (see 6 June 1939, n. 11); later he taught at the Camberwell School of Arts and Crafts and the Slade School.

3 Henri Hayden's exhibition of recent works at the Galerie Suillerot, 8 Rue d'Argenson, Paris 8, was held from 4 to 31 May; Edouard Roditi's overview of recent exhibitions mentioned that the show "should have attracted more attention; his recent landscapes and still-life compositions are perhaps too subtle in their effects for many to realize the masterly quality of his color and composition" ("A Market Report," *Arts Magazine* 36.10 [September 1962] 32). On 8 May, Joan Mitchell's "double" exhibition opened at the Galerie Lawrence, 18 Rue de Seine, Paris 5, at 4 p.m., and the Galerie Jacques Dubourg, 126 Boulevard Haussmann, Paris 8, at 5 p.m. ("C'est arrivé aujourd'hui," *Le Figaro* 8 May 1962: 23).

HENRI LEFEBVRE
BRUSSELS

12.5.62

Ussy sur Marne
38 Bld St Jacques
Paris 14me

Cher ami

Merci de vos lettres et de votre main.

J'ai beaucoup de mal à écrire et crains toujours de dire quelque chose qui vous navre qui êtes déjà si navré.

Vous m'êtes très ombre. Je ne sais pas ce qui ne va pas (je veux dire pour que vous soyez à l'hôpital) ni comment vous aider.

Je suis à la campagne pour quelques jours et me dis qu'il faut que je m'y installe à demeure – et bientôt.

J'essaie de traduire Comment c'est en anglais. Ça ne donne rien.

J'ai une idée pour un acte (une heure maximum) avec trois visages blancs (bouches) et des lumières. Mais mes idées . . .

C'est ici encore l'Ile de France, mais au seuil de la Brie et de la Champagne. J'ai une petite bicoque tout à fait isolée au milieu des champs. Je ne devrais plus la quitter.

Dites-moi que vous allez mieux et en quoi je peux vous être utile.

Bien amicalement

Sam. Beckett

ALS; 1 leaf, 1 side; *env to* Monsieur Henri Le[febvre], 20 Place Anneessens, Bruxelles, Belgique; *pm and corner of env torn*; De Staël Collection.

12.5.62

Ussy sur Marne
38 Bld St Jacques
Paris 14

Dear Henri Lefebvre

Thank you for your letter, and your hand.

I am finding it very hard to write, and am constantly in fear of saying something that will distress you who are already so distressed.

To me you are very much shadow. I do not know what is wrong (for you to be in hospital, I mean) nor how to help you.

I am in the country for a few days, and telling myself that I must settle in here for good – and soon.

I am trying to translate *Comment c'est* into English. Getting nowhere.

I have an idea for a one-acter (an hour at the outside) with three white faces (mouths) and lights. But my ideas . . .

It is still the Ile-de-France here, but at the edge of the Brie and the Champagne regions. I have got a little shack here, totally isolated, in the middle of the countryside. I ought never again to leave it.

Do tell me that you are feeling better, and what way I can be useful.

Warmest good wishes
Sam. Beckett

JACOBA VAN VELDE
AMSTERDAM

12.5.62 Ussy

Chère Tonny

Merci de ton coup de téléphone, merci de ta lettre.

Je t'écris bien fatigué et ce sera une pauvre lettre.

Content d'avoir les bonnes nouvelles de Varsovie.[1]

Pour ta pièce, pas de conseil à te donner.[2] Pour moi il s'agit de plus en plus de savoir à tout instant exactement ce qui se passe sur la scène, de tout voir et entendre exactement et depuis l'auditoire. Mais je suis maniaque et n'ai pas à recommander mes besoins.

Pas encore revu Geneviève ni Nadeau. Je te promets de m'en occuper dès mon retour à Paris.[3]

Ici depuis quelques jours seulement et obligé de rappliquer à Paris bientôt pour l'arrivée de Kaća et Rade.[4]

Vu ni Bram ni Geer. Attends toujours le retour de ma peinture.[5]

Belles expositions Hayden et Joan Mitchell.

Un avion s'écrase sur une île déserte. Survivent l'hôtesse et 3 passagers. Le temps passe. L'hôtesse en meurt. Le temps passe. Les passagers: "Ça ne peut plus continuer comme ça, enterrons-la." Ils l'enterrent. Le temps passe. Les passagers: "Ça ne peut plus continuer comme ça, déterrons-la."

Mal raconté.

Sonny et Mimi sont passés avec les enfants. Soûlographie.[6]

Amitiés à Fritz. Je t'embrasse bien affectueusement

Sam

ALS; 1 leaf, 1 side; BNF, 19794/88.

12.5.62 Ussy

Dear Tonny

Thanks for your telephone call, thanks for your letter.

I'm very tired as I write, and it will be a poor letter.

Glad to have the good news from Warsaw.[1]

For your play, no advice to give you.[2] For me what matters more and more is knowing at every moment *exactly* what is happening on stage, seeing and hearing *exactly*, from the auditorium. But I am obsessional and have no call to recommend my needs.

Haven't seen Geneviève or Nadeau yet. I promise I'll deal with it as soon as I'm back in Paris.[3]

Been here only a few days, having to scuttle back to Paris soon for Kaća and Rade's arrival.[4]

Seen neither Bram nor Geer. Still waiting to get my picture back.[5]

Lovely Hayden and Joan Mitchell exhibitions.

A plane crashes on a desert island. Air hostess and 3 passengers survive. Time passes. The hostess dies of the effects. Time passes. The passengers: "Can't go on like this, let's bury her." They bury her. Time passes. The passengers: "Can't go on like this, let's dig her up."

Didn't tell it right.

Sonny and Mimi dropped in with the children. Orgy of drinking.[6]

Best to Fritz, a loving kiss to you

Sam

1 Jacoba van Velde's 1953 novel *De Grote zaal* (*The Big Ward*) had been published in Krakow by Wydawnictwo Literackie in 1961, translated by Ola Watowa as *Duża sala*. It is possible that her 1961 novel *Een Blad in de wind* (*A Leaf in the Wind*) was under consideration.

2 Jacoba van Velde's play has not been identified.

3 SB's promise to contact Geneviève Serreau and Maurice Nadeau on Van Velde's behalf: 9 March 1962.

4 SB would write to Kaća Samardžić and Radomir Konstantinović on 30 May that he planned to be out of Paris for a few days, but he proposed that they have lunch on Sunday 3 June (Konstantinović, *Beket prijatelj*, 78–79).

5 SB's Bram van Velde painting taken for the New York exhibition: 7 February 1962, n. 7.

6 Sonny and Hermina Sinclair, with their children Frank and Anne, had visited SB in Paris before 4 May, when SB wrote: "It was good being with you again" (Sinclair Collection).

ROBERT PINGET
PARIS

15.4.62 [*for* 15 May 1962] Ussy

Cher Robert

Merci de ta lettre.

Je suis bien content que tu fasses une suite à L'Inquisitoire. Je sens qu'avec ce travail tu arrives dans une grande période et qu'il y aura de grands textes de toi dans les années qui viennent. J'en suis même sûr – et très heureux, pour toi et pour nous.

Où en est-tu [sic] de la pièce BBC? Newby m'en a parlé – et de toi avec beaucoup de chaleur.[1]

Barbara te l'aura dit, on va donner Architruc à un Festival en Angleterre, j'oublie le nom. C'est très réputé en tout cas. Je m'en réjouis pour toi.[2]

Une lettre de Devine. M^c^Whinnie ne peut pas diriger Happy Days. Rien de M^c^W., aucune explication. Devine veut le remplacer. Je sais que Plowright tient à Devine. Je n'ai encore rien décidé. Il faut que je le voie.

Je suis ici depuis 8 jours et donnerais cher pour pouvoir rester toujours. Ce n'est pas encore possible, mais il va falloir que ça se fasse, je ne peux plus continuer comme ça.

Diner [sic] chez Jérôme avec les Borchardt. [. . .][3]

Vernissages Hayden et Joan Mitchell – très beaux – suivis des foires d'usage. Riopelle m'a donné une plume-aquarelle de cette année, très fine, mais pas pour toi, je ne crois pas.[4]

Je ne fais rien. Dix faux départs – de je ne sais quoi. Une idée pour un acte – trois visages et des lumières. Ça me tient un petit peu chaud. Très difficile mais je pense y arriver. J'aimerais à t'en parler.[5]

La gouache d'Avigdor est partie à la Biennale (il a le tiers de la section israëlienne). La peinture de Bram n'est pas encore rentrée.[6]

Edward a raté son examen de solfège. Il est maintenant chez la mère de Jean. Je l'ai entendu jouer un concerto de Quantz dans une église adventiste à Neuilly. Il semble avoir horreur de Paris.[7]

Voilà, j'entends le café qui bout, bon courage et bien affectueusement

Sam

ALS; 1 leaf, 2 sides; Burns Library, Samuel Beckett Collection, SB-RP. *Dating:* Joan Mitchell's double exhibition opened on 8 May; SB was in Ussy from 9 May, hence the present letter must have been written after that date.

15.4.62 [*for* 15 May 1962] Ussy

Dear Robert

Thank you for your letter.

I am very glad that you are writing a follow-up to *L'Inquisitoire*. I feel that with this work you have come into a great period, and that there will be great texts by you in the coming years. I am even very sure of it – and very happy, for you and for us.

How are you getting on with the BBC play? Newby talked to me about it – and about you, with great warmth.[1]

Barbara will have told you, they are putting on *Architruc* at a Festival in England, I don't remember the name. It's very well thought of, in any case. I am delighted for you.[2]

A letter from Devine. McWhinnie cannot direct *Happy Days*. Nothing from McW., no explanation. Devine wants to take over. I know that Plowright favours Devine. I have taken no decision yet. I must see him.

I have been here for a week and would give a great deal to stay forever. It is not possible yet, but it will have to happen; I cannot go on like this.

Dinner at Jérôme's with the Borchardts. [. . .][3]

Hayden and Joan Mitchell private views – lovely – followed by the usual silly nonsense. Riopelle has given me a pen-watercolour from this year, very delicate, but not for you, I don't think.[4]

I am doing nothing. Ten false starts on – I don't know what. An idea for one act: three faces, and lights. That keeps me warm a little. Very difficult, but I think I can get there. I'd like to talk to you about it.[5]

Avigdor's gouache has gone off to the Biennale (he has a third of the Israeli section). Bram's picture has not come back yet.[6]

Edward has failed his solfège exam. At the moment he is staying with Jean's mother. I heard him playing a concerto by Quantz in an Adventist church in Neuilly. He seems to loathe Paris.[7]

That's it, I can hear the coffee boiling, keep your courage up, with all fondness

Sam

1 P. H. Newby had met SB earlier in the month; Newby was considering Pinget's "Interview II" for broadcast on the BBC.

2 Pinget's play *Architruc* was published in 1961 (in a Minuit collection with *Ici et ailleurs* and *L'Hypothèse*). It would be performed in England on 23 June at the Workmen's Club, Thorpeness, Suffolk, as part of the 1962 Aldeburgh Festival of Music and the Arts.

3 On 12 February 1961, SB reported to Judith Schmidt that literary agent Georges Borchardt (b. 1928) had "been here and produced a contract for performance rights of Old Tune in some small off-Broadway, to be presented with Duras her Square." SB explains that he signed this contract as it was "important for Pinget after misadventure here – La Manivelle withdrawn from programme after CRRRRitics' night!" (NSyU; see 28 January 1961). With his wife Anne, Borchardt would found their own agency, Georges Borchardt, Inc., New York, in 1967, which became responsible for introducing numerous French writers to American publishers.

4 This untitled work by Jean-Paul Riopelle in private hands measures 65 × 50 cm.

5 SB wrote to Alan Schneider of the play: "The idea excites me immoderately and the difficulties appal ditto. Have not yet begun writing. Shall tell you more about it if it comes to anything" (12 May 1962; Burns Library, Samuel Beckett Collection, SB-AS; previous publication Beckett and Schneider, *No Author Better Served*, 122).

6 SB is referring to the Arikha gouache given to him by the artist, entitled "Rouge-bleue" (Private Collection). A second gouache, bought at the Arikha exhibition at the Galerie Karl Flinker (see 23 October 1961), remained in his home. He comments on it in a letter to the artist: "C'est une gouache de première" (6 July 1962; InU, Arikha) (It's a first-rate gouache). The 31st Biennale Internazionale d'Arte Venezia would take place between 16 June and 7 October; of the five artists representing Israel, Arikha would be the youngest, with ten of his works on show (see *Catalogo della XXXI Esposizione Biennale Internazionale d'Arte Venezia* [Venice: Stamperia di Venezia, 1962] 191–194).

7 Edward Beckett was lodging with Jean Martin's mother, 5 Rue Léon Delagrange, Paris 15. He played the Concerto for flute and strings in G, No. 161 (QV5:174) by Johann Joachim Quantz (1669–1773) at the Adventist church of Neuilly-sur-Seine, 81 Boulevard Bineau.

SIEGFRIED UNSELD
SUHRKAMP VERLAG, FRANKFURT

le 4 juin 1962 | 38 Bld. St.-Jacques
Paris 14me

Cher Dr Unseld

Merci de votre lettre du 1er juin.

J'ai bien reçu les deux volumes du Théâtre de Frisch et vous en remercie vivement. Leur présentation ne [*for* me] plaît beaucoup.[1]

Votre projet d'une édition d'ensemble trilingue de mon théâtre me fait naturellement grand plaisir. La disposition de pièces selon la langue originale me semble préférable à celle par ordre chronologique. Des trois présentations que vous envisagez je préfère de beaucoup la seconde (traduction française ou anglaise en appendice).

Je suis incapable de me rappeler en quelle langue j'ai rédigé les deux mimes. Ce ne sont pas des textes "écrits" et peuvent figurer dans l'un ou l'autre volume, à votre convenance.[2]

La traduction de HAPPY DAYS n'est pas encore commencée.

J'ai une idée pour une autre pièce (un acte). Si j'arrive à l'écrire, ce sera en anglais.

Je serais heureux de rencontrer Peter Weiss. Je m'en vais pour quelques jours. Nous pourrions nous voir à partir du 13 juin, si ça lui convient. Il n'a qu'à me faire signe.[3]

Amitiés.
s/ Sam. Beckett
Samuel Beckett

TLS; 1 leaf, 1 side; DLA, Suhrkamp, VL, Samuel Beckett: 1962–1964; TLcc 1 leaf, 2 sides; GEU, MSS 1221.

4 June 1962

38 Bld. St.-Jacques
Paris 14

Dear Dr Unseld

Thank you for your letter of 1st June.

I have received the two volumes of the Frisch plays, and I thank you most warmly. I very much like the layout.[1]

Naturally I am delighted with your project of a complete trilingual edition of my plays. Grouping the plays by their original language seems to me preferable to a chronological grouping. Of the three layouts you have in mind I much prefer the second (French or English translation in an Appendix).

I am unable to remember which language I wrote the two mimes down in. They are not "written" texts, and may appear in either volume, as you see fit.[2]

The translation of *Happy Days* has not yet been started.

I have an idea for another play (one act). If I manage to write it, it will be in English.

I should be glad to meet Peter Weiss. I am going away for a few days.

We might meet some time after the 13th of June, if that suits him. He has only to get in touch.[3]

Best wishes
s/Sam Beckett
Samuel Beckett

1 Unseld had sent SB *Stück*, a two-volume set of the plays of Max Frisch published by Suhrkamp Verlag earlier in the year.

2 Suhrkamp's trilingual edition of Beckett's plays, *Dramatische Dichtungen*, would follow SB's proposal: Volume I (1963) presented the plays that originated in French with the French text on one page and the German on the facing page, and the English translation as an appendix; Volume II (1964) presented the plays that originated in English, with the English text on one page and the German on the facing page, and the French translation as an appendix. The mimes were presented in Volume I, since they had been written in French.

3 SB wrote to playwright Peter Weiss proposing that they meet at SB's apartment on 16 June (14 June 1962; AdK, Peter Weiss Archiv, 78).

ALAN SCHNEIDER
NEW YORK

16.6.62 Paris

Dear Alan

Thanks for your letter. Very disappointed. Do hope you'll make it in August.[1]

Saw Devine. Donald can't direct H.D. Some other engagement. Hard to understand, but there it is. Position now is that George will direct & with whatever help I can give him. Plowright as Winnie. Willie not yet cast. Set by Jocelyn Herbert.[2] Opening 1st week October. I'll go to London for last 10 days of rehearsals. Great if you could be there then.

Smothered in visitors. Very tired indeed. Shall have to try & organise things differently – if it's not too late.

Thanks for receiving Obie. I read V.V. account and some description from Judith, including your "I shall abstain etc . . . Walter Kerr." Good for you.[3]

New play festers away on the way to, back from & during rendez-vous. Have got 3 pages down – more or less acceptable. No pillars – pace Esslin.[4] Difficult to write about. Keep it till we meet. Know who's going with me, but not where I'm going. Endless possibilities in idea. In great fear of spooking them.

Affectionately to you all

Sam

ALS; 1 leaf, 1 side; Burns Library, Samuel Beckett Collection, SB-AS. Previous publication, Beckett and Schneider, *No Author Better Served*, 123.

1 SB had expected to meet Schneider in Paris during the second week of June, but when Schneider next wrote to SB, on 21 June, it was from the University of Wisconsin, Milwaukee, where he was directing Pinter's *The Dumb Waiter*, Thornton Wilder's *Pullman Car Hiawatha*, and SB's *Act Without Words II* (Burns Library, Samuel Beckett Collection, SB-AS; Beckett and Schneider, *No Author Better Served*, 124; Schneider, *Entrances*, 396).

2 Set designer Jocelyn Herbert* (1917–2003) joined the English Stage Company at the Royal Court Theatre in 1956.

3 *The Village Voice* awarded an Obie to *Happy Days* for the Best Foreign Play "'with judge Walter Kerr wishing to be announced as abstaining.' After a moment's hush, there came a scattering of hisses, boos, and some small applause. On the podium

co-judge Edward Albee indulged in a brief dry smile." ("Top 'Obies' to Harris, Jones; Huge Crowd Cheers Lenya," *The Village Voice* 7.32 [31 May 1962] 1.) Judith Schmidt wrote to SB on 8 June describing Schneider's acceptance of the award:

> Alan made a very nice short speech, with a preliminary remark "I abstain from stating what I think of Walter Kerr" or some similar words. [. . .] The night H.D. opened [. . .] someone read the Times and Tribune reviews aloud. At the end of the reading of the Kerr review, Ruth White said "he just wouldn't let himself be moved", which I think was the perfect comment. (NSyU.)

4 In an essay on Beckett, Martin Esslin had written that SB discarded "layer after layer of accidental qualities . . . to reach the innermost core" and that for SB the novel was "a shaft driven deep down into the core of the self." Esslin compared SB to Michelangelo who chipped away at a piece of marble to release the figure within ("Samuel Beckett," *The Novelist as Philosopher: Studies in French Fiction 1935–1960*, ed. John Cruickshank [London: Oxford University Press, 1962] 129, 145).

JÉRÔME LINDON
EDITIONS DE MINUIT, PARIS

30.6.62 Paris

Cher Jérôme

La radio de Cologne, qui fait une émission sur toi, m'a demandé, par l'intermédiaire de Tophoven, d'y contribuer.

D'où le pauvre petit hommage que voici.

Je n'écrirai à Tophoven pour traduction que lorsque tu m'auras donné le feu vert.[1]

Bien amicalement

Sam

Enclosure

Hommage à Jérôme Lindon

Jérôme Lindon a été pour moi l'éditeur de la dernière chance.

C'est en 50 ou 51 qu'ont échoué chez lui, criblés d'éconduites, les manuscrits de Molloy, Malone Meurt et L'Innommable.[2]

Je réclamais, ni plus ni moins, un contrat pour les trois ouvrages. Un seul four m'eût laissé sur ma faim. Tout juste si je n'exigeais pas leur parution en un volume.

Il ne me manquait plus que ce dernier petit non merci pour qu'enfin je me le tienne pour dit.

C'est comme j'ai l'honneur de vous le redire.

Ce fut le grand oui.

Ensuite un vrai travail de vrai éditeur, de celui qui, en défendant ce qu'il imprime, ne fait que défendre ce qu'il aime.

Je lui dois tout.

Mais je ne lui devrais rien, ou plutôt rien en dehors de ce que nous lui devons tous, que je n'en dirais pas moins, devant tant de pureté, de noblesse et de courage[:] C'est un grand éditeur et un grand bonhomme.

Samuel Beckett

Juin 1962

ALS; 1 leaf, 1 side; IMEC-Fonds Samuel Beckett, Boîte 4: Correspondance 1962–1963 [Affaire S.T. 1951]; enclosure TMS; 1 leaf, 1 side; for Radio de Cologne; IMEC-Fonds Beckett, Boîte 4: Correspondence 1962–64.

30.6.62 Paris

Dear Jérôme

Cologne Radio, which is doing a programme about you, has asked me, via Tophoven, to contribute something.

Hence this poor little homage.

I shall only write to Tophoven for a translation when you have given the go-ahead.[1]

All best

Sam

Homage to Jérôme Lindon

For me, Jérôme Lindon was the last-chance publisher.

It was in 50 or 51 that there fetched up on his desk the manuscripts, riddled with rejection notes, of *Molloy*, *Malone meurt*, and *L'Innommable*.[2]

I was asking for nothing less than a contract for the three works. One rebuff and that was it. I wasn't all that far from asking that they should be brought out in one volume.

It would have taken only this last little no thank you for me finally to see that that was it.

It was as I am honoured to be able to say again.

It was the great yes.

Then real work by a real publisher, someone who, defending what he prints, is simply defending what he loves.

I owe him everything.

But should I have owed him nothing, or rather nothing beyond what we all owe him, I would still be saying, before such purity, such nobility of character, such courage, he is a great publisher and a great man.

Samuel Beckett

June 1962

1 Details of the broadcast for which this homage was written have not been found at Westdeutscher Rundfunk, Cologne.

2 On Minuit's contract with Beckett for the three novels, see 11 December 1950.

BARBARA BRAY
BATH

4.8.62 Paris

Dear Barbara

Sitting here this morning window gazing from within after garrubibulous evening with Schmidt & Meged in course of which seem to have lost yet another watch.[1] To console a letter from George announcing that Lady Olivier is putting the weight again in January and her Winnie now subject to gynaecologist's report timed to pop next Monday. I couldn't care less. But shall write to George suggesting he postpone production till she is past the age or the baronet has them removed.[2]

Going to Manivelle - Architruc Sunday tomorrow instead of Monday with the swells which is a relief. Ça a l'air de se présenter on ne peut plus mal.[3]

Request for permission to include Lucky's meditation in a programme of excerpts from various writers entitled FOR CRYING OUT

LOUD to be performed by Sylvia Read and William Fry in churches at the Edinburgh Festival and subsequently all over the islands. "A Kaleidoscope of Christian Witness. Equally Suitable for Church or Stage performance." You'll never guess what I said.[4]

Read the unread ¾. Shall be able thank God to stutter something friendly about the TV one.[5]

Watch just reappeared. Oh yes great mercies.

Love

S.

ALI; 1 leaf, 1 side; *env to* M[rs] Bray, Ardenne, Lyncombe Vale, Bath, Somerset, Angleterre; *pm* 4-8-62, Paris; TCD, MS 10948/1/187.

1 Judith Schmidt and Mati Meged (later spelled Matti Megged).

2 As SB explained to Lawrence Harvey on 4 August:

> Joan Plowright is in the family way again, baby due in January, and not sure now if we can open with her in October as planned. But no question of waiting for her any longer. Her first baby, end of last year I think, has already held up things long enough. George Devine seems rather upset – & very surprised. (NhD, Beckett Collection, MS 122/1.6.)

Exasperated though he was, SB wrote to Devine on 4 August wondering whether he might invite Ruth White to play the role of Winnie (V and A, THM2374118 Production File).

3 Pinget's *Architruc* was to have opened on 6 August at the Comédie de Paris with two short plays by René de Obaldia, *Poivre de Cayenne* and *Le Défunt*; by 8 August, Pinget's *La Manivelle* was on the double bill instead. The press opening of *Architruc* was deferred until September (SB to Bray, [2 August 1962]; TCD, MS 10948/1/186). Later, Bertrand Poirot-Delpech reviewed both Pinget plays ("'Architruc' et 'La Manivelle'," *Le Monde* 5 September 1962: 11). "Ça a l'air de se présenter on ne peut plus mal" (looks to be shaping up the worst way possible).

4 SB quotes from a letter from John Barber, Curtis Brown; here SB adds the initial capitalizations to the description given in the program. SB's response to Barber on 3 August: "I don't want Lucky in churches in Edinburgh or anywhere else and should be obliged if you would refuse permission for this" (AL draft, verso of John Barber, Curtis Brown, to SB, 31 July 1962; GEU, MSS 1221).

5 Jean Reavey had given SB a typescript of one or more plays, of which SB wrote to Bray: "Reaveys back, MSS unread, miserere me" ([2 August 1962]; TCD, MS 10948/1/186). Jean Reavey's play *Adora* had been presented by the New York Theatre Ensemble in May and June, but it is not known whether this was one of the typescripts left with SB. In her memoir "How It Is With Sam," Jean Reavey writes: "There was one moment in Paris in that 1962 summer when I ventured to ask Sam about the craft of playwrighting. He spent a long time over this with me." (1972; TxU, Reavey; see also Deirdre Bair, *Samuel Beckett* [New York: Summit Books, 1990] 550–555.) To Bray, SB reported later: "Saw the Reaveys and she took very nicely the little there was to give" (9 August 1962; TCD, MS 10948/1/188).

BARBARA BRAY
BATH

Monday 13.8.62

HOTEL EHRENBACHHOEHE
KITZBUEHEL-
HAHNENKAMM-TIROL

Dear Barbara

First clatter of mail here this morning including your welcome letter.

Beautiful weather after first cold days. Work in the morning. Walk all afternoon. Marvellous walks. Hocks, calves, thighs, & ankles destroyed with descending - over 1000 metres to the valley & Kitzbühel. Hotel people quite charming. Too many yelping galloping brats. Too many froggies.

Have worked a lot on Play. You'll notice a lot of changes. Half-light a bit longer & new theme. Still confused and - to me - confusing. Fear it must be like that. Don't know - as usual - any better than my wretched creatures what it's all about. Typescript a shambles. Better leave it now till I get back to a typewriter. And correct Cascando. And start on How It Is.[1]

No drink only bad weak beer and not much of that. But smoke like a fish.

No news from Devine. Hope Ruth White suggestion shook him. Hope Plowright plays and aborts in second act. Hope the whole thing called off.

Robert now in England. He writes that A. was a success first night & La M. a fiasco. Second night audience of 16. Plans to stagger somehow thro' August and open with press beginning September replacing La M. by L'Hypothèse with (possibly) Raimbourg. Writes us to pray God he don't follow in footsteps of Marilyn.[2]

Escaping it belle in Paris with various invites to meet - from Blau & Simpson among others and a female student I used to know out of my class in 30-31![3]

Bed at 10 under that awful Pflaumdecke that always leaves something uncovered and the rest incandescent.[4] Shudder at the sound of the German that I dribble when compelled. But the Tyrolese have heard worse.

Reading Enzensberger's Einzelheiten which might as well be entitled Kleinigkeiten. How a poet can bother about the heinosities of the Frankfurter Allgemeine defeats me.[5]

Grüss Gott![6]

Love

Sam

ALS; 1 leaf, 2 sides; *letterhead*; *env to* Mrs Bray, Ardenne, Lyncombe Vale, Bath, Somerset, ENGLAND; *pm* 13-8-62, Kitzbühel, Austria; TCD, MS 10948/1/189.

1 The changes to *Play* are to the manuscript marked "4," noted: "Corrected Ehrenbachhöhe," and dated August 1962 (MoSW [Admussen E]; photocopy, UoR, BIF MS 1528/4). In this manuscript, the boxes have been changed to "large white urns"; speech is "provoked by spotlights," and passages are added (Bryden, Garforth, and Mills, eds., *Samuel Beckett Catalogue*, 76; Admussen, *The Samuel Beckett Manuscripts*, 79).

SB had written earlier to Bray: "Finished yesterday in cold last English Cascando. Usual shambles." ([2 August 1962]; TCD, MS 10948/1/185.)

2 *La Manivelle* would continue on the program in September, with Pinget's *Architruc*. Marilyn Monroe had died of a drug overdose on 5 August.

3 "Escaping it belle," a Gallicisim from "l'échapper belle" (to have a lucky escape). Herbert Blau, Alan Simpson. SB's former student was probably Elliseva Sayers.

4 With "Pflaumdecke" SB combines the word for a down-filled quilt or duvet (Daunendecke) with a – presumably humorous – version of the word for softest down or fluff (Flaum).

5 Hans Magnus Enzensberger, *Einzelheiten* (Frankfurt: Suhrkamp Verlag, 1962). "Kleinigkeiten" (small, trivial matters) as opposed to the title word "Einzelheiten" (details). In his chapter "Journalismus als Eiertanz: Beschreibung einer Allgemeinen Zeitung für Deutschland" (16–61), Enzensberger presents a detailed and ultimately devastating critique of the German press after 1945, and of the *Frankfurter Allgemeine Zeitung* in particular.

6 "Grüss Gott" (Good day; literally, God greet/bless you).

BARBARA BRAY
BATH

16.8.62 Kitzbühel

Dear Barbara

Nothing here in last bunch of mail yesterday. Hope all well with you.

Nothing from London either.

All well here. 4 or 5 marvellous days, but now barometer falling fast and thick mist this morning, no going out under pain of Beinbruch.

Sore knee with all the plunging downward – piè fermo sempre il più alto – but trundle along just the same.[1]

Fear I've over-fiddled with the play Play, pace te, but found at least apex theme for half light, i.e. are they being heard, are they as much as being seen – "Mere eye, quite unintelligent, opening & closing on me". But still worried about that part. Hope now to have the sense to let it lie till I get back to sea level and typewriter. Had a look at Cascando – good enough as it stands, not worth fussing about. So suppose must now turn disgusted eyes on How It Is.[2]

Don't think Meged your Genesis man. He spoke only of a book of essays and a novel jettisoned. Nice rugged handsome revolted imbibbing Israel-haunted chap.[3] Enzensberger now fussing about the Spiegel, having demonstrated villa[i]nies of Frankfurter A. Z. für Deutschland. Think I better move on to Bloch's Deutsche Menschen. Don't think Austen possible at this altitude. Next time I'm in Bath.[4]

Flying back, fog permitting, on 25th. Innsbruck-Zürich always very chancy.

Glad to hear Arts not ausgeschlossen. Was hoping to hear from Schneider that he could come over next month, but nothing so far. A note from Seaver asking that we get together, on his way to the Fair, to work on his translation of Le Calmant.[5]

Your Observer article reads fine, in spite of scissors, and I liked very much your straws in hair & wind.[6]

{WAYWARD
{Unruly Head & Heart[7]

?

Love

S

ALI; 1 leaf, 2 sides; *env to* Mrs Bray, Ardenne, Lyncombe Vale, Bath, Somerset, ENGLAND; *pm* 17-8-62, Kitzbühel, Austria; TCD MS 10948/1/190.

1 "Beinbruch" (breaking a leg).

SB adapts a line from Dante's *Inferno*, I.30: "sì che 'l piè fermo sempre il più basso" (keeping always the lower foot firm), replacing "basso" by "alto" (high, or here, upper).

2 In the second section of *Play* ("when first this change") the action becomes self-reflective rather than narrative; the light that calls forth speech is "Mere eye, No mind. Opening & closing on me." (Beckett, *Play*, 15, 21.) "Pace te" (with due deference to you).

3 SB had recently seen Matti Megged, author of *Or Be-Sorag* (*Light in the Cell*, 1953) and of an unpublished novel (1962); his elder brother Aharon Meged (b. 1920) was the author of *Genesis* (1962).

4 In his chapter "Die Sprache des *Spiegel*" (62–87), Enzensberger criticizes *Der Spiegel* for obscuring what it describes, for blurring the line between information and commentary, for replacing news with anecdotes, for taking no clear stance, for presenting pseudo-critical instead of critical perspectives, for disorienting its readers, and for perpetuating anti-intellectual language.

A series of letters between well-known German writers had initially been published by Walter Benjamin in the *Frankfurter Zeitung* when Benjamin was writing for the paper in the 1930s; a selection from these letters was published as a single volume, *Deutsche Menschen, eine Folge von Briefen*, in Lucerne in 1936, not under Benjamin's name, but under the pseudonym Detlev Holz. SB was reading the 1962 Suhrkamp Verlag edition which restored Benjamin's name to the title page, as well as one of the letters cut from the 1936 edition, namely the letter from Schlegel to Schleiermacher that SB cites in his next letter to Bray, of 22 August. SB here misnames the author/editor of the volume as Ernst Bloch (1885–1977).

5 The Arts Theatre Club had been threatened with closure; its lease had been purchased in March by film producer Nathan Cohn who planned to run late-night plays, following the evening film showing ("Arts Theatre Sold," *The Times* 13 March 1962: 15). The Royal Shakespeare Company announced on 26 July that their lease of the Arts Theatre Club would end in September ("An Experiment Abandoned," *The Times*, 5). On 2 August, The New Arts Theatre Club declared a new program as an arts center to start in October, as well as renovations; conversion for film performances had already been completed ("Arts Theatre's New Policy," *The Times*, 7). "Ausgeschlossen" (ruled out).

Richard Seaver had written to SB on 8 August about his plans to be in Paris prior to the Frankfurt Book Fair in September (NSyU).

6 Bray's column, Paris Notebook, closes with these words ("Advance in all directions," *The Observer Weekend Review* 5 August 1962: 15).

7 Bray was working on a translation of *Les Egarements du cœur et de l'esprit, ou Mémoires de M. de Meilcour* (1736–1738) by Crébillon fils; it would be published with a title derived from SB's suggestion: *The Wayward Head and Heart* (Oxford: Oxford University Press, 1963).

BARBARA BRAY
PARIS

22.8.62

HOTEL EHRENBACHHOEHE
KITZBUEHEL-
HAHNENKAMM-TIROL

Dear Barbara

Glad to have your letter into today's bundle and to hear good news of Wilts and critics. Welcome back to the quarter of the Star.[1]

Tomorrow is the last day here, Friday to Innsbruck and to Paris Saturday. I don't know when I'll be able to get round, but shall telephone. By the same mail a letter from George sounding worried if not too hot, saying he had approached "a very clever["] English (?) actress called Eileen Herlie, who also (Ref. to Ruth White dont il ne veut pas. At least Eileen has that to be said for her, that she lives in the same country as Ruth) lives in America and seems to be interested. Know nothing about her so replied to do as he pleased. No question of reverting to Donald now. It's shaping to be one grand mess - yet another. Whatever happens, unless the whole thing flops, it means I shall probably have to go to London earlier than I expected - if I go at all. Thought of sending enclosed to Lady O. - or a Nürnberg chastity belt.[2] Have finished Cascando - not worth fussing over - and am translating Happy Days like mad, nearing end of Act I. Very difficult, but not quite beyond my declining powers. Great help having no dictionary. Can't see Play any more till I get to a type-writer. M now hiccups, not sure that this is right. Perhaps the two W's should belch and yawn respectively.[3] A long letter from Yod, posted in Brighton! Little obviously did he suspect.[4] Jackie's secretary at him for a copy of More --> s (to put it mildly), but he doesn't seem to be playing ball.[5] Avow that this mountain air ... Marvellous quotation from Schlegel in a letter to Schleiermacher about understanding & not understanding, right in my barrow, ideal epigraph for Suhrkamp ed. of plays, remind me to croak it.[6] Fischer seems to be selling out, great to-do in the despicable Frankfurter. Unseld naturally madder now than ever for the performance rights (for the few pfennigs they earn).[7] Letter from Barber too esteeming George's idea judicious. You know about her I expect, but it's too late to veto now or do anything but smirk and murmur, Go ahead, my dear man, go ahead.[8] You don't comment on my beautiful Crébillon title, which is most ulcerating, perhaps that was another letter.[9] Left knee half torn from socket with slithering down 1 in 3 or is it 3 in 1 inclines, but won't misquote Dante again.

See you then soon, love to the children and love.

S.

ALI; 1 leaf, 2 sides; *letterhead*; *env to* Mrs Bray, 14 Rue le Sueur, Paris 16me, FRANKREICH; *pm* 23-8-62, Kitzbühel, Austria; TCD, MS 10948/1/191.

1 Bray had been working for the BBC in London on *The Critics* for several weeks. "Quarter of the Star," a literal translation of "Quartier de l'Etoile," to which Bray had moved.

2 George Devine's letter to SB suggested the possibility of Eileen Herlie (1920–2008) for the role of Winnie in the Royal Court Theatre production of *Happy Days*; she refused Devine's offer (Eileen Herlie to George Devine, 18 August 1962; V and A, THM/237/4/1/18 Production File).

SB writes his afterthought in the right margin: "Ref. to Ruth White ... country as Ruth." "Dont il ne veut pas" (whom he is keen not to have).

SB's enclosure is not known.

3 The three characters in *Play* are W1 and W2 and M (Woman 1, Woman 2, Man).

4 Leslie Daiken had written with news that his radio play *The Circular Road* had been accepted for broadcast by the BBC Third Programme.

5 Jack MacGowran was preparing his one-man Beckett show, *End of Day*. No passage from *More Pricks than Kicks* is included in this selection from SB's works.

6 "Avow that," a Gallicism from "avoue que" (you must admit).

The letter from Schlegel to Schleiermacher refers to a conversation that took place on 19 June 1799, when the two had irritated each other.

> Es ist mir ja eben nichts verhaßter als diesen ganzen Verstandes und Mißverstandes Wesen und Unwesen. Ich freue mich herzlich, wenn irgendeiner, den ich liebe oder achte, einigermaßen ahndet [sic], was ich will, oder sieht, was ich bin ... Geben Dir meine Schriften nur Anlaß, Dich mit einem hohlen Gespenst von Verstehen und Nichtverstehen herumzuschlagen, so lege sie noch beiseite. (Walter Benjamin, ed., *Deutsche Menschen: eine Folge von Briefen* [Frankfurt: Suhrkamp Verlag, 1962] 44.) (Indeed there is nothing more loathsome to me than the nature and the nuisance of all this understanding and misunderstanding. I am delighted when someone whom I love and respect has a reasonable notion of what I want or sees who I am ... If my writings give you only cause to battle the hollow ghost of understanding or not understanding, put them aside.)

7 Siegfried Unseld confirmed to SB that Dr. Rudolph Hirsch (1906–1996) planned to leave S. Fischer Verlag on 15 September (Siegfried Unseld to SB, 3 September 1962; DLA, Suhrkamp Verlag).

8 Frank Barber, Curtis Brown.

9 On SB's suggested title, see 16 August 1962.

H. ALAN CLODD
LONDON

26.8.62 Paris

Dear Mr Clodd

Thanks for your letter.

There will be no film script of Godot. Their intention is to respect as far as possible the existing text. What a talky it will be.[1]

Sincerely

Sam Beckett

ACS; 1 leaf, 1 side; *env to* H. Alan Clodd Esq, 22 Huntingdon Rd, East Finchley, London N.2, Angleterre; *pm* 26–8–62, Paris; NLI, Clodd MS 35,293/1.

1 Keep Films (a company formed by actor Peter O'Toole and producer Jules Buck) planned to make a film of *Waiting for Godot* on the west coast of Ireland in October; it was to star O'Toole and José Ferrer, with Jack MacGowran, and Kenneth Griffith. Ultimately, the film was not made.

GEORGE DEVINE
ROYAL COURT THEATRE, LONDON

September 4th 1962

Ussy-sur-Marne
Seine-et-Marne

Dear George

Thank you for your letter and Jocelyn's excellent sketches which I am returning at once. I have marked with a cross the one I prefer (where Winnie has her head on the mound). I like it very much and if this effect can be obtained when the set is lit I think it is just about right. The sky might perhaps be a little hotter (slightly more orange at the top only). Blue sky I'm afraid simply won't work – tant pis for the word in the text.[1]

Structurally what is important is that the mound be as little noticeable as possible and Winnie's imbeddedness as noticeable as possible. In some photos of sets I have seen the impression is of a completely artificial elevation pour les besoins de la cause, with a Winnie not in but behind it. The problem essentially is how to bring her up to conveniently visible level, and hide Willie, inconspicuously. I know the thing could be approached in quite a different spirit, but I think we should aim at the maximum of naturalness.[2]

Details, the bag is higher and more to her left so that she has to turn strongly to get at it. She never takes it up or moves it from its place. The parasol might be striped (quartered) the same colours as ribbon of Willie's hat (red and white?). The handle is of rather too unexpected length. I don't think yellow is right for Winnie's bodice, with so much of it about. The best colour here is the one that makes her most visible and enhances her fleshiness, perhaps pink.

I have never seen Joyce Redman, but heard good accounts of her. I understand your reluctance to invite Ruth White. I suggested her because I have heard nothing but praise of her performance and know she is lepping to play the part again. I don't think she would be unamenable to redirection.[3]

I am up to my ears in work and shall stay here as long as I can, but of course can meet you in Paris whenever it suits you and at short notice.

Greetings and compliments to Jocelyn.

Yours

s/ Sam

TLS; 1 leaf, 1 side; UAL Wimbledon, JH/1/15.

1 The sketch of Winnie with her head on the mound is published in Jocelyn Herbert, *Jocelyn Herbert*, 52. "Tant pis" (too bad).

2 SB inserts "is" in the right margin, to read: "the impression is of a completely artificial elevation"; SB inserts "aim" in the right margin, to read: "we should aim at the maximum of naturalness."

"Pour les besoins de la cause" (for practical reasons).

3 Irish actress Joyce Redman (1918–2012) was now proposed by Devine for the role of Winnie.

BARBARA BRAY
PARIS

Wednesday [12 September 1962] Ussy

Dear Barbara

Thanks for your letter this morning.

Herewith the last state of this unhappy work. It has me dizzy. If you could have a look at it before Friday evening I'd be grateful.

Try and take it at it's [sic] word and see the jumping light. It should all be over à peine commencé. It's my only hope.[1]

No more now.

Love – à vendredi

Sam

ALS; 1 leaf, 1 side; enclosure: TMS with AN of *Play*, 16 pages; *env to* Mrs Bray, 14 Rue le Sueur, Paris 16me; *pm* 13–9–62, La Ferté-sous-Jouarre; TCD, MS 10948/1/195.

1 SB sent Bray a typed draft of *Play, An Act* (TCD, MS 10948/1/195a). It has sixteen pages, including the unnumbered title page; there are eight handwritten notes to correct typos. This is an intermediate draft, between the drafts 5 and 6 (MoSW, described as E and G by Admussen, *The Samuel Beckett Manuscripts*, 79; photocopies, UoR, BIF, MS 1528/6 and 1528/7, described by Bryden, Garforth, and Mills, eds., *Samuel Beckett Catalogue*, 77). SB's next letter to Bray (19 September; TCD, MS 10948/1/197) details changes reflected in the following draft, Admussen G, photocopy UoR, BIF, MS 1528/7.

SB indicates the paragraph order presented here using an arrow. "A peine commencé" (when it's hardly begun).

PATRICK MAGEE
LONDON

17.9.62

38 Bld. St. Jacques
Paris 14me

Dear Pat

Thanks for your letter.

My only Jugoslav contact is the writer

RADE KONSTAATINOVICI [sic]
BEOGRAD
29 Novembra 22 / VI

He is a nice chap and a good friend and would I know do all in his power to help you and show you round & introduce you to the theatre crowd etc. His wife Kaća Samardžic has translated some of my works. Rade is probably the most interesting of the younger Jugoslav writers. They have a seaside place in Istria.

Rovinj
Augusto Ferrari 36

where they may be now, I'm not sure. Don't hesitate to look them up or write, wherever they are, they'll give you a great welcome. Sorry I have no other addresses to offer.[1]

Most kind of you to offer to put me up when in London, but I have arranged to stay with Calder – if I go at all. Things are in such a mess at the Court – no Winnie decided on yet, and opening scheduled for Oct. 18th! – that it may not come off at all. I shall know this week one way or another. If it does come off I shall be there for rehearsals this day week. Will you still be in London then?

So glad you like Words & Music. John went through Paris, but I missed him.[2]

Barbara is in Nice with the children for a fortnight.

I stumble along with diminishing impetuosity and I hope shall soon just lie down and refuse to move.

Yours ever

Sam

ALS; 1 leaf, 1 side; TCD, MS 11313/6.

1 Magee was going to Yugoslavia to make a film.

2 Magee had recorded *Words and Music* for the BBC Third Programme on 10 September (BBCWAC, RCONT1, Barbara Bray, Scriptwriter I). SB wrote to Barbara Bray on 17 September that Magee "seems pleased with W. & M. but has to re record the songs, John objecting that he [had] sung too well!" (TCD, MS 10948/1/196).

THOMAS MACGREEVY
DUBLIN

30.9.62 Paris

Dear Tom

Good to have your letter.

Things have been a bit wearing here since our return from the Tyrol, with people to be seen and work not working. We wish we could join you in Venice next month, but I'm afraid no chance. I go to London tomorrow week for rehearsals of Happy Days and will be there till the opening Nov. 1st. While I'm away Suzanne will have to hold the fort here. She is in pretty good form, though the old cough is still there. I'm off tomorrow for a breather at Ussy before going to London. One Brenda Bruce, of whom I know nothing but who I am told is good, has been engaged to play Winnie. Lady O. went all pregnant again, the Redgrave wouldn't take it on, the Ashcroft neither, and Ruth White wasn't free. On verra.[1] In London I'll stay with John Calder - who publishes the novels - and hope to break away towards middle of rehearsals for a few days with Sheila.

Edward is back in Paris after a 3 weeks "Masters Course" in Cologne which seems to have done him good and got him on his toes again after the Dublin inertia. He starts at the Conservatoire on Monday.[2] John passed through on his way back from Spain, but I missed him. He has done his Words & Music music and recorded it and says he is pleased. Broadcast in November I think. Chip & Monique are still at Ascona, but back now any moment. She had a triumph at the Lucerne Festival and I heard her over [the radio] play superbly - Strawinsky's Capriccio at the Festival of Holland with the Gebouw orchestra conducted by Rosbaud.[3] I saw the Strawinskys again on the eve of their departure for Russia and was very surprised and moved when he embraced me coming & going![4]

I can't & won't believe that your retirement from Gallery wd. mean retreat to Tarbert - when it should mean liberation for this old mainland where you belong and are most happy. Tell me I've got it wrong.[5]

I do hope you'll stop going or coming or both in Paris and see Suzanne & Marthe & in London. Calder's address is 56 Wimpole St.

Much love from us both

Sam

ALS; 2 leaves, 2 sides; TCD, MS 10402, MacGreevy.

1 On 21 September, SB wrote to Barbara Bray: "A telegram from Devine last night. He has engaged Brenda Bruce (brrr!) 'a very good actress' for Winnie and letter to follow which not so far. I don't know her of course, is she as butterscotch as she sounds?" (TCD, MS 10948/1/198.) Brenda Bruce (1918–1996) was born in Manchester, had trained at the Birmingham Rep, and had acted with the Royal Shakespeare Company. By "Lady O" SB intends Joan Plowright; Vanessa Redgrave had been proposed as a possible Winnie, as had Peggy Ashcroft.

"On verra" (We'll see).

2 Edward Beckett had taken a summer course at the Museum Morsbroich, in Leverkusen near Cologne, with the Italian flautist Severino Gazzelloni (1919–1992).

3 Monique Haas was the piano soloist on 9 September 1962 in the Lucerne Festival; she played Maurice Ravel's Concerto for Piano and Orchestra in G major, with the Philharmonic Orchestra of the RTF directed by Jean Fournet (Lucerne Festival program). She performed Stravinsky's *Capriccio* in the Holland Festival on 28 June 1962, with Amsterdam's Concertgebouw Orchestra, guest-conducted by Hans Rosbaud (1895–1962). The concert was broadcast in Paris on "Haute Fidélité," France 4, on 11 September. Haas later recorded both of these works with other orchestras for Deutsche Grammophon.

4 On 21 September, SB wrote to Barbara Bray of his meeting the day before: "Lunch with Lieberson (most exquisite shirt & tie formation I ever saw) and the Strawinskys, off to Moscow today. He embraced me coming & going! Lieberson very witty & entertaining. S. scotching & hors d'oeuvring and murmuring to me inaudible things in the reverberating hubbub of the Plaza-Athénée dining room." (TCD, MS 10948/1/198.)

5 The village of Tarbert, Co. Kerry, was the McGreevy family home.

LAWRENCE HARVEY
HANOVER, NEW HAMPSHIRE

3.10.62 Ussy

Dear Larry

Herewith your queries answered to the best of my lamentable ability. I have read your French essay with great interest, the French seems to me excellent. I find it as difficult to comment on writing on the work as on the work itself – and these old bones are so bleached now. I feel as you know that they are not worth so close investigation and do not support it. I think perhaps you make too much of their relation to my "life" – I really never had any. And that you are over-eager in your pursuit of an intentionality which is not always there. But these are trifles and I think it is a good and scholarly essay and I am grateful for it. Just a few remarks, would you mind removing Frank's lung cancer (unimportant & private) and the bit about Ethna's accident and my reaction to it. (I wd. have quit in any case).[1] The "secret things" are Dante's "cose segrete". I haven't the reference here, but it's in the Inferno, early on, before he penetrates into Hell's "Secret things".[2] "The Weeds" in Malacoda are the Widow herself

("Widow's Weeds").[3] Forgive such broken sticks. I'm completely confused and tired and – after reading Ruby Cohn's book – more than ever accablé by the whole thing.[4] I haven't got Cascando (now translated) or Words & Music here. I'll send you the former as soon as I make more copies. The latter no point, as it will be appearing shortly in Evergreen Review. It has now been recorded by BBC and will be broadcast next month. John is pleased with his music (which I don't know). Pat Magee plays Words.[5] I saw Barney Rosset last week and gave him the new play (PLAY). It's loupé, but I can't do any more and after usual hesitation decided to let it go. Very short (15–20 mins.)[6] I sent Alan S. your letter and hope he has been in touch with you. Afraid not much chance of an opening in Dartmouth. I don't know what they'll do with it, but must abide by whatever they decide. I'll send it to you in due (!) course.[7] Things in London now definite at last and I go there this week for rehearsals. Opening Nov. 1st. Winnie: Brenda Bruce. Know nothing of her but am told she is good. Nearly fell through altogether – for want of a Winnie. Ruth White was not available. Thanks for all your news. I hope you'll work out your professional quandary in the way most happy for you all and am impatient to hear what you decide. Good rest in the Tyrol mountains and worked on translation of Happy Days. When back from London in November I'll have to finish that and then HOW IT IS. Before I can think of anything new. Here for a few days and final breather before taking off.

Forgive this sorry scrawl. Falling further and further behind – I know not what.

Affectionately to you all

Sam

ALS; 2 leaves, 2 sides; *env to* Mr Lawrence Harvey, Dartmouth College, Department of Romance Languages & Literature, Hanover, New Hampshire, U.S.A., *upper left corner* PAR AVION; *pm* 4-10-62, La Ferté-sous-Jouarre; NhD, Beckett Collection, MS 122/1.6.

1 Harvey's essay on SB's early poems and *Echo's Bones and Other Precipitates*, "Samuel Beckett: Initiation du poète," was published in *La Revue des Lettres Modernes: Histoire des Idées et des Littératures* 100.8 (1964) 153–168. The essay includes references to events in SB's life. The essay as published includes neither the reference to SB's automobile

accident in December 1931 (which injured his passenger Ethna MacCarthy, and which precipitated SB's abrupt resignation from Trinity College Dublin), nor details of Frank Beckett's illness and death in 1954.

2 SB's invoking of "le segrete cose": 22 April 1958, n. 6.

3 Beckett, "Malacoda," *Echo's Bones and Other Precipitates* [33–34].

4 Ruby Cohn, *Samuel Beckett: The Comic Gamut* (New Brunswick, NJ: Rutgers University Press, 1962). "Accablé" (overwhelmed).

5 *Words and Music* would appear in *Evergreen Review* 6.27 (November–December 1962) 34–43; the BBC Third Programme would broadcast the play on 13 November.

6 "It's loupé" (It doesn't work).

7 On 24 July, Harvey had reported to SB that there was enthusiasm at Dartmouth College about the possibility that SB's newest play ("incidentally is it still to be called Must It?") might be produced during an Arts Festival in Winter or Spring of 1963. Beckett had responded, "whatever you arrange with Alan will be acceptable to me. Rosset of course will have to be consulted also." (4 August 1962; NhD, Beckett Collection, MS 122/1.6.)

BARBARA BRAY
PARIS

Monday [8 October 1962] [London]

Dear Barbara

I'm in the pub next the theatre drinking Guinness waiting for it to be time to go to the Devines for dinner & see her models. Have just had a few with Barber.[1] Worked with George & BB this morning & afternoon. Feel I might slip under table and give up any moment. B.B. most encouraging. I saw her last night in a bad TV play (The Stepfather) & realized she might have the needful.[2] There's a tremendous way to go but I think she can do it. Very sympathetic, keen & quick. The inflexions were quite wrong. Got them I hope on the right track. Felt her English voice was wrong and for her to give an edge of her semi-native Scots. Great improvement. George very nice as always and I foresee pleasant rehearsals. But I feel really shaky. Terrible departure from Paris, impossible to find a taxi and had to rescue car from garage at 11th hour and leave it to its fate at Orly. Then English customs took half my cigarettes away from me – leaving me 200 free as a favour. John Calder not back till this evening.[3] Remember me in yr. orisons.[4] Love to the children.

Love

Sam

ALS (lettercard); 1 leaf, 1 side; *to* Mrs Bray, 14 Rue Le Sueur, Paris 16me, France; *pm* 8-10-62, London; TCD, MS 10948/1/200.

1 SB had met John Barber, Curtis Brown, in what he describes in his letter the next day to Bray as a "lousy King's Rd. pub" near the Royal Court Theatre, 50-51 Sloane Square, London SW1 (9 October 1962; TCD, MS 10948/1/201). SB inserts "time" in the left margin.

2 SB here refers to Brenda Bruce, who acted in J. J. Crisp's play on BBC Television; a review of the production indicated that the supporting actors, including Bruce, "could hardly have played better" ("Formula Well Applied," *The Times* 8 October 1962: 16).

3 SB, of staying with John and Bettina Calder: "Calders very kind - comfortable there. Except for yapping toy poodle." (9 October 1962; TCD, MS 10948/1/201.)

4 At the end of his most renowned soliloquy, as Ophelia enters, Hamlet utters, "Nymph, in thy orisons / Be all my sins rememb'red" (William Shakespeare, *Hamlet*, III.i.88-89).

AVIGDOR ARIKHA AND ANNE ATIK
PARIS

9.10.62 Londres

Chers amis

Après deux jours de répétitions j'ai très bon espoir. Elle a des choses très bien. C'était plutôt mal parti - voix et inflexions fausses. Ça va déjà beaucoup mieux. Elle est petite, blonde, assez jolie, sourire très prenant, un peu trop mince, 44 ans. Moitié écossaise, moitié Cockney, et élevée à Manchester! Elle prend maintenant un petit accent écossais, c'est fou ce que ça bonifie. Pige très vite, travaille beaucoup. Devine très gentil et bonne atmosphère de travail. Si elle continue à progresser à la même cadence ça doit vraiment donner quelque chose. Je vous dirai plus tard si ça vaut le déplacement. Willie bien aussi. Et décor, d'après maquettes vues, à peu près juste il me semble.[1] A la bonne vôtre. Affectueusement Sam

ALS (lettercard); 1 leaf, 2 sides; *to* Monsieur et Madame Avigdor Arikha, 10 Villa d'Alésia, Paris 14me, FRANCE; *uncancelled* [British stamps]; InU, Arikha.

9.10.62 London

Dear Both

After two days' rehearsing I'm very hopeful. There are some good things about her. It had started off badly – voice and inflexions all wrong. Now much better. She is small, blonde, quite pretty, very engaging smile, a little too thin, 44. Half Scots, half Cockney, and brought up in Manchester! Now she puts on a touch of a Scots accent, amazing what an improvement it makes. Quick on the uptake, works hard. Devine very nice, good working atmosphere. If she goes on progressing at the same rate it should be really quite something. I'll let you know later if it's worth coming over. Willie good too. And set, to go by the maquettes I've seen, just about right I think.[1] Here's to you.

Love

Sam

1 Peter Duguid (1923–2009) played Willie. Set design: 16 June 1962.

BARBARA BRAY
PARIS

11.10.62 London

Dear Barbara

Poor rehearsal yesterday, B. B. quite lost in text & business. When I went to theatre this morning George asked me (nicely) to let them work alone today. I seem to be upsetting her. That is, failing in what I came to do. I'll let them get on with it without me now & then, every now & then. I'm not worrying. If she can't do it she can't. Just another of those old things.[1]

Not going down to the country this w.e. because of Jacky's run-through at the Arts Sunday afternoon. I'll see Donald then too. If it's bad I'll be in the nice fix again.[2]

John C. handed me his Kenner this morning. He has decided to do Miller and is flying to Berlin (and back) Monday to see him.[3]

Good evening with John, Ann & Vera in Hampstead yesterday. He's fine, but limping more than I'd been given to think. He showed me his W. & M. score and I'm to hear the replay on Thursday. It looks very good.

George rang me after sine me rehearsals to tell me how it had gone, obviously upset at having had to dismiss me. In a burst of maximanimity I suggested I shd. leave them in peace on Monday again & only renew intrusion on the Tuesday.[4]

Mind your step with Josette.

Love

Sam

ALS; 1 leaf, 1 side; *env to* Madame Bray, 14 Rue Le Sueur, Paris 16$^{\underline{me}}$, FRANCE; *pm* 13–10–62, London; TCD, MS 10948/1/202.

1 SB brought to the rehearsals expectations of "metronomically strict rhythm" and gave "microscopically detailed notes" which unsettled Brenda Bruce (see Knowlson, *Damned to Fame*, 447–448).

2 SB described the run-through of Jack MacGowran's *End of Day* to Bray: "Thought it pretty ghastly but didn't say so. Some good moments. Bits & scraps from all over the place within framework of mime, which first stops and then resumes after line said. Aïe!" (15 October 1962; TCD, MS 10948/1/203.)

3 Hugh Kenner, *Samuel Beckett: A Critical Study* (London: Calder, 1962). Calder would publish Henry Miller's *Tropic of Cancer* (1963).

4 "Sine me" (without me).

AVIGDOR ARIKHA
PARIS

20.10.62 Londres

Cher Avigdor

Merci de ta lettre.

Ici rien ne va plus. Sans miracle cette semaine c'est le désastre. Je m'étais trompé. Je ne comprends pas ce qui s'est passé. Pourquoi je n'ai rien pu – ou su – faire. Je vais reprendre tout ça avec Devine aujourd'hui. Trop déprimé pour en dire davantage.

Très content pour toi que le travail marche un peu et que l'exposition soit remise.[1] Encaisse ce foutu chèque pour l'amour de Dieu, je n'en ai pas besoin.

Je rentrerai avant la première - peut-être bien avant si ça continue comme ça.

Affectueusement à vous 2

Sam

ALS; 1 leaf, 1 side; InU, Arikha.

20.10.62 London

Dear Avigdor

Thank you for your letter.

Here everything's gone wrong. Failing a miracle this week it will be a disaster. I had got it all wrong. I don't understand what has happened. Why I couldn't, or didn't know how to do something. I'm going to go over it all with Devine today. Too depressed to say any more about it.

Very pleased for you that the work is making some headway and that the exhibition has been postponed.[1] Cash that bloody cheque - for God's sake, I don't need it.

I shall come back before the first night, maybe much sooner if things go on the way they're going.

Love to you both

Sam

1 Whatever the envisaged exhibition may have been, it did not take place (Avigdor Arikha to the editors, 5 December 2009).

BARBARA BRAY
PARIS

Sunday [21 October 1962] Hampshire (somewhere in)

Dear Barbara

Down here with George & Jocelyn & divers children since yesterday till tomorrow.[1]

Saw the Bruce again Friday. She went through. Disastrous. Stuttered a few groans and fled. Shall have it out here with G. today.

But fear nothing to be done. He has her back on her puke English – only dead flat – if you know what I mean. I'll get the Scots back or perish in the attempt. And slow! Jesus. Haven't suffered & sweated so much for decades. Je crois que c'est foutu. Quoi qu'on fasse. If it goes on like that I won't stay.[2]

Rang up Jacky who seems pleased with the way his salade is going. Only saw Times notice. He says Financial Times good. Wondering what to put in place of Lucky.[3]

Quite exhausted. Dread this week. Due with Sheila next Friday to Monday. Little red agenda black with commitments.

Mine took a long time to get to you.

Oh to be in Paris now that the fug is here.[4]

Love to all 3

S.

Read & liked the interviews. I think perhaps the two "its" at the opening of the first should be "hims"[.][5]

ALI; 1 leaf, 2 sides; *env to* Madame Bray, 14 Rue Le Sueur, Paris 16$^{\underline{me}}$, FRANCE; *pm* 22-10-62, London; TCD, MS 10948/1/206.

1 Andrews Farm, the country home of Jocelyn Herbert and George Devine, was in Long Sutton, near Basingstoke, Hampshire. Herbert's four children from her marriage to Anthony Lousada (1907–1994): Sandra (b. 1938), Jenny (b. 1940), and twins Julian and Olivia (b. 1944); Devine's daughter from his marriage to Sophie Harris (1900–1966): Harriet (b. 1942).

2 "Je crois que c'est foutu. Quoi qu'on fasse." (I think it's hopeless. Whatever we do.)

3 MacGowran's *End of Day* opened on 16 October at the New Arts Theatre. The reviewer in *The Times* noted that the "snippets from various works of Mr. Beckett inserted into a framework of the first '*Act Without Words*'" was not an entirely successful choice: "one tends to lose track of the mime as soon as Mr. MacGowran breaks off to speak some of Mr. Beckett's marvellously evocative prose" ("Late-Night Show from Beckett," *The Times* 18 October 1962: 18). Tom Stoppard observed that MacGowran "uses the mime play *Act Without Words* as an active unity recurring throughout the evening. It does not simply interrupt the extracts but cues them in." ("Crying till you Laugh," *Scene* 7.25 [October 1962] 19.) T. C. Worsley reviewed the evening in "New Arts Theatre, End of Day," *The Financial Times* 18 October 1962: 20; Harold Hobson's review was "Man in his Loneliness," *The Sunday Times* 21 October 1962: 41. The one-man show included Lucky's monologue from *Waiting for Godot*. "Salade" (hotch-potch).

4 SB had written of London to Jacoba van Velde: "J'ai horreur de cette ville. La vieille frénésie de marche à pied me reprend. Espèce de fuite en rond." (12 October

1962; BNF, 19794/91.) (I loathe this town. The old walking frenzy gets hold of me again. Some sort of escape, running in circles.)

5 Bray translated Robert Pinget's *Interview One*, and *Interview Two*, both about the character Mortin (contract 25 October 1962; BBCWAC, RCONT1, Barbara Bray, Scriptwriter I); the two interviews would be broadcast by the BBC in May 1963.

ARLAND USSHER
DUBLIN

6.11.62 — 38 Bld. St. Jacques
Paris 14me

Dear Arland

I have read your meditations with great pleasure.[1] I wish I had something intelligent to offer in return. But it has fled this long time vers le ciel noir – mind I mean.[2] So have nothing wherewith either to agree or disagree with what you say about my work, with which my unique relation – and it a tenuous one – is the making relation. I am with it a little in the dark and fumbling of making, as long as that lasts, then no more. I have no light to throw on it myself and it seems a stranger in the light that others throw.

I read your ghostly table-talk always with the same pleasure. A wry musing that is quite unique, and lit always with a courtesy quite gone from writing & thought. It is a shame it is not published. I wd. contribute with joy to a Dolmen (for ex.) volume.[3]

I had a gruelling time in London with rehearsals & encounters and am worn out. I had a brief glimpse of Con the last day – indomitable as always under new adversity.

Hommages to Emily,

Ever your

SAM

Do you want MS back?

ALS; 1 leaf, 1 side; *env to* Arland Ussher Esq, 18 Green Road, Blackrock, Co. Dublin, IRLANDE, *pm* 7-11-62, Paris; TCD, MS 9031/56/1-2.

1 On 12 October, Ussher had written to SB: "I send you a few pages from the JOURNAL à propos of Godot, Beckettism and all that. A dangerous thing to do

perhaps – and you must indeed be tired of having people interpret Godot to you! But you might be interested in my reactions and reflections, though they are probably very wide of the mark." (TCD, MS 9031/54.)

Adrian Kenny writes in the introduction to his selection from Ussher's journal: "Arland Ussher began this journal in 1943. When he stopped it in 1977 there were fourteen volumes" (*The Journal of Arland Ussher*, ed. Adrian Kenny [Dublin: Raven Arts, 1980] 3.) It is not known which selections Ussher sent to SB, but the entry of 21 April 1956 from this published selection states:

> Godot is sentimental pessimism – almost like Barrie's sentimental optimism. "Waiting . . ." is always a sentimental note.
>
> Godot is a mood, a half-truth; but art can only express moods and half-truths – though it suggests Whole Truths through them. Philosophy (in the old sense), in attempting to state a Whole Truth, produces something less, something unreal (the "Great Paradox"). But the artist must have a mind. (15.)

Ussher shared further observations on *Waiting for Godot* in his letters to Aidan Higgins (TCD, MSS 9331–9041/1499, 1503, 1505, 1508).

2 SB quotes from the seventh stanza of Paul Verlaine's poem "Colloque sentimental":

> – Qu'il était bleu, le ciel, et grand, l'espoir!
> – L'espoir a fui, vaincu, vers le ciel noir.
> (How high our hopes, how blue the sky, outspread!
> Dark now the sky, and, humbled, hope has fled!)

(Paul Verlaine, *One Hundred and One Poems by Paul Verlaine: A Bilingual Edition*, tr. Norman R. Shapiro [Chicago: University of Chicago Press, 1999] 62–63.)

3 Ussher thanked SB, "for liking the Table-Talk. ('Stool-Talk' it should perhaps rather be called, since I have generally no one to bore with it – except, sometimes myself! The relation, as you say of your work, is tenuous.)" (25 November 1962; TCD, MS 9031/57.) Two further books of selections from Ussher's journals were published: *From a Dark Lantern*, ed. Roger Nyle Parisious (Dalkey: Cuala Press, 1978), and *The Juggler: Selections from a Journal*, selected by Roger Nyle Parisious (Dublin: The Dolmen Press, 1982). The Dolmen Press, founded by Liam Miller (1924–1987) and his wife Josephine in Dublin in 1951, published, among many works by Irish artists and writers, Thomas MacGreevy's book, *Nicolas Poussin*.

ALAN SCHNEIDER
NEW YORK

7.11.62 Paris

Dear Alan

Good to hear from you after so long.

Congratulations and to Albee on hit with Who's Afraid. I am pleased. Devine said he was inviting you to direct it at the Court. Great news too.[1]

So glad you like Play. It seems to me only difficult technically (how to work spots). Have thought how it might be done and will discuss it when the time comes. In fact I think by far the easiest play of mine you have had. What I should like to know from you and Barney is whether or not I am free to make arrangements in London & Europe. I mean, do you want the world première or merely the new world? I have given the script to Devine. I have decided to give Royal Court first option on all my work in the future, this applying both to revivals & to new work. Devine is the nicest and most decent man one could meet and this is very important to me. He is not a great director, but most conscientious and painstaking and will always let me be in on production. Happy Days opened Nov 1, with Brenda Bruce & Peter Duguid. I don't think she carries the guns for the part, but she has done well and got – I am told – great praise. Excellent set by Jocelyn Herbert. I haven't read the critics and don't intend to read any more notices of my work. Friendly or not it's all misunderstanding. Hobson for as usual, Tynan as usual against. My friends tell me.[2] Suzanne came over with a party and was very pleased with the production – said it was infinitely superior to the 2 German productions she had seen at Cologne & Düsseldorf.[3] I worked very hard on it on and off, with George, and got back to Paris last week more tired and shaky than I ever remember having been. Bit better now. I saw neither dress-rehearsal nor première – simply can't take it anymore.

Faced now with ever more than the usual wilderness of self-translation – Comment c'est into English, H.D. & Play into French. I.e. all real work blocked for at least 6 months. A chacun son petit enfer.[4] I'll go to Ussy in a few days and start getting down to it – and drinking a little more water!

I do hope you'll be able to ease off a bit after the Pinter opening.[5] Why don't you come over here for a week or so. Perhaps you will have seen Devine in N.Y. on his way to Brazil where he is to lecture.[6] I didn't see Harold Pinter in London I'm sorry to say.

Affectionately to you all

Sam

ALS; 1 leaf, 2 sides; Burns Library, Samuel Beckett Collection, SB-AS. Previous publication: Beckett and Schneider, *No Author Better Served*, 131.

1 Schneider was grateful for the opportunity given to him by Edward Albee to direct *Who's Afraid of Virginia Woolf*, and had thanked SB for his part in this; the play opened on 13 October at the Billy Rose Theatre, New York, to "fantastic notices" and an extended run which necessitated rehearsing a second cast for matinees (Schneider to SB, 4 November 1962; Burns Library, Samuel Beckett Collection, AS-SB; Beckett and Schneider, *No Author Better Served*, 129–130). The New York cast would perform Albee's play in London from 23 January 1964, at the Piccadilly Theatre.

2 Harold Hobson, "The Really Happy Woman," *The Sunday Times* 4 November 1962: 41. Kenneth Tynan, "Intimations of Mortality," *The Observer* 4 November 1962: 29.

3 SB wrote to his cousin Sheila Page: "I saw Suzanne and party including Edward safely stowed on Thursday night and then fled. [. . .] They had a good party afterwards with the Calders & other friends in Chelsea." (6 November 1962; Jill Babcock Collection.) The Cologne and the Düsseldorf productions: 4 December 1961, n. 4.

4 "A chacun son petit enfer" (To each his own little hell).

5 Schneider was directing Harold Pinter's plays, *The Dumb Waiter* and *The Collection*, which would open on 26 November at the Cherry Lane Theatre, New York (Schneider, *Entrances*, 395).

6 George Devine had given a series of lectures in Brazil, one of which may have been at the Conservatório Nacional de Teatro, Rio de Janeiro. Later he was asked to teach there (Harriet Devine to the editors, 23 January 2013).

JOCELYN HERBERT
LONDON

8.11.62 Paris

Dear Jocelyn

Thanks for your letter.

The Paris party were all very pleased with Brenda and the play. Suzanne, who is hard to please, was quite enthusiastic. I was in no fit state, at the end, to judge anything.

I haven't read any of the notices and don't want to. I'm not going to read anything any more about [illeg 1 word] my work. Things are hard enough without that.

Thank you and George again for all your kindness and concern with the play. I never said sufficiently how much I liked and admired your set.[1] It's my fault if it wasn't quite right from the stalls. A lower mound would have worked in the Royal Court. From the circles it was perfect. But perhaps any lower you couldn't have hidden Willie. Awful English this.

I wrote to Barber to tell him what I told George that evening in Chelsea, viz. first option on everything, revivals or new, to Royal Court in future.[2] I feel happy about this.

I seem to have lost Jenny's adress [sic] Rue Jacob (the number). Could you please let me have it - and the nom de famille which I'm ashamed to say has also flown.[3]

Bon repos et bonne peinture & bon voyage to George if he has not already departed.[4] Remember me to the young.

Affectionately
Sam

ALS; 1 leaf, 2 sides; *env to* Jocelyn Herbert <Royal Court Theatre, Sloane Square, London S.W.1, Angleterre> *AN AH* 6 Rossetti Studios, Flood Street, SW3; *pm* 8–11–62, Paris; *pm* 12–11–62, London; UoR, BIF, MS 5200/1.

1 The unsigned review in *The Times* closed with: "Miss Jocelyn's Herbert's set, a bare blazing arena of scorched grass, has the atmosphere of a primitive altar" ("One-Sided Dialogue by Half-Buried Wife," 2 November 1962: 6).

2 John Barber, Curtis Brown, London.

3 Jenny Lousada was studying printmaking with Stanley William Hayter in Paris; she lived not with a family but in a chambre de bonne in a building on Rue Saint-Jacques (Sandra Lousada to the editors, 23 January and 29 January 2013). "Nom de famille" (surname).

4 "Bon repos et bonne peinture & bon voyage" (Have a good rest and a good trip and enjoy your painting).

STEFANI HUNZINGER
S. FISCHER VERLAG, FRANKFURT

le 18 novembre 1962

38 Boulevard Saint-Jacques
Paris 14me

Chère Stefani Hunzinger

Merci de votre lettre du 14 novembre.

Je suis désolé que vous réagissiez de cette façon à ma proposition. J'étais persuadé que vous en verriez le bien-fondé.[1]

Je ne sais comment j'ai pu vous donner l'impression de méconnaître ce que vous avez fait pour mon travail, d'autant que, dans ma lettre du 11 novembre, je vous en renouvelle l'expression de ma reconnaissance.[2]

Il n'est pas dans mes habitudes de m'occuper de ces questions. Elles ne m'intéressent pas et j'ai autre chose à faire. Si j'interviens aujourd'hui, c'est que je m'y vois forcé par l'impossibilité où je me trouve de supporter plus longtemps que les Editions Suhrkamp, étant donné ce qu'elles ont fait, et ce qu'elles se proposent à faire, pour mon théâtre sur le plan de l'édition, ne bénéficient en aucune façon de sa réalisation théâtrale.

Je suis donc obligé de maintenir les termes de ma lettre du 11 novembre.

J'écris à Dr Unseld pour le mettre au courant de ma démarche, dont jusqu'ici il ignore tout. Il n'est même pas certain qu'il partage entièrement ma façon de voir.[3] La solution que je propose me semble à la fois la plus simple et la plus juste. Mais il peut y en avoir d'autres. Je souhaite vivement que vous puissiez en discuter au plus tôt avec lui. Si votre conversation devait aboutir à un accommodement autre que celui que j'envisage, il va sans dire que j'y suis acquis d'avance.

Je serai en voyage lors du passage à Paris de Dr Fischer et ne pourrai donc, à mon grand regret, avoir le plaisir de le recontrer.[4]

Croyez, chère Stefani Hunzinger, à mes sentiments sincèrement amicaux.

Samuel Beckett

TLcc; 1 leaf, 1 side; GEU, MSS 1221.

18 November 1962 — 38 Boulevard Saint-Jacques
Paris 14

Dear Stefani Hunzinger

Thank you for your letter of 14th November.

I feel very sad at your reacting in this way to my proposal. I was persuaded that you would see the strength of my case.[1]

I cannot think how I can have given you the impression of not recognising what you have done for my work, the more so since in my letter of the 11th I once again give expression to my gratitude.[2]

It is not my habit to concern myself with these matters. They do not interest me, and I have other things to do. If I am intervening today, it is because I see myself as forced to do so by what I see as the impossibility for me, of continuing to put up with a situation in which, given all that Suhrkamp Editions have done, and intend to do for my plays in publishing terms, they should draw no benefit whatever from their performance in the theatre.

I am therefore obliged to maintain the terms of my letter of the 11th November.

I am writing to Dr Unseld to inform him of my actions, of which he is wholly unaware. It is not even certain that he will entirely share my view.[3] The solution that I am proposing seems to me both the simplest and the fairest. But there may be others. My earnest wish is that you will be able to discuss this with him as soon as possible. If your conversation were to end up in an agreement other than the one that I am envisaging, it goes without saying that I agree to it in advance.

I shall be travelling abroad during Dr Fischer's visit to Paris, and will be therefore, to my great regret, unable to have the pleasure of meeting him.[4]

I send you my sincere good wishes.

Samuel Beckett

1 SB had written to Stefani Hunzinger on 11 November, to indicate that he felt it only right that Suhrkamp Verlag have a share in the profit from the performance of those plays for which they held the rights. He proposed that Fischer Verlag keep the rights for the plays that they currently represented (*Warten auf Godot* to *Glücklichte Tage*), "mais pour ce qui est de mes pièces à venir, qu'elles soient pour le théâtre ou radionphoniques [sic], que tous le droits, aussi bien de représentation que de publication, soient réservés aux Editions Suhrkamp" (GEU, MSS 1221). (But that where my future plays are concerned, whether for stage or radio, all rights, for performance and publication alike, should be reserved for Suhrkamp Editions.) Her response on 14 November expressed consternation (DLA, Hunzinger, MS.0016.27/5).

2 SB had assured Hunzinger: "Ne voyez surtout pas, chère Stefani Hunzinger, dans cette lettre la moindre critique de ce que vous avez fait pour la diffusion de mon travail

en Allemagne et dont je vous serais toujours reconnaissant" (11 November 1962; GEU, MSS 1221) (Above all, dear Stefani Hunzinger, do not see in this letter the slightest criticism of what you have done for the promotion of my work in German, for which I shall always be grateful).

3 Siegfried Unseld and SB had discussed the matter when they met in Paris on 28 July. On 6 September, SB had written to Unseld that, as he had told him in Paris, "le problème des Editions Fischer me dépasse complètement" (the problem of Fischer Editions is altogether beyond me) (DLA, Suhrkamp, VL, Samuel Beckett: 1962–1964).

4 On 16 November, Dr. Gottfried Bermann-Fischer had written to SB to arrange an appointment to discuss the matter; he planned to be in Paris on 24–25 November: "Dr. Unseld tries again and again in a rather unfair way behind our back to take the stage rights away from us" (S. Fischer Verlag).

MATTI MEGGED
KIRYAT-TIVON, ISRAEL

3.12.62 38 Bld. St.-Jacques
Paris 14me

Dear Mati

Many thanks for your long letter. It was a great pleasure to see you again in Paris and no thanks whatever are due to me. I do hope you will be back soon, under your own steam. There is very little chance, I am afraid, of my ever going to Israel – or to any other distant place. Up and down between Left Bank and Marne Valley is all I ever want to move again. And I'm pretty sure the time will come when I'll settle down in the former and call Paris a day.[1]

I have not met Dr Spitzer, but have had great accounts of him from Avigdor and have seen some of his editions. I am very pleased that he is to do a book of my plays and that you are to do the translation. of [sic] course I am at your disposal for any help it is in my power to give.[2] How difficult the transfer is, even into a kindred tongue, I know only too well. And I, when I can't translate, have the right to try and reinvent. You are taking on the hell of a job and I do hope you won't regret it. I should like to think that there will be more in it for you than just hard work and that the doing will shed some light on your own problems. Writing I suppose for some of us – though most certainly not for all – is only possible in the last ditch and in complete désespoir de cause and at a depth where one's "living" not only is gone, but never was.[3] Either it comes to that or it doesn't – and one couldn't wish it for anyone.

I had a bad time in London with rehearsals of Happy Days and came back rather ill, but am better now. It ran a month with a certain success – I mean succes [sic] in certain quarters. The actress was competent – without more. I didn't read the critics. Avigdor and Anne went the second last night and telephoned from London very pleased. I have just finished the French translation. Also competent – without more![4]

Not a word from Judith since Paris apart from business notes. I hope she is not too sad.

When you see Dr Spitzer tell him how pleased I am that he is doing this edition – and honoured – and that I hope we may meet next time he comes to Paris.

Bon courage, bon travail.[5]

Yours ever

s/ Sam Beckett

What news of your back?

TLS, with APS; 1 leaf, 1 side; GEU, Ashton, MSS 1068.

1 SB had seen Megged in August in Paris. SB presumably intends "the latter" since to "call Paris a day" would mean renouncing the Left Bank.

2 Moritz Spitzer (also Moshe, Maurice; 1900–1982), a close friend of Arikha's, was a Sanskrit specialist who had studied in Kiel, Germany, and Vienna, and collaborated with Martin Buber on his translation of the Hebrew Bible into German; he had worked at Schocken Verlag in the 1930s, until he was ordered to close the press by the Nazis in November 1938. In 1939, Spitzer emigrated to Palestine and founded Tarshish Books, where he was designer as well as publisher. (Daniel Spitzer to the editors; Israel Soifer, "The Pioneer Work of Maurice Spitzer," *The Penrose Annual 1970*, ed. Herbert Spencer [London: Lund Humphries, 1970] 126–142.)

3 "Désespoir de cause" (utter hopelessness).

4 "Without more," a Gallicism from "sans plus" (nothing more).

5 "Bon courage, bon travail" (Courage, and work well!)

BARBARA BRAY
LONDON

29.12.62 Paris

Dear Barbara

Thanks for your letter from Bath & letter card received together yesterday. Also for your article on Ionesco. I saw the play with George & Jocelyn. I thought it was a hideous production and obscuring of the work. Moved notwithstanding – passim.[1] Next night went with Robert to see Maison d'os which I liked very much indeed, particularly first half.[2] George & Jocelyn & daughter Jenny in good form, we noctambulated deep into morning. Con arrived yesterday – after usual hellish barless wait at Invalides. The same old invincible, perhaps a little more gone in the feet. We went to Multicolor and made the price of our dinner at the Iles.[3] The Hayden as well as possible. I spent Xmas Eve (his 80th) with them. Sad evening. He has done half a dozen gouaches since his return. No question of his going out for the moment. The Tate finally bought a good red landscape from this summer I think. He presented me with a small one and an ink done while still in hospital.[4] About time I began selling my little collection. Lindon has given O.L.B.J. to printer and Blin to Madeleine Renaud who it seems wants to do it.[5] Jacky rang up. He wanted to see me on his way through to Spain. It wd. have meant going out to Orly and it couldn't be arranged. He was very nice on phone. I told him I wasn't happy about End of Day and would rather he dropped it if he isn't too far committed by Moreduck [*for* Morduch]. I said I wd. try and write something for him to make up for it. He agreed immediately so ouf. I suspect you y es pour quelque chose & am grateful if so.[5] Bitter cold here but no snow. Streets look murderous today, so may have a bit of fun later on[.] Glad to hear about Esslin & shall congratulate sometime I suppose. Had a card signed by him – Michael & Newby.[6] Tired to the core and why still standing and how God knows, punctilio perhaps.[7]

Corrected groaning Murphy proofs for Calder.[8] George brought more Irish & beautiful gloves from Mary Hutchinson. You can bring me a nice warm dark blue scarf if you like, of the kind that doesn't itch the neck. I am tired trying yellow. Terrible Lindon party in honour of Robert next Friday, des Bosquet aux Mauriac en passant par la Sarraute. All the pros. Impossible to mitch.[9]

Love

Sam

ALS; 1 leaf, 2 sides; *env to* Mrs Bray, c/o Miss Pearson, 24 Hallam Court, Hallam Street, London W.1, Angleterre; *pm* 30-12-62, Paris; TCD, MS 10948/1/216.

1 *Le roi se meurt* (*Exit the King*) by Eugène Ionesco opened on 15 December at the Théâtre de l'Alliance Française, Paris, directed by Jacques Mauclair. Bray's article "Ionesco takes a New Turning" compared the play with *Endgame* (*The Observer Weekend Review* 23 December 1962: 20).

2 *La Maison d'os* (*House of Bones*) by Roland Dubillard (1923–2011) opened at the Théâtre de Lutèce, Paris, directed and acted by Arlette Reinerg (pseud., an anagram of her family name Grenier, 1926–2012).

3 Multicolor is a game similar to roulette; it is played in billiard clubs rather than in casinos (which were not - and are still not - allowed within a radius of 100 km. of Paris).

4 Henri Hayden's birthday was on 24 December. His painting at the Tate Britain Museum is *La Plaine rouge* (*The Red Plain*, 1962; T00559). SB wrote to Mary Hutchinson that Hayden had given him "a smaller red landscape and a fine drawing made in hospital"; both are in a private collection.

5 *Oh les beaux jours*. On 19 December, Jérôme Lindon wrote to SB that he had read the second act:

> Que te dire que je ne t'ai déjà dit vingt fois: après Godot, Fin de Partie, Krapp, il est de plus en plus difficile de trouver les mots exprimant l'émotion du lecteur-spectateur. Mais cette pièce-ci est sûrement l'une des plus grandes [. . .]. Pourvu que Roger la monte, et vite. (IMEC-Fonds Samuel Beckett, Boîte 5, Affaire Curtis Brown-Godot film [1960–1964].) (What to tell you that I haven't told you twenty times: after *Godot*, *Fin de partie*, *Krapp*, it's harder and harder to find the words expressing the feelings of the reader-spectator. But this play is assuredly one of the greatest [. . .]. Let's hope that Roger puts it on, and soon.)

6 The agent for Jack MacGowran's show *End of Day* was Irina Morduch (1927–2003), Centaur Productions, London. She wrote to SB on 30 December for his approval of offers for *End of Day*; SB replied, to explain the circumstances:

> I cannot go on with END OF DAY. There is nothing to be done with such a piece. I should have realised this sooner. I have been on the phone to Jack and he has very understanding[ly] agreed to call it off. I have promised, by way of amends, to try and write for him in the course of this year a coherent mime with text. I am exceedingly sorry and apologize for the inconvenience I have caused you, through sheer obtuseness. It was not till I got down to trying to improve the piece that I realised what an impossible hotch-potch it was and how irretrievably wrong. (3 January 1963; GEU, MSS 1221.)

"[Tu] y es pour quelque chose" (you had a hand in it).

7 Martin Esslin was named to succeed Val Gielgud, who planned to retire as Head of Drama at the BBC in April 1963. The card sent jointly by Esslin, Michael Bakewell, and P. H. Newby was probably a New Year greeting "expressing the hope that he would write something for us in the coming year" (Michael Bakewell to the editors, 30 January 2013).

8 On 17 December, Calder had sent proofs for the paperback edition of *Murphy* (Jupiter Books, 1963); this edition was set from the Grove Press text, which Calder also enclosed. SB replied on 22 December: "I have found no mistake so far. But my corrected copy is in the country and I should like to check with it." (InU, C&B, Beckett.)

9 At the party for Robert Pinget on 4 January 1963: "des Bosquet aux Mauriac en passant par la Sarraute" (from the Bosquets to the Mauriacs not forgetting the Sarraute woman): Alain Bosquet and Norma Caplan Bosquet (d. 2011), Claude Mauriac (1914–1996) and Marie-Claude Mante Mauriac (b. 1932), Nathalie Sarraute. "Mitch" (school slang: dodge, play truant).

CHRONOLOGY 1963

1963	4 January	SB attends party in honor of Pinget at the home of the Lindons.
	25 January	*Tous ceux qui tombent* broadcast on French television with an introduction by Georges Belmont.
	25 February	SB accepts Barney Rosset's commission to write a film.
	20 March	Grove Press publish *Poems in English.*
	22 March	SB attends Ramón Valle-Inclán's play *Divines paroles* at the Théâtre de l'Odéon, directed by Roger Blin.
	27 March	Jean-Jacques Mayoux speaks on SB's work on France III radio.
	5 April	SB begins a manuscript notebook of *Film.*
	13 April	Completes first draft of *Film.*
	week of 15 April	Works with Jean-Marie Serreau on *Comédie.*
	10 May	Attends *King Lear* directed by Peter Brook at the Théâtre Sarah-Bernhardt.
	13 May	Agrees to an embargo against performance of his plays before segregated audiences in South Africa.
	16 May–6 June	Attends rehearsals and recordings of *Cascando,* RTF studios.
	30 May	With Alan Schneider, attends two rehearsals of *Spiel* in Ulm, Germany.
	3 June	Death of Pope John XXIII.
	14 June	Premiere of *Spiel* at the Ulmer-Theater, Ulm-Donau, directed by Deryk Mendel.

before 17 June	SB rehearses *Comédie* with Madeleine Renaud and Roger Blin.
17 June – 16 July	Holidays with Suzanne in Zell-am-See, Austria, leaving on 15 July via Innsbruck to arrive in Paris on 16 July.
21 June	Election of Cardinal Montini as Pope Paul VI.
4 July	SB begins to translate "Texte pour rien 13."
29 July	A. J. Leventhal moves from Dublin to Paris.
before 20 August	SB writes a brief tribute to Richard Aldington.
24 August	Begins a play for a lit face ("Kilcool").
27 September	*Oh les beaux jours* has its premiere at the Teatro del Ridotto, directed by Roger Blin, with Madeleine Renaud, as part of the Venice Festival.
30 September	*Happy Days* opens at the Eblana Theatre, Dublin, directed by John Beary, with Marie Kean.
13 October	RTF broadcasts *Cascando*.
15 November	SB asks Faber and Faber to publish the unexpurgated version of *Waiting for Godot*.
22 November	Assassination of John F. Kennedy. Lyndon B. Johnson becomes President of the United States.

BARBARA BRAY
PARIS

16.1.63 Ussy

Dear Barbara

Have just finished part one and am writing this before rereading French proofs with narrower eye. It reads very flat to me, perhaps it's being so drenched in it.[1] Bitter cold again, bright sun, & though a few carts, tractors & lorries pass I'm doubtful if the fuel Tankwagen will make it all the way from Château (Thierry), with the roads so slippy. Enough food for 3 or 4 days, but not so sure of the oil. 500 litres when I gauged it last, two days ago, & it goes without ceasing day & night. Improved C. C. a bit I think and caught up on some bad slips, but it remains unreadable which is a great beauty. The yellow tits come for their margarine, though they clearly prefer butter. If this weather continues I may not be able to get in on Monday. No news of interest. A wire from Einaudi requesting a wire of sympathy on his Spanish troubles with which I obliged. "Indignation & solidarity!" Tu parles.[2] Grove Press proofs in Paris, God knows of what. PLAY I suppose. Let them wait.[3] Nothing from Blin needless to say, but rumours uncontrollable of the Renaud eager to take it on and looking for a little Théâtre de France.[4] A letter from Con safely home and pleased with his diversions. I gave him Joyce's father's embroidered waistcoat for the Tower and he was hoping for trouble with the customs, but none.[5] Poor Jane has got herself in a mess at the end of S. & S., the big scene between Elinor & Willoughby could hardly be worse. Perhaps irony is not quite the right word.[6] I go to bed at 11 and get up at 9 and should be feeling all right were it not that the nature of the beast [is] never to do so. Bendon writes pleased with the picture I switched him to which would relieve if anything could.[7] Avigdor & Anne are off to Israel by boat on Sunday, free aller-retour.[8] With luck I should be half way through With Pim by the time I leave, leaving only second half & how it is.[9] Then retype all and off before end of Feb. with more luck. And then what? Translate Textes Pr Rien? Play? Merde.

Love

Sam

ALS; 1 leaf, 2 sides; *env to* Madame Bray, 14 Rue Le Sueur, Paris 16me; *pm* 18-1-63, La Ferté-sous-Jouarre; TCD, MS 10948/1/220.

1 SB had written to A. J. Leventhal the previous day: "Have just corrected proofs of Oh les B. J. which seems flat in French, but I'm too saturated with it to be able to judge."

2 In 1962, Einaudi published *Canti della nuova resistenza spagnola, 1939–1961* (Songs of the New Spanish Resistance) by Sergio Liberovici and Michele L. Straniero, with Margot Galante. On 8 January, the Spanish government declared that Giulio Einaudi and three of his editors were "undesirable" and "barred from Spain" for publishing this book which was "judged to be insulting to Spain" ("Spain, Angered by Article, Bars an Italian Publisher," *The New York Times* 9 January 1963: 7). In Rome, on 11 January, Einaudi called a press conference to protest against Franco's action. A protest document was signed by representatives of publishing houses in Madrid with plans to send it to publishers in Barcelona and then to "the secretariat of the International Union of Publishers at Zurich" ("Madrid Protest," *The Times* 12 January 1963: 8). "Tu parles" (Some hope).

3 SB received proofs of *Murphy* and *Watt* to be published by John Calder in paperback editions (SB to Lawrence Harvey, 27 January 1963; NhD, Beckett Collection, MS 122/1.6).

4 For Blin's production of *Oh les beaux jours*, "the large Théâtre de l'Odéon was gigantic, and the Petit-Odéon was too small. The solution was to reduce the size of the large theatre to the orchestra and the first balcony by curtaining off the second and third balconies." (Aslan, *Roger Blin*, 52.)

5 The waistcoat of the father of James Joyce was taken by Con Leventhal for the exhibition and readings to be held at the Joyce Tower and Museum, Sandycove, Co. Dublin; it remains on exhibit there (Robert Nicholson, Director, to the editors, 5 February 2013).

6 In Chapter 44 of Jane Austen's novel *Sense and Sensibility*, Willoughby, the suitor of Elinor's sister Marianne, confesses to Elinor the reason for his apparent disaffection.

7 Mick Bendon was a friend and neighbor of Sheila and Donald Page; the pictures exchanged have not been identified.

8 "Aller-retour" (round trip).

9 "With Pim" is the second section of *How It Is*. SB sets out the structure of *How It Is* in the opening line of the book: "how it was I quote before Pim with Pim after Pim how it is three parts I say it as I hear it" (*How It Is* [Grove Press] 7; section two: 49–99).

ROGER BLIN
PARIS

31.1.63 Ussy sur Marne

Cher Roger

Ci-joint un travail que j'ai fait pour Mihalovici et la R.T.F. M. a terminé sa musique et nous avons vu Dutilleux hier pour parler de la réalisation.[1] Nous avons proposé:

réalisateur - Blin
l'ouvreur - "
la voix - Martin.

Que tu n'aies pas ta licence n'est pas, paraît-il, rédhibitoire. Il suffirait de t'adjoindre un metteur en scene [sic] agréé - Dutilleux a suggéré Jean-Jacques Vierne.[2]

Ce serait pour mars - avril au + tard.

Ça ne t'intéressera peut-être pas. Et je sais que tu est [sic] très pris avec la pièce de V. I.[3] Enfin voilà ce que nous avons voulu.

Affectueusement

Sam

ALS; 1 leaf, 1 side; *env* to Monsieur Roger Blin, 264 Rue St.-Honoré, Paris 1er; pm 31-1-63, La Ferté-sous-Jouarre; IMEC-Fonds Roger Blin.

31.1.63 Ussy sur Marne

Dear Roger

Enclosed something I did for Mihalovici and French radio. M. has finished his music and we saw Dutilleux yesterday to talk about getting it performed.[1] We have proposed:

director - Blin
the opener - "
the voice - Martin.

The fact that you haven't a licence is not, apparently, a serious obstacle. All you would have to do is appoint a deputy director who has one. Dutilleux suggested Jean-Jacques Vierne.[2]

It would be for March–April at the latest.

Perhaps you won't be interested. And I know that you are very busy with V.I.'s play.[3] Anyhow, that is what we wanted.

Affectionately

Sam

1 On 27 January, SB wrote to Lawrence Harvey: "Mihalovici has finished his Cascando music and it shd. be on the air before long. We are conferring with Dutilleux tomorrow." (NhD, Beckett Collection, MS 122/1.6.) Composer Henri Dutilleux (1916–2013) was Director of Musical Productions from 1945 to 1963 at RTF (French Radio). About the *Cascando* broadcast, see Ruby Cohn, *A Beckett Canon* (Ann Arbor: University of Michigan Press, 2001) 271–272.

2 Jean-Jacques Vierne (1921–2003) began his radio career by adapting literary texts; in 1946 he became a radio director, and later directed in television and film. Paul Ventre produced *Cascando* on the France-Culture service of the ORTF (see Zilliacus, *Beckett and Broadcasting*, 143–144).

3 Blin was in rehearsal as director of Robert Marrast's adaptation of Ramón del Valle-Inclán's play translated as *Divines paroles* (*Divine Words*) which would open on 21 March at the Odéon-Théâtre de France; in this play he also took the role of Pedro Gailo.

ALAN SCHNEIDER
NEW YORK

6.2.63 Ussy sur Marne

Dear Alan

It was good to hear you again and to know I shall be seeing you again soon.

Many thanks for Who's Afraid. safely arrived.[1]

Jean-Marie Serreau was on the phone about it a few days ago, wondering if I wd. translate or supervise translation and wanting my opinion on the play. As I told you I am too submerged with my own work to be able to take on anything else – and as I have not yet read the play I had no reaction for Serreau. But from the glance I took and from what I know of it, adapation is going to be a big problem here. I shall be meeting Serreau in a week or so to have a talk about it. But as translator I'm definitely out. Please tell Albee I'm sorry. I know he'll understand.

Finished French translation of Happy Days & gave it to Blin. Madeleine Renaud wants to do it – it appears. Blin is more communicative – and very busy at the moment with his Valle-Inclán production for Barrault.

The German first of Play will probably be in April at Ulm (small theatre) – in conjunction with the two mimes and perhaps stage production of my radio play WORDS & MUSIC. No plans so far for English production as far as I know. Vague possibility at Edinburgh Festival.[2]

All That Fall was done on French TV. Badly I thought – but well received.[3]

Hope to finish this week revision of Comment C'est translation and get it off to Barney before end of month. Then take a bit of a rest from translation and try and do a spoken mime for Jackie McGowran. Had to promise this for reasons too complicated to explain here.[4] Shall tell you all about it when we meet and report progress if any!

More or less marooned out here with bitter cold and state of roads. Couldn't be better pleased! Absolute silence and peace 24 hours out of 24. Suppposed to be going to Ionesco opening on Friday (Le Piéton de L'Air), but probably won't make it. Saw Le Roi Se Meurt and liked it – though a poor production. Dubillard's Maison d'Os is most remarkable – best evening in the theatre for years. It was to have come off last week – but the last night the house was packed and it's continuing. Beautifully written, produced, acted and set.[5]

Love to Jean and the children.

Yours ever

Sam

ALS; 1 leaf, 2 sides; Burns Library, Samuel Beckett Collection, SB-AS. Previous publication, Beckett and Schneider, *No Author Better Served*, 134–135.

1 Schneider, who had directed Edward Albee's *Who's Afraid of Virginia Woolf* in New York, had sent a copy of the play to SB (New York: Atheneum, 1962). Schneider had written to SB on 17 December 1962 to ask whether he had received the book, adding: "I have a secret vision of you translating it into French and you and I coming over this winter working on it in Paris" (Burns Library, Samuel Beckett Collection, AS-SB; Beckett and Schneider, *No Author Better Served*, 132–133).

2 Deryk Mendel would direct *Spiel* at the Ulmer Theater, Ulm-Donau, Germany, in June, with SB's mimes *Akte ohne Worte I und II*. No staged reading of *Words and Music* would occur.

John Calder had proposed that George Devine's production of *Play* might open at the Traverse Theatre during the Edinburgh International Festival, but Devine felt that this arena-style playing space was inappropriate (SB to John Calder, 16 February 1963; InU, C&B, Beckett; SB to Mary Hutchinson, 26 February 1963; TxU, Hutchinson, 2.6).

3 Michel Mitrani directed the television production of *Tous ceux qui tombent* that aired on Télévision Française 1 on 25 January.

4 SB's promise to write a new piece for Jack MacGowran: 29 December 1962 and n. 6.

5 Eugène Ionesco's play *Le Piéton de l'air* (*A Stroll in the Air*) opened on 6 February at the Odéon-Théâtre de France, directed by Jean-Louis Barrault. SB had planned to attend on Friday 8 February. SB on *Le Roi se meurt* and Roland Dubillard's play *La Maison d'os*: 29 December 1962 and n. 1, n. 2.

JOHN CALDER
JOHN CALDER (PUBLISHER) LTD., LONDON

12.2.63 Ussy

Dear John

I am sending you today corrected proofs of Watt. The snags are p. 169 and last page. I do hope it will be possible to (1) set the table in its proper place and (2) not break up the chorus.[1]

Other point: I have asked throughout for hyphenated "ground-floor, first-floor, second-floor". If this is too much of a nuisance, it is not indispensable.

I started to suppress colons & semi-colons, having forgotten "how hideous is the semi-colon" page 156. So they all go back as indicated. Sorry for this stupidity.[2]

I hope to get How It Is off to you tomorrow. Just have to go through it quickly once. It has been an awful job. I really can't do any more with it now. I may better it a little in proof.

Should be grateful if you would deal with enclosed.[3]

Back to Paris Thursday more dead than alive.

Hope Anastasia is taking kindly to this strange place.[4]

Affectionately to you both

Sam

ALS; 1 leaf, 1 side; *datestamped* 15.FEB.1963; InU, C&B, Beckett.

13. John Calder

1 In response to SB's request, the estimate of Louit's expenses for his research in County Clare is typeset as a table on page 169 of the Calder edition of *Watt* (1963). The chorus of the "descant heard by Watt on way to station" is set without interruption on page 254.

2 Hyphens are supplied, and both the semi-colons and colons are restored in the Calder edition of *Watt*.

3 On 8 February, Judith Schmidt wrote to Dr. G. Drudi, who had inquired about the Italian rights for SB's *Poems in English*; a copy of this letter was sent to SB,

who, with this letter, forwarded the inquiry to John Calder (InU, C&B, General Correspondence).

4 SB had congratulated the Calders on the birth of their daughter Anastasia: "may all the good fairies attend her always" (9 February 1963; InU, C&B, Beckett).

ELMAR AND ERIKA TOPHOVEN RUEIL-MALMAISON, NEAR PARIS

2.3.63 Ussy

Chers Top et Kiki

Voulez-vous regarder, dans PLAY, la réplique "At home all heart to heart, new leaf and bygones bygones." Je me demande si vous avez bien traduit "new leaf". L'expression anglaise est "to turn over a new leaf", c'est à dire, tourner la page, s'amender, changer de conduite, recommencer de zéro, etc. Rien à voir avec la feuille de l'arbre![1] Je n'ai pas votre texte ici. Il est bien possible que votre traduction soit juste. Pardonnez-moi en ce cas de vous avoir alerté pour rien.

Bien amicalement

Sam

ALS; 1 leaf, 1 side; Tophoven Collection.

2.3.63 Ussy

Dear Top and Kiki

Would you have a look, in *Play*, at the line: "At home all heart to heart, *new leaf* and bygones bygones." I wonder if you have translated "new leaf" right. The English expression is "to turn over a new leaf", that is, turn the page, mend one's ways, change behaviour, make a fresh start, etc. Nothing to do with the leaf on the tree![1] I haven't got your text here. It is quite possible that your translation is accurate. In that case forgive me for pointlessly asking for your attention.

All the best

Sam

1 In the acting version of *Spiel* (prepared from the typescript for stage production and not for general sale), the line reads: "Zuhause alles ein Herz und eine Seele, junges Grün, das Alte tot und begrabent" (Samuel Beckett, *Spiel: ein Akt*, tr. Erika and Elmar Tophoven [Frankfurt: Surhkamp Verlag, 1963] 16). "Junges Grün" (new shoots). In the next publication of the play, in *Theater heute* (July 1963), the phrase was corrected to read: "Zuhause alles ein Herz und eine Seele, ein neues Blatt, das Alte tot und begrabent" (III). "Ein neues Blatt" (a new leaf).

C. G. BJURSTRÖM
PARIS

25.3.63 Paris

Cher Monsieur

Spinal dog:

il ne s'agit pas d'une race de chiens, mais d'un chien de laboratoire dont on mutile le cerveau et système nerveux pour les besoins d'expériences du genre de celles de Pavlov.[1]

Cordialement votre

Sam. Beckett

ALS; 1 leaf, 1 side; NLS.

25.3.63 Paris

Dear Monsieur Bjurström

Spinal dog:

it is not a breed of dog, but a laboratory dog whose brain and nervous system are mutilated for experimental purposes of the Pavlovian kind.[1]

Yours sincerely

Sam. Beckett

1 Carl Gustaf Bjurström (1919–2001; Profile, II) was the Swedish translator of SB's works. The passage in *Comment c'est*: "mon chien spinal ou spinal dog" (105). On 4 January, SB had already responded to Bjurström's highly detailed questions on his translation of *Comment c'est*; in this letter he judged this work to be, of all his works, "by far the most difficult" (NLS).

AVIGDOR ARIKHA AND ANNE ATIK
PARIS

31.3.63 Paris

Chers amis

Merci de tout coeur pour les pièces de Yeats. Je suis très très content de les avoir.[1]

Rien à faire, pas la moindre chose. Je m'en vais lundi comme prévu pour une dizaine de jours j'espère. McGowran très compréhensif.[2] Je laisse tomber le mime pour le moment et vais essayer de voir le film – ou de traduire PLAY.[3]

Bon courage, bon travail.

Affectueusement

Sam

ALS; 1 leaf, 1 side; InU, Arikha.

31.3.63 Paris

Dear Both

Heartfelt thanks for the Yeats plays. I'm very very pleased to have them.[1]

Nothing to be done, not the smallest thing. I'm off on Monday as planned, for ten days or so, I hope. MacGowran very understanding.[2] I'm dropping the mime for the moment and am going to try to see the film – or translate *Play*.[3]

Bon courage, bon travail.

Love

Sam

1 The gift was the two-volume *Collected Plays of W. B. Yeats*, second edition (London: Macmillan, 1960).

2 SB's promise to write what he calls a "spoken mime" for MacGowran: 29 December 1962 and n. 6; 6 February 1963, n. 4.

3 On 27 February, SB wrote to A. J. Leventhal: "Rosset is here for a few days with a tempting offer for a 30 min. film which I'll probably have a shot at if they leave me enough time" (TxU, Leventhal Collection, 1.4). The television production company Four Star had approached Rosset with the suggestion that he ask some of Grove's authors to write a screenplay (for which they provided initial funding). Jean Genet

refused the offer, but Rosset commissioned scripts from SB, Marguerite Duras, Eugène Ionesco, Harold Pinter, and Alain Robbe-Grillet (Seaver, *The Tender Hour of Twilight*, 318).

JACOBA VAN VELDE
AMSTERDAM

11.4.63 Paris

Chère Tonny

D'abord tes questions

"Celui (le bruit) de la combustion". Je ne saisis pas la difficulté. Il entend un bruit qui est peut-être celui de quelque chose qui brûle - un bruit de flammes si tu veux[.][1]

"Vases de Galilée" = vases communicants. C'est une expérience inventée par Galileo Galilei, avec des vases de différentes formes reliés entre eux, pour rechercher les conditions d'équilibre des liquides. Tout changement dans un vase (densité, niveau) se répercute dans tout le système.[2]

Tu as été gentille de me téléphoner - et moi très coupable de par mon long silence. A part le travail, de + en + dur et exigeant, d'innombrables riens dévorent ma vie. Et la fatigue montante.

Je me réjouis à l'idée que tu viendras peut-être à Paris, t'installer. Mais le moindre logement coûte effroyablement cher. J'ai trouvé pour l'ami Leventhal, qui vient vivre à Paris, un 2 pièces meublé à Montparnasse - 400 francs (40.000 anciens) par mois, et il paraît que c'est une occasion extraordinaire.[3]

Avigdor Arikha a vu Bram qui a été, parait-il, assez malade, mais il va mieux.

Vu Geneviève enfin, qui aurait bien voulu te voir lors de ton dernier passage. La jeune Les Lettres Nouvelles disparait, au profit d'une grande machine internationale, titre à trouver encore. Nadeau et Geneviève préparent déjà l'édition française du 1er numéro.[4]

J'irai peut-être à Ulm fin mai pour quelques répétitions. Nous irons probablement 3 semaines en Autriche (Tyrol) au mois de juin. On m'invite à Edimbourg pour le Festival, mais je ne sais pas si j'irai.

Il ne me reste qu'un seul exemplaire de PLAY et ne pourrai te l'envoyer avant d'avoir fait ou fait faire des copies. Top l'a bien traduit. Je vais m'y mettre bientôt.

Toujours question de Renaud pour Winnie. Elle y tient et Barrault aussi. Roger somnole comme d'habitude. Pas à l'Odéon bien sûr.[5]

J'ai donné PLAY à Serreau. Envie de travailler une fois avec lui.

Amitiés à Fritz.

Je t'embrasse

Sam

ALS; 1 leaf, 2 sides; BNF, 19794/93.

11.4.63 Paris

Dear Tonny

First, your questions.

"Celui (le bruit) de la combustion" / "That (the sound) of burning". I don't get the difficulty. He hears a sound which is perhaps that of something burning – *a sound of flames* if you like.[1]

"Vases de Galilée" = communicating vessels. This was an experiment invented by Galileo Galilei, with interconnected vessels of different shapes, to carry out research into the conditions of equilibrium of liquids. Any change in one vessel (density, level) is felt throughout the whole system.[2]

It was kind of you to telephone me – and on my side guilty, with my long silence. Apart from work, harder and harder, more demanding, countless silly little things are eating up my life. And growing fatigue.

I am delighted at the thought that you may be coming to settle in Paris. But the smallest flat costs a fearful amount. I found, for my friend Leventhal who is coming to live in Paris, a two-roomed furnished flat in Montparnasse: 400 francs (40,000 old francs) per month – and apparently it is an extraordinary bargain.[3]

Avigdor Arikha has seen Bram who, it appears, has been rather ill, but is on the mend.

Have finally seen Geneviève, who would have loved to see you when you were last here. The young review *Les Lettres Nouvelles* is folding up, swallowed up by some big international affair, name not yet decided on. Nadeau and Geneviève are already preparing the French edition of the first issue.[4]

I may go to Ulm at the end of May for a few rehearsals. We shall probably have 3 weeks in Austria (Tyrol) in June. I am invited to Edinburgh for the Festival, but I don't know if I will go.

I have only one copy of *Play* left and won't be able to send it to you until I've made copies of it, or had them made. Top has translated it well. I shall set about it soon.

There is still talk of Renaud for Winnie. She is keen, and Barrault too. Roger is dozing as usual. Not at the Odéon of course.[5]

I gave *Play* to Serreau. Feel like working with him some time.

Best to Fritz.

Love

Sam

1 SB is assisting Van Velde in her translation of *Molloy* into Dutch. The sentence puzzling her contains what SB himself translates into English as "the sound of burning" (*Molloy* [New York: Grove Press, 1955] 69). The passage comes from the section describing Molloy's residence at Lousse's house:

> Car je n'aidais ni dans la maison ni dans le jardin et ne savais rien des travaux qui s'y effectuaient, jour et nuit, et dont les bruits me parvenaient, bruits sourds et secs aussi et puis souvent celui de l'air brassé avec force, à ce qu'il me semblait, et qui était peut-être tout simplement celui de la combustion (*Molloy* [Paris: Editions de Minuit, 1951] 77–78).

This becomes, in Van Velde's translation:

> Want ik hielp noch in het huis noch in de tuin en wist niets van het werk dat er dag en nacht omging en waarvan de geluiden tot me doordrongen, doffe geluiden en ook scherpe, en dan dikwijls het geloei van hevig warrelende lucht dat misschien gewoon van het stoken afkomstig was. (*Molloy*, tr. Jacoba van Velde [Amsterdam: Uitgeverij De Bezige Bij, 1963] 67).

2 As Molloy is attempting to account for how to describe the phenomenon of change, while being interviewed by the police sergeant near the end of *Molloy* part 1, SB writes of "Galileo's vessels" in his own English translation (*Molloy*, 119). In the French original from which Van Velde is working, the passage is: "Et ce sont ces petits ajustements, comme entre les vases de Galilée, que je ne peux exprimer qu'en disant, Je craignais que, ou J'espérais que" (*Molloy* [Minuit] 135). Van Velde renders this:

"En die kleine vereffeningen, zoals tussen de buizen van Galileï, kan ik slechts uitdrukken door bij voorbeeld te zeggen: Ik vreesde dat, of: Ik hoopte dat, of" (117).

3 Describing the flat he has found for Leventhal, SB writes to him: "Gas radiators in bedroom & sitting room. You won't have any of the usual exasperating signing-on formalities (gas, electricity, telephone) as they are all in the name of landlord (Monsieur Bürger [sic], avocat au barreau de Paris). You have your own meters. The address 144 Bld du Montparnasse, Paris 14me. The stairs aren't too stiff." (18 April 1963, TxU, Leventhal Collection, 1.4.)

4 Plans for this new review, to be published in French, Italian, and German, were gestating from 1961, as will be explained in the editorial to *Les Lettres Nouvelles* (nouvelle série [3] 12 [June–July–August 1964]): The different writers' groups

> entendaient mettre sur pied une revue aux sommaires semblables publiée (au début) en trois langues, dans trois pays en même temps, par trois éditeurs différents, et qui aurait été rédigée par un collège unique formé d'écrivains des trois pays. Les textes pour un premier numéro ont même été réunis. (5.) (planned to set up a review, with similar summaries of contents, published (initially) in three languages, in three countries at the same time, by three different publishers, and written by a single editorial body made up of writers from the three countries. The texts for a first issue have even been put together.)

The editorial goes on to explain that the plans failed to materialize because of a difference of perspective on what constituted writers' common ground ("l'écriture commune"); as a result, "Nous décidâmes alors de reprendre notre liberté, en même temps que la publication des *Lettres Nouvelles*, interrompue pendant plusieurs mois, pour tenter de constituer par nos seules forces un lieu de rassemblement et de travail pour une revue internationale" (7) (We therefore decided to resume our freedom of action, as well as publication of the *Lettres Nouvelles*, which had been interrupted for several months, in order to try to set up, drawing only on our own resources, a shared environment, personal and literary, for an international review).

5 Odette Aslan wrote: "Roger Blin did not want to be known as the director of the production. 'What would people say? It's a play without entrances and exits. My work consisted of seeking, with Madeleine Renaud, a stylized diction for a text built on the head of a needle'." (*Roger Blin*, 53, citing *Le Figaro Littéraire* 14 October 1963.) "Pas à l'Odéon bien sûr" is added in the right margin.

BARNEY ROSSET
GROVE PRESS, NEW YORK

13.4.63 Paris

Dear Barney

I have finished a first project for the film, with a certain amount of detail which I won't set forth here, as I'm not at all sure of it.[1] This is merely to give you some idea of material requirements.

The film is in three parts:

1) Street in a town. Early morning. People going to work. No cars. One bicycle with passenger. One cab. O (principal character, he who would not be seen), hastens along followed by E (eye). One incident with an elderly couple and a pet monkey. About 10 minutes in all.
2) Stairs of a house. O mounts towards room, followed by E. One incident with an old flower seller (woman). About five minutes in all.
3) Small room poorly furnished. O and E together, but the former still observed with sufficient obliquity to allow him to feel unseen. Animals: cat, dog, parrot and goldfish. This in three parts:
    a) Occultations by O (window, mirror, pets' eyes).
    b) Inspection and destruction of photographs by O.
    c) Final investment of O by E. Last shots: O at last seen fully, and E seen. E = O.

About 15 minutes in all.

Period: about 1939.[2]

No speech. Perhaps sounds (breath, feet, creak of rocking-chair, etc.). But not sure yet.

I'm letting it lie now for a bit and beginning to feel already the desolemnizing climate it needs – sort of silent film comedy, but not broad.

Shall tell you all I know in May and let you have a detailed outline (untechnical) in first week of June, as promised, after I've seen Alan.[3]

Best always.

s/ Sam

TLS; 1 leaf, 2 sides (notes and sketch on verso, missing); CUSD, MSS 103/1/22.

1 The film project: 31 March 1963, n. 3.

2 In the published text, the period setting is changed to "1929" (Samuel Beckett, *Film: Complete Scenario, Illustrations, Production Shots* [New York: Grove Press, 1969] 12).

3 SB wrote to Alan Schneider on 15 March: "The film thing has me petrified with fright. To talk with you about it would be a great help. About that and all the text." (Burns Library, Samuel Beckett Collection, SB-AS; previous publication, Beckett and Schneider, *No Author Better Served*, 136).

AVIGDOR ARIKHA
PARIS

25.4.63 Ussy

Cher Avigdor

Merci de ta lettre.

Ci-joint. Dis-moi si ce n'est pas assez.[1]

C'est dans la collection "Petits Atlas Payot, Lausanne". Il s'agit d'un très joli oiseau vert foncé, vert clair, jaune-vert et rouge – le pic vert. Il en vient quelquefois toute une bande picorer sur la pelouse.[2]

Oui, trop de main nuit, trop de tête aussi, trop de trop peu sans doute aussi, mais c'est par là la seule chance qui nous reste.

Je ne fais rien. Drift about, la tête à mille lieues. Ah si je pouvais ne plus jamais bouger.

Affectueusement à vous 2

Sam

ALS; 1 leaf, 1 side; InU, Arikha.

25.4.63 Ussy

Dear Avigdor

Thank you for your letter.

Enclosed. Tell me if it isn't enough.[1]

It's in the "Petits Atlas Payot, Lausanne" collection. It's the very pretty bird, dark green, light green, green-yellow and red – the green woodpecker. Sometimes a whole flock of them comes and pecks all over the lawn.[2]

Yes, too much hand does harm, too much head as well, no doubt too much too little does as well – but it's our one remaining chance.

I am doing nothing. Drift about, my head miles away. Oh if only I could never make another move.

Love to you both

Sam

1 Although Arikha never requested money from SB, the letters he received from him often came accompanied by a check; when Arikha would repay what he saw as a loan, SB almost invariably objected.

2 The pic vert (green woodpecker), described as being "sédentaire et erratique" (sedentary and erratic), is depicted climbing a tree in the *Petit Atlas de Poche Payot: Oiseaux I* by C. A. W. Guggisberg and R. Hainard ([Lausanne: Librairie Payot, n.d.] 32–33).

MAURICE SAILLET
PARIS

2.5.63 38 Bld St Jacques

Cher Maurice Saillet

J'ai un mal infernal à m'aligner en ce moment - depuis longtemps. Je m'acharne voulant vous faire plaisir. Si j'y arrive, ça ne pourra être que moche et bref. Pardonnez-moi. Les mots ne sont plus tenables - et avec ça elle m'échappe complètement.[1]

Très cordialement
Sam. Beckett

ACS; 1 leaf, 1 side; *env to* Monsieur Maurice Saillet, 12 Rue de l'Odéon, Paris 6me; *pm* 2-5-63, Paris; TxU, Saillet Collection, 265.1.

2.5.63 38 Bld St Jacques

Dear Maurice Saillet

I am having a dreadful time trying to do my bit, and have been for a long time now. I am working away hard at it, wanting to please you. If I do manage something, it can only be messy and short. Forgive me. Words elude me - and with that she disappears from me altogether.[1]

Yours very sincerely
Sam. Beckett

1 Maurice Saillet (1914–1990) had met Sylvia Beach in the 1930s when working at Adrienne Monnier's La Maison des Amis des Livres. In the 1950s, with Maurice Nadeau, he founded *Les Lettres Nouvelles*. After Sylvia Beach's death on 14 October 1962, Saillet had invited SB and others to write a tribute to her. On 21 November, SB had replied to Saillet: "Je m'associe bien volontiers à l'Hommage à Sylvia Beach. Ce sera des lignes plutôt que des pages. Je vous enverrai ça bientôt." (TxU, Saillet

Collection, 265.1.) (I am very happy to join in the Homage to Sylvia Beach. It will be lines rather than pages. I'll send it to you soon.)

On the same day that he wrote to Saillet, SB wrote to Cyril Connolly in Sussex: "Saillet keeps chivvying for a hommage to Sylvia Beach & you too I suppose. Even 5 lines seems for some reason a mountain." (Tulsa, Cyril Connolly Collection, 2.3.) The volume, entitled *Sylvia Beach (1887–1962)*, published later in 1963 (Paris: Mercure de France), did not include an entry from SB.

DERYK MENDEL
ULM, GERMANY

13.5.63 Paris

Dear Derek [*for* Deryk]

Thanks for yr. letter. Pity about pudding face.[1] Abstractize, abstractize. Translating it into French last week I realised that "black out" – "Finsternis" – is imprecise. In French it becomes "noir = obscurité presque totale du début", i.e. when curtain goes up stage in almost complete darkness. In the 5 seconds before weak spots come on one should just be able to make out presence of urns – and whenever stage direction is "blackout", "noir", "Finsternis", it is this opening more than penumbra which is required, awful English this.

By all means left to right as in Comment C'est.[2]

The Observer wants to do a photographic reportage for their number of June 16th. The material would have to be in Friday 14th at latest. Barbara Bray would be on the job. What date would suit you best for the photos.[3] My motions so erratic I suggest you write to her directly

14 Rue LESUEUR

Paris 16me

Jacky McGowran just done 1st mime for Irish TV, well I am told.[4]

Just back from week of frenzied work at Ussy. Serreau now threatens to come to Ulm with Schneider & me. Can you face this? Franchement.[5]

Best of best.

Sam

ACS; 1 leaf, 2 sides; *env to* Herrn. Dr. Deryk Mendel, Ulm-Donau, Ulmer Theater, Allemagne; *pm* 14–5–63, Paris; Overbeck Collection.

1 In the text, W1 says of W2: "pudding face" (Samuel Beckett, *Play, and Two Short Pieces for Radio* [London: Faber and Faber, 1964] 13). In the Ulm production, Sigrid Pfeiffer who played W2 was "a young healthy girl, very pretty" (Deryk Mendel to the editors, October 2003).

2 SB notes in the text that the "heads are those, from left to right as seen from the auditorium, of W2, M. and W1" (9). Movement in *Comment c'est* from left to right occurs on eight occasions (*Comment c'est* [Minuit] 109, 140, 186, 192, 194, 197, 205, 213).

3 Jack Nisberg (1922–1980), an American freelance photographer, who worked for *Life*, *Look*, *Newsweek*, *The Observer*, *The New York Times*, *The Sunday Times*, *Elle Magazine*, and *Vogue*, took the photos for Barbara Bray's article ("The New Beckett," *The Observer, Weekend Review* 16 June 1963: 29).

4 Jack MacGowran appeared in *Act Without Words I*, directed by Jim FitzGerald (1929–2003) on 9 May, for *Spectrum* on Telefís Éireann (RTE), Dublin (Young, *The Beckett Actor*, 193, 81). FitzGerald, A. J. Leventhal, Emile Arnould, and Alec Reid introduced the production; G. A. Olden observed that the man was "heroically played by Jack MacGowran" ("Beckett Here, Beckett There . . .," *The Irish Times* 16 May 1963: 8).

5 "Franchement" (Tell me honestly).

FREDA TROUP
LONDON

13.5.63 — 38 Boulevard Saint-Jacques
Paris 14[me]

Dear Miss (or M[rs]) Troup

Thank you for your letter.[1]

I am in entire agreement with your views and prepared to refuse performance of my plays except before non-segregated audiences.

My agents are:

Grove Press
64 University Place
New York, N.Y.

and

Curtis Brown Ltd.
13 King Street
London W. C. 2

the latter controlling South African performing rights.
Yours sincerely
Samuel Beckett

ALS; 1 leaf, 1 side; *datestamped* 15 MAY 1963; BL, Add. 80776/9.

1 Freda Troup (1911–2004) was a writer and anti-apartheid activist. She had asked SB and many other writers to sign a public declaration to promote performances for "mixed audiences in all theatres":

> While not wishing to exercise any political censorship over their own or other works of art, but feeling colour discrimination transcends the purely political, the following playwrights, after consultation with the Anti-Apartheid Movement and with South African artists and writers, as an expression of their personal repugnance to the policies of apartheid and their sympathy with those writers and others in the Republic of South Africa now suffering under evil legislation, have instructed their agents to insert a clause in all future contracts automatically refusing performing rights in any theatre where discrimination is made among audiences on grounds of colour.

Among the signatories were SB, Ronald Duncan, Arthur Miller, Spike Milligan, Iris Murdoch, John Osborne, Harold Pinter, C. P. Snow, Muriel Spark, Arnold Wesker, and Angus Wilson ("48 Playwrights in Apartheid Protest," *The Times* 26 June 1963: 12).

GOTTFRIED BÜTTNER
KASSEL, GERMANY

le 24 mai 1963

38 Bld. St.-Jacques
Paris 14me

Cher Docteur

J'ai bien reçu votre aimable lettre et vous en remercie vivement.[1]

J'ai vu Menetti [*for* Minetti] dans quelques scènes de Krapp, voici deux ans environ, pas au théâtre, mais sur l'écran de la TV. Je me trouvais à ce moment-là à Bielefeld, pour la première de l'opéra Krapp de Mihalovici. C'est un théâtre de Cologne, si je ne me trompe, qui présentait la pièce et avait eu l'idée, à l'occasion de l'opéra, d'en donner des extraits télévisés. Menetti m'a fait très bonne impression.[2]

Je suis flatté et touché par ce que vous dites de mon travail. Moi je suis tout à fait incapable d'en parler. Je ne le vois et ne le vis que du dedans. Là il fait toujours sombre et il n'y est jamais question ni de diagnostic, ni de prognostic [sic], ni de traitement.

J'ai de très bons souvenirs de Kassel et notamment de Wilhelmshöhe. J'y allais assez souvent fin des années 20 début des années 30.[3]

Croyez, cher Docteur, à mes sentiments très cordiaux.

s/

Samuel Beckett

TLS; 1 leaf, 1 side; T *env to* Herrn Dr. Gottfried Büttner, Kassel, Feldbergstrasse 6, Allemagne; *pm* 25-5-63, Paris; Büttner Collection. Previous publication: Martin Brunkhorst, Gerd Rohmann, and Konrad Schoell, eds., *Beckett und die Literatur der Gegenwart*, Anglistische Forschungen (Heidelberg: C. Winter, 1988) facing 293.

May 24th 1963

38 Bld. St.-Jacques
Paris 14me

Dear Dr Büttner

I have received your kind letter, for which I am most grateful.[1]

I saw Minetti in some scenes from *Krapp*, about two years ago, not in the theatre but on the TV. I happened to be in Bielefeld at the time, for the première of the Mihalovici opera *Krapp*. It was a Cologne theatre, if I am not mistaken, that was putting on the play and had had the idea, when the opera opened, of giving televised extracts. I was very favourably impressed by Minetti.[2]

I am flattered and touched by what you say of my work. I myself am quite incapable of talking about it. I see it and live it only from the inside. There it is always dark, and in that dark no question ever of diagnosis, or prognosis, or treatment.

I have very good memories of Kassel, notably of Wilhelmshöhe. I used to go there quite often in the late 20s and early 30s.[3]

Yours sincerely

s/

Samuel Beckett

1 Gottfried Büttner (1926–2002) practiced medicine in Kassel; his interests in literature and the anthroposophical teachings of Rudolf Steiner led to a second doctorate from the Gesamthochschule Kassel on *Watt* (later published as *Samuel Becketts Roman "Watt,"* 1981).

2 Bernhard Minetti (1905–2003) had performed the role of Krapp in 1960–1961 at the Städtische Bühnen, Cologne, directed by Karl Zeiser. In his memoir, Minetti writes that Zeiser: "Er hat mich dazu gebracht, Krapps Situation unerbittlich hart erdulden zu können, den Blick in den Abgrund dieses Lebens auszuhalten und den winzigen Rest von Bewußtheit mit der allerletzten, reduzierten Kraft zum Ausdruck zu bringen; dabei äußerste Präzision" (*Erinnerungen eines Schauspielers*, ed. Günther Rühle [Stuttgart: Deutsche Verlags Anstalt, 1985] 230) (Got me to the point of being able to suffer Krapp's situation without flinching, to withstand the look into the abyss of life, and to express the tiny remainder of consciousness with the very last ounce of strength; and to do this with extreme precision). Minetti adds: "Aber in der Darstellung des Krapp spürte ich eine hohe, illusionslose Wahrhaftigkeit" (233) (But in portraying Krapp, I felt an intense truthfulness, devoid of any illusion).

3 SB had spent several extended periods in Kassel visiting his cousin Peggy Sinclair and her family; her mother was SB's paternal aunt Frances Sinclair. Gottfried Büttner lived in the suburb of Wilhelmshöhe, site of the Bergpark and Palace which houses a museum of Old Masters.

JOHN CALDER
JOHN CALDER (PUBLISHER) LTD., LONDON

4.6.63 Paris

Dear John

Thanks for your letter, accounts, enclosure of handsome cheque and proof covers which that old gob notwithstanding I like.[1]

Hope corrected galleys of How It Is arrived safely.[2]

I went to Ulm with Alan Schneider and saw two rough rehearsals. Derek [*for* Deryk] Mendel and his actors doing their damnedest, but still far from right. It will be a very careful and conscientious production and no director's big ideas, which is a rare thing in Germany. The theatre had just been into bad trouble with the municipality because of their production of Vaut[h]ier's Nouvelle Mandragore.[3]

Two nice cards from Bettina who seems to be liking Ireland. So pleased she is to sing John's songs on Irish radio.[4]

We leave for Innsbruck & environs June 17th for about a month. Afraid Scotland very doubtful this year, with the accumulation of trouble I'm sure to find on my return and then rehearsals of Oh les

B. J. Last session with Madeleine R. and Blin most encouraging. Before opening here in October they are to give a few performances in Venice, at the Ridotto I think.[5]

Got the film outline down at last, showed it to Alan who approved and then sent it to Barney.[6]

Up to our eyes at the moment with recording of Cascando in undesirable confusion of R.T.F. Studios. Three 4 hour sessions have not been enough. Another this evening and probably another again.[7] God knows when I'll get to Ussy.

Translated PLAY (COMEDIE) and gave it, with Blin's consent, to Serreau. Now the Barrault ask that the two plays should not be on at the same time. More trouble.[8]

A good short text from Nick ("Crawled towards the grey carcass"), but very difficult. Suppose you saw Nadeau's write-up of Higgins in the Express.[9]

Love to Bettina

yrs ever

Sam

ALS; 1 leaf, 2 sides; *datestamped* 5.JUN.1963; InU, C&B, Beckett.

1 John Calder had sent royalty statements and payment on 31 May; with his letter he enclosed proof covers for the Jupiter paperbound editions of *Murphy* (1963) and *Watt* (1963), each with images of SB on the front cover (InU, C&B, Beckett).

2 Calder acknowledged the corrected galleys of *How It Is* in his letter of 17 June (InU, C&B, Beckett).

3 SB and Alan Schneider had traveled to Ulm on an overnight train from Paris, leaving 29 May; in his telegram to Deryk Mendel on 28 May, SB indicated that he planned to "ARRIVE WITH SCHNEIDER THURSDAY 7.13 A.M. AND LEAVE SOMETIME FRIDAY" (Overbeck Collection). Mendel countered: "TELEVISION HAS WIND OF YOUR ARRIVAL ULM BAHNHOF. PLEASE LEAVE TRAIN AT STUTTGART 6.05 A.M. SHALL MEET YOU WITH CAR" (Overbeck Collection).

The Ulmer Theater produced *La Nouvelle Mandragore* (1952) by Jean Vauthier in June; it incited public outrage: "Skandolöser Höhepunkt ist eine im Innern einer Kirche spielende Szene, bei der es zu Handgreiflichkeiten zwischen der junger Ehefrau, ihrer enkelwütigen Mutter und einem korruptem Mönch kommt" ("Fast nur solches," *Der Spiegel* 24.63, 12 June 1963: np) (The scandalous high point is a scene inside the church where a physical altercation occurs between the young wife, her mother who desperately wants a grandchild, and a corrupt monk). Audience members walked out of the premiere, and some members of the City Council threatened to withdraw funding if the play continued ("'Die neue Mandragor,' von Jean Vauthier," *Die Zeit* 28 June 1963: 16; "Fast nur solches," np).

4 In his letter of 31 May to SB, Calder writes: "Bettina is going to sing John Beckett's songs on the Irish radio"; however, the broadcast did not occur (Bettina Jonić to the editors, 8 March 2011).

5 Roger Blin directed Madeleine Renaud and Jean-Louis Barrault in *Oh les beaux jours*, which would open at the Venice Festival on 28 September at the Teatro del Ridotto, and at the Odéon-Théâtre de France on 21 October.

6 SB sent the film outline to Barney Rosset on 2 June: "We went through it carefully together. I don't think I can do any more without technical help. Alan made a lot of excellent points." (CUSD, MSS 103/1/22.)

7 Rehearsals for *Cascando* had begun on 16 May, with time that day and on 18 May for recording the music by Mihalovici (SB to A. J. Leventhal, 30 April 1963; TxU, Leventhal Collection, 1.4). The sessions were difficult primarily for technical reasons, as SB reported to Lawrence Harvey on 2 July:

> Cascando was recorded before I left in the crazy RTF studios. Different studio every time (in a different recording ambience) & different technicians. A 4 hour session boiled down to 2 hours work, the other two devoted to finding tape, unwinding it, repairing apparatus, answering phone, etc. Disastrous. Mihalovici's music is fine, but the result most disappointing. Not rehearsed, nor prepared, realised "Comme je te pousse". (NhD, Beckett Collection, MS 122/1.6.)

"Comme je te pousse" (any old how).

8 Although Jean-Marie Serreau's production of *Comédie* would make a brief appearance at the Théâtre du Pavillon de Marsan from 10 June 1964, the premiere would not take place until 28 February 1966, directed by Serreau and produced by the Compagnie Renaud-Barrault.

9 Nick Rawson's short text has not been found in the Calder and Boyars archives at the Lilly Library, Indiana University. Maurice Nadeau reviewed *Felo de Se* by Aidan Higgins in Edith Fournier's French translation *La mort que l'on se donne* ("Ces critiques égoïstes," *L'Express* 30 May 1963: 29–30).

MICHAEL BAKEWELL
BBC, LONDON

11.6.63 Paris

Dear Michael

Thanks for your letter.[1]

If they have not replaced Bob and Joe by Swedish names there is no need to seek a Swedish equivalent for Croak. It is the man's name. But if they are transposing proper names, and if the ambiguity of croaking voice and dying man is not possible in Swedish, then Krax is all right with me. But I should prefer the three names to be left as they stand.[2]

With best wishes,

Yours ever

s/ Sam

Samuel Beckett

TLS; 1 leaf, 1 side; BBCWAC, RCONT 12, Samuel Beckett, Scriptwriter II.

1 On 6 June, Michael Bakewell wrote to SB that he had just produced *Words and Music* for Swedish Radio, using the Swedish translation *Ord och Musik* by Göran O. Eriksson in which the character of Croak was named "Krax" ("which is, I gather a kind of noise that frogs make"). Bakewell continued that Swedish Radio was "very worried as to whether the idea of a man on the point of death is what you wish the name to convey." (BBCWAC, RCONT12, Samuel Beckett, Scriptwriter II.)

2 Bakewell would write again to SB on 21 June saying that he had suggested that they simply use "Croak" (BBCWAC, RCONT12, Samuel Beckett, Scriptwriter II).

BARNEY ROSSET
GROVE PRESS, NEW YORK

21.6.63

Berghotel
Zell-am-See
Austria

Dear Barney

Dick told me you would like a plainer statement of what the film is about, or a brief restatement in plainer language.[1] Here goes to try, though I doubt if I can get it any plainer than in the outline (of which a friend to whom I showed it said it reminded him of Lucky's monologue).

The point of departure is the old metaphysical doctrine to the effect that being consists in being perceived and that without some perceiving intelligence there would be nothing – the counter-doctrine being that objective reality is an absolute independent of any such intelligence and existing indestructibly whether apprehended or not.[2]

I often imagine a naive human being involved in the first situation, so unphilosophically minded as to take it literally, seeking ingenuously to be as nothing by withdrawal within a space stripped of all perceiving organs and running foul of himself as perceiving organ.

It is this innocent literal-mindedness that makes him a comic figure and conditions the whole style and atmosphere of the film.

It is therefore the old theme of split personality, except that here the split is not in ethical terms, as in Stevenson, nor in affective as in Schubert, nor in psychological, as in Freud, but in naive metaphysical – not between good and evil being, nor between past and present being, but between conscious and non-conscious being, but between the being that is perceived and the being that perceives.[3] And in order that this may be shown (on a screen) the two halves are given shape, as legitimately or illegitimately as Stevenson's two halves, in the form of a fleeing object and a pursuing eye.

I hope this does not sound like more Lucky.

Best always.
s/ Sam

TLS; 1 leaf, 1 side; CUSD, MSS 103/1/22.

1 SB saw Richard Seaver on 13 June (SB to Lüfti Özkök, 13 June 1963; Özkök Collection).

2 SB refers to a central tenet of George Berkeley's "immaterialism": "esse est percipi" (to be is to be perceived) (George Berkeley, *A Treatise Concerning the Principles of Human Knowledge*, ed. Kenneth P. Winkler [Indianapolis: Hackett Publishing, 1982], 24).

3 Robert Louis Stevenson explores "two halves" in many of his works, not least in *The Strange Case of Dr. Jekyll and Mr. Hyde* (1886) and *The Master of Ballantrae* (1889). SB may be referring to the affective divide reflected in Franz Schubert's music; or to the thought of Gotthilf Heinrich von Schubert (1780–1860). Freud is invoked because of his view of the human psyche as irremediably divided.

BARBARA BRAY
PARIS

27.6.63 Zell am See

Dear Barbara

Second slug of mail yesterday with your 2 letters. Glad to have them, to know you are all right, busy & in demand.

Uninformative note from Deryk with programme & long article in some small gazette. All serious & interesting texts. From article I learnt at least that whistles and boos had not been wanting.[1]

Beautiful walk yesterday right down into valley through the pines, a bit hamstrung after the long descent. Slopes covered with alpine roses & anemones. Sharp air and burning sun.

Labouring at final text of Comédie or no doubt Que comédie. Should get it off by end of week.[2]

Lost burberry turned up having been to Berchtesgaden or thereabouts.[3]

Hard to write a letter with nothing within and without only alpine & lacustrian [*for* lacustrine] splendours. Perhaps I should stop trying to work in the morning & walk all day. From 9 to 12 and 14 to 19.

Finishing in bedtime snatches Guns in August, then your Chekhov volume. Found two Serie Noire in the bar. But not yet back on the booze.[4]

Thanks of [*for* for] Montherlant. Had already read (and rather liked) it, for its parody.[5]

Pen empty, penman too.

Love

Sam

ALS; 1 leaf, 1 side; *env to* Madame Bray, 14 Rue Le Sueur, Paris 16me, Frankreich; *pm* 27-6-63, Zell am See; TCD, MS 10948/1/234.

1 *Spiel* had opened on 14 June in Ulm. SB had reported to Bray on 19 June that Mendel had sent a wire: "all did our best apparently successfully" (TCD, MS 10948/1/230). The program of *Drei Stücke von Samuel Beckett* by the Ulmer Theater included an article by Wolfgang Hildesheimer, "Becketts Spiel" ([2–3]) (rpt. *Spectaculum* 6 [1963] 321–323 and *Theater heute* 4.7 [1963] 57/I), and one by Dieter Henrich, "'Spiel' in Becketts Werk" ([4–6]). Joachim Kaiser's article about the premiere in Ulm "Spiel in Urnen" (6–9) was in the same issue of *Theater heute*; it was followed by an interview with Deryk Mendel, "Dirigent für Becketts Partitur" (9–10). Beckett had also seen the article by Bray in *The Observer* (29); he commented to Bray, in the letter of 19 June: "The urns in Observer picture excruciated me."

2 SB had mentioned to Bray in his letter of 23 June that he had "Finished revising PLAY yesterday, adding a note on light, and send it to London today" (TCD MS 10948/1/232). He needed to make similar changes in the French script, as well as determine a title. "Que comédie" (Just Play).

3 In his travel from Paris, via Innsbruck, to Zell am See, SB had lost his raincoat (SB to Bray, 23 June).

4 Barbara Tuchman, *The Guns of August* (1962). It is not known what SB was reading by Anton Chekhov, but he did own *The Brute and Other Stories*, ed. Eric Bentley and Theodor Hoffmann (New York: Grove Press, 1958). SB enjoyed reading Série Noire crime fiction.

5 Henry de Montherlant, *Le Chaos et la nuit* (1963); Bray had reviewed this as well as Julien Green's *Partir avant le jour* (1963) in "Re-enter two French Elders," *The Observer, Weekend Review* 5 May 1963: 25.

JÉRÔME LINDON
EDITIONS DE MINUIT, PARIS

30.6.63

Berghotel
Zell am See
Autriche

Cher Jérome

Voici la pièce – enfin quelque chose d'approchant.

Je tiens beaucoup à ce que la publication ne devance pas la représentation – et je crois que tu seras de mon avis. La mise cette fois n'est pas sur un texte, mais tout entière sur le choc de la chose vue, qu'amortirait forcément une lecture préalable. C'est l'unique raison pour laquelle je te prie d'attendre. Je n'ai aucune nouvelle de Serreau et ignore s'il veut passer outre à la demande des Barrault ou s'il accepte de remettre ça au mois de janvier.[1]

Pour le titre j'ai hésité entre Comédie, Que Comédie et Que Jeu, ce dernier entraînant un changement page 7, à savoir "que jeu" à la place de "que comédie", deux fois.[2] Qu'en penses-tu?

Nous nous plaisons bien ici. Le temps s'améliore et nous faisons des promenades magnifiques. Retour vers le 20 juillet.

Bien amicalement

Sam

ALS; 1 leaf, 1 side; IMEC-Fonds Samuel Beckett, Boîte 4, Correspondance 1962–64.

30.6.63 Berghotel
Zell am See
Austria

Dear Jérôme

Here is the play - well, something close to it.

I am very keen that publication should not come before performance; and I think you will be of the same mind. This time we are putting our money, not on a text, but entirely on the shock of the seen, something which would be deadened by a preliminary reading. That is the only reason why I am asking you to wait. I have heard nothing from Serreau, and have no idea whether he intends to hold out against the Barraults' request or accepts to postpone it till January.[1]

For the title, I have been hesitating between *Comédie*, *Que comédie*, and *Que jeu*, this last involving a change on p. 7, namely "que jeu" instead of "que comédie", twice.[2] What do you think?

We are enjoying ourselves here. The weather is improving and we are going for wonderful walks. Back round the 20th of July.

All best

Sam

1 Jean-Louis Barrault's wish that *Oh les beaux jours* be the only SB play in Paris at the time during which it was produced would, if fulfilled, delay the opening of *Comédie* by Jean-Marie Serreau (see 4 June 1963).

2 If the title were to change from *Comédie*, the mention of "Que comédie" in the text would require a change to "Que jeu" ("Just play" or "Just playing").

AVIGDOR ARIKHA AND ANNE ATIK
PARIS

1.7.63 Berghotel

Chers amis

Merci de vos deux lettres. Je suis très content que ça marche pour la tapisserie - pourvu que ça ne bloque pas la peinture encore une fois.[1] Mais ce sera plus vite liquidé que les vitraux.[2]

Ici ça va. Temps incertain, mais très beau quand il s'y met. Promenades merveilleuses dans la montagne, moins belles dans la vallée. Alpenrose et anémones jaunes partout. Surpris par un orage en rase montagne je viens de prendre une douche pas ordinaire – et Suzanne de perdre ses lunettes. Nous sommes seuls à l'hotel, les lune de mielleux Anversois étant repartis chez eux. On annonce des arrivées de Beyrouth. A tort j'espère. A partir de 17.30 pas âme qui vive en dehors du personnel. Après le dîner on se tape la TV autrichienne. Au pieu à 10 heures et debout à 7½. Travail jusqu'à midi, puis marche ou crève (Galliéni).[3] J'en ai terminé avec PLAY et COMEDIE, fait quelques petits changements et ajouté une note sur l'éclairage. Sur Ulm quelques maigres échos me parviennent peu à peu. Ça semble avoir marché pas mal. Le da capo a déplu. Possible que ce soit une connerie. Je verrai bien avec Serreau. Je crois que c'est une question de tempo. J'ai demandé à Lindon de ne pas publier avant la représentation.[4]

J'aimerais bien apprendre que vous avez réussi à trouver un logement – atelier, ou les deux séparés. J'espère que le petit hôtel allait faire [*for* a fait] l'affaire.[5] Et New York? Toujours sur le tapis? J'espère bien que non.

Peu joué aux échecs. Une partie contre Alekhine (championnat).[6]

Rien de Con. Il doit être très occupé à bazarder. Enfin il peut s'amener quand il voudra. De la literie sur le lit, whiskey et slivovic dans le buffet et les clefs chez la concierge.

Affectueusement

Sam

ALS; 1 leaf, 2 sides; InU, Arikha.

1.7.63 Berghotel

Dear Both

Thank you for your two letters. I'm very pleased that it's working out for the tapestry – just so long as it doesn't block the painting again.[1] But it will be quicker to deal with than the stained-glass windows.[2]

Here everything all right. Weather uncertain, but very fine when it puts its mind to it. Marvellous walks in the mountains. Less good in the valley. Alpenrose and yellow anemones everywhere. Caught by a storm in open ground on the mountain I've just had a shower, of no ordinary kind, and Suzanne just lost her glasses. We're on our own in the hotel, the honeymooners from Antwerp having gone home. There is talk of people from Beirut. Inaccurate I hope. From 5.30 on not a soul apart from the staff. After dinner we treat ourselves to Austrian TV. In bed by 10 and up at 7½. Work till noon, then march or die (Galliéni).[3] I've finished with *Play* and *Comédie*, made a few changes and added a note about the lighting. About Ulm a few faint echoes come through little by little. It seems to have gone off OK. The da capo went down badly. Maybe it is a stupid mistake. I'll see with Serreau all right. I think it's a question of tempo. I've asked Lindon not to publish before the performance.[4]

I would like to hear that you've succeeded in finding somewhere to live – a flat with studio, or two separate places. I hope that the little hotel did the trick.[5] And what about New York? Still on the cards? I do hope not.

Not much chess. One championship game against Alekhine.[6]

Nothing from Con. He must be busy clearing things out. Anyhow he can come when he wants. Bedding on the bed, whiskey and slivovic in the sideboard, and the keys with the concierge.

Love

Sam

1 Arikha's tapestry was commissioned for an Israeli luxury liner, the SS *Shalom*, belonging to Zim Lines. It was completed in the same year, woven by Aubusson; the ship, built at the Saint-Nazaire docks in France, entered commercial service in 1964 (Arikha to the editors, January 2010).

2 Arikha's work in stained glass: 17 February 1962, n. 2.

3 SB attributes the expression "marche ou crève" to the French officer Joseph Galliéni (1849–1916) who, between 1896 and 1905, was Governor General of Madagascar; according to Pierre Montagnon, in *Histoire de la Légion*, this well-known unofficial motto of the Légion Etrangère was created rather by soldiers of the column of the Légion led by General Jacques Duchesne (1837–1918) during the Madagascar campaign of 1895 (Paris: Flammarion, 1999) 185.

4 The *da capo* ending of *Spiel* was a repetition of the whole play, and then, a further suggestion of a third repeat. Siegfried Unseld had reported to SB immediately after the premiere in Ulm, on 14 June, sending his impressions of the production:

> Die Widerholung des SPIELS verlief im gleichen Tempo, vollkommen identisch mit dem ersten Durchlauf, mit sehr kleinen, geringfügigen Schwankungen. Das Publickum ermüdete bei den Wiederholungen, wurde etwas unruhig. Dem allgemeinen Eindruck nach war die Wiederholung keine Steigerung. ("Uraufführung SPIEL von Samuel Beckett am Ulmer theater, 14.6.1963," GEU, MSS 1221.) (The repetition of *Spiel* ran at the same tempo, fully identical to the first performance, with very small, insignificant variations. The audience grew tired during the repetitions and a bit restless. The general impression was that the repetition was not an intensification.)

John Calder notes that SB's visit to Ulm had led to "many changes to his original play," including the decision to "repeat the action a second time. Derrick [*for* Deryk] suggested that as the play was so short, it might be repeated more often still, indeed why not go on until the last member of the audience had left? Sam thought a minute. 'No,' he said finally. 'This is Germany. They'll still be here at breakfast.'" (Calder, *Pursuit*, 299.)

5 Arikha had lived from 1955 in a small apartment at 10 Villa d'Alésia. Having been asked to vacate it, for several months he and Anne Atik lived at the Hôtel de Scandinavie, 27 rue de Tournon, Paris 6.

6 Alexander Alekhine (1892–1946) became World Chess Champion in 1927. SB owned a copy of Alekhine's *My Best Games of Chess 1924–1937* (London: G. Bell & Sons, 1949), and it is probable that it is from this book that he was playing.

BARBARA BRAY
PARIS

1.7.63 Zell am See

Dear Barbara

Thanks for your letters, enclosures & Ulm programme.[1]

I return M.'s letter as I think you may wish to keep it.[2]

I shall keep the programme in case you want it back. The texts seem to me quite good, especially Hildesheimer's.

The answer to your man about Portora should be, I think, that you don't know, think it most unlikely and advise him to ask me. I won't of course.[3]

Poor Jack and his one-man me, if only I could do something.[4]

Unseld (Suhrkamp) wrote about Ulm – a regular report. Favourable to the production & with good points – such as mistake of so characterizing faces.[5] Doubts about utility of da capo – general impression that not needed. Perhaps its [sic] wrong. I still feel that taken at right speed it is valid. Got both PLAY & COMEDIE off. Added a note on spot and changed – which may amuse you – "Age and appearance indifferent" to "Faces so lost to age and aspect as to seem almost part of urns. But masks forbidden." and "slice of lemon" to "squeeze of lemon".[6]

Remarkable study in Australian University Review AUMLA, "B's Brinkmanship" by Ross Chambers whom I once met. Shall keep to show you.[7]

Here ça va.[8] Weather better. Mountain lovely with Alprosen [sic] and yellow anemones. Long tortuous up & down walks. Taking the cabin down to the valley this afternoon and walking back up – to see can I. Three pubs on the way, but if I use them it will be for tea with lemon. Should take about 5 hours with breath like mine.

Should have written card to children but stupidly neglected. They'll be gone by now.

Getting a bit brown walking with only a short.[9] Still only guests in hotel, great quiet. Mountains of good food, can't eat the quarter. Chef came along very worried to know what on earth could be the matter. Boots marvellous, never trudged in such comfort.

Doze after dinner in front of TV, finishing every evening on reportage on Tour de France.[10]

So it goes and will go till time to go home.

Bon courage.

Love

Sam

ALS; 1 leaf, 2 sides; *env to* Madame Bray, 14 Rue Le Sueur, Paris 16$^{\underline{me}}$, Frankreich; *pm* 2-7-63, Zell am See; TCD, MS 10948/1/235.

1 Having been at the opening on 14 June, Bray had accumulated early cuttings as well as the program for *Spiel*.

2 "M's letter" refers, most probably, to a letter of appreciation from Deryk Mendel related to Bray's review of the production in *The Observer*.

3 Neither the question about Portora nor the questioner's identity is known.

4 SB hoped to create a new work for Jack MacGowran (see 29 December 1962, and n. 6).

5 Siegfied Unseld reported on the production of *Spiel* at Ulm:

> Die drei Köpfe, die aus drei schön geformten Urnen (Michel Raffaelli), ragten, waren (im Gegensatz zu den Regieanweisungen) individualisiert: der halb-intellektuelle Ehemann mit Brille, blinzelnd im Licht, die rothaarige, ältere, sehr monotone Ehefrau, und ein weißblondes, schmollmündiges Girl. Nur dem Aussehen nach waren es drei verschiedene Menschen: ihre Sprache war monoton, ziemlich starkes, rhythmisches Stakkato, eher schnell als langsam. ("Uraufführung SPIEL von Samuel Beckett am Ulmer Theater," 14 June 1963; GEU, MS 1221.) (The three heads, which protruded out of three beautifully shaped urns (Michel Raffaelli), were individualized (in contrast to the stage directions): the quasi-intellectual husband with glasses, blinking in the light; the red-haired, older, very monotone wife; and a pale-blond girl with a pouting mouth. Only by their appearance were they differentiated: their language was monotonous, a fairly strong, rhythmic staccato, fast, rather than slow.)

6 The other change indicated by SB: "squeeze of lemon" (*Play*, 17); "zeste de citron" ("Comédie," 23).

7 Ross Chambers, "Beckett's Brinkmanship," *AUMLA* (*Journal of the Australasian Universities Language and Literature Association*) 19 (May 1963) 57–75.

8 "Ça va" (Everything OK).

9 "Short": Gallicism for shorts.

10 The Tour de France took place between 23 June and 14 July in 1963.

SIEGFRIED UNSELD
SUHRKAMP VERLAG, FRANKFURT

Le 1er juillet 1963

Berghotel
Zell-am-See
Autriche

Cher Dr Unseld

Merci de votre lettre du 21 juin qui m'est parvenue hier. Vos impressions de SPIEL à Ulm m'ont vivement intéressé. On m'a envoyé une critique parue dans un journal local. En dehors de ça je ne sais rien. J'apprécie beaucoup votre souci de me tenir au courant. Il est possible en effet que le da capo soit une erreur. Il se justifiait dans mon idée, techniquement parlant, par l'intelligence forcément imparfaite, au bout d'une seule écoute, d'un discours à ce point cassé et précipité. Il est évident que si le mouvement n'a pas la rapidité requise la répétition risque d'être fastidieuse. Il faut que ça soit un véritable affolement de lumière et de bribes vocales. Souhaitable aussi, au lieu de trois projecteurs fixes, un seul mobile. J'espérais qu'ils allaient y arriver à Ulm, mais finalement non. Voir plus loin les indications à ce sujet qui figureront dans les éditions anglaise et française. Vous avez raison en disant qu'il ne fallait pas caractériser les visages. Mais à cet égard mon texte n'était pas assez clair et je pense l'avoir amélioré en mettant à la place de "age and appearance indifferent" "faces so lost to age and aspect as to appear almost part of urns. But masks forbidden (!)." En français: "Visages sans âge et pour ainsi dire sans aspect, à peine plus différenciés que les jarres." C'est seulement de retour d'Ulm que j'ai fait ce changement et rédigé la note sur l'éclairage. Je ne les ai pas encore communiqués à Tophoven, mais ne tarderai pas à le faire, trop tard hélas pour votre édition.[1]

Il est difficile à des comédiens privés de leurs moyens normaux (voix atones, visages impassibles) d'exprimer cette Qual dont vous parlez et de faire sentir, dans les deux second[e]s dont ils disposent, que la parole leur est littéralement extorquée.[2] Possible sans doute, mais horriblement difficile.

Nous sommes ici depuis quinze jours et pensons rester jusqu'au milieu du mois. L'endroit est magnifique et nous nous y plaisons beaucoup.

Je regrette énormément d'avoir manqué Boehlich lors de son passage à Paris.[3]

Bien amicalement
s/ Sam Beckett

TLS; 1 leaf, 1 side; DLA, Suhrkamp, VL, Beckett Samuel: 1962–1964; AL draft; 1 leaf, 2 sides *on* Siegfried Unseld to SB on 21 June 1963 (TLS, 1 leaf, 1 side); GEU, MSS 1221.

1st July 1963

Berghotel
Zell-am-See
Autriche

Dear Dr Unseld

Thank you for your letter of 21st June which reached me yesterday. Your impressions of *Play* in Ulm greatly interested me. I was sent a review in a local paper. I know nothing beyond that. I am very grateful for your concern to keep me informed. It may be that the *da capo* is a mistake. It was justified in my mind, technically speaking, by the necessarily imperfect understanding, on a single hearing, of such broken and rushed speech. It is obvious that if the delivery does not have the required speed, repetition is likely to be wearisome. There has to be a bewildering outburst of light and speech fragments. Desirable too, instead of three fixed spots, one single mobile spot. I hoped that they would manage this in Ulm, but in the end they didn't. See later the instructions about this which will appear in the English and French editions. You are right to say that the faces must not be characterised, but the text in this connection was not clear enough, and I think I have improved on it by putting, instead of "age and appearance indifferent", "faces so lost to age and aspect as to appear almost part of urns. But masks forbidden (!)." In French: "Visages sans âge et pour ainsi dire sans aspect, à peine plus différenciés que les jarres". It was only after getting back from Ulm that I made this change and wrote the note about the lighting. I have not yet passed them on to Tophoven, but shall do so forthwith - too late, alas, for your edition.[1]

It is difficult for actors, deprived of their normal means (toneless voices, expressionless faces) to express this Qual that you speak of, and to put across, in the 2 seconds at their disposal, the idea that speech is being literally wrung from them.[2] Certainly possible, but horribly difficult.

We have been here for a fortnight and are thinking of staying on until the middle of the month. The site is magnificent and we are very happy here.

I very much regret having missed Boehlich when he was passing through Paris.[3]

All good wishes
s/ Sam Beckett

1 After returning from rehearsals in Ulm where SB saw the play performed with three separate spotlights, one for each figure in its urn, he decided to change the stage direction to one single swivelling spotlight; a copy of the note about this change can be

found with 22 September 1963 to Christian Ludvigsen, below. SB also decided there to use the da capo ending, and to shorten the pauses.

The light change was made in "Spiel" as published in *Spectaculum* 6 (1963).

2 "Qual" (Ger., agony).

3 Walter Boehlich (1921–2006) was a senior editor at Suhrkamp Verlag until 1968; later, he was a literary editor and journalist. According to his letter of 19 June, Boehlich expected to be in Paris for a few hours on 26 June (Suhrkamp Verlag).

EDWARD BECKETT
DUBLIN

12.7.63 Zell am See

Dear Edward

Thanks for your letter. So sorry you didn't get the scholarship. But, as you say, the type-setter needs it more. But the confusion between musical & human merit is irritating and we can understand how fed-up you must be.[1]

I wrote to Belgrade and learn that my plays have earned for me there – & elsewhere – the sum of 72.094 dinars. This seems enormous to me, but I have no idea what it represents in £ or F. I don't think the dinar is quoted on exchange market.[2] However I'll find out roughly what it works out at. I have now written to the Jugoslav National Bank at Rijeka (Fiume) requesting that this sum be paid to you, at Rijeka, first fortnight of September, on presentation of your passport. They may not accept for the total amount, but there should be a good whack available. I'll let you know as soon as I hear from them.

There was a moment I feared French Happy Days might be down the drain because of PLAY, which the Barrault do not want running (?) at the same time & which Serreau insists on putting on in October. However to judge from a letter from Roger received yesterday things seem to have been settled and the Venice performances definite. There is also an invitation from Belgrade for two performances 1st week in October which can probably be accepted.

You should have sent Daro's bill straight away. I had a letter from the director threatening to put the law on me because I hadn't yet paid! I sent him the cheque from here, with a good stinker! Nice way to treat an old customer who always paid on the nail.[3]

Suzanne thinks you should be careful about taking lessons elsewhere, because of Crunelle's reaction should he hear of it. She may be right. I wouldn't know. Think about it before you do anything.

The weather has been poisonous, in spite of good days & good intervals, in the sense that we don't dare venture far in the mountains because of the sudden violent storms almost daily. And grand walks all the same, down by the lake when it's too dirty up here. Leaving Monday 15th, spending that night at Innsbruck, and back to Paris following afternoon – weather permitting tricky Innsbruck-Zürich flight. Rest of week in Paris and then I hope Ussy till the painter drives me away.

Remember me to Jimmy B. when next you're up and ask for news of his mother and sister. If the former dead (I suppose so) who's living in the little house?[4]

Much love to you all from us both.

s/Sam

ALS; 1 leaf, 2 sides; Edward Beckett Collection.

1 The bursary of the Musicians' Union of Ireland was awarded to a young clarinettist, who was working as an apprentice typesetter for a Dublin newspaper at that time (Edward Beckett to the editors, 17 May 2011).

2 In 1963, Yugoslavia accepted exchanges at a premium of 150 percent added to the official exchange rate; 1 pound equalled 840 dinars at the Official Exchange rate, and 2,100 dinars at the Uniform Exchange Rate (*Statistical Pocket-Book of Yugoslavia* [Beograd: Federal Institute for Statistics, May 1963] 227).

3 The travel agency Daro Voyages was situated near the Place de la Madeleine, Paris 8. Edward Beckett assumed, when he collected his tickets for Yugoslavia, that his uncle would be billed directly.

4 "Jimmy B" (1919–2008), son of James Barrett the golf professional at Carrickmines Golf Club (see Thursday [12 August 1948], n. 2), held what had been his father's post from 1959 to 1984. Golf Cottage, a small house beside the club house, was intended for the professional, but as James Barrett was married and lived elsewhere, his mother Mary Barrett (d. 1971) and her daughter Eleanor (known as Addie, d. 1983), who served as the Steward in the club, lived there.

ROMAN HAUBENSTOCK-RAMATI

le 31 juillet 1963

38 Bld. St. Jacques
Paris 14me

Cher Monsieur

J'ai bien reçu votre lettre du 25 juillet, votre partition CREDENTIALS et la bande magnétique de l'enregistrement. Je vous en remercie vivement.[1]

N'étant pas possesseur d'un magnétophone je n'ai pas pu encore écouter votre ouvrage. Je le ferai à la première occasion et vous écrirai de nouveau à ce moment-là.

Je suis très impressionné par l'organisation et par la beauté graphique de la partition, sans pouvoir hélas, d'une notation si nouvelle pour moi, dégager la moindre audition mentale.

Plutôt que de vous parler de la petite pièce donnée pour la première fois à Ulm et à laquelle vous me faites l'honneur de vous intéresser, je vais demander à mon éditeur allemand de vous envoyer la brochure. Les indications sur l'emploi du projecteur ne sont pas assez précises et seront corrigées lors de sa parution en librairie.

En vous renouvelant mes remerciements de votre envoi et de votre si gentille lettre, je vous prie de croire, cher Monsieur, à mes sentiments très cordialement dévoués.

s/ Samuel Beckett

TLS; 1 leaf, 1 side; *datestamped* 02.AUG.1963; Roman Haubenstock-Ramati Collection, Paul Sacher.

31 July 1963

38 Bld. St. Jacques
Paris 14

Dear Monsieur Haubenstock-Ramati

I have received your letter of 25th July, your score of *Credentials*, and the tape of the recording. I am most grateful.[1]

Not owning a tape recorder I have not yet been able to listen to your work. I shall do so at the earliest opportunity, and will then write to you again.

I am much impressed by the organisation and graphic beauty of the score, while alas unable, from so unfamiliar a notation, to arrive at even the faintest auditory representation of the piece as a whole.

Rather than talk to you about the little play, put on for the first time in Ulm, in which you do me the honour of showing an interest, I shall ask my German publisher to send you the booklet. The directions for the use of the spotlight are not precise enough, and will be corrected by the time it is out in the bookshops.

With my thanks again for your score and your kind letter, I am

Yours most sincerely
s/ Samuel Beckett

1 Roman Haubenstock-Ramati (1919–1994) composed *Credentials, or, "Think, think Lucky"* for voice and eight players; based on *Waiting for Godot*, it was written in 1961 and published by Universal Edition in Vienna in 1963.

MARY HUTCHINSON
LONDON

31.7.63 Paris

Dear Mary

Thanks for your letter.

Here it's the procession. Higgins, Nick, Caroline & girlfriends, Con Leventhal, Jacoba van Velde – et j'en passe.[1]

I had a week at Ussy cleaning up after the long absence. Saw quite a lot of Henri & Josette in good form – & his work getting under way. They told me about their evening with you which they greatly enjoyed.

I have seen nothing of Nadeau or Geneviève Serreau and don't know much about their set-up (new magazine). So fear I can't be much help. It boils down to finding the writers.[2] John Barber of Curtis Brown showed me an interesting TV play by a young

Australian Peter Kenna. You might ask him to show it to you and propose it to Nadeau if you like it.[3] Everybody will be away here all next month. But later on if I can be of any help I'll be only too pleased.

Rehearsals of Happy Days with Madeleine R. begin in about a fortnight. They open at Venice Theatre Festival Sept. 27th. Working with her & Blin should be interesting.[4] French PLAY (COMEDIE) will probably have its first series at Lausanne (Les Faux Nez) Jan. 64, before opening in Paris. Directed by Serreau whose double bill Les Bonnes with current actresses & Ionesco's Le Tableau is transferring to Théâtre de l'Oeuvre next month.[5]

No chance of getting to Scotland this year. Perhaps leaving for a week late October. I'll certainly be in Paris rehearsing at the time you mention – look forward to seeing you then.[6]

The National Theatre has approached George with a suggestion he should produce PLAY for them next Spring, with a Sophocles play. I like the idea and have asked for further details. I wd. of course be there for those rehearsals.[7]

Mendel is invited to do another production of Spiel for the Schiller Theater Werkstatt (Berlin), probably early next year, I don't yet know with what. His other production seems to have been more than creditable and I know exactly the mistakes that were made & which can be corrected.[8]

Edward missed his first scholarship, but he can manage without it. He will be going for a jaunt in Jugoslavia in September and will be in Venice for opening there. I was invited officially by Biennale people, but needless to say declined.

Take care of yourself.

Affectionately

Sam

ALS; 1 leaf, 2 sides; *env to* Mrs Hutchinson, 21 Hyde Park Square, London W.2, Angleterre; *pm* 1-8-63, Paris; TxU, Hutchinson, 2.6.

1 SB expected to see Aidan Higgins, Nick Rawson, his niece Caroline Murphy and other friends in Paris in the coming weeks. "Et j'en passe" (to name but a few).

2 In an undated draft of a letter to SB, Mary Hutchinson wrote that Geneviève Serreau had encouraged her to see Jean-Marie Serreau's production of Genet's *Les Bonnes*. She also told SB that she had been appointed to the Comité for English contributions to *Les Lettres Nouvelles*; her primary responsibility would be to suggest manuscripts for publication, and she invited SB's suggestions (TxU, Hutchinson Collection, drafts Mary Hutchinson to SB, n.d. [before 31 July]).

3 The play that SB had been shown, written by Peter Joseph Kenna (1930–1987), has not been identified. Nothing by him was published in *Les Lettres Nouvelles*.

4 The premiere of *Oh les beaux jours* was in Venice.

5 *Comédie* would not open in Lausanne. Serreau's production of *Les Bonnes* had opened with *Le Tableau* (*The Picture*) at the Théâtre de la Gaîté-Montparnasse in June; this production of *Les Bonnes* featured black actresses Morena Casamano, Toto Bissainthe, and Danielle Van Berchyche. The productions moved to the Théâtre de L'Œuvre from 24 August to 28 September.

6 Hutchinson had remarked (in her undated draft letter to SB mentioned in n. 2 above) that she frequently saw Marion Boyars Lobbenberg who had said that John Calder had invited SB to Scotland. Hutchinson planned to be in Paris from 30 August.

7 It was planned that George Devine would direct *Play* at the National Theatre (Old Vic) as a curtain raiser for Sophocles' *Philoctetes*.

8 Deryk Mendel would direct *Spiel* in Berlin in November.

BARBARA BRAY
LONDON

26.8.63 Paris

Dear Barbara

Your letter of Friday this morning.

Thursday evening is out, but Friday if that suits you, hour depending on rehearsal arrangements. I'll ring you Friday morning. Rehearsals not yet begun and no sign from either Blin or Madeleine. It's going to be Xmas after all I'm afraid, even if she does come almost word perfect. Not for Paris, but for Venice, which no doubt they regard as more rehearsals.[1] I saw Con Friday evening and drove him to Multicolor. We lost 200 cash. Having backed the star in vain for two hours it kicked us in the arse as we were crawling out.[2] Dinner last night with the Arikha. Dined in and then music. Bartok's piano concerto which I thought a bit flashy, then Haydn quartets, and Mozart's Dissenzen [*for* Dissonanzen] dedicated to him. He suddenly started drawing me slumped in the old fauteuil, in senseless absence. Gave me a very fine one.[3] Was hoping to have gone to Ussy Saturday & yesterday to fix up house, but paint not dry and at earliest tomorrow.[4] Shall have to switch rehearsals for this, if they begin tomorrow. Have started fiddling round with the lit face with nothing to show but notes & abandons. However something begun.[5] News from Schneider. Mostel interested in film & no companion yet found for play. Alan wd. like to do it with Harold's Lover but Harold wants this with something else of his own, how right he is.[6] Gloria rang after your evening with them to know could I see Jacky & Meredith Saturday 7th. Mais comment donc![7] Said you were looking flourishing. Shall not write again now before I see you. Reread Purdy's short stories – with intermittent pleasure.[8]

Love

Sam

surclassant

J'ai plus de souvenirs etc[9]

ALS; 1 leaf, 2 sides; *to* Mrs Bray, 24 Hallam Court, Hallam St., London W.1, Angleterre; *pm* 26-8-63, Paris; TCD, MS 10948/1/245.

1 SB overstates the delay in rehearsals, which he had expected to begin in the middle of August; he reported to Alan Schneider on 20 July, "Madeleine still very keen and according to Blin knows the text already!" (Burns Library, Samuel Beckett Collection, SB-AS; Beckett and Schneider, *No Author Better Served*, 138).

2 The roulette-like game of Multicolor has a star (étoile) which earns 24 times the stake.

3 Bartók wrote three piano concertos, and Haydn sixty-seven quartets. In 1785, Mozart published the String Quartets (nos. 14–19, written from 1782 to 1785) which he dedicated to Joseph Haydn. The last of these is Quartet no. 19 in C major ("Dissonance"), K. 465.

4 SB had removed furniture to prepare the cottage at Ussy for painting before 4 August, and now was anxious to put everything back in place (SB to Barbara Bray, 9 July 1963; TCD, MS 10948/1/239).

5 The lit face suggests SB's abandoned play *Kilcool* which describes a "Woman's face alone in constant light." S. E. Gontarski writes at length about the manuscript (TCD, MS 4664) in *The Intent of Undoing in Samuel Beckett's Dramatic Texts* (Bloomington: Indiana University Press, 1985) 134–142. SB wrote about his efforts to Alan Schneider on 25 August:

> I have started these last few days scratching round like an old hen in the desert for the structures and text of that face play I told you about. Nothing so far but dubious notes and false starts. Impossible to get down to it properly till rehearsals are out of the way and I can get to Ussy. I have never undertaken anything so tenuous and at the same time so complex. It may take years. So no point in suggesting you wait for it to do with PLAY. It will probably be so short in any case that you would still need something to send them full empty away. (Burns Library, Samuel Beckett Collection, SB-AS; Beckett and Schneider, *No Author Better Served*, 139–140.)

6 Zero Mostel had read the script of SB's *Film* with Alan Schneider (NYPL, Billy Rose, T MSS 1993-007, Box 16, F 2, 5).

Harold Pinter's *The Lover* (1962) is a one-act play in which a couple indulges their fantasy of a love triangle where the husband also assumes the role of a lover.

7 SB wrote to Bray on 5 July that Schneider had offered to present MacGowran in the United States with Burgess Meredith and Mel Ferrer. "This all pending my new piece for him." (TCD, MS 10948/1/237.) Meredith also had plans to direct recordings of Beckett's texts with Jack MacGowran and Patrick Magee for Columbia Records, which SB had approved on 2 June (SB to John Barber, Curtis Brown; GEU, MSS 1221; SB to Alan Schneider, 20 July; Burns Library, Samuel Beckett Collection, SB-AS; Beckett and Schneider, *No Author Better Served*, 139). By 20 August, however, this recording project had been cancelled by Curtis Brown (SB to Barbara Bray; TCD, MS 10498/1/243).

"Mais comment donc!" (Well of course I would).

8 James Purdy (1914–2009) had sent SB his collection of stories, *Color of Darkness* (1957); SB thanked Purdy: "I think it is very fine and I look forward keenly to your next work" (2 August 1958; CtY, Beinecke, MS 44, 1.4). Purdy's most recent collection was *Children is All* (1962).

9 "Surclassant" (outdoing). "J'ai plus de souvenirs. . . "("I have more memories . . .") is the opening line from Charles Baudelaire's poem "Spleen" (Baudelaire, *Œuvres complètes*, I, 73; Baudelaire, *Les Fleurs du Mal: The Complete Text of The Flowers of Evil*, 75).

BARBARA BRAY
LONDON

8.9.63 Paris

Dear Barbara

Thanks for yours of Friday.

Rose grey nags. But jades is what I meant. Take them over day after tomorrow.[1]

Very shaky this morning after two late nights, one very, very pleasant evening yesterday with Jacky & Con. Didn't get much work done with Jacky, but pulled out of the old black bag an idea for his show which should help. He had come straight from Louis M^{c}N.

memorial service at St John's, alleviated by Sussex v. Middlesex at Lord's. I think he is off with Con to Longchamp this afternoon.[2] I have to crawl out now to lunch with Mary Hutchinson, and this evening billiards & dinner with Trochee again. Have found for him a charming little 2 vol. edition of Sophocles in Greek that belonged to Herriot.[3]

Rehearsals going comme ci comme ça. The impossible vivacity gets me down a bit. Yesterday feeling like death I did Willie's 4 stage journey for them, with nose & balls in the dust. They enjoyed it. Barrault crawls too high.[4]

9.9.63

Waked by Alan Schneider calling from London. He can't get over. Asked him to send us the musical box. He spoke of some play by Martin Walser as a possible companion piece to PLAY.[5] Got through evening without encombre.[6] Billiards & the Iles. Then drive to Montmartre & home.

AL; 1 leaf, 1 side; *env to* Mrs Bray, 24 Hallam Court, Hallam St., London W.1, Angleterre; *pm* 9-9-63, Paris; TCD, MS 10948/1/248.

1 SB was to take delivery of a new Citroën 2CV which he refers to in a previous letter to Bray as "rose grey nags," and here as "jades" (4 September 1963; TCD, MS 10948/2/246).

2 A later letter to MacGowran throws some light on SB's suggestion: "That idea needs working out more fully, but it should be useful. I have asked Grove Press (Dick Seaver) to send you a copy of The End." (17 September 1963; TxU, Beckett Collection, 9.3.)

SB wrote to Bray on 6 September: "Saw of MacNeice's death in Monde. Con upset. Knew first wife & daughter." (TCD, MS 10948/1/247.) Louis MacNeice (1907–1963), poet, playwright, and BBC producer, died on 3 September; his funeral was held at St. John's Wood Church on 7 September. On the same day, Sussex played Worcestershire (not Middlesex) at Lord's Cricket Ground ("Final Abounds in Promise," *The Times* 7 September 1963: 4). Longchamp Racecourse is in the Bois de Boulogne.

3 SB had given the classicist Stuart Maguinness the nickname of Trochee after a scholarly study that he had done: "Very good burst from MacGuinness [sic] on dactyls & trochees" (SB to Barbara Bray, [9 December 1962]; TCD, MS 10948/213; Stuart Maguinness, "Petit Plaidoyer pour la poésie trochaïque," *Rivista di cultura classica e medioevale*, II [Rome: Edizioni del'Ateneo, 1963]).

French politician and bibliophile Edouard Herriot (1872–1957).

4 Speaking of Madeleine Renaud's Winnie, SB wrote to Herbert Myron, also on 8 September: "She'll make something of it in her own way – i.e. on the light side for this hardened sorrower" (MBU, Myron). When Willie emerges from his hole, he does so in a series of movements and halts (Beckett, *Happy Days*, 61).

5 Alan Schneider was in London to make arrangements for a production of Edward Albee's *Who's Afraid of Virginia Woolf* at the Piccadilly Theatre. He and Albee had been at the Edinburgh International Festival where *The Rabbit Race*, a play by Martin Walser (b. 1927), had its British premiere; it was published in 1963 by John Calder.

6 "Encombre" (hitch).

RUBY COHN
SAN FRANCISCO

9.9.63 Paris

Dear Ruby Cohn

Thanks for your letter.

"Il n'a pas souvent retourné du coeur. ." "There hasn't been much talk about the heart". Derived from the common "de quoi retourne-t-il?" A very hasardous [sic] tournure which no French man would commit.[1]

"Et qui a honte etc." Yes, its "le" refers to the question or questions as to who is the one who "a honte etc" and who the one "Tout le silence etc".[2]

Feminine insignes is an error.[3]

I presume you know that Krapp's Last Tape was written in English & that "La dernière Bande" is my translation.

With all good wishes,

Yrs. sincerely

Sam. Beckett

ALS; 1 leaf, 1 side; UoR, BIF, MS 5100/6.

1 In *Textes pour rien* (XIII) SB writes: "Vrai il n'a pas souvent retourné du cœur, au propre, au figuré, mais ce n'est pas une raison pour espérer" (*Nouvelles et Textes pour rien* [Paris: Editions de Minuit, 1955] 218); in "Texts for Nothing 13," untranslated as yet, this line becomes: "True there was never much talk of the heart, literal or figurative, but that's no reason for hoping" (*Stories and Texts for Nothing* [Grove] 138–139).

2 In *Textes pour rien* (XIII) SB writes:

> Et qui a honte, à chaque muet millionième de syllabe, et inextinguible infini de remords se creusant, morsure dans morsure, de devoir entendre, de devoir dire, en deçà du moindre murmure, tant de mensonges, tant de fois le même mensonge et mensongèrement démenti, qui dont le silence hurlant est plaie de oui et couteau de non, elle se le demande (219).

In *Texts for Nothing* 13:

> And whose the shame, at every mute micromillisyllable, and unslakable infinity of remorse delving ever deeper in its bite, as having to hear, having to say, fainter than the faintest murmur, so many lies, so many times the same lie lyingly denied, whose the screaming silence of no's knife in yes's wound, it wonders (139).

3 In *Textes pour rien* (VIII), SB writes: "Ces insignes, si j'ose dire, avancent de concert, comme reliées par le traditionnel excipient humain, s'immobilisent, repartent, confirmées par les vastes vitrines" (137). The error stands uncorrected in subsequent printings of the text.

HERBERT MYRON
CAMBRIDGE, MASSACHUSETTS

18.9.63 Paris

Dear Herbert

I have made a French translation of PLAY (Comédie), but it will not be published before performance probably early next year. I have given it to Serreau. Faber will publish it about same time, together with Cascando & WORDS & Music, 2 short pieces for radio comportant musique by Mihalovici & John Beckett respectively.[1] In London the National Theatre has invited Devine to direct PLAY for them in March, in a double bill with Sophocles' Philoctetes. That's all I can tell you about French & English publication & performance set-up. In N.Y. talk of its production with a wild affair by a young negro entitled Funnyhouse of a Negro, possibly in November, more likely next year. Barr sent me MS of Funnyhouse to read. I told him it was beyond me, but by all means to go ahead.[2]

Crawling out now in the Homer mauve for a coupe and a blather at the Closerie.[3]

Rehearsals going well. Madeleine a cross between Agnès & Mme Sans-Gêne.[4]

Best ever

Sam

I gave yr. address to Pinget who will be seeking your advice on a lecture tour on Max Jacob. Do your best for him[.][5]

ALS; 1 leaf, 1 side; *env to* Mr Herbert Myron, 8 Plympton St., Cambridge, Mass, USA; *pm* 19-9-63, Paris; MHU: bMS Thr 32.

1 Publication of *Play*: SB to Avigdor Arikha and Anne Atik, 1 July 1963, n. 4. The first publication of *Comédie* would be in *Les Lettres Nouvelles* nouvelle série (3) 12 (June-July-August 1964) 10–31. *Play, and Two Short Pieces for Radio* would be published by Faber and Faber on 26 March 1964, a slim volume of 48 pages.

2 SB wrote on this date to both the New York Producer Richard Barr and Alan Schneider about *Funnyhouse of a Negro* by Adrienne Kennedy (b. 1931). The play would open on 14 January 1964 at the East End Theatre, New York, directed by Michael Kahn; it would receive the Obie award for "Most Distinguished Play" in 1964.

3 The person whom SB met at the Closerie des Lilas has not been identified.

4 Agnès is the ingenue in Molière's *L'Ecole des femmes*. Madame Sans-Gêne is the sobriquet given to Catherine Hubscher (1753–1835), who came to court as the wife of François Joseph Lefebvre (Marshal of France and Duke of Dantzig). Her lack of courtly manners led to this nickname. Victorien Sardou and Emile Moreau wrote a play entitled *Madame Sans-Gêne* (1893) that was made into a silent film starring Gloria Swanson (1924), later remade with Arletty (1941), and again with Sophia Loren (1961).

5 The postscript is hand-written horizontally across the left margin. Robert Pinget planned to make a tour in the US to speak on French writer and painter Max Jacob (1876–1944), including a lecture at La Maison Française, New York University, on 2 April 1964 ("Events Today," *New York Times* 2 April 1964: 29).

14. Suzanne Beckett, Thomas MacGreevy, Matias, in Venice for the premiere of *Oh les beaux jours*, September 1963

CHRISTIAN LUDVIGSEN
GENTOFTE, DENMARK

22.9.63 Paris

Dear Chr. Ludvigsen

Ash and Snodland: simple place names. In French: par Sept-Sorts et Signy-Signet.[1]

Hellish half-light: half way through the play the spot is reduced to half previous strength, with corresponding lowering of voices. This is the half-light that W1 finds hellish. Cf. her lines: "Dying for dark – and the darker the worse . . ." No quotation involved.[2]

Bonfire: associated with Nov. 5th (Guy Fawkes Day) when they "burn the guy". But no allusion to this here. It is a simple fire lit in gardens at this season to burn fallen leaves and which commonly smoulders on for days.[3]

Never woke together: Related to his previous line: "To think we (all three) were never together (on earth) . . ." He has this fantasy of how they might all three have lived together, slept and woke together, gone rowing together on the river on a May morning. Because they never did – "we were not civilized". French: Nous ne savions pas vivre.[4]

Why go down: In the second part they all speak to the light as to an animated being. This should be quite clear from text. M's question is interrupted by the spot leaving him and resumed when he next speaks. The same effect exactly is obtained in German translation. Cf. W2's "You might get angry and blaze me clean out of my wits". It is the loss of reason theme.[5]

Light: The light may be thought of as an inquisitorial intelligence. Throughout the second part the three characters speculating on its nature and exigencies, address it directly What does it want of them? Why does it go down? Why does it go out? Is it not mere mindless eye? Etc.[6]

It should be clear from the text that each one thinks that he or she is alone in this place and the other two left behind in the light of the sun. When the light leaves W1 for example, and until it solicits her again, there is for her complete dark and silence. Light on the others is no light for her and the voices of the others make no sound for her. The same for the other two.

The light should have a probing quality, like an accusing finger levelled at them one after another. This is obtained by a single pivoting spot and not, as in Ulm, by three fixed independent spots, one for each face, switching on and off as required.[7] This mobile spot should be set mechanically once and for all so as to strike full on its successive targets without fumbling and move from one to another at maximum speed. It should be worked by an invisible operator with perfect knowledge of text, either by electric control from wings or manually from a kind of prompter's box below footlights. The ideal position for spot is at centre of footlights. It belongs to world of characters and cannot emanate from any part of auditorium space. My first idea was to have it incorporated in some way in the urns and operated by actors themselves. This is unsatisfactory because of additional strain on them and because it is not enough merely to illuminate the faces, they must be "fusillés" by a visible swivelling beam.[8]

I enclose note on light to be incorporated in published text, in case you do not have it.

Da capo: its efficacy depends on speed at which the piece is taken. Everything must be sacrificed to this. Reduce pauses if necessary. The fragments of speech should follow on one another so fast, and the light extort them with such urgency, in a kind of feverish discontinuity, as to leave the audience confused, at the end of the first time through, and not averse to a restatement. If the pace is too deliberate and comprehension too easy, the repeat will be irksome.

Kind regards to your wife and to your father.

Yours

s/ Sam Beckett

Note on light

The source of light is single and must not be situated outside the ideal space (starge [*for* stage]) occupied by its victims.

The optimum position for spot is at centre of footlights, the faces being thus lit at close quarters and from below.

When exceptionally three spots are required to light the three faces simultansouly [sic], they should be as a single spot branching into three.

The method consisting in assigning to each face a separate fixed spot is unsati[s]factory in that it is less expressive than the single pivoting spot of a unique inquisitor.

TLS; 3 leaves, 3 sides; T *env to* Chr. Ludvigsen <Vangede Bygade 82, Gentofte, Danemark> *forwarded to* P.T. Hoffungarde, Aumborg, Heiming; *pm* 23-9-63, Paris; Ludvigsen Collection.

1 The English text is from the Faber and Faber edition of *Play*; "Comédie" is from the first publication in *Les Lettres Nouvelles*, 10–31.
Play, 14. *Comédie*, 19.

2 *Play*, 15, 16: "Hellish half-light." *Comédie*, 20, 29: "Lueur infernale."

3 *Play*, 15. *Comédie*, 29: "les feuilles mortes."

4 *Play*, 20, 21. *Comédie*, 28, 29.

5 *Play*, 19. *Comédie*, 26–27. Beckett, *Spiel; ein Akt*, 14–15.
Play, 16. *Comédie*, 21–22.

6 *Play*, 15. *Comédie*, 19.

7 The change in the stage directions for the lights from those used at the premiere of *Spiel* in Ulm: SB to Siegfried Unseld, 1 July 1963.

8 "Fusillés" (shot).

DULAN BARBER
JOHN CALDER (PUBLISHER) LTD., LONDON

October 20th 1963 38 Bld. St.-Jacques
Paris 14me

Dear Mr Barber

Thank you for letter and proofs which I shall return to you tomorrow.[1]

Take first example (A.20). If the line is carried over in the way you suggest, it is not clear – typographically – whether <u>since</u> belongs to the line beginning "I pissed" or is a separate element. There must always appear at foot of page either a line less than full or a line carried over by a hyphen to following page. The only way in which this line may be carried over is therefore:

foot of page

I pissed and shat in my crib never so clean sin-

top of following page

ce

This being unsightly, only two solutions are possible: either that the line be brought back by resetting so as to gain at least one point, making clear its separation from what follows at top of next page, or that I shorten the line by correction. This holds for all the other examples of this error, the final word of the line involved lending itself in no case to hyphenation.[2]

If it is possible to shorten all these lines by resetting, this is the solution I prefer. But in case it is not, you may correct them as follows:

"I pissed and shat another image in my crib never so clean since" (A-20)

Replace clean by pure.

"I don't like to touch myself they haven't left me that this time" (A-22)

Replace don't like by am loath.

"wafted straight to Abraham's bosom I'd tell him to stick it up" (A-31)

Replace wafted by rapt.

"the signal for the mud to open under me and then close again" (A-31)

Replace signal by sign.

"news of my mishap wherewith to spew him out another week" (A-35)

Replace spew him out by vomit him.

"the circle of friends in their white dhotis without going that far" (A-37)

Replace circle by knot.

"lousy same as three eight encore same as one or two as may be" (A-42)

Replace lousy by crap.

"all I didn't say it I didn't know it then my own I didn't say it" (A-51)

Replace I don't know by didn't know.

"now the third fourth and first now the second third and fourth" (A-64)

Replace now the third by now third and now the second by now second, and correct similarly previous "paragraph" to read "now first second and third now fourth first and second".

Yours sincerely
s/ Sam. Beckett
Samuel Beckett

TLS; 2 leaves, 2 sides; InU, C&B, Beckett.

1 Dulan Barber was responsible for communication with the printer, in this case on corrections of page proofs for *How It Is*. Page proofs: C&B, Beckett, 60.18–20.

2 *How It Is* introduced two oddities that presented typesetting problems: no end punctuation, and stanzas of text divided by an extra line space. All of the concerns were resolved typographically in the Calder edition, without resort to changes of wording.

LAWRENCE HARVEY
HANOVER, NEW HAMPSHIRE

28.10.63 Paris

Dear Larry

Glad to have your letter with all your news.

Your essay on my "aesthetics" seems to me the very best and most indulgent that could be made of such wild and wretched material. There is no comment I wish to make, except to confirm that "Les 2 Besoins" has never been (and never will be) published and to suggest that you seem to have slipped up, most pardonably, on the "grand Thomas", by whom I meant Masaccio (Tommaso Guidi).[1] All my critical work, including Joyce and Proust essays, was à mon corps défendant, which may go to explain, if not to excuse, its prevailing tone of cantankerous overstatement.[2] Grove have not published, so far as I know, any of the texts you quote, so no problemn [sic] of copyright there.

I saw Rosset. He said that his plans for the triple film are developing. My script is in long ago, Ionesco's now, Pinter's not yet. Mostel would like to play mine if his commitments permit. Actual shooting still remote I should think.[3] N.Y. production of my new short play PLAY will probably be next March, with Pinter's THE LOVER, at the Cherry Lane.[4] Madeleine opened well last Monday and Tuesday, has her third avant-première tonight and faces what she calls "les affreux" (crrritics) tomorrow.[5] I have no new work in hand or in view. I must get to Ussy for a long spell. This Paris life is just a long tottering by the wayside.

I look forward to seeing you all again 64–65. I have no advice worth offering as to where you should make your head-quarters, but agree that if one can't be right in Paris it is better to be way out. I would of course be at your disposal at any time, for talk I hope about any old thing under the sun but me.

Affectionately to you all.
s/ Sam

The Hayden are in good form. His summer in the country produced 40 paintings and a dozen gouaches!

TLS; 1 leaf, 1 side; T *env to* Mr L., *upper left corner* Par Avion; Harvey, 3 Tyler Road, Hanover, New Hampshire, USA; *pm* 30–10–63, Paris; NhD, Beckett Collection, MS 122/1.6.

1 SB refers to Lawrence Harvey's article "Samuel Beckett on Life, Art, and Criticism," *Modern Language Notes (MLN)*, 80 (December 1965) 545–562. Harvey had asked about permissions for quotations from "Les Deux Besoins," "La Peinture des van Velde ou le monde et le pantalon," "Peintres de l'empêchement," and "Three Dialogues." Harvey's reference to "grand Thomas" does not appear in the published text, nor is there a reference to Masaccio.

2 "A mon corps défendant" (wrung out of me).

3 Ionesco's script for the film project "The Hard Boiled Egg"

> was written in a Manhattan hotel room on 57th Street during a blizzard, and represents Ionesco's bemused reaction to American television commercials. Interspersed with an attractive model's instructions on how to hard-boil an egg, pease porridge transforms into lava cascading down a mountainside, carrots grow to monumental size, rivers burst into flame and a two-headed eagle is sautéed alive.

Pinter's contribution would be "The Compartment"; this was later expanded and filmed in 1967 by the BBC as *The Basement*" (Paul Cullum, "Samuel Beckett is Ready for his Close-up," *The New York Times*, 4 December 2005, section 2: 15.)

Mostel's interest in SB's *Film*: 26 August 1963 and n. 6.

4 Harold Pinter wrote to Alan Schneider on 18 October: "Well, I'm very glad indeed that everyone seems happy about 'The Lover' and 'Play'. Incidentally, what about sending me a copy of 'Play'. I haven't read it. But, needless to say, I'm happy about the arrangement without reading it." (NyPL, Billy Rose, Barr-Wilder T-MSS 1978–002, Box 1, Folder 5.)

5 Madeleine Renaud played *Oh les beaux jours* at the Odéon-Théâtre de France, with the opening for the critics on 29 October. "Les affreux" (the horrors).

MADELEINE RENAUD
PARIS

1.11.63 Paris

Bien chère Madeleine

Merci de tout coeur pour votre mot qui m'a profondément ému. Vous avez été merveilleuse. Je vous dis brava bravissima et vous embrasse bien affectueusement, en attendant de pouvoir le faire mardi prochain.[1]

Sam

ACS; 1 leaf, 1 side; BNF, Arts-Spectacles, Compagnie Madeleine Renaud – Jean-Louis Barrault.

1.11.63 Paris

My dear Madeleine

Thank you with all my heart for your note, which affected me deeply. You have been marvellous. I'm saying to you "brava, bravissima", and I'm giving you an affectionate hug – till I can actually do it in person next Tuesday.[1]

Sam

1 On the same day, 1 November, SB wrote to Patrick Magee: "The opening of Happy Days went well, Madeleine had her triumph and the press was good with the gratifying exception of Monsieur Gauthier [sic]" (TCD, MS 11313/9). Jean-Jacques Gautier wrote: "Tel est ce festival d'abjection. Jamais nous n'avions atteint à tant de complaisance dans l'horrible. Lucidité? Non. Sadisme." ("'Oh! Les beaux jours' de Samuel Beckett, à l'Odéon," *Le Figaro* 30 October 1963: 20.) (Such is this festival of abjectness. Never before had we sunk to such easy indulgence in the horrible. Lucidity? No. Sadism.)

CHARLES MONTEITH
FABER AND FABER, LONDON

November 15th 1963 38 Bld. St.-Jacques
Paris 14me

Dear Charles

Thanks for your letter of November 7th.

I alone am responsible for the bowlers and the note concerning them.[1]

While on the subject of GODOT there is something I should like to ask you. The version published by you is the playing version authorized by the Lord Chamberlain and differs considerably from the unexpurgated version published by Grove. I appreciate the necessity of there being available in England a text securing theatre managements from trouble with the censorship. At the same time one is depressed by the mutilations involved and which so weaken the meaning in certain places as to make it scarcely intelligible. I have been wondering recently if it would not be possible, now that there seems to be a more liberal view of what may be said on the stage than when GODOT was first purified, to bring your version closer to the original. I suppose this would involve resubmission of the play Grove edition to the Lord Chamberlain's office with the suggestion that they deal with it less puritanically than – is it 7 years ago already? If such an application were ever partially successful it would mean a completely new edition of the work and this perhaps – and very understandably – you might not feel inclined to undertake. The whole question was brought forcibly to my mind by the first volume just published of Suhrkamp's trilingual edition of my plays in which he has used quite unnecessarily your text instead of the integral one.[2] I should be grateful if you would talk the matter over with Peter and let me know what you think.[3] If you feel things are better left as they are I shall not bring it up again.

I received yesterday the proofs of PLAY etc. and hope to let you have them back by the end of next week. I am afraid I shall have to make some rather important changes in the stage directions of

PLAY. If they seem to you excessive please charge them to my account.

With best greetings to Peter,

Yours ever

s/ Sam

TLS; 1 leaf, 1 side; The Faber Archive.

1 On behalf of Professor John Lawlor of Keele University (1918–1999), Charles Monteith had written to SB on 7 November to ask if he had written the footnote "All four wear bowlers" in the 1956 Faber and Faber edition of *Waiting for Godot* (33; the Faber and Faber Archive).

2 *Dramatische Dichtungen 1*: 4 June 1962, n. 2. On 10 November, SB had reviewed the English and the French texts in this volume, and wrote to Siegfried Unseld:

> Il y a une erreur majeure, cher ami, que je suis désolé d'avoir à vous signaler. Pour le texte anglais de GODOT vous avez suivi l'édition de Faber. Or cette version est celle autorisée par le Lord Chamberlain et comporte d'assez nombreux changements et coupures, au point d'être par moments à peine intelligible. Une telle édition a sa raison d'être uniquement en Angleterre, dans la mesure où les théâtres anglais désirant monter la pièce savent qu'ils peuvent l'utiliser sans risque d'histoires avec la censure, alors qu'ils ne pourraient présenter le texte intégral, tel que Grove Press le publie, sans le soumettre de nouveau à l'approbation du Lord Chamberlain. C'est bien entendu le texte de Grove Press qui aurait dû figurer dans votre édition. (DLA, Suhrkamp, VL Samuel Beckett: 1962–1964.)
>
> (There is one major error which I am very sorry to have to point out to you. For the English text of *Godot* you have followed the Faber edition. But this version is the one authorised by the Lord Chamberlain, and contains a good many changes and cuts, so many indeed as to be at moments barely intelligible. An edition of this sort has no raison d'être outside England, in so far as English theatres wanting to stage the play know that they may use it without running into trouble with the censors, whereas they could not stage the uncut text, as published by Grove Press, without once again submitting it for the Lord Chamberlain's approval. It is of course the Grove Press text which should have appeared in your edition.)

3 When Faber and Faber published *Waiting for Godot*, SB had expressed disappointment that the edition was truncated (see 27 February 1956). On 3 February 1957, SB had again raised the matter with Monteith: "I fully appreciate the difficult position you were in last year with the publication of Godot – n'en parlons plus. Perhaps some day you may print the complete version" (The Faber Archive). "N'en parlons plus" (Let's hear no more about it).

On 18 November 1963, prompted by SB's recent letter, Charles Monteith suggested to Peter du Sautoy that the next theatre group wishing to perform *Waiting for Godot* approach the Lord Chamberlain's office for permission to use the original version, and that, if this was successful, Faber and Faber consider publishing the unexpurgated text (The Faber Archive). A new edition would be under way by 13 January 1964, when SB sent a copy of the 1954 Grove Press edition indicating words to restore. (This copy, inscribed as owned by Monteith, is now held by Columbia University's Rare Book Library [SB to Monteith, 13 January 1964; The Faber Archive]).

ALAN SCHNEIDER
HASTINGS-ON-HUDSON, NEW YORK

November 19th 1963 Paris

My very dear Alan

I know your sorrow and I know that for the likes of us there is no ease for the heart to be had from words or reason and that in the very assurance of sorrow's fading there is more sorrow. So I offer you only my deeply affectionate and compassionate thoughts and wish for you only that the strange thing may never fail you, whatever it is, that gives us the strength to live on and on with our wounds.[1]

Ever
s/ Sam

TLS; 1 leaf, 1 side; Burns Library, Samuel Beckett Collection, SB-AS. TL copy; 1 leaf, 1 side; CUSD, MSS 103/1/22. Previous publication: Schneider, *Entrances*, 340; Beckett and Schneider, *No Author Better Served*, 142.

1 Alan Schneider's father died on 12 November. In his letter of 27 November to SB, Schneider responded: "I shall never be able to tell you what your letter meant to me – especially as it happened to come the day president Kennedy was killed. All I can say is thank you for understanding so well." (Burns Library, Samuel Beckett Collection, AS-SB; Beckett and Schneider, *No Author Better Served*, 146.)

ALAN SCHNEIDER
HASTINGS-ON-HUDSON, NEW YORK

26.11.63 Paris

Dear Alan

Thanks for your letter. I did not know that you yourself had been ill and am greatly relieved to know you are better. You drive yourself too hard.

I am perplexed about PLAY and so find this letter very difficult to write. I realize that no final script is possible till I have had work on rehearsals. And as those with Serreau will not begin till after yours, all I can do is try and tell you my doubts and leave final decisions to you.

Suzanne went to Berlin for Deryk's second production and did not like it. But when I saw Deryk himself on his return he was very pleased. It seems in any case to have been well received. They arrived at the incredible speed of 25 minutes, with repeat.[1]

The problems still are:

1. Urns
2. Lighting.
3. Faces
4. Voices.
5. Da capo.

1. Deryk's urns have their unpleasant bulging shape because the actors are sitting. The ideal is urns trapped and actors standing. If this not possible I am coming round to the idea of actors standing and full length urns as closely fitting as possible and mounted or not on hollow plinth about knee height.

Possibly by means of painting (darkened contours) reduce apparent volume of urns.

Disadvantage: they will no longer appear to be touching. Urns open of course behind. If full length bring them back from front toward midstage. Obviously the smaller the actors the better.

2. Deryk said he had got his spot pivoting and moving fast. Suzanne did not feel much speed and said there was little visible beam. There should be a pencil (finger) of light snapping from face to face. But we have been through all this. Deryk worked out some system which I don't understand and can't explain. The man on the light should be regarded as a fourth player and must know the text inside and out. I don't mind if the spot hits from above, provided it does not involve auditorium space. Light, W1, W2 and M belong to the same separate world.

When the play begins, and before spots provoke opening "chorus", there is faint general light in which the urns are just discernible as vague shapes. Enough of this behind them would help kill the shadows. The best background is that which best suggests empty unlit space.

3. Suzanne found the faces excessively made up and characterized: aging missus and exciting mistress, etc. This would be completely wrong. There [*for* they] are all in the same dinghy at last and should be as little differentiated as possible. Three grey disks.

4. I don't see much to add to what I tried to explain when we talked about it. I ask for complete expressionless[ness] except for W2's two laughs and W1's single vehemence.[2] This may be excessive. I simply can't know till I work on it in the theatre. You must feel yourself free to mitigate it if it seems to you desirable. Voices grey and abstract as the faces, grey as cinders – that is what seems to me right. I may be wrong.

5. I still am not absolutely sure that this is right. I think it is, if the movement is fast enough. I asked Deryk to cut all the pauses. Speech reaction to light stimulus now instantaneous, i.e. all those three second pauses cancelled with sacrifice of effect of <u>effort to speak</u> and all the five seconds reduced to two or three.[3] Everything for the sake of speed if you adopt the da capo. If you decide against it then obviously you should play it slower.

I find it practically impossible to write such a letter. What matters is that you feel the spirit of the thing and the intention as you do. Give them that as best you can, even if it involves certain deviations from what I have written and said.

The actual lines to be spoken are practically without change. I shall send you this week the latest "final" text.

London rehearsals begin May 9th. George has not been well, but is better.

Enthusiastically in favour of McGowran if Mostel falls through.[4]

Bon courage.

Yours ever

s/ Sam

TLS; 2 leaves, 2 sides; Burns Library, Samuel Beckett Collection, SB-AS. ALS draft; 1 side, 1 leaf; GEU, MS 1221. T transcription; 2 leaves, 2 sides; NSyU: Grove Press Records [with errors of transcription]. Previous publication: Beckett and Schneider, *No Author Better Served*, 144–146.

1 Deryk Mendel directed *Spiel* at the Schiller-Theater-Werkstatt, Berlin; it opened on 16 November.

2 W2 laughs at two points: (Faber, 21). W1's vehement retort: "Get off me!" (Faber, 16).

3 SB underscored "effort to speak" in blue ink.

4 Zero Mostel was willing to play in *Film* if his schedule permitted, but Schneider had written to SB on 21 November: "What do you think of Jack MacGowran if we can't pin down Mr. M.?" (Burns Library, Samuel Beckett Collection, AS-SB; Beckett and Schneider, *No Author Better Served*, 143).

RUBY COHN
SAN FRANCISCO

7.12.63 Paris

Dear Miss Cohn

Thank you for your letter of December 1st.

"Et qui a honte etc." I don't grasp your difficulty. "Honte" and "inextinguible infini de remords se creusant" are objects of "qui a". "Morsure" because "remords" is a bite. "A chaque millionième etc" a subordinate of occasion (my expression). A rough free translation would be: "And who burns with shame, at every mute millionth of every syllable, and with inextinguishable infinite of remorse delving deeper and deeper in its bites, to have to hear etc."[1]

By all means quote me on "... retourné du coeur".[2]

Krapp's Effie is indeed Effie [*for* Effi] Briest.[3]

PLAY was written in English, The French title is COMEDIE.

I look forward greatly to meeting you next summer.

Yours sincerely
s/ Sam. Beckett
Samuel Beckett

TLS; 1 leaf, 1 side; UoR, BIF, MS 5100/7.

1 For the source of SB's text, see 9 September 1963, n. 1.

2 No record has been found in Cohn's published works that she quoted SB about "retourné du coeur."

3 Krapp recollects reading Theodor Fontane's novel *Effi Briest*: "Scalded the eyes out of me reading *Effie* again, a page a day, with tears again" (Beckett, *Krapp's Last Tape* [Grove Press] 25).

CHRONOLOGY 1964

1964	4 January	*Play* opens at the Cherry Lane Theatre, New York, directed by Alan Schneider, on a double bill with Pinter's *The Lover*.
	16 January – 5 February	SB in London for rehearsals of *Endgame* with Patrick Magee and Jack MacGowran.
	25 January	Attends playback of *Cascando*, recorded in Stuttgart.
	28 January	Attends the opening night of Max Frisch's play *Andorra* at the Old Vic.
	29 January	Attends *Theatre of Cruelty* productions organized by Charles Marowitz and Peter Brook, at LAMDA.
	4 February	Attends dress rehearsal of *Who's Afraid of Virginia Woolf*, directed by Alan Schneider, Piccadilly Theatre.
	17 February	*Endgame* with MacGowran and Magee opens at the Studio des Champs-Elysées.
	24 February	SB declines Goddard Lieberson's invitation to contribute to a homage to John F. Kennedy.
	14 March	In London for rehearsals of *Play*.
	21–22 March	Spends weekend with George Devine and Jocelyn Herbert at their farm, "Andrews," in Hampshire.
	7 April	*Play* opens at the National Theatre, Old Vic, on a double bill with Sophocles' *Philoctetes*.
	8 April	SB returns from London to Paris.
	10 April	Writes tribute to Brendan Behan for *Theater heute*.

14 April	Resumes rehearsals of *Comédie*, directed by Serreau.
21 April	Gisèle Freund photographs SB.
30 April	John Calder (Publisher) Ltd. publish *How It Is*.
20 May	Henri Cartier-Bresson photographs SB.
June	*Les Lettres Nouvelles* publish *Comédie*.
11 June	*Comédie* opens at the Pavillon de Marsan, as part of the Estival 1964, directed by Jean-Marie Serreau assisted by SB.
12 June	Nelson Mandela sentenced to life imprisonment in South Africa.
29 June	SB in London to assist director Donald McWhinnie with rehearsals of *Endgame* for the Aldwych Theatre.
9 July	*Endgame* opens at the Aldwych produced by the Royal Shakespeare Company.
10 July	SB flies from London to New York for work on *Film*. *Murphy*, published by John Calder (Publisher) Ltd., is banned in Ireland.
11–12 July	SB stays at Barney Rosset's home in East Hampton, works with Alan Schneider and cameraman Boris Kaufman on plans for *Film*.
20 July	Shooting of *Film* begins on location in New York.
23 July	SB attends *Dutchman* by LeRoi Jones (later Amiri Baraka) and *The American Dream* by Edward Albee at the Cherry Lane Theatre.
30 July	Final day of shooting of *Film*.
1 and 2 August	SB works with Sidney Meyers, the editor of *Film*.
6 August	Flies to Paris.
15 August	Death of Leslie Daiken, in London.
by 21 August	SB has begun to write first of four pieces which will later be called "Faux départs."

18 September	Death of Sean O'Casey.
6 October	BBC Third Programme broadcasts *Cascando*, with Patrick Magee and Denys Hawthorne.
20 October	SB halts publication of *More Pricks Than Kicks* by Grove Press and Calder.
9 December	SB in London for rehearsals of *Waiting for Godot*, directed by Anthony Page at the Royal Court Theatre.
10 December	Jean-Paul Sartre refuses the Nobel Prize in Literature.
30 December	*Waiting for Godot* opens at the Royal Court Theatre with Jack MacGowran and Nicol Williamson.
31 December	SB returns to Paris from London.

AVIGDOR ARIKHA AND ANNE ATIK
PARIS

27.1.64 [London]

C'est dur. McGowran excellent, Magee pas encore - les 2 N. quelconques.[1] Je pense rentrer lundi.

Affectueusement

Sam

APCS; 1 leaf, 1 side; "Royal Hospital, Chelsea"; *to* Monsieur & Madame Avigdor Arikha, 19 Avenue de Tourville, Paris 7$^{\underline{me}}$, FRANCE; *pm* 27-1-64, London; InU, Arikha.

27.1.64 [London]

It's tough going. McGowran excellent, Magee not yet - the 2 Ns pretty ordinary.[1] Am thinking of coming back on Monday.

Love

Sam

1 SB was rehearsing *Endgame* in London for a production by The English Theatre, produced by Philippe Staib (b. 1941) and directed by Michael Blake (b. 1929); it would open at the Studio des Champs-Elysées on 17 February. Jack MacGowran played Clov; Patrick Magee played Hamm; Sydney Bromley (1909–1987) played Nagg. Patricia Leventon (n.d.) had been cast as Nell, but could not be released from a BBC Radio commitment, leaving the understudy Nancy Cole to take up the role in rehearsal in London. On 2 February, SB would write to Barbara Bray: "Nell out. Looking for another." (TCD, MS 10948/1/264.)

BARBARA BRAY
PARIS

28.1.64 Hallam Court [London]

Dear Barbara

Thanks for your letters.

I can't think who your Bill is who so cooed to you.

I weaken. Bad day yesterday on top of Royal Court - 3$^{\underline{rd}}$ rehearsal room since we started, cold & hideous, it was better above the pub in

Conway St.[1] Then dinner with Devines & St Denis.[2] Got very drunk Sat. at Pat's party. Harold dropped in after 2/3 of Chronicles & shall see him again Friday.[3] Met Vicky at lunch Sunday.[4] Played chess with Frisch & lost. This evening opening of Andorra with Calders. Tomorrow Lamda with Frisch.[5] Expect to return Monday. Do on me Sunday at Arts or Criterion with readings by Jack & Pat, then discussion.[6] Lunch with Hobson tomorrow. Calders want me back Thursday but hope to stay here. Staggered up late Sunday to find Barbara ? sculpting Miss P.'s neice [sic] in kitchen, can't spell neice. Most comfortable & peaceful place here, but don't take advantage of it as you did.[7] Feel utterly abolished as always in London. Evening with John & Vera Sunday. Playback on German Cascando Sat. at BBC with Esslin & Bakewell, much better than French, then back to Esslin's for drinks & to meet squinty doaty.[8] Off now to Sloane Square.[9] Shall take tomorrow morning off to book flight, etc. Whole thing looks like a mistake, yet another. Dread accumulation of trouble in Paris on return. Glad you liked the Mayoux. Que faire que faire.[10]

Love

Sam

ALS; 1 leaf, 2 sides; *env to* Madame Bray, 14 Rue Le Sueur, Paris 16me, FRANCE; *pm* __-1-64, London; TCD, MS 10948/1/262.

1 According to a rehearsal diary published by Clancy Sigal, rehearsals moved from what was then the Adams Arms, a pub-hotel at 4 Conway Street, near Fitzroy Square, to "an empty night-club on one of the upper floors" of the Royal Court Theatre, with red walls and a low black ceiling ("Is This the Person to Murder Me?" *Sunday Times Colour Magazine* 1 March 1964: 22).

2 George Devine, Jocelyn Herbert, Michel St. Denis.

3 Pinter dropped in on the rehearsal during Hamm's "Chronicles" (*Endgame*, Grove, 50–54). Pinter remarked to Jack MacGowran and Patrick Magee: "'You know, it's not what you were saying to each other, it's what was happening in between that gave me tickles up my spine'" (Richard Toscan, "MacGowran on Beckett," Theatre Quarterly 3.4 [July–September 1973] 8; rpt. McMillan and Fehsenfeld, *Beckett in the Theatre*, 174).

SB would write to Barbara Bray on 2 February: "Good evening Friday with Harold, Albee, Schneider & Pat" (TCD, MS 10948/1/264).

4 SB met Victor Weisz (1913–1966), a political cartoonist who drew under the name of "Vicky," at John Calder's home. When describing the Sunday afternoon lunch with SB, Max Frisch, and Weiss, during which they all played chess, Calder recalls "the conviviality and the brilliance" (*Pursuit*, 287).

5 Max Frisch was a guest of the Calders during the rehearsals of his play *Andorra* at the Old Vic Theatre (John Calder to SB, 3 January 1964; InU, C&B, Beckett). At the New LAMDA Theatre Club, Peter Brook and Charles Marowitz produced *The Theatre of Cruelty* in a workshop-performance that juxtaposed classical texts and contemporary events ("Audience Inside the Workshop," *The Times* 13 January 1964: 12; "The Theatre of Cruelty: An Experimental Programme," *The Times* 1 January 1964: 13).

6 No details have been found about the readings.

7 During the time that Max Frisch was a guest of the Calders, SB had moved to Hallam Court. Mrs. Pearson was the resident landlady there. The identity of the sculptress has not been established. Mrs. Pearson's niece has not been identified.

8 On 25 January, SB heard the playback of the Stuttgart recording of *Cascando* directed by Imo Wilimzig, with Fred C. Siebeck and Robert Michal, and produced by SDR/NDR; it had been broadcast on SDR (now SWR) on 16 October 1963, and NDR on 20 October 1963. The radio play was translated into German by Elmar Tophoven, and first published in *Dramatische Dichtungen*, I (Frankfurt: Suhrkamp Verlag, 1963). "Squinty doaty," from *Whoroscope*, here possibly referring to a member of Esslin's family.

9 The Royal Court Theatre is on Sloane Square.

10 "Que faire que faire" (What *are* we to do?).

JUDITH SCHMIDT
GROVE PRESS, NEW YORK

25.2.64 Paris

Dear Judith

Many thanks for your so moving and affectionate letter. I do of course want all those I am fond of to stay with me and my work on our way out. But I'm the first to wonder how they can and the last to love them less if they can't. I don't know what to think of PLAY myself. It seemed to function on my dim mental stage when I did it, enough at least to justify my letting it go. And I felt it had something the others had not, nothing to do with writing (no attempt at writing there) or with more or less compassion or humour, but simply in the way of theatrical contrivance and attitude.[1] I won't know how hard to kick myself till I'm through with rehearsals in Paris, beginning now, and in London, beginning next month.

Saw Alan last night just arrived from Zürich, and again today. Good form and good news of finger and mother.[2]

Looking forward to seeing you this summer. We'll drink champagne on a terrasse and laugh at unhappiness.

Best always

Sam

ALS; 1 leaf, 1 side; Burns Library, Samuel Beckett Collection, SB-JD.

1 On 22 January, Judith Schmidt wrote to SB, having seen *Play* twice: "It wasn't, of course, a question of not 'liking' it. It was funny in part; the language was beautiful. [. . .] But I felt, in the main, that it was the most bitter Beckett I had ever seen, and that it had the least compassion. And I was not deeply touched." Yet, after seeing *Play* a third time:

> And last night something broke [. . .] something came through that I had not felt before. I cannot say what it was. I got a sense of the language, and the breaking of the language between the three, and between each and the light, which struck me at moments as if it were a miracle – and I do not know what the miracle was. (Douw Collection.)

2 Schneider's mother, Rebecka Schneider.

GEORGE DEVINE
ROYAL COURT THEATRE, LONDON

9.3.64 Paris

Dear George

The last rehearsals with Serreau have led us to a view of the da capo which I think you should know about. According to the text it is rigorously identical with the first statement.[1] We now think it would be dramatically more effective to have it express a slight weakening, both of question and of response, by means of less and perhaps slower light and correspondingly less volume and speed of voice. To consider only strength of light and voice, if we call C the minimum and A the maximum the first time round we would get something like this:[2]

	1
C	Opening chorus.
A	First part of 1.
B	Second part of 1.

	11
Less than C	Second chorus.
B or B plus	First part of 11.
C or C plus	Second part of 11.
	111
C or C plus	

The impression of falling off which this would give, with suggestion of conceivable dark and silence in the end, or of an indefinite approximating towards it, would be reinforced if we obtained also, in the repeat, a quality of hesitancy, of both question and answer, perhaps not so much in a slowing down of actual débit as in a less confident movement of spot from one face to another and less immediate reaction of the voices.[3] The whole idea involves a spot mechanism of greater flexibility than has seemed necessary so far. The inquirer (light) begins to emerge as no less a victim of his inquiry than they and as needing to be free, within narrow limits, literally to act the part, i.e. to vary if only slightly his speeds and intensities.

This is all new and will yield more as we go into it. Thought I had better submit it to you without delay.

See you Monday. If they could be word perfect by then it would be marvellous.[4]

Love to Jocelyn

yours ever

s/ Sam

Perhaps some form of manual control after all.

TLS with APS; 1 leaf, 1 side; NTA, Play and Philoctetes, Old Vic 1964. Previous publication: *New Theatre Magazine*, Samuel Beckett Issue, 11.3 (1971) 16–17; *Samuel Beckett: An Exhibition*, ed. James Knowlson (London: Turret Books, 1971) 92; Beckett, *Disjecta*, 111–112.

1 SB had begun to rehearse the Paris production of *Comédie*, directed by Jean-Marie Serreau, with Eléonore Hirt, Delphine Seyrig, and Michael Lonsdale; this production would open at the Pavillon de Marsan on 14 June.

2 SB cancelled "sound" and inserted in the right margin, "light."

3 "Débit" (speed of delivery).

4 SB wrote to Bettina Jonič Calder on 1 March that he expected to arrive at Calder's home, 76 Wimpole Street, London, on 14 March, to assist with the rehearsals of *Play* produced by the National Theatre (TCD, MS 110990/15).

BARBARA BRAY
PARIS

17.3 [1964] 76 Wimpole [London]

Dear Barbara

All well. Horribly cold. Good first contact yesterday with cast. All wrong, but word perfect. Very keen and will I think be pleasant to work with. Got them pointing in right direction.[1] Ken Tynan snooping round.[2] Rehearsals morning with George, then individually with me afternoon. Decided to improve things further by changing order of répliques in repeat.[3] Won't matter to them as they are not cueing one another, but will to poor Spot. Seen no one so far except David Jones from Aldwych: Elvi & Sidney can't be used,

15. Edward Beckett, Samuel Beckett, and Patrick Magee, after the opening night of *Endgame* at the Studio des Champs-Elysées, 17 February 1964

Midgley to direct, Koltai to do set, opening about July 7.[4] Going to George's "farm" next weekend & following to Sheila. Hope all well with you & children.

Love

Sam

ALS (lettercard); 1 leaf, 2 sides; *to* Madame Bray, 14 Rue Le Sueur, Paris 16$^{\underline{me}}$, FRANCE; *pm* 17-3-64 London; TCD, MS 10948/1/265.

1 SB describes his first rehearsal at the National Theatre production of *Play* at the Old Vic Theatre, directed by George Devine, with Rosemary Harris (b. 1930), Billie Whitelaw (b. 1932), and Robert Stephens (1931–1995).

2 Kenneth Tynan, who had been Drama Critic of *The Observer*, was now Literary Manager of the National Theatre Company.

3 "Répliques" (speeches).

4 The operator of the spot has not been identified, but the Chief Electrician David Read would have worked out the lighting design with Donald McWhinnie (Victoria Lawston and Robert Howells, The Shakespeare Centre, to the editors, 8 July 2013). David Hugh Jones (1934–2008) was Artistic Controller of The Royal Shakespeare Company at the Aldwych Theatre. The Paris production of *Endgame* with Jack MacGowran and Patrick Magee was to be transferred there. The actors who had played Nell and Nagg in Paris were Elvi Hale (b. 1931) and Sydney Bromley. Robin Midgely (1935–2007) was to direct the London production; the Associate Designer of the Royal Shakespeare Company, Ralph Koltai (b. 1924), would do the set.

SIEGFRIED UNSELD
SUHRKAMP VERLAG, FRANKFURT

19.3.64

chez Calder
76 Wimpole St.
London W.1

Dear D$^{\underline{r}}$ Suhrkamp

Thanks for your letter of March 13 received yesterday.

Back as you see in London for rehearsals of PLAY at the Old Vic.

As far as I can judge away from my books your list is complete and correct. I do not think there was any Lord Chamberlain interference in any of these texts, but it is safer to use the American edition in all cases. PLAY and WORDS & Music have not yet been published in

America and you should use the Faber edition (PLAY, WORDS & Music & Cascando) which has just appeared. I have translated PLAY into French under title of Comédie and shall send you the text when I get back to Paris next month. It has not yet been published by Minuit. Words & Music I have not translated and don't know if I can because of the poems.[1]

I began rehearsals of Comédie in Paris with Serreau before leaving. In the light of these, and of my work here on PLAY, the stage directions of original script are no longer valid. The actual speech of the actors remains unchanged. The German text will have to be corrected therefore and Faber's text, published before these rehearsals, is not accurate as far as stage directions go. I shall make the necessary corrections when I get back and give them to Tophoven. The order of the actors' speeches in the repeat is changed, making it necessary to print the entire repeat.[2] Sorry for these complications. I shall never give another theatre text, if there ever is another, to be published until I have worked on it in the theatre.

I don't think you should set up this 2nd volume until I have gone through all original texts & French texts, correcting them if necessary and I should be very grateful if you would let me have proofs of all at a later stage.

Andorra doing very well. So glad.[3]

Yours ever

Sam B.

ALS; 2 leaves, 2 sides; DLA, Suhrkamp, VL, Samuel Beckett: 1962–1964; AL draft *on* Siegfried Unseld to SB, 13 March 1964; GEU, MSS 1221.

1 Siegfried Unseld asked SB to confirm the list of his plays written originally in English in preparation of Suhrkamp's second volume of *Dramatische Dichtungen*. SB refers to *Play, and Two Short Pieces for Radio*. There are two poems in *Words and Music*: "Age is when to a man . . ." and "Then down a little way . . ." (32, 35).

2 In the Suhrkamp edition of *Spiel*, the repetition of the play had been indicated in the final stage direction, "und so weiter, bis" (and so on, thus) (Beckett, *Spiel: Ein Akt*, 19).

3 SB reports on the London production of Max Frisch's play *Andorra*, which Suhrkamp had published in 1961.

BARBARA BRAY
LONDON

21.4.64 Paris

Dear Barbara

Thanks for your letter. Grateful to the Critics.[1]

Dined with Arikhas last night. Then out with Avigdor. Anne not too well. Not more drink than usual but suddenly drunk. Don't remember driving home, him & self. Went down this morning to see if car there. Never better parked. Ran into Con & his white lipped Marion at one stage. Also Alberto with his latest.[2] Checked & despatched all texts for Suhrkamp save Happy Days, Play & Words & Music which I must try & translate.[3]

Dreadful session all yesterday afternoon on Madeleine's record (very bad) of Oh les B. J. that wd. be good but - unending recording studio.[4]

Have not seen Comédie anew since last Wed.[5] Tomorrow. Bastards.

Dined with Hayden & Leslie Waddington who had just purchased another 4 1/2 millions "worth". Silly talk about "success". Started screaming.[6]

Off now to walk in Paris and bring Comédie to Lettres Nouvelles. Gisèle Freund this afternoon. Jesus.[7]

Session with Jean on Krapp. Not encouraging.[8]

Blin, Nicole & Manolo this evening.

Jesus.

Sam

ALS; 1 leaf, 1 side; *env to* Mrs Bray, c/o Pearson, Hallam Court, Hallam Street, London W.1, Angleterre; *pm* __-4-64 Paris; TCD, MS 10948/1/270.

1 *The Critics* of 19 April featured Harold Hobson on the National Theatre productions of SB's *Play* and Sophocles' *Philoctetes* (BBCWAC, Programme as Broadcast: Home Service).

2 A. J. Leventhal was with Marion Leigh, later his wife. SB mentions Alberto Giacometti and a companion.

3 SB and Leventhal had gone through all the texts for the second volume of *Dramatische Dichtungen* (SB to Siegfried Unseld, 10 April 1964; DLA, Suhrkamp VL, Samuel Beckett: 1962–1964).

4 Madeleine Renaud recorded *Oh, les beaux jours* live at the Théâtre de France on 5 and 6 February for *Avant-Scène 33 tours*, Disques Adès (TS 30 LA 568); the studio work that SB mentions here may have involved editing or augmenting the live recording. A brief section of this recording is included in *L'Univers scénique de Samuel Beckett*, Théâtre aujourd'hui, 3 (Paris: CNDP, 1994).

5 Jean-Marie Serreau was rehearsing *Comédie* for production at the Théâtre de Marsan. SB rejoined the rehearsals after his time in London, but the sessions were interrupted by Serreau's having to travel to Salzburg. SB had written to Robert Pinget: "Reprise avec Serreau décourageante, fouille-merdeuse à souhait, les acteurs ayant perdu le peu qu'ils savaient il y a un mois" (16 April 1964; Burns Library, Samuel Beckett Collection, SB-RP) (Revival with Serreau discouraging: the worst kind of nitpicking, the actors having lost the little they knew a month ago).

6 Leslie Waddington was Henri Hayden's London agent.

7 The first publication of *Comédie*: 18 September 1963, n. 1. Gisèle Freund (1912–2000) wished to photograph SB for her book on James Joyce (Gisèle Freund and Verna Carleton, *James Joyce in Paris: His Final Years* [New York: Harcourt, Brace and World, 1965] 56).

8 Jean Martin was preparing the role of Krapp for a double bill featuring *La dernière bande* and Robert Pinget's *L'Hypothèse*.

JEAN SCHLUMBERGER
PARIS

27.4.64 — 38 Bld. St. Jacques
Paris

Cher Jean Schlumberger

Absent de Paris tous ces temps-ci je n'ai pu assister qu'avant-hier à votre spectacle aux Mathurins.[1] Ca a été ma meilleure soirée au théâtre depuis La Maison d'Os de Dubillard. Laissez-nous, ma femme et moi, vous en dire un grand merci. Oui, même et surtout perdant, il n'y a que l'esprit qui vaille. Nous sommes sortis du vôtre comme remis debout.

Croyez, cher Jean Schlumberger, à mes hommages émus.[2]

Samuel Beckett

ACS; 1 leaf, 1 side; *env to* Monsieur Jean Schlumberger, 78 Rue d'Assas, Paris 6$^{\underline{me}}$; *verso*: Ex Beckett, 38 Bld St. Jacques, Paris 14; *pm* 28–4–64, Paris; Doucet, Schlumberger, Ms. 14847.

27.4.64 38 Bld. St. Jacques
Paris

Dear Jean Schlumberger

Having been away from Paris this past while I haven't been able to get to your show at the Mathurins till the day before yesterday.[1] For me it was the best evening's theatre since Dubillard's *La Maison d'os*. Let my wife and me send you special thanks. Yes, even and above all when it is defeated, only the spirit counts. We came out of yours buoyed up.

Our deeply felt homage[2]

Samuel Beckett

1 Jean Schlumberger* (1877–1968), novelist, dramatist, critic. SB had seen a "Spectacle Jean Schlumberger," which opened at the Théâtre des Mathurins on 9 April, directed by Jean-Paul Cisife, and which comprised *Césaire ou la Puissance de l'esprit*, *Les Yeux de dix-huit ans*, and *Le Marchand de cercueils*.

2 Three days later, SB would have to write to Schlumberger in response to the latter's wish to make public parts of the present letter, stating: "Le petit mot que je vous ai adressé est d'ordre purement personnel et je ne tiens pas à ce qu'il soit publié" (Doucet, Schlumberger, Ms. 14848) (The little note that I sent you is entirely private in nature, and I would not wish it to be published).

EURÓPA KÖNYVKIADÓ
BUDAPEST

[after 3 May 1964] [Paris]

Thank you for your letter of May 3rd.[1] As a writer I have no feeling of any national attachment. I am an Irishman (Irish passport) living in France for the past 27 years who has written part of his work in English and part in French. The following plays were written in French:

En attendant Godot

Fin de Partie

Actes sans Paroles I & II

and the following in English

Cascando (Radio)

Krapp's Last Tape

All That Fall }
Embers } Radio
Words & Music }
Happy Days
Play

If you should see fit to include one of the latter in your British Anthology and one of the former in your French I should be pleased. If this is not possible and a choice must be made, I should prefer to figure in your French anthology.[2]

A draft; 1 leaf, 1 side; *on* Európa Könyvkiadó 3 May 1964 *to* SB (TLS; 1 leaf, 1 side); *letterhead*; GEU, MS 1221.

1 The Budapest literary publisher Európa Könyvkiadó has, since 1957, specialized in publishing world classics and contemporary literature in Hungarian translation. The firm was planning to publish an anthology of contemporary British drama and wished to include a work by SB, but wondered whether SB's work belonged in an anthology of French or English drama. Over the signature of Jenó Simó (d. 1994), a letter had been sent to SB on 3 May asking him to specify his literary citizenship (András Barkóczi, Director, Európa Könyvkiadó, to the editors, 18 March 2013).

2 *Krapp's Last Tape* was translated into Hungarian as *Az utolsó tekercs* by László Szenczei and published in the English anthology *Mai angol drámák* (1965). No Beckett writing was included in the French anthology *A harag éjszakái* (1965). *Endgame*, translated into Hungarian as *A játszma vége* by Emil Kolozsvári Grandpierre, was published in a two-volume anthology entitled *A játszma vége I–II / Modern egyfelvonásosok* (1969). (András Barkóczi to the editors, 18 March 2013.)

ALAN SCHNEIDER
NEW YORK

13.6.64 Paris

Dear Alan

Thanks for your letter of June 9.

Every problem of image in the film is to be solved by reference to the one or other vision. The street is as E sees it. He is looking for O and if there were other people in the street besides the 6 couples he would be bound to fix his gaze on them as he does on the couples. So one must assume that these couples are the only people in the opening scene. There may of course be registered very briefly, as he switches from one couple to another, the normal street objects (whatever they are), one or more of which (tree, lamppost) could help to indicate, when the pursuit begins, the direction it is taking, i.e. against the stream.

This same principle obtains during pursuit sequence, with this difference, that E having fastened on O may now legitimately record, blurredly, other human elements, without the question arising as to why he does not scrutinize them as well. The only [sic] to be seen clearly are O and the 7th couple, the latter first by O, then by E, but if you wish there may be a confused presence of other couples all of course moving with the stream, i.e. in direction opposed to that of E and O.[1]

The question of transfers should be clear from the further notes.[2] The point I tried to make was that the two visions are to be distinguished, not only on the plane of absolute quality, but also dynamically, i.e. in their manner of transferring from one object to the next. It is therefore necessary that the samples of O's vision given before the room sequences should involve such transfers, and I specify them, both in the case of the 7th couple and in that of the flower-woman, in the latter case O's eye moving from her face to the tray, from the tray to her hand, from the hand back to tray, from the tray back to face, more slowly than E's eye a moment later effecting same transfers.

In the midst of apprehension at thought of N.Y. joy at prospect of seeing you all so soon.

Best always.
s/ Sam

TLS; 1 leaf, 1 side; *AN AH left margin, paragraph 3 & 4:* OK; Burns Library, Samuel Beckett Collection, SB-AS; AL draft; 1 leaf, 1 side; GEU, MS 1221. Previous publication: Beckett and Schneider, *No Author Better Served*, 158.

1 In *Film* there are two points of view, which correlate to camera views: E = eye; O = Object. E, the camera, follows O, at "an angle of immunity," which never allows the camera to be seen by O (Beckett, *Film*, 11). This angle is maintained throughout by keeping the camera behind the back of O, until the last frames of the film.

2 By "transfers," SB means shifts from one point of view to another.

30 June 1964, Barbara Bray

BARBARA BRAY
PARIS

30.6 [1964] 76 Wimpole W1 [London]

Dear B.

Arrived. Bettina away. Bachelor confusion.[1]

First contact today. Unpleasant rehearsal room in Covent G.[2] N. & N. all wrong, hardly to be got right in the time. J. & P. much forgotten, but they'll be all right. Donald helpful, nice about my inrushes. Not on stage before Sunday. L.-C. continues to refuse bastard & pee. Trying leak for latter. But arses accepted. Bollocks overlooked.[3] Felt dull & dim about it all today. But actors seemed pleased. Back to Wimpole early to look at Wimbledon on TV, then long walk Mayfair way with dog.[4] Letter from Grove, with 50 photos of Buster. Alan's darling camera man not available till later, possibility of further postponement if acceptable replacement not found.[5] Mime 2 Thursday in "Expeditions". Dread to contemplate.[6] Pat to play divine marquis in Weiss Marat.[7] Could lie down & give up which shortly I shall do so now.

Love

Sam

ALS (lettercard); 1 leaf, 2 sides; *to* Madame Bray, 14 Rue Le Sueur, Paris 16$^{\underline{me}}$, FRANCE; *pm* __-__-64, London; TCD, MS 10948/1/282.

1 SB was staying with the Calders in London.

2 The renewed rehearsals of *Endgame* for the Aldwych Theatre were held in a Covent Garden space. Nell and Nagg were played by Bryan Pringle (1935–2002) and Patsy Byrne (b. 1933), both new to their parts. Jack MacGowran and Patrick Magee continued in their roles as Clov and Hamm. Donald McWhinnie, rather than Robin Midgley, was director.

3 As in previous London productions of *Endgame*, the Lord Chamberlain's Office objected to some of the language of the play. The outcome of a series of communications was that "balls," "pee," and "bastard" were refused; "swine" was accepted as a substitute for "bastard," and "leak" as a substitute for "pee." The Lord Chamberlain's Office preferred "a bunch of the fly" to "a botch of the fly" (Michael Hallifax, London Manager, The Royal Shakespeare Theatre, to Lt.-Col. Eric Penn, OBE, MC, The Lord Chamberlain's Office, 1 July 1964; BL 58/57B).

4 The Wimbledon Championships were played from 22 June to 3 July in 1964.

5 Grove Press collected photos from Buster Keaton in order to find images that might be used in *Film* (Judith Schmidt, Grove Press, to SB, 22 June 1964; NSyU). The original cameraman was "lost . . . to some Hollywood epic" (Alan Schneider, "On Directing *Film*," 66).

6 *Act Without Words II* was grouped together in a short program under the title *Expeditions One*, produced by the Royal Shakespeare Company in repertoire at the Aldwych Theatre.

7 Patrick Magee acted the role of the Marquis de Sade in Peter Weiss's play *The Persecution and Murder of Marat as performed by the Inmates of the Asylum of Charenton under the Direction of the Marquis de Sade*. It was directed by Peter Brook at the Aldwych Theatre from 20 August ("Lively Summer Plans for the Aldwych," *The Times* 29 April 1964: 8).

AVIGDOR ARIKHA AND ANNE ATIK
PARIS

1.7 [1964] London

Chers amis

Bien arrivé. Faiblesse du côté des poubelles. Tout à refaire et très peu de temps. Travail sur le plateau à partir de dimanche. Pat et Jack – beaucoup de perdu mais pas d'inquiétude. Complications à N.Y. Possible que ça soit de nouveau remis. J'espère que non. En finir. Très beau temps. Vu personne. Aucune envie. Sors le soir avec la chienne Calder. Elle me promène – Hyde Park et Mayfair. Du bon tennis à la TV. Un rêve tout ça, ininterprétable.

Affectueusement

Sam

ALS (lettercard); 1 leaf, 2 sides; *to* Monsieur et Madame Avigdor Arikha, 19 Avenue de Tourville, Paris 7me, France: *pm* 1-7-64, London; InU, Arikha. Previous publication, with variant, Atik, *How It Was*, 98–99.

1.7 [1964] London

Dear Both

Got here all right. Bins part rather weak. All needs redoing in short order. Work on stage from Sunday on. Pat and Jack – a lot lost, but no anxiety. Complications in N.Y. Possible it will be postponed again. Hope not. Oh to have done with it. Very fine weather. Seen no one. No desire to. Go out in the evening with the Calders' bitch. She takes me for walks - Hyde Park and Mayfair. Good tennis on the TV. Whole business a dream, uninterpretable.

Love

Sam

BARBARA BRAY
PARIS

Monday [6 July 1964] [London]

Dear B. 7 p.m., Guinnessing in Mooney's Strand before going back to theatre.[1] All well more or less, but dull. Can't listen to the play any longer. N. & N. have progressed & will be all right. Set fussy, lighting banal.[2] Departure for N.Y. now practically certain. Cameraman found, celui d'Atalante & Zero de Conduite (vague shooting script arrived, haven't looked at it[)].[3] Seen noone except John briefly. If I could drag myself down to the sea.. Bettina due back today to a proper shambles. Take care of yourself.

Love

Sam

ALS (lettercard); 1 leaf, 2 sides; *to* M[me] Bray, 14 Rue Le Sueur, Paris 16, France; *pm* illeg, London; TCD, MS 10948/1/284. *Dating*: London rehearsals began on 30 June; SB arrived in New York on 10 July.

1 The Irish firm of J. G. Mooney & Co. Ltd. operated a pub at 315 The Strand, near the Aldwych Theatre.

2 SB had rehearsed with Patsy Byrne and Bryan Pringle, Nell and Nagg, on their own (SB to Barbara Bray, [4 July 1964]; TCD, MS 10948/1/283).

3 The cinematographer for *Film* was Boris Kaufman (1906–1980). He had filmed *Zéro de Conduite* (1933, *Zero for Conduct*) and *L'Atalante* (1934), both directed by Jean Vigo. The cameraman for *Film* was Joe Coffey (1915–2000).

BARBARA BRAY
PARIS

10.7.64 [Paris - New York]

Dear Barbara

Writing about 1/2 way across the pond, devant un cognac et même pas la mort dans l'âme.[1] A tooth fell out this morning at breakfast but flatter myself foolishly that noone noticed. Not a good performance last night, Donald dixit, but all very pleased with reactions, including P. Brooke's [sic]. Mad night in the Opera, Catherine St. This morning they all came round, Pat, Jack, Gloria, Donald, for the last embrace, very touching. Because of strike at London A. P. had to land at Shannon to refuel. Irish drizzle & misery.[2]

Good morning. Slam from Evening News's 2nd string and Murphy banned in Ireland.[3] Unimaginable kindness from John Calder, cd. never have got through it without him. The simple things the nascent (?) senile can't cope with.[4] Wrote cards to J. & Ch. Got books on Sade from Mary H. for Pat.[5] No one likes set, fussy self-opinionated bastard.[6] Feels good up here, queer joy at slowing laws of time. Saw George yest.[7] Tired & disillusioned. Yes! Decided to refuse Berlin & N.Y. Season.[8] Not biting any more. Window & foolscap, doesn't matter what happens now.

Love

Sam

ALS; 1 leaf, 2 sides; *env to* Madame Bray, 14 Rue Le Sueur, Paris 16, France; *pm* uncancelled; *upper left corner* AIR; TCD, MS 10948/1/287.

1 "Devant un cognac et même pas la mort dans l'âme" (in front of a brandy, and not even with heavy heart).

2 Reviews of *Endgame* were positive: for example, "An Early Failure is Now almost a Riot," *The Times* 10 July 1964: 7. SB writes "P. Brooke," referring to Peter Brook, who was Co-Director of the Royal Shakespeare Company at this time. The company gathered at the Opera Tavern, 23 Catherine Street, Covent Garden, after the opening performance. The group send-off in the morning included Gloria MacGowran.

An airport fuel strike at London Airport began on 10 July.

3 Details of the "slam" and of censorship of *Murphy* have not been found.

4 SB wrote to the Calders: "Thank you with all my old rags of heart for your great kindness to the old man I am becoming so fast now. This morning at breakfast a tooth fell out, did you notice?" (TCD, MSS 11090/17.)

5 Julia and Checchina (Francesca) Bray. Hutchinson's notes for 8 July mentioned that SB had borrowed three books from her for Magee, including *The Revolutionary Ideas of the Marquis de Sade* by Geoffrey Gorer (London: Wishart, 1934) (TxU, Hutchinson, 1.4).

6 SB refers to the set designer Ralph Koltai.

7 The Royal Court Theatre was under renovation from March through August, so during this time its productions were held at the Queen's Theatre. Their production of Bertolt Brecht's *St. Joan of the Stockyards* opened there on 11 June, but received such poor reviews that it was taken off weeks later. Devine's declining health led him, gradually, to withdraw from day-to-day management; this was difficult because he was trying to establish a new production team at the Royal Court and determine the Fall repertory. Devine would resign on 14 October, though this did not become effective (or public) until 5 January 1965: "When a man begins to feel he is a part of the fixtures and fittings, it is time he left. I am deeply tired." (Wardle, *The Theatres of George Devine*, 256–265; Philip Roberts, *The Royal Court Theatre and the Modern Stage* [Cambridge: Cambridge University Press, 1999] 99.)

8 The Barr, Wilder, and Albee production company, Theatre 1965, had proposed a Beckett season for 1965: "The idea is to have a season of say 6–8 weeks at a time when Pat and Jackie and the theatre are all available" (Alan Schneider to SB, 10 March 1964; NYPL, The Billy Rose, Barr-Wilder T-MS 1978-002, Box 1, F. 5, Schneider Correspondence with Beckett, Pinter).

The Berlin invitation has not been identified.

PATRICK MAGEE
LONDON

10.7.64 Plane

Dear Pat

Wish you were beside me here in this old losing game with the sun. All I couldn't say and that's nearly all take it from this for said. Your coming round this morning moved me mightily. Deep thanks for your great Hamm & fond love to you both. May we get together soon.[1]

Sam

ALS; 1 leaf, 1 side; *env to* Patrick Magee Esq, 1A W. Cromwell Rd., London S.W.5, England, *upper left corner* AIRMAIL; uncancelled; TCD MS 11313/11.

1 SB also sent notes to Jack MacGowran and Donald McWhinnie (TxU, Beckett Collection, 9.3; OSU, Spec.rare.124, McWhinnie).

BARBARA BRAY
PARIS

13.7.64 [New York]

Dear Barbara - by the train between Long I. & N.Y., early morning. Very busy week-end with Alan & Kaufman, got a lot done and clarified a lot. K. impressive. He did also 12 Angry Men.[1] Broke down entire scenario into about 170 shots & begin to know something of cuts, pans & setups. Won't start shooting before this day week and hope to finish it in a week though I doubt it. All this week to decide about exteriors, build the room, find the hallway, see the actors (Keaton already in N.Y.), get the E-O distinction right with Kaufman, et more work on analysis of scenario. Voilà.[2]

Marvellous flight all the way, then in a little Piper yoke to L. I.[3] Don't feel too grand but suppose will make it somehow. One tooth fell out. Another broke, & now a molar wobbling like mad. No further news of Endgame. May see the Sundays in N.Y. The Friday dailies weren't too bad. All seems very remote.[4]

Saw Albee last night in his beautiful place at end of the Island, right on the ocean.[5]

Hope all well with you & the children & the job not too painful. Shall write again soon.

Love

S.

ALI; 1 leaf, 2 sides; *env to* Madame Bray, 14 Rue Le Sueur, Paris 16, FRANCE; *pm* 1_-7-64, Jamaica, N.Y.; *upper left corner* AIRMAIL; TCD, MS 10948/1/288.

1 SB had spent the weekend working with Alan Schneider and Boris Kaufman at Barney Rosset's home in East Hampton, Long Island. Kaufman had been the cinematographer of *Twelve Angry Men* (1957) directed by Sidney Lumet.

2 Concerning the planning of *Film*, Alan Schneider writes:

> For three days we talked, walked and sat. (We also played tennis.) Sam explained the necessary camera positions and angles to all concerned (nor did he budge from his fundamental position in the face of some highly sophisticated arguments about the new-found flexibility and mobility of the film medium), and tried to explain the exact difference of intensity he wanted in the separate visions of O and E. The rough shooting script got revised into an exact shooting script. ("On Directing *Film*," 68, 71.)

3 SB and Judith Schmidt had flown from Idlewild Airport (now J. F. Kennedy) to East Hampton in a private four-seater Piper Cub airplane "hardly large enough to hold his long legs" (Schneider, "On Directing *Film*," 68).

4 In the *Weekend Review* of *The Observer*, Bamber Gascoigne wrote of *Endgame* at the Aldwych Theatre: "The relentless mathematical repetitions of the script are played for maximum irritation ... Stripped of all poetry and humour, we are left only with Beckett's facile pessimism." ("All the Riches of the Incas," 12 July 1964: 22.)

5 Edward Albee had a home in Montauk, Long Island, "on a cliff 60 feet above the ocean with 200 yards of beach" (Elaine Dundy, "Who's Afraid of Edward Albee," *The Sunday Times* 2 February 1964: 26[S]-27[S]).

AVIGDOR ARIKHA AND ANNE ATIK
PARIS

[15 July 1964]

c/o Grove Press
64 University Place
N.Y.

Chers amis

Petit mot en vitesse pour vous dire que ça va à peu près et que le travail se présente bien. Trouvé la rue (près de Brooklyn Br., côté Manhattan) et le vestibule dans le Village.[1] La chambre est en train de se faire, on commence à tourner lundi.[2] Rencontré Keaton hier avec sa femme, il sera très bien, une gueule de [*for* du] tonnerre et le reste à l'avenant.[3] Je me sens perdu et étourdi, il s'agit de tenir encore 10 jours. Enorme gentillesse de tout le monde, impossible de dépenser un sou. Très bien logé chez Rosset.[4] Cameraman formidable - celui de Vigo - Boris Kaufman. Passé le weekend chez Rosset à East Hampton à discuter le coup avec lui et Alan et autres intéressés. Excellent découpage technique de Schneider déjà terminé.

Affectueusement

S.

ALI; 1 leaf, 1 side; *env to* M^{r} & Mme Avigdor Arikha, 19 Av. de Tourville, Paris 7, France; *pm* 15-7-64, New York; InU, Arikha.

[15 July 1964]

c/o Grove Press
64 University Place
N.Y.

Dear Both

Hasty little note to let you know that all more or less well and work shaping up well. Found the street (near Brooklyn Br., Manhattan side) and the hall in the Village.[1] The room is being done. We start shooting on Monday.[2] Met Keaton with his wife yesterday. He'll be really good; great face and rest to match.[3] I feel a bit lost and dazed – got to hold out for another 10 days. Enormous kindness from everyone, impossible to pay for anything. Have a lovely room at Rosset's.[4] Great cameraman – the one Vigo used – Boris Kaufman. Spent the weekend with Rosset in East Hampton chewing the fat with him and Alan and other interested parties. Excellent sequencing by Schneider, already done.

Love

S.

16. Alan Schneider, Samuel Beckett, and Joe Coffey, on the set of *Film*, New York, 1964

1 Richard Seaver writes:

> Back in the city, Alan and Beckett walked endlessly, scouting for locations. Though he was apparently affected by the heat and humidity, never having experienced the equivalent of New York summer weather, Beckett never complained. One day in lower Manhattan, Beckett's eyes brightened as we came in sight of a dilapidated old wall hard by the Brooklyn Bridge. He nodded and indicated that this is where the opening sequence should be shot, no question. The wall, part of a building slated for demolition, was pure Beckett: sagging, uneven, its cement flaking and crumbling. (*The Tender Hour of Twilight*, 320.)

2 Seaver writes: "the following days' shooting went almost without a hitch, especially once we were off the street and into the studio on the Upper East Side of Manhattan, where the interior room had been built to Beckett's specifications" (*The Tender Hour of Twilight*, 321).

3 Alan Schneider recounts the first meeting of SB and Keaton:

> When Sam and I arrived, Keaton was drinking a can of beer and watching a baseball game on TV; his wife was in the other room. The greetings were mild, slightly awkward somehow, without meaning to be. The two exchanged a few general words, most of them coming from Sam, then proceeded to sit there in silence while Keaton kept watching the game. I don't even think he offered us a beer. Not out of ill will; he just didn't think of it. Or else maybe he thought that a man like Beckett didn't drink beer.

After giving a sample of their broken conversation, Schneider concludes: "They simply had nothing to say to each other, no worlds of any kind to share. And all of Sam's good will and my own flailing efforts to get something started failed to bring them together on any level. It was a disaster." ("On Directing *Film*," 71–72.)

Keaton's (third) wife was Eleanor Norris (1918–1998).

4 Rosset lived at 196 West Houston Street, Manhattan.

BARBARA BRAY
PARIS

Wed [29 July 1964] N. Y.

Dear B.

Thanks for your letter. This in haste 6.30 a.m. before rushes of yesterday-today's shooting. Great stuff in film. Keaton marvellous. Finish shooting today with luck. Staying into next week to help with rough cut and to get an idea of ensemble.[1] Working morning noon night. T'will have been worth it. Home prob. middle of next week. Have seen none save Reaveys, exhausting session after work with poems & manuscripts. No more now. Alan who sleeps in next room clamouring to be off. Too busy to be too shaky. Take care of yourself and sack those Europhonamiers.[2]

Love

Sam

ALS; 1 leaf, 1 side; *env to* Mme. Bray, 14 Rue Le Sueur, Paris 16, France; *pm* 29-7-64, New York; TCD, MS 10948/1/292.

1 SB had written to Bray on 24 July: "'Crew' better & better & B. K. actually getting involved? Beautiful things in the rushes. Cutting vitally important. Good contact with cutter thanks be to G." (TCD, MS 10948/1/291.)

2 Europhon was an Italian company producing radiophonic equipment.

AVIGDOR ARIKHA AND ANNE ATIK
PARIS

31.7.64 [New York]

Chers amis

Merci pr. votre lettre. Ici ça va. Tournage terminé hier. Suis content du résultat. Il reste à dégrossir le montage et je rentre, vers le milieu de la semaine prochaine j'espère. Ce sera un simple bout à bout, il s'agit surtout de trouver des principes organisateurs. Le monteur, Sidney Meyers, est un type très bien, ex-altiste professionnel, je peux compter sur lui pour la musique définitive.[1] Vu personne sauf les Reavey 1 fois. Dans le boulot depuis 8 heures du matin jusqu'au soir. N'ai vu N.Y. que par la bande. Tout le monde formidablement gentil. Espère voir le Frick et le Modern Art avant de partir – à l'heure du déjeuner! Il fait très chaud mais j'aime assez. Je crois qu'on [va] l'appeler FILM tout court. Inutile de se fatiguer inutilement.

Affectueusement

Sam

Horace Gregory a téléphoné, mais je ne sais si je pourrai le voir. Il habite en dehors de N.Y.[2]

ALS; 1 leaf, 1 side; *env to* Monsieur et Madame Avigdor Arikha, 19 Avenue de Tourville, Paris 7, FRANCE; *pm* 31-7-64, New York; InU, Arikha.

31.7.64 [New York]

Dear Both

Thanks for your letter. All OK here. Filming finished yesterday. Am pleased with result. Remains to polish the montage and I'll come back, toward the middle of next week I hope. It will just be a rough cut. What matters above all is to hit on organising principles. The editor, Sidney Meyers, is a great bloke, a former professional viola player, I can rely on him for the final music.[1] Seen nobody except the Reaveys, once. At work from 8 in the morning till evening. Seen nothing of N.Y. except glimpses while busy with other things. Everybody amazingly nice. Hoping to see the Frick and the Modern Art before leaving – at lunch-time! It's very hot, but I quite like it. I think it will be called just *FILM*. No point in tiring oneself pointlessly.

Love

Sam

Horace Gregory phoned but I don't know if I'll be able to see him. He lives outside N.Y.[2]

1 Sidney Meyers (1906–1969) was a documentary film-maker and film editor, celebrated for several works, including *The Quiet One* (1948), *Edge of the City* (1957), and *The Savage Eye* (1959); for three years he had played viola with the Cincinnati Symphony Orchestra.

2 This postscript is inserted at the top of the handwritten letter. Horace Gregory had been Anne Atik's professor at Sarah Lawrence College, Bronxville, New York.

AVIGDOR ARIKHA AND ANNE ATIK
PARIS

<u>Mardi</u> [4 August 1964] [New York]

Chers amis,

Terminé, je rentre. Vu ce matin projection du "bout à bout". Pas mal. Reste à fignoler aux autres. Ça a été dur. Je m'étonne un peu d'être encore à peu près debout. Lit[t]éralement rien fait d'autre depuis l'arrivée. Vu personne sauf les Reavey 1 fois. Horace G. trop loin pour que je puisse espérer le voir. Je lui téléphonerai demain, et à un tas d'autres que je n'ai pas pu voir. Une dernière séance avec Alan pour dresser la liste des choses à revoir. Timing encore à préciser, je fais confiance à Sidney Meyers, type merveilleux, ex-altiste professionnel et grand amateur de peinture. Visité aujourd'hui avec [? lui] le Modern Art Mus, formidable collection. Voilà! Je vous appellerai cette semaine.

Affectueusement

Sam

ALS; 1 leaf, 1 side; *env to* Monsieur et Madame Avigdor Arikha, 19 Avenue de Tourville, Paris 7me, FRANCE; *pm* 4-8-64, New York; InU, Arikha. Previous publication: (facsimile and transcription) Atik, *How It Was*, 46, 47; transcribed here with variants.

Tuesday [4 August 1964] [New York]

Dear Both

All done, am on my way back. This morning saw screening of the rough cut. Not bad. Final touches to be done by the others. It's been hard. I'm quite surprised to be still on my feet, just about. Done literally nothing else since arriving. Seen no one except the Reaveys, once. Horace G. too far away for me to hope to see him. I'll phone him tomorrow, and a whole load of other people I haven't been able to see. One last session with Alan to draw up the list of things to be looked over again. Timing still to be settled, I can trust Sidney Meyers, a great bloke, ex-professional viola player, and a great lover of painting. Visited today the Modern Art Mus with [? him], tremendous collection. That's it! I'll call you this week.

Love

Sam

ROBERT PINGET
NICE

14.8.64 Ussy

Cher Robert

Merci de ton mot. Je suis arrivé d'hier et espère rester jusqu'à la fin du mois. Il fait assez beau.

Moi aussi au pied de la feuille-falaise. Sans une lueur et sans espoir, mais d'accord toujours avec le Gd. Taciturne.[1]

Je pense beaucoup à N.Y. et remettrais ça volontiers. N'ai vu la ville que par la bande, en courant pour les besoins du travail. Harlem et Bowery plusieurs fois en voiture. 1 heure au Guggenheim (assez) itou au Modern Art (pas assez). Ball game (nocturne) à Queens. Fascinant.[2] Aucuns amis que les Reavey (1 fois). Gorki et increvable dramaturgie.[3] Très gentils. Chaleur et humidité assommantes. Je m'accrochais aux étranges boîtes aux lettres. Merveilleuses giclées le long des fleuves en Morgan Sport ouverte. Pagodes téléphoniques dans Chinatown. Férocité des chauffeurs de taxi.

Affectueusement

et à bientôt.

Sam

ALS; 1 leaf, 1 side; *env to* Monsieur Robert Pinget, Résidence Négresco, Nice, A.-M.; *pm* 14–8–64, La Ferté-sous-Jouarre; Burns Library, Samuel Beckett Collection, SB-RP.

14.8.64 [Ussy]

Dear Robert

Thank you for your note. I arrived just yesterday and hope to stay until the end of the month. Weather quite good.

I too at the foot of the cliff-blank-sheet. Without a glimmer, without a hope, but always in agreement with the Great Silent One.[1]

I think a great deal about N.Y., and would gladly do it again. Only had odd glimpses of the city as we raced about for work reasons. Harlem and Bowery a few times by car. One hour in the Guggenheim (enough) and the same in the Modern Art (not enough). Evening ball game in Queens. Fascinating.[2] By way of friends only the Reaveys (once): Gorki and the undefeatable dramaturgy.[3] Really nice. Wearisome heat and humidity. I used to hang on to the strange letter boxes. Wonderful spurts along the rivers in open-topped Morgan Sport. Telephone pagodas in Chinatown. Ferocity of the taxi-drivers.

Affectionately

and till soon.

Sam

1 Pinget's family owned an apartment in the Hôtel Negresco in Nice, to which the author would retire when seeking to concentrate. It is probable he was working on what would become the novel *Quelqu'un*, published the following year.

2 Richard Seaver took SB to the recently built Shea Stadium in Queens to see the New York Mets beat the Houston Colt .45s in a double header (3–0 and 6–2). He recounts of SB:

> As the game progressed, he asked key questions, wondering why, for instance, when a batter hit the ball so weakly he nonetheless ran as if his life depended on it. And why in the world on what you called a passed ball, the batter didn't run, just stood there. Balls and strikes he understood immediately, and was especially impressed by the blue-suited umpires, who acted with such histrionic authority.

After the first game, Seaver asked SB if he wished to leave. SB asked, "'Is it over then?'" Seaver explained about the double header, and SB replied, "'So there's a whole other game? . . . Then we should stay.'" (*The Tender Hour of Twilight*, 322–323.)

3 Reavey had worked on a thesis on Maxim Gorky (see 9 May 1950, n. 8), and in 1961 had edited and translated *Modern Soviet Short Stories* (New York: Grosset and Dunlap), which contained Gorky's story "The Nightingale." Jean Reavey as a dramatist: 16 January 1962.

BARBARA BRAY
LONDON

Friday [21 August 1964] Ussy

Dear Barbara

Nothing to say, here goes. The tomb will be lively after here and no pen and paper. J'ai découvert que tout le malheur des hommes vient d'une seule chose, qui est de savoir demeurer au repos dans une chambre.[1] Bossuet hailed the Revocation of the Edict of Nantes as the greatest political achievement since Constantinus and shat in his old age on the memory of Molière.[2] Beginning the Journal of Delacroix.[3] Edward rang up. He's giving a recital with John in Wexford (Festival) in October, three Bach sonatas. Seems all laid on.[4] Work quite hopeless. Thirty abortive beginnings like: "Plus signe de vie, dites-vous, dis-je, bah, qu'à cela ne tienne, imagination pas morte, et derechef, plus fort, trop fort, Imagination pas morte." Trop fort, en effet.[5] Hope the journey went well and the evening prospect up to expectations. No mail of interest. Henri's eye reconsultation & biological examination postponed, so no more Meaux for the moment.[6] Invitation from Zürcher Werkbühne to write a Vorspiel to Spiel. Sent them packing.[7] Nothing to say, c'est chose faite, give my love to the lovable, ce sera vite fait.[8]

Love

Sam

ALS; 1 leaf, 1 side; *env to* Mrs Barbara Bray, c/o Pearson, Hallam Court, Hallam Street, London W.1, Angleterre; *pm* 22-8-64, La Ferté-sous-Jouarre; TCD, MS 10948/1/294.

1 SB adapts a line from Blaise Pascal's *Pensées*: "J'ai découvert que tout le malheur des hommes vient d'une seule chose, qui est de ne savoir pas demeurer en repos dans une chambre" (*Pensées* [Paris: Jean-Claude Lattès, 1988] 60) ("I have often said that man's unhappiness springs from one thing alone, his incapacity to stay quietly in one room" (*Pensées and Other Writings*, tr. Honor Levi [Oxford: Oxford University Press, 1995] 44). SB changes "ne savoir pas" (incapacity) into "savoir" (capacity).

2 Jacques-Bénigne Bossuet (1627–1704), Bishop of Meaux, was the single most influential cleric of the age, not least because he was well looked on by the increasingly conservative Louis XIV. He wrote extensively, not only on religious topics proper but on political and cultural matters. His views, always forcefully expressed, were rigorously orthodox, opposed to anything which he saw as weakening the Church. His enthusiasm for the Revocation (1685) of the Edict of Nantes (1598) is typical, even though the Edict itself had been sponsored by Louis's ancestor, the great Henri IV, in order to put an end to the religious wars (Catholic versus Protestant) that had marked his reign. His disapproval of what he saw as Molière's dangerously freethinking work was again typical. In his *Maximes et réflexions sur la comédie* (1694), Bossuet wrote:

> Il faudra donc que nous passions pour honnêtes les impiétés et les infamies dont sont pleines les comédies de Molière, ou qu'on ne veuille pas ranger parmi les pièces d'aujourd'hui, celles d'un auteur qui a expiré, pour ainsi dire, à nos yeux, et qui remplit encore à présent tous les théâtres des équivoques les plus grossières, dont on ait jamais infecté les oreilles des chrétiens (*L'Eglise et le théâtre*, ed. C. Urbain and E. Levesque [Paris: Bernard Grasset, 1930] 172) (So we are to let pass as decent the impieties and infamies that abound in the plays of Molière, or else refuse to include among the plays of today those of an author who has, as it were, expired before our very eyes, who yet still fills theatres everywhere with the coarsest and most suggestive meanings that have ever defiled the ears of Christian folk).

SB's amused contempt is unsurprising. SB inserts "in his old age" in the right margin.

3 Eugène Delacroix's *Journal* encompassed the years 1822–1863 (*Journal de Eugène Delacroix*, 3 vols. [Paris: E. Plon, Nourrit, 1893]). The edition that SB was reading has not been identified.

4 Edward Beckett, John Beckett, and Betty Sullivan would present "A Recital of Music by Johann Sebastian Bach" in the 1964 Wexford Festival on 26 October (NLI, Charles Acton Collection, Box 71).

5 This is the opening of the first line of SB's "Faux Départs," first published in *Kursbuch* 1 (June 1965) 1–5 (rpt. *Samuel Beckett, Complete Short Prose, 1929–1989*, ed. S. E. Gontarski [New York; Grove Press, 1995] 271–273).

6 Henri Hayden had a cottage in Reuil-en-Brie, near Ussy, and SB drove him to the central town of Meaux for his eye appointments.

7 The Zürcher Werkbühne was an experimental theatre company organized in 1962 by Director Georg S. Müller (b. 1935). In 1965, he directed SB's *Spiel* at the Theater am Neumarkt in Zurich. "Vorspiel" (Prologue).

8 "C'est chose faite" (job done). "Ce sera vite fait" (that won't take long).

BARBARA BRAY
LONDON

29.8.64 Paris

Dear Barbara

Thanks for your letter and good news of Endgame, Jack & Pat. There was an article in the Monde on the anti-Aldwych outcry.[1]

Got back yesterday, just as great heat breaking. Last days at Ussy were marvellous (when I condescended to enter them). Henri all right, but eye still hazy. He saw the occulist [sic] yesterday & I am to call them today. It doesn't stop him from working – or driving. Corrected more proofs for Suhrkamp.[2] Fear your noble suggestion for further squirms beyond my powers. Not a subject for romance. Literally nothing to show for that fortnight of mornings, hand to yawned off head. But for your entertainment enclosed abortion which I'd be obliged if you wd. destroy. Shall try to continue trying here.[3] Delacroix's Journal very disappointing & [illeg.1 word] wd. be foolish I think to take it on. When it's not unbearable dissertations it[']s fascinating but untranslatable technicalities – peering at Rubens from tops of ladders. Avigdor rang this morning, said the American teaching jobs had come to naught. He sounded dim. Letter from Esslin with agreement to sign for use of Transition "dialogues" for his anthology. He mentioned that in absence of Michael [illeg.1 word] he had invited Donald to produce Cascando and that he will – with inevitable Jack & Pat.[4] Nothing from Staib so far. Thinking of joining the abonnés absents.[5] Don't yet know when Madeleine wants her regisseurs but I suppose in about a week.[6] Rosset here on way back from Fair Sept. 20. No further news of film. I suppose they haven't done a tap since I left – or reshot the peasant inserts.[7] Many thanks in advance for Petrarch not yet to hand. Looking forward to a sniff of that old decency. A student I used to pin up sonnets on walls of my chamber in different coloured inks for the rime pattern.[8] Did I tell you Bossuet's co-students' nickname for him, he was such a bûcheur: Bos suetus aratro.[9] Whole lit. page of Combat on Flaubert and analogy with Sartre (!) – to [? come] clear one fine day when his "éblouissant personnage" will have ceased to dazzle us.[10] Bosquet rang. Biannual literary agapes not far removed.[11]

Love

Sam

Enclosure

Plus signe de vie, dites-vous, dis-je, bah, qu'à cela ne tienne, imagination pas morte, et derechef, plus fort, trop fort, Imagination pas morte, et le soir même m'enfermai sous les huées et m'y mis, sans autre appui que les Syntaxes de Jolly et de Draeger.

Mon cabinet à [*for* a] ceci de particulier, ou plutôt moi, que j'y ai fait aménager une stalle à ma taille. C'est là, au fond, face au mur, dans la pénombre, que j'imagine, tantôt assis, tantôt debout, au besoin à genoux. Je cale au préalable la porte qui y donne, sans quoi, étant munie d'un groom, elle se refermerait sur moi.

Dois-je me présenter? Bah.

Première nuit. Je m'abîme dans le lieu, à partir de ce que j'en crois savoir. Je sens dans mon dos le jour poignant. Je ne suis plus que silence, noir et vide, ce dernier toutefois encore insuffisamment à mon gré. Une pauvre question se fait jour, Sont-ils définitifs?

Deuxième nuit. Suite du vide et de là sus au sol et à l'air. Repoussé je trébuche sur la question, Toujours les mêmes? Les mêmes partout? Comme s'il pouvait y avoir changement sans bruit! L'est s'avivait d'orange déjà qu'à peine je commençais à rougir de moi.

Troisième nuit. Echaudé je m'unis au silence et finis par trouver. Sol mou. Température et humidité élevées. Exhortations. Gare le géomorphisme! Varier les attaques!

Par nuit j'entends la naturelle, celle qui s'étend du coucher du soleil jusqu'à son prochain lever. Or nous descendons vers l'hiver.

Quatrième nuit. Etendue. Vers quatre ou cinq heures du matin je renonce à ma méthode et recours à la logique. Éclair. Toute limite inconcevable. La raison me dégoûte. Mais il est des joints qu'elle arrive à remplir, Donc je la souffre. C'est ce qui fait ma supériorité.

Je me sens rarement seul. Comment le pourrais-je? J'ai un geste si cela m'arrive. J'envoie contre la cloison le joint médian de mon médius droit replié à cet effet. C'est là le nord, puisque j'ai l'est dans le dos. Jamais le sud. Jamais l'ouest. La cloison nord. Je dégage la main, fais saillir le joint et frappe. Cela sonne faux, je n'y peux rien.

ALS; 2 leaves, 2 sides; *enclosure* TMS, 1 leaf, 1 side; *env to* Mrs Barbara Bray, c/o Pearson, Hallam Court, Hallam Street, London W.1, Angleterre; *pm* 29-8-64, Paris; TCD, MS 10948/1/296 and 296a.

1 The Royal Shakespeare Company's production of *Endgame* continued in repertory at the Aldwych Theatre. One reviewer compared it to that done Off-Broadway: "The greater abstractness of the recent interpretations has been traced to the direct influence of Mr. Beckett, who seems to be taking more of a hand in supervising the staging of his plays" ("American Clowns with a Weakness for Beckett," *The Times* 1 August 1964: 10).

Emile Littler (1903–1985), a member of the executive council of the Royal Shakespeare Company for twenty-five years, had complained that the Aldwych Theatre's *Season of Cruelty* was a mistake and that the plays had no place in the tradition of the company ("Theatre Criticism 'Not Personal': Mr. Littler Explains his Attack," *The Times* 26 August 1964: 6). Against Mr. Littler's claim that the experimental season of Peter Hall and Peter Brook was "ruining our Stratford image," Peter Hall pointed out that the plays were a financial success (*The Times* 26 August 1964: 6).

2 SB continued to correct proofs for the second volume of *Dramatische Dichtungen*.

3 SB's enclosure here, and the enclosures with SB's letter to Bray of 1 September 1964, are draft material "taken from the initial *Imaginez morte imaginez* notebook kept at TCD as MS 11223, but amended" (Mark Nixon to the editors, 9 June 2013).

4 Martin Esslin sent SB contracts for permission to include "Three Dialogues" by SB and Georges Duthuit in his book *Samuel Beckett* to be published by Prentice-Hall in their Twentieth Century Views series. When SB wrote to Esslin to return the signed contracts on 28 August, he added: "it is good news indeed that Donald is available to do Cascando. With Pat (the Voice I presume) and Jack." (Private Collection.) Jack MacGowran did not play the role of the Opener. Michael Bakewell had moved to BBC TV, so he was no longer available to produce radio dramas (Michael Bakewell to the editors, 13 March 2013).

5 Philippe (not Francis) Staib wished to make a film of *Fin de partie* for TV. By 1 October he had met Jérôme Lindon as well as SB, who would write to Lindon on 15 October:

> Je ne veux pas m'opposer au projet de Staib à condition qu'il ne soit pas question d'une adaptation pour la TV, mais d'un simple document filmé aussi proche que possible d'une représentation normale, et à condition aussi bien entendu que toi et Roger soyez d'accord (IMEC-Fonds Samuel Beckett, Boîte 11, *Fin de partie*, contrats, représentation [2]). (I have no wish to stand out against the Staib project provided there is no question of an adaptation for TV, but a simple filmed document as close as possible to a normal performance, and provided also, of course, that you and Roger agree).

"Abonnés absents" (absent subscribers).

6 "Regisseurs" (here: directors). SB refers to Roger Blin and himself.

7 Barney Rosset was expected in Paris following the Frankfurt Book Fair. By "peasant inserts," SB may be referring to the facial reactions of the elderly couple and the flower woman when they view O (Beckett, *Film*, 15–16, 21).

8 SB owned a copy of Petrarch's *Rime*. It is not certain what book on or by Petrarch may have been sent by Bray. A new introduction to Petrarch had been published by Chatto and Windus in April, namely Morris Bishop's *Petrarch and his World*. Newly in paperback was *Life of Petrarch* by Ernest Hatch Wilkins, originally published by the University of Chicago Press (1961).

9 Bossuet was nicknamed "Bos suetus aratro" (ox accustomed to the plough) by his fellow students at the Collège des Godrans in Dijon.

10 On 27 August, under the heading "Au temps du bovarysme des foules, redécouvrons Flaubert . . .," *Combat* published several articles (p. 4): "Flaubert contemporain," "Flaubert et Valéry," and an excerpt, "Maurice Nadeau juge de Flaubert," from Maurice Nadeau's preface to the *Œuvres complètes de Flaubert*, 18 vols. (Lausanne: Editions Rencontre, 1964–1983).
"Eblouissant personnage" (dazzling personage).

11 Alain Bosquet. SB anticipates the "rentrée littéraire" (autumn publishing season).

BARBARA BRAY
LONDON

1.9.64 Paris

Dear Barbara

Your letter would encourage a corpse. Here two more gasps for yr. collection. I'll go quite mad if it goes on much longer – & who can doubt it?[1] No, I did not see what H. H. wrote about me. Keep it for some day when I complain of my boots.[2] Four large photos, plus gruesomes les unes que les autres, in Theater 1964, with usual diarrhoea, including translation of Clancy Segal. In same issue strange photo of Pat tearing strips in B.P. and article on him by Esslin. Am keeping it for you.[3] Edward left this morning for Munich in Triumph with co-competing girl. Dined him at old Dôme last night and billiards at the 3 Musketeers, won on the Bo[a]st with 7 e[x]quisite & successive cannons.[4] No news of film. Also contributions from Brook, Pinter and Hall.[5] I should be able to manage an evening over week-end if you come. Been browsing in Renard again. Not what he was, but marvellous things, like the pigeon helping with its wing the too frail branch on which it lights.[6] Bos (ox) suetus (p.p. of suesco, accustomed) aratro (to the plough).[7] Don't know what you mean by Beckett Ms and thirst for the homonym's fjords.[8] Invitation from Cuban Embassy to Latin-American Theatre Festival at Havana September-October. Tempted but won't.[9] Series of wonderful days (weather), seldom (if ever) saw the light so beautiful. Shall walk this afternoon to Place de la Convention to lodge a few rubbishy cheques, through the old unrecognisable haunts.[10] Rang the Hayden – all well and ophthalmologist's report encouraging. Blood also fluider. Neighbours back with brats. Let a roar out of me this morning & they seemed to move away. Have seen no papers so nothing for you. Expecting a sign from Madeleine (also in Theater 64) but nothing yet. Nothing from Staib or Serreau.[11]

Love

Sam

Enclosures

His refuge now is a kind of cupboard in a wall. He talks to himself of himself – that always! – in the last person, he says, Now he has taken refuge in what seems to be a wall cupboard. Let it measure four feet in width by six in depth by five in height. Here he squats, on a low stool, stands, kneels and moves about, on all fours and upright. When he stands still his hat brushes the ceiling, when he moves upright it does not. This discordancy is due to ancient habit, that of walking crouched and, when brought to a stand, of drawing himeslf [sic] up to his full height. The longer he lives, he says, and therefore the further he goes, the smaller they grow, and there will be smaller still, if he continues to be spared. And this is logical, the reasoning being, The more he fills the space, the less room etc. And similarly the barer they grow, the longer he lives, and the bitterer his experience of recesses. And one day there will be one, if he is spared till then, empty of all but of him. Here there is this unindispensable stool and on the walls, when he turns on the light, women's faces, including one he is pleased to think of as his mother's. Light, did he say light? Yes, and this is new, but it was bound to come. For if darkness was his ally always, and remains so, undispellable it can harm, he knows that now and is by so much the wiser. What is less accountable, if at all, is this voice that prattles on, normally loud and with seldom a pause for breath or reflection. Did he not literally hold his breath, he says, for what seemed an eternity, and then, for what seemed another, barely venture an occasional murmur, not so much emboldened – that never! – as to keep his courage up. And now he projects for all the world as if he were out of all earshot for ever, or in the depths of the earth. No, there is no accounting for this. And while there was a time he would not have admitted this without long struggle and debate, that time too is no more.

On my return, once clean, I looked to satisfy my mind that all was as I had left it. There was in me that which could not have got in here, faces, strips of sky. Once clean of these I looked, scrupulous as always, to satisfy myself that all was well. I went on the basis of from five to ten more years of reason. This figure was not arrived at lightly, in a dismal spirit of foreboding, it was an inference from more than half a century of progress, now brisk, now sluggish, but never discontinued. So oceanward through mounting storm a body of diminishing mass. Be that as it may, this figure was in my mind, not less than five, not more than ten, and the problem of how it might be put to best account, the day I looked to make certain that nothing was changed in the situation I had left behind me.[12]

ALS; 2 leaves, 2 sides; *enclosure* TMSS, 2 leaves, 2 sides; *env to* M$^{\underline{rs}}$ Bray, c/o Pearson, Hallam Court, Hallam Street, London W.1, Angleterre; *pm* 1-9-64, Paris; TCD, MS 10948/1/297 and 297a, 297b.

1 On SB's enclosures, see 29 August 1964, n. 3.

2 Harold Hobson defended the experimental program at the Aldwych Theatre, writing: "The Royal Shakespeare Company is the most alert and exploratory theatrical

organisation in Britain ... It is they who discovered for England Samuel Beckett, the noblest, the gentlest, the most saintly spirit now working in the theatre." (Harold Hobson, "In Defence of Peter Hall, The Aldwych Affair," *The Sunday Times* 30 August 1964: 25.)

3 "Plus gruesomes les unes que les autres" (each more gruesome than the next; SB dresses up the English "gruesome" as a French plural). *Theater 1964: Chronik und Bilanz des Bühnenjahres* (1 September 1964), published as an annual supplement by *Theater heute*; it offered a preview of the coming theatre season. The section "Wer ist Samuel Beckett?" includes three articles (Adam Seide, "Besuch bei Beckett," 85; Georg Hensel, "Die Weltbühne des Samuel Beckett," 85–89; and a translation of Clancy Sigal's notes on the rehearsals of *Endgame*, "Beckett auf der Probe," 90–92) as well as four full-page photos of SB by Vera Mertz Spoerri (b. 1936) (83, 84, 88–89, 93). Martin Esslin's essay "Der Ire Patrick Magee" includes a photo of Magee in Harold Pinter's *The Birthday Party* taken by David Sim (109–110). SB inserts an arrow indicating where he mentions other essays in this issue (see n. 5).

4 Edward Beckett traveled to the Munich International Competition sponsored by the Bayerische Rundfunk (held each year for a different instrument, in 1964 for flute) with an American who owned a Triumph TR4 sports car. Les Trois Mousquetaires is at 77 Avenue du Maine, Paris 14. (Edward Beckett to the editors, 14 March 2013.)

5 Also included in *Theater 1964*: Peter Brook, "Radikale Experimente" (19–21); Martin Esslin's essay "Der Ire Patrick Magee" which is about Harold Pinter, but not by him; Christina Pesch's essay "Arbeit in Stratford: Ein Bericht von den Proben" which is about Peter Hall (114–116).

6 Jules Renard's *Journal*: 12 January 1957, n. 5. SB owned a four-volume edition (Paris: F. Bernouard, 1928; Dirk van Hulle and Mark Nixon, *Samuel Beckett's Library* [Cambridge: Cambridge University Press, 2013] 282). SB refers to Renard's entry of 16 April 1908: "Le vol d'un pigeon qui se pose sur une branche trop faible. De l'aile, il aide la branche." (*Journal 1887–1910*, ed. Léon Guichard and Gilbert Sigaux, Bibliothèque de la Pléiade [Paris: Gallimard, 1960] 1172.) (The flight of the pigeon which lights on a branch that is too weak. With its wing it helps the branch.)

7 SB translates the nickname of Bossuet, "Bos suetus aratro" (see 29 August 1964, n. 9); p.p.: past participle.

8 Possibly Bray had made a reference to Samuel J. Beckett, *The Fjords and Folk of Norway* (London: Methuen, 1915).

9 The Latin-American Theatre Festival (El Festival de Teatro Latinoamericano) was founded in 1961 to stage Latin American playwrights; in 1964, it assumed an international character by instituting a meeting that invited playwrights, actors, directors, and critics to convene in Havana during the Festival (September–October) (www.casadelasamericas.org/teatro.php, accessed 7 May 2013; "Festival de Teatro Latinoamericano Casa de las Americas 1964," *Conjunto* 1.2 [1964] 66).

10 SB will be revisiting his former quartier, that of Rue des Favorites.

11 Madeleine Renaud in *Oh les beaux jours* was mentioned in "Revue der Schauspieler" in *Theater 1964*, with a full-page photograph (107). Jean-Marie Serreau had directed *Comédie* at the Pavillon de Marsan, from 14 June, and was expected to arrange further productions.

12 There are two enclosures: TCD, MS 10948/1/297a and TCD, MS 10948/1/297b.

HENRY WENNING
NEW HAVEN, CONNECTICUT

8.9.64 Paris

Dear Henry

Phoned you yesterday but no reply. Perhaps Labour Day.[1]

Rightly or wrongly have decided not to let Godot go yet. Neither sentimental nor financial, probably peak of market now and never such another offer. Can't explain.[2]

Molloy is a good MS. and I know you'll handle it for the best. I wouldn't need the money this year.[3]

I have suppressed fairly successfully all memories of dealing with Schwartz, but now a faint one assails me of having done for him a transcript of Godot from the published text. I don't know how this wd. affect value of original MS.[4]

Best always,

Sam

ALS; 1 leaf, 1 side; *AN AH bottom margin:* 38, Boulevard St. Jacques, Paris 14; MoSW, Samuel Beckett Papers, MSS 008, 1.9.

1 The American holiday of Labor Day occurred on Monday 7 September in 1964. SB sent a telegram to Wenning on 8 September when he could not reach him by telephone: "DECIDED NOT SELL GODOT SENDING YOU MOLLOY 4 CAHIERS AIRMAIL TODAY WRITING" (MoSW, Samuel Beckett Papers, MSS 008, 1.9).

2 After SB's death, the manuscript of *En attendant Godot* was donated to the Bibliothèque Nationale.

3 Henry Wenning contacted F. W. Roberts, then Director of the Humanities Research Center, University of Texas, on 12 September; Roberts responded on 14 September that he would "look forward with eagerness to the receipt of the manuscript of Samuel Beckett's Molloy" (Beckett Collection, Box 5, General Correspondence). The four cahiers of the manuscript of *Molloy* in French are there (TxU, Beckett Collection, Box 4, F 5–7).

4 Jake Schwartz had indeed asked SB to make a transcription of *En attendant Godot*, (see 5 November 1959, and n. 3). In his letter of 14 September to Henry Wenning, F. W. Roberts wrote: "The other manuscript of Godot which I mentioned is undoubtedly a transcript which Beckett must have prepared when he was dealing with Mr. Schwartz; it is now in a private collection, and I suspect the least said the better." This transcription is now at the Humanities Research Center, University of Texas (Beckett Collection, 7.5–6).

MARY HUTCHINSON
LONDON

14.9.64 Paris

Dear Mary

I am sorry you are hurt by my not have [sic] replied to your last letter. I intended no unfriendliness.

If you knew what my life has been these last months, and indeed since the beginning of the year, you would perhaps be more indulgent.

The claims on me have become so ferocious, and the disproportion so acute between what I have to do and the time and energy required to do it, that I neglect things which normally I would attend to.

Some of those foolish enough to care for me understand this and do not reproach me with indifference. But it is normal that friendship should be withdrawn, and this is what I expect.

Yours affectionately

Sam

ALS; 1 leaf, 1 side; *env to* M[rs] Hutchinson, 21 Hyde Park Square, London W.1, Angleterre; *pm* 15-9-64, Paris; TxU, Hutchinson, 2.6.

BARBARA BRAY
LONDON

22 [September 1964] Paris

Dear Barbara

Thanks for your Bath letter.

I was up all night with the one and the other and am still drunk. Wobbling home in the car in the morning was in Winnie's light or flying above clouds into N.Y. with sun trying to set.

Saw screening of Film latest cut yesterday & with Barney u. Frauenzimmerchen & Hodeir. C'est raté. Laying on movieola for next Sunday, silly attempt to improve. Thinking in desperation of possible sound – tick tick tick tick – tock tock tock tock – to reinforce 2 visions. Knowing all in vain.[1]

Have now 3 pages shit to my credit. Going to pull chain on now.[2]

Please thank Checchina for beautiful German. Only found one Fehlerchen.[3]

Meant to see Madeleine last night but fell by wayside.[4]

Most beautiful day today.

This evening the Riopelle. Tomorrow the Lindon. Thursday the Arikha.

Letter, no, picture P.C., from Con from Cagnes (sur Mer).

Invitation from inconnu (s?) (e?) (es?) to spend xmas in Bavarian Schloss expenses paid. From Cuba embassy to congress in Habana (?) Havana (?). From N.-W. University for next spring to celebrate W.B.Y.'s birth too soon to be influenced. All expenses always paid & in case N.Y. 1500 $. Petty pocket money cash.[5]

Oh spark decency blaze.

Never seldom saw more beautiful day. Out now prowl out soon prowl mind stumble unseeing glare lifetime of.

Herzlichst[6]

S

on verso[7]

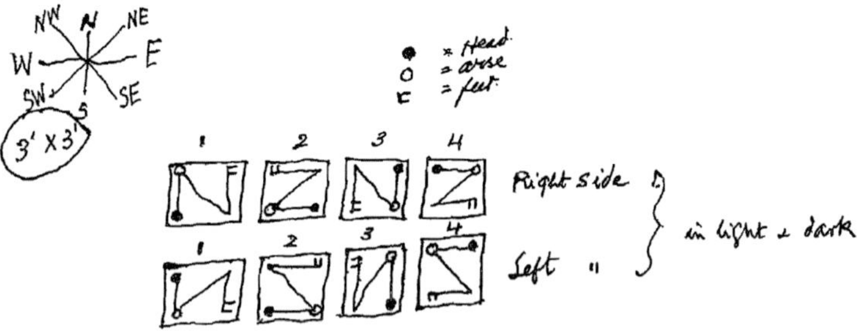

ALI; 1 leaf, 2 sides; *env to* Mrs Bray, c/o Pearson, Hallam Court, Hallam Street, London W. 1, Angleterre; *pm* 22–9–64, Paris; TCD, MS 10948/1/303.

1 "U[nd] Frauenzimmerchen" (and little dame), the unnamed woman managing the space and operating the movieola.

André Hodeir (1921–2011).

2 This writing is related to fragments enclosed with SB's letters to Bray of 29 August and 1 September.

3 Francesca Bray had been studying in Germany and had written to SB. "Fehlerchen" (small mistake).

4 Madeleine Renaud was preparing to open in *Oh les beaux jours* at the Odéon-Théâtre de France on 21 October.

5 "Inconnu (s?) (e?) (es?)" (unknown man /men? / woman? / women?). The invitation to attend Drama Festival in Cuba: 1 September 1964, n. 9. SB had refused the invitation of Richard Ellmann to participate in a conference at Northwestern University, Evanston, Illinois, in celebration of the centenary of W. B. Yeats in 1965: "to my sorrow I cannot accept because of galloping exhaustion and inability to speak a word worth having" (21 September 1964; OkTU, Richard Ellmann Papers).

6 "Herzlichst" (warmest wishes).

7 The drawing on verso is a schematic of body positions, presented with permutations. These may be related to SB's later text *Le Dépeupleur*.

SIDNEY MEYERS
NEW YORK

29.9.64 — Ussy-sur-Marne
Seine-et-Marne

Dear Sidney

I have now had two screenings of the new cut and a session with such a deficient movieola and in such absence and need of a bottle that I had difficulty in functioning.[1] Hence inadequacy of notes herewith.[2] In a few weeks time I'm getting a better machine and should have something more worth having for you then, if you are not in a hurry to make final cut. But I feel there is not much more you can do. And realize it is not really possible to be of use to you from a distance. We should need to be all together again in room 312. All five.[3]

I am on the whole pleased with the film, having accepted its imperfections, for the most part perceptible only to the insiders, and discerned how in some strange way it gains by its deviations from the strict intention and develops something better. The last time I found myself submitting, far from the big crazy idea, to a strangeness and beauty of pure image. The few reactions I have had from others are strongly positive. All sound is definitely out as far as I am concerned, except for the hssh.[4]

I have fled here for as long as I can bear it, with empty head and empty page. There's poles for you.

Love to Nina.[5]

Yours ever

s/ Sam

TLS; 1 leaf, 1 side; Meyers Collection.

1 SB had viewed the rough cut of *Film* on 21 September. After a second viewing, SB wrote to Richard Seaver: "I feel better about it. I forget my little idea and let the images go over me. Sound definitely out." (26 September 1964; TxU, Seaver, R 16501.)

2 SB's enclosed notes are not with this letter in the Meyers Collection, nor with the letter sent to Alan Schneider on the same day in the Burns Library Collection. An undated typed list of notes about cutting adjustments can be found in the Alan Schneider Papers at the University of California, San Diego (TMScc; 1 leaf, 1 side; CUSD, MS 103/19/10; photocopy UoR, BIF, MS 1227/7/6/2). This undated list belongs to the letters of 29 September 1964 to both Sidney Meyers and Alan Schneider. It predates the typed list SB sent to Sidney Meyers with his letter of 28 October 1964 (Meyers Collection); internal evidence (for example the flower scene) confirms this. None of the lists mentioned is reproduced in the present text, referring as they do to a cut of the film not currently available (see http://filmbysamuelbeckett.com, accessed 24 April 2014; Ross Lipman to the editors, 20-21 April 2014).

3 By "all five," SB means Barney Rosset, Alan Schneider, Boris Kaufman, Sidney Meyers, and himself. Meyers had a studio in Room 312, Screen Building, 1600 Broadway, New York.

4 In the opening episode with the couple, each looks at the other, the man opens his mouth as if to speak, but the wife "checks him with a gesture and soft 'sssh!'" (16).

5 Nina Feinberg was assistant to Sidney Meyers on *Film*.

ALAN SCHNEIDER
NEW YORK

29.9.64 Ussy

Dear Alan

Forgive delay in sending these notes.[1] They are no more than suggestions. Don't act on them if you don't agree. The movieola here was bad and I in poor form. I'm getting the use of a better one in a few weeks and shall write again then. But don't hold up final cut on that account if you are in a hurry to get it done or for any other reason. I don't expect to have much better to offer.

I have had two screenings here, the first with Barney, Christina and Hodeir, the second with Suzanne, the movieola girl and again Hodeir (most helpful).[2] After the first I was not too happy, after the second I felt it really was something. Not quite in the way intended, but as sheer beauty, power and strangeness of image. The problem of the double vision for example is not really solved, but the attempt to solve it has given the film a plastic value which it would not have otherwise. In other words and generally speaking, from having been troubled by a certain failure to communicate fully by purely visual means the basic intention, I now begin to feel that this is unimportant and that the images obtained probably gain in force what they lose as ideograms and that the whole idea behind the film, while sufficiently expressed for those so minded, has been chiefly of value on the formal and structural level. After the first screening I though[t] again a lot, and spoke with Hodeir, about the possibility of reinforcing the E-O distinction by means of sound. Now I am definitely and finally opposed to any sound whatever apart from the "hssh" which I think should be as brief and uninsistent as possible. Suzanne, Hodeir and Miss Movieola were all I think genuinely impressed. When I get back to Paris I'll show it, with Barney's permission, to a few close (but outspeaking) friends and let you have reactions. I described it to Barney after the first screening as an "interesting failure". This I now see is much too severe. It does I suppose in a sense fail with reference to a purely intellectual schema, that is in a sense which only you and I and a few others can discern, but in so doing has acquired a dimension and a validity of its own that are worth far more than any merely efficient translation of intention.

Thank you again for all you have done. Love to Jean and the kids.[3]

Ever

s/ Sam

TLS; 1 leaf, 1 side; Burns Library, Samuel Beckett Collection, SB-AS. Previous publication, Beckett and Schneider, *No Author Better Served*, 166–167. Maurice Harmon includes the filmscript, rather than the notes made by SB after two viewings of *Film*, with this letter in *No Author Better Served* (167–176).

1 SB's notes can be found only in the Alan Schneider Collection (TMScc; 1 leaf, 1 side; CUSD, MS 103/19/10; photocopy UoR, BIF, MS 1227/7/6/2). In them, OPOV = O's point of view; EPOV = E's point of view; because the notes are hermetic, referring as they do to a cut of *Film* which may no longer exist, they have not been included in full here.

2 Barney and Christina Rosset were in Paris. André Hodeir was a classical violinist and composer, as well as a noted jazz musicologist. Grove Press published translations of several of his studies: *Jazz: Its Evolution and Essence* (1956), *Toward Jazz* (1962), and *The Worlds of Jazz* (1972). Rosset introduced SB to Hodeir, who composed a jazz cantata, *Anna Livia Plurabelle* (1966), and a jazz quintet, *Bitter Ending* (1972), both based on *Finnegans Wake*.

3 The problem of the "double vision" is most acute in the final frames of *Film* when, for the first time, E is seen by O. In note 13 of the enclosure SB writes: "13. Agree that last view of E by O a little long. Perhaps cut just before eye opens wider. Also feel last E of O too long after rocking stops. But alone in this opinion." SB adds: "Query: How do we end? Dissolve or just cut off? I liked the latter followed by announcement THE END. But open mind."

SB further refines his thoughts on these final frames, in a list sent to Sidney Meyers on 28 October (Meyers Collection).

9. First full face of O in E vision closes on open mouth, second opens with mouth opening. Cut opening frames of latter so that shot opens on open mouth.

10. Cut opening frames of second and final shot of E in O vision so that opening of shot not static but already moving in.

PETER HALL
ROYAL SHAKESPEARE COMPANY,
STRATFORD-UPON-AVON

[after 5 October 1964] [Ussy]

Thank you for your letter. I am so glad you are pleased with the Endgame production.[1]

A season of my work at the Aldwych would of course give me great pleasure. It would be necessary to get the consent of George Devine who has the priority. The play I should like most of all to be revived is Krapp's Last Tape with Pat Magee directed by McWhinnie.[2]

With best wishes to you all,

Yours ever

Sam

ALS draft; 1 leaf, 1 side; *on* Peter Hall to SB, 5 October 1964 (TLS; 1 leaf, 1 side; *letterhead* ROYAL SHAKESPEARE COMPANY); GEU, MS 1221.

1 Peter Hall wrote to SB on 5 October with the news that *Endgame* would remain in the Aldwych Theatre repertory until 3 December, and that the Royal Shakespeare Company would keep the set so that the play could be revived. "We all feel here that it is one of the best things this theatre has ever done" (Peter Hall to SB, 5 October 1964; GEU, MS 1221). Hall proposed a Beckett season: *Endgame*, *Happy Days* with Peggy Ashcroft, *Waiting for Godot*, and a new play.

2 SB had designated George Devine and the Royal Court as his preferred London director and venue (see 8 November 1962). McWhinnie had directed Magee in the London premiere of *Krapp's Last Tape* in 1958.

BARNEY ROSSET
GROVE PRESS, NEW YORK

October 20th 1964 38 Bld. St.-Jacques
Paris 14me

Dear Barney

I have broken down half way through galleys of More Pricks than Kicks. I simply can't bear it. It was a ghastly mistake on my part to imagine, not having looked at it for a quarter of a century, that this old shit was revivable. I'm terribly sorry, but I simply have to ask you to stop production. I return herewith advance on royalties and ask you to charge to my account with Grove whatever expenses whatever entailed by this beginning of production. I'll be talking to John today to the same humiliating effect. Please forgive me.[1]

Yours ever
s/ Sam

TLS; 1 leaf, 1 side; NSyU.

1 SB had written to Barbara Bray on 27 April that he had given in to Calder and Rosset on publication of *More Pricks Than Kicks*: "But publication date my decision" (TCD, MS 10948/1/272). The next day, SB warned Calder, "Better send me that contract before I start weakening backwards or before I have time to reread the muck"; SB returned the signed contract to Calder on 22 May (InU, C&B, Beckett).

ALAN SCHNEIDER
NEW YORK

20.11.64 Paris

Dear Alan

Thanks for your letter.

I have thought a lot about that distressing couple. Of course the "ssh" without the look has no meaning. And I don't see how we can eliminate them completely. Again my feeling is to reduce them to their essential functions, the "sssh" & the look, cutting out O's inspection of them and their actual exit from frame.[1]

Harold rang from London very warm about the film & with some good points. He finds Buster[']s look of horror at the end unconvincing and thinks it might be shortened. I'm inclined to agree.[2] With his suggestions for a sound track ("selective natural sounds") I disagree entirely, as with Fred Jordan[']s arguments in favour of some kind of sound. I have quite decided now that I want it silent.[3]

I look forward to Tiny Alice.[4] There is talk of a revival of Godot very soon at the Royal Court, directed by Anthony Page. He is coming to see me this weekend. I am very sceptical, but George sounds keen and so it will probably come off.[5]

It's great news I'll be seeing you next Spring. I've been having bad trouble with my mouth, but the worst is over and I'll be all right.[6]

Happy & successful rehearsals. Greetings to all.

Yours ever

Sam

ACS; 1 leaf, 2 sides; Burns Library, Samuel Beckett Collection, SB-AS. Previous publication: Beckett and Schneider, *No Author Better Served*, 178–179.

1 SB wishes to cut the shots, taken from O's point of view, of the jostled couple's reaction to him and as they leave his field of vision (Beckett, *Film*, 15–16).

2 SB refers to Buster Keaton's "look of horror" at the end of *Film* when his character becomes aware that the camera fully perceives him (Beckett, *Film*, 43–44).

3 From its inception, SB treated *Film* as a silent film. Fred Jordan (b. 1925) had begun his career at Grove Press in 1956 and "stayed for most of the next thirty years"

(Ken Jordan interview with Barney Rosset, "The Art of Publishing II," *The Paris Review* 39.145 [Winter 1997/1998] 173).

4 Schneider directed Edward Albee's play *Tiny Alice*, with John Gielgud and Irene Worth; it would open on 29 December at the Billy Rose Theatre, New York.

5 SB wrote to Susan Findley at Curtis Brown:

> I saw Anthony Page and have agreed in principle to Godot at the Court in Jan. with Williamson & Lynch. I feel dubious about it, but want to please George. I suggested McGowran & Magee for Lucky & Pozzo, but doubt if they will be free, or if Jacky would accept any role but Vladimir. However they must be asked. I would have to go over for part of rehearsals, though I don't feel up to it. ([after 20 November 1964]; GEU, MS 1221.)

6 SB had undergone surgery for a cyst on his jaw.

JOHN FLETCHER
DURHAM, ENGLAND

21.11.64 Paris

Dear Mr Fletcher

Herewith your queries answered as best I can and French Cascando. It is a R.T.F. typescript and very imperfect. If you decide to use it you should refer to the Faber volume (PLAY) for the correct mise en page. Jérôme Lindon has no objection to its appearing in your student review. There should be some form of acknowledgement to Editions de Minuit.[1]

Yours sincerely

Samuel Beckett

The first poem in Echo's Bones was suggested by the opening of Goethe's Harzreise im Winter

Dem Geier gleich,

Etc __ __ __

__ __ __ __

Schwebe mein Lied.[2]

1) What is Nancy Cunard's present address, which you said you'd give me so that I can ask for details about the manifesto on Spain you signed?

last address known to me: La MOTHE FÉNELON
LOT
FRANCE[3]

2) What was the date of the recent French première of Comédie at the Pavillon de Marsan?

I think June 14 of this year. If you want to check this you should write to André Perinetti, Théâtre du Pavillon de Marsan, 109 Rue de Rivoli, Paris 1er [4]

3) Why did you submit L'Expulsé to Fontaine and Suite to Les Temps Modernes in 1946? Had you any contacts with the editors?

I knew Sartre but not Max-Pol Fouchet at the time. They must have seemed to me the most likely reviews.[5]

4) In my book I give the chronological order of your writings after 1945 as Nouvelles – Mercier et Camier – Molloy, etc. This was the order you gave me in 1961. As there seems to be some disagreement among the critics, could you tell me whether you still maintain that order? (E.g., Gessner puts Eleuthéria before Molloy and Godot before Malone meurt, and Kenner puts Mercier et Camier before Nouvelles and Eleuthéria before Molloy, but Godot after Malone meurt). This is the order you told me:

La Fin	This is the correct order to the best of my
L'Expulsé	recollection. I have no means of checking it.
Le Calmant	Godot is without any doubt between Malone &
Premier Amour	L'Innommable. Mercier & Camier was first attempt
Mercier et Camier	at novel in French & cannot have preceded
Molloy	Nouvelles. It is possible Eleuthéria preceded
Eleuthéria	Molloy, but I think not.[6]
Malone meurt	
En attendant Godot	
L'Innommable	
Textes pour rien	

Perhaps you could arrow modifications, if any.

5) Could you tell me again what quatrain it is of Hölderlin's that Dieppe *is based on, as far as its form is concerned? I can't recall what you told me on the point.*

Ihr lieblichen Bilder im Tale,
Zum Beispiel Gärten und Baum,
Und dann der Steg, der schmale,
Der Bach zu sehen kaum.
(Der Spaziergang)[7]

6) On the last page (p. 255) of the Calder 1963 ed. of Watt*, a gap is left and the score omitted after "The soprano sang". Is this your modification or the publisher's lapse? (Same question for the fact that "Watt looking as though nearing the end of a course of injections of sterile pus" is displaced to just before "parole non ci appulcro"). In a general way, do you tend to make alterations in the case of reprints such as the recent ones of* Murphy *and* Watt*?*

Unintentional on my part. No alterations in reprints, except spelling mistakes, as e.g. "hölder" in Proust which should be "holder". May interest you to know that I have just restored Faber's Lord Chamberlain text of Godot which will henceforward appear with them as written.[8]

7) Do you remember having seen Dullin's production of Balzac's Le Faiseur *in 1936?*

Did not see it.[9]

8) Has the paper you read to the Modern Languages Society in Dublin in late 20's on Le Convergisme *[for* Concentrisme*] survived or is it, as far as you know, lost? It was never published, was it?*

Lost, please God. Never published.[10]

9) Do you recall translating any of the following, unsigned, in post-war Transition*?*

On a journey to the land of the Tarahumaras, by A. Artaud	
Introduction to Akara, by Yves le Gall	
Akara, Act III, by Romain Weingarten	Certainly trans-
Introduction to the Works of Francis Ponge, by Pierre Schneider	lated the Bove.
Armand, by Emmanuel Bove	
Apollinaire, by Gabrielle Picabia	No recollection
The Work of The Painter – To Picasso, by Paul Eluard	of the others.[11]

10) After detailed search in The Bookman, etc., no sign of the review of a late work by W.B. Yeats you told me of. Since The Bookman amalgamated with the London Mercury in Jan. '35, just after your reviews of Pound etc. appeared in the former, do you think it possible that the review was commissioned, and written by you, but never published? If you have any other clues I can follow up, e.g. any recollection of what work was reviewed, I shall not give up yet.

Can't help you at all with this.[12]

ALS; 1 leaf, 1 side; *env to* D[r] J. W. Fletcher, Department of French, University of Durham, 48 Old Elvet, Durham, Angleterre; *pm* 23-11-64, Paris; T *enclosure*, TMScc with AN by SB (3 leaves, 3 sides); TxU, Beckett (Lake) Collection, 18.8.

1 *Cascando* had been published in English (Beckett, *Play*, 37–48). SB had written to John Fletcher (b. 1937) on 20 November with appreciation of his book *The Novels of Samuel Beckett* (1964) and had granted permission for *New Durham* to publish *Cascando*, pending Jérôme Lindon's agreement (TxU, Beckett [Lake] Collection, 18.8). It was not published.

2 SB quotes the first stanza of Goethe's poem "Harzreise im Winter" (see 16 April 1958, n. 2). Beckett's poem is "The Vulture" (*Echo's Bones and Other Precipitates*, [11]).

3 Nancy Cunard had requested that SB contribute to *Authors Take Sides on the Spanish War* (see 7 July 1937, and n. 6).

4 *Comédie* directed by Jean-Marie Serreau premiered at the Théâtre du Pavillon de Marsan, 109 Rue de Rivoli, Paris 1, on 10 June; André-Louis Perinetti (b. 1933) would later collaborate with Serreau (Compagnie Serreau–Perinetti). He became the Director of the Théâtre des Nations in 1966.

5 The submission of Beckett's story "L'Expulsé" to *Fontaine*: 15 May 1946 and n. 3. SB's introduction to Max-Pol Fouchet was through André-Charles Gervais, Editions Bordas (see 8 November 1949).

6 SB began "Suite / La Fin" on 17 February 1946, and *Mercier et Camier* on 5 July; he wrote "L'Expulsé" from 6 to 14 October. SB began "Premier amour" on 28 October and "Le Calmant" on 23 December. (See Chronology 1946.)

SB began *Eleutheria* on 18 January and finished the play on 24 February 1947. He wrote *Molloy* between 2 May and 1 November. He began *Malone meurt* on 27 November 1947 and finished a draft on 30 May 1948, although he revised the novel through 29 September. He began *En attendant Godot* on 9 October 1948 and finished it on 29 January 1949. He began *L'Innommable* on 29 March 1949, and completed it in January 1950. (See Chronology 1947 - Chronology 1949.)

The first "Texte pour rien" was begun on 24 December 1950, and the last, "Texte pour rien XIII," was finished on 20 December 1951. (See Chronology 1950 - Chronology 1951.) Niklaus Gessner, *Die Unzulänglichkeit der Sprache: Eine Untersuchung über Formzerlfall und Beziehungslosigkeit bei Samuel Beckett (Zurich: Juris, 1957)*. Kenner, *Samuel Beckett*.

7 SB cites lines 9–12 of Hölderlin's poem "Der Spaziergang" in relation to his poem "Dieppe" (Samuel Beckett, *Selected Poems 1930–1989*, ed. David Wheatley, [London: Faber and Faber, 2009] 46). Translated as "The Walk," these lines read:

You graceful views in the valley,
For instance garden and tree
And then the footbridge, the narrow,
The stream one can hardly see

Friedrich Hölderlin, "Der Spaziergang" ("The Walk"), in *Friedrich Hölderlin: Poems and Fragments*, tr. Michael Hamburger [Ann Arbor: University of Michigan Press, 1967] 576–577).

8 SB did ask Calder to address some matters of typesetting in his edition of *Watt* (see 12 December 1963, and n. 1). The spelling error in *Proust*, "hölder Wahnsinn," remains in the 1957 Grove edition (70), which photographically reproduced the 1931 first edition; it is corrected in the 1970 Calder edition (Samuel Beckett, *Proust*; Samuel Beckett, *Proust and Three Dialogues with Georges Duthuit* ([London: Calder and Boyars, 1970] 91). Faber and Faber's plans to publish the unexpurgated *Waiting for Godot*: 15 November 1963 and n. 3, and SB to Charles Monteith, 13 January 1964 (The Faber Archive, 17/50).

9 Charles Dullin performed in Balzac's *Le Faiseur* from 29 November 1935 at the Théâtre de l'Atelier, Paris.

10 What Fletcher here refers to as *Le Convergisme* is SB's spoof on literary movements and criticism that he read to the Modern Language Society of Trinity College in 1930, *Le Concentrisme or Jean du Chas*. SB gave a copy of the typed manuscript to Nuala Costello (1907–1984; Profile, I) (UoR, BIF, MS 1396/4/15); it was published, with an inadvertent omission of four lines, in Beckett, *Disjecta*, 35–42. (Cohn, *A Beckett Canon*, 21–22.)

11 SB did not sign his translations for *Transition*, and he often reviewed the translations done by others, as well as reading materials under consideration for inclusion. Of those listed by Fletcher, SB had a hand in or did the translation of the works that follow: *Yves Le Gall*, "Introduction to Akara," *Transition Forty-Eight*, no. 4 (January 1949) 40–41 (see 30 July 1949); Romain Weingarten, "*Akara*, Act III," *Transition Forty-Eight*, no. 4, 42–59 (see 30 July 1949); Pierre Schneider, "Introduction to the Works of Francis Ponge," *Transition Fifty*, no. 6 (October 1950) 68–74 (see 1 March 1949, and n. 3); Emmanuel Bove, "Armand," *Transition Fifty*, no. 6, 99–104; Gabrielle Picabia, "Apollinaire," *Transition Fifty*, no. 6, 110–125, as well as Guillaume Apollinaire's "Zone" in the same issue, 126–131 (see 1 March 1949, and n. 20); Paul Eluard, "The Work of The Painter - To Picasso," *Transition Forty-Nine*, no. 5 (December 1949) 6–13 (see 17 January 1949). For other mentions of SB's translations for *Transition*, see 27 May 1948, 12 August 1948, 17 January 1949, 1 March 1949, 27 March 1949, [on or after 30 April, before 26 May 1949], and 19 May 1953, n. 3.

12 Reviews by SB for *The Bookman*, 87 (December 1934), included: "Ex Cathezra" on Ezra Pound's *Make It New* (10), "Papini's Dante" on *Dante Vivo* by Giovanni Papini (14), and "The Essential and the Incidental," on Sean O'Casey's *Windfalls* (111). SB's article written under the pseudonym Andrew Belis, "Recent Irish Poetry," does mention W. B. Yeats; however, this is not a review of Yeats's work, but, rather, an assessment of the state of Irish poetry (*The Bookman*, 86 [August 1934] 235–236).

PETER BROOK
ROYAL SHAKESPEARE THEATRE, LONDON

[after 24 November 1964]
Dear Peter Brooke [sic]

Thank you for your letter and for your proposal by which I am greatly honoured. I have never done any adaptations and feel unqualified for such work. I'll refresh my memory of the play & think it over and probably decide it is beyond me. I'll let you have a definitive answer before the end of the year.[1]

In the second half of December I'll be in London rehearsing Godot for the Court and hope to have the pleasure of seeing you then.

Yours sincerely

AL draft; 1 leaf, 1 side; the first of two AL draft letters on the verso of Peter Brook to SB, 24 November 1964 (TLS; 1 leaf, 1 side; *letterhead*: THE ROYAL SHAKESPEARE THEATRE); GEU, MS 1221.

1 On 24 November, Peter Brook had asked SB to consider doing an adaptation of *La Vida es Sueño* (*Life is a Dream*) by Calderón. Brook had written: "As you are the only person in the world who could recreate this play from its core, I wonder if such a work might appeal to you" (24 November 1964; GEU, MS 1221).

BARBARA BRAY
PARIS

Tues. [15 December 1964] London

Dear Barbara

It's difficult. Jack, with whom I haven't had more than 3 hours work since I came, called off today (flu?), & Williamson did not turn up this morning (out all night). We plotted Act I Pozzo scenes as best we could with substitutes. Text not known, nothing done on 2nd act, & we open tomorrow fortnight! Paul Curran working very hard & will be excellent. Lynch light weight but adequate. O'Brien seems to understand. Page enclined [sic] to inopportune stringing of pearls but pleasant

17. Samuel Beckett and Jack MacGowran

to work with.[1] Dining with George & Jocelyn this evening, tomorrow with Jack, Pat & Donald. First sorties since I came. Cold still there & hole wide open, but not too much discomfort.[2] Lot of evening rehearsals will be necessary if we are to make it. Caesar off, no booking, so we have the theatre all the time.[3] Writing this during lunch break in King's Road Kardomah.[4] Bright cold day. Impossible to find a pair of brown boot-laces. Bought a black. No mail of interest. Calders very kind. Bettina off to Scotland this week with baby & barking bitch.[5] Love to children.

Love

Sam

ALS (lettercard); 1 leaf, 2 sides; *to* Madame Bray, 14 Rue Le Sueur, Paris 16me, FRANCE; *pm* __-12-64, Paris; TCD, MS 10948/1/310. *Dating*: *Waiting for Godot* opened at the Royal Court Theatre on 30 December.

1 SB was assisting Anthony Page in rehearsals of his production of *Godot* for the Royal Court Theatre. The cast included Jack MacGowran as Lucky, Nicol Williamson (1936–2011) as Vladimir, Alfred Lynch (1931–2003) as Estragon, Paul Curran (1913–1986) as Pozzo, and Kirk Martin as the Boy. Curran worked with SB to block his scenes. Timothy O'Brien (b. 1929) was the set designer for the play; at this time he

was Head of Design for ABC (American Broadcasting Company). Anthony Page said: "'Sam had a very clear picture of the way it should be in his head, but he was very open-minded; he cut little things that weren't working. There was a lot of experimenting on *Godot*, trying things out. Beckett had the most energy of all of us; he never wanted to stop working.'" (Young, *The Beckett Actor*, 96.)

2 SB's jaw could not heal without further surgery (SB to Thomas MacGreevy, 30 January 1965; TCD, MS 10402/263).

3 The final performances of *Julius Caesar* at the Royal Court Theatre were on 19 December; the show closed a week ahead of schedule ([classified advertising], *The Times* 19 December 1964: 2; Wardle, *The Theatres of George Devine*, 265).

4 Kardomah Cafés were a chain of coffee shops popular in England and Wales from the 1900s through the 1960s.

5 For the third time this year, SB was staying with John and Bettina Calder.

AVIGDOR ARIKHA AND ANNE ATIK
PARIS

Jeudi [17 December 1964] Londres

Chers amis

J'apprends de Barbara qu'Avigdor est tombé d'une échelle et s'est blessé au pied. J'espère que ce n'est pas grave et qu'il sera bientôt tout à fait remis.[1]

Ici travail épuisant, matin, après[-]midi et soir. Les crises et pépins habituels. Beaucoup de retard. Bons acteurs individuellement, excellent climat de travail. Mais ils n'y sont pas encore. Content surtout du Pozzo, beaucoup de technique et de force – joue César en ce moment![2] Ils ne savent pas encore la brochure et on passe en [*for* dans] moins de 15 jours! Pas encore seulement filé la pièce! Par moments j'ai bon espoir quand même, puis – sinon le contraire – le contradictoire? Vu personne, pas même le cousin.[3] Temps affreux, froid et brume. Comme cicatrisant il y a mieux. Ce sera quand même une mise en scène convenable, peut-être plus que ça, si l'étincelle vient. Bien affectueusement et qu'Avig. se remette vite

Sam

ALS (lettercard); 1 leaf, 2 sides; *to* Monsieur et Madame Avigdor Arikha, 19 Avenue de Tourville, Paris 7$^{\underline{me}}$, France; *pm* 17-12-64, London; InU, Arikha.

Thursday [17 December 1964] London

Dear Both

I hear from Barbara that Avigdor has fallen off a ladder and injured his foot. I do hope it's not serious, and that he'll soon be over it.[1]

Here exhausting work morning, noon and night. The usual crises and things going wrong. Badly behind time. Actors individually good, working atmosphere excellent. But they're not there yet. Pleased above all with Pozzo, great technique, strength – playing Caesar at the moment![2] They don't know the text yet, and we're due on in less than a fortnight! Haven't even rehearsed right through the play yet! There are times when I have hopes even so, then, if not the contrary, the contradictory? Seen no one, not even the cousin.[3] Dreadful weather, cold, mist. Not what you'd recommend for healing wounds. All the same it will be a decent production, maybe more than that if the spark comes. Love to both, and hoping Avig. gets better soon.

Sam

1 Arikha had broken three metatarsal bones when he fell 6 meters from a ladder (Arikha to the editors, 5 December 2009).

2 Paul Curran was currently playing the lead in Lindsay Anderson's production of Shakespeare's *Julius Caesar* at the Royal Court Theatre which had opened on 26 November; Curran dominated the stage with "a physical presence that confirms and enhances the textbook presentation of a dictator whose murder was an act of moral mercy" ("Caesar as Enormous, Ugly Tyrant," *The Times* 27 November 1964: 15).

3 SB's cousin John Beckett lived in London.

CHRONOLOGY 1965

1965	21 January	SB sends completed manuscript of *Come and Go* to Barbara Bray.
	5 February	SB called to Berlin to help with Schiller-Theater production of *Warten auf Godot*, directed by Deryk Mendel.
	18 February	Flies from Berlin to London to assist with rehearsals of Jack MacGowran's *Beginning to End*.
	19 February	Attends *Marat/Sade*, by Peter Weiss, directed by Peter Brook, with Patrick Magee as the Marquis de Sade.
	21 February	Returns to Berlin from London to resume rehearsals of *Warten auf Godot*.
	27 February	Flies from Berlin to Paris.
	28 February	Learns that Italian actress Clara Colosimo has gone on hunger strike because she cannot obtain permission to perform *Giorni felici* (*Happy Days*).
	2 March	Launch of Operation Rolling Thunder, a sustained American bombing campaign of North Vietnam that lasts until November 1968
	11 March	SB views latest cut of *Film* and sends his notes on to Schneider the following day.
	17 March	Death of Nancy Cunard in Paris.
	21 March	SB completes a draft of *Va-et-vient*, French translation of *Come and Go*.
	7 April	Sends third and fourth (final) draft of *How It Is* to Henry Wenning as a gift to the Boston University Beckett collection.

13 April	Begins draft of *Eh Joe* for television.
6 May	Faber and Faber publish unexpurgated edition of *Waiting for Godot.*
15 May	SB completes *Eh Joe* and sends to MacGowran, Donald McWhinnie, and Curtis Brown.
20 June	SB and Suzanne fly to Turin, travelling on to Courmayeur on 22 June for a holiday.
3 July	SB completes the French translation *Dis Joe.*
4–8 July	Translates *Imagination morte imaginez* into English.
14 July	Returns to Paris from Courmayeur via Turin.
16 July	Opening of the Mont Blanc Tunnel.
19 July	SB has surgery on jaw.
8 August	Begins French translation of *Words and Music;* draft translation completed on 14 August.
4 September	Premiere of *Film* at the Venice Film Festival. SB begins draft of *Assez.*
11 and 13 October	SB attends rehearsals of Pinget's *L'Hypothèse* performed by Pierre Chabert.
16 October	Begins revisions of *Assez.*
18 October	Pinget's *L'Hypothèse* performed by Pierre Chabert at the Musée d'Art Moderne (Biennale de Paris).
November	*Annales* (Toulouse) publish an extract from *Mercier et Camier* (hitherto unpublished novel, 1946).
mid-November – 5 December	SB in Ussy, resting and working on *Le Dépeupleur.* Completes first draft on 28 November.
7 December	Begins work with director Marin Karmitz on a film of *Comédie.*
11 December	Attends performance of *Des journées entières dans les arbres* by Marguerite Duras.
12 December	Charles de Gaulle is reelected as French President, defeating François Mitterrand.

SHIVAUN O'CASEY
? LONDON

13.1.65

38 Bld. St.-Jacques
Paris 14me

Dear Shivaun

Thanks for your letter of Jan 9.

You have my permission to do From an Abandoned Work in the States and there should be no difficulty with the agents.[1]

This is not at all the kind of dramatic writing I had in mind when we talked in Paris and I think the spotlit face presentation would be wrong here. The face is irrelevant. I feel also that no form of monologue technique will work for this text and that it should somehow be presented as a document for which the speaker is not responsible. At the same time a completely straight undramatized reading is hard to manage in an evening of theatre with Shaw and O'Casey.[2] What would you think of the following setup? Moonlight. Ashcan a little left of centre. Enter man left, limping, with stick, shadowy in faint general lighting alone. Advances to can, raises lid, fishes about inside with crook of stick, inspects and rejects (puts back in can) unidentifiable refuse, fishes out finally tattered copy or MS of FAAW, reads aloud standing "Up bright and early that day, I was young then, feeling awful, and out – " and a little further in silence, lowers text, stands motionless, finally closes ashcan, sits down on it, hooks stick round neck and reads text through from beginning, i.e. including what he has read standing.[3] Finishes, sits a moment motionless, gets up, replaces text in ashcan and limps off right. Reads with maximum of simplicity. Only effect to be sought a slight hesitation now and then at places where most effective, due to strangeness of text and imperfect light and state of MS. If you like this idea you'll be able to improve on it. But keep it cool.

Hope you received cheque I sent via Jack. It might be worth your while to consult him about rhythms of text, we did a little work on it together once.[4]

Love

s/ Sam

TLS; 1 leaf, 1 side; Private Collection (offered by Sotheby's July 1996).

1 Actress and director Shivaun O'Casey (b. 1939), daughter of Sean O'Casey, organized Theatre Group 20 with Gordon Taylor and Mary Evans; the troupe, composed of recent graduates from the Drama Centre in London, planned a four-month tour of the United States from 25 January to 8 May (NRU, Theatre Group 20 Papers, Box 1, F8). They planned to present three programs, including a triple bill with Beckett's "From an Abandoned Work," Sean O'Casey's *Figure in the Night*, and G. B. Shaw's *The Inca of Perusalem: An Almost Historical Comedietta*; as it turned out, the Beckett piece was not produced by the company because the Shaw play was too long (NRU, Theatre Group 20 Papers; "12 British Actors Start Campus Tour," *The New York Times* 30 January 1965: 17 [with errors of identification]).

2 SB had talked with Shivaun O'Casey about *Play* when they met in Paris (Shivaun O'Casey to the editors, 19 March 2005).

3 SB quotes the opening line of "From an Abandoned Work," *Evergreen Review*, 83.

4 Theatre Group 20 had raised funds from individuals; SB is listed as a subscriber (NRU, Theatre Group 20, 1.7).

PATRICK MAGEE
LONDON

24.1.65 Ussy-sur-Marne

Dear Pat

Thanks for your letter. Glad the books arrived safely and that you found the Godot OK. Nicol W. as you say has something very special. Both Curran and Lynch are very disturbed about something there and play all tense & controlled. I could never make out what it was. They both have it in them to be good in the parts.[1]

I had a pleasant evening with Peter and his wife in their Paris flat. I have not seen Encore with his article, but Jack will be bringing it next Sunday when he comes over about his Monitor programme.[2]

I have written a tiny playlet for John Calder's new theatre in Soho, one page and a half, 4 minutes misery. He has been over with

Bettina and hopes to have the theatre in May. This means perhaps in the Fall. Three old faggots, golden yellow, bishop violet, Bordeaux red, in the gloom.[3]

You must have your bellyful of Sade by now. I read Harold's Homecoming and was impressed. Pity you can't do Max. It's about the most beautiful part he has written.[4]

Much love, dear Pat, and to Belle and the children.[5]

Sam

ALS; 1 leaf, 1 side; TCD, MS 11313/12.

1 Magee had written to SB about the Royal Court Theatre production of *Waiting for Godot* with Nicol Williamson, Paul Curran, and Alfred Lynch.

2 Peter Brook's wife is the actress Natasha Parry (b. 1930). SB later thanked Jack MacGowran for Peter Brook's article "Endgame as King Lear, or how to stop worrying and love Beckett," *Encore* 12.1 (January–February 1965) 8–12 (3 February 1965; TxU, Beckett Collection, 9.3).

Jack MacGowran met SB in Paris on 31 January, to discuss the former's show due to be broadcast on the BBC television program *Monitor*. With him were Patrick Garland (b. 1935), Director of *Beginning to End*, and Jonathan Miller (b. 1934), Editor of *Monitor* (Jonathan Miller to H.D. M.P., 25 January 1965; BBCWAC, T32/1089/1, Beginning to End).

3 *Come and Go* was written for John Calder's proposed theatre on Bateman Street in Soho, London. "The theatre would have seated about a hundred, just right for the kind of play I had in mind" (Calder, *Pursuit*, 335). Calder's project did not come about. The three women in *Come and Go*, each dressed in a different color, wear nearly identical coats and hats.

4 Magee was continuing to play the role of the Marquis de Sade in the repertory of the Royal Shakespeare Company at the Aldwych Theatre. Max is the father in Harold Pinter's *The Homecoming*; Peter Hall would direct the play in the RSC's London repertoire due to begin on 22 March.

5 Magee's wife was Belle Sherry McGee (1922–2006); their children are twins Caroline and Mark (b. 1961).

HAROLD PINTER
LONDON

27.1.65 Ussy sur Marne

Dear Harold

Forgive my not having written before now to tell you how impressed I am by the Homecoming. It seems to me the best you have done since the Caretaker & perhaps the best of all – best meaning of course nothing here, but you know what I mean. The part of the father is tremendous and should play like a bomb. I wish Pat could do it. Wish I could tell you better how I feel about it and how glad I am. But too tired and stupid and have been waiting too long to be less so, before writing, to wait any longer. So just – chapeau! and may it soon [sic] to be seen.[1]

Affectionately

Sam

ALS; 1 leaf, 1 side; BL, Add MS 88880/7/2/5.

1 Paul Rogers (1917–2013) played Max in the first production of *The Homecoming*. "Chapeau!" (hats off to you!).

LAWRENCE HARVEY
RIPOLI, NEAR FLORENCE

30.1.65 Ussy

Dear Larry

My compliments on this long unmerited study of Echo's Bones.[1] I am greatly touched by such scholarship and research and depth and patience of investigation – and embarrassed as you know by the disproportion I cannot help feeling between this scrutiny and its object. But you've had enough from me on that. And it would ill become me to murmur that you make too much of this old clutching at old straws, and missing of them mostly, since what emerges is a poetry richer than it is. I have scribbled a few notes in the margin that may be of use. Forgive me if I have nothing better to offer. You know and I think have accepted that I am as lost in such matters as the mole above ground or the owl in broad daylight.

I hope you got home comfortably and found all well at the Villa. It was good seeing you here again and I am sorry I was not in better form. The wine you so kindly burdened yourself with all that long way was excellent, especially the Verdicchio I thought. And I have read the Barzini book with much enjoyment.[2] I go back to Paris tomorrow, but hope to get back here about mid-February for another good spell. I finished the little play we talked about in that desperate sala de espera, but simplified down to next to nothing, one page and a quarter, three minutes "theatre".[3] And started again for the 20th time, this time in French again, on what will not be written. Imagination morte imaginez.[4]

Again congratulations and thanks and affectionately to you all.

s/ Sam

TLS; 1 leaf, 1 side; NhD, Beckett Collection, MS 122/1.6.

1 Lawrence E. Harvey, "Samuel Beckett: Initiation du poète," *La Revue des Lettres Modernes: Histoire des Idées et des Littératures* 100.8 (1964) 153–168.

2 Harvey was living at the Villa Bisarno, Ripoli, outside Florence, during his sabbatical. He had brought SB Italian wine, including Verdicchio from the Marche region of central Italy. Luigi Giorgio Barzini (1908–1984) wrote *The Italians* (New York: Atheneum, 1964; London, Hamish Hamilton, 1964); *Gli Italiani* (Verona: Mondadori, 1965).

3 *Come and Go*. "Sala de espera" (Sp., waiting area).

4 For the composition of *Imagination morte imaginez*, see Cohn, *A Beckett Canon*, 292–293.

BARBARA BRAY
PARIS

8.2.65

Akakakakademie der
Kükükükükünste
Hanseatenweg 10
Berlin 21

Dear Barbara

Never found myself in such a Goddam bloody mess. 2nd rehearsal this evening. Total confusion. Haven't yet begun to clean up 1st act, nor yet started on second. Actors willing but 3rd rate, miscast, lost & worried to death. The great Minetti, who has played Krapp & Hamm all over Germany, & whom I saw so good the other night as Marat in the Weiss play, incredibly wrong as Pozzo – and stubborn (another Beckett specialist). Set all haywire. Shall keep on trying this week and if still no hope after that shall go.[1]

Fairly comfortable in this kind of artists' centre in the Tiergarten.[2] Room beside Deryk. Snow when I arrived. Bitter cold. Better off in bed.

Going to the Oper this evening to hear Brahms' German Requiem. Only one rehearsal a day from 10 to 14, actors playing most evenings. After we are supposed to open 25th![3]

Dead tired & confused, mouth squelching more & more with loosening plate, no eatable food so far, one bellyful of bad Beaujolais, bought a bottle of Tullamore Dew today, which to every man his.[4]

Love

Sam

ALS; 1 leaf, 1 side; *env to* Mrs Barbara Bray, 15 Rue Séguier, Paris 6me, Frankreich; *pm* __-__-65, Berlin; TCD, MS 10948/1/314.

1 Klaus Herm (1925–2014), who played Lucky in the Schiller-Theater production of *Warten auf Godot*, described the situation that led to SB coming to Berlin to assist Deryk Mendel with the rehearsals. The cast also included Horst Bollmann (Vladimir), Stefan Wigger (Estragon), and Bernhard Minetti (Pozzo).

> Mendel was having problems working with Minetti. Bollmann suggested "But the author is living! We could ask and maybe he'll come." That's how it happened that Beckett came to Berlin. None of us knew Samuel Beckett yet. He came about fourteen days before the premiere. Beckett held back, didn't want to interfere. He only emphasized decisive points; in particular, he wanted the comic aspect to be done somewhat differently – he wanted everything to be as simple as possible. Wigger, Bollmann and I understood what Beckett meant; Minetti couldn't understand. [. . .] Minetti was known as a Beckett specialist in Germany, so it was especially frustrating or sad for him that he had a hard time understanding Beckett. Minetti really loved Beckett's work, but Minetti is, of course, a star. (Klaus Herm interview with Martha Fehsenfeld, 12 December 1996, translated by Laura Barlament.)

Minetti had played Marat in Peter Weiss's *Die Verfolgung und Ermordung Jean Paul Marats* (*The Persecution and Assassination of Jean-Paul Marat*) at the Schiller-Theater, Berlin; the play had been in repertory since 29 April 1964.

Minetti recalls the rehearsals of *Warten auf Godot* and his difficulties with the role of Pozzo: "Ich wußte nicht, was er wollte, und er wurde mit mir nicht fertig . . . Ich war ihnen nicht phantastisch genug, hatte zu große Hemmungen, die realistische Kontur der Figur aufzugeben." (Minetti, *Erinnerungen eines Schauspielers*, 308.) (I did not know what he wanted, and he could not deal with me . . . I was not imaginative enough for them, was too inhibited to give up the realistic contours of the character.)

2 SB stayed at the Akademie der Künste at the northwestern edge of Berlin's Tiergarten; his joke with its name in the header of his letter reflects the stutter in Lucky's speech: "the Acacacacademy of Anthropopopometry" (*Waiting for Godot* [Grove] 29).

3 The *German Requiem*, Op. 45, by Brahms was performed on 7 and 8 February by the choir of the Singakademie with the Radio-Symphonie Orchestra at the Philharmonie.

4 SB's jaw had not fully healed, which affected his ability to chew. Tullamore. Dew is a brand of Irish whiskey whose famous advertising slogan was "Give every man his Dew."

AVIGDOR ARIKHA AND ANNE ATIK
PARIS

10.2.65 [Berlin]

Chers amis

C'est trop pour un seul homme. Tout à refaire. Acteurs quelconques. Une répétition de 4 heures par jour. 1ère dans 15 jours! De la folie. Je m'en vais la semaine. J'irai peut-être directement à Londres. Assez bien logé ici, mais trop loin du centre et du théâtre. Froid de chien. C'est gai. J'espère que le pied va mieux et qu'il y a de bonnes nouvelles de Boston.[1] Vous embrasse

Sam

APCS; 1 leaf, 1 side; "Berlin, Hansaviertel, Akademie der Künste"; *to* Monsieur et Madame Avigdor Arikha, 19 Av. de Tourville, Paris 7me, Frankreich; *pm* 11-2-65, Berlin; InU, Arikha.

10.2.65 [Berlin]

Dear Both

It's too much for one man. Everything needs redoing. Actors pretty ordinary. One 4-hour rehearsal a day. First night in a fortnight! Lunacy. I'm off next week. I shall go direct to London. Quite good room here, but too far from the centre and the theatre. Cold as hell. Some prospect. I hope the foot is better and that there's good news from Boston.[1] Big hug

Sam

1 Arikha's injury: [17 December 1964]. The good news related to a gouache being sold to a friend of Boston-based architect Samuel Glaser (Avigdor Arikha to the editors, 5 December 2009).

BARBARA BRAY
PARIS

10.2.65 Akademie der Künste

Dear Barbara

Your letter begun Sunday & posted Tuesday received safely today. You will have had mine Wednesday latest. Here things are pretty bloody, mainly because of Minetti (Pozzo), an undirectable neurotic. He has us all exasperated. There is some pleasure & hope with the other three. I have had to ask for complete change of set – only the tree more or less ok.[1] So tired after 4 hours morning rehearsal that just wander back & stay in till dinner in nearest pub – then back bath bed. Called in at Zoo Aquarium on way home today. Envied them. Went one evening to Philharmonie (Brahms' German Requiem). Dull mostly. Plan to wander East Berlin Saturday. Unless I throw my hat at it between now & then shall fly direct to London for Jack next Thursday. Back to Paris following Sun. or Mon. Shall stay with Calders if they can have me.[2] Have had no mail forwarded and dread thought of what there must be accumulating. All very quiet, no invitations, no journalists (choked off by Bessler). Deryk buoyant. Very good on cleanness of movement & so on. But difficult for us both.[3] Tullamore Dew helps a little. Thanks for cutting. Had seen it. How glad I'll be to get away. Even to London. Sorry to hear of Wendt chore. The friends one has.[4] Glad you like the Homecoming a bit more. What's sad? Still cold, grey, sporadic snow. Nothing to read. A German treatise on suicide. Statistics. Unexciting. Uninformative. Unhelpful. Courthouse USA. Leopold-Loeb. Hiss.[5] Dull. Should have brought Dante. Just missed Rauschenberg originals at Amerika-Haus.[6] Sent a card to Arikha u. a. Shall write again before I leave, that you may know what I've decided. Food uneatable. Beaujolais scarce. Bref Hundesleben [*for* Hundeleben].[7]

Love

Sam

ALS; 1 leaf, 1 side; *env to* Madame Bray, 15 Rue Séguier, Paris 6$^{\underline{me}}$, Frankreich; *pm* 12-[2]-65, Berlin; TCD, MS 10948/1/316.

1 The set and costume designer was H. W. Lenneweit (b. 1925).

2 Jack MacGowran was rehearsing his one-man show *Beginning to End* in London for the BBC program *Monitor* (see 24 January 1965, n. 2).

3 Albert Bessler was chief dramaturg of the Schiller-Theater. The clarity of Mendel's directing of the actors' movement reflected his experience as a mime and dancer.

4 Stephen and Alison Wendt were close friends of Bray and her children in Paris. An Austrian, Stephen Wendt wrote in English, and Barbara Bray helped him. Alison Wendt worked for UNESCO. Either may have asked Bray to assist (Francesca Bray, 20 August 2013).

5 SB was reading *Courtroom U.S.A.* 2 by Rupert Furneaux (Harmondsworth: Penguin Books, 1963); he misremembers the title. It contained a chapter on the 1924 murder trial of Nathan Leopold and Richard Loeb and their defense by Clarence Darrow (9–65), and another on Alger Hiss who, in 1948, was charged with perjury for denying under oath that he had given secret government documents to Soviet Russia (118–156).

6 Robert Rauschenberg: Bilder, Zeichnungen, Lithos was the exhibition at the Amerikahaus, from 8 January to 4 February.

7 "U. a." for "unter anderem" (among others). "Bref" (in a word); "Hundeleben" (dog's life).

BARBARA BRAY
PARIS

Saturday [13 February 1965] Berlin

Dear Barbara

Your Thursday letter today. It is not inspiriting. You do not change. You know that the situation you complain of and suffer from to the point of falling ill is bound to recur very often. The inference has been drawn so often that there is no point in drawing it again.

Another painful rehearsal today with the impossible Minetti. With the others there is something (not much) to be done. I have decided to stay till Thursday & then fly direct to London. I rang up the Calders and they can put me up for the few days I shall be there.

Another rehearsal, exceptionally, this evening with Didi & Gogo alone.

I do nothing & go nowhere. Wander round after the late lunch, then back here to read till time to go out for dinner, then back & bed. Bought some paperbacks – & more Dew. Keep working thanks be to ____. Meant to go over to Berlin East this afternoon, but weather too miserable.

Deryk bearing up very well, we have a good relationship.

One theory of why Crippen murdered his wife very reminiscent of Play. But it is considered erroneous.[1]

Had no mail forwarded and now a bit late. Dread to think of what is piling up. Pity I couldn't train Con.

Going to see The General (Buster) on Monday – 1926.[2]

Nothing all day tomorrow. Try and work possibly.

Love to the children.

Love

Sam

ALS; 1 leaf, 1 side; *env to* Madame Bray, 15 Rue Séguier, Paris 6$^{\underline{me}}$, Frankreich; *pm* 14-2-65, Berlin; TCD, MS 10948/1/317.

1 Hawley Harvey Crippen (1862–1910) was tried for the murder of his wife in 1910; purportedly he poisoned her, disposed of her dismembered body, and fled to Canada with his mistress Ethel Le Neve. He was captured in Quebec and returned to London for trial. Crippen was executed, but doubts were raised, and continue to be raised, about his guilt.

2 Buster Keaton starred in *The General*, a silent film about a locomotive (named "The General") which was stolen by Union spies during the Civil War; he plays the role of the engineer who crosses enemy lines to pursue, and eventually recover, his locomotive.

AVIGDOR ARIKHA AND ANNE ATIK
PARIS

17.2.65 [Berlin]

Chers amis

M'en vais à Londres demain, reviens ici dimanche terminer les répétitions, serai à Paris jeudi ou vendredi de la semaine prochaine. Ça va mal. Ils auraient besoin de 15 jours de +. Et encore. Et ils travaillent ça depuis le début janvier! Savent le texte à moitié à peu près. Un Pozzo à s'arracher yeux et oreilles. Les autres quelconques. Non combustibles. C'est gai.

Amitiés

Sam

APCS; 1 leaf, 1 side; "Berlin, Dom und Schloss"; *to* Monsieur et Madame Avigdor Arikha, 19 Av. de Tourville, Paris 7me, Frankreich; *pm* 18-2-65, Berlin; InU, Arikha.

17.2.65 [Berlin]

Dear Both

Off to London tomorrow, back here on Sunday to finish the rehearsals, will be in Paris on Thursday or Friday of next week. Things are not going well. They'd need another fortnight. Maybe not even then. And they've been working on it since early January! They just about half know the text. A Pozzo that would make you tear your hair out and your ears off. The others pretty ordinary. Not likely to catch fire. Some prospect.

All best

Sam

BARBARA BRAY
PARIS

Sunday 21.2.65 [Berlin]

Dear Barbara

Got back here this afternoon - direct flight from London.

Thanks for yr letter in London. Had bad news while there, death of my uncle Howard in Dublin hospital, 2nd heart attack - not to be confused with amputee.[1]

Got something done with Jack & Garland, but time too short. They record today. It may be all right. At least he looks marvellous.[2]

Saw actors between matinée & evening performance yesterday. All in good form & pleased. Alfie Lynch transformed.[3]

Dinner with John & Vera yesterday.[4] It was good to be with John a little again. Finished evening at Calders. Very late to bed. Crept in here this afternoon & went to bed. No sign of Deryk. Dread resumption tomorrow. Going out now for my cold fillet of hake.

Expect to be back Thursday on principle that when no more work possible go __ & with these no urge to see them after opening.

Saw Sade-Marat and Pat in Opera afterwards. Rather disappointed. Production gone very sloppy. Perhaps was always. Excellent moments & incomprehensible lapses. Pat wrong I thought except in whipping scene.[5]

Lunched with Jocelyn yesterday but missed George gone to country. Missed Stephen Frears also and still don't know exactly what George wants of me.[6]

Good houses continue at R.C. Last week now. Miller turned up at rehearsing room with sweatshirt decorated with Beethoven's head lifesize. Said he had asked for a Schönberg - but sold out. Garland so slow & gentle could sleep on feet.[7]

Calders kindness itself as always but Hallam wd. have had advantages.

Shall send a card before I leave & call you when I get in.

Love

Sam

ALS; 1 leaf, 1 side; *env to* Madame Bray, 15 Rue Séguier, Paris 6$^{\underline{me}}$, Frankreich; *pm* 22-2-65, Berlin; TCD, MS 10948/1/319.

1 Howard Beckett, the youngest of SB's paternal uncles, had died in Adelaide Hospital on 14 February. He was known as the family comic; he often took the young SB to the cinema, as well as spending evenings in Cooldrinagh. To Edward Beckett who had written to SB with the news, SB replied: "Nothing to be said. Try and write tomorrow the usual useless note to Enid." (21 February 1965; Edward Beckett Collection.) SB's uncle James Beckett was a double amputee.

2 Jack MacGowran's *Beginning to End* was directed by Patrick Garland for *Monitor*. Their rehearsals with SB are described by Michael Ratcliffe: "The true collaboration at this stage is between player and author . . . Beckett demonstrates the rhythms he requires, the whispered tensions, the precise patterns of exasperation." ("The Collaborators," *The Sunday Times* 28 February 1965: 49.) SB had been sufficiently taken by his idea for staging "From an Abandoned Work" (see 13 January 1965) that he suggested the idea to Jack

MacGowran, who used it as part of his *Monitor* presentation (SB to Barbara Bray, Friday [15 January 1965]; TCD, MS 10948/1/312; BBCWAC, T32/1089/1, Beginning to End).

3 SB visited the actors in the Royal Court Theatre production of *Waiting for Godot*. Alfred Lynch played Estragon.

4 John and Vera Beckett.

5 Patrick Magee would continue in the role of Sade at the Aldwych Theatre until 18 March. The Opera Tavern: 10 July 1964, n. 2.

6 Stephen Frears (b. 1941), British film director, began his career working at the Royal Court Theatre, assisting George Devine. Devine's letter to SB of 17 March offers details about his project: "I am going to bring out the book which will be partly a record of the ten years' work in various fields and partly contributions from various writers with whom we have been associated in the last ten years, on any subject that they like" (UAL Wimbledon, JH/1/15).

7 R.C. (Royal Court) production of *Waiting for Godot*. Jonathan Miller.

BARBARA BRAY
PARIS

Tuesday [23 February 1965] [Berlin]

Dear Barbara

Thanks for Sunday letter.

TV & photographers this morning, so without me. Do. tomorrow morning, when Theaterfreunde, so only staying for a few hours with them Wed. evening and again Thurs. morning - foolishly no doubt.[1] Desperate run through yest., nearly screamed. Deryk continues to smile, joke and sing. Shall take off with relief from this failure, mine & all of ours.

Sitting room looking at feeble snowing. Nothing to do, nothing to read, too early for Dew. Trying to read Creeley's <u>The Island</u>. Jesus what prose. Trying to read <u>Henri Brulard</u>. Crawl out now and buy some paperbacks and book flight. Then to Kantine to show no ill feeling.[2]

The boy is 21 and towers over Vladimir![3]

Every time Pozzo jerks on rope Lucky's hat falls off. Pozzo gets tied up in rope. If it wasn't too late would add a skipping scene. Yesterday Lucky tripped & fell on his arse, dropping basket which flew open emitting bottle. They use an enormous crank to hoist moon which rises with creaks and rattle. All this organized by veritable gangs of technicians. Vive Hitler.

Love

Sam

ALS; 1 leaf, 1 side; *env to* Madame Bray, 15 Rue Séguier, Paris 6me, Frankreich; *pm* 23-2-65, Berlin; TCD, MS 10948/1/320. *Dating*: from pm.

1 "Theaterfreunde" (Friends of the Theatre). "Do." (ditto).

2 Stendhal, *La Vie de Henri Brulard* (*The Life of Henri Brulard*) was written in 1835–1836. A novel by the American poet Robert Creeley (1926–2005), *The Island* (New York: Scribners, 1963; London: John Calder, 1964).

3 The Boy was played by Gerhard Sprunkel.

UNIONE NAZIONALE SCRITTORI TRIESTE, ITALY

le 28 février 1965

Editions de Minuit
Paris

Unione Nazionale Scrittori
Giuliani e Dalmati
Piazza Vittorio Veneto
Trieste

Messieurs

Rentré hier à Paris je trouve en même temps:

1e. Une lettre de Madame Colosimo en date du 12 février.

2e. Votre lettre du 24 février.

3e. Le Corriere della Sera du 21 février contenant l'entrefilet sur l'action entreprise par Madame Colosimo, avec l'aimable précision qu'elle aurait fait appel à moi en vain.[1]

Il n'y a dans tout cela rien qui me renseigne sur la nature du conflit qui oppose Madame Colosimo aux détenteurs des droits de représentation en Italie. On me demande d'intervenir auprès de ceux-ci en faveur de Madame Colosimo sans que j'aie la moindre donnée qui me permette de me faire une opinion. Je serais heureux que cette actrice puisse jouer ma pièce librement et comme elle l'entend, mais dans l'ignorance totale où je suis des raisons pour lesquelles on le lui interdit comment voulez-vous que je prenne parti pour elle? Je déplore la voie violente où elle s'est engagée pour faire pression sur ses adversaires, et sans doute sur moi, et je renouvelle instamment ici les termes de mon télégramme où je vous priais de faire en sorte qu'il y soit mis fin.[2]

Il me sera peut-être facile, quand je saurai en quoi consiste ce litige, d'obtenir de qui de droit que satisfaction soit donnée à Madame Colosimo. Qu'elle arrête d'abord cette action indéfendable et qu'ensuite me soient communiqués, ou à mon éditeur, dans le calme, les vrais éléments du problème.

Veuillez agréer, Messieurs, l'assurance de mes sentiments les meilleurs.

Samuel Beckett

TL; 1 leaf, 1 side; and A draft; IMEC-Fonds Samuel Beckett, Boîte 4, Correspondance 1965.

28 February 1965

Editions de Minuit
Paris

Unione Nazionale Scrittori
Giuliani e Dalmati
Piazza Vittorio Veneto
Trieste

Gentlemen,

On my return to Paris yesterday I find at one and the same time:

1. A letter from Madame Colosimo, dated 12th February
2. Your letter of 24th February.
3. The *Corriere della Sera* for 21st February with its paragraph on the action being brought by Madame Colosimo, together with the nice detail that she had appealed to me in vain.[1]

In none of this is there anything that enlightens me as to the nature of the conflict between Madame Colosimo and those who hold the performance rights in Italy. I am being asked to intervene with the latter in favour of Madame Colosimo without having a single fact on which I might base an opinion. I should be happy if this actress could perform my play freely and in the way that she sees it, but, knowing nothing of the reasons why she is being forbidden to do so, how do you imagine I could take up her cause? I deplore the violent path that she has chosen in order to put pressure on her opponents, and no doubt on myself as well, and I hereby restate with some force the terms of my telegram, in which I asked you to act in such a way as to put an end to this.[2]

It will perhaps be easy for me, when I have found out what is involved in this litigation, to obtain from the appropriate people that satisfaction be given to Madame Colosimo. Let her first of all put a stop to this indefensible action, and let me or my publisher be supplied with the true elements of the problem in a calm state of mind.

Yours

Samuel Beckett

1 Italian actress Clara Colosimo (1922–1994) had written to SB on 12 February, because she had not been granted permission by the holder of the Italian rights to play Winnie in *Giorni felici* (*Happy Days*) at the Teatro Piccola Commenda in Milan, although she had previously played the role in several other Italian towns. She had begun a hunger strike in protest. SB returned to Paris on 25 February to find her letter. Colosimo's condition had deteriorated in the meanwhile, according to a newspaper article, "Sciopero della fame di una attrice" (*Corriere della Sera* 21 February), that made public her distress. (Knowlson, *Damned to Fame*, 470–471, 718.) On 24 February, the Unione Nazionale Scrittori wrote to SB to implore him to take action.

The authorized agent of the Italian rights was Connie Ricono; she had granted Clara Colosimo and her director Giuseppe Babic permission to perform the play only in the region of Tre Venezie (Connie Ricono to Jérôme Lindon, 5 April 1965 and enclosures; IMEC-Fonds Samuel Beckett, Boîte 4, Correspondance 1965; Anna Maria Cascetta and Laura Pejà, "Winnie and the Tradition of the Actor: From the Old Italian Style Theatre to the Experimental Stage," tr. Mark Pietralunga, *The Journal of Beckett Studies* 13.1 [2004] 73–97).

2 SB drafted a telegram on 28 February: "Prière intervenir auprès Colosimo pour qu'elle arrête cette grève lettre suit. Beckett" (IMEC-Fonds Samuel Beckett, Boîte 4, Correspondance 1965.) (Please press Colosimo to stop strike letter follows. Beckett.) The present letter is what followed. On the same day, SB wrote to Jacoba van Velde: "Drame en Italie – une actrice qui fait à Trieste la grève de la faim parce qu'on lui interdit de jouer Les Beaux Jours! Il ne me manquait que quelques morts sur la conscience." (BNF, 19794/105.) (Drama in Italy – an actress in Trieste who has gone on hunger strike because she is not being allowed to perform *Oh les beaux jours*! All I needed: a few corpses on my conscience.)

GEORGE DEVINE
ROYAL COURT THEATRE, LONDON

7.3.65 Ussy

Dear George

I wish I could have seen you in London last month, for the pleasure of being with you and to know the kind of thing you would like from me for your book (Stephen could not tell me) and to talk with you about the matter which is the burden of this letter.[1]

Peter Hall writes: "What I would like is to build up a selection of your work in our repertory so that we could regard as usual to have a work by you in our bill. You remember I wrote to you with such an idea some months ago. I wanted to start off with GODOT – but I was too late."[2]

He knows of my commitment to the Court. I have always regarded the Court as you and our understanding as essentially a personal one between you and me rather than with the Society. The theatre will never be the same for me with you gone and quite frankly I am not interested in maintaining its priority in your absence. If you agree with this view I shall be free to consider whether or not to accept Hall's offer. If on the other hand you ask me to maintain the priority after your departure I shall bow to that view and reply to Hall accordingly.[3]

I had a bad time in Berlin. Only a fortnight in which to straighten things out, very bewildered and anxious actors and an utterly impossible Pozzo (the highly esteemed Minetti).[4]

Here for a few days only, rummaging for wits to collect.

Much love to you both.

s/ Sam

TLS; 1 leaf, 1 side; UAL Wimbledon, JH/1/15.

1 On a possible contribution by SB to Devine's proposed book: 21 February 1965 and n. 6. Devine would later write to SB:

> I have been rather diffident about this whole matter, as I know the difficulty that you have in writing and I feel that I am imposing a burden by asking you. I was hoping that I was making the burden less by leaving you free to write anything you liked. Things like the making of the film, for instance, could be very interesting, so that's what it is all about. (17 March 1965; UAL Wimbledon, JH/1/15.)

SB replied on 29 March: "I am so utterly hopeless at occasional writing that I suggest for your book one of my old theatre texts (inédits) begun and abandoned. I think there are some not without interest. If this is all right for you I'll start rummaging." (UAL Wimbledon, JH/1/17/1.)

2 Peter Hall wished to incorporate SB's plays in the repertory of The Royal Shakespeare Company (see SB to Hall, after 5 October 1964). Peter Hall's more recent letter has not been found. SB had explained to Patrick Magee:

> I should be happy for the Royal Shakespeare to have my work if I can clear up things with George [. . .] If he wants the priority to continue after he has left it will be difficult to refuse [. . .] Please tell Hall in any case that I have nothing for him but friendly feelings and admiration for what he has achieved and that to be in rep in his theatre again would give me much pleasure. (1 March 1965; TCD, MS 11313/13.)

3 SB shared with Devine his worries about the consequences of accepting the RSC offer, to which Devine responded:

> I personally feel that it would be a pity if you were to give Hall an exclusive right to produce your plays [. . .]
>
> I know that Gaskill, who is taking over here in September, will want to do your work and indeed I have told him to write to you and say so [. . .] I will, of course, be only too ready to give you the best advice that I can [. . .] but as I am leaving the Court I do not want to exercise any pressure on you, as far as the Court is concerned, after I have left. I hope this is clear. (17 March 1965; UAL Wimbledon, JH/1/15.)

SB would report to John Calder: "After correspondence with George and Peter Hall I have decided that my commitment to the former ends in September when he leaves and not to commit myself to the Royal Shakespeare, though welcoming any proposal from them." (SB to John Calder, 9 April 1965; InU, C&B, Beckett.)

4 SB had written to Mary Hutchinson on 1 March: "The Pozzo was quite undirectable & gave the worst performance I have ever seen by any actor" (TxU, Hutchinson, 2.6).

PETER DU SAUTOY
FABER AND FABER, LONDON

April 17th 1965 | 38 Bld. St.-Jacques
Paris 14me

Dear Peter

Thank you for your letter of April 12th.

It is very good of you to allow John Calder to publish COME AND GO which I wrote for the opening of his new theatre and dedicated to him. It is understood of course that this does not preclude eventual publication by you.[1]

I am not keen on bilingual edition either of the novels or the plays, but would not oppose it if my publishers agree it is desirable. It suggests an invitation to consider the work as a linguistic curiosity, or an adventure in self-translation, which does not appeal to me. I am sure there would be no difficulty in getting permission to use the French texts.

I am trying to write in English a short work for TV. It would be the first. I don't know if it will come to anything. Another full length stage play seems to me unlikely. I don't think there is much work left in me, I mean I don't think I can get it out. Everything I try aborts. I'll keep trying.

Warm regards to Charles.

Yours ever

s/ Sam

TLS; 1 leaf, 1 side; The Faber Archive.

1 Although Faber and Faber were the publisher of SB's plays, Peter du Sautoy had agreed to allow John Calder to publish *Come and Go* "by itself," as long as Faber and Faber had "an opportunity of publishing it together with any other short pieces" that SB might write in the future (Peter du Sautoy to SB, 12 April 1965; The Faber Archive).

BARBARA BRAY
LONDON

15.5.65 Ussy

Dear Barbara

Thanks for your second letter received here yesterday.

All well here. Feeling much better than on arrival. But a few days in Paris will correct that. Beautiful days. First integral sunbath today, behind my arras. Have been working within and without. Finished (?) Eh Joe and got it off today to Jack, Donald & M$^{\underline{rs}}$ McL, before either I threw it away or overfignoled. It's not what it could be but not bad for a weary old drunk[1]. Tomorrow Imagination... & perhaps Va et V.[2]

Clan gathering last weekend of month, Sunny & kids, John & Vera, latter staying over for Edward's concours the 1st.[3]

Hope you got to Bath quand même.[4] Next Friday shd. be all right. To come not too late & leave not too early.

Must fish out now Cahier for Tara MacG. aged ½ & get Avigdor on job next week. Going back, with H's naturally, prob. next Tuesday.[5]

Sex-obsessed nightingales all night & part of day. Vive le merle.[6]

Madeleine success in Switz. Zürich, Lausanne, Geneva.[7] Jérôme showed film to unhappy few. Before sending it back. Success, with Blin notably.[8]

Can't think of triplex now. But next or nothing.[9]

More work on Play with Serreau in store. No word from Gaskill, Galligaskill.[10]

Shall ring children when I feel less shy. Love

Sam

ALS; 1 leaf, 1 side; *env to* Mrs Bray, c/o Miss Pearson, Hallam Court, Hallam Street, London W.1, Angleterre; *pm* 17-5-65, La Ferté-sous-Jouarre; TCD MS 10948/1/327.

1 SB sent the script of *Eh Joe* to Jack MacGowran, for whom it was written; Donald McWhinnie, who was the intended director of the TV play; and Margaret McLaren, Curtis Brown, who would handle the rights. "Overfignoled": SB invents a word combining English "over-" and part of the French verb "fignoler" (to polish). To MacGowran SB wrote on the same day: "I hope I did not seem to assume that you would necessarily want to do it because it comes from me. I assure you I don't. I do hope you will take it on. But if on reading it again and thinking it over you decide it is not for you, no one will better understand than me." (TxU, Beckett Collection, 9.3.)

2 *Imagination morte imaginez. Va et vient.*

3 Family of Morris Sinclair and John Beckett planned to attend Edward Beckett's final concours at the Conservatoire.

4 "Quand même" (all the same).

5 SB wrote the same day (15 May) to Jack MacGowran: "I'll have Tara's Ms with me when I go back to Paris in a few days." Tara (b. 1964), daughter of Jack MacGowran and Eileen Gloria Nugent, received a notebook including a draft of "From an Abandoned Work," part of the English translation of *Molloy* and *En attendant Godot*, as a gift from SB (OSU, Irish Collection, Spec.rare.115). MacGowran wished to have a portrait of SB by Avigdor Arikha on the cover of the recording he was planning to make of his readings from SB's work for Claddagh Records. "H's" are the Haydens.

6 "Vive le merle" (Long live the blackbird).

7 Madeleine Renaud's tour of *Oh les beaux jours*.

8 SB had written to Lindon on 10 May: "Si tu montres le film tu serais gentil d'inviter mon ami Peter Lennon – malgré qu'il soit journaliste!" (Lennon Collection, Archives *Guardian/Observer*, 2001–098.) "If you do show the film, it would be nice if you would invite my friend Peter Lennon, even if he is a journalist!" Peter Lennon (1930–2011) wrote for *The Guardian* as a film critic.

9 By "triplex" SB may be referring to the evening of plays by three playwrights proposed for the Odéon-Théâtre de France, comprising his own *Comédie* and *Va et Vient*, Robert Pinget's *L'Hypothèse*, and Eugène Ionesco's *La Lacune* and *Délire à deux*, which would open together the following year, on 28 February.

10 *Comédie*, directed by Jean-Marie Serreau; *Play*, to be presented at the National Theatre, produced by the Royal Court and directed by William Gaskill (b. 1930).

JOHN FLETCHER
DURHAM, ENGLAND

28.5.65 Paris

Dear Mr Fletcher

You may of course include the V. Velde piece. "Abstenez" should of course read "s'abstenir".[1] The thing on Miller was supplied to Calder at his request when there was a risk of action against the publication. It was designed only to be read – if necessary – in court and shd. not have been used in back of paperback.[2] I did not know. Plot for bibliographers.

Sincerely

Sam. Beckett

ALS; 1 leaf, 1 side; TxU, Beckett (Lake) Collection, 18.9.

1 John Fletcher had requested permission to publish SB's text for the invitation to Bram van Velde's exhibition at the Galerie Maeght in 1952 (see SB's letter of [before February 1952]). The final two lines read: "Peinture de vie et de mort. / Amateurs de natron, abstenez" (Painting of life and death. / Those who like their natron should keep away).

2 John Calder had solicited letters in support of the publication of Henry Miller's *Tropic of Cancer* from a great many writers, including SB, should these letters be necessary in a court case. He asked that the letters respond to two questions: "1) do you consider the book of sufficient literary merit to warrant publication? 2) do you consider publication to be in the public interest?" Although SB's response was enclosed with his letter of 14 February 1963 to Calder, it has not been found (InU, C&B, Beckett). A phrase from SB's testimony was printed on the back jacket of Calder's edition of *Tropic of Cancer* (1963): "'A momentous event in the history of modern writing.'" There was no prosecution of the novel.

RUBY COHN
SAN FRANCISCO

27.6.65 Courmayeur

Dear Ruby

Thanks for your letter of Father's Day.

I used to like Ussher, but no longer so. Indeed wish I never had. God knows what is in those letters.[1]

I was fascinated for years by idea of a play on D[r] J. & M[rs] Thrale (1781–84) and accumulated a mass of notes which I still have. Actually started first act. Then gave up – chiefly but not only because of language difficulty.[2]

I translated the dog doggerel myself, from what I could remember of the German, into both French and English.[3]

I am not going to Berkeley.[4]

As well as Come & Go there is my first attempt at a TV play called EH JOE. I wrote it for the Irish actor Jack MacGowran. For a face and a voice. It will be done in London probably this year. I gave it to Alan Schneider the other day. He came through Paris on his way to Israel.

In Italy for about another 10 days. Then back to Paris to try and face it all.

Yours ever

Sam

ALS; 1 leaf, 1 side; UoR, BIF MS 5100/14.

1 SB and Suzanne are on holiday in the Italian Alps.

Ruby Cohn may have noted the acquisition by the Humanities Research Center, University of Texas in Austin, of a group of letters from SB to Arland Ussher written between 1935 and 1950; they had been purchased in 1957 (TxU, Samuel Beckett Collection, Box 9.5). Ussher's papers at Trinity College Dublin include SB's letters written between 1953 and 1977, but these were not held by the archive until 1981 (MS 9031–41/45–77).

2 SB's abandoned play *Human Wishes*: 13 December 1936, 3 July 1937, 4 August 1937 to McGreevy. For the manuscript, see UoR, BIF, MS 3458–3461.

3 The dog song in *En attendant Godot*.

4 The previous day, 26 June, Cohn had written to Raymond Federman: "There are rumors around here that Beckett is coming to be Regents lecturer at Berkeley, but I

can't believe it. I wrote to ask him, but he hasn't answered yet. He has, however, thrown cold water on my idea for a 60th birthday Festschrift for him. I might have guessed, but I'm disappointed." (InU, Federman Collection.)

AVIGDOR ARIKHA AND ANNE ATIK
PARIS

30.6.65 Courmayeur

Chers amis

Merci de votre lettre.

J'attends avec impatience des nouvelles de la visite de Robertson.[1]

J'ai prévenu le garage et vous n'aurez aucune difficulté pour la clef.

Ici ça va. Temps magnifique toujours. Dehors tout le temps. Presque pas travaillé. Un peu sur Dis Joe. Aucune envie. Abruti de soleil, d'altitude et d'air pur. . . et d'eau minérale.

Visité Aoste hier. Ville très prenante. Vestiges romains impressionnants. Maison natale d'Anselme! [2]

Pense être de retour vers le 13. S'agit de ne pas faire le con avant la greffe.[3]

Question de Londres au mois d'août pour Come & Go. A condition de pouvoir articuler.

Affectueusement à vous deux.

Sam

ALS; 1 leaf, 1 side; InU, Arikha.

30.6.65 Courmayeur

Dear Both

Thank you for your letter.

I await impatiently news of Robertson's visit.[1]

I have warned the garage and you will have no difficulty over the key.

Here all well. Weather still wonderful. Out all the time. Hardly done any work. A little on *Dis Joe*. No wish to. Dazed by sun, altitude, and pure air . . . and mineral water.

Visited Aosta yesterday. Very engaging town. Impressive Roman remains. House where Anselm was born![2]

Think I'll be back round the 13th. Mustn't do anything silly before the graft.[3]

Talk of London in August for *Come & Go*. Provided I can make recognisable sounds.

Love to you both.

Sam

1 Bryan Robertson (1925–2002), then curator of the Whitechapel Gallery in London, would write enthusiastically to Arikha on 13 July, offering to explore the possibility of an Arikha show (Arikha Collection).

2 The Italian town of Aosta was the birthplace of the theologian Archbishop Anselm of Canterbury (1033–1109).

3 SB had written to Barbara Bray five days earlier: "Am here, then a day or so in Turin, then Paris, mouth, slops and odonto-daemonology" (25 June 1965; TCD, MS 10948/1/337).

BARBARA BRAY
PARIS

7.7.65 Courmayeur

Dear Barbara

Your Robertson letter just now, just from day in open. So glad it has been fairly successful. Letter from Avigdor same post. Curious R. not more taken with the drawings. It looks anyhow as if it may produce something. If all the paintings were as good as mine a show in London could make a noise. But I'm afraid they're not.[1]

No recollection of having helped N.C. with Auden MS.[2]

Finished first go at Dis Joe. Half way through Imagination ... Putting in plenty of Gallicisms. Reads weird.[3]

Letter from L. Waddington to introduce a "young French dealer called Claude Givaudan" who wants to do a limited edition of Molloy illustrated by English sculptor Bernard Meadows. Ring any bells. Says "I enclose photos of M's work", but none with letter.[4]

Feel I suppose the better of all the sun, clear air, walking and sobriety. Weather now not so good. Place full of flics and gorilles &

French & Italian huiles getting ready for the 16th. None at this hotel that I can smell happily.[5]

Enclosed cheque for 2000. Please don't thank. Thank you for letting me.

No news from Hayden since I left. Hope nothing wrong. Have written more than once.

Beckett Festival in Rome according to Stampa. Some young group. Première nouvelle.[6]

Abandoned B. et P. [? quel pion].[7]

Read X. de Maistre's Prisonnier de la Tour. Tour du lépreux at Aosta. Awful.[8]

Elie Faure on Egyptian art. Awful.[9]

Stampa & Stampa Sera daily from cover to cover. Great stuff. All crimes still unsolved. Tour de France comme si on y était.[10]

Bought six pairs of socks today in the Wednesday market. Very colourful. Not the socks. 5 francs a pair.

London in August most uncertain. Considering Calder & palate. Hope not that I can't but that I don't have to.

Take it easy in the empty flat. Don't worry about silly money.

Love

Sam

ALS; 2 leaves, 2 sides; *env to* Madame Bray, 15 Rue Séguier, Paris 6me, Francia; *pm* 8-7-65, Courmayeur; TCD, MS 10948/1/341.

1 Bray had conveyed further information about Bryan Robertson's interest in Avigdor Arikha's work. SB owned three abstract paintings by Arikha: *Composition* (1959), *Composition* (1961), and *Noir et blancheur* (1965); this last is reproduced in Thomson, ed., *Arikha*, 36.

2 Nancy Cunard published W. H. Auden's poem "Spain" in *Deux poèmes* (the other was "Madrid," a poem by Raúl González Tuñón) in the series that she and Pablo Neruda edited, Poètes du monde défendent le peuple espagnol (Madrid, 1937). It is possible that SB had helped Cunard when she experienced difficulties deciphering the manuscript of Auden's poem (see Anne Chisholm, *Nancy Cunard: A Biography* [New York, Alfred A. Knopf, 1979] 239).

3 The French translation of *Eh Joe*, entitled *Dis Joe*, is in a notebook held by Washington University, St. Louis; this is dated as "finished 3 Jul 1965" (Photocopy, UoR, BIF, MS1538/2). A manuscript draft of *Imagination Dead Imagine*, the English translation of *Imagination morte imaginez*, is in the same notebook; it is dated as "Started 4 Jul 1965, finished 8 July 1965" (Photocopy, UoR, BIF, MS 1541/1).

4 Leslie Waddington (b. 1934) introduced to SB the publisher and gallery director Claude Givaudan (n.d.) from Geneva. He planned to open the Galerie Givaudan, 201 Boulevard Saint-Germain, in January 1966. Givaudan had seen the work of sculptor Bernard Meadows (1915–2005) in the 1952 Venice Biennale and asked him to exhibit at his new gallery. Meadows chose to create a "livre objet" (book object) after SB's *Molloy*.

5 On 16 July, the Mont Blanc Tunnel linking Italy and France was to be inaugurated by Presidents Charles de Gaulle and Giuseppe Saragat; this appearance by dignitaries from each country led to a strong security presence in the area. "Flics" (sl., police); "gorilles" (sl., heavies); "huiles" (sl., bigwigs).

6 The Beckett Festival in Rome mentioned by *La Stampa* has not been identified. "Première nouvelle" (First I've heard of it).

7 SB had written to Barbara Bray about *Bouvard et Pécuchet* by Flaubert: "Reading with relish opening of Bouvard & P. Pity one can't want any more in that direction." (30 June 1965; TCD, MS 10948/1/336.) If the editors' reading "quel pion" is correct, then: "what a drudge" if referring to Flaubert; "what a useless creature" if referring to SB himself.

8 SB was probably reading *Le Lépreux de la cité d'Aoste* (1811) by Xavier de Maistre (1763–1852). The work was inspired by the imprisonment in this tower, in the late eighteenth century, of a leper named Pierre-Bernard Guasco.

9 Elie Faure (1873–1937) was the author of *Histoire de l'art* (1920–1921), published in five volumes. The first of these was a history of ancient art.

10 *La Stampa* and *Stampa Sera* are published in Turin. "Tour de France comme si on y était" ("Tour de France as if you were there").

GEORGE DEVINE
LONDON

27.8.65 Ussy

Bien cher George

Just to say how grieved I am to hear you are ill and how I long to hear you are over it all and back at Andrews getting strong again.[1] I send you my deeply affectionate thoughts. In my old head I have your hand in both of mine.

Always

Sam

ACS; 1 leaf, 1 side; *env to* George Devine Esq, William King Ward, St. George's Hospital, London S.W.1, Angleterre; *pm* 27–8–65, La Ferté-sous-Jouarre; UoR, BIF, MS 5200/2.

1 On 7 August, George Devine had suffered a heart attack while on stage, and this was followed by a stroke ten days later. Only in mid-October was he discharged from the hospital. (Wardle, *The Theatres of George Devine*, 277–278.)

JOCELYN HERBERT
LONDON

15.9.65 Paris

Dear Jocelyn

I'm very grateful to you for having written, in the midst of all your trouble, and distressed that the news is not better. I do

18. Jocelyn Herbert

hope this week is easier and the signs of recovery now definite. You know what's in my heart for you and George, so I needn't try and say it. But you do, to you both, for me. You're with me here and I'm wishing for you hard. All loving thoughts, dear George and Jocelyn.

Sam

ALS; 1 leaf, 1 side; *env to* Jocelyn Herbert, 6 Rossetti Studios, Flood Street, London S.W.3, Angleterre; *pm* 15-9-65, Paris; UoR, BIF, MS 5200/4.

PATRICK MAGEE
LONDON

17.9.65 Paris

Dear Pat

So glad to hear from you.

Re film of mime the simplest for all would be for me to see it when I am next in London which may well be next month for TV venture with Jack and Donald. There are 2 mimes and I wonder which he has done. Foolish as you say without permission.[1] Same thing a few days ago with Murphy or similar. Film script by some woman out of the blue which no question of at any price.[2]

Had dinner last night with the Searles whom I had never met. Very enjoyable.[3]

Had a letter from David Jones about late evening performance of Krapp in December before you go to USA. I suppose this is all right with you. I replied saying it was with me on condition Donald was consulted. If there is ever a regular revival I would ask for the old set up, as I did Gaskill awful English when question of doing it again at the Court. Have a few ideas of how the three of us together might gain another inch or so.[4]

Yes, my mouth has been giving trouble, as though to atone for all the solace it has conveyed to me for so long, and still does, in the form of nicotine and alcohol. The trouble isn't serious, just uncomfortable and a nuisance.

Hope greatly to see you before you leave.[5]

Love to you all

Sam

ALS; 1 leaf, 1 side; TCD, MS 11313/15.

1 SB planned to be available in London for work on *Eh Joe* with Donald McWhinnie and Jack MacGowran.

Magee had reported that Paul Joyce (b. 1952) had made a film of *Act Without Words II*, with actors Freddie Jones (b. 1927) and Geoffrey Hinsliff (b. 1937). Joyce had not sought SB's permission. Joyce admitted to SB: "I was hoping [Magee] might like the film, and perhaps mention it to you" (Paul Joyce to SB, 29 November [1965]; Paul Joyce Collection). SB saw the film when he was next in London, and retroactively granted permission for *The Goad, adapted from Act Without Words, by Samuel Beckett* (4 December 1965 and 5 February [1966]; Paul Joyce Collection). Joyce's filmscript was published in *Nothing Doing in London* 1 (November 1966) 124–131.

2 The person who proposed to film *Murphy* has not been identified.

3 The British composer Humphrey Searle (1913–1982) and his second wife Fiona Nicolson. Searle studied at the Royal College of Music and at the New Vienna Conservatory under Anton Webern. In 1951, Searle had composed *The Riverrun*, a setting of James Joyce's *Finnegans Wake*.

4 SB assented to the request of David Jones, the Royal Shakespeare Company (RSC), for a short run of *Krapp's Last Tape*, adding: "If there is ever a normal revival of this piece, I shd. want to do it again with Donald & Pat and think I know how the original production at the Court can be pushed a bit further" (12 September 1965; GEU, MS 1221).

5 Magee was due to perform in New York as Sade in the RSC production of Peter Weiss's play *Marat/Sade*, opening at the Martin Beck Theatre on 27 December.

REINHART MÜLLER-FREIENFELS
SÜDDEUTSCHER RUNDFUNK, STUTTGART

October 22nd 1965

38 Boulevard St. Jacques
Paris 14me

Dear Dr Müller-Freienfels

Thank you for your letter of October 18th.[1]

When I accepted your kind invitation to work on your production of EH JOE there was no thought of payment in my mind. My only concern is with helping to have the work presented as I see it. So please forgive me if I have to decline the very generous fee you propose.

The dates you give for rehearsal and recording are quite convenient to me. I should of course welcome a meeting in Paris with our decorator Matias. Any time in the second half of January would suit me.[2]

Thank you for your promise of competent technical assistance. I assure you I shall need it, having no experience of TV production. But I hope to have the advantage of working with my London director before going to Stuttgart.[3]

With all good wishes,

yours sincerely

s/

Samuel Beckett

TLS; 1 leaf, 1 side; SWR Historisches Archiv, Bestand SDR 19/1342. AL draft on R. Müller-Freienfels's letter to SB, 18 October 1965 (TLS, 2 leaves, 2 sides); GEU, MS 1221.

1 German art historian Werner Spies (b. 1937) was at this time a Paris correspondent for Süddeutscher Rundfunk (SDR) in Stuttgart; Spies had negotiated arrangements with SB for his work to be produced by SDR, therefore the letter of 18 October from SDR's Artistic Director Reinhart Müller-Freienfels (1925–2010) was his first direct communication with SB.

2 Rehearsals were scheduled from 14 to 29 March; studio time had been reserved for 30 March through 1 April for recording the play. "Decorator": Gallicism for "set-designer."

3 SB assumed that he would already have worked with Donald McWhinnie on the BBC production of *Eh Joe* beforehand.

BARBARA BRAY
PARIS

Sat. [? 23 October 1965] Ussy

Dear Barbara

Thanks for your letter.

I still have no phone 24 hours after having signalled derangement – yesterday was hellish.[1] It rang all day. When I pick it up it goes on ringing in my ear. No one hears what I say & I hear nothing just the ringing. I asked them this morning to cut if off if they couldn't fix it. Perhaps I'll get rid of it altogether.

Country charm not working. Feel exhausted & exasperated. Want to stay alone. Sorry. Perhaps I'll come back before Thursday. Reading Quelqu'un. Prefer L'Inquisitoire.[2] Burning leaves. Levelling molehills. Mooching about. Afraid to go for a walk in case tel. man arrives. Dined with Hayden 1st evening. Mortel.[3] Tottered back in mist. Shan't go again. Turn out in the dark & cold. Did work on All That Fall. Mrs R. represented by an animated line. Looked at nothing else. Piles of letters. All no. Refused Stuttgart fee. Refused Duthuit dialogues BBC. Wrote crankily to Calder about his readings.[4] Time they buried me.

Love

S.

ALI; 1 leaf, 1 side; *env to* Madame Bray, 15 Rue Séguier, Paris 6me; *pm* _5-10-65, La Ferté-sous-Jouarre; TCD, MS 10948/1/345. *Dating*: after letters mentioned below in n. 4.

1 "Dérangement" (faulty connection).

2 SB was reading Pinget's recently published novel *Quelqu'un* (*Someone*); Pinget's novel *L'Inquisitoire* had been published by Editions de Minuit in 1962.

3 "Mortel" (deadly).

4 SB refused a fee for *Eh Joe* at Süddeutscher Rundfunk (see 22 October).

Martin Esslin had asked that copyright be cleared for a reading of the *Three Dialogues* on the Third Programme on 5 October (BBCWAC, RCONT12, Samuel Beckett, Scriptwriter II); Margaret McLaren, Curtis Brown, refused permission on 27 October.

SB had written to John Calder on 23 October: "Please go easy with these readings. Imagination.. should not be read now. Why that passage from Molloy? I don't want to interfere with anything under way, but please no more without my knowing what extracts and read how & by whom. Forgive if I sound cantankerous." (InU, C&B, Beckett.)

MARTIN ESSLIN
LONDON

9.11.65 Paris

Dear Martin

Thanks for your letter.

I should like to hear the Rothwell Group recording of PLAY. Perhaps you would play it back for me in London where I expect to be soon. If I find it possible I'll withdraw my opposition.[1]

Rightly or wrongly I regret the Duthuit Dialogues and prefer not to have them broadcast.[2]

Best always

Yours

Sam

ACS; 1 leaf, 1 side; *env to* Martin Esslin Esq, Broadcasting House, London W.1, Angleterre; *pm* 8-11-65, Paris; Private Collection.

1 In a letter to SB of 3 November, Martin Esslin explained that *Play* was prepared by the Rothwell Group: "an experimental group among our actors who are such enthusiasts for radio that they record plays for their own amusement and without a thought of broadcast [...] I advised them against it [*Play*] because I was convinced that the essence of the play lies in the operation of the light on the faces emerging from the urns. But they went ahead anyway just for the hell of it." (BBCWAC, RCONT12, Samuel Beckett, Scriptwriter II.)

To establish an aural equivalent for the light in *Play*, director Bennett Maxwell (b. 1934) created "a continuum of sound ... which would be abruptly interrupted each time one of the characters was jerked into speech." According to Martin Esslin, SB explained that the Chorus, the Narration, and the Meditation must be distinguished from each other, and that with each repeat "there must be a clear progression by which each subsection is both faster and softer than the preceding one." The effect is that "the same text will go on *ad infinitum*, ever faster and ever softer without quite ceasing altogether." SB's modification of the sequence of the speeches in the repeat led to his suggestion "that each character's part should be recorded separately and that these permutations of exactly the same words spoken in exactly the same way be achieved by cutting the tape together like the takes of a film." (Martin Esslin, "Samuel Beckett & the Art of Broadcasting," *Encounter* 45 [September 1975] 44.)

2 Esslin had heard the *Three Dialogues* read at John Calder's Beckett evening at the Traverse Theatre in Edinburgh and wrote to SB that "these seem to me to be excellent radio and an important statement about modern art." Since they were now available in print, Esslin wondered why SB was against broadcast (Esslin to SB, 3 November 1965).

JOHN CALDER
CALDER AND BOYARS, LONDON

23.11.65 Ussy

Dear John

Thanks for yours of 17th.

I don't want the Dialogues to go any further, i.e. no translations, and definitely don't want Proust to appear in French. Please forgive me.[1]

I'm dead tired and hoping now TV production not too imminent. The more so as PLAY film with Serreau signed and due any day (to make).[2]

Seaver texts of Nouvelles on their way. Shall try and clear them up fast.[3]

Working laboriously. Prose in French. About 3000 words so far. Looks as if it might continue.[4] May it for my little ever.

Yours ever

Sam

ALS; 1 leaf, 1 side; *datestamped* 25.NOV.1965; InU, C&B, Beckett.

1 John Calder published SB's *Proust and Three Dialogues with Georges Duthuit* in 1965; he had interested other publishers in the reprint rights for France and Italy. In his letter to SB of 17 November, Calder asked him whether he would like the *Three Dialogues* published in Italian by Sugar Editore or Einaudi. He also mentioned that Gallimard was interested in publishing *Proust and Three Dialogues* in French. (InU, C&B, Beckett.)

2 SB was awaiting a date for the rehearsal and production of *Eh Joe* at the BBC with Jack MacGowran. Also pending was a film related to Jean-Marie Serreau's theatre production of *Comédie* with Delphine Seyrig, Michael Lonsdale, and Eléonore Hirt (Graley Herren, "Different Music: Karmitz and Beckett's Film Adaptation of Comédie," *Journal of Beckett Studies* 18.1–2 [September 2009] 10–31; Marin Karmitz and Samuel Beckett, *Comédie* [Paris: Editions du Regard, 2001]).

3 SB had written to Richard Seaver, Grove Press, to ask him for "the short stories including rough draft of Le Calmant."

4 SB would write to Jocelyn Herbert on 7 December, "Just back from a spell at Ussy, in the raging wind living mostly inside a cylinder of my imagining with 200 others" (UoR, BIF, MSS 5200/6). SB was working on prose in French that would, in time, become *Le Dépeupleur*; the first draft in a notebook, later marked in SB's hand "DEPEUPLEUR I," is dated as begun "31 Oct 1965 (Paris), finished 28 Nov 1965 (Ussy)" (Admussen, *The Samuel Beckett Manuscripts*, 35).

JACOBA VAN VELDE
AMSTERDAM

3.12.65 Ussy

Chère Tonny

1. Le chuchotement porte chaque fois sur l'état de santé de celle qui vient de sortir. Elles sont "condamnées" toutes les 3.[1]

2. J'imagine un lion de pierre dans la cour de l'école. Elles avaient l'habitude de s'asseoir dessus côte à côte. "Bûche" ou "tronc d'arbre" ne vont pas en français. Mais "lion" n'est pas bon non plus. Je le changerai probablement sur les épreuves.[2]

3. Cascando, droits radio: Editions de Minuit

4. Words & Music " ": Curtis Brown.

5. Actes sans Paroles 1 et 2, droits théâtre: Ed. de Minuit

6. Come & Go, droits théâtre: Curtis Brown.

7. Eh Joe, droits TV: Curtis Brown.

J'ai écrit aujourd'hui à Curtis Brown en leur demandant de faire des copies de Eh Joe et de t'en envoyer une. Je t'enverrai la traduction française dès que j'aurai recupéré [sic] le ms. J'ai demandé à Top de t'envoyer la traduction allemande. Elle n'est pas encore prête.

Je n'ai toujours pas la date de la BBC et ne sais pas encore quand j'irai à Londres. Mais probablement dans le courant de ce mois-ci. Je commence la semaine prochaine à préparer avec Serreau et son équipe le film de Comédie.

A ma grande surprise je suis ici depuis quinze jours. Pas mal de repos. Un peu de travail. Je rentre après-demain.

Bien affectueusement

Sam

ALS; 1 leaf, 1 side; BNF, 19794/107.

3.12.65 Ussy

Dear Tonny

1. Each time the whispering touches on the state of health of the woman who has just exited. All three of them are "condemned".[1]

2. I am imagining a stone lion in the schoolyard. It was their habit to sit on it side by side. "Bûche" or "tronc d'arbre" doesn't work in French. But "lion" isn't good either. I shall probably change it in the proofs.[2]

3. *Cascando*, radio rights: Editions de Minuit.

4. *Words & Music*: radio rights: Curtis Brown.
5. *Actes sans paroles 1 and 2*, theatre rights: Ed. de Minuit
6. *Come & Go*, theatre rights: Curtis Brown.
7. *Eh Joe*, TV rights: Curtis Brown.

I have today written to Curtis Brown asking them to have copies made of *Eh Joe* and to send you one. I shall send the French translation as soon as I have got the MS back. I have asked Top to send you the German translation. It's not ready yet.

I still have no date for the BBC, and don't know when I'll be going to London. But probably some time this month. Next week I begin preparing with Serreau and his team the film of *Comédie*.

To my great surprise I've been here for a fortnight. Quite a lot of rest. A little work. I go back the day after tomorrow.

Much love

Sam

1 SB refers to *Come and Go*. Van Velde's translation, *Komen en gaan*, would be published in a collection of her translations of SB's short plays in 1967: *Hé, Joe; Sintels; Woorden en muziek; Cascando; Komen en gaan; Allen die vallen; Spel zonder woorden 1; Spel zonder woorden 2* (Amsterdam: Uitgeverij de Bezige Bij).

2 The "benchlike seat" accommodating the three women in *Come and Go* is featureless and "as little visible as possible" in the published version (*CSP*, 196). On the manuscript development of the play, see Breon Mitchell, "Art in Microcosm: The Manuscript Pages of Beckett's *Come and Go*" (*Modern Drama* 19.3 [September 1976] 245–254).

JOCELYN HERBERT
LONDON

7.12.65 Paris

Très chers amis

I have been thinking of you and wondering how things were and was so glad to have your news today and to know that George is making progress. It would be a great thing and help to put up with the slowness of it all if he could get on with his writing.[1] I am still waiting for a date from that B.F.B.B.C. Nothing to be extracted so far from Stonewall Bakewell. But I am hoping it will be towards the end of the month. McWhinnie not forthcoming either, only Jacky panting to get at it.[2] En attendant I start work today with Serreau & his merry men on film of PLAY, which should be amusing (for us). Just back from a spell at Ussy, in the raging wind living mostly inside a cylinder of my imagining with 200 others.[3] Triumph of Madeleine in Duras's Des Journeés Entières . . . Going on Saturday.[4] Shall get in touch as soon as I get to London and be in Flood St. as soon as you can have me.

Courage and much love.

Sam

ALS; 1 leaf, 1 side; *env to* M[r] and Mrs George Devine, 6 Rossetti Studios, Flood Street, London S.W.3, Angleterre; *pm* 7-12-65, Paris; UoR BIF MS 5200/6.

1 When George Devine's daughter Harriet later wrote about celebrating her father's birthday on 20 November, she observed: "inside that semi-useless body was a mind, as quick and alert as ever, which was wild with frustration and disappointment at being trapped inside, unable to use the energy and activity to which it was so accustomed" (Harriet Devine, *Being George Devine's Daughter* [London: Barkus Books, 2006] 166).

2 The BBC's delay in setting a date to record *Eh Joe* had been an irritation, hence SB's reference to BBC TV producer Michael Bakewell as "Stonewall" and the BBC as "B.F.B.B.C." (Bloody Fool BBC).

3 "En attendant" (meanwhile).
SB had been working on the manuscript of what becomes *Le Dépeupleur*.

4 Madeleine Renaud was performing in Marguerite Duras's *Des journées entières dans les arbres* that opened on 1 December at the Odéon-Théâtre de France.

NICHOLAS RAWSON
HAMBURG

25.12.65 Paris

Dear Nick

Thanks for your card.

Herewith the poems. Re-reading confirms impression that they are the best you have done so far. Odd things here and there that the cold eye crueller cast will better. Compliments.[1]

Have not seen L.N. But when so shall as you ask.[2]

Making a little film of Play with young technique hogs. Not unexciting. London soon for a TV thump with Jack MacG. Looking forward to seeing[.] George home from sea very diminished improving slowly.

Mary appears from time to time in the 4 seasons fountain. Good form.[3]

So tired channel swim from margin to margin so forgive more now.

All best to you both for the in store & pickle.

Ever

Sam

ALS; 1 leaf, 1 side; TCD, MS 10513/1.

1 Nicholas Rawson had received several earlier cards and letters from SB, but these are lost; the present letter is the first from SB in the collection at Trinity College Dublin (Rawson to the editors, 22 September 1991). The poems by Rawson have not been identified, but they may have been those enclosed with his letter of 27 December to Marion Boyars, Calder and Boyars, two days later: "Vatnajökull," "Know surely," and "Let." In his letter, Rawson wishes Marion Boyars to ask her husband Arthur Boyars (b. 1925), poet and Editor of *Transatlantic Review*, to read them. Rawson had placed a poem in that journal two years earlier: "Indoor View" (*Transatlantic Review* 12 [Spring 1963] 73–79).

2 Rawson may have submitted some of his work to *Les Lettres Nouvelles*; however, nothing was published there (Rawson to the editors, 22 September 1991).

3 Mary Hutchinson's daughter Barbara (d. 1989) was married to artist Nikos Ghika (1906–1994); the couple lived at 59 Rue de Grenelle, Paris 7, which is where the Fontaine des Quatre-Saisons is located. Mary Hutchinson visited her daughter in Paris several times a year.

MARY MANNING HOWE
CAMBRIDGE, MASSACHUSETTS

25.12.65 Paris

Dear Mary

Good to have your annual. Don't suppose you can read this but can't face the machine.

De nobis silemus. Jean has been seriously ill. Three ops. in Monkstown hospital by Cooldrinagh Wheeler I think. Successful removal reported. Home at last very weak and shaky. Edward stuck in Dublin all summer and autumn in consequence. Looking forward to moving to London now and getting going professionally with help of John. Caroline married to Paddy Murphy prosperously selling biscuits for Bolands. Living in Sorrento Terrace.[1]

Have not been back since 59 and completely out of touch. What little I hear sounds grim. Con Leventhal here for the old memories. Happy in Montparnasse. Nice little flat. Paris letters for the Irish Press.[2]

Why don't you come over for the James Joyce do here Feb. 2 at 21 hours with the Gilberts, Mme Léon and Mayoux among others and Gisèle Freund pictures. You'll find me sitting mute in a corner and then drinking somewhere in vain.[3]

Did you hear about the Zürich jinks next Bloomsday? The separated remains to be dug up, united and crowned by an American bust. Giorgio wrote asking me to unveil. No. But shall probably go, cower in a corn[er] and drink in vain at the Kronenhalle. Why don't you come over for that?[4]

Invited to go to Finnegan film, replied for neither love nor even money.[5]

Glad you liked Jean-Jacques. I do extremely. Had a good dinner with them all the other day and Nadeau.

Jim has lost a leg above the knee, same kind of thing as Gerald. Howard dead. Peggy and Ann still driving on in Field Place. Things a bit better for John in London. Sonny embourgeoisé in WHO Geneva. Ralph Cusack dead. But all this you must know.[6]

Yes, people keep giving me money for vinegar. That they continue a few more years is all I ask.

London soon for a TV prod. with MacGowran. Then ditto in Stuttgart. At presenter [sic] making a little film of Play with a horde of demented technicians.[7]

I enjoyed N.Y. Heat & humidity desperate. Had to stop every four yards and hold on to things, chiefly pillar boxes. Saw Kay Boyle one evening. All the rest with Grove and the crew.

Much love and a happy recirculation.

Sam

ALS; 2 leaves, 2 sides; TxU, Beckett Collection, 8.10.

1 "De nobis [ipsis] silemus" (Of ourselves we are silent), the epigraph of Immanuel Kant's *First Critique of Reason* (*Immanuel Kants Werke* III, *Kritik der Reinen Vernunft*, ed. Albert Görland [Berlin: Bruno Cassirer, 1913] [unpaginated]).

Dr. Desmond de Courcy Wheeler: 6 February 1959.

Patrick J. Murphy (b. 1925) became a Director of Bolands. Sorrento Terrace, Co. Dublin, on the northern-most point of Killiney Bay, had stunning views over the Bay and toward the mountains beyond.

2 A. J. Leventhal's column "Letters from Paris" had appeared in *The Irish Press* roughly twice a month beginning on 12 September 1963.

3 With Lucie Léon, Maria Jolas was organizing "A Birthday Tribute" to Joyce to be held on 2 February 1966 at The American Centre for Students and Artists, 261 Boulevard Raspail, Paris 14. A discussion, "Yesterday, Today, Tomorrow," was planned with Jean-Jacques Mayoux, Michel Butor, A. J. Leventhal, George Steiner, and Hélène Berger, moderated by Stuart Gilbert and herself. It would be followed by "Joyce and His Contemporaries," a "screen projection" by Gisèle Freund of her photographs of Joyce and his contemporaries (see 21 April 1964, n. 7). There would also be three exhibitions: Freund's photographs of Joyce, Joyce's books, and Joyce's papers. The program would "close with excerpts from recordings made by Joyce of his works" (Program, University of Tulsa, Paul and Lucie Léon Collection of James Joyce, Box 1.1).

4 Nora Joyce had wished to bury James Joyce in Ireland after his death in Zurich on 13 January 1941, but this was not possible during the War. There were later attempts to repatriate his remains (see 27 July 1948, and 26 September [1948]). Both the Joyces had been buried in the Fluntern Cemetery, Zurich. On Bloomsday (16 June) in 1966, they were to be reburied together in a permanent plot there. The monument was a life-size sculpture of Joyce reading, to be set behind the author's grave, by Milton Hebald (b. 1917). The Kronenhalle Bar, Ramistrasse 4, Zürich.

5 *Passages from Finnegans Wake* (1965), directed by Mary Ellen Bute (1906–1983), was based on Mary Manning's script, *The Voice of Shem*; it was shown at the Cannes Film Festival in 1965, and was distributed by Grove Press (Dilys Powell, "Finnegan's funferall," *Sunday Times* 20 January 1966: 45).

6 SB mentions his paternal uncles and other family members in his letter to Molly Roe, 6 February 1959 (see n. 5). James Beckett, an anaesthetist and an athlete, had had both legs amputated (see 21 February 1965, n. 1). Gerald Beckett: 26 April 1937, n. 9. Howard Beckett: 21 February 1965, n. 1. Peggy Beckett and her daughter Ann. Sonny Sinclair worked in the office of Public Information of the World Health Organization, Geneva, from 1952. Ralph Cusack's illness and death: 2 June 1958 to Ethna MacCarthy-Leventhal, n. 6.

7 Both the BBC production of the television play *Eh Joe* and that with SDR in Stuttgart were planned for early in the coming year.

THOMAS MACGREEVY
DUBLIN

25.12.65 Paris

Dear Tom

It seems a very long time since I wrote or heard. I hope you are not vexed with me. I feel tired and speechless. But I don't want the year to end without telling you how often there is thought of you and simply being with you in my mind and wondering how you are. Jean was very moved by your visit to her in Monkstown Hospital and your generosity. The poor woman has had an awful time. Home now at last but very shaky and weak. Nothing of interest to tell you here. I pass my time, or most of it with mechanical things and the work that might matter doesn't get done. Suzanne is brave and well and enjoys her own circle – Marthe & Manolo & Jean and Madeleine.[1] I haven't seen much of Chip & Monique but dine with them tomorrow. His Krapp sung by the same American was very badly received in Berlin and I think he was simply wounded by the critics.[2] I suppose you have heard about the Joyce nonsense next Bloomsday in Zurich – the separate remains to be exhumed and united and crowned by American sculpture! Giorgio wrote asking me to perform. I said no but that I'd try to be with him. Maria J. is organizing a do at the American centre on Feb 2nd for 25th Anniversary of his death. Same answer from me, can't help but shall try and be there, with Lucie Léon, the Gilberts, Mayoux, Butor, and a film of Gisèle Freund. Perhaps you got the invitation.

Have you been getting on with your memoirs? Did you try the tape-recorder?[3] Will you still let me get you one?

Through the open window I hear the Santé prisoners howling like beasts. And see beyond the Val de Grâce and Panthéon illuminated.

Much love from us both, dear Tom, and the best of whatever is to come.

Sam

ALS; 1 leaf, 2 sides; *env to* Dr Thomas M^ac^Greevy, 49 Morehampton Rd., Dublin, Irlande; *pm* 27-12-65, Paris; TCD, MS 10402/268.

1 Marthe Gautier, Manolo Fandos, Jean Martin, and Madeleine Renaud.

2 Marcel Mihalovici's opera *Krapp, oder Das letzte Band* was performed by the Akademie der Künste at the Berlin Festival on 25 September and again on 11 and 12 October. William Dooley's acting and singing received universal praise: Walther Kaempfer wrote: "Ihm und seinen beiden Helfern dem Regisseur und dem Dirigenten galt der starke Beifall eines interessierten und sachverständigen Publikums" ("Warum Liu-Tung der Welt entsagen wird . . . Kann man Beckett vertonen?" *Saarbrücker Zeitung* 1 October 1965: 5) (The warm applause of an interested and educated audience was for him and his two helpers, the director and the conductor). The response to the music was largely negative: "Die Musik ist teils illustrativ untermalend, teils ausführlich lärmend, aber jedenfalls schwächer als das Wortdrama für sich" (Wolfgang Schimming, "Halb und Halbe," *Der Abend* 17 September 1965: np) (The music in part underscores the text in an illustrative fashion, in part it is thoroughly noisy, but it is certainly weaker than the play by itself). Anita Laeseck wrote: "Mihalovicis Musik ist ganz geschickt, nicht ohne Phantasie, aber sie erschöpft sich sehr schnell und stagniert über weitere Strecken. Sie ist dem höchst originellen Einfall Becketts in keiner Weise adäquat." ("Der Traum des Lieu-Tung," *Das Berliner Wort* 16 October 1965: np.) (Mihalovici's music is rather clever, not without vision, but it quickly exhausts itself and languishes over long periods. It is in no way comparable to Beckett's highly original idea.)

SB would write later to MacGreevy: "Suzanne went and thought Dooley remarkable, but a characteristically frightful German mise en scène" (16 February 1966; TCD, MS 10402/269).

3 MacGreevy had begun, but did not complete, his memoirs; sixty pages of autobiographical fragments are among his papers at Trinity College Dublin (TCD, MS 8054).

APPENDIX

PROFILES

Fernando Arrabal (b. 1932) was born in Spain, which he left for France in 1955, a decision made easier by his detestation of Franco's regime; he has lived for the most part in France ever since. His literary output is prodigious: it is doubtful if any Spanish playwright since Lope de Vega in the sixteenth century has written more for the stage – his Collected Plays run to over 2,000 pages. Then there are novels and poetry in abundance, film scripts, essays. He has always been politically active, on the optimistic, anarcho-revolutionary left, and his writing is just as forcefully challenging. Attempts to describe or define his work usually fall back on other names (Sade, Artaud, Jarry) or groupings (the Surrealists, the Collège de Pataphysique), but he was no imitator. He wanted above all to challenge consensus, of whatever kind, and was as ready to deal in cruelty and death as in gaiety and hope. Nor were these attitudes confined to his writing, and it is to this total commitment that his wife, the highly intelligent Luce Moreau Arrabal, pays tribute, saying of him that he had "never sought the favour of the powerful or lowered his guard before them," nor "hidden the generosity of his public interventions to allow himself private abuses."

In short, it would be difficult to imagine any writer more different from Samuel Beckett. Twenty years after Beckett's death, Arrabal himself wrote, "Je n'ai jamais rien eu de commun avec lui" (I never had anything in common with him), though in a Festschrift prepared for SB's sixtieth birthday he would say, "I am always fascinated by the magic mirror of his work," and "In the everyday presence of the fantastic, Beckett, jumping out from behind the tombstones, brings us to the initiation, the hope and the despair. YES."[1] What made a connection possible between the two men was something neither literary nor political: the fascination that chess held for both of them. (Chess must have been the only context in which Arrabal

1 Fernando Arrabal, "Beckett," *Atelier du Roman* 59 (21 September 2009) 3; Fernando Arrabal, "In Connection with Samuel Beckett," in John Calder, ed., *Beckett at 60: A Festschrift* (London: Calder and Boyars, 1967) 88.

tolerated rules.) The two men passed chess news to each other, discussed tournaments, exchanged problems and solutions. If SB recognised chess expertise, Arrabal greatly respected the older man, and was to discover how justified that respect was when Beckett took up his cause after his arrest in 1967 by the Spanish authorities on charges of blasphemy, and sent a "Letter to the judges of Spain in defence of Fernando Arrabal."

Anne Atik (b. 1932), poet, wife of Avigdor Arikha, and close friend of SB, was born the third of five children in Palestine. At the age of six, she emigrated with her family, which had been resident in Palestine since the early 1800s, to Brooklyn, where her father worked as a printer. Strongly religious until her fifteenth year, she continued to be active in Zionist groups, and it was when on her way to Israel in 1959 that she decided to stop in Paris and there, through a common friend, met Avigdor Arikha, who was already a good friend of SB. The couple married in 1963 and remained together until Arikha's death in 2010, dividing their time between short stays in Jerusalem and New York, and residence in Paris. Fluent in Hebrew and French, Atik is the author of several collections of poetry, including *Words in Hock* (1974) and *Offshore* (1997). She was the principal subject of the portraits by Arikha, and with him had two daughters, Alba, for whom SB was godfather, and Noga. She is the author of *How It Was: A Memoir of Samuel Beckett*.

Edward Beckett (b. 1943), musician, SB's nephew, is Literary Executor of the Beckett Estate. The combination - musician and executor - is a heavy one: distinguished career as a flautist, concert and orchestral, and teacher, later professor, at the Guildhall School of Music and Drama. His musical gifts were apparent by the end of his schooldays at St. Columba's, near Dublin. He briefly considered studying Engineering at Trinity College Dublin, and indeed took one year of the course, but soon followed his instincts. SB always encouraged him in pursuit of his musical career, and Suzanne Beckett coached him in his studies. After a highly successful training at the Paris Conservatoire, he emerged, with highest honors, as a gifted flautist, went on to work with the great Jean-Pierre Rampal, and was soon in demand as a concert performer, with special interest in French Romantic and Post-Romantic music. In artistic terms there are only tenuous links with SB, notably the fact that SB was a music lover.

Managing the Beckett Estate is an onerous task, as one SB revival succeeds another. As the years go by, and as SB's work has taken on an almost legendary importance, all and sundry feel free to adapt it to their convictions or hunches. It is Edward Beckett who must deal with this.

Alain Bosquet (1919–1998), poet, novelist, and regular reviewer for *Combat*, was early drawn to SB, who reciprocated: the connection lasted lifelong. He was one of the first critics to recognize SB's specific originality, writing, as early as July 1953 "Deux Portraits du Néant?", and "Samuel Beckett ou l'écriture abstraite" (December 1955). There were to be many such pieces, not least his powerful review of *Fin de partie* (February 1957).

SB, never at ease at public occasions devoted to his work, found an ideal ally in Bosquet, who sat in for him at the "Beckett-Abend" at the Schiller-Theater in Berlin in October 1959, part of the series "Matineen im Schiller-Theater."

Bosquet himself was a prolific writer, and he found in SB an eager reader. The connection was formalized when SB translated three of Bosquet's poems, from his *Deuxième Testament* (1959): "En moi, c'est la guerre civile," "Achetez mes soupirs," and "Couteau." His translations ("In me, civil war," "Fresh sighs for sale," and "Knife") were published in Alain Bosquet, *Selected Poems* (New York: New Directions, 1963). Characteristically, SB worried about the translations, writing to Bosquet "Les poèmes vont être difficiles à traduire" (The poems are going to be hard to translate), and then, when the translations were done, adding the note "Trop peu 'littéraires', sans doute" (Not "literary" enough, no doubt).[2]

Bosquet, loyal friend and shrewd critic, was one of the few members of the French literary "establishment" with whom SB felt totally at ease.

Kay Boyle (1902–1992), writer, teacher, and political activist, was born in St. Paul, Minnesota, and educated in the United States, but from 1923 spent more than twenty years living and working in Europe, almost all of them in France. Her determination to be a writer encouraged her to join the expatriate, largely American, literary community of Paris, where she met, among others, Eugene and Maria Jolas, and Robert McAlmon, with whom she wrote *Being Geniuses Together*, a light-hearted, insider's view of that world. Unlike many in it, such as

2 SB to Alain Bosquet, 21 September 1959; DLA, Bosquet in A: Wiedemann, S. Beckett, 92.51.26; SB to Alain Bosquet, 20 October 1959; Doucet MS. Série-Ms 47.200/35.

Djuna Barnes or Nancy Cunard, she was a prolific writer: novels, short story collections, and books of verse (her *Collected Poems* was published in 1991), as well as essays and newspaper articles. She was on good terms with Beckett. Both were contributors in the 1930s to *transition*, the ambitiously avant-garde review edited by the Jolases. As well as occasionally meeting, they corresponded on literary matters. In 1943, she married a German, Joseph von Franckenstein, and after the War they moved to Germany.

Boyle shared political views with Beckett, but the difference too began there: Boyle was above all an activist, something barely imaginable for Beckett. Largely on account of her political involvements, she returned to the United States in the early 1950s, taking up a post in San Francisco State College, where she was Professor of English from 1963 to 1979. A misunderstanding over a lecture (on a Joyce short story, "The Boarding House") that she had sent to Beckett, had, when cleared up, the effect of bringing them closer together again, as the increasing range and warmth of the letters clearly shows. Beckett was deeply impressed by the warmth and humanity of her politics – she was an early and vociferous opponent of McCarthyism and of American policy in Vietnam – and by the more surprising fact that she never lost touch with the literary. The letters move in style from the cautious and distance-preserving ("Dear Kay Boyle") to the deeply affectionate and sympathetic, whether about her health or changes in her personal circumstances – changes, including prison sentences, that were often the consequence of her political activism. SB's fondness increased with age, in spite of the huge differences between their lives. They finished on the best of terms.

Barbara Bray (1924–2010), producer, translator, critic, found her way into radio after graduating from Cambridge University. She worked mostly for the BBC Radio Drama Department, where for years she was a key figure. Life was not always kind to her. She was widowed early, leaving her with sole care of her two daughters, Francesca (Checchina) and Julia. She met SB over his first venture in radio, *All That Fall*, which she produced for the BBC Third Programme in February 1958. Few people can have come so close to SB. Lively, inventive, and with a strong literary sensibility, she was the ideal person to help him through his characteristic lack of confidence about the new medium – not least because she saw at once that it was perhaps, of all the media, the one best suited to his gifts. SB was soon to feel totally at home with the BBC

Sound Drama team (the others at that time were Donald McWhinnie and John Morris), but his connection with Bray, while unfailingly and productively professional, went well beyond that. There should be no surprise there: this unambiguously warm and attractive woman was passionately concerned with words. Her literary and linguistic gifts and her many interests equipped her to stand the test of his wariness as few people could. He came to trust her as well as loving her, and the measure of this trust was that he could and did, over the years, talk and write to her without reservations about his work, current or projected – and could receive what she had to say. It was a powerful combination. So close indeed were they in their qualities and concerns that, in anyone less unpretentious than Bray, there might have been the risk of rivalrous feelings, conscious or unconscious – they were, after all, both translators. In fact, she never saw herself as a writer, and was aware from the beginning that, for SB, translating was simply one of the directions his writing would take, and by no means the most important.

In 1960, she left her position in the BBC following a change of regime, and in 1961 moved with her daughters to Paris. By now her own career was taking shape: translations, from writers as various as Anouilh, Duras, Genet, Kristeva, and Robbe-Grillet; editorial work; productions for radio; broadcasting in her own right (she was an occasional contributor to the admirable and long-running Sunday radio series *The Critics*). Her companionship with SB was intensely lived and durable: he never lost his affection and respect for her. They had much to give each other, and gave it, even though, by SB's choice, they never lived together.

John Calder (b. 1927) is the founder of John Calder (Publisher) Ltd., later Calder and Boyars during the years of his partnership with Marion Boyars (1963–1975). Calder became the British publisher of SB's prose and poetry, beginning in 1958 with SB's novels *Murphy*, *Molloy*, and *Malone Dies*. He published one play, *Come and Go*, which SB wrote for a theatre project Calder was planning in Soho. Calder was introduced to SB's work following the success of *Waiting for Godot*. When he met the writer himself, the two began what became a life-long friendship. Beckett suggested several young writers to Calder, including Aidan Higgins and Nick Rawson.

John Calder was an inveterate promoter-impresario; he could be found meeting booksellers in their shops and promoting his list personally, as well as traversing Europe and the United States seeking out new and promising writers. With his second wife, the Croatian singer

Bettina Jonič, he launched the Ledlanet Nights, a general arts festival (1963–1973). He frequently created opportunities for SB's work to be read and performed in festivals and special events; at times, SB had to slow him down.

Calder was born into a prominent Scottish family. He secured a place at Oxford, but his stepfather prevailed on him to study Economics at Zurich University. For a time he worked with his uncle in the family timber business. Calder's passion for opera led him into a career in publishing, at first distributing opera annuals and the British Film Institute's journal *Sight and Sound*. Unafraid of controversy, Calder began publishing books critical of French and British colonialism, including a collection of articles edited by Beckett's French publisher, Jérôme Lindon. In the 1960s, he published such "obscene" works as Henry Miller's *Tropic of Cancer*, Alexander Trocchi's *Cain's Book*, and William Burroughs's *The Naked Lunch*, joined in this by his colleague, SB's American publisher, Barney Rosset at Grove Press. By the end of the 1960s, Calder and Boyars had introduced to English readers many of the radically innovative authors of modern Europe. Near the end of his years in publishing John Calder sold his Beckett list to Faber and Faber, publisher of SB's plays. He wrote *Pursuit: The Uncensored Memoirs of John Calder* and *The Philosophy of Samuel Beckett* (both published in 2001).

Ruby Cohn (1922–2011) was a theatre scholar and Beckett specialist who published the first full-length monograph on Beckett's work, *Samuel Beckett: the Comic Gamut* (1962). Cohn graduated from Hunter College, then served as a member of the WAVES division of the US Navy in World War II, installing radar on battle ships. She pursued a degree at the University of Paris after the War, and while in Paris attended a performance of *En attendant Godot* in 1953, setting the course of her life-long study of SB's work. She returned to the US and began a doctorate in literature, at Washington University in St. Louis, where she wrote a dissertation on Samuel Beckett. In 1961, she taught at San Francisco State University (where she was an office-mate of Herbert Blau), until she resigned in 1968 to protest against the university administration. She taught at the California Institute of the Arts from 1969 to 1972, and then joined the faculty at the University of California, Davis, for the remaining twenty years of her academic life.

Cohn's studies of SB's writing and modern theatre put her in frequent correspondence with SB. They met in London, Paris, and Berlin. Cohn continued to publish on theatre, but returned most frequently to Beckett as her chief interest, with a *Casebook on Waiting for Godot* (1967), *Back to Beckett* (1973), and *Just Play: Beckett's Theatre* (1980). SB allowed her to edit his shorter unpublished or little-known works in *Disjecta: Miscellaneous Writings* (1984). Cohn's capstone study of his oeuvre was *A Beckett Canon* (2001). Cohn explored the full range of theatre in modern British and American drama in her many monographs and collections of essays; she formed close friendships with Beckett directors, actors, and theatre groups, including Herbert Blau, Joseph Chakin, and Mabou Mines.

Martin Esslin (1918–2002), director, writer, radio producer, and academic, was head of BBC Radio Drama and author of *The Theatre of the Absurd* (1961), an influential study of contemporary theatre; the book linked SB to Jean Genet, Arthur Adamov, Eugène Ionesco, Harold Pinter, and other playwrights in a tragicomic view of what Esslin called "the senselessness of the human condition."[3] Born in Budapest and educated in Vienna, Esslin fled to London and joined the BBC in 1940, becoming a scriptwriter and producer. From 1963 to 1977, Esslin was head of the Radio Drama Department at the BBC and commissioned readings and productions of SB's work, including *Lessness* (1971) and *Rough for Radio II* (1976), which he also directed. Throughout his career, he wrote extensively on modern theatre: on Brecht, Pinter, Artaud, and SB. His writing led to a second career as an academic in the United States, first as Visiting Professor at Florida State University and, after he retired from the BBC, as Professor of Drama at Stanford University.

Marthe Gautier (b. 1925) received her medical degree at the Sorbonne (1955), did post-doctoral research at Harvard University (1955–1956), and returned to Paris to become head of the laboratory of Jérôme Lejeune and Raymond Turpin, contributing to the discovery in 1959 of the chromosome abnormality that causes Down's syndrome. She was a friend of Jean Martin, who had asked her for advice on how to play Lucky; she had suggested that he observe patients with Parkinson's disease. She was a close friend of Suzanne Beckett and the two often traveled together. Suzanne frequently used Gautier's grand piano for practice.

3 Esslin, *The Theatre of the Absurd*, 24.

Jocelyn Herbert (1917–2003), theatre designer, saw, through her long professional life (she was still working in her eighties) and largely through her own efforts, the gradual transformation of theatre design from a support service to an integral part of any production. The key to this was her long association with the inventive director George Devine at the Royal Court Theatre. For this work she had three crucial qualities: a powerful imagination, total respect for text and author, and great warmth. The resolutely innovative culture of the Royal Court allowed these to flourish.

For someone as little at ease with theatre people as SB, this was ideal, and it was not long before he was offering the Royal Court first option on his plays. *Endgame, Krapp's Last Tape, and Happy Days* all had their first performance at the Royal Court. Other writers – among them Eugène Ionesco, Arnold Wesker, John Osborne, David Storey, and, later, Tony Harrison – were comparably impressed and grateful. The connection with SB, first signaled by a postcard co-signed to him in 1934, endured after Devine's death and indeed developed into an intimate and intensely lived relationship. On the professional side of this, Herbert continued to design for SB's plays. What SB and the others all saw in her was her ability to identify the imaginative reality that the author sought, and find a way of expressing it in visual terms. Their response – their readiness, so to speak, to come back for more – was proof, if proof were needed, that she could and would do it. A constant of that way was its rigorous simplicity, its avoidance of clutter – as if inspired by SB's search for the fewest words in which to say what he wanted to say.

Henri Lefebvre (?1925–?1972) was a Belgian artist who, in the 1950s, corresponded with, and promoted the work of, André du Bouchet and Maurice Blanchot; the former suggested to him that he contact SB, though, being reclusive and depressive, Lefebvre never met any of his three correspondents. Information on his life has been very hard to come by. He published only one piece in his lifetime, under the pseudonym Henri Demasnuy (his birthplace being Masnuy Saint-Jean): "Phases de la poésie d'André du Bouchet."[4] In 1975, *Argile* published Lefebvre's "Ecritures Dessins (1958–1972)," and, in 1976, *Luna-Park* published three of Lefebvre's "graphies" and a brief

4 [Henri Lefebvre] Henri Demasnuy, pseud., "Phases de la poésie d'André du Bouchet," *Synthèses* 190 (March 1962) 434–440.

biographical profile.[5] Lefebvre's article on André du Bouchet was republished, with added accompanying notes and six examples of his calligraphic drawings (his "graphies") as "'Scintillation' – écritures," in *L'Ire des Vents*.[6] Virtually unknown by the public during his lifetime, Lefebvre's posthumous reputation was boosted by his becoming the subject of a story by Roberto Balaño, "Vagabond in France and Belgium," in *Last Evenings on Earth*.[7] It is unclear just how much of Balaño's story is invention: while he is accurate in having Lefebvre commit suicide, he follows the *Luna-Park* indication that this event took place in 1973.

Jack MacGowran (1918–1973) gained much of his early stage experience with the Abbey Theatre in his native Dublin; in spite of many appearances on the English stage and in films, he was to remain a thoroughly Irish actor. It was not only a matter of personal style or vocal range – some of his best work was in two of Sean O'Casey's greatest plays: *Juno and the Paycock*, in which he played Joxer Daly; and *The Plough and the Stars*, in which, as a young man, he played the Young Covey, and, later in his life, Fluther Good. The combination of impishness and something closer to roguery was one that suited him perfectly, and it drew the attention of film-makers, notably John Huston, who put him in *The Quiet Man*. He appeared too in the caricaturally Irish *Darby O'Gill and the Little People*. But his qualities went beyond Irishness, and he was to have a very different kind of film success as the Fool to Paul Scofield's King in Peter Brook's *King Lear* (1971). Later he impressed Roman Polanski, who cast him in two of his films.

He came to England in 1954, and joined the Royal Shakespeare Company. When, in 1957, he met SB, the two men took to each other straight away; his voice was familiar to SB, who had heard it in the original broadcast of *All That Fall*. In 1964 he played Lucky in *Waiting for Godot* at the Royal Court Theatre, and went on to play Clov in the Paris and London productions of *Endgame*, to Patrick Magee's Hamm. It was a formidable combination, continued in *Embers*, and in *The Old Tune* (SB's translation of Robert Pinget's *La Manivelle*). MacGowran devised a one-man show of excerpts from SB's work, *End of Day*. SB, to his own

5 Henri Lefebvre, "Ecritures Dessins (1958–1972)," *Argile* 8 (Autumn 1975) 111–139. Henri Lefebvre, "Graphies," *Luna-Park* 2 (1976) np.

6 Henri Lefebvre, "'Scintillation' – écritures," *L'Ire des Vents* 6–8 (1983) 54–71.

7 Roberto Balaño, "Vagabond in France and Belgium," in *Last Evenings on Earth*, tr. Chris Andrews (New York: New Directions, 2006) 172–187.

distress, disliked the result and wrote his first venture in television, *Eh Joe*, partly to overcome this difficulty in their relationship. In fact MacGowran, with SB's help, revised the one-man show which achieved great success in the United States. MacGowran was a man of formidable energy, and the list of his parts in theatre and film is enormous. He was also a heavy drinker, even by the standards of SB, himself no abstainer. This may well have taken its toll: he was only fifty-four when he died.

Patrick Magee (1922–1973), actor, born in Armagh, Northern Ireland, was soon drawn to theatre, and for some years worked in the Ireland-based touring company of Anew McMaster, one of the last of the line of actor-managers. This meant playing in towns and villages all over Ireland: extracts from Shakespeare for the most part, but with occasional ventures into terrain as recondite as Sophocles. The effect on young provincial audiences was electrifying. This work and the hierarchical nature of the company shaped Magee's apprenticeship. It was during this time that he met Harold Pinter, who recognized his talent, and who would later seek him out.

Magee was invited over to England by Tyrone Guthrie, and appeared in a series of Irish plays. Then, in 1957, came the crucial encounter with SB. Magee was asked to record for the BBC Third Programme a reading of extracts from SB's prose: *Molloy, Malone Dies, The Unnamable,* and *From an Abandoned Work*. His powerful, gravelly voice not only impressed SB, but fired his creative imagination. The range of possibilities that this voice opened up set SB thinking of a text that might harness them: that text was *Krapp's Last Tape*. Magee gave the first performance in 1958 at the Royal Court Theatre, where it was presented as a curtain-raiser (!) for *Endgame*. From that point on, he was always SB's first choice for certain parts, notably Hamm in *Endgame* in 1964. In that year he joined the Royal Shakespeare Company, appearing, at Pinter's insistent request, as McCann in *The Birthday Party*. His many subsequent engagements included *Marat/Sade* (stage and film versions), and, with Paul Scofield, Charles Dyer's *Staircase*. SB not only admired him as a performer but liked him greatly, as the letters make clear.

Matti Megged (1923–2003) was born in Poland; his family moved to Israel when he was a child. Megged changed the spelling of his family name to the Latin spelling in order to differentiate his work from that of his brother Aharon Meged (b. 1920). In 1962, Megged wrote a novel in

English, which remained unpublished. Megged later translated *Endgame* and *Happy Days* into Hebrew, and wrote *Dialogue in the Void: Beckett and Giacometti* (New York: Lumen Press, 1985). In 1960, Judith Schmidt introduced him to SB, in whom Megged found a sympathetic sounding board.

Marcel Mihalovici (1898–1985), composer, moved from Romania to study in Paris after World War I, where he became a pupil of Vincent d'Indy, and where he spent the rest of his life. With fellow émigré composers Bohuslav Martinů, Conrad Beck, and Tibor Harsányi, he set up the "Ecole de Paris," and eventually took French citizenship. He married the concert pianist Monique Haas, an enthusiastic proponent of twentieth-century French composers, particularly Debussy and Ravel. It was her friendship with Suzanne Deschevaux-Dumesnil that brought about a meeting with SB. The two men got on well from the start, and remained friends.

Much of Mihalovici's musical output is small-scale: chamber works, songs, works for solo instruments, church music; but there are also five symphonies. There is also an opera, *Phèdre*, and it is to opera that Mihalovici turned as he grew to know SB's work. He himself was deeply impressed by SB's musicality, saying of him "Beckett is a remarkable musician ... he possesses an astonishing musical intuition." The two men collaborated in the making of an opera based on *La dernière bande*, and called *Krapp ou la derniere bande*. Of it, Mihalovici said: "I shall always remember the astonishment of Beckett ... who looked at the ten pages of his text spread out over an orchestral score of nearly 260 pages of music!" Score, setting, and performance (by the young tenor William Dooley) drew high praise from René Dumesnil in *Le Monde*, although, inevitably, not everyone was so enthusiastic. There would be one further collaborative venture: the music Mihalovici wrote for the 1963 "radiophonic invention" *Cascando.*[8]

Harold Pinter (1930–2008) figures in the letters of the present volume not as the prolific and admired writer, still less as the Nobel laureate, but rather as an eager, hopeful, and ambitious young actor and dramatist for whom discovering SB was a crucial experience. Even in England, in spite of remarkable and original early work (such as the radio play *A Night Out*, or, in theatre, *The Birthday Party*), it was not until 1960 and *The Caretaker* that his career really took off. SB writes to him of

8 Marcel Mihalovici, "My Collaboration with Samuel Beckett," in Calder, ed., *Beckett at 60*, 20.

his pleasure in reading the play, but when, translated as *Le Gardien*, it was put on in Paris in 1961, critical reception was little short of disastrous. SB's is virtually the only voice from France to offer comfort and understanding, and he continues to write approvingly as Pinter's reputation in England grows, on the strength of such plays as *The Lover* and *The Homecoming*. Where the early work had depended for its force on unspecified menace, these and other later plays such as *Betrayal* presented clearly defined human situations riven by desire and fear. But Pinter struck out too in a very different direction, in work concerned above all with power and its abuses, such as *One for the Road*, and *Mountain Language*, the latter having unmistakable echoes of the Turkish treatment of the Kurds and their language.

Pinter saw himself as a kindred spirit of SB, although with the years his increasing concern with political issues moved him farther and farther from Beckett's world. It is in the earlier work that we come closer to that world: work such as *The Dumb Waiter*, in which dialogue, represented in the language of the street, reveals above all the distance which separates people. Pinter retained a deep respect for SB, and was an eager contributor to celebratory presentations of his work. As late as 2006, when he was already seriously ill, he performed *Krapp's Last Tape*, at the Royal Court Theatre.

Judith Schmidt (b. 1926) started at Grove Press in 1956 as Barney Rosset's secretary and assistant. She was also responsible for permissions, rights, and royalties, and managed correspondence with SB on these matters. Schmidt met SB for the first time in 1959 during a trip to Paris, and their business correspondence soon reflected their friendship. Schmidt met Beckett whenever she travelled to Europe. She accompanied him during much of his visit to New York in 1964 for the making of *Film*, and took *Film* to the Venice Film Festival in September 1965. She introduced her lover, the Israeli writer Matti Megged, to Beckett. Schmidt left Grove Press in 1970 and married John Douw in that year. She maintained a personal correspondence with SB until his death.

Jacob Schwartz (n.d.), a dentist from Brooklyn, operated the Ulysses Bookshop in London during the 1920s. He occasionally published books under the Ulysses imprint but primarily ran a successful rare book business, later based in Brighton. Schwartz amassed a collection of primary materials from writers including George Bernard Shaw,

Nancy Cunard, James Joyce, Dylan Thomas, Ezra Pound, and T. S. Eliot. Schwartz contacted SB in the 1950s in order to purchase his manuscripts. Schwartz was given the nickname "The Great Extractor" for his abilities to extract rotten teeth as well as first editions and literary manuscripts. Much of the Schwartz Collection is archived at The Harry Ransom Center at the University of Texas, Austin.

Siegfried Unseld (1924–2002) was publisher of Suhrkamp Verlag from 1959 to 2002. He is considered one of the leading figures in twentieth-century German literary publishing. Unseld served three years in the German Army during World War II before he studied German, Philosophy, and Library Studies at the University of Tübingen. In 1952, he entered Suhrkamp Verlag, shortly after earning his doctorate on Hermann Hesse. One year later, Elmar Tophoven translated *En attendant Godot* as *Warten auf Godot*, the first of SB's works to be published by Suhrkamp. Suhrkamp's associate from 1958, Unseld became the Director upon Peter Suhrkamp's death in 1959. Over the course of the following decades, Unseld created a publishing empire; in 1999, he obtained the majority of the shares in Suhrkamp. Along with SB, major writers published by Suhrkamp during Unseld's tenure included Thomas Bernhard, Bertolt Brecht, Max Frisch, Jürgen Habermas, and Claude Lévi-Strauss. Unseld first met SB in 1960 in Paris; the following year, SB came to Frankfurt. Unseld held SB in high regard and would often discuss literary news, translations, and questions concerning publication rights with him. Joachim Kaiser called Unseld the most influential German publisher after World War II.

Marc Wilkinson (b. 1929) is a French-born Australian composer who studied at Columbia and at Princeton Universities. He was the Director of Music at the National Theatre in London from 1965 to 1975. He composed and conducted for the Royal Shakespeare Theatre, the Royal Court Theatre, and for films and Broadway performances. Wilkinson composed music to accompany a selection from Beckett's *Waiting for Godot* entitled *Voices* which premiered in London's Festival Hall in March 1960. As a member of the Music Today group, which performed a series of concerts in 1960, Wilkinson arranged a reading of Beckett's "From an Unabandoned Work" by Patrick Magee for a concert in April of the same year. Wilkinson also conducted film scores and concert productions for the BBC. He composed scores for a number of feature films, including *If...* and *The Hireling*, both honored at the Cannes Film Festival.

X, A Quarterly Review, whose uncompromising title already suggests something of the spirited independence that marked this literary and artistic journal throughout its short life, was published in seven issues from 1959 to 1962. The unofficial subtitle was the definition of X given in the *Oxford English Dictionary*: "unknown quantity, incalculable or mysterious fact or influence." But the "unknown quantity" was to become very well known indeed, thanks to the review's unvarying policy of making space for the work of new writers and artists and ignoring reputation or convention – even the conventionally "official" avant-garde. It owed its existence to the enthusiasm of SB's friend Mary Hutchinson and the financial support of Michael Berry (later Lord Hartwell), owner of the *Daily Telegraph*. The review was edited by the South African poet David Wright and the Irish painter Patrick Swift, themselves regular contributors (and indeed the only permanent "staff"), with Swift responsible for layout and illustration. Poets such as Patrick Kavanagh, Hugh MacDiarmid, C. H. Sisson, Stevie Smith, Geoffrey Hill; artists such as Lucian Freud, Alberto Giacometti, Francis Bacon, Frank Auerbach – these and others, all barely known at the time, found an ideal outlet in *X*. The articles were often explicitly critical of current cultural fashion. Even the format of the review was determined by unexpected considerations: Swift, reaching in a London café for something on which to sketch his idea for a cover, picked up a menu card. That settled the dimensions. Perhaps the best summary of the review's power and relevance was given by Philip Toynbee, who hailed it in *The Observer* as "an event, if only because a literary magazine of this kind has not existed for a long time. The admirable impression of a review devoted to attacking both the corruptions of an established avant-garde and the dreary 'retrenchments' of the age is reinforced by every article and poem which appear here."

BIBLIOGRAPHY OF WORKS CITED

Ackerley, C. J., and S. E. Gontarski. *The Grove Companion to Samuel Beckett: A Reader's Guide to his Works, Life, and Thought*. New York: Grove Press, 2004.

Admussen, Richard L. *The Samuel Beckett Manuscripts: A Study*. Ed. Jackson Bryer. A Reference Publication in Literature. Boston: G. K. Hall, 1979.

Adorno, Theodor W. *Can One Live After Auschwitz? A Philosophical Reader*. Tr. Rodney Livingstone, *et al*. Ed. Rolf Tiedemann. Stanford: Stanford University Press, 2003.

Noten zur Literatur II. Bibliothek Suhrkamp. Frankfurt: Suhrkamp Verlag, 1961. 1958–1974. 4 vols.

Albers, Patricia. *Joan Mitchell, Lady Painter: A Life*. New York: Alfred A. Knopf, 2011.

"Ash Can School of Drama." *Life* 42 (22 April 1957) 143.

Aslan, Odette. *Roger Blin and Twentieth-Century Playwrights*. Tr. Ruby Cohn. Cambridge: Cambridge University Press, 1988.

Atik, Anne. *How It Was: A Memoir of Samuel Beckett*. London: Faber and Faber, 2003.

Barrault, Jean-Louis. *Memories for Tomorrow: The Memoirs of Jean-Louis Barrault*. Tr. Jonathan Griffin. New York: E. P. Dutton, 1974.

Souvenirs pour demain. Paris: Editions du Seuil, 1972.

Baudelaire, Charles. *Les Fleurs du Mal: The Complete Text of The Flowers of Evil*. Tr. Richard Howard. Illus. Michael Mazur. Boston: David R. Godine, 1982.

Œuvres complètes. Ed. Claude Pichois and Jean Ziegler. Bibliothèque de la Pléiade. Paris: Gallimard, 1975–1976. 2 vols.

Beach, Sylvia. *Shakespeare and Company*. New York: Harcourt, Brace, 1959.

Beckett, Samuel. "Accul." Avigdor Arikha. *Paintings, Gouaches and Drawings*. London: Matthiesen Gallery, 1959. [2].

"Alle, die da fallen." Tr. Erika Schöningh and Elmar Tophoven. *Die Neue Rundschau* 68.2 (1957) 255–282.

"The Calmative." Tr. by the author. *No's Knife*. London: Calder and Boyars, 1967. 25–42.

"Cascando." *Dublin Magazine* 11.4 (October–December 1936) 3–4.

Čekajući Godoa. Tr. Andreja Milicevic. Beograd: Srpska književna zadruga, 1964.

"Cendres." Tr. Robert Pinget. *Les Lettres Nouvelles,* nouvelle série (2) 36 (December 1959) 3–14.

Collected Poems 1930–1978. London: John Calder, 1984.

The Collected Shorter Plays of Samuel Beckett. New York: Grove Weidenfeld, 1984.

"Comédie, un acte de Samuel Beckett." Tr. by the author. *Les Lettres Nouvelles,* nouvelle série (3) 12 (June–July–August 1964) 10–31.

Comment c'est. Paris: Editions de Minuit, 1961.

"Dante and the Lobster." *Evergreen Review* 1.1 (December 1957) 24–36.

"Dante and the Lobster." *This Quarter* 5.2 (December 1932) 222–236.

"Dante . . . Bruno. Vico. . Joyce." *Our Exagmination Round His Factification for Incamination of Work in Progress*. Ed. Sylvia Beach. Paris: Shakespeare and Company, 1929. 1–22.

"La dernière bande." *Les Lettres Nouvelles,* nouvelle série (2) 1 (March 1959) 5–13.

La dernière bande. Paris: Editions de Minuit, 1959.

Disjecta: Miscellaneous Writings and A Dramatic Fragment. Ed. Ruby Cohn. New York: Grove Press, 1984.

Dramatische Dichtungen. Tr. Elmar Tophoven. Frankfurt: Suhrkamp Verlag, 1963–1964. 2 vols.

"Echo's Bones" [a selection]. *Evergreen Review* 1.1 (1957) 179–192.

Echo's Bones and Other Precipitates. Paris: Europa Press, 1935.

"The End." Tr. Richard Seaver. *Evergreen Review* 4.15 (November–December 1960) 22–41.

"The End." Tr. Richard Seaver with the author. *Merlin* 2.3 (Summer–Autumn 1954) 144–159.

Endgame, followed by Act without Words. Tr. by the author. London: Faber and Faber, 1958.

Endgame, followed by Act without Words. Tr. by the author. New York: Grove Press, 1958.

Endgame, With a Revised Text. Ed. S. E. Gontarski. New York: Grove Press, 1992. The Theatrical Notebooks of Samuel Beckett. Ed. James Knowlson. Vol. II. 1992–1999. 4 vols.

"Endspiel." *Spectaculum* 2 (1959) 7–42.

Erzählungen und Texte um Nichts. Tr. Elmar Tophoven. Frankfurt: Suhrkamp Verlag, 1997.

"The Essential and the Incidental." *The Bookman* 87 (December 1934) 111.

"Ex Cathezra." *The Bookman* 87 (December 1934) 10.

"L'Expulsé." *Fontaine* 8.57 (December 1946–January 1947) 685–708.

"Faux Départs." *Kursbuch* 1 (June 1965) 1–5.

Film: Complete Scenario, Illustrations, Production Shots. New York: Grove Press, 1969.

Fin de partie. Ed. John Fletcher, Beryl S. Fletcher, Barry Smith, and Walter Bachem. Methuen's Twentieth Century Texts. Gen. Ed. W. J. Strachan. London: Methuen Educational, 1970.
Fin de partie. Paris: Editions de Minuit, 1957.
"From an Abandoned Work." *Evergreen Review* 1.3 (1957) 83–91.
"From an Abandoned Work." *Trinity News* 3.17 (7 June 1956) 4.
"From an Unabandoned Work." *Evergreen Review* 4.14 (September–October 1960) 58–65.
Gedichte. Tr. Eva Hesse and Elmar Tophoven. Wiesbaden: Limes Verlag, 1959.
Gelukkige dagen: een toneelstuk in twee bedrijven. Tr. Jacoba van Velde. Amsterdam: Uitgeverij de Bezige Bij, 1962.
Giorni felici. Tr. Carlo Fruttero. Turin: Einaudi, 1961.
Glückliche Tage: ein Stück in zwei Akten. Tr. Elmar Tophoven and Erika Tophoven. Frankfurt: Fischer Verlag, 1961.
Happy Days. New York: Grove Press, 1961.
Hé, Joe; Sintels; Woorden en muziek; Cascando; Komen en gaan; Allen die vallen; Spel zonder woorden 1; Spel zonder woorden 2. Tr. Jacoba van Velde. Amsterdam: Uitgeverij de Bezige Bij, 1967.
"Henri Hayden, homme peintre." *Henri Hayden: 1883–1970*. Cherbourg: Musée Thomas-Henry, 1997. 12–15.
"Henri Hayden, homme peintre." *Henri Hayden: Recent Paintings, 12th February – 7th March 1959*. London: The Waddington Galleries, 1959. [2].
"Henri Hayden, homme peintre." *Les Cahiers d'Art – Documents* (Geneva) 22 (November 1955) 2.
How It Is. Tr. from the French by the author. New York: Grove Press, 1961.
"L'Image." *X, A Quarterly Review* (November 1959) 35–37.
L'Innommable. Paris: Editions de Minuit, 1953.
[Invitation to Bram van Velde's exhibition at the Galerie Maeght 1952]. *Bram van Velde: Stedelijk Museum, Amsterdam, December 1959 – Januari 1960*. Amsterdam: Stedelijk Museum, 1959.
"Krapp's laatste band." Tr. Jacoba van Velde. *Randstad* 1 (Autumn 1961) 8–18.
"Krapp's Last Tape." *Evergreen Review* 2.5 (Summer 1958) 13–24.
Krapp's Last Tape. New York: Grove Press, 1958.
Krapp's Last Tape and Embers. London: Faber and Faber, 1959.
Krapp's Last Tape and Other Dramatic Pieces. New York: Grove Press, 1960.
Krapp's Last Tape with a Revised Text. Ed. James Knowlson. New York: Grove Press, 1992. The Theatrical Notebooks of Samuel Beckett. Ed. James Knowlson. Vol III. 1992–1999. 4 vols.
"Letter from Samuel Beckett Concerning Manuscript of Story 'Killachter Meadow'." *Review of Contemporary Fiction* 3.1 (1983) 156–157.

The Letters of Samuel Beckett: 1929–1940. Vol. I. Ed. Martha Dow Fehsenfeld, Lois More Overbeck, George Craig, and Dan Gunn. Cambridge: Cambridge University Press, 2009.
The Letters of Samuel Beckett: 1941–1956. Vol. II. Ed. George Craig, Martha Dow Fehsenfeld, Dan Gunn, and Lois More Overbeck. Cambridge: Cambridge University Press, 2011.
Malone Dies. Tr. from the French by the author. London: John Calder, 1958.
Molloy. Paris: Editions de Minuit, 1951.
Molloy. Tr. by Patrick Bowles in collaboration with the author. Paris: Olympia Press, 1955.
Molloy. Tr. from the French by the author. New York: Grove Press, 1955.
Molloy. Tr. Jacoba van Velde. Amsterdam: Uitgeverij de Bezige Bij, 1963.
More Pricks Than Kicks. Hors commerce mimeograph edition. London: Calder and Boyars, 1966.
More Pricks Than Kicks. London: Chatto and Windus, 1934.
More Pricks Than Kicks. New York: Grove Press, 1972.
Murphy. London: Calder and Boyars, Jupiter Books, 1963.
Murphy. New York: Grove Press, 1957.
Murphy: Roman. Tr. Elmar Tophoven. Hamburg: Rowohlt Verlag, 1959.
Nouvelles et Textes pour rien. Paris: Editions de Minuit, 1955.
Nouvelles et Textes pour rien [with six illustrations by Avigdor Arikha]. Paris: Editions de Minuit, 1958.
"Ooftish." *transition* 27 (April–May 1938) 33.
"Papini's Dante." *The Bookman* 87 (December 1934) 14.
"Peintres de l'empêchement." *Derrière le miroir [Pierre à feu]* 11–12 (June 1948) 3, 4, 7.
"Peintres de l'empêchement [extract from]." *Bram van Velde: Stedelijk Museum, Amsterdam, December 1959 – Januari 1960*. Amsterdam: Stedelijk Museum, 1959. [4–6].
"La Peinture des van Velde ou le monde et le pantalon." *Cahiers d'Art* 20–21 (1945–1946) 349–356.
Play, and Two Short Pieces for Radio. London: Faber and Faber, 1964.
Poems in English. London: John Calder, 1961.
Proust. The Dolphin Books. London: Chatto and Windus, 1931. Rpt. New York: Grove Press, 1957.
Proust and Three Dialogues with Georges Duthuit. London: Calder and Boyars, 1965.
Proust and Three Dialogues with Georges Duthuit. London: Calder and Boyars, 1970.
Samuel Beckett, Complete Short Prose, 1929–1989. Ed. S. E. Gontarski. New York: Grove Press, 1995.
Selected Poems: 1930–1989. Ed. David Wheatley. London: Faber and Faber, 2009.

"Skraldespandsduetten: Scene af Skuespillet 'Fin de partie'." Tr. Christian Ludvigsen. *Perspectiv* 4.7 (1957) 14–16.
Slutspil; og, Scene uden ord. Tr. Christian Ludvigsen. Fredensborg: Arena, 1959.
"The Smeraldina's Billet Doux." *Zero Anthology* no. 8. Ed. Themistocles Hoetis. New York: Zero Press, 1956. 56–61.
"Spiel." Tr. Elmar Tophoven. *Spectaculum* 6 (1963) 321–323.
"Spiel." Tr. Elmar Tophoven. *Theater heute* 4.7 (July 1963) 57/II–IV.
Spiel; ein Akt. Tr. Erika and Elmar Tophoven. Frankfurt: Suhrkamp Verlag, 1963.
Stories and Texts for Nothing. New York: Grove Press, 1967.
"Stories and Texts for Nothing, III." Tr. Anthony Bonner and Samuel Beckett. *Great French Short Stories*. Ed. Germaine Brée. New York: Dell, 1960. 311–317.
Three Novels: Molloy, Malone Dies, The Unnamable. New York: Grove Press, 1959.
"Three Poems" ("my way is in the sand flowing," "what would I do without this world faceless incurious," and "I would like my love to die"). *Transition Forty-Eight* no. 2 (June 1948) 96–97.
"Tous ceux qui tombent." *Les Lettres Nouvelles* 5.47 (March 1957) 321–351.
The Unnamable. New York: Grove Press, 1958.
Wachten op Godot; Eindspel; Krapp's laatste band; Gelukkige dagen; Spel. Tr. Jacoba van Velde. Amsterdam: Uitgeverij de Bezige Bij, 1965.
Waiting for Godot. London: Faber and Faber, 1956.
Waiting for Godot. New York: Grove Press, 1954.
Watt. London: John Calder, 1963.
Watt. New York: Grove Press, 1959.
Words and Music. *Evergreen Review* 6.27 (November–December 1962) 34–43.
"Yellow." *New World Writing* 10 (November 1956) 108–119.
[Beckett, Samuel] Andrew Belis, pseud. "Recent Irish Poetry." *The Bookman* 86.515 (August 1934) 235–236.
Beckett, Samuel, and Georges Duthuit. "Dialogue avec Georges Duthuit." [Third Dialogue]. *Georges Duthuit*. Paris: Flammarion, 1976 [Limited Edition]. 57–62.
"Three Dialogues [extract from]." *Bram van Velde: Stedelijk Museum, Amsterdam, December 1959 – Januari 1960*. Amsterdam: Stedelijk Museum, 1959.
"Three Dialogues: Samuel Beckett and Georges Duthuit." Extract: Third Dialogue. Tr. Samuel Beckett. *Bulletin de la Galerie Michel Warren* (Paris, 1957) np.
"Three Dialogues: Samuel Beckett and Georges Duthuit." *Transition Forty-Nine* 5 (December 1949) 97–103.
See also Beckett, *Proust and Three Dialogues with Georges Duthuit*.

Beckett, Samuel, Georges Duthuit, Jacques Putman, and Bram van Velde. *Bram van Velde*. Musée de Poche. Paris: Editions Georges Fall, 1958.
Bram van Velde. Tr. Samuel Beckett and Olive Classe. New York: Grove Press, 1960.
Beckett, Samuel, and Marin Karmitz. *Comédie*. Paris: Editions du Regard, 2001.
Beckett, Samuel, and Marcel Mihalovici. *Krapp, ou la dernière bande*. Paris: Heugel, 1961.
Beckett, Samuel, and Alan Schneider. *No Author Better Served: The Correspondence of Samuel Beckett and Alan Schneider*. Ed. Maurice Harmon. Cambridge, MA: Harvard University Press, 1998.
"On Endgame." *Village Voice Reader: A Mixed Bag from the Greenwich Village Newspaper*. Ed. Daniel Wolf and Edwin Fancher. Garden City, NY: Doubleday, 1962. 182–186.
Beckett, Samuel, and Marc Wilkinson. *Voices: From the Play Waiting for Godot*. London: Universal Edition, 1960.
Behan, Beatrice, with Des Hickey and Gus Smith. *My Life with Brendan*. Los Angeles: Nash Publishing, 1974.
Benjamin, Walter, ed. *Deutsche Menschen: eine Folge von Briefen*. Frankfurt: Suhrkamp Verlag, 1962.
Berkeley, George. *A Treatise Concerning the Principles of Human Knowledge*. Ed. Kenneth P. Winkler. Indianapolis: Hackett Publishing, 1982.
Blubacher, Thomas. *Gustaf Gründgens*. Hamburg: Ellert and Richter, 2011.
Bosquet, Alain. *Les Fruits de l'an dernier*. Paris: Grasset, 1996.
Bossuet, Jacques-Bénigne. *L'Eglise et le théâtre*. Ed. C. Urbain and E. Levesque. Paris: Bernard Grasset, 1930.
Bowles, Patrick. "How Samuel Beckett Sees the Universe." *The Listener* 59 (19 June 1958) 1011–1012.
"How to Fail: Notes on Talks with Samuel Beckett." *PN Review* 20.4 (March–April 1994) 24–38.
Boyle, Kay. "All Mankind is Us." *Samuel Beckett: A Collection of Criticism*. Ed. Ruby Cohn. New York: McGraw-Hill, 1975. 15–19.
Briscoe, Desmond, and Roy Curtis-Bramwell. *The BBC Radiophonic Workshop: The First 25 Years*. London: The British Broadcasting Corporation, 1983.
Browning, Robert. *The Poetical Works of Robert Browning*. Vol. I. Ed. Ian Jack and Margaret Smith. Oxford: Clarendon Press, 1983. 1983–2009. 15 vols.
Bryden, Mary, Julian Garforth, and Peter Mills, eds. *Beckett at Reading: Catalogue of The Beckett Manuscript Collection at The University of Reading*. Reading: Whiteknights Press and the Beckett International Foundation, 1998.
Butler, Alban. *Butler's Lives of the Saints*. Ed. Herbert Thurston and Donald Attwater. New York: P. J. Kenedy and Sons, 1956. 4 vols.

Cabianca, Jacopo. *Il Torquato Tasso: Canti Dodici*. Venice: Tip. del commercio, 1858.
Calder, John. *Pursuit: The Uncensored Memoirs of John Calder*. London: Calder Publications, 2001.
Calder, John, ed. *Beckett at 60: A Festschrift*. London; Calder and Boyars, 1967.
Carpenter, Humphrey. *The Envy of the World: Fifty Years of the BBC Third Programme and Radio 3, 1946–1996*. London: Weidenfeld and Nicolson, 1996.
Cascetta, Anna Maria, and Laura Pejà. "Winnie and the Tradition of the Actor: From the Old Italian Style Theatre to the Experimental Stage." Tr. Mark Pietralunga. *The Journal of Beckett Studies* 13.1 (2004) 73–97.
Catalogo della XXXI Esposizione Biennale Internazionale d'Arte Venezia. Venice: Stamperia di Venezia, 1962.
"Le challenge 1960 au Berliner Ensemble." *Les Lettres Françaises* 834 (21–27 July 1960) 6.
Chessman, Caryl. *Cell 2455, Death Row*. New York: Carroll and Graf, 1954.
Chisholm, Anne. *Nancy Cunard: A Biography*. New York: Alfred A. Knopf, 1979.
Claudius, Matthias. "Der Tod (Death)." Tr. Robert M. Browning. *German Poetry from 1750 to 1900*. Vol. XXXIX. Ed. Robert M. Browning. New York: Continuum, 1984. 12–13. The German Library. Gen. Ed. Volkmar Sander. 1982–2007. 100 vols.
Claussen, Detlev. *Theodor W. Adorno: One Last Genius*. Cambridge, MA: Harvard University Press, 2008.
Coffey, Brian. "Memory's Murphy Maker." *Threshold* 17.20 (1962) 28–36.
Cohn, Ruby. *A Beckett Canon*. Ann Arbor: University of Michigan Press, 2001.
Craig, George. *Writing Beckett's Letters*. Paris and London: Center for Writers and Translators, The American University of Paris, with Sylph Editions, 2011.
Craig, H. A. L. "Poetry in the Theatre." *The New Statesman* 60.1548 (12 November 1960) 734, 736.
Dante Alighieri. *Convivio*. Ed. Piero Cudini. Milan: Garzanti, 1980.
The Divine Comedy of Dante Alighieri. Tr. and ed. John D. Sinclair. London: John Lane The Bodley Head, 1948. 1939–1948, rev. 1948. 3 vols.
The Inferno. New York: Anchor Books, 2002.
Inferno. New York: Bantam Classics, 1980.
Deschevaux-Dumesnil, Suzanne. "F –." *Transition Forty-Eight* no. 4 (January 1949) 19–21.
"Deux cent trente intellectuels assurent J. Lindon de leur solidarité." *Les Lettres Françaises* 906 (21–27 December 1961) 4.
Devine, Harriet. *Being George Devine's Daughter*. London: Barkus Books, 2006.
Driver, Tom Faw. "Beckett at the Madeleine." *Columbia University Forum* 4.3 (Summer 1961) 21–25.

Duckworth, Colin. "Beckett's Early Background: A New Zealand Biographical Appendix." *New Zealand Journal of French Studies* 1.2 (October 1970) 59–67.

Duras, Marguerite. *Romans, cinéma, théâtre, un parcours (1943–1993)*. Paris: Gallimard, 1997.

Duthuit, Georges. "Maille à partir avec Bram van Velde." *Bram van Velde*. Ed. Claire Stoullig and Nathalie Schoeller. Paris: Editions du Centre Georges- Pompidou, 1989. 180.

"Maille à partir avec Bram van Velde." *Cahiers d'Art* 27.1 (July 1952) 79–81.

Le Musée inimaginable: Essai. II. Paris: Librairie José Corti, 1956. 2 vols.

Eliot, George. *The Mill on the Floss*. Ed. Carol T. Christ. New York: Norton, 1994.

Eliot, T. S. *Four Quartets*. New York: Harcourt, Brace and World, 1962.

Ellmann, Richard. *James Joyce, New and Revised Edition*. Oxford: Oxford University Press, 1982.

Enzensberger, Hans Magnus. *Einzelheiten*. Frankfurt am Main: Suhrkamp Verlag, 1962.

Esslin, Martin. "Samuel Beckett." *The Novelist as Philosopher: Studies in French Fiction 1935–1960*. Ed. John Cruickshank. London: Oxford University Press, 1962. 128–146.

"Samuel Beckett and the Art of Broadcasting." *Encounter* 45 (September 1975) 38–46.

The Theatre of the Absurd. London: Eyre and Spottiswoode, 1961. Rpt. Garden City, NY: Anchor Books, Doubleday, 1961.

"Fast nur solches." *Der Spiegel* 24.63 (12 June 1963) np.

Federman, Raymond, and John Fletcher. *Samuel Beckett: His Works and His Critics*. Berkeley: University of California Press, 1970.

Fernández, José Francisco. "Surrounding the Void: Samuel Beckett and Spain." *Estudios Irlandeses* 9 (2014) 44–53.

"Festival de Teatro Latinoamericano Casa de las Americas 1964." *Conjunto* 1.2 (1964) 66.

Findlater, Richard, ed. *At the Royal Court: 25 Years of the English Stage Company*. New York: Grove Press, 1981.

Ford, John. *The Lover's Melancholy*. London: 1629. Rpt. *The English Experience: Its Records in Early Printed Books Published in Facsimile*. Vol. CCLXXI. Ed. N. J. Norwood and W. J. Johnson. New York: Da Capo Press, 1970. 1900–1979. 964 vols.

Fournier, Edith. "Pour que la boue me soit contée . . ." *Critique* 17.168 (May 1961) 412–418.

Fowler, F. M. "Günter Eich." *Essays on Contemporary German Literature*. German Men of Letters. Ed. Brian Keith-Smith. London: Oswald Wolff, 1966. 89–107. 1961–1972. 6 vols.

Freund, Gisèle, and Verna Carleton. *James Joyce in Paris: His Final Years*. New York: Harcourt, Brace and World, 1965.

Furneaux, Rupert. *Courtroom U. S. A.* Harmondsworth: Penguin Books, 1963. 2 vols.

Galey, Matthieu. "Des limbes et des rêves." *Arts, Lettres, Spectacles* 806 (25–31 January 1961) 4.

Genêt [Janet Flanner]. "Letter from Paris." *The New Yorker* 37.11 (29 April 1961) 132–134, 137–140.

Gilgenkrantz, S., and E. M. Rivera. "A History of Cytogenetics: Portraits of Some Pioneers." *Annales de Génétique* 46.4 (October–December 2003) 433–442.

Goethe, Johann Wolfgang von. *Goethe: With Plain Prose Translations of Each Poem.* Tr. and ed. David Luke. London: Penguin Books, 1964.

Poems of Goethe. Tr. Edwin H. Zeydel. University of North Carolina Studies in The Germanic Languages and Literatures. New York: AMS Press, 1966.

The Sorrows of Young Werther; Elective Affinities; Novella. Tr. Victor Lange and Judith Ryan. Ed. David E. Wellbery. New York: Suhrkamp Publishers, 1988. Goethe's Collected Works. Vol. XI. Ed. Victor Lange, Eric A. Blackall, and Cyrus Hamlin. 1983–1989. 12 vols.

"Goings on About Town." *The New Yorker* 37.38 (4 November 1961) 4.

Gontarski, S. E. *The Intent of Undoing in Samuel Beckett's Dramatic Texts.* Bloomington: Indiana University Press, 1985.

Gray, Thomas. *The Complete Poems of Thomas Gray.* Ed. H. W. Starr and J. R. Henrickson. Oxford: Clarendon Press, 1966.

Griffiths, Dennis, ed. *The Encyclopedia of the British Press: 1422–1992.* London: Macmillan Press; New York: St. Martin's Press, 1992.

Guggisberg, C. A. W., and R. Hainard. *Petit Atlas de Poche Payot: Oiseaux I.* Lausanne: Libraire Payot, n.d.

Gussow, Mel. *Conversations with Pinter.* New York: Grove Press, 1994.

Harvey, Lawrence. "Samuel Beckett: Initiation du poète." *La Revue des Lettres Modernes: Histoire des Idées et des Littératures* 100.8 (1964) 153–168.

"Samuel Beckett on Life, Art, and Criticism." *Modern Language Notes* 80 (December 1965) 545–562.

Samuel Beckett: Poet and Critic. Princeton, NJ: Princeton University Press, 1970.

Haubenstock-Ramati, Roman. *Credentials, or, "Think, Think Lucky."* Vienna: Universal Edition, 1963.

Hayden, Henri. *Henri Hayden: His Cézannesque and Cubist Period.* London: Roland, Browse and Delbanco, 1966.

Henrich, Dieter. "'Spiel' in Becketts Werk." *Drei Stücke von Samuel Beckett.* Ulm: Ulmer Theater, 1963. [4–6].

Herbert, Jocelyn. *Jocelyn Herbert: A Theatre Workbook.* Ed. Cathy Courtney. London: Art Books International, 1993.

Herren, Graley. "Different Music: Karmitz and Beckett's Film Adaptation of Comédie." *Journal of Beckett Studies* 18.1–2 (September 2009) 10–31.

Higgins, Aidan. *Donkey's Years: Memories of a Life as Story Told*. London: Secker and Warburg, 1995.

Killachter Meadow. New York: Grove Press, 1960.

The Whole Hog. London: Secker and Warburg, 2000.

Hildesheimer, Wolfgang. "Becketts Spiel." *Drei Stücke von Samuel Beckett*. Ulm: Ulmer Theater, 1963. [2–3]. Rpt. *Spectaculum* 6 (1963) 321–323; *Theater heute* 4.7 (1963) 57/I.

Hogarth, William. *The Analysis of Beauty, Written with a View of Fixing the Fluctuating Ideas of Taste*. London: J. Reaves, 1753. Rpt. *The Analysis of Beauty*. Ed. Ronald Paulson. New Haven and London: Yale University Press: 1997.

Hölderlin, Friedrich. *Friedrich Hölderlin: Poems and Fragments*. Tr. Michael Hamburger. Ann Arbor: University of Michigan Press, 1967.

Huxley, Aldous. *The Doors of Perception, and, Heaven and Hell*. London: Chatto and Windus; Harmondsworth: Penguin Books, 1959.

Johnson, Samuel. *Diaries, Prayers, Annals*. Ed. E. L. McAdam, Jr., with Donald Hyde and Mary Hyde. New Haven: Yale University Press, 1958. The Yale Edition of the Works of Samuel Johnson, Vol. I. 1958– . 23 vols.

Jones, Ernest. *Sigmund Freud: The Life and Work*. Vol. III. *The Last Phase, 1919–1939*. London: Hogarth Press, 1957. 1953–1957. 3 vols.

Jordan, Ken. "The Art of Publishing II." Interview with Barney Rosset. *The Paris Review* 39.145 (Winter 1997/1998) 170–215.

Joyce, Paul. "The Goad, Adapted from Act Without Words, by Samuel Beckett." *Nothing Doing in London* 1 (November 1966) 124–131.

Kaiser, Joachim. "Spiel in Urnen." *Theater heute* 4.7 (1963) 6–9.

Kant, Immanuel. *Kritik der Reinen Vernunft*. Ed. Albert Görland. Berlin: Bruno Cassirer, 1913. *Immanuel Kants Werke*. Vol III. Ed. Ernst Cassirer. 1911–1923. 11 vols.

Keats, John. *Complete Poems*. Ed. Jack Stillinger. Cambridge, MA: Belknap Press of Harvard University Press, 1982.

Kenner, Hugh. "The Cartesian Centaur." *Perspective: A Quarterly of Literature and the Arts* 11.3 (Autumn 1959) 132–141.

Kenny, Adrian. Introduction. *The Journal of Arland Ussher*. Ed. Adrian Kenny. Dublin: Raven Arts, 1980. 3.

Knowlson, James. *Damned to Fame: The Life of Samuel Beckett*. New York: Grove Press, 2004.

Knowlson, James, ed. *Samuel Beckett: An Exhibition*. London: Turret Books, 1971.

Konstantinović, Radomir. *Beket prijatelj*. Beograd: Otkrovenje, 2000.

Kramer, Andreas, and Robert Vilain. *Yvan Goll: A Bibliography of the Primary Works*. Oxford: Peter Lang, 2006.

Lake, Carlton, ed., with the assistance of Linda Eichhorn and Sally Leach. *No Symbols Where None Intended: A Catalogue of Books, Manuscripts, and Other*

Material Relating to Samuel Beckett in the Collections of the Humanities Research Center. Austin: Humanities Research Center, University of Texas at Austin, 1984.

Laws, Frederick. "Drama, Producers." *The Listener 65.1652* (24 November 1960) 953.

Leab, Katharine Kyes, Daniel J. Leab, Marie-Luise Frings, Abigail Leab, and Kathleen Thorp, eds. *American Book Prices Current, 1994–1995*. Washington, CT: Bancroft-Parkman, 1995.

Leopardi. *Selected Prose and Poetry*. Ed. and tr. Iris Origo and John Heath-Stubbs. Oxford Library of Italian Classics. London: Oxford University Press, 1966.

Levasseur, Catherine. *Dans l'intimité des Renaud-Barrault*. Ed. Jean Desailly and Simone Valère. Paris: Pygmalion, 2003.

Leventhal, A. J. "Close of Play: Reflections on Samuel Beckett's New Work for the French Theatre." *Dublin Magazine* 32.2 (April–June 1957) 18–22.

"Dramatic Commentary." *Dublin Magazine* 32.4 (October–December 1957) 42–43.

"Samuel Beckett, Poet and Pessimist." *The Listener* 57 (9 May 1957) 746–747.

Lewis, Jeremy. *Cyril Connolly: A Life*. London: Jonathan Cape, 1997.

Lidderdale, Jane, and Mary Nicholson. *Dear Miss Weaver: Harriet Shaw Weaver 1876–1961*. London: Faber and Faber, 1970.

Logue, Christopher. *Prince Charming: A Memoir*. London: Faber and Faber, 1999.

Louange et Prière: Psaumes, chorals, cantiques, chants liturgiques. Paris: Editions Delachaux et Niestlé, 1939.

Ludvigsen, Christian. *Det begyndte med Beckett – min egen teaterhistorie*. Aktuelle teaterproblemer. Vol. 42. Aarhus: Institut for Dramaturgi, 1997. 1979–2003. 51 vols.

MacGreevy, Thomas. "Breton Oracle." *Poetry* 99.2 (November 1961) 85–89.

"Moments Musicaux." *Poetry* 99.2 (November 1961) 85. Rpt. *Collected Poems of Thomas MacGreevy: An Annotated Edition*. Ed. Susan Schreibman. Dublin: Anna Livia Press; Washington: The Catholic University of America Press, 1991.

Nicolas Poussin. Dublin: The Dolmen Press, 1960.

McMillan, Dougald, and Martha Fehsenfeld. *Beckett in the Theatre: The Author as Practical Playwright and Director*. London: John Calder; New York: Riverrun Press, 1988.

Mallarmé, Stéphane. *Œuvres complètes*. Ed. Bertrand Marchal. Bibliothèque de la Pléiade. Paris: Gallimard, 1998–2003. 2 vols.

Stéphane Mallarmé: Poems. Tr. Roger Fry. New York: New Directions Books, 1951.

Mander, Raymond, and Joe Mitchenson. *The Theatres of London*. London: Rupert Hart-Davis, 1961.

Mask, Ahmad Kamyabi. *Qu'attendent Eugène Ionesco et Samuel Beckett?* Paris: A. Kamyabi Mask, 1991.

Mason, Rainer Michael, and Sylvie Ramond, eds. *Bram et Geer van Velde: Deux peintres, Un nom.* Paris: Editions Hazan, 2010.

Mayoux, Jean-Jacques. "Le Théâtre de Samuel Beckett." *Etudes Anglaises* 10.4 (October–November, 1957) 350–366.

Vivants piliers: le roman anglo-saxon et les symboles. Paris: Les Lettres Nouvelles, 1960.

Mellen, Joan. *Kay Boyle: Author of Herself.* New York: Farrar, Straus and Giroux, 1994.

Mendel, Deryk. "Dirigent für Becketts Partitur." *Theater heute* 4.7 (1963) 9–10.

Miller, Henry. *Tropic of Cancer.* London: Calder and Boyars, 1963.

Minetti, Bernhard. *Erinnerungen eines Schauspielers.* Ed. Günther Rühle. Stuttgart: Deutsche Verlags Anstalt, 1985.

Mitchell, Breon. "Art in Microcosm: The Manuscript Pages of Beckett's *Come and Go.*" *Modern Drama* 19.3 (September 1976) 245–254.

Montagnon, Pierre. *Histoire de la Légion.* Paris: Flammarion, 1999.

Montgomery, Niall. "No Symbols Where None Intended." *New World Writing* 5 (1954) 324–337.

Müller-Doohm, Stefan. *Adorno: A Biography.* Tr. Rodney Livingstone. Cambridge: Polity Press, 2005.

[Nadeau, Maurice. "Editorial"]. *Les Lettres Nouvelles*, nouvelle série (3) 12 (June–July–August 1964) 3–9.

"Maurice Nadeau in 'Express'." Tr. Larysa Mykyta and Mark Schumacher. *Samuel Beckett: The Critical Heritage.* Ed. Lawrence Graver and Raymond Federman. London: Routledge and Kegan Paul, 1979. 224–229.

Special issue on Reverzy, *Les Lettres Nouvelles,* nouvelle série (2) 7.21 (16 September 1959).

"Notes About Contributors." *Transition Forty-Eight* no. 4 (January 1949) 151.

"Obituaries: A. C. M. Elman." *The British Medical Journal* (26 August 1978) 643.

O'Casey, Sean. *Juno and the Paycock.* London and New York: Samuel French, 1932.

Officiel des Spectacles 785 (29 November – 5 December 1961) 53.

O'Grady, Desmond. "Desmond O'Grady Recalls Beckett in Paris." *Poetry Ireland Review* 37 (Winter 1992–1993) 126–132.

Olivier, Claude. "Je ne sais quel charme." *Les Lettres Françaises* 721 (8 May 1958) 10.

Pascal, Blaise. *Pensées.* Paris: Jean-Claude Lattès, 1988.

Pensées and Other Writings. Tr. Honor Levi. Oxford: Oxford University Press, 1995.

Paz, Octavio, ed. *Anthology of Mexican Poetry.* Tr. Samuel Beckett. London: Thames and Hudson, 1958; UNESCO Collection of Representative

Works: Latin American Series. Bloomington: Indiana University Press, 1958.

Peslin, Daniela. *Le Théâtre des Nations: Une aventure théâtrale à redécouvrir*. Paris: L'Harmattan, 2009.

Petrarch. *Petrarch's Lyric Poems: The Rime sparse and Other Poems*. Tr. and ed. Robert Durling. Cambridge, MA: Harvard University Press, 1976.

Pinget, Robert. *La Manivelle, suivi de Lettre morte*. Texte anglais, Samuel Beckett. Paris: Editions de Minuit, 1960.

Pope, Alexander. *Moral Essays: Epistles to Several Persons*. Ed. F. W. Bateson. The Twickenham Edition of the Poems of Alexander Pope. London: Methuen, 1951.

Pritchett, V. S. "An Irish Oblomov." *New Statesman* 59 (2 April 1960) 489.

Pryce-Jones, Alan. "The Anti-Novel in France." *Times Literary Supplement* 2972 (13 February 1959) 82.

Pyle, Hilary. *Jack B. Yeats: A Biography*. London: Routledge and Kegan Paul, 1970.

Jack B. Yeats: His Watercolours, Drawings and Pastels. Blackrock: Irish Academic Press, 1993.

Rawson, Nicholas. "Indoor View." *Transtlantic Review* 12 (April 1963) 73–79.

Renard, Jules. *Journal 1887–1910*. Ed. Léon Guichard and Gilbert Sigaux. Bibliothèque de la Pléiade. Paris: Gallimard, 1960.

Rewald, John. *The Paintings of Paul Cézanne: A Catalogue Raisonné*. New York: Harry N. Abrams, 1996. 2 vols.

Rimbaud, Arthur. *Œuvres complètes*. Ed. André Guyaux and Aurélia Cervoni. Bibliothèque de la Pléiade. Paris: Gallimard, 2009.

Roberts, Philip. *The Royal Court Theatre and the Modern Stage*. Cambridge: Cambridge University Press, 1999.

Roditi, Edouard. "A Market Report." *Arts Magazine* 36.10 (September 1962) 32.

Ronsard, Pierre de. *Œuvres complètes*. Ed. Gustave Cohen. Bibliothèque de la Pléiade. Paris: Gallimard, 1958. 2 vols.

Saiu, Octavian. "Samuel Beckett Behind the Iron Curtain: The Reception in Eastern Europe." *The International Reception of Samuel Beckett*. Ed. Matthew Feldman and Mark Nixon. London: Continuum International Publishing, 2009.

Savane, Paule. *Samuel Beckett à Ussy sur Marne*. Ussy-sur-Marne: Association pour la sauvegarde d'Ussy-sur-Marne, 2001.

Sayers, Elliseva. "The Irish Mavericks." *The World of Hibernia* 1.2 (Autumn 1995) 121–129.

Schneider, Alan. *Entrances: An American Director's Journey*. New York: Viking Press, 1986.

"On Directing *Film*." In Samuel Beckett, *Film: Complete Scenario, Illustrations, Production Shots*. New York: Grove Press, 1969. 62–94.

"Waiting for Beckett: A Personal Chronicle." *Chelsea Review* 2 (Autumn 1958) 3–20.

Schneider, Pierre, and Jean-Paul Riopelle. *Bronzes de Riopelle: la sculpture de peintre*. Paris: Jacques Dubourg, 1962.

Schulz, Kathryn. *Being Wrong: Adventures in the Margin of Error*. New York: HarperCollins, 2013.

Seaver, Richard. *The Tender Hour of Twilight*. New York: Farrar, Straus and Giroux, 2012.

Shakespeare, William. *The Riverside Shakespeare: The Complete Works*. Ed. G. Blakemore Evans. Assisted by J. J. M. Tobin. 2nd edition. Boston: Houghton Mifflin, 1997.

Sigal, Clancy. "Is This the Person to Murder Me?" *Sunday Times Colour Magazine* (1 March 1964) 22.

Soifer, Israel. "The Pioneer Work of Maurice Spitzer." *The Penrose Annual 1970*. Ed. Herbert Spencer. London: Lund Humphries, 1970. 126–142.

Spanier, Sandra Whipple. *Kay Boyle: Artist and Activist*. Carbondale: Southern Illinois University Press, 1986.

Statistical Pocket-Book of Yugoslavia. Beograd: Federal Institute for Statistics, 1963.

Stoppard, Tom. "Crying Till you Laugh." *Scene* 7.25 (October 1962) 19.

Stoullig, Claire, and Nathalie Schoeller, eds. *Bram van Velde*. Paris: Editions du Centre Georges Pompidou, 1989.

Swan, Michael. "The Spoken Word: Language and Culture." *The Listener* 57 (14 March 1957) 452.

Swift, Carolyn. *Stage by Stage*. Dublin: Poolbeg Press, 1985.

Swift, Jonathan. *Journal to Stella*. Ed. Harold Williams. Oxford: Clarendon Press, 1948. 2 vols.

Swinburne, Algernon Charles. *The Complete Works*. Ed. Sir Edmund Gosse and Thomas James Wise. Vol. VI. London: William Heinemann, 1925. 1925–1927. 20 vols.

Thom's Directory of Ireland for the Year 1934. Dublin: Alex Thom, 1934.

Thomson, Duncan. *Arikha*. London: Phaidon Press, 1994.

Thomson, James. *The Complete Poetical Works of James Thomson*. Ed. J. Logie Robertson. Oxford: Oxford University Press, 1908.

Tindall, William York. *Beckett's Bums*. London: Shenvel Press, 1960.

Todorović, Pedrag. "Godot in Belgrade." *The Beckett Circle* 34.2 (Fall 2011) 8–10.

Ulloa, Marie-Pierre. *Francis Jeanson: A Dissident Intellectual from the French Resistance to the Algerian War*. Tr. Jane Marie Todd. Stanford, CA: Stanford University Press, 2007.

Ussher, Arland. *The Journal of Arland Ussher*. Ed. Adrian Kenny. Dublin: Raven Arts, 1980.

Van Hulle, Dirk, and Mark Nixon. *Samuel Beckett's Library*. Cambridge: Cambridge University Press, 2013.

Verlaine, Paul. *One Hundred and One Poems by Paul Verlaine: A Bilingual Edition*. Tr. Norman R. Shapiro. Chicago: University of Chicago Press, 1999.

Wakeman, John, ed. *World Film Directors II: 1945–1985*. New York: H. W. Wilson, 1988.

Walker, Roy. "Judge not . . . ." *The Listener* 57 (9 May 1957) 767–768.

Wardle, Irving. *The Theatres of George Devine*. London: Jonathan Cape, 1978.

"Workshop Players Score Hit Here." *San Quentin News* 17.24 (26 November 1958) 1, 3.

Young, Jordan R. *The Beckett Actor: Jack MacGowran, Beginning to End*. Beverly Hills, CA: Moonstone Press, 1987.

Zilliacus, Clas. "'Act Without Words I' as Cartoon and Codicil." *Samuel Beckett Today / Aujourd'hui* 2 (1993) 295–304.

Beckett and Broadcasting: A Study of the Works of Samuel Beckett for and in Radio and Television. Acta Academiae Aboensis, series A humaniora, 51.2. Aabo, Sweden: Aabo Akademi, 1976.

ELECTRONIC WORKS CITED

Beckett, Samuel. Italia Prize Acceptance Speech. Accessed 14 September 2012. www.ubumexico.centro.org.mx/sound/beckett_samuel/various/Beckett-Samuel_Acceptance-Speech-Italy-Prize_Sorrento_1959.mp3.

Census of Ireland 1901/1911. National Archives of Ireland. Accessed 9 August 2013. http://www.census.nationalarchives.ie/pages/1911/Dublin/Ballybrack/Kerrymount/96663/.

"Dirección de Teatro." *Casa de las Americas*. Accessed 7 May 2013. www.casadelasamericas.org/teatro.php.

Hartwig, Edward. Photos of the Teatr Współczesny production of *Czekając na Godota*. Accessed 3 October 2013. www.wspolczesny.pl/archiwum/spektakle/czekajac-na-godota.

Hourican, Bridget. "Ó Faracháin, Roibeárd (Farren, Robert)." *Dictionary of Irish Biography*. Ed. James McGuire and James Quinn. Cambridge: Cambridge University Press, 2009. Accessed 6 August 2013. www.dib.cambridge.org/.

Lundy, Darryl. The Peerage: A Genealogical Survey of the Peerage of Britain as Well as the Royal Families of Europe. Accessed 15 October 2012. www.thepeerage.com/p37747.htm#377463.

"Palmarès de Roger Godeau." Mémoire du cyclisme. Accessed 6 August 2013. www.memoire-du-cyclisme.eu/palmares/godeau_roger.php.

"The San Francisco Actor's Workshop: 1952–1965." Accessed 15 March 2012. www.sanfranciscoactorsworkshop.com/.

Wildemeersch, Georges. "Biografie: 1960–1970." De Plicht van der Dichter: Hugo Claus ed de Politiek. Universiteit Antwerpen. Accessed 2 August 2012. www.ua.ac.be/main.aspx?c=*CLAUS&n=24734.

"Wisden's Five Cricketers of the Year." Wisden Almanack. Accessed 2 July 2013. www.espncricinfo.com/wisdenalmanack/content/story/209422.html.

INDEX OF RECIPIENTS

The first page number of each letter is listed by recipient.

INDEX OF FIRST NAMES

The following index of first names is supplied in order to reduce the need for identifications in the notes. Where first names are shared and if context does not make a reference clear, full names are given in the annotations.

SUMMARY LISTING OF SAMUEL BECKETT'S WORKS, MENTIONED IN VOLUME III

Works are listed below by original title. Individual poems or stories are indexed by collection unless published separately. Translations are listed following the title of the original here, but in the General Index are listed by translated title.

"Accul" (earlier title, "bon bon il est un pays")

Acte sans paroles I (*Act Without Words I; Akt bez słów I; Akte ohne Worte I; Drama i 1 akt*)

Acte sans paroles II (*Act Without Words II; Akte ohne Worte II*)

All That Fall (*Alle, die da fallen; Allen die vallen; Hvo som falder; Tous ceux qui tombent*)

Assez

"Le Calmant" ("The Calmative," see *Nouvelles; Nouvelles et Textes pour rien*)

"Cascando" (poem)

Cascando (radio play, same title in translation)

Come and Go (*Va-et-vient; Kommen und gehen*)

Comment c'est (also "Pim") (*How It Is; Wie es ist*)

Le Concentrisme, ou Jean du Chas

"Dante and the Lobster" (see *More Pricks Than Kicks*)

"Dante . . . Bruno . Vico .. Joyce"

Le Dépeupleur

"Les Deux Besoins"

"Dieppe" (see "Poèmes 38–39")

Echo's Bones and other Precipitates ("Alba," "Dortmunder," "Echo's Bones," "Enueg I," "Enueg II," "Malacoda," "Sanies I," "Sanies II," "Serena I," "Serena II," "Serena III," "The Vulture")

Eh Joe (*Dis Joe*; *He, Joe*; *Słuchaj, Joe*)
Eleutheria
Embers (*Aschenglut*; *Cendres*)
En attendant Godot (*Čekajući Godoa*; *Czekając na Godota*; *Vi venter på Godot*; *Wachten op Godot*; *Waiting for Godot*; *Warten auf Godot*)
"The Essential and the Incidental"
"Ex Cathezra"
"L'Expulsé" ("The Expelled"; see *Nouvelles*; *Nouvelles et Textes pour rien*)

"Faux départs"
Film
Fin de partie (provisional title *Haam*; *Endgame*; *Endspiel*; *A játszma vége*; *Końcówka*; *Slutspil*; *og Scene uden ord*)
"From an Abandoned Work" ("Aus einem aufgegebenenWerk")
"From an Unabandoned Work"
"The Gloaming" (later, *Rough for Theatre I*)

Happy Days (*Gelukkige dagen*; *Giorni felici*; *Glückliche Tage*; *Oh les beaux jours*)
"Henri Hayden, homme peintre"
"Hommage à Jack B. Yeats"
Human Wishes

Imagination morte imaginez (*Imagination Dead Imagine*)
L'Innommable (*Der Namenlose*; *The Unnamable*)

"Kilcool" (precursor to *Not I* and *That Time*)
Krapp's Last Tape (*La dernière bande*; *Krapp's laatste band*; *Krapps sidste bånd*; *Das letzte Band*; *Az utolsó tekercs*)

Malone meurt (*Malone Dies*; *Malone stirbt*)
Mercier et Camier
Molloy (same title in translation)
More Pricks Than Kicks ("Dante and the Lobster"; "The Smeraldina's Billet Doux"; "Yellow")
Murphy (same title in translation)

Nouvelles (see *Nouvelles et Textes pour rien*): "Le Calmant" ("The Calmative"); "L'Expulsé" ("The Expelled"); "Suite" (later entitled "La Fin") ("The End")

"Ooftish"

"Papini's Dante"
"Peintres de l'empêchement"
"La Peinture des Van Velde ou le monde et le pantalon"
Play (*Comédie*; *Spel*; *Spiel*; *Spil*)
"Poèmes 38–39" ("Ascension"; "Dieppe"; "La Mouche")
"Premier amour" (see *Nouvelles*)
Proust

"Recent Irish Poetry" (pseud. Andrew Belis)
Rough for Theatre I
Rough for Theatre II (*Fragment de théâtre II*)

"Saint-Lô"
"Sanies I" (see *Echo's Bones and other Precipitates*)
"Sedendo et Quiescendo"
"Serena I" (see *Echo's Bones and other Precipitates*)
"The Smeraldina's Billet Doux" (see *More Pricks Than Kicks*)
"Suite" (later re-entitled "La Fin" [translated as "The End"]; see *Nouvelles*; *Nouvelles et Textes pour rien*)

Textes pour rien (see also *Nouvelles et Textes pour rien*)
"Three Dialogues" (also "Three Dialogues with Georges Duthuit")
"Trois poèmes": "Accul"; "Mort de A. D."; "vive morte ma seule saison"
"Trois Poèmes – Three Poems": "je suis ce cours de sable qui glisse" ("my way is in the sand flowing"); "que ferais-je sans ce monde sans visages sans questions" ("what would I do without this world faceless incurious"); "je voudrais que mon amour meure" ("I would like my love to die")

"The Vulture" (see *Echo's Bones and other Precipitates*)

Watt (same title in translation)
Whoroscope
Words and Music (*Ord och Music*; *Paroles et musique*)

"Yellow" (see *More Pricks Than Kicks*)

GENERAL INDEX

Names of persons and publications with a profile in this volume are marked with an asterisk; those with a profile in a previous volume are noted with an asterisk and with that volume number (II). The titles of SB's works are given in the summary listing above; individual titles (including translations) are indexed separately, as are poems and stories if they appeared independently; poems or stories that appeared in a collection are indexed by the title of that collection.